PHILOSOPHY
AND
ITS
OTHERS

SUNY Series in Systematic Philosophy
Robert C. Neville, Editor

Whether systematic philosophies are intended as true pictures of the world, as hypotheses, as the dialectic of history, or as heuristic devices for relating rationally to a multitude of things, they each constitute articulated ways by which experience can be ordered, and as such they are contributions to culture. One does not have to choose between Plato and Aristotle to appreciate that Western civilization is enriched by the Platonic as well as Aristotelian ways of seeing things.

The term "systematic philosophy" can be applied to any philosophical enterprise that functions with a perspective from which everything can be addressed. Sometimes this takes the form of an attempt to spell out the basic features of things in a system. Other times it means the examination of a limited subject from the many angles of a context formed by a systematic perspective. In either case systematic philosophy takes explicit or implicit responsibility for the assessment of its unifying perspective and for what is seen from it. The styles of philosophy according to which systematic philosophy can be practiced are as diverse as the achievements of the great philosophers in history, and doubtless new styles are needed for our time.

Yet systematic philosophy has not been a popular approach during this century of philosophical professionalism. It is the purpose of this series to stimulate and publish new systematic works employing the techniques and advances in philosophical reflection made during this century. The series is committed to no philosophical school or doctrine, nor to any limited style of systematic thinking. Whether the systematic achievements of previous centuries can be equalled in the twentieth depends on the emergence of forms of systematic philosophy appropriate to our times. The current resurgence of interest in the project deserves the cultivation it may receive from the SUNY Series in Systematic Philosophy.

PHILOSOPHY AND ITS OTHERS

Ways of Being and Mind

William Desmond

State University of New York Press

Published by
State University of New York Press, Albany

© 1990 State University of New York

For information, address State University of New York
Press, State University Plaza, Albany, N.Y., 12246

Library of Congress Cataloging-in-Publication Data

Desmond, William, 1951–
    Philosophy and its others : ways of being and mind / William Desmond.
        p.   cm. — (SUNY series in systematic philosophy)
    Includes bibliographical references.
    ISBN 0-7914-0307-6. — ISBN 0-7914-0308-4 (pbk.)
    1. Philosophy.   2. Aesthetics.   3. Philosophy and religion.   4. Ethics.   5. Logic.
  I. Title.   II. Series.
  B53.D476   1990
  101—dc20   89-37872
                                                                              CIP

10   9   8   7   6   5   4   3   2   1

For Hugh and Oisín
The New Ones

ψυχῆς πείρατα ἰὼν οὐκ ἂν
ἐξεύροιο, πᾶσαν ἐπιπορευόμενος ὁδόν· οὕτω βαθὺν λόγον ἔχει.

You could not search out the furthest limits of the soul,
even if you traversed all of the ways; so unfathomable is its
logos.

—Heraclitus, Fragment 45

Civilization is hooped together, brought
Under a rule, under the semblance of peace
By manifold illusion; but man's life is thought,
And he, despite his terror, cannot cease
Ravening through century after century,
Ravening, raging, and uprooting that he may come
Into the desolation of reality.

—W.B. Yeats, *Meru*

. . . God of Heaven theres nothing like nature the wild
mountains then the sea and the waves rushing then the
beautiful country with fields of oats and wheat and all kinds
of things and all the fine cattle going about that would do
your heart good to see rivers and lakes and flowers all sorts
of shapes and smells and colours springing up even out of
the ditches primroses and violets nature it is as for them
saying theres no God I wouldnt give a snap of my two
fingers for all their learning why dont they go and create
something I often asked him atheists or whatever they call
themselves go and wash the cobblers off themselves first . . .

—Molly Bloom, James Joyce's *Ulysses*

Contents

Preface

A philosopher discovers himself repeatedly asking the mocking question: Why philosophize at all? The convenient comforts fail: scholarly advance, scientific curiosity, intellectual glory; or less flatteringly, careerism, inquisitiveness, vanity. These are not inconsiderable, but none touches the hardest question: Is the game worth the candle? I do not have an easy answer. I do know that one does not simply choose to philosophize. Over a time one finds oneself haunted by certain recurrent thoughts that refuse to let one be. When time threatens to deaden our early astonishment before being, exasperation with such importunate thoughts takes over. One philosophizes because now and then a quiet of mind comes from thought itself to allay this very insomnia of thought. Mind contradicts itself to be in harmony with itself, disturbs itself to make peace with itself and being. One finds oneself thrust into an adventure of mind in the middle between this rupture and this peace.

Stretches of this book may strike some as written by a philosopher for philosophers, but it was composed in the conviction that philosophy is not only for technical specialists. Thinking selves have sometimes hoped that this might be true, though the hope is not always met. My sense is that philosophy today is increasingly restless with the confined emptiness of all conceptual ghettos, and hopeful of renewing its intellectual community with what is other to itself. This need imply no diminution of the hardness of philosophical thought and its distinctiveness. The great thinkers of the tradition may sometimes seem unapproachable, but the singularity of their thought, even in its most abstract articulations, is nurtured on sources of perplexity that confront the basic concrete issues of being and human being.

The present work is written on more than one level. This may discomfit some readers who expect that thought should pare itself down to univocal prose. The reader will find different forms of philosophical writing, ranging from the aphorism through abstract dialectic to more lyrical thought. Here Aristotle is my guide when he said: We should expect as much precision as the matter dictates; the matter itself should be allowed to dictate the appropriate mode of discourse. One does not insist that the matter itself conform to a mode of discourse or conceptual scheme canonized in advance for reasons which may have nothing to do with the matter at stake and its inherent requirements. Univocal prose can console thought, but sometimes its comforting clarity is exacted by a sacrifice of richness of content. Such clarity, thinned of recalcitrant content, becomes a blindness, albeit one that tries intellectually to justify itself. But unlike Oedipus, this self-blinding has not solved the riddle of the Sphinx; it has merely run away from it.

While the work has a strong systematic side, some things I want to say resist being conceptually systematized in a total way. This does not mean one does not try to articulate them, but the appropriate form of expression need not always be domestic, monolinear prose. If being is said in many ways, this has to be enacted, not just said in lip-service. The range of linguistic resources in this book reflects the belief that there is not just one privileged language. I strive for a certain conguence of form and content. There is no abstract content that floats in separation from the form in which it comes to manifestation or expression. The form of manifestation is the shaping of the content; our mode of expression should try not to betray this form of manifestation. There are some forms that misshape the content.

Since I do not want to write in a language whose form gives the lie to the content proclaimed, sometimes the appropriate language has to remain true to an element of necessary discontinuity. But this too must not be canonized into the sort of strategy, celebrated and endlessly repeated by the Corybantic deconstructionist. If the expectation of an absorbing conceptual totality is not to the point, even less to the point is the identification of plurality with the dissemination of fragmentation. Sometimes what is at stake is a process of naming, not conceptual mastering, nor anti-conceptual refusal of meaning. If one is not to betray philosophical openness to otherness, one has to let the voice of the other speak in its otherness. This reflects the need for a certain honesty in the naming of certain elemental disclosures of being. Such simple honesty may be betrayed by the narrowness of the univocal analyst, the hubris of the conceptual totalizer and the avant-garde braggadocio of the deconstructive disseminator.

So if one says: There is not one univocal voice in this work, therefore the author wanders, let one recall Aristotle and also ask: Are the discourses open to the matter, even as unmastered? Why are the discourses more than polysemic babble but mindful of philosophy's others? The philosopher simply wants to ask the hardest questions and make the best sense possible. If making a fetish of one way of talking or thinking hinders this, then philosophical thought should smash the idol. But the point is not to smash, but to release better thought in relation to the matter itself. And this is to offer no hints as to the things that are left unsaid.

For reading the manuscript in part or as a whole and for their helpful comments, I want to thank Louis Dupré, Richard Kearney, George Kline, Brian Martine, Carl Vaught, and Merold Westphal. I want to thank Robert Neville for his generous editorial encouragement, encouragement that came from a philosophical mind that itself is plurivocal. A person I especially want to thank is Robert O'Donoghue. About ten years ago or so, Robert O'Donoghue—a writer and poet himself—said to me that Ireland was saturated with poets but lacked for philosophers. He edited an arts and studies page for the *The Cork Examiner*, and invited my contribution. I contributed over a number of years. Some of the present themes then received a first voicing. If on occasion the voice of the poet breaks through, the reader will trace it at least to one source. Whether the lack of philosophy has been remedied, I must leave to the reader's judgment. For his generous support over these sometimes difficult years, I gratefully mark my debt to Robert O'Donoghue.

Without the innumerable and often nameless acts of support of Maria, my wife, and without the daily familial solidarity of Maria, William Óg, Hugh and now Oisín, this book would not have been possible. My gratitude—not said often enough—to them.

A version of the third meditation of chapter 5 appeared under the title "Philosophy and Failure" in *The Journal of Speculative Philosophy*, vol. II, no. 4, 1988.

Introduction

Unity and Plurality: The Wittgensteinian and Hegelian Option

A significant part of the current ferment about philosophy's contemporary task turns on the question of philosophy's relation to its others. The extremes might be broadly defined thus. On one hand, we find those who advocate breaking down the barriers between philosophy and its others in the interests of philosophy's relevance to the wider human whole. On the other hand, we find those who think of philosophy as a specialized technical activity, essentially insulated from, or to be insulated from, any contaminating otherness. Some hold that philosophy has a stake in the larger culture and criticize (let us call it) nitpicker thought; others countercharge that philosophy (so to speak) must not fly by night. Some reject anorexic analysis in the shadowless glare of technique; others spurn the speculative rhapsody of metaphysics sung in poetry's blue light.

In general, traditional philosophy is criticized as lacking sufficient respect for what is other to its system of categories. This we see in the two main "camps" of contemporary philosophy, namely, Anglo-American analysis and Continental thought. The Continentalist often criticizes the "logocentric" bias of the metaphysical tradition, imputing to it a secret imperialistic urge to reduce everything to a conceptual whole. By contrast, the analytical philosopher is suspicious of what he sees as the grandiose constructions of past metaphysicians. Under the influence of the later Wittgenstein, among others, he is content with a more modest role for philosophy, with a putative tolerance for the plurality of language games, even in their otherness to philosophical thought.

I find myself dissatisfied with these options. First, philosophical thought can speak to certain fundamental questions without either nitpicking or flying by night. Second, the voice of philosophical discourse has in the past been hospitable, and can in the present be welcoming, to the voices of modes of mindfulness that are other to philosophical analysis, understood in a narrower sense. Third, our relation to earlier thinkers can be informed as much by hermeneutical generosity as by suspicion; reserves of thought, as of

1

"unthought," may still remain unmined in the metaphysical tradition. Hence this book considers how philosophy has taken and can continue to take seriously the ways of being that are other to itself, without itself ceasing to be philosophical in a manner recognizable to its traditional practitioner. At its richest, philosophy has always been defined by its interplay with its others. Nor need it evidence the totalizing conceptual imperialism that is reductive of otherness and the plurality of essential ways of being. This is especially true of the others I will take with seriousness: namely, the aesthetic, the ethical and the religious, each considered as a significant way of being and a distinctive mode of what I call being mindful.

There are two extremes I want to avoid. In a shorthand way I will call these the "Wittgensteinian" and "Hegelian" options. The Wittgensteinian option emphasizes that human meaning is marked by a pluralism of different forms, the manyness of which cannot be reduced to some simple unifying "essence." To seek the latter is to be guilty of the so-called essentialist fallacy. The original impetus of the later Wittgensteinian view was a reaction to the monistic and possibly totalizing pretensions of some traditional metaphysics and especially scientism—traces of which even the early Wittgenstein showed. In fact, there are a number of different "forms of life" and "language games" that cannot be reduced to one overarching form or underlying essence. What is to prevent this plurality from becoming a mere aggregate of diversified forms? Wittgenstein uses the metaphor of "family resemblance." This implies a certain togetherness in the diversity, I would say a community in the different ways of being mindful. The complex character of this togetherness or community is not satisfactorily spelt out. It is not incidental that some commentators have pointed to a similarity between the fragmentariness of Wittgenstein's later thought and the sense of disunity strongly marking modernist art and literature.

The Hegelian option is perhaps the other extreme. I am reluctant to label Hegel with a misleading monist tag, for he seeks a certain dialectical balance of unity and plurality. Nevertheless, I will speak of the Hegelian option, give the history of Hegel interpretation and his undoubted propensity to subordinate difference to identity, otherness to sameness in the final *dialectical*, that is, philosophical reckoning. These qualifications granted, the Hegelian option sees the plurality of configurations of meaning as interrelated by a dialectical necessity that must culminate in philosophy as the crowning mode of mind. This philosophical culmination claims to incorporate whatever is to be retained as meaningful in the other ways of being. Thus, some of the most important and standard criticisms of Hegel concern his view of philosophy's relation to art and religion. Philosophy for Hegel is the highest mode of absolute spirit. Art and religion also belong in absolute spirit, but while they exhibit the absolute content, their mode of exhibition lacks the absolute form. Philosophy displays both absolute content and absolute form. Hence art and religion have to acquiesce in a finally subordinate position, even despite Hegel's ascription to them of absolute content.[1]

The divergent stresses of these two options are clear. In the Hegelian option unity seems to dialectically reduce plurality, while in the Wittgensteinian option the emphasis on discontinuous plurality seems to make problematic the possibility of any unity. The question to be put to the Hegelian option concerns the character of unity it seeks and which indeed it claims is attained, at least in Hegel's own case. The question to be put to the Wittgensteinian option concerns the very possibility of unity at all, given that our ways of being seems to be dispersed into a plurality of radically discontinuous activities. Can we find a different balance of sameness and otherness, unity and plurality, human wholeness and variousness?

Unity and Plurality: The Metaxological View

I think one can.

I have systematically developed a view in *Desire, Dialectic and Otherness*[2] which tries to do justice to this different balance. This view turns on the meaning of what I have called the "metaxological" sense of being. The term derives from the Greek *metaxu*, meaning middle, intermediate, between, and *logos*, meaning discourse, speech, articulate account. The metaxological concerns a *logos* of the *metaxu*, a discourse of the "between," the middle. Philosophically we need to understand how this middle articulates itself, both ontologically and in relation to mind. Our being is essentially intermediate, this is, midway between the totalizing wholeness represented by the Hegelian option and the discontinuous plurality of the Wittgensteinian option. A qualified defense of human wholeness is necessary against Wittgensteinian discontinuity. Against Hegelian totality, a greater respect is required for the plurality of ways of being and mind, in their very *otherness* to philosophy itself. My emphasis on this "middle," here and elsewhere, speaks to the contemporary sense of plurality but dissents from its sometimes unfruitful proclamation of discontinuity. This is not to sleepily subscribe to worn clichés but to reawaken some of the affirmative promise dormant in some traditional views and to wrest them free from any equally unfruitful sense of totalizing unity.

In this work, I explore how the metaxological sense is instantiated in the relation of philosophy to its others, and also in those others themselves as ways of being. Hence I need to briefly outline what I mean by it. The present work can be read on its own term, though a familiarity with *Desire, Dialectic and Otherness* would certainly facilitate a surer grasp of my overall aims.

Being brief at the risk of enigma, the following is a skeletal sketch of what the metaxological implies.

Running throughout this work will be the following fourfold sense of being. I define the metaxological sense of being in it dynamic interrelation to three other senses: namely, the "univocal," the "equivocal," and the "dialectical" senses of being. The first sense, the *univocal* puts the emphasis on simple sameness, hence on the unmediated unity of the self and the other. The univocal sense has its place in our efforts to make sense of being but its unmediated sense of unity cannot do proper justice to the complex *differences* between philosophy and its others. By contrast, the *equivocal* sense breaks with the ideal of univocal unity and stresses those aspects of unmediated *difference* between the self and the other. While rightly getting at a certain rich ambiguity of intermediate being, the danger with the equivocal sense is that it tempts one to give up on the search for the mindful mediation of difference. We acquiesce in a sense of plurality which, lacking a deeper relatedness, is indistinguishable from fragmenting dispersal. I find a drift in this direction, for example, in deconstructionist thought: *différance* deconstructs univocal unity, only to disseminate itself in equivocal thinking.

The third sense of being, namely, the *dialectical* sense, criticizes univocal unity: being is more complex and rich than any simple unmediated unity. But unlike deconstructionist thought, and even though it too criticizes the limits of univocal unity, dialectical thinking still tries to mediate equivocal difference. Unmediated difference is not enough. Dialectic rightly seeks to address the mediation between philosophy and its others and so to overcome difference as merely dispersing fragmentation. But the dialectical sense of being shows an ambiguous tendency to interpret *all* mediation primarily in terms of *self-mediation*. So its mediation of dispersing difference runs the risk of reducing *all otherness* to something that must be dialectically subordinated to the putative primacy of self-mediation. Thus it faces the problem of avoiding a final reduction of the other ways of being mindful to the self-mediation of philosophy's own thought (this tends to happen with Hegel). The upshot then is that philosophy only mediates with *itself* in mediating with its others.

The fourth sense of being, the metaxological, is not per se antagonistic to dialectic, but it does resist any such dialectical reduction. For the metaxological sense tries to name the space of the middle as also open to mediation, not only from the side of the dialectical self, but also from the side of an otherness that can never be reduced to a moment of self-mediation, not even philosophy's own self-mediation. It follows that the "inter," the "between" is not to be interpreted solely in terms of dialectical self-mediation. This "between" grants certain forms of otherness as irreducible; if these forms are to be mediated at all, this must be done in terms other than dialectical self-mediation. Dialectical self-mediation risks reducing the plurality of forms of mediation to one essential form that encompasses the others. By contrast, metaxological intermediation is itself plural. It is significantly double in that the mediation of the between cannot be reduced either to the mediation of the self or the mediation of the other, should either of these two sides claim to mediate entirely the complex between. Relative to philosophical thought this implies that philosophy cannot just hold a conceptual monologue with itself in which it rests satisfied to merely reformulate the voices of its others in its own terms. It must listen to the voices of the others. Wherever appropriate it must let its own voice be reformulated under the impact of their otherness. When it does reflectively try to voice these others, it must genuinely try to respect what these other voices *on their own terms* bring to the metaxological between.

In the present case, this double mediation of the metaxological means that genuine philosophical thinking must be *both* self-mediating and also open to the intermediation between thought and what is other to thought, precisely as other. This does not entail a rejection of the univocal, equivocal and dialectical senses; it is rather to plot their limits, to avoid the dangers previously noted, while yet doing justice to what they rightly emphasize. But the ultimate closure of thought by itself and in itself is impossible. The metaxological resists this closure, though it does not entirely jettison the notion of wholeness. A metaxological web of relations articulates the differences of the ways of being, yet also holds them together. "Holding together" is part of the meaning of human wholeness. The human being is not the whole, nor can one of its ways of being completely overreach all being in its otherness. And this point applies as much to the others as to philosophy. The human being as intermediate is the promise of an open wholeness that is midway between completed totality and sheerly indefinite imcompleteness.[3] The community of being includes the possibility of an open wholeness that calls for a defense and recovery of a dialectical self-mediation sufficiently qualified to avoid closure.

One might say that the metaxological sense of being asks us to take seriously the *dia* of *dia*lect, for this *dia*, dyad, recalls us to a doubleness, recalls us to the middle as itself plural. Dialectic must become dynamically dyadic because ultimately it finds itself in the interplay of the middle as metaxological. Thus, in deference to a certain traditional usage, I will sometimes speak of an *open* dialectic, in that the metaxological sense opens dialectic to the pluralized middle and its demand of pluralized mediation. The openness of every whole is precisely the internal eruption of the charge of otherness within that whole itself. Thus, while the others of philosophy are distinctive ways of being and mind, they are not just strange opposites but are family others, intimate others. Likewise they have a certain internal relatedness to philosophy itself. Far from this internal relatedness implying any dialectical *reduction* of these others to philosophy, rather philosophical thought is deprived of any simple univocal "identity." It requires a pluralized, metaxological "identity" in so far as philosophy is defined by thought about this community of others in familial interplay. Nor is this interplay devoid of conflict, for family quarrels are often the most bitter.

Ways of Being and Mind

All of this is to take seriously Aristotle's saying that *to on legetai pollachōs*, being is said in many ways. I want to interpret this saying metaxologically. There are many ways of being, each of which is also a distinctive mode of being mindful. In so far as philosophy is concerned with the mindful thought of being, and in so far as the mindful thought of being must be metaxological, philosophy finds itself charged with a double imperative. First, it has to remain faithful to the exigency of its own form of mindfulness. Again Aristotle's classic formulation captures this requirement: the ultimate energeia of being is that of *noēsis noēseōs*, thought thinking itself. That is, genuine thought mediates with itself, tries to be as internally coherent and consistent as possible. Put in the above terms: philosophy is dialectically self-mediating in thinking through the apparent equivocality of being in search of a unity, community of meaning more complex than univocal identity.

But now a fundamental tension begins to emerge: in so far as thought thinking itself pursues only its own internal self-coherence, philosophy is tempted to renege on the plurality of the ways of being and ways of saying being, especially in that these ways present themselves to mind as other to philosophical thought. In modern philosophy this temptation is epitomized in Descartes' classic phrase *cogito me cogitare* (the subjectivistic version of Aristotle's *noēsis noēseōs*) and the subsequent history of mind's alienation from being's otherness, now alternatively reduced to a mindless dualistic opposite or dialectically dominated by an idealistic self-mediation.[4]

Against this temptation of thought to close on itself in seamless self-mediation, we find this second exigency of thought beyond complete dialectical mediation: self-mediating thought must be genuinely open to the otherness of the ways of being. Hence, philosophy as metaxological finds itself charged not only with the self-mediation of thought but also with the *intermediation* between thought and what is other to thought. It seems to me that the current accusations against traditional philosophy stem from its tendency to privilege the first exigency, namely, thought thinking itself, such that it harbors the danger of logocentrism, or else the will to create grand structures of conceptual abstractions that have severed their connection with being in its otherness. I will say that thought as metaxological is a self-mediating openness to otherness, where the second charge breaks open the tendency to closure on the part of self-mediation. Stronger, thought is so charged with metaxological intermediation with otherness that it may sometimes find itself breaking on forms of otherness it cannot completely master in terms of its mediating categories.

This double exigency is broadly reflected in the history of philosophy. In ancient and medieval thought, first philosophy (*prōtē philosophia*) was conceived metaphysically, hence we find respect for thought thinking being in its otherness. Modern, post-Cartesian philosophy contracts metaphysics into epistemology as first philosophy, and pushes thought thinking *itself* to an extreme. Thus, the legacy of Descartes' *cogito me cogitare* produces the so-called "way of ideas," according to which all we directly know are our own ideas. Dualism is then unavoidable, as the "way of ideas" insists on carrying through the project of reducing philosophy to the completion of thought thinking itself. Dualism produces an impoverished form of the double requirement of thought: the otherness of being is reduced to dualistic opposition, while self-mediation is elevated into a putative self-sufficient subjectivity. This is reflected in Kant's transcendental philosophy. Kant claims that the founders of the modern scientific revolution "learned that reason has insight only into what it produces after a plan of its own . . ." (*Critique of Pure Reason*, B xiii–xv). This is mind elevating its own self-mediation into a position of originative primacy over being's otherness. The latter becomes mere unformed stuff to be worked into articulate shape by the categories and constitutive activities of the transcendental self.

Hegel is even more consistent in trying to carry though this project of elevating self-mediation to primacy. He is also more sophisticated in that he recognizes a dialectic of self and other. But true to the project of thought thinking itself, the primacy of *self-mediation* dominates his sense of dialectic. Thus, he reduces metaxological intermediation to dialectical self-mediation: the interplay of self and other is not properly safeguarded against its closure into singular self-mediation. As avoiding this closure, metaxological intermediation opens dialectic, is an "open" dialectic in a sense reminiscent of Platonic dialectic as dialogical. Indeed, in so far as Hegel allows for a dynamic interplay of self and other, even while thinking in terms of the primacy of self-mediation, his philosophy, despite any putative closure, yields its own equivocal openness to otherness. Despite the intention of completing the project of thought thinking itself, Hegel does, must inhabit the middle. His dialectical being in the middle inevitably calls for an explicit metaxological inhabitation of the middle and a less equivocal openness to the other as other.

Thus, in an important sense, all significant post-Hegelian philosophy is concerned with forms of otherness that resist the closure of Hegelian dialectic. In the nineteenth century, Schelling, Kierkegaard, Marx, Nietzsche, are ambiguous explorers of otherness against any dominating Hegelian self-mediation. In the twentieth century, Husserl's transcendental subjectivity is the acme of thought thinking itself; being's otherness is suspended in the epochē, "put in parentheses," while transcendental subjectivity occupies itself with itself. Heidegger, existentialism, hermeneutics, deconstruction, exhibit countermovements to thought thinking only itself; all are explorers of potentially disruptive otherness. In all the latter, Hegelian dialectic provides a kind of logicist shadow that hovers near their thinking of otherness. Thus, the movement of modern philosophy can be said to exemplify historically the metaxological sense of being in its twofold requirement of thought thinking itself and its other. For what we first find in modern philosophy is a progressive radicalization from Descartes to Hegel of self-mediation or of thought thinking itself; then from Hegel to current philosophy, we find the countermovement to thought thinking only itself, namely, a progressive shift to thought thinking its other, or philosophy's interplay with its significant others. At the end of this double movement, we need to reiterate that the metaxological sense of being, as developed here and elsewhere, requires *both* self-mediation and intermediation with otherness.

In citing Aristotle (being is said in many ways), I imply no radical dualism between the many ways being is articulated and our attempts to bespeak mindfully the significance of those ways. There is a metaxological community between being and mindfulness. Being *articulates itself* in a plurality of ways marked by affinity and divergence. To make sense of being is to try to do justice to the togetherness and differentiation of this plurality of ways. The ways of being constitute a metaxological community, a family; but a family is held together, both in the differences of its members and in their non-reductive relatedness, by reference to a common genesis or origin, even though that origin be itself irreducible to any of its offspring. As we shall see, it is the original power of being that is the common source of their articulation, but this originating energy is not univocally identical with any of the particular ways in which it may be expressed. The original power of being is common precisely because it constitutes the metaxological *community* of being and may indeed be said to necessitate a plurality of possible articulations in order to do justice to its own power. Thus, the irreducibility of the different forms to one another does not preclude their relativity and dynamic interplay as each a way of being, outcome of the dynamic power of being as this comes to articulation in the mindful human being. The traditional image of the tree of philosophy now becomes the family tree of philosophy and its others.

Beyond the discontinuity of Wittgensteinian forms of life, or the absorption of plurality in a Hegelian conceptual totality, we must do justice to the sense of ontological origin implied by this, namely, being as a metaxological community. Wittgensteinian plurality seems simply to acquiesce in a manyness, de facto given in the middle, a manyness accepted as a manyness, with too much uncritical respect for commonsense. One cannot simply acquiesce thus in the middle, for if the human being as intermediate is a dynamic articulation of the originative power of being, then the middle is a moving one, and the forms of life emergent there must be critically sifted. By contrast, Hegelian totality, refusing to accept uncritically that intermediate plurality, interprets the dynamism of human being as the dialectical thrust towards an encompassing end, interpreted as philosophical knowledge of the Whole within which are to be situated the other ways of being. In this the Hegelian has more *philosophical* persuasiveness on his side than does the Wittgensteinian. However, this dialectical thrust of the Hegelian for an encompassing end does not do justice to the overdetermined power of being as origin, and in a manner that may easily lend itself to the distortion of our own intermediate being. For the Hegelian end claims to incorporate the mediation of the original power of being within the dialectical self-mediation of philosophy, with the resultant subordination of being's otherness to thought thinking its own categories. The double exigency of thought is collapsed into the first exigency of thought thinking itself. The result is that the second exigency of thought thinking its other is distorted by being dialectically domesticated. My understanding of our intermediate being as itself the issue of the original power of being in its metaxological otherness is intended to guard philosophical thought against this danger, without the less than philosophical respect for unreflective commonsense that seems to mark Wittgenstein's heirs.

Structure of the Work

This sense of the intermediate and the doubleness of mediation it requires will be variously seen in the chapters to follow. Each way of being and mind concretizes the metaxological in its own way. I do not want heavy-handedly to insist on the point, as if the metaxological sense of being were a dominating conceptual scheme to be imposed on self and otherness ab extra. I will try to let each way of being speak for itself. Thus, in chapter 1, I will address the current perplexity about the "identity" of philosophy and claim that philosophy as inhabiting the middle must instantiate a certain metaxological mindfulness. The above sense of the double middle forms the context for the treatment of a family of significant others, relative to which philosophy has defined itself. These others shape the self-images of philosophy and include the scholar, scientist, technician, poet, priest, revolutionary, hero, and sage. Each of these is a distinctive inhabitant of the middle, both akin and yet other to the philosopher.

In chapter 2, I turn to the aesthetic as a significant other to philosophy that reveals the metaxological sense of being. I look at the emergence of mindfulness from bodily origins, its specialization in art, the resistance of the aesthetic to conceptualizing and its own tolerance of otherness. In chapter 3, I discuss the metaxological as embodied in being religious and the overdetermined ambiguity of the interplay we find there between selfness and sacred otherness. In chapter 4, I consider the ethical as evidencing a complex metaxological mediation of value in selfhood itself that culminates in a valuing of the ethical other as other. I will say that ethical community involves a metaxological respect, even love of the worthy being of the other.[5]

In each of these three chapters, we will see a development of mindfulness from immediacy, through dialectical self-mediation to metaxological intermediation. In each of these three, as indeed in philosophy itself, I also want to understand the possible loss of a sense of metaxological being. As allowing a dynamic interrelating of self and other, the metaxological allows its own potential deformation. The middle allows the self to disfigure the middle, when the self hubristically asserts its will-to-power over otherness. This "dissolution" of the middle allows us to situate the so-called end of philosophy, the "death" of art, the "death of God," the fragility of the ethical. These results are not to be endorsed but they must be understood. They all follow from a reduction of the doubleness of the metaxological to a singular self-mediation that tries to dominate all otherness.

Given the explorations of the other ways of being, in the final two chapters I return to philosophy itself as a mode of being mindful, but now one that does not see the other ways of being as merely opposites set over against it. Its community with these others entails its willingness to break any claims to its own absolute self-sufficiency. In chapter 5, I am concerned with mindfulness as thought thinking its other. Here I will be concerned with a sense of philosophical mindfulness that is other to instrumental reason, revealed through discussions of being logical, solitude and failure. What will be at stake here are the limits of thought as self-mediation, indeed forms of limiting otherness on which thought sometimes breaks.

The "breakdown" of claims to complete self-mediation in chapter 5 is complemented by the possible "breakthrough," beyond all instrumentalization, of a more affirmative energy of thought and being in chapter 6. We follow the possible loss of the double middle through to a turning point in negation where an elemental love of being springs up again and calls for a renewal or recreation of mindfulness of the metaxological. Thus, the negative process of chapter 5 is not a negative result, but the essential preparation for chapter 6, where I am concerned with (as I will put it) being mindful as thought singing its other. Where chapter 5 speaks of a limiting otherness on which thought can break, this final chapter will ask about the possibility of a breakthrough into more affirmative thought, even in this breakdown. I will speak of golden being, song and the elemental, death and time and reversal, breakthrough, festive being, folly and idiot wisdom. These are others to thought that reveal certain aporiai of logos, yet such aporiai teach thought a deeper mindfulness, particularly in relation to the intrinsic worth of being itself. Together these last two chapters try to respond to philosophy's respect of the double exigency of thought and the voices of its others.

This is outline but let me underscore the recurrence of the following major themes. As already suggested, I will be concerned with a movement from immediacy to self-mediation to metaxological intermediation in the different ways of being. Moreover, I will acknowledge the need to becomes free of what Vico calls the "conceit of scholars"—namely, mistaking the developed actuality for the original phenomenon—this will be continuous with an emphasis on meaning as emergent from origins that are initially inchoate and hence resistant to simple philosophical conceptualization. Further, I will be concerned with the insufficiency of instrumental reason to account for philosophical thought and the significance of its others. Further again, I will take seriously the challenge to philosophy of the sense of charged otherness as revealed by the aesthetic, the religious and the ethical. Finally, I will insist on the need for a philosophical thought that acknowledges such resistant otherness in order not to betray *its own* rational openness.

I am aware that an entire book might have been devoted to each of the different ways of being. What I say about each is not the last word, nor my last word. But I deem it important to try to think of philosophy in its complex *togetherness* with its others. If it is charged that this is too ambitious, I think it is part of the nature of philosophical thought to be ambitious, even in its humble openness to being's otherness. If philosophy involves the mindful thought of being as metaxological, it deals with what as *other* is always, as it were, too much for it. But it is just this excess of otherness that we must patiently try to think. Likewise, since I see philosophical thought together with its others, I find it impossible hermetically to seal the mode of philosophical discourse itself. If philosophy is thought thinking itself and its others, just to that extent to be truly welcoming of the voice of the other means on occasion to be willing to voice one's own thought in the voice of the other. Then the voice of philosophy itself becomes plurivocal. Hence, in the voicing of philosophical thought, the voices of the aesthetic, the religious, and the ethical will inevitably sound through, even in their imagistic, urgent and singing form. In its own way this work tries to instantiate philosophically such a plurivocal thinking.[6]

I cannot now dwell on the complicated and important issue of the nature of philosophical language. Beyond what I said in the preface, I will say that there are no a priori limits on the character of this language. To insist on such limits is already to give expression to a secret will to conceptual domination, to insist that *the* voice is the voice of philosophy thinking itself and thinking of the others only in terms of itself. I see this as a betrayal of philosophy itself, in so far as it too requires the openness to otherness that is inherent in all genuine thinking. If someone should insist: this is not how philosophy *should* speak, one must reply: Who says so? The point surely is to become properly mindful of the ways of being and mind. Nor need such mindfulness exclude the laughter of thought, and indeed the willingness of philosophers to laugh at themselves.[7]

It is logicist dogmatism to insist that only a certain sparse diet of univocal categories is appropriate to aid us in the pursuit of philosophical mindfulness. If language must speak for and to the *Sache selbst*, and if this is metaxological, genuine language, including philosophical logos must always be potentially plurivocal. Moreover, our choice is not just between the frozen clarity of univocity and the flux-like confusion of equivocity. Dialectical logos is already richer and more complex than either of these two alternatives. We must expect as much from, indeed more from, the plurivocal thought that answers to the metaxological sense of being. It seems to me in fact that the great thinkers of the metaphysical tradition in their richest discourse always broke through the sterile alternation between a dogmatism of univocity and a skepticism of equivocity in their radical renewal of the double requirement of genuine thinking. Language that seeks to articulate philosophical fidelity to the energy of thought, not only tries to constitute its own integrity but also finds any drift to closure challenged by the matter itself, and hence is driven to acknowledge without intellectual rancor what may continue to resist its best efforts. And if some readers find my introduction too heavy, I plead the excuse that presently I am merely weighing anchor. My desire is to philosophize with a little *sprezzatura*. I hope to redeem this promise in the chapters to follow.

The reader will find at the end that the whole point is to return to certain elemental things that reveal being's intrinsic worth but that I cannot here anticipate. The work will be unabashedly philosophical but I remain convinced that genuine philosophical thought remains true to what is deepest in our humanity as articulated in the fundamental ways of being. The philosopher is himself a participant in the metaxological and as humanly participant cannot conceptually objectify in an absolute way the ontological ground that makes possible his own way of being and mind. This participation again imposes a plurivocal task on thought and discourse.[8]

Despite all the recent talk of philosophy's place in the conversation of mankind, a great difficulty with contemporary philosophy is that the human voice has become muffled in the conversation of the professionals. This is ironical since quite a bit of that professional talk ostensibly concerns itself with philosophy's relation to its others. The self-mediation of professional talk swamps the originary perplexity before otherness. Pascal has words to the effect that he sought an author but to his delight he found a human being. I know it is hard for philosophers to remain human beings, but in the intricate twistings of thought in this work as a whole, I have sought this hard simplicity.

Philosophy and Its Others:
On Ways of Being Philosophical

Philosophy's *Felo De Se*

Today thought is tempted to give itself up for lost in the dusk of philosophy's *felo de se*. I prefer to light a candle rather than curse the dark. We find a pervasive perplexity concerning the self-images of the philosopher as a plurality of possible paradigms vie for influence.[1] First I focus on a family of images by which philosophy, past and present, has defined itself. Philosophers have always been obsessed, critics will say narcissistically, with the question: What is philosophy? I do not want to ask the question merely abstractly, as if we could isolate philosophy from its interplay with its others. In a sense there is no "pure" philosophy, if this detaches it from all intermingling with other significant ways of being. Philosophical thought must do more than think itself, mediate with *itself*; it must try to think its others, enact its own metaxological intermediation with otherness. Certain individuals, like Socrates or Spinoza, have exemplified philosophical possibility, but I want to portray different configurations of human possibility that have been and still are crucial for philosophy. These are: the scholar, technician, scientist, poet, priest, revolutionary, hero, and sage.

These figures are illuminating in their own right and not as merely parasitical on philosophy. But philosophy does not just have *one* other, say science or religion, the two most often named. When it does restrict its concern to just one other, the risk it runs is malnourished thought. To be robust again it must allow that these figures make up a family of significant others, each an embodiment of mind as implicated in the quest of the ideal of philosophical wisdom. This chapter will be, as it were, a family album of sketches of philosophy and its others. While not unsystematic, it does not offer any closed system wherein plurality is reducible to one principle. Each figure is an inhabitant of the metaxological community of being, each is a flowering of the original energy of the human being as mindful, each is itself a potential mediator of the metaxological community of being. If philosophy

15

is defined in interplay with its others, it has no static univocal identity, but is potentially plurivocal in a metaxological way. There are a plurality of ways of being philosophical. We need to be reminded of this plurivocity of philosophy itself. In the following sketches I offer no complete account but enough to break open any freezing of philosophy into a univocal identity. This breaking open will also be an expansion of philosophy's "identity" by a remembrance of both its ancestral voices and its present practitioners.

As a mediating participant in the metaxological community of being, each of the figures mentioned (the scholar, technician, and so forth) exhibits something of the doubleness of thought as outlined in the introduction. All are in the middle, and the middle has a certain immediate otherness of being that calls for mediation. But this mediation is potentially double, namely, both self-mediation and intermediation with otherness. Each figure, we might say, is an image that both reveals and distorts the original, both captures and caricatures the wise man—meaning by the latter someone whose mindfulness is marked by the double mediation. This twofoldness will be reflected in a doubleness in the portraits. I will mark both an affinity and difference between philosophy and its others. Thus, we may avoid reducing the richness of human diversity, deny that philosophy ever completely discharges its debt to its others, while yet preserving the irreducibility of philosophy itself.

The point is not to ascribe defect to the others, but to see the contribution and limit of their mediation of the between. In the middle all figures are configurations of being mindful, but none covers or encapsulates the middle entirely. This is to be expected, but the danger with every configuration of mindful being is that it is tempted to reduce the middle to its own self-mediation. Such a reduction inevitably breaks down both in terms of the otherness of the others and the otherness of the middle itself. So in my portraits we will see this double movement: the immediate otherness of the middle as particularly mediated by a particular figure (e.g. the scientist); the impossibility that any self-mediation can be total, including philosophy's own mediations. I will say that philosophy has a special charge to be mindful of the open space of the between, the irreducible "inter" wherein all self-mediation and intermediation occurs.

My aim is to respond, sometimes directly, sometimes obliquely, to the striking feature of contemporary philosophy which is, as I said, a corrosive unsureness about its own very enterprise. Its practitioners appear to lack deep confidence in their calling, its procedures and purposes. Philosophy seems fatigued with itself. There have always been outside detractors, and traditionally philosophers have never lacked skepticism about themselves, but now they are their own most virulent scoffers. They wonder if their questions, as traditionally posed, are really genuine questions at all. Not surprisingly, the outsider ceases to take seriously what the insider seems to mock. In a self-reversion of skepticism, philosophy brings itself low, even contemplating the hara-kiri of thought, as least as traditionally conceived. One hears of a "post-philosophical" philosophy, as if philosophy were trying to outlive its own suicide—though as with such suicides, one wonders how serious they are, whether their dying is obliquely a pathetic plea for notice.

This fatigue with traditional thought surfaces regardless of scholastic allegiances. In Continental thought, many thinkers follow Heidegger and speak of the end of philosophy (this question actually stems from Hegel's legacy). In Anglo-American analysis, after an initial barrage against traditional metaphysics and a long infatuation with the new techniques of logic, the bloom finally fades from analytical thought, as its practitioners begin to question themselves, even to the point of philosophical euthanasia (Ernest Gellner's apt word). Philosophy becomes a problem to itself. It does so more radically in the Continental camp. In analytical thought the technicist nature of its practices can serve to muffle the urgency of the issue.[2]

This matter is not a mere indulgence of "metaphilosophy." If philosophers know not what they do, the suspicion surfaces of sham. What do philosophers do? The question looks elementary, even banal. Are there not many professionals who go by the title "philosopher"? Yet this excess of professionals is part of the problem. The professional is an initiate into a defined role; it is often custom and habit that make one such. The philosophical mind may atrophy in just this outward perfection of the professional ritual. At its best philosophy, I will say, is a way of being, a way of metaxological mindfulness. The difficulty is how to recognize those on this way. We do not call a person "religious" because he places "reverend" before his name, or honor as "poet" someone who produces much charming verse. We reserve the name "poet," "philosopher," "holy one" for those who exhibit the essentials of their calling, for those who epitomize its possibility. Their calling can be usurped by impersonators— versifiers, false prophets, sophists. The difficulty is not just one of abstract, general definition, but of the concrete discrimination of a kind of self: not what is the philosopher, but who is?[3]

Philosophy as Middle Mindfulness

Before turning more directly to the different figures, I remark on the traditional ideal of wisdom that is related to the sense of intermediate being I stress and to being mindful, the meaning of which will become clearer in the work as a whole. This ideal is not the exclusive concern of a "pure" philosophy, since every essential human possibility has a bearing on life as a whole, on the making meaningful of the whole, and so is implicated, as a mode of mindfulness, in the quest for wisdom. Being mindful, as thought thinking both itself and its other, is not identical with self-reflection, though of course, philosophy has claimed to pursue this quest in its own reflective terms. Here, on the one hand, guardians of the tradition make play with the etymology of *philosophia* and point out that *philos* and *sophia,* translate as "lover" (in the sense of *friend*) and "wisdom." Philosophy becomes a love of wisdom and the philosopher its friend. What marks him then is not the possession of wisdom but the mindful courting of it: the eros of thought is in scarch. On the other hand, those tired of the tradition will now dismiss this search of thought as a wild goose chase; the ideal will evoke a yawn; it is an old day dream. Some say: we want science, not wisdom. Others say: we seek revolution, not wisdom. Others again say: give us excitement, not boring wisdom. Wisdom is a stale ideal, old truth turned tedious.

Nevertheless, a mindful self must grant that something essential is here at stake. We want to discriminate—between the better and worse, the true, the sham, the philosopher, the sophist, the doctor, the quack. What grounds our discrimination? Can we know the false without some sense of the true? Can we separate worse and better without a sense, initially vague and indeterminate perhaps, of the best? Can we know imperfection except by contrast with the fullness it lacks, namely, perfection? We call on some implicit standard or standards by which we judge. Undoubtedly, we argue about their nature, but our argument itself is futile if not grounded in some presupposition of the ideal. It is the exigency of the enigmatic, implicit ideal that drives, articulates and makes reflectively intelligible our powers of discrimination. This is but to reiterate what thoughtful human beings have always held, namely, that some implicit ideal of wisdom is inherent in our humanness. Though it be difficult to say explicitly what philosophical wisdom exactly is, nevertheless we are haunted by its call.

Here philosophy has always had problems about beginning in a noncircular way. My response is that we are always already in the middle, where the immediate otherness of being is in some measure mediated. We *find ourselves* in the middle, having already begun. Yet we are capable of both beginning again and being mindful of the actuality that is to be mediated in the middle. Philosophy is an attempt at mindfulness of what is at work in the middle, considered as the metaxological community of being. Nor need this attempt be circular in a vicious way, in that being's otherness may always break into, break down the insufficiencies of all our self-mediations. The problem of beginning is one of becoming mindful of what is already at work in the middle.

But the contemporary skeptic shifts uneasily at words like "the best," "the perfect," even "the true." He has long breathed the acid air of post-Nietzschean nihilism and his eye for ideals has grown jaundiced. He is a "master of modern suspicion" or a deconstructionist, or a Rortian weary of those voices in the "conversation of mankind" whose inexcusable fault is that they spoke *earlier* in the philosophical tradition. He pours sour milk not only on the existence of philosophical wisdom but also on its very possibility. He says: it does not, it cannot exist; we must give it up. But this philosophical denial of philosophy harbors incoherence. Must one not have some sense of the denied ideal to justify one's denial of it to everyone else? Must not this skeptical negation sprout from some concealed comprehension of what is really at stake in the middle, that is, from a hidden wise mindfulness? Indeed, the skeptic should not be able to distinguish the philosopher and sophist, were it not that he plays the philosopher's part himself. We must presume him to have in mind something of the standard of discrimination he denies to others.

Or suppose you object: the ideal is only "in the mind," only an ideal; it does not, cannot exist in "reality." This objection is beside the point, or rather it confirms the point in this essential respect: it is just in the nature of mind as participant in middle being, in being mindful, and not elsewhere, that we are to look for this ideal. Nor can you say every philosophy is a fake unless you know the real thing. Otherwise your skepticism is really dogmatism: skepticism in regard to others, dogmatism in regard to yourself. For *you* must be the genuine philosopher, if you say all others are phony. Or are you willing to turn skepticism back on yourself, carry your misology to its logical conclusion, and concede that you must be included in the company of fakes? Very well then, I talk to someone else.[4]

To carry misology to its logical conclusion is already to reveal the self-contradiction in practice. Indeed, there is no properly consistent logical reason why skeptical misology should be thus logically consistent. The dogmatism of this skepticism consists in applying the standard of logical consistency to others, while allowing oneself the privilege of a misology that inconsistently tries to exempt itself. When this contradiction is pointed out to the skeptical misologist, too often all he does is squirm logically—that is to say, squirm illogically. However, my main point is not to dismiss skepticism *simpliciter* but the secretly dogmatic skepticism that in effect closes thought to otherness. There is a *fertile skepticism* that opens thought to otherness in the very act of its own self-questioning. Such skepticism is metaxological. For it says: I might be wrong, hence I listen to the other. By contrast, a fruitless skeptic only validates the barrenness of thought he anticipates in the other when he says: the *other* is always in principle suspect of wrong, hence all I will hear is the clever voice of my own thought, congratulating itself on its own debunking powers.

We can be more than sterile skeptics without becoming equally sterile dogmatists. We know we do not possess the truth, yet the truth is somehow already with us, showing us that we belong to what we lack, for otherwise we could not search it out. If we are seekers, we must have some sense of what we seek. We do not merely lack our other; we long for it, and so already love it, even though not claiming it. Philosophy is such a longing, indeed belonging, in which we are already friends of truth, companions. Truth is never a possession, a property—we do not lay claim to it; it claims us. This again mirrors our nature as in-between beings, beings in the intermediate. One cannot either dogmatically assert wisdom, nor be skeptically void of it. Between its complete absence and full presence, we are gifted with its promise. The quest of philosophy emerges in this middle, the metaxological community of being, where we can either renege on the ideal or remain loyal to what, after all, constitutes our perplexing core.[5]

This intermediate character is evident in that one can *recognize*, be *struck* by perfection, even though one does not realize it oneself, nor possess the power to attain it. At once we are bound to the ideal and separated from it. We move back and forth between our poverty here and our hunger to be full. We are a commingling of these extremities, weaving together the opposites in our being. Caught in a tension between extremes, tugged in both directions, our being is both dynamic and ambiguous, centered between the limits of negation and affirmation, at once capable of apathy and ecstasy. One can betray this tension and settle for a contentment less complex. The middle becomes mid-dling in the sense of mediocre. We do not possess perfection, so we refuse even to dream of it; we desert the struggle and make a tired peace with our shabby selves. But that one does not realize perfection is no cause to disparage it and dismiss it as empty impossibility. This is to excuse oneself from the search and to belittle greatness because one lacks it oneself. Such a repudiation can spring from rancor: what one lacks, one will allow to no one else. Not even the promise of greatness is granted. One concedes failure before even attempting the deed. Those who dare to dream of perfection find themselves obstructed by the discouragements of the already defeated.

We may be unsure about absolute answers, but we still have the mindful asking of the fundamental questions. Philosophy is just this mindful asking. Out of the complex ambiguity of the middle, fundamental questioning emerges. As a self-reflecting openness to otherness, as thought thinking *doubly,* that is, of both itself and its other, fundamental questioning extends to both beginnings and ends, first and final things. Though its reach be limited, its aim is to be as comprehensive as possible, reaching out towards the whole of being in its otherness. Some thinkers have denied that we can answer such questions, but no such denial will ever still their asking. For the point is not to amass the minutiae of things but to comprehend, and if this is not possible, at least to name the essential.

As Jaspers reminds us, philosophy poses *limit* questions. The most elemental of these concern the middle and its extremes. They put the question to the origin (*archē*), the end or perfection (*telos*), as manifest from the complex middle, the *metaxu*. Why something rather than nothing? In the between I was not mindfully there at my own origin, and may not be mindfully there at my ceasing. Nevertheless I must ask about these recalcitrant others that show the potential nothingness of middle being. Why then our struggle for significance at all, when we encounter in the middle such surds that always seem conquering, always in excess of our small clearing of light? Are we privileged guests of being or merely the quintessence of dust? Such questions do not seek infinite information about things but ponder the being of all beings, the intelligibility of being, the benevolence of being.

As mindful of ultimacy, such questions call for more than the lip serviced reiteration of truths already domesticated. The philosopher has to ask the extreme questions, discontented till perplexity is pushed to the boundary, either to be answered there, to be exhausted there, or perhaps closed to further pursuit. As a self-reflecting openness to the otherness of being, indeed as struck into openness by this otherness, philosophy in the intermediate is at war with the idols of closed thought. So it is double in this way too: it is both the sheer disquiet of thought, a not-being-at-home with being, and also a quest of ultimacy, of a radical being-at-home with being. The situation is perhaps more complex in this sense: as tending towards the extremes of thought, philosophy cannot be such as to desert the truth of the middle. Hence its questions are not merely theoretical, abstract speculations that soar beyond the heavens and descend beneath our earth, as in the charge of the Athenians against Socrates. Its questions cannot be severed from where we are ethically placed. Some fit is asked between the thought of a self and its doing. We rightly expect the deed of a genuine self somehow to exemplify its deepest and most essential thoughts. Philosophy is not only a metaxological way of thinking about being, but a metaxological way of being according to thought.

Nietzsche said that the philosopher should be the chief example of his thinking. Wisdom demands the truthfulness of the self, not just an inventory of abstract, disembodied "truths." It calls out to be embodied, calls on the self to be true, hold true. It insists on witness. Mindfulness of human ends is necessary, discriminating and just judgment about better and worse. To be justified is to be willing to offer an accounting of oneself. Wisdom demands that, when necessary and so far as is possible, the self give the reason, articulate the grounds of its judgment (*logon didonai*). It communicates itself not by the power of force, not by dogmatic insistence, but by the justice of its reason.

Philosophy and the Scholar

The first figure I consider, the scholar, has been seen in the past as a realization of the ideal, an embodiment of wisdom. Often he belonged to a privileged, esoteric caste and was not always separated from the poet and priest—all were enveloped in the aura of sacred learning and speech. With the post-scientific scholar, this aura has vanished. I will work my way back to these archaic others but, in its present professionalization, philosophy is sometimes identified with academic scholarship. One thinks of the nineteenth century humanist scholar who was swept along in the wash of post-Hegelian historicism; for him philosophy is the history of philosophy. In the twentieth century a more up-to-date version can be found among hermeneutical philosophers. By contrast with the sober philology of these more conservative historians of ideas, we find the Corybantic textualists among the deconstructionists. Yet these too remain textual scholars, albeit chic "postmodern" terrorist scholars, philological guerrillas armed with the catchcries of the avant-garde. This species is avid to be seem as *scholasticus exoticus*. In this frenzy of Dionysian hermeneutics we do detect again the fatigue of philosophy?

In the last century, Schopenhauer and his philosophical son Nietzsche (his word for the fatigue was "decadence") attacked the confusion of philosophy and historical scholarship. With all due respect for the latest research techniques, their strong words are still green. The savant is not the pedant—not even when masked as a deconstructionist son of Nietzsche. For middle being manifests a certain immediate otherness: the complex otherness of being is given and we are in its midst. The scholar too inhabits the middle but he comes on the scene late—that is when the middle has already been massively mediated by human texts. He does not look on the immediate givenness of the middle with the originating ontological perplexity before being's otherness: his mind is already mediated through the mediations, that is books, of others. His mind lives in these mediations that now become *his* middle: that they are mediations of *being's otherness* is not always to the fore. The textual mediation (book) or participant mediator (the scholar himself) stand in the place of the ontological middle.

But lest my own text begins in too mediated a way, let me sketch a contrast with a little more immediacy to it. Consider this contrast of thinker and scholar. The first opens straight on life and thinks through his direct encounter with what is; the world perplexes him, precipitates his questioning. As he thinks from his own being, so also he judges; if he did not think for himself, he would not think at all. He stands or falls on the genuineness of his thought about being. He does not garner his insights at a remove, but prides himself on the firsthand character of his concerns. He is able to say "I think" and need not always quote another.

The second individual does not go directly to life but to his library. This is the book philosopher. Between being and the scholar falls the book. He must think at a distance, that is, through the intermediary of what he reads.

(This "reading" now preens itself with the title: "the textual revolution.") The book becomes a repository of wisdom, a treasury into which he dips to rouse and quiet his queries. If this mandarin lacked a text to think about, he might not think at all. An elemental question is something unsheltering, but the book is a fine buffer—one wraps one's cogitations in the warm wool of scholarship. The thinker stamps thought with a peculiar vision; the scholar researches the opinions of others, appeals to the authorities and vanishes in quotation. The first kind speaks with witness, for his thought is in his heart and soul and mind; the other is nothing without his notes.

When philosophy and scholarship are identified, the former becomes a body of doctrines written down and preserved in the books of past thinkers. We must study these works with the scholar as our mentor, for his immense learning gives him authority. Soaked in erudition, master of minutiae, he has status as the specialist. Laymen stand in silent awe, like the rustic idiots of Goldsmith's poem: "And still they gaz'd, and still their wonder grew /That one small head could carry all he knew." Is this enough? Arrogant Heraclitus was one of the first to say no, contemptuously dismissing learning without wisdom.[6] Book lore will not do. (I searched myself, Heraclitus said.) Scholarly studies of other's texts offer us encyclopedic surveys of positions, past and present. But such massive studies can still be void of philosophic spirit, like colossal temples full of expectant worshippers but empty of real presence.

It would be stupid to disparage such study. But for the thinker it is a means to an end, namely, that of thinking for himself of being's otherness; for the scholar it can become an end in itself. The great thinkers are the philosophical originals. They are models of what below I will call "heroic thinking": voices that still ring strongly in the "conversation of mankind," voices to be heard in the spirit, not of antiquarian devotion but a blend of critical and monumental history (to use Nietzsche's terms). They open the mind to its most elemental perplexity before being in its otherness, inviting us to participate critically, perhaps creatively in that ontological perplexity. The scholar usefully delves into secret corners, expands acquaintance with quirky and exotic things, secretly feels he discharges a noble office. He is duty-bound, working according to a restrained, economical order. Compared to this, there is a kind of profound uselessness about the great philosophers. Here we find spirits generous with thought beyond utilitarian concerns, willing to spend themselves lavishly, not measure out thought parsimoniously. Thought thinking its other is moved by excess, by love of transcendence. Safety and caution mark the scholar, risk and adventure the thinker. Scholarship can dilute this suffering of thought, but also can dim its exuberant audacity.

But scholars will stiffen at being teased. In the mask of irony they fear the face of mischief.[7] Very well, let the mockery fall on me. I look at myself and laugh. What caricature do I see? I see the solemn face, the grave countenance. Does this face hide reserves of depth? I see the eyes, strained after long looking. But I notice an owlish aspect. Why should I be disconcerted? After all, philosophy's ancient symbol was the owl of Minerva, that nocturnal bird that, in Hegel's famous phrase, only takes flight at dusk. But are these scholar's eyes owlish, wise, from a weary peering into the dark night itself? Unlike the owl's dead stare, these eyes blink too much. It is the dust of archives that irritates these eyes. These eyes blink with weary alertness, nor for vigilance in the dark, but for the ceaseless inspection of texts.

The scholar is often made a figure of fun amid a gathering of the unlearned. Awkward, shy, hesitant, we sigh for the study where texts can be handled after our time and will. We can restrain the great books from retorting impertinently. We are at home, however, at a congress of the learned; among our own, we breathe freer; if we alight on a fellow specialist, we soar. But even here we are watchful. We do not want to be neglected by our colleagues, those rivals for position we also fear. Our publications are our weapons; both a means to promotion and a soother of vanity. We jealously guard our specialty. We will admit new workers to our vineyard, but these must first be initiated, "trained": this means, wayward impulses must be smothered; the student must learn reverence for the teacher. Other rivals must be met in duels of words. The scholar practices for combat by becoming an expert in the short, sarcastic put down.

We stand on respectabilities. Writings, too, must observe the respectabilities: footnotes, bibliography, all to standard form. We are not the flamboyant monarchs of mind's realm but its sober and solid civil servants. We are at ease with the already accepted, the already canonized; we are not always best to judge the emergence of the new. It is a delight to watch our faces relaxing when someone brings up an old chestnut. It affords the opportunity for a favorite form of boldness: to improvise a variation on the familiar. How does this affect philosophy? Philosophers who were originals when alive later risk becoming dead models for imitation. When a living original appears, if he is not killed with silence, first he is described as an upstart. When times makes him less startling, he is slowly fitted into the pantheon of past philosophers, that is, he is mumified. This is perhaps to be expected. How else can we make philosophy into an "object of research"?

The danger here is that the double movement of mind in the metaxological—as thought thinking itself and its other—gets reduced to a simpler, *scholastic* self-mediation. The result can be a *closed self-mediating circle* of initiated professionals whose talk smothers the originating astonishment of thought's self-reflective openness to otherness. The elemental perplexity that opens the mind to the otherness of being gets caught in an endless circulation of texts out of which the real question never breaks. Even the very otherness of great texts is tamed.[8]

Strangely enough with the terrorist textualist, the deconstructionist, we get something similar. We get a parody of Aristotle's thought thinking itself: texts think themselves through the proxy specialist, the textualist. There is no outside, no other to the text, *il n'y a pas de hors-texte,* it is said; nor indeed can we find the perplexed "I" thinking being's otherness (for the textualist puts *himself* "under erasure"). But this is to put the cart before the horse. What is other to the text? The other of the text is the originating astonishment of thinking in its encounter with being's otherness: it is the mindful encounter with being's otherness that grounds and waters the stunning articulation of great philosophical texts. Without this intermediation with being's otherness, there would be no texts at all in the first place and the textualist himself would have nothing to do. He would be properly "under erasure," that is, actually be nothing.

The scholar comes *after*: when the original work is done, we sift the remains. Our task is commentary, not creation. As a kind of simulacrum of the philosopher, we do not set to thinking on our own; first we need to read. Mind is reactive, not creative; at best it conserves the traces of creation. We do not sit besides a blazing fire but stoke the dying embers with a long poker. Satisfied with a gentle, soothing warmth, we have no wish to be set on fire ourselves. But philosophy is not the cultivation of polite letters. It is a living of dangerous perplexity that might be consumed, reduced to ashes by its own doubt (I think of Kierkegaard's Johannes Climacus).[9] It is absolutely essential to know the thought of others, for philosophy is thought thinking both itself and its other. But the philosopher is never just an historian: other philosophers are his spiritual kin, not "objects of research." Philosophers themselves belong to a metaxological community of thought about being in which they are *philoi*, friends of truth. Such a community of others cannot be objectified without remainder into an "object of research." Nor, for that matter, can the plurivocity of metaxological thought be identified with the endless dissemination of textual interpretations. The "between" of the metaxological is not the "inter" of intertextuality.

The scholar often has modest thought on his own behalf, and so follows like an acolyte the philosopher he makes his "life work" (as the Germans say). To be a philosopher is to insist that no one else does one's thinking for one, that, as Kant defined enlightenment, one dares to know (*sapere aude!*). The scholar is a halfway house between the desire to think for himself and the necessity he undergoes of having to react to the work of others. It is easier to comment on, indeed deconstruct, the work of others than to create one's own. Scholars are the valets of thinkers. They are like those who smoke only when they can borrow someone else's cigarettes. Scholars school like those pilot fish that live to service a shark. The deconstructionist pilot thinks he is the shark.[10]

Philosophy and the Technician

A second self-image for philosophy, as prevalent today as the scholar (though perhaps the latter's antipode), is the technician. Its prevalence is related to the "cybernetic revolution," though its roots are much older. Indeed it testifies to a recurring possibility of thought. Initially what drives us to philosophize is not that we have the answers but that we are nagged by fundamental questions. We find ourselves inhabitants of an ambiguous world where being's otherness initially hides its meaning and puts us at a loss. We are forced to question its significance, forced to question ourselves. Within the enveloping opaqueness of the middle there breaks forth the desire to know. Nor does this first arise from some act of self-conscious choice; it surges up spontaneously and unbidden, an imperative of our being as an ineluctable orientation to truth. But our rejoinder to the given opaqueness of being can be developed diversely. In one development thinking becomes a matter of technique.

Thus, the technicist mind begins by granting the givenness of being as posing a problem and even grants ambiguity as its starting point. But, for its end, it aims to be rid of ambiguity. Impatient with all obscurity, and especially the resistance of the middle to conceptualization, it devises its techniques to eradicate the darkness of being, indeed to subject the world to an order of mind's own invention. It wills to subordinate being's otherness to the self-mediation of instrumental mind. So it seeks to change our initial condition of confusion into clarity—clarity controlled and exploited by our own will. It may even hold out the promise to be the royal road to rational enlightenment. The technicist mind seduces us with secure, definite procedures for tackling issues, procedures to *guarantee* univocal solutions to troubling ambiguity, unambiguous rules which, if only we follow them, will lead us from the labyrinth of perplexity. In terms of the fourfold sense of being I outlined in the introduction, it wants to put *univocal* clarity in place of what it sees as the *equivocity* of our being in the middle.

For reasons such as these philosophers have always been tempted by technique, and particularly in our era. The line of thought runs like this. There are many specialized techniques for dealing with different problems; but suppose there was one supreme technique, the technique of techniques, as it were, the instrumental thought of all thought? Would not such a supreme technique provide the skeleton key to unclose every lock, to master all the opaque otherness of being? If we possessed the mastery of this supreme technique would we not have the capability of becoming wise, in fact, be virtually wise? Thus the technician aspires to become a cybernetic god.[11] Indeed, at the beginning of contemporary philosophy, there was widespread faith that logic might provide this supreme technique. Logic might encompass all the fundamental questions; those it could not encompass could be dismissed as unimportant. Philosophers have always been attracted to logic to the degree that equivocation disturbs them and univocal thought consoles them. Logic is rigorous in its application, imposes its conclusions on all, purges thought of every trace of eccentricity, is imperiously brusque with otherness that resists its univocal categories. If we submit to it, our minds are placed under restraints which, in turn, necessitate conclusions on which all can, indeed must come to agreement.

Other, more human motives drew the philosopher to logic in our time. For one, it rescued him from the scholar's archives and allowed mind a freer play with intellectual puzzles.[12] It also assured him of a position of cultural importance, since now he might claim to have the key common to all structures of meaning. So, too, it gave him confidence that he was not wasting his time on inconclusive and perhaps empty "metaphysical" debates. Not surprisingly he willingly takes on the cast of the technical specialist. Thus, we find a proliferation of journals of "technical" philosophy, of "exact" philosophy, as if philosophy were like an esoteric branch of higher mathematics or computer science. Exact knowing replaces absolute knowing. In other cases, the philosopher takes his cue from the technological character of modern society and models himself on the engineer. He becomes an operator imbued with purpose: to reduce the equivocations of the everyday world, to dispel its confusion, and to reconstruct, notably like Carnap, the world according to the austere univocity of his logical techniques.[13]

From one point of view philosopher and technician are not dissimilar. The former tries to understand being rationally, while technique itself seems to epitomize rationality. A technique is an ordered procedure, governed by well defined rules, efficient and precise in its operations. Indeed, when we speak of "rationalizing," say, an industrial process, this equation of technique and reason is clear. Here to "rationalize" ("to make rational") means just to subject the process to technique, and so to shear it of excess (the "irrational") and control it more economically and methodically. And is this not what the philosopher claims to do: to rationalize what is, to make rational sense of being in its thereness? Under the aegis of technique, to think philosophically would mean to reduce being to conformity with rational rules, spare and simple, to conformity with a kind of logical calculus. Such rules would appear to be the "essentials" of rationality, while the excess pruned off by technique would be merely "accidental," that is, irrelevant in the final reckoning of reason. A notable example is Leibniz who sought all his life, unsuccessfully as it turned out, for a *mathesis universalis* that would provide the basis to explain all things.

The desire for such explanation has been a recurring dream. It has a nobility as mind's search for lucidity, when technique does not tyrannize over philosophical vision, when rather the vision shines through the technique, using it in the services of a larger view (as it does in Leibniz, indeed in Plato).[14] But what if technique *reduces* the complex otherness of being in the middle? Why must mindful lucidity be identified with conceptual univocity? In the middle our choice of logos is not exhausted by an "either/or" between univocity and equivocity. What if the technician swallows the philosopher and ceases to be mindful of the larger, perhaps incalculable issues, issues that resist reduction to univocity? Is not philosophical vision blurred just in this excess of univocal clarity?

Two such issues arising in the middle concern origins and ends. Thus, if we ask what *originates* any technique, we must answer: never just another technique. Rather it is mind's inventiveness acting *before* the rules of technique have been formalized. The origin of technique is itself nontechnical. Philosophy first helps produce technical rationality, technique does not first produce philosophy. Technique, of course, may be an instrument of philosophy (*organon* is Aristotle's word for logic). But this means that there is a sense of reason, philosophical mindfulness, that is *prior* to and *exceeds* technical rationality and its predeliction for univocity. This sense of reason tends to remain unexamined if we just confine ourselves within technique's domain. Mind's metaxological intermediation with otherness is reduced to technicist thought thinking itself in the self-mediation of instrumental reason. The technical mind, be it programmed in a controlled, faultless fashion, must still live off the leap of creation that strikes out into new, uncharted territory. Once reason has been reduced to technique, the technical mind cannot rationally explain that leap, for that leap is outside or other to technique.

In this sense, there is something blind about technical reason, since to even function at all, it must presuppose, indeed be parasitical upon a nontechnical sense of mind (see chapters 5 and 6). The univocal mind is grounded in a mindfulness, ultimately metaxological, that is not, cannot be reduced to univocity; if the univocal mind denies this ground, it undercuts itself—as tends to happen when the will to reduce all being to univocity tries to be comprehensive, that is, totalizing. When the philosopher is only a technician, we sense that despite the surface of precision, the spirit has fled. We catch the faint sound of philosophy giving off a cybernetic death rattle. This is part of what Heidegger meant by the end of philosophy.

A similar consideration applies to ends. Technique gives us "know how," but not, as it were, "know why." It tells us how we can do certain things but not why we should. "Know how" is by no means incompatible with philosophical mindfulness but alone it cannot realize this. The mind as metaxologically mediating is not a mere instrumentality; it is, let us call it, a "finality." I may possess all the techniques in the world but may still use them unwisely. Wisdom, in its ethical sense, I must already possess in order to get the genuinely best from the technique. Thus, when asked about the good, the technician tends to answer in accord with the prevailing opinion, that is, uncritically. He easily becomes a lackey of ideology, not the guardian of free mind. We expect of the philosopher a certain truthfulness and integrity. No technique will ever originate the potential for these ideals nor constitute their actuality. Not surprisingly, modern technology has no ethical difficulty serving equally the rival ideologies of communism and capitalism. It offers itself neutrally as an instrument. It is a means to an end, not an end itself; the end is dictated from elsewhere. I am not saying that technique is absolutely neutral, morally speaking, for its very essence fosters a mentality that has serious ethical repercussions. Nevertheless it has the character of a chameleon, making it so plastic to alternative ethical views as to indicate that its lack, at core, is the absence of guiding philosophical mindfulness.[15] Indeed this chameleon character is strangely the opposite of the rigidity of its insistence on univocity. The univocal mind, as it were, harbors its own *internal other*, namely, a susceptibility to a secret equivocity that it mistakenly believed it has conquered.

Often the technician is motivated by fear of failure (see chapter 5); more than anything else "results" are required. But excessive anxiety about "results" can be antithetical to philosophical thinking. Certainly in the past philosophers have been willing to risk failure to raise the essential questions, no matter how intractable they prove to be. Indeed there may be questions concerning being's recalcitrant otherness on which thought must *break*, questions nevertheless essential to pursue (as will emerge in this work as a whole). There is a thinking in excess of technique, a thinking that metaxologically opens to the excess of otherness. Wonder (*thaumazein*), Plato said, is the pathos, the passion of philosophy and its very source, but the instrumental mind tends to stifle this source. Nietzsche claimed to philosophize with a hammer; the technician is other. He thinks with a metallic, better, microchip mind; he philosophizes with a word processor.

Philosophy and the Scientist

A third significant other is the scientist. The technician and scientist are especially linked in our time, hence some of my previous remarks apply here too. Thus when we invoke "science," its twin, "technology," trips invariably behind, as if they were bonded by a marriage of sorts. This is to be expected in that modern science is the theoretical side of an outlook on being, the practical side of which finds expression in modern technology. The desire to reduce being's otherness to clear and distinct univocity is at work in both. This outlook was envisaged by sixteenth and seventeenth century thinkers like Descartes and Bacon who helped initiate and consolidate the spirit of modern science. At its inception modern science intended to be not just speculative but useful. If we can scientifically understand nature's secrets, we can intervene in nature, control its otherness, redirect its course in accordance with desire. Clearly Bacon puts it: knowledge is power. Similarly, Descartes dreamed that the new science would make man, in his famous phrase, "the master and possessor of nature." The marriage of science and technology was not made in heaven, but it was made with the vision of a surrogate heaven on earth. The priest promises perfection in an afterwards, in an elsewhere. The scientist and technician seek to redeem this promise differently by harnessing our native powers and engineering their betterment here and now in the middle, and perhaps even their perfection.

With Descartes this was still a dream; *now* due to science's success, the scientist, like the technician, has come to enjoy enormous prestige. If the technician is taken to epitomize efficient making, the scientist is seen as the new high priest of valid knowing. Science seems to provide the touchstone of all knowledge; not unnaturally, the philosopher feels the urge to remake himself in the scientist's image. The wish to realize science in pursuit of wisdom is as old as Plato's *epistēmē*; the claim to realize science and so to possess wisdom is as recent as Hegel's *Wissenschaft*. In the twentieth century, both analytical and Continental philosophy are different heirs of Kant's will to set philosophy on the secure path of science. Analytical philosophy, at least in its earlier phases, sought to emulate the "hard" sciences like mathematics and physics. In Continental philosophy, the most strenuous advocate is perhaps Husserl with his desideratum of philosophy *als strenge Wissenschaft*. But the prevalence of the scientific paradigm is nowhere more evident than in orthodox Anglo-American thought, where the philosophy of science has been a cottage industry for decades.

There is an irony here. Originally science referred simply to organized knowledge, and in ways was coextensive with philosophy. But what we now call "science" is a more specialized activity that began to emerge around the seventeenth century. Modern science is originally a creation of modern philosophy, such that up to recently natural science was called "natural philosophy." But if science is an offspring of modern philosophy, it is one which in time threatened its parent. Eventually, in a reversal of priority, the parent wanted to imitate the child. Comtean positivism even held that philosophy was but a passing phase in the growth of mind, to be made obsolescent when science came to maturity.[16] The scientifically enlightened child displaces the parent still in thrall to residual metaphysical obscurantism and cellared piety.

The philosopher looks to find a place for himself, but often this is a diminished place, compared to its ancient privileges. Indeed, when he presents himself as a kind of scientist, he is often vehemently opposed to what was traditional, ancient in philosophy. The great philosophers of the past cease to the heroes of thought and become like dinosaurs: monumental creatures of their time but doomed to extinction, outsize creatures we can now reconstruct only as skeletons. Since now science is the core, philosophy becomes a fringe activity. Technically it is called a "meta" discipline; but this means that the real truth is an *always elsewhere other*. The closest the philosopher gets to the scientist is to provide some second-order analysis of the concepts scientists use. He has no vision of his own to offer, no outlook on being justified in its own right. The scientist alone has eyes for reality, while he, the philosopher, has eyes only for the scientist. Inevitably he succumbs to an inferiority complex before science's success.

A stock explanation often offered for this success is *method*. Scientific method offers ordered and common procedures for meeting difficulties, and so provides a pledge of progress. Result can be added to result, and a gradual accumulation of knowledge can ensue. Again this is tied to the ideal of univocity. Thus, science shies off imponderables that may never be resolved; by observation and experiment, it tackles definable problems it can solve. Traditionally, philosophy seemed to lack such a method, and to be always racked with garrulous disputes. It does not yield any progressive accumulation of information and wastes mind in questions recalcitrant to rationalization. Since Descartes the search for a philosophical method has been a major preoccupation. Descartes' strategy was: reduce the complex to the simple. The irreducible simples are then treated like univocal atoms, perfectly perspicuous to the light of reason. Having extruded all equivocation or ambiguity by complete enumeration, later Descartes wants to reconstruct the complex out of the now methodologically univocalized simples. The complex whole, as scientifically reconstructed, becomes a synthesized univocal complex. To the extent that scientific method tries to cover the totality of our being in the middle, the metaxological community of being is reconstructed as such a synthetic univocal complex. This may give us the sense (ultimately spurious) that we are masters and possessors of nature; in face we are "masters" only of being as a univocally reduced objectification, not of being in its full metaxological otherness.

This obsession with method has been recently attacked, by Gadamer in Continental thought, by Feyerabend in Anglo-American analysis, to cite but two well-known instances. The charge of lack of progress can also be equivocal. If philosophy is the mindful asking of essential questions, perhaps there are never ready-made answers that can be encapsulated in univocal categories, hence packaged and transmitted through time, like mail handled through the post. Even the hermeneutical mail we receive from the past is ambiguous and requires mindful interpretation. It is an accomplishment even to properly ask the essential questions that mediate the opening of thought to being in its metaxological otherness. No genuine philosopher can accept answers ready-made from others: this is simply the nature of the philosophical enterprise as a metaxological dialogue. This may seem to confirm the prejudice that philosophy is just sophisticated, not to say sophistical garrulousness. The deeper meaning is that each age and every individual must struggle, in the overdetermined ambiguity of the middle, to renew for itself a mindfulness of the essential questions. Nothing, not even scientific method, can stand proxy for this struggle.[17]

I am far from denying the genuine bond between philosopher and scientist. This lies in their common commitment to the spirit of questioning. Both place great store by our powers of mind; both hold that we can, ought to, and must attempt to understand the world; both willingly open themselves to the world as it presents itself to mind. Each is skeptical of the scholar's predilection for being predigested in texts; neither is satisfied to question at a too textually mediated remove. Again, both share a common refusal to bow the neck before absurdity. Both are inquiring approaches to being which do not degrade intelligence, and which embody the hope that, should we exercise intelligence, the world may show itself as intelligible. Yet even in their kinship, the spirit of philosophical questioning takes on a different twist. Science is a complex blend of mediating reason and immediate experience; philosophy does not repudiate either reason or experience, but arising from the different questions it asks, it constitutes a different synthesis of the two, and hence a different mindfulness of metaxological being.

If we return to questions of origins and ends, a philosopher is potentially a radical and extremist. Consider the philosophical inquiry into the grounds of science itself. The scientist trusts that the world is intelligible and that, in the long run, it will reveal its latent intelligibility. The philosopher need be no enemy of reason but he does query the status of this trust in reason. For mind itself may be pluriform. What significance does mind as scientific reason possess? Might it be just one net of abstractions we throw over being to buffer ourselves against nonsense? Or alternatively: why do thinking selves, human beings as reflectively mindful, find it all but impossible to rest content when things appear absurd? More radically still with Nietzsche: what is the value of truth itself? Immediately we ask such questions about the significance of science we cease to be scientists and are marked by a mindfulness other than the scientific. We inhabit the middle with this different mindfulness. Where the scientist tries to be rationally conscious about things in the world, the philosopher tries to be rationally self-conscious, not only of things, not only of himself, but of other human activities, including science itself. The concern of philosophy is not primarily an objective investigation of finite things within the middle, but of what it means to mindfully inhabit the middle, a habitation as much aesthetic, religious and ethical, as scientific.

For all the scientist's curiosity, his questioning stops before the very being of the world. He takes that being as given and confines himself to discovering the workings of beings as there. ("Workings" is a blatant understatement of the astonishingly intricate structures, patterns, regularities and so forth that things exhibit in themselves and in relation to other things, and that science lays bare.) His is not the metaphysical astonishment at the sheer fact that in the middle there is anything at all, being rather than nothing. Heidegger is entirely correct to try to reawaken mindfulness of this very old and always new wonder, this ageless astonishment at being that is prior to and outlives all scientific objectifications. Despite his complex probing and exploration of the world, the scientist takes its being for granted. *What* things are, not *that* they are: this engages his interest.

In addition to being's otherness in its sheer ontological givenness as opposed to ontic working, there is also an *inward* otherness to selfhood, an excess of the thinking "I." In the metaxological we are also questions to *ourselves*. In accounting for the complex intelligibility of things, can the scientist account for himself?[18] Can he qua scientist give self-knowledge? He teases out the riddles of nature, but he cannot account for himself in exactly the same way. The reason is this. The scientist himself, as thinking about things, is not just another thing that can be subjected to science, as can the objects in the world. The thinking of the scientist is not itself an object of scientific thinking. I am not saying that the scientist cannot be investigated scientifically. He can, but only in the third person and not in the first person, as a "what," not a "who," as an "It" and not as the "I" itself that is thinking the scientific self. The thinking "I" as thinking scientifically is not, cannot be, the object scientifically thought. The scientist's greatest strength, namely, his objectivism, runs this great risk, namely, the self-forgetfulness of the scientist himself. Neither the otherness of being that surrounds us in the middle, nor the self's own inward otherness can be completely objectified.

Further, science might describe the world but can it prescribe how we ought to be or act? Science is not ethics but rather the product of a certain kind of ethics: one which holds that we *ought* to be rational, *ought* to be faithful to observation, *ought* to follow scientific method. There is no univocal science of science itself nor of the ends of man; to consider these an other mindfulness is required. It is not surprising that, contrary to its critical beginnings, contemporary science can sometimes coexist with a conformist attitude. In the Communist block, for instance, the mathematical and natural sciences can be seriously pursued without challenge to the status quo but the humanities and liberal arts are not so neutral. From this results the suspicion of science as being a one-sided rationalism that attenuates a sense of the whole. By contrast, philosophy makes a claim on the self, contests the ideals by which it lives and so implicates it as a whole. Science need not always so challenge us, especially when, as now, it is in the ascendancy. Of itself, it does not create certain values but is itself the product of values that are accepted on grounds which are nonscientific, precisely because they are prior to science. What is sometimes called the "scientific world-view" or "scientism" is not an example of science. It is a philosophy that accepts the values that generate science, and the philosophical consequences it thinks follow for us. Without some philosophy, science is inarticulate about its own significance within the economy of life. For science too is *within* the middle, and as one formation of mind there, it, too, is defined by *its others* and its metaxological relation to them.

Though implicitly open to the whole after an objectivistic fashion, science is always a theoretical abstraction, never an absolute facsimile of the whole. This has been recognized by analytical philosophers, indeed mirrored in the difference between the early and late Wittgenstein. In reaction to the "scientism" of positivism and even earlier efforts to logically reconstruct all of meaning, the justified recalcitrance of the "ordinary" world to such logicist imperialism is granted. Likewise, in Continental philosophy the ideal of *strenge Wissenschaft*, indeed with Husserl himself, has had to concede its originary ground in the *Lebenswelt*.[19] Science is a development of mind in the middle that emerges out of the dense promiscuous world, the given otherness of being that is prior to it. It builds itself on the prescientific otherness but it never totally circumscribes it. The abstract findings it gains in the controlled, artificial conditions of the laboratory conceal something of the same world science also intends to reveal. The scientific mind wills to be rational, but to be fully rational means to reroot reason in the concrete otherness of metaxological being that precedes and exceeds science. This philosophical rerooting is to be guided not only by science but by the mindfulness of wisdom. A wise man might be a scientist, but a complete scientist might not be wise.

Philosophy and the Poet

The scholar, technician, and scientist are all specialists: this is both their strength and limit. A specialist tends to privilege his own particular expertise as the most adequate mediation of being in the middle. But no one configuration of mind exhausts the plenitude of given being, nor can one be an "expert" of intermediate being. No one "specialty" within the metaxological entirely encapsulates the intermediation of self and other. Yet if there is no specialist of the between, there are figures that allow a freer play to the exigency of human wholeness, and a different openness to otherness, even down to the thisness of concrete things as recalcitrant to complete conceptualization.

The poet is one such. By poet here is not meant a post-Kantian aesthete, the specialist of "aesthetic experience." The poet is an archaic image of the wise man. In many premodern societies, say with the Greek and Celtic peoples, the poet was carrier of the traditional wisdom, guardian of the images of the divine. In Celtic society the poet was conserver of law, member of a privileged caste, invested with the dangerous power of the holy. Unlike the modern aesthete, the poet was priestly, regal, heroic, sage, as Vico rightly recalls.

If we consider poetry and philosophy as modes of mindfulness, we are familiar with their "ancient quarrel." Often conflict alone is stressed. For each seems the representative of a fundamental power: imagination and reason. Uplifted by imagination the poet soars beyond reason's restrictions; the philosopher, by contrast, seems to clip imagination's wings and bridle its flight with categories. Art and logic, image and concept: are these at war? Nietzsche thought so when he said: Homer versus Plato—this is life's fundamental antithesis. We might say that the poet is closer than the philosopher to the *lived texture* of the middle in the particularity of its concreteness. Yet many thinkers have mingled image and concept. Parmenides, the philosophical father, was a strange conceptualist poet. Plato—for artists the arch enemy—voiced the eros of philosophy in dramatic dialogues, some of which show the perfection of artworks. Augustine was suspicious of the senses, but he was a master rhetorician, an African rhapsodist of the religious. Hegel, Schelling, and Schopenhauer, in different ways, acknowledged the kinship of philosopher and poet, each according to art a profound metaphysical significance.

Nietzsche himself is very instructive, for in his own practice, he undercuts his antithesis of Plato and Homer, even calling for an "artistic Socrates." Nietzsche is the epitome of the poet-philosopher: his vigor of thought springs from a fertile confluence of image and concept. But many others—Heidegger, Marcel, Sartre, to name some—have cradled their reflections in the inspirations of the artist. It is highly revealing that Heidegger's dialogue of poet and thinker follows directly in the wake of Husserl's view of philosophy as rigorous science. A like transition in analytical thought is recently evident in Rorty's shift from philosophy as scientific system to "hermeneutical edification." Significantly, the paradigms of human possibility replacing the scientist and technician are the strong poet and the utopian revolutionary.[20]

We need the power of the image and not only the abstraction of the concept to remain true to the concreteness of the middle. Yet philosopher and poet are at one in their common care for language.[21] As guardians of the sources of articulation both muse on what can be spoken with significance; both are impelled to the boundaries of the "sayable," driven by perplexity whether the "unsayable" can be said after all, if only indirectly or falteringly or deviously. The stock contrast of the two implies that philosophers write only "plain prose." This is clearly false: philosophical discourse is sometimes more outlandish, full of somersaulting dialectic, that is, more imaginative than anything a surrealistic poet might devise. Far from "plain prose" such discourse can be as cunning as the poet's, sometimes even more crooked, more foxy.[22] For like the poet, the philosopher can be a kind of adventurer of mind, a thinker of otherness. Mind runs against the wall of ordinary thereness, but its energy is not thereby exhausted. Being cannot be reduced to univocity, nor is it merely equivocal. In one sense it is in excess of all our articulations. Philosophy and poetry both feed on this surplus of mind as face to face with being's surplus. Each seeks some articulation of what is "more," what is beyond the reach of scholarly research, the utilitarian concerns of technique, or the theoretical objectifications of science. Both are mediators between what is immediately given and what mindfulness divines is other or more.

What provokes thought in the poet's work is that it offers an image of possible wholeness without denying its origins in human incompleteness, or closing us off from otherness. Thus, the poetic image resists reduction, indeed invites repeated reinterpretation. It is beyond the simple unity of univocity and the scattered plurality of equivocity. As an open dialectical whole, the poem presents a conjunction of opposites, a communion in the intermediate of the sensuous and spiritual, an aesthetic middle that resists logicist reduction. It need not shirk conflicts, but in trying to contain contraries, it may offer for mindfulness a place of turbulent rest. The poet is not wise in being able to quiet all questions, but he can shake awake the concrete mindfulness of essential perplexity. He may release our wonder through the inexhaustible image his work offers. The wonder he releases is the same wonder at the origin of philosophy. In this respect, philosophy and poetry are each a non-instrumental mode of middle mindfulness.

The poet's language is richly resonant and concrete. As a mode of discourse drenched with meaning, it presents to us a certain linguistic otherness. This can disquiet the philosopher about the limits of analysis and the poverty of his abstractions. Philosophy, to be true to being's otherness, must take this challenge seriously. Indeed, its temptation to conceptual caution can be put to shame by the spiritual seriousness of great poetry.[23] Philosophy finds this hard to admit. Some poets think that this is reason enough to jettison reason, but we need not be seduced by this, the poet's specious reasoning. Instead of reneging on reason, we need a more complex conception of it, one closer to the fullness of articulation the artwork images. The philosopher, too, can be open to the contrary otherness of being, as well as to its concreteness and intelligibility. He can be impressed by the poet's power to place form in being where chaos was before, admire him for not being timid in mind before the to-be-articulated thereness of things, for his struggle to see, in an originative way, the significance of the thereness. Philosopher and poet, both can be originators of deeper mindfulness in this sense: each may envisage possibilities of being undreamt within the narrows of commonsense, otherness out of the ordinary in the very ordinary. Ontological astonishment at being in the middle is never exhausted.

The metaxological sense implies the possibility of a two-way interplay between poet and philosopher: if the poet can be philosophical, the philosopher can be poetic. This is to resist any dialectical reduction of poetry to philosophy. The philosopher must also bear within his own mindfulness the poet's voice, for without imaginative power he could not body forth the thought of the possibly other.[24] This is very evident with, say Plato and Nietzsche. The present work, in its desire to be plurivocal, follows their lead.

When commonsense consults its cribbed thought, its quick conclusion on otherness is: impossible! It shuns speculating what might still be possible were our horizon on being enlarged or our dwelling in the midst of things deepened. What imaginative envisagement is to the poet, speculative mind is to the philosopher. In this sense, philosophy's speculations are the poetry of reason. Why does one imagine, the other speculate? Here we can detect a secret desire to transfigure being by the unfolding of its latent power, a pursuit of the perfection of existence, indeed the hope to participate through their work in that perfection. We discover the alchemist's wish: to make gold of dross. To see the world as golden would be to speak well of being, despite even its darkness and disfigurement (see chapter 6). Thus, the philosopher's "God" can be a metaphysical mnemonic that enshrines such a blessing of being, a thinker's attempt at amen.[25]

There is a kinship then between these others, but there is also tension. Philosophy cannot escape its old familiar—that nagging bitch—doubt. Does the dream wander into more mindless sleep or to an awakening? We cannot avoid interrogating the truth of the image. Does art's image conceal as well as reveal? Is there another way—without images—to overcome conceal-ment? Does the poetic image resolve a riddle by another riddle? Through the free play of imagination, the poet opens up a new articulation of being in the middle and releases for thought an enlarged range of possibility.

Philosophical speculation cannot consent to just any possibility, but fundamental possibility consonant with being's recalcitrant otherness. For free thought is vacuous in the end if not somehow in accord with the necessities of being. Poetry can disport with images for their own sake; philosophy must reflectively think on their truth, seek to reconcile image and original being. This means hermeneutically sifting images that may be empty, images of nothing. The poet can dream up possible worlds in his works, images of being as other; the speculative philosopher must ask how dreams of possible otherness square with the world of being as actual.

Both want to remain true to the middle; to remain thus true we need the image but we also need more than the image. In this respect, the philosopher is other to the poet in wanting to account in more reflective terms, sometimes more abstractly mediated terms, for the poet's genuine significance. To create an image is one thing; it is another to reflect on how it mediates our sense of being. We must sometimes look elsewhere than the vision to interpret its riddles. There is also the fact that the poet's image casts its spell and seduces, but the visionary gleam does not always glow. When it fades, skepticism brings the suspicion that it was mere play, a child's game. Philosophy need not lack its charm and it, too, shows the face of the ugly: witness the uncouth Silenus face of Socrates. It nevertheless is true that the "wisdom" of some poets seems to be little more than the sanctification of their own eccentricity. There are great exceptions, but we find that in life the artist does not always live up to the fullness of meaning he embodies in his work. And aesthetes to the contrary, art is not for art's sake: the richness of art is for the enrichment of life. Yeats, a true high priest of poetry, said we may have to choose between perfection of the work and perfection of the life. Fidelity to the complex mediation of the metaxological and to the call of human wholeness makes one reluctant to acquiesce in this choice as an "either/or" that cannot be surpassed.

I hear the rising indignation of the Nietzschean accusation: anyway, philosophers are defectives in imagination, hence rancorous about the poet! The charge must be admitted — against some philosophers. And yet why do we still love to *play* logically with Zeno's mad paradoxes.[26] Are some poets not as deficient, as pedestrian where flights of *thought* are concerned, as tied to the apron strings of platitude. The poet murmurs: this is Plato *redivivus*, the old foe who would exile us from his perfect polis. But Plato was too subtle for the accusers who note no irony when assaulting him with all the righteous ire of fundamentalist priests. Do they mark Plato's playfulness, his irony, all those tricks of poetry up his sleeve? Have the kings of imagination read Plato so literalistically, so unimaginatively, as if he wrote bald newspaper reports of boxing bouts?

But the point is not at all to give philosophy the laurels. Not at all.

Philosophy and poetry are others in interplay, complementary mediators of being's otherness, each with its unique strength. If we recall the double movement of thought demanded by the metaxological (see introduction), we must say: Philosophy's shame for the poet is when thought so *thinks only itself* as to cut itself off from otherness, when it becomes a *closed formal self-mediation of abstractions* that circle around other abstractions whose logical coherence serves to buffer mind against being. By contrast, the limit of poetry for philosophy is when its celebration of otherness abbreviates or short-circuits the necessity of reflectively *thinking through* the otherness: for thought can think, indeed sing its other (as we will see in chapter 6).

Being aesthetic (we will also see in chapter 2) is a fundamental way of being. But if the poet is the image-maker, sometimes one must be image-breaker, especially when the image is mistaken for the absolute original. The image becomes an idol, and mind's iconoclastic (literally: image-breaking) power appears. The poet ties us to the earth with images; the philosopher may strain against these ties, against being bound by images. He poses questions that perhaps no image can ever encapsulate. Dreaming beyond the images of the earth, he sometimes shows the twin face of the priest.

Philosophy and the Priest

Though placed in the middle of things, the human being is nevertheless driven in search of what is ultimate. The ensemble of finite objects do not exhaust this drive. Something other, beyond the finite, though mediated through the finite, will be sought. The metaxological community of finite beings will suggest its own ultimate ground. Likewise the self's energy of being strains against the middle, risks so driving to the extremes as to desert the middle and seek the "more" of otherness beyond finite being. This quest of the ultimate ground joins philosopher and priest together in the middle.

Indeed there were times when philosophy was just one activity of the priest, as with the clerics of Christendom. Likewise the two have been associated in their quarrels. Thus, for his commitment to thought, Socrates was condemned for impiety, and sent to death. Priest and philosopher are blood relations, and for that their wars are all the sharper. Here I broadly take the priest as representative of being religious, to which I will return more fully in chapter 3.

The priest occupies the middle between finite beings and their ultimate ground as other. Thus, his way in the world is not worldly in any simple univocal sense. Practical people care for the body's necessities but he is said to be the caretaker of the spirit. Though traditionally he went among his people, he was not just one of them. He was set apart, testament to more ultimate things amidst the mundane harry. As a dealer with the divine, minister for the absolute, he is other to everyday life, but his otherness as a self is said to represent the more radical otherness of the divine. So he is a creature of tension, midway between sense and spirit. He must show the spirit to those who live the body. He is intermediary between finitude and infinitude and must reconcile these opposites, that is, make spirit incarnate. Of course, because of this, some find him a living contradiction: neither here nor there, neither one thing nor the other, "in the world but not of it," a hybrid contradiction. There are priests who glory in this ambiguous, contrary nature, in being "a sign of contradiction."

Either way, whether we evaluate the case critically or positively, the priestly nature is complex. Being a contradiction is to be other to logicist univocity, but this need not mean the priest is just a living equivocation. This complexity has been seen as a twisted duplicity (see Nietzsche), but it can also be seen as an affirmative doubleness, both dialectical and metaxological (see chapter 3). Not unexpectedly, to enter the priestly caste require long initiation. Here one does not choose a profession; one answers a call. By becoming the servant of the god, one pursues the path of blessedness. After preparation and purification, one walks a way of sacred being. I speak of the one called to the Holy; I do not speak of the power priest; I do not speak of the mushy trendy.

Traditionally these considerations have bolstered the belief that, as representative of the Most High, the priest is someone higher—a servant of the sacred, the chief carrier of wisdom. As a sacred intermediary, he is privileged to know the sacred scriptures. He consecrates the ordinary things, reunites estranged selves with the sacred order. He heals the fragmentary, makes whole what is incomplete, elevates what is falling, ushers muddled man into the awesome presence of the Holy. Like the poet's transfiguration of thereness, the religious power to transfigure the profane reveals again a concern with the alchemist's dream of golden being: bread and wine are not to be just bread and wine; they are to be the flesh of the god. The ritual of worship tries to mediate the presence of the divine, restore participation in the sacred otherness of the cosmos. True being is a Sabbath, a holiday, a day of divine festivity—intermediate being revealed and enjoyed in relatedness to sacred otherness.

Though the parallel is seldom noted today, anyone familiar with the philosophical tradition repeatedly comes across this parallel between priest and philosopher. For instance, at the origin of philosophy Parmenides appears as a kind of sacerdotal father of logos who recounts the revelation of the goddess in his poem. Even Aristotle, dutiful son of logic, reminds us of the priestly caste of Egypt: mathematics, all theoretical knowing, he says, originates with the priests, who had leisure, *skolē*. Hegel spoke of philosophy and art as divine service (*Gottesdienst*) and echoed a long tradition. Even in our own secular age, a kind of sacerdotal aura sometimes surrounds two heroes of twentieth century thought—namely Heidegger and Wittgenstein. Heidegger himself studied for the priesthood. And at one point in his life, after World War I, Wittgenstein thought seriously of becoming a priest.

The philosopher undergoes the discipline, not of spiritual exercise, but of mindful thought. Similarly, he is concerned with ignorance, stupidity and estrangement, reason's counterparts to "sin." He reflects in the face of contradiction, but trusts that his pathway of thought may yield the illumination of insight, an end to bless a long and often solitary road. Analogous to purification by prayer, thought must sometimes withdraw from the outer otherness to the inner, to comprehend being by means other than the senses. Thus, Socrates spoke of philosophy as catharsis (as did the Pythagoreans and Empedocles). One thinks here also of Descartes locked up within himself simply to think. Descartes wanted to found a scientific philosophy, but the meditations required for such a founding have about them a vague air of, so to say, mathematical prayer. One thinks of Husserl invoking Augustine: *noli foras ire, in te redi, in interiore homine habitat veritas* (Do not go outside, return into yourself, truth dwells in the inner man). Nor need the philosopher be a blasphemer of mysteries; he can have his piety too. His crowning insight may appear like a revelation: struck by a sudden lightning bolt, being ready and long prepared, at last passing from shadow to brightness. Then he will hold, as Plato held, that something inexpressible shines forth. One cannot write it down, but one might be witness to it; one cannot bespeak it fully, but one might be a reminder of it. Just as Socrates' life was a kind of living memorial of the ideal in its otherness, so the philosopher can be an intermediary between our ignorance and what is beyond profane ken. It was Plato who also taught: the philosopher seeks to become as like the god as is possible for a human being.[27]

There is this kinship of priest and philosopher, yet as in interplay there is also difference. Standing on the same middle ground, these two can also join battle there. I intend no rationalist Enlightenment cliché about "priestcraft" and "superstition." Even Nietzsche, in his hyperbolic hatred of the priest, knew that he dealt with a *significant* other.[28] Often the need for philosophy is only felt with the *decay* of religion, as in philosophy's very emergence in Greece from mythological origins. Philosophy feeds on the carrion of religion; it is a scavenger that gets nourishment in what, while living, was great. But as claiming to stand for the ultimate, the priest's claim sometimes will brook no rival: he is the minister of the absolute, and he alone. In his otherness he stands in the place of the ultimate otherness; rival pretenders to ultimacy (philosophic, poetic, scientific) can then become interpreted as *suspect* others. The priest often justifies his claim by appeal to authority and faith; he asks us to believe the revelation he communicates. And indeed philosophy sometimes greets this appeal for trust with its brand of suspicion—rational refusal. Doubt cannot be put aside by assuming the pose of pretended faith. As wanting to answer for himself, the philosopher will seems a blasphemer. In this sense, the Athenians were quite right to accuse Socrates of inventing a new god, since his way of being amounted to an argument with the religious oracle, a refusal. The new god?—logos.[29]

The priest preaches humility: submit to the will of the god revealed through the will of the priest. This can lead to a belittling of mindfulness, the assertion of mind's impotence with respect to the essential questions. We must believe the answers given by the sacred tradition, not drive ourselves to distraction with doubt. By contrast, the philosopher seems guilty of stubborn pride, vaingloriously insisting that the truth be evident to his mind. The "reason" of the arrogant thinker is then suspected as only a subterfuge for insolence. But here the tale takes a twist. The priest advises submission; yet such self-belittlement is paradoxically an *elevation* through faith. Through self-negation, the previously insignificant individual becomes absolutely significant in the god's eyes. Self-deprecation and vanity, self-abasement and pride come to light side by side. Luther's diatribe against the "whore Reason," Kierkegaard's sometimes absurd glorying in the absurdity of faith, are instances of such fideistic insolence to thought.[30] God is said to be a mystery, remote and unknown; yet we are to act as if intimate with the Remote, in fact, so familiar as to be on first name terms with the Most High. Is it the philosopher who alone is proud?

The priest does not *logically* reduce the otherness of being in the middle, nor confine our deepest perplexity within univocal categories. He divines that the otherness in the middle points to an ultimate other, and allays our perplexity by appeal to this ultimate other. But this appeal can become *inverted* into a religious (not logicist) reduction of middle being. Then something like this following difficulty can emerge. The priest holds much *power* by being guardian of a sacred tradition. Yet he can fall from his calling and turn worship into a magic hocus-pocus show. He manipulates the bones of the dead to give him power over the god, exploits his flock's awe to palm it in his power. His guardianship degenerates into a policing of the perplexing middle, a policing sanctioned by the sacred. He becomes anxious to avoid any aberration from the sacred tradition. His witness to God is transmuted into being a custodianship of orthodoxy—this becomes *the closed frame* within which all thinking must be mediated. Trust in the absolute becomes the absolute distrust of everything else. Doubt's repressed disquiet reappears as a fury of anxiety about orthodoxy. The custodian of absolute faith now proves to be actually of little faith and thus quick to suspect any deviation. Soon he beats the bushes for lurking heretics, fanatical in his fear that God might be dishonored by diversity. Instead of gentle reverence for the Holy we find the religious rage of the Inquisitor. In a vile parody of witnessing, the Inquisitor establishes the divine truth on a rack.

The threat of orthodoxy and the sanction imposed on the heretic conspire to make one at once cautious and dogmatic of mind, in a word, unphilosophical. The priest then becomes a provisioner of comforting assurance who gives out the answer before the question has been asked. The courage to question is undermined, mind is kept within the bounds of a domesticated salvation, the otherness of the divine itself is domesticated. Churches become the bureaucracies of redemption. Again my point is not to "attack" religion but to remind us that being's plenitude cannot be reduced, whether religiously, scientistically, philosophically, aesthetically. What must be fought is the contraction of mindfulness that is coupled with such reductions.

And there are philosophers, I know, in whom the Inquisitor lies in wait. They work within the confines of a certain orthodoxy. Should a member of the school depart from the received teaching, he might be met with responses varying from devious disagreement to blunt assault. Philosophers, too, swarm in crowds, and hunt the renegade who leaves the pack. I mention Marxism, though there are other schools. For all its revolutionary origins, Marxism quickly congealed into a stale dogmatism. As Thomism was the "official" philosophy of the Catholic Church, Marxism is the "official" philosophy of the Communist state. But an "official" philosophy, a philosophy for "officials": do not these two terms cancel each other out? Sometimes Marxists are latter day scholastics, and their internal wranglings have the tone of theological disputes about what multitude of counterrevolutionary devils might dance on pinheads. Of all philosophical schools, Marxism has been most racked by splits into orthodoxies and heresies. It has not been wanting in its Inquisitors either, willing to murder the apostate not alone in logic but in blood. Marxists originally made a name for themselves by hating the priests and everything they stood for. But this hatred is that of a rival. The Marxist is the minister of a different idol.

Philosophy and the Revolutionary

The reader will notice how, the more we advance, the less possible it is to pigeonhole in tight univocal categories the different figures of mind. These figures, though others, exists and are defined in an interplay that is not only dialectical but also metaxological and hence irreducible to any singular form, as each figure itself is irreducible to any single univocal identity. (In the next section on the hero I will suggest how *human eros* in the middle helps hold together the plurality of figures.) The "identity" of any figure thus shows the presence of its interplay with the others. Thus, beneath the "official" identity of each, a plurality of other possible "identities" will be evident. The figures are others, not opposites; and their dialectical and metaxological *porosity* becomes the more evident as we consider more *archaic* images of the wise man (see the move to the poet). In modernity we are mesmerized by the specialization of functions, but this breaks down, or proves less than ultimate, in terms of the metaxological sense of being. If we consider philosophy as trying to think the "whole," there is no specialty of the "whole," especially if we understand that "whole" not as a univocal totality but a metaxological community of being. The plurality exhibits the interplay of each figure as contributing to a community of others, each of whose "identity" itself carries the mark of its intermediation with figures other than itself. With these remarks in mind, let us return to the priest and revolutionary.

The Marxist is a rival of the priest because he harbors a strain of the priestly character. At best priest and revolutionary are bound together in their common concern for the realization of our full promise. So if we swivel the priest slightly, away from the other world to this one, he can easily mutate into the revolutionary. We see this clearly where religion and revolution are wedded under the banner of Liberation Theology. For though these two seem antithetical, one a conserver of the sacred tradition, the other a trumpet blast of the future utopia, beneath the antithesis is a common origin. Both have their genesis in their sense of human existence as *alienated*; each is a different response to this common predicament, namely, our self-estrangement. The otherness of present being is conceived as literally *alien*: life now in the middle is alienating. Similarly, both claim to overcome this estranged condition. Each has its dream of perfection and desires to remake human beings in accord with its ideal. The philosophical power of both is that they dream of being as differently other, of the human being as the promise of otherness beyond alienation; they dream how to make human beings whole. Of course in the struggle for ascendancy over the total man, the dream of wholeness can degenerate into its night terror, namely, totalitarianism. The kingdom of heaven on earth becomes the idol of the state.[31]

Just as philosophy and religion have been akin, so also have revolution and philosophy. There has never been a revolution without some philosophy preparing for it and guiding its direction. Philosophy is the mother of revolutionaries, who are her warrior sons. Without it there would be no revolutions, only uprisings or rebellions, protests always limited in extent and temporary in duration. Compared to these, revolution tends to be extremist. As philosophy is ambitious for a "holistic" view of being, revolution is intent on a total transformation of being. What then is revolution but an attempt to embody, realize a philosophy in action?[32]

Consider the course of philosophy in recent centuries. The kinship of philosophy and revolution needs hardly to be recalled in the case of Marxism. Modernity generally, with its future-oriented sense of temporality, is saturated with the rhetoric of revolution. This is reflected in philosophy: Descartes initiates modern philosophy with a claim to a radically new beginning in thought thinking itself; Kant then claimed a Copernican revolution; later again German idealism claimed to complete this Copernican revolution in thought; then logical analysis claimed to be revolutionary in relation to idealism; and now in the iron age of analysis, Richard Rorty comforts us with the paradigm of the utopian revolutionary, as if *that* were new. Likewise in twentieth century Continental thought, Husserlian phenomenology claimed to initiate a philosophical revolution; Heidegger made claims to an unprecedented thinking that was to overcome the traditional categories of all past metaphysics; now deconstruction (one heir of phenomenology out of post-Heideggerian hermeneutics, but grown skeptical with excessive, albeit exotic, philological fastidiousness) exults in the self-proclaimed "textual revolution" or the post-structuralist revolution in forced search of further "originality." When we have revolutions every ten years or so, the reiterated rhetoric of absolute originality and difference instead arouses one's suspicion of the return of the *same*, only now naively buoyed up by new generational energy.

Yet philosophy *does* tend to be revolutionary—this is simply the need of thought to be open to otherness, indeed open to its own rupturing by otherness. Philosophy deals with the questioning of being, with testing the effect of thought on being in the very disruptions of being. Traditionally it saw itself as revolving the self, turning it around from ignorance to knowing. Plato speaks of enlightenment as a *periagōgē*, a rotation of our soul bringing it full circle from illusion to truth. Dissolving with doubt all naiveté, it is critical of what is unreflectively taken as true. It puts reality to the test, searching out what falls short of perfection. But it also sets forth an ideal. Like the revolutionary, the philosopher might not be at home with present being. He need not expire in weary resignation, but rather envisage the good and labor for its implementation. This dual movement of thought—criticism of what is and construction of what should be—is found in thinkers as far apart as Plato and Marx.

If we recall the double need of metaxological thought, namely, to think both itself and its other, we must say that revolutionary thought is never self-contained thinking. It always faces recalcitrant being. That is, thought itself must become other to itself as abstract thought, and as the mind's *praxis*, it must grapple with being as other to thought. This is why Plato

famously forces those philosophers who have seen the Sun back into the
Cave. The Cave is the temporal other of the pure Ideas, but it must be
ethically transformed by those enlightened ones who have thought the
otherness of the Ideas. We see something similar in Marx's critique of
Hegel's so-called panlogism. If we take Hegel's panlogism as a form of
thought thinking only itself, for Marx revolutionary philosophy must not only
think its other (socioeconomic history, etc.) but it must participate in that
other in an interventionist way, that is, as disruptive and transfigurative, as
thought willing the *new* other of future revolutionary society.

This disruptive side is related to the breakdown of the univocal categorization of human function, a breakdown that is potentially "creative" of a
"breakthrough." For while launching an assault on the old world, the revolutionary looks forward to a new world. In working for this transfiguration, there
is something of the poet in him. We might say that he rolls poet and priest into
one—he is their synthesis. Like the poet, he creates an image—the ideal order
he projects; like the priest, he is concerned with perfecting his ideal (Christians
call perfection "the kingdom of heaven"). Thus, he tries to unite the image with
its perfection, the ideal with its realization. But unlike the poet, he is not
satisfied with the image as image, or with a vision of new otherness as only
imaginative: he wants to transform the image into actuality, actualize the promise of new otherness. Unlike the priest, he is not content with a faith that
perfection is an elsewhere, an otherworldly other ("the kingdom of heaven is
not of this world"). He wants to create the perfection here and now. His New
Jerusalem is not a Lotus Land for dandies, nor an empire for an always elsewhere God, but the Kingdom of Man, fought for and won, here and now.

Like the poet, the revolutionary is a dreamer, and like the priest, he has a
dream of perfection (a "new creation"). But unlike them, he is more impatient
to realize the dream here and now. The artist is happy with the dream of the
artwork; the priest is comforted with the hope of perfection. The revolutionary
wants to go further: complete the poet and priest, and so abolish both as
distinct.[33] As the revolutionary mingles poet and priest, so also he unites aspects
of priest and philosopher. He is a peculiar mixture of doubt (the philosopher)
and faith (the priest): doubt about the established order, faith in the future order.
In fact, the power of the revolutionary impulse springs from its combination of
disillusioned realism and uncompromising idealism. Disillusioned realism: the
revolutionary is utterly discontented with reality as it now is and would destroy
it. Extreme idealism: he also has an urgent desire for absolute change and the
realization of the ideal. Revolutionary power explodes in and is carried forward
by an amalgam of cynicism and enthusiasm, hatred and hope.

It is necessary to remember the extreme dangers here. The revolutionary
urgency for transforming otherness can degenerate into a deformation of the
otherness of being, already at work in the middle. The origin of revolution is
dream and imagination, but since dreams can sour, revolution needs more

than imagination to remain significant. The revolutionary often resorts to force to remold reality in the image of his hope; but should his hope be unwise, his force is brute power, mere violence. If the revolutionary thinker lacks the leavening power of nuanced philosophical mindfulness, he becomes the "militant intellectual" who, in turn, is indistinguishable from a conceptual terrorist. Revolutionary impatience gets the better of philosophical subtlety. It tries to create the dreamt otherness by destroying all given otherness. In the extreme—we moderns have witnessed too many instances—the revolutionary becomes a butcher.

The modern revolutionary tends to make politics and philosophy inseparable; politics becomes the whole, with philosophy a subordinate means to revolution. Marx, not Plato, stalks his mind. Politics emerges *in medias res* but spreads its wings of ambition for revolutionary change to the extremes—in becoming extremist it risks being totalitarian. But Plato had his point: while teaching the necessity of politics, he also taught its limits. To ennoble politics, philosophy must transcend politics. The difference between philosophy and politics has to be kept open: there is a community of affinity, never an identity between them. The revolutionary side of philosophy cannot be univocally reduced to political revolution, for before politics can be revolutionized, we need first to undergo a philosophical revolution. The political master, be he conservative or revolutionary, is often a slave to the illusion of the day. Without a vision larger than politics, the politician risks being only a huckster.

Some consequences of univocally identifying philosophy and politics are evident with Marxism, the most important modern effort to reconcile theory and praxis. As its best in theory Marxism seeks a *dialectical* relationship between philosophy and politics, but in the press of practicalities, dialectical complexity gets flattened to totalitarian univocity. The philosopher ceases to be a free thinker and becomes a party ideologist—a priest of the party, now turned into a new church, a closed self-mediating sect (see chapter 3), complete with the sacred scriptures of prophets such as Marx, Lenin, and Mao. As the party becomes inviolable and immune from criticism, party hack attacks party hack, often with political motives, imputing suspect politics to opponents. The others are branded as counterrevolutionaries, revisionists, running dogs of reaction, that is, apostates to be excommunicated. In the suspicious fury of orthodoxy, all otherness becomes criminal, philosophy is reduced to an instrument of power and wisdom becomes might. A freer mindfulness is stifled in the gulag. The strongest in the struggle is crowned as a provisional god. When it becomes the vassal of such politics, a revolutionary philosophy degrades itself into an ideological dogmatism. Then once the revolutionary gains power, the pharisee in him buds. The "Party line" becomes sacrosanct, in other words, a pathway to a privileged stupidity. Politics degenerates when not challenged from an independent position, and when it subordinates its others. When philosophy marries with such politics too incestuously, its offspring end up mongoloid.

Thus, there is benefit and drawback here. The benefit is showing that philosophy has to do with concrete being in community, that it is not just abstract doctrine but a call for some embodiment in a way of being. The drawback is that sometimes instead of politics being elevated, philosophy simply sinks: life is not ennobled by philosophy but the soul of thought is sold for a shortsighted relevance to life. Then the revolutionary cannot endure the tension of otherness between philosophy and being; he reneges on philosophy in the full, and tailors it to the noise of the day, or if you will, the noise of the day after tomorrow. His courage to live the solitariness, singleness of philosophy falters. In the end he renounces philosophy and finds his reconciliation in crowds.

Once again the complexities of our relatedness to otherness are at stake. The modern revolutionary refuses the pathos of distance coming from the otherness between man and God, or put reflectively, the difference between philosophy and its rational dream of perfection. Revolutionary impatience becomes an eros for otherness somewhere over the rainbow, but in the process this eros dialectically reverses into a hatred of present otherness, or rather reveals the power of that hatred at work all along. The ancient Platonic dream of the philosopher-king expressed a revolutionary concept of philosophy and a philosophical concept of revolution. But where the modern revolutionary is intoxicated with the dream, Plato reminds us that the dream was still that, a dream. Mindfulness must induce the temperance of revolutionary intoxication, for being's otherness remains unmastered.

Philosopher and revolutionary both are skeptical about the common pieties; commonsense is often riddled with common nonsense, and a warlike attitude is needed. In their unease with the pieties, both lose innocence; enlightenment is always disillusioning. The revolutionary sometimes fails to regain reverence: his discontent with reality can become an indictment, a hatred of being; suspicion and disgust remain lodged in his soul. Can one come to a different acceptance on the other side of innocence lost? A *pietas* of being, purged of naiveté? Can disillusion be cleansed of disgust? Recalcitrant otherness chastises hubris, but one can be happy knowing what to expect, knowing when not to expect much. The revolutionary expects too much and too little, misses the wise middle, and continues to rage against the loss of innocence. His atheism is disappointed piety, his cynicism soured idealism. Or will the grapes of Marx's wrath yet ferment into palatable vintage?[34]

Philosophy and the Hero

The scholar, technician, revolutionary, scientist have provided images of the philosopher acceptable to many moderns. Poet and priest are older paradigms. While the poet now wins more respectability in reaction to technicist and scientific models, the priest finds less acceptability. This is traceable partly to the Enlightenment debunking of religion ("superstition" and "priestcraft"), whose shadow still hovers over us, partly to the conflict of science and religion that has repeatedly flared up in the modern era. The poet's acceptability and the priest's repudiation is epitomized by Nietzsche, a paradigm figure for many contemporaries, and is a revealing mixture of readiness for the aesthetic and reluctance towards the religious. One need not subscribe to this reductionistic repudiation while granting the ambiguity of the priest (as indeed of the others). I return to being aesthetic and religious in subsequent chapters, but in the rest of this chapter, I concentrate on two final figures, namely, the hero and sage. These are significant others of philosophy, even more archaic, "primitive," than the revolutionary, priest, poet, scientist, technician, and scholar.

This is appropriate since the "hero" lets us see philosophy and its others as bound together in the middle by the eros of dynamic humanness, the original energy of being that erupts in us and that diversifies itself into a plurality of configurations. This original energy of being is figured forth in all, but the "hero" may serve as a metaphor for a singular instantiation or exemplification of human possibility in its richest embodiments. Hence, my sketch will be a little fuller. First, I consider this eros in relation to our intermediate being and the role of heroic individuals as originals. Second, I remark on the neglect of the hero today, a neglect that disguises a continued need for the figure. Third, I consider philosophers and heroes.

Human beings inhabit the metaxological community of being differently. Animals search out and fight, driven by necessity, but nature being appeased, and granting the absence of external threats, the animal rests, peculiarly at peace with itself and the world, gentle even with other animals that shortly again will become its prey. The animal is simply content to be. We are more intricate, sometimes more twisted and perverse—we are not satisfied just to be. We do not dwell in the middle with simple immediacy; we dwell as beings that mediate being. In extreme cases we even revolt against the conditions of being and refuse what, from the vantage of the rest of nature, should content a healthy animal. We are capable of a revolt more comprehensive than political revolt: ontological revolt against being itself.

We go beyond. Ontological revolt itself reveals the negative face of our freedom to transcend. Over and above animal need and gratification, we expend ourselves in an excess of energy. This excess is the prodigal power of our inward otherness that originates all culture, all efforts to beautify being outside us, and the beast within. When this excess cannot find constructive expression, it may instead discharge itself in destruction: what generates culture lies also at the origin of war—blocked excess that does not mediate being but explodes against being as a barrier, now in blind fury, now in calculated cruelty. We are both the flamboyant animal *par excellence* and the ape given to excess.

The promise of the middle is thus powerful and dangerous and resists reduction to unambiguous mediocrity. Hence, there is nothing as miserable as the self with an anaemic soul. Such a one, echoing Dante,[35] we might call the "neutral." The neutral is one who cultivates a flattening of desire, a thinning of the strength of loves and hates. The neutral is an *existential reduction to univocity* of the ambiguity of intermediate being, here skirted as an unsettling equivocalness. Reminding us of Nietzsche's last man, the neutral is a half-self, parsimonious with passion, feeble with the generous gesture. It settles for a negative goal: the mere absence of evil. The contentment of the neutral one is not even the animal's peace. For the neutral wants not to be ill, as opposed to possessing a vigorous health; it tries not to make mistakes as opposed to any bold but dangerous quest for excellence. John Donne sums up the condition in *An Anatomie of the World*: "There is no health;/ Physitians say that wee/ At best, enjoy but a neutralitee./ And can there be worst sicknesse, than to know/ That we are never well, nor can be so?" In the neutral the thrust for transcendence is dimmed; the excess of our energy of being is pared away at both its extremities, the higher and the lower, and we are left with a manageable median, a fallow simulacrum of our intermediate being.

The fate of such a neutral is always, if only in moments of crisis, to find its univocal equilibrium upset. A richer possibility of being has only to flare up briefly for us afterwards to become uneasy and equivocal about our habitual poverty. Again and again the excess of energy will express itself, it will out. Otherwise the self can only successively contract its outreaching, and ultimately it will collapse into itself, like a black hole.

These few words about the neutral intend to let us see the "hero." I use hero as a metaphor for this insistent striving of desire, our thrust beyond for transcendence, as epitomizing our excess of energy. What is important is not the hero as some univocal identity but the self-transcending drive that powers us beyond present limits and reaches out from the middle to its ultimate extremes. For this promise of otherness (both in the self and beyond the self) is not confined to a chosen few but implicates all. The same excess of energy that drives the hero, also drives the scholar's dedication, the technician's calculation, the scientist's curiosity, the poet's imagining, the priest's hope, the agitation of the revolutionary. Each is a particular formation of the energy of human being as it mediates with itself and relates to otherness. Each crystallizes its indeterminate dynamism into a determinate human figure.[36]

What is at issue is the definition of our ontological promise in the middle. Our intermediate being is more than univocal identity, more than equivocal difference. As transcending power, it is both dialectically self-mediating and metaxologically open to otherness. In that sense, the heroic figure has an essential, structural place in the self-becoming of the human, the place that is, of an *original*. We realize our promise and become ourselves, not like Athena springing complete from the head of Zeus, but by initially imitating exemplary selves who, as other, manifest the ideal we seek. The beginner looks to the adept other and falters to repeat his accomplished gesture. Every self who turns out an original in itself begins its course to perfection as a humble imitation of another. Where, then, are we to get originals to first set the process in motion? A human can become an eventual original if only there are first originals to inspire and emulate.[37] But from where are these first other originals to come? Whom do they imitate? Still other originals? Then the question goes on and still we have not hit on any first originals. Is every self then an imitation of an imitation . . . and so on to infinity? But then we have a hall of mirrors in which there is nothing original to be reflected. The self becomes an image of nothing. Beneath the palace of shimmering images there lies but desert; we ourselves, seemingly solid, are hardly even wind-blown dust. (This happens in the desert of deconstruction where there is no original self. The self is "under erasure," not a formation of the original energy of being.)

Or should we say that the first originals generated themselves, not in the sense of a creation *ex nihilo*, but as dialectically self-mediating? We grow into accomplishment by emulating some model, and the question is: What do these models emulate? The suggestion is that such models do not so much emulate another model external to themselves as *exemplify* something internal to their own being. As dynamic beings pregnant with possibility, we become ourselves by realizing some of this possibility. By the nature of the case, it is impossible to realize our every possibility; to realize one possibility means to repress another; every fulfillment entails a corresponding exclusion. There is always *more* to us than what we actually become; that is, in our self-mediation, we are *other to ourselves*, we are our own otherness. We exhibit an inward otherness, the unmastered depth of what in *Desire, Dialectic and Otherness* I call "original selfhood." Now and then individuals emerge who manifest something of this "more," this otherness in excess of univocal identity, selves who more richly realize essential human possibility. They live by inclusion not exclusion, embracing as much as possible of human promise. Abundance is their mark, and from their plenty they pour themselves forth. We say such selves are "larger than life"—other and more prodigal in spirit than the normal average. They come to assume the stature of heroic selves.

Such selves harness the teeming energy of our being, rescue it from its amorphous vehemence and give it form. They do not imitate an external model; they exemplify this energy, this original power of being that first lies slumbering in us. They reveal its vigor, sometimes its cruelty, at other times its fullness, but always its delight. These first originals become the heroes who, in struggling to bring themselves to perfection, become the exemplars of human promise. They live on in memory as a reminder of what this individual once was, and as an example of what others might become again. When we look retrospectively, we gild them with a false serenity and repose. In truth they were more tortured figures, but time works to erase the traces of their struggle.

Why then (this is my second point) has the "hero" suffered a certain eclipse today? In theory we democratically hold all to be equal, while in praxis we have eyes inordinately attentive to utility. The egalitarian and utilitarian spirit conspire to make us suspicious of the hero. The age of nobility is past, and in our dramas the shoe salesman and suburban housewife play the king and queen. Likewise the long leavening effect of religion leads to an apotheosis of the common man: one may be poor in privilege, a beggar in social status but, naked before God, one has a worth surpassing human hierarchies. History shows the slow dawning that it degrades our dignity, not alone to be treated as slave but to treat another as slave. It also shows the exploitation of the rhetoric of heroics to sanctify a long and bloody stupidity, namely, the Great War. Emperors may entice their masses to this massacre but in the process they become divested of their glorious divinity and stand revealed in their imbecile humanity. We who once reverenced the vestments of the hero now perceive only the rags.[38]

Consciously we shudder at heroics, yet unconsciously we crave a guide. We want to be equal but we also want to be led. We are caught in the middle between hating the idea of the hero while yet longing for a leader. This middle makes space for many a charlatan, though into it a demagogue does not always step. The Revolution, which inaugurates the era of equality, the French Revolution, also produced its Napoleon. Or consider communism and Western democracy, as each in part a descendent in spirit of that Revolution and its ideals. Communism proclaims all to be equal, yet it repeatedly throws up "the cult of personality." Then the leader of the masses is temporarily canonized as a five year deity, that is, until he makes himself into a godhead for life, a tyrant. Western democracy, too, announces the equality of all. But when the democratic leader imitates the man in the street in plebian fashion, the people themselves, in patrician fashion, quickly vote him out of office. When choosing his leader, democratic man is a little like a valet—a servant with aristocratic tastes. Communist man, democratic man, each secretly loves a lord.

Invariably we find distinctions of rank, even when the dominant rhetoric is egalitarian. Consider the previous figures in this light. The revolution of the masses casts up its avant-garde, who by their exceptional powers, do not melt into the masses. Similarly, though all be equal in God's sight, a priestly caste will emerge claiming special authorization. Poets, too, will license themselves with the privilege of a special sensibility. The great scientist even assumes a heroic aura—ecce Einstein! Some concession to the hero, be it sly or chagrined, is unavoidable. Even failing the emergence of exemplary genius in politics, religion, art or science, the spirit of the *snob* is always there to miserably meet our need for distinction.

How traditionally has the heroic figure been portrayed? Like Aristotle's great-souled man, the hero is not he who thinks much of himself but who asks more of himself. His danger lies in being haughty and arrogant, but he makes pride a virtue, not a vice; his pride is in excellence, not in vanity. He is charged with elitism, but this charge can be democratized. Democracy is an exoteric egalitarianism but an esoteric elitism: publicly everyone is said to be the same, but privately each is held, or holds himself, to be a unique individual. In its heart every self thinks itself to be different and special; it is the others who are all the same. We form for ourselves a hidden elite of which we are the only member. Hence, the rankest soil that roots the tyrant is our very inwardness itself: the inward otherness usurps God, the absolutely other.

The hero is seen in the fact that here and there nature and circumstances give birth to a few, favored ones. They bear the talents fortune gives them, but fortune, in its cruel benignity, demands the more of them. Blessed with more, more is exacted. Should they betray the talent, their fall is all the more precipitous. It is less dangerous to be solidly placed on the horizontal plane, a stranger alike to heights and to abysses, to greatness and degeneracy, a man and nothing but a man. The self driven by the more to the more finds its vision constrained by the vertical. It must look up or look down, seeking poise between the peak and pit.

The hero inhabits a middle between higher ideals and a limited present: the tension of extremes provides the spring of his self-transcendence. Harnessing this tension, stretching it to the breaking point, the heroic figure can evidence a certain cruelty, almost hatred: hatred of the halting and mediocre; cruelty, hardness toward the second rate and weak. Love of excellence makes him despise himself for falling short; his self-contempt in his spur. Every great joy he wins, he pays for by a passage through pain. Normally we stifle the stirrings of such restlessness and grow ashamed of our longings when these are jeered at by others and are not quickly fulfilled. We lose patience with our deepest desire, and make a show of being well pleased with nothings. The hero's passion is more enduring. More restless, it is also more patient. His struggle is not to betray the hope of perfection, though he be forced to send this hope underground. He is willing to watch and wait for what is absent: the blaze of divine fire. In the interim his vigilant eyes inwardly tear his own starched mask into tatters.

If the neutral ever became a philosopher, his thought would be anorexic analysis. To this anorexic analysis of the neutral thinker, the above sketch is already a rhapsody of excess. And (turning to my third point) we do often contrast philosopher and hero, one all calmness and cool reason, the other ardor and the vehement will. But against the neutralization of philosophical thought and in deference to the affinity of philosopher and hero, we can recall the famous story about father Thales, one of the Seven Sages of ancient Greece.[39] One evening Thales was strolling out, his head thrown back in contemplation of the stars, so absorbed in the world above that he was blind to the ground beneath; he was pitched into a ditch. The passing Thracian maid upbraided the comedy of contemplation with scoffing laughter. Perhaps the story is apocryphal but it carries the point. One self is so firmly rooted to the ground that anything higher is a lost world; the girl epitomizes everything familiar, domesticated, close to hand and pragmatic. Another self will be stargazer, dreamer, contemplative beyond commonsense. Unpracticed, negligent and useless, it will be in the minority, driven to solitude, made silent by the mocking majority for whom the earth is closer than a star.

Thales and the Thracian girl: is this a parting of the ways? Each has its justification, each its deficiencies. Strains of each will be found in the other: the girl will idle and daydream, the thinker must eat. As intermediate beings we are *both* sides, caught in the tension of this fork, at one time making a foray into this side of the split, at other times forced out along the other line. We are not just tensed in this fork; we are this fork. In the intermediate we are tugged in contrary directions between limited realities and higher idealities, if you like, between finiteness and infinitude. It is the heroic figure who lets loose the insistence of the latter. He breaks through the crust of finite contentments, and is harshly honest about our infinite restlessness. For this restlessness not only serves to develop our own self-mediation, but also radically opens us to all otherness and spurs us beyond.

I suggest again (as I hinted in my sketch of the scholar) that the great philosophers of the tradition epitomize heroic thinking in that their thought provides exceptional (literally, outstanding) mediations of this openness. A frequent charge leveled today against the ambitious thought of the great thinkers is that it is conceptually imperialistic. But heroic thought need not be thus tyrannical. It may just be this self-transcending openness to otherness. We find again the double mediation of thought. The inward otherness of the philosophic self breaks through its own domesticated selfhood (dialectical self-mediation), in thought's restless search of more radical otherness (metaxological intermediation). Every closure of self-mediation is inevitably broken open, whether it be the insipid whole of the neutral, or the high-minded wholeness of spiritual self-sufficiency, or indeed that of a philosophical system claiming absolute conceptual completeness. The same applies to all the figures of mind previously sketched: It applies to the closed circle of scholars of ideas, to the technicist, scientistic imperialism of instrumental mind. It applies to the closure of the aesthetic coterie with its chant of *l'art pour l'art*, and to the religious totalizing of ultimacy by any sect claiming false catholicity. It applies to the idolatrous totalitarian state of the modern revolutionary.

Hence, such a radical restlessness, as the dynamic power of thought potentially open to *all* being, whether inward or other, has been repeatedly recognized as a chief energy driving the philosophical search. Let me name a few exemplary instances. Plato saw philosophical thinking as emergent with the insistent thrust of eros in the *metaxu*; the philosopher, model of sanity, is no adversary of divine madness. Aristotle, for all his respect for the cautions of commonsense, saw *prōtē philosophia* as thought in excess of humanity.[40] Giordano Bruno, to name an exemplary Renaissance figure, spoke of the philosophical individual as cast out from the common run, driven by heroic furor. Bruno himself gave his life up to philosophy, both figuratively and literally; he ended up a sacrifice on the inquisitor's bonfire, a burnt offering to his unorthodox god. Or consider the peculiar case of Spinoza. Beneath the geometrical, neutral surface of his austere writing, Spinoza disguises a hunger for the absolute such that, not inappropriately, Novalis called him a "God-intoxicated" philosopher (*der Gottvertrunkene Mann*). Even Husserl calls for a "heroism of reason" at the end of *Philosophy and the Crisis of European Man*. More generally, the hero is philosophically underscored in Vico's sense of aboriginal selves, autochthonous human beings, in Hegel's view of world-historical individuals, in the stress on genius by Schelling and Schopenhauer. Nietzsche revives the need to break through the barriers of domesticated being in the middle by harbinging the *Übermensch* and celebrating the god of drunken excess, Dionysus. Heroic thought can be thought thinking, perhaps even singing, its other.

Philosophy and the Sage

I turn finally to the sage, the most archaic and recurrent image of wisdom. Again any reduction of the family of figures to a univocal category breaks down. Thus, the sage is intimately related to the priest and poet, in that he was often seen as marked by a "holiness" or as the privileged speaker of the gnostic word. In some cases, he is related to the scholar, if he has access to the sacred books or secret lore from which the many are excluded. He has a metaphorical bond with the scientist as purportedly possessing insight into the nature of things. Likewise, the technician is an echo of the sage, in that the latter was sometimes seen as a magus, a magician, someone with superhuman power over the rough elements. The technician, through the power of the machine, has an effective magic, or better, effects the dream of the magician: control of nature, gratification of desire at will. Nor is the sage unrelated to the revolutionary, though perhaps the relation is an inversion: in traditional societies the sage embodied political wisdom, but most often in a conservative dress, hence, as a guardian of continuity, not as an agent of rupture.

The sage stands out most clearly in contrast to the hero. Though the hero might strive for the heights, he is not necessarily the highest. Though he closes on being a rich exemplar of human possibility in relation to intermediate being, he is not immune from flaw. In repudiating the feeble equilibrium of the neutral one, the hero risks a different imbalance, namely, hubris. This, too, is undoubtedly the danger of all great thought. Hence, the accusation against heroic thought (Lyotard calls this a "Grand Narrative") of the anti-philosophical philosopher, or the modest scholar or the technician, is both right and wrong. Right—overreaching is always the risk; wrong— thought as excess, as self-transcending, as radical openness to otherness, cannot be indefinitely neutralized. But every hero is human, and in releasing the divine dunamis in himself, he can forget this fact. As Montaigne said: Sit we on the highest throne in the world, yet sit we only on our own tail.

In reaching out beyond, the hero can overreach. Pride comes before a fall, the saying has it. At the tip of his utmost reach, Nemesis is the just power that reminds the great man that he is still a man. The otherness he thought he had mastered strikes back as other than mastered. Any pretension to be the absolute whole is shattered in failure. (Post-Hegelian reminders of finitude are here relevant.) But Nemesis works cunningly, for often the fall does not come from powers above, but originates in things he thought beneath him. The hero is single minded (manic in Plato's sense) in pursuit of his particular excellence, but others love excellence more ambivalently. If we loved it wholeheartedly, we would emulate it. But we are terrified by excellence: the greatness we lack secretly shames us when we meet it. To assuage this shame, we may attack excellence. Give a mob time and it will turn against its hero. It will hate him for what before made it revere him: his being above it. The king who does not pander is dethroned. Only the seducer survives.

What makes the heroic self different is that it is an exaggeration: an existential extravagance of certain human powers. This is a source of strength but also cause of blindness. Overcomings in one thing are mortgaged by shortcomings in others. Everything great initially grows out of an extremist intention, which discards, as accidental, many aspects essential to a less intoxicated life in the middle. Time will let flower again these cast off concerns, causing the heroic figure, in its concentrated intensity, to stand out all the more isolated and single, like a beached whale, a stranded Leviathan. Everything great is earned with great sacrifice, but some sacrificial victims have their rights and return to reassert themselves. The complexity of our being in the middle reasserts itself against any insistent exaggeration of extremes.

A chief difficulty is: what *goal* is to be given to the excess driving the heroic figure? Without a goal the energy of our being goes nowhere, expends itself to no purpose. This energy is an insistent thrust for transcendence. However, at what should this thrust aim? Without appropriate direction, it dissipates itself in aimless dissemination. The heroic figure epitomizes the surge of enthusiasm for something more, but without a wise harnessing or mediation of the surge, it becomes a blind busyness, intense work spent on worthless nothings. The excess of energy remains mere excess, a violent impatience with intermediate being, a dark fertility that fructifies into nothing. The question presses because the excess may discharge itself in destruction as well as creation. What tells the difference between destructive and constructive power? Sheer energy and power is not enough. To avoid the negative outcome, the hero needs the corrective of something other. Every conqueror needs his counsellor, every Alexander his Aristotle. The hero needs the balance of the sage.

For the sage tries to filter a middle wisdom into the hero's extremist enthusiasm. Where the hero is heart, the sage is head; one is youthful will, the other aged mind; one the impulse to extremes and romantic restlessness, the other moderating equilibrium and the harmony of the classical. The hero is divine intoxication and surging eros, the sage is the divine temperance that has suffered mourning time. Our relatedness to otherness is again at issue. Where the hero articulates the impatience of inward otherness, the sage counsels mediating respect for the larger otherness of being—otherness that can never be "mine."[41] Our intermediate being as itself double needs both. Perfection requires harmony without tedium, dynamism without delirium.

How is the sage traditionally portrayed? The sage is thought to offer us a portrait of a certain perfection. Every people has its images of what constitutes sound sense.[42] The sage is the one who personifies, concretizes this sound sense. Moreover, this exemplification has an ethical character— the sage is identified with the image of the good man. Nor need his range be narrow. A people does not only act in pursuit of its practical goals; it ponders on these acts and their worth. The sage will be the one singled out for the depth and embrace of his thoughtfulness. As the Preacher in *Ecclesiastes* asks: How can a man get wisdom whose talk is only of bullocks?

The sage will be the very expression of discriminating mindfulness, discerning between nobility and baseness. He will disentangle himself from petty things, the time's beguiling baubles. Where others gossip, he will be conspicuous by his reticence. He rejects envy and spite, vices needful for everyday vivacity. Cultivating the courage to abide with essential things, no novelty turns his head, since in elementals he finds nothing new under the sun. Baseness remains a constant, while nobility is never guaranteed. Not many, if any at all, may complete the course, yet all may run the race; to do one's generous best is enough. It is better to fail in a higher endeavor demanding everything than to succeed in an inferior task where little is required. Is not this how the sage talks? But such pithy counsels seem to indicate that wisdom verges on *platitude*. Is this all? But what is platitude but the rough gem of essential thought worn smooth to shining obviousness. And there is *deep* platitude: not in what is said, but in how it is said and in who says it.

But the sage need not be bland. Plato says there are two basic patterns (*paradeigma*): the human and divine. The sage is man in excess of man in seeking to be likened or assimilated to the divine pattern. Conducting himself in concord with this order, he looks towards transfiguring otherness in order to be in the middle its living mimesis. Again as the Preacher says: wisdom makes one's face to shine, and the hardness of one's countenance is changed. As imaging the two paradigms the sage is *double*: a self that is other, different, and yet representative in the middle of more ultimate otherness; a human self that in its own otherness lives the respect of this second ultimate otherness. As *self-mediating*, the sage is neither despot nor slave but the freeman. As *intermediating with otherness*, he bears neither rage towards being, nor rancor, but gratitude and goodwill.

Nor does he shirk the blunt terror of death's otherness. Like Spinoza's sage,[43] his thoughts concentrate on the essentials of life. He quietly dismisses distraction, bypasses the wasting detours of chatter and enters into conversation with the ultimate things. The sage is the Heraclitean watchman of the night, awaiting those moments of breakthrough when the sleepwalkers will wake. Alas, the cynic is scoffing at this idealized portrait—this sage, the cynic says, is a solemn as an owl and as dull. But was Nietzsche alone in giving ear to the laughing sage? An eerie laughter rings in the night, laughter of derision and delight. Was Montaigne right again:[44] "The chief sign of wisdom is a constant rejoicing (*esjouissance*). Its state is like that of things above the moon: always serene." Yes. But we must also sing *below* the moon.

If the sage personifies sound sense, epitomizes a discerning mindfulness, philosophy cannot hush that cynic cry. There is an affinity with the philosopher but also a non-identity. The sage embodies wisdom—a concrete exemplar of wise thinking in action. Philosophy should be stunned into thought by the astonishing actuality of the good man, be challenged to match in its own thought the doubleness there embodied: thought thinking itself in rich self-mediation, thought thinking its other in respect of what resists conceptual encapsulation. Yet one can embody an ideal, and be unable to account fully for it. I may be a good man, but when asked to account for this goodness, I may be at a loss to reply. The case is similar with poet and priest: they manifest a rich meaning for which reflectively, they find it difficult to fully account. I may embody, live the logos but be put to the test in trying to account for the logos (*logon didonai*). What the sage reveals in practice, the philosopher wants to comprehend in thought. One makes an ideal concrete in the very flesh, as it were. The other thinks through the significance of this meaningful incarnation. There are many ways of being mindful. The sage embodies mindfulness through the particularities of his deeds and enigmatic words; philosophy may articulate the meaning of this way in language that strains further for reflective universality.

Such reflective universality seems abstract and remote, but this is not a decisive difficulty. Even the most abstracted of philosophers now and then feels the stir of the sage in himself, and will seek to show the relevance of his universal concepts to particular cases. The fuller the philosopher is, the less his universality is merely abstract, and the more the mediating power of his thought is able to move back and forth in intermediate being between universal and particular. The sage communicates by metaxological presence; the philosopher communicates by the truthfulness of metaxological thought.

Since this presence of the sage is ambiguous, pronouncing itself in riddles, proverbs, parables, inevitably the *critical* spirit, the cynic's cry, will rouse. Is the riddle a shell without secret kernel? Are these vatic utterances really vacuous oracles? Are the deep platitudes of the sage indistinguishable from idiot wisdom (see chapter 6)—a strange serenity unnervingly free of the metaphysical stress of the middle? And when the philosopher sees the *disciples* sitting rapt, the skeptic in him squirms. Doubt has wormed its way to the center, and ousts discipleship; he declines to sit at another's feet. Unlike some sages, the philosopher is disquieted at his *own* disciples, embarrassed when they sit at his feet. If disciples must attach themselves to him, he would prefer followers with fight.

It would be wrong not to acknowledge that on occasion the philosopher will yield to the sage in himself and riddle. For shorthand let me just name two heroes of contemporary thought who riddle: first the later Heidegger; and lest analysts smirk in condescension at the "wooly" Continentalist— Wittgenstein.[45] But besides the riddling self, there will always be another self to laugh and refuse the riddle. The speaking self riddles, the listening self refuses. Often the philosopher is both speaking and listening, uttering and refusing rolled in one. This is part of the double nature of thinking: the intermediation between affirmation and negation, proposing and disposing, with here and there a peppering of perhaps. The philosopher knows middle thought to be an incessant alternation between extremes, an endless conversation between thought and its others. Thinking mediates with itself but also makes war on itself, on its own perennial seduction to closure against otherness. Failing incitement from elsewhere, from external others, the philosopher is the type who picks a quarrel with himself. He makes himself other.

Philosophy as Metaxological

Who then is the philosopher? The answer emerging is: no-one and every-one. The philosopher is all and none of the figures above portrayed. He is the thinker of the interstices and connections, the spaces of intermediaton between thought and its others, between pluriform mind and the plenitude of being. The philosopher is the thinker of the middle. He has no univocal identity in the middle, even in the act of metaxologically "identifying" the shapes of others and their relations. But the result of this is not equivocal, in that in the ambiguity of the middle, philosophy as middle mindfulness is both dialectically self-mediating and metaxologically intermediating with otherness. This double mediation sifts the ambiguity of the middle, but precisely in order to remain true to its truth. Thus, *the* philosophical voice does not exist; there are many voices and philosophy itself is plurivocal. To vary the metaphor and slyly borrow from Nietzsche and Hegel: the philosopher is no one-eyed Cyclops, but a thousand-eyed Argus. One sees and yet there is more to see and other ways to be seeing. There is no totalizing closure or closed totality.

The philosopher need not reduce being and mind to univocal unity; nor need he scatter, disseminate being and mind into an equivocal plurality without deeper community; nor need he dialectically reduce being and mind to moments within a closed totality. The philosopher thinks the metaxological community of being and mind. Plurivocity is here the promise of communivocity—a promise sometimes redeemed in the babble that also always threatens. So as we moved from scholar, to technician, and so on, we have seen the double mediation of mind variously at work in a complex community of others in which the philosopher is also participant. As we move towards the sage, we move towards the *existential living* of the double mediation. The sage wins respect for a rich equilibrium of being, for resolving the lived contradictions we confront without dissolving the dynamism of our being. The sage lives this vigorous resolution; the philosopher reflects on its sources, forms and goals to clarify its ultimate efficacy. He distances himself from the sage only to sharpen this lived resolution at the level of reflective mind. Still in the middle, the skeptic in him is the devil's advocate that asks even the divine to prove itself. Devil's advocacy is the absolutely necessary negative side of philosophy, without which any affirmation would be bland and untrue. Philosophy as middle mindfulness mingles yes and no, openness and critical reflection. In subsequent chapters, I want to consider this doubleness of the metaxological in relation to being aesthetic, being religious, being ethical and being mindful itself.

C H A P T E R 2

Being Aesthetic

The previous portraits make up a family of figures concerned with the significance of being in the middle, each also metaphorical of a mode of mindfulness. In turning to being aesthetic, I intend no mere aestheticism but a crucial comportment towards being, a way of being with ontological weight. The poet may be its most concentrated configuration, but what he concentrates individually is continuous with a way of being that human beings, simply as human, reveal. Hence I use the term "aesthetic" in its widest traditional sense, that is, as relating to sensuous apppearance (*to aisthētikon*) and the modes of mindfulness bound to sensuous apearance. I am concerned with being aesthetic as showing the appearance of mind within our sensuous placement in the metaxological community of being. There is no argument for the appearance of mind that does not itself presuppose mind, for every argument is a form of mind. But this circle is not malign; instead of a logicist deduction of mind from non-mind, it demands of us a phenomenological fidelity to appearing mind.

The aesthetic is this encompassing sense brings home to us an otherness that challenges philosophy to a different mindfulness of thereness in the middle. Being becomes drab prose when a merely utilitarian mentality neutralizes the thereness for purposes of exploitation. The aesthetic asks for our recovery of the *poiēsis* of intermediate being. This cannot be confined to its artistic expressions, even granting these as frequently its most exemplary articulations. We are pointed to an origin of meaning as coming to articulation in sensuous being, in that this is more than mere neutral matter, in that we desire to transfigure any valueless thereness of bodily being, in that we cannot renege on the exigency to beautify being. Against art's idolization as in *l'art pour l'art*, against such cultural compartmentalizing, the aesthetic is not an insulated whole but an opening to the otherness of the whole.[1]

In what follows we will look at the metaxological community between self and other in being aesthetic. We are immediate participants in the metaxological where we spontaneously live a certain intimacy with being.

The metaxological bond of self and other emerges in immediacy, but with its mediation we are allowed to stress, sometimes overstress, either the self or the other. In that the human self is dialectically self-mediating, it can inflate its own power to dominate the aesthetic middle. Thus, we may lose sight of the inherent community of self and other in aesthetic being. We can cease to participate properly in the metaxological, with aesthetic consequences such as we see in the so-called death of art. Despite this, the promise of the metaxological always persists. Art is essential to this promise and the recovery of a metaxological mindfulness of otherness at its richest.

In accord with the metaxological sense of being, my reflections will pass through these stages: from the immediacy of aesthetic being, through its dialectical self-mediation, to its express metaxological intermediation. This involves a progressive articulation of the complex senses of selfness and otherness in being aesthetic. First, I look at the wider sense of being aesthetic in its immediacy, where we discover the emergence of self-mediation in the human body itself. Second, I discuss beauty in relation to the self's *own otherness* and the ethical aspect of its aesthetic self-mediation. Third, I turn to art as a further, more concentrated emergence of articulation. Here I claim that imagination reveals the double mediation required by metaxological being: imagination is metaxological in revealing *both* the self's own inward otherness and the opening of the self to otherness beyond itself. I relate this doubleness to the two major ways in which art has been traditionally understood: first as imitation (which stresses an otherness beyond the self), second as creation (which stresses the self's own inward otherness). I claim that a certain balance of the two is demanded by the metaxological.

Since we can lose this balance and with it a sense of the aesthetic middle, I discuss—fourthly—this loss in relation to the modern notion of "creativity." This loss makes us attend to the cultured doomsayers who have proclaimed the "end of art." Such latecomers are properly mindful of the inhospitality of late modernity to the spirit of great art. But as we questioned philosophy's *felo de se*, so we cannot take such inhospitality as an unquestionable fate.[2] I will say that an undue dominance of the self leads to a forgetfulness of the metaxological but also that aesthetic mindfulness requires a reawakening to our being in the middle and its rerooting of selfhood in the otherness of being. Fifth, I discuss this rerooting of mind in the metaxological in terms of what I call art's tolerance of otherness.

I. THE IMMEDIACY OF THE AESTHETIC

Dualism, the Body and Being's Intimacy

I begin where all the grand dreams of art originate, namely, in our bodily rootedness. Great culture rises from a home that is humbly elemental—our fleshed humanness. Here we find the rudiments of being aesthetic, for here we live an elemental, yet elusive intimacy with being. We find ourselves as incarnate inhabitants of the metaxological, which itself is present to us with an intimate, inarticulate immediacy. In the immediate givenness of aesthetic being, that is, in our sensuous beginnings, we are not self-possessed solitudes, deliberately soliciting contact with others. We are spontaneous thrustings into an enigmatic world, surges of the energy of being responsive to the being of otherness as it touches us in the flesh. On our release to the earth we introduce ourselves by crying out, but we still enjoy an initially inarticulate intimacy with the body and in it with being. Our body as inhabiting the middle is a compacted, aesthetic intimation of the meaning of being. So also our embodied difference from the otherness of being reveals a fluid space of incessant interchange. If we neglect this primary intimacy and freeze our difference from things into an ontological gulf, the result is dualism, whether of a Platonic or Cartesian form. Set apart from the other, our estrangement from creation assumes priority over our intimacy. Our first crying out ceases to signify our calling on others. It becomes the gesture of our metaphysical grief.

Dualistic doctrines retard mindfulness of the aesthetic by oscillating between an *equivocal* and *univocal* sense of being. Hence these remarks are needed. Platonic and Cartesian dualisms have been especially influential. They dualize the doubleness of the middle and turn the otherness of being into an *opposition* between us and things. The overdetermined ambiguity of intermediate being is seen as equivocal, and thence reduced to univocity. Thus, instead of letting dialectical self-mediation and metaxological intermediation flower, dualism sets up division *within* the self and separates it into two different substances: mind and matter.

Consider the Cartesian *cogito*: it is thought thinking *itself*, but as set in opposition to its own machine-like body and to nature's otherness as an aggregate of soulless objects. Mind as spiritual is utterly unlike its opposite, the sensuous body. Our glassy essence, the superior substance is the abstracted mind, while the body is relegated to an inferior adjunct—so much mortal trash, a fleshed prison whence the soul pines for deliverance (Plato).[3] Thus, we lose our immediate intimacy with ourselves, for such ascetic doctrines look with suspicion, even hatred on the split body. Likewise, our bond with *others* is attenuated. If I am essentially a separable mind, my essence is invisible. To reveal self I must perforce resort to the body, but this is now a lifeless go-between, manipulable at will in a middle that is itself lifeless. Like a puppet, the strings jerking it into life are pulled from elsewhere by a detached mind, hovering voyeuristically outside the middle.

Dualisms risk identifying our essence with a condition of estrangement and are persuasive only because we are not simple. But we can be single without being simple. Mind and body are not two separate substances but different articulations of a singleness of being that is itself neither mental nor material. A certain wholeness of singular being as placed in the middle is originary; what normally are named as "mind" and "body" give expression to this origin but neither separately exhausts it.

Consider how we actually live the middle in, say, the sensuous intimacy of conversation: the gestures of hands, the volatility of faces, the flushed excitement of attentive eyes, the total expression of charged bodily presence—these are not the ventriloquizing of voyeuristic minds or the gauche embrace of scarecrows. Rather, the body is shaped, shapes itself, as the very presence of self, better, the selving of presence. It is a revelation of self to the other, to itself, an articulation of its being. The original disclosure of self is rooted in bodily expression (here is the half truth of behaviorism). Mind is not pure spirit entombed in the lifeless externality of flesh, ventriloquizing through a dummy. Self-expression is an act of significant embodiment. Bodily image is not a disposable extra but tends towards coincidence with expression. Being aesthetic is a living refutation of dualism in showing us *bodied mind* as activating its own self-mediation and intermediation with otherness—an activation grounded in our immediate intimacy with being.

These remarks apply to the biases of rationalistic philosophy, but similar considerations, and a complementary tendency to "neutralize" being, apply to the empiricist's view of experience. The power of empiricism resides in its insistence that experience opens up for us the world. Experience is something we accumulate with age, and depending on the quality of individual alertness, it is richer in some, more bare in others. But at the most basic level, it reveals that our body is not self-enclosed but inhabits the middle and brings us into touch with things. At its most rudimentary, experience is feeling, sensation, intimation. As with other sensitive animals, our consciousness is first bodily, what the Greeks called the *"aisthētikos"* (though very importantly Aristotle in *De Anima* says that *aisthēsis* is a *logos*).

But in their analysis, empiricists and behaviorists view experience as primarily descriptive of "objects." They are heirs to the scientific reduction of the flow of experience to primary and secondary qualities. The world offers a set of discrete sensory stimuli or impressions; experience is bodily response to discrete, atomic things. These latter are said to originate experience, impressing themselves on consciousness like a seal stamping itself on blank wax (a traditional mindless metaphor for mind). The objects are just "neutrally there," detached, indifferent entities; experience becomes a kind of neutral transaction between objects and us. Likewise, sensation becomes stripped of all "emotional values." Red is just red; it is not warm or terrifying, or reassuring or seductive; red is indifferently red. Its warmth or provocativeness is merely an emotional projection we impose on indifferent things. Experience is reduced to "pure" sensation, void of emotion. Notice how this projection must presuppose (as with dualism) the human being as essentially separable, detached, alienated from things. This is, our need to "project" is the reversed, reactive side, turned active, of our *lack* of intimacy with being in its otherness.

Contrary to this empiricist account, being aesthetic reveals a radically richer sense of immediate experience. In a sense there is no pure immediacy: all experience is already in some sense mediated. Sense-data are not pure immediacy but already differentiations from the originary intimacy of being, hence mediated results. The issue is really: what mediations remain true to what is given in or promised by the originary intimacy. Some mediations are abstractions and objectifications. Art, too, is a mediation but one close to the concrete appearing of being in its lived immediacy. Phenomenological fidelity to aesthetic being induces suspicion of the epistemological doctrine of "primary" and "secondary" qualities. I do not yet want to dwell with art, but since empiricism is influenced by a certain scientific abstraction of experience which it identifies with what is immediately given, I will anticipate and refer to art as an aesthetic naming that importantly points us to this originary richness of experience.

If we look at an artwork as "object," like a Van Gogh painting, the thing we behold is never emotionally neutral. These yellows are not neutrally there; these blues are genuinely somber; the golden sunlight is God's gaiety. These so-called "emotional values" belong to the thing before us. If the empiricist analysis is correct, the painting is just an inert strip of canvas, crowded with blots and blurs; the emotional values are merely subjective "projections" that we impose on the object and are not intimate to the thing itself. But, phenomenologically speaking, this analysis is very artificial. We do not experience the artwork as set apart into sensation on the one side and something subjective on the other. We experience, stronger, we are stunned by something sensuous that is richly charged with expressive power. We witness the emergence of charged presence, at once stirring and elusive. This point can be generalized to the extent that *all* experience originates in the aesthetic body.

In fact, there is something not only artificial but impoverished about the empiricist analysis. If experience is an *interplay* or *intermediation* between us and being in its otherness, the primary stress must be on their relatedness, on their coming together, not on their abstraction and separation. There is an aesthetic *community* between the body and being in its otherness: sense-data are abstractions derivative from this community. Experience is a complex conjunction of self and world into which emotion is inextricably woven.

Experience and emotion are not subsequently pieced together from essentially different things. From the start experience is charged with emotion through and through. Even emotional neutrality is itself an emotional mood, not itself entirely neutral. Emotion defines our feeling for the world, how we are attuned to it, what Heidegger calls *"Befindlichkeit."* Even the most desiccated abstractions of philosophy never entirely escape this.[4]

Thus, the neutralization of our world into an "It," indifferently there, is an abstraction from the originary abundance of being. The neuter "It" is a reduction to univocity of being seen as equivocal; it is not itself original being. Against any scientific abstraction, art prompts us to repudiate the dualisms productive of this reduction. Again my focus is not yet on art *per se*, but on art as especially revealing concerning originary experience. It is out of an original indeterminate matrix that being mindful comes to embodiment, analogous to the way the artwork comes to form. So for a bodied being art is especially fitting; it shows us, we might say, a sort of acme of embodiment. We clarify consciousness by articulating it, and the consciousness art clarifies is not experience sterilized of its emotional energy, nor severed from its bodily origins. Prior to this articulation, ordinarily our *rapport* with being is dimly defined and, like the drifting of the ocean, is all but impossible to fix or map. It is an amorphous flux, a tangle of immediacies, thoughts, haunting anxieties, unnamed longings. We are tumbled around *inside* this tangle; the ocean of feeling in which we swim surrounds us. (I use the metaphor of the ocean for the maternal indeterminacy and the originary intimacy with thereness that is being aesthetic. Thus *"mater"* is related to *"materia,"* matter: the metaxological as material is maternal.) We feel our being, have an inarticulate, sensuous sense of what it is to be, prior to becoming self-conscious of what and how and why we feel. This sense has an enveloping, enfolding character, difficult to name, for we *live* this envelopment by aesthetic being.

Art recalls us to this envelopment even in the very struggle to articulate this envelopment. The artist divines the secret shape of our attunement. Out of the tumult of fleeting impressions, out of the pandemonium of impulses, he singles out, or may be singled out by, particular objects or events that are steeped with significance. Significant particulars come to singularly bespeak a sense of the whole, a *rapport* with creation. What I stress is that this aesthetic *rapport* implies a bond of communication, a charged affinity between us and beings. This bond is immediately given in our aesthetic inhabitation of the metaxological community of being. Relative to it, the world may still be other but it is not a dualistic opposite. Where dualistic opposition engenders animosity towards being, by contrast, such otherness may arouse our admiration (*admirare* implies our being stunned into marveling, into praise and appreciation of what is before us). *Rapport* brings to mind our conjunction with creation, our elemental intimacy with the thereness of what is, made concrete in our being aesthetic. This brimming of experience with excess, this our intimacy with aesthetic concreteness, is clearly evident in the body's beauty, in how we beautify it. I turn now to this.

Purposeless Preening: The Celebrating Body

The hostility to the body harbored by monkist moralists, and sundry puritan sages responds to our undeniable finitude. The body epitomizes our finiteness: it suffers, it decays, it dies; ascetic contempt for flesh is also a refusal of finitude. Socrates, upheld by many as a philosophical exemplar, calls philosophy a "lifelong preparation for death"; death, like enlightenment, brings release from the fetters of flesh, liberating the real self, the soul out of its carnal coffin. Inevitably the ascetic, ill at ease with being aesthetic, casts an evil on sensuous beauty. The seductive body in its splendor, and especially woman in her allure might lead pure spirit astray. The artist, by contrast, celebrant of the aesthetic, repeatedly searches out strategies to reaffirm the body in its beauty. He brings to it a proper festive wisdom; the body is not to be reproached as impoverished matter; it has an inherent claim to respect. I now consider the body as an abundance of presence, as the appearing of mind in sensuous immediacy, in terms of what we may call functional, aesthetic, and expressive form.

Consider first the living body at the elemental level of *functional form*. The body's form is precisely molded to the functions it must perform to survive and perpetuate itself in health. Illness indicates a breakdown in functional form, with the accompanying deformation, invalidity of bodily activity. Functional form defines the body's plasticity and adaptability in its environment. The particular parts cooperate, coalesce into an intricate dynamic unity, even though this living organic community of the parts is often invisible on the surface. The body, as it were, hides its organic art. An other greets us with a broad smile, but we do not discern the community of facial muscles effecting this seemingly simple act. With increasing complexity of functional form, the body may also grow in its range of freedom. A plant is rooted in one place; perhaps only its seed floats loose, carried elsewhere by wind and air. An animal, through itself, moves about in its habitat and forages. But the human body not only moves through its environment; it mindfully surveys its world. In its self-activating freedom from its immediate surroundings, it begins to master what it surveys. The very environment is itself appropriated as an extension of the human body. Thus, in our tools, we bridge the gap between the body and external otherness, mediating in the world between an expansion and freeing of our own bodily power.

Beyond functional form there emerges a dimension of sheet *aesthetic form*. Perhaps in parrakeets and others birds, in insects, beasts and fishes, the dazzling display of color, markings, feathers, hair is linked with reproduction and the rituals of mating. But even nonhuman nature is prodigiously generous with what seems biologically useless beauty. Nature might be much more aesthetically drab, and its many species might still manage to survive and prosper. But nature is a peacock that struts and swaggers beyond any evident pragmatic intent. It preens itself purposelessly.[5] The human being is the animal who carries to an extreme this purposeless preening.

In this sense, the human body is singularly revealing of sheer aesthetic form. Consider the erect posture. The human body does not crawl or wriggle or slouch or merely squat like a toad. It directs itself upward and out, like a vector of transcendence, an embodied arrow to a beyond. In our posture we *stand out*: the human body is an ecstasy (*ec-stasis*) in the middle. Just as we notice and admire those gracefully carrying themselves with flowing posture, so within nature our bodily presence can carry a singular grace. When we recoil at deformation or ugliness, what shocks is the absence of this grace, normally taken for granted. In recalling this grace, I put myself at odds with a certain metaphysical resentment that denies us any singular beauty, a denial that justifies itself by reducing the human being to an indifferent thing among other things. Beauty is sneered at as the outworn piety of a tired humanism or a mummified religion. A common aesthetic posture now is to be anti-aesthetic, to seek to shock jaded sensitivities with the affront of the ugly. Is this a post-religious, post-humanist revenge on the body; is its secular skepticism simply a profane mirror-image of the traditional contempt of the religious ascetic?

Beauty, I shall argue, is linked with our sense of a singular dignity. In all its beauty the upright posture of the human body is densely ambiguous. It might be seen as the corporeal image of *adventure*: it looks out, it stretches out, it risks itself in all the dangers of the unexpected universe. If may be like an arrow to the beyond, but an arrow might be a communication or a weapon. The human body is both. That the human body is double follows from its mindful presence in the metaxological: that is, it is *both* self-mediating and open to otherness, concerned with its own intrinsic requirements of being and necessarily defined by relatedness to all other being. Thus, it carries our contact with what is other; is also makes us warriors. The erect posture is this ambiguous message of communication and aggression: an articulation in flesh of our organic wholeness, the openness of that wholeness in our desire for others, yet also our vulnerable trepidation before their very otherness.

Let us look more closely at the human body as appearing mind. If we attend to the head, ambiguous subteties are revealed. The nose alone might be the subject of a study. Think of how we screw up our nose to express an attitude—the thing itself is there: disdain! The nose is also a symbol of suspicion: like Hamlet we smell out the imposters. A certain wrinkling of the nose—this is no mere motion; it is a miniature drama whose motif is haughtiness. The nose is often associated with a negative evaluation or demeanor. To "cock a snout" is to communicate one's negation of the other, one's impertinence perhaps, or insolence or arrogant dismissal. We speak too of someone with a "nose for something," like a connoisseur. The nose is a symbol of spiritual powers, the powers of one "in the know," not just merely animal capacities like those of keen hounds for foxes. As we all know, the human nose, simply as an animal power, is pretty poor compared to that of even the most pampered poodle.

In signifying power the mouth is perhaps richer. It is not just a grinding maw for food but as the bodily organ of the voice, it expressly communicates the entire self, in its innerness and outerness. It speaks with fullest power of incarnate mind. A play of delight haunts these lips; other lips are twisted in scorn. And this is not just on one occasion: the *whole self* is there. One sees a mouth tight set and hard—an embodied refusal of openness, a warning that wards off every gesture of friendship, even before they have been offered. Another mouth twitches—a self verging on uncontrol and frenzied dissolve.

The eyes are strange globes of silence; but this silence shows a peculiar power to speak worlds. Thus, a glance can be swift or furtive or penetrating or evasive or modest or wrathful or stony or dead. The eyes are called the "windows of the soul": the intimate vulnerable inwardness of selfness comes to emergence in the body. Sometimes eyes are the show of troubled spirit, sometimes just a delicate gloss on darkness. This is partly why we experience it as a violence if another holds one's eyes for too long. Eye contact is fraught with ambiguity, dangerous ambiguity. It is to show respect for another not to bore into their eyes with one's own, threatening the fragile intimacy with a harsh, brazen look. This intimacy of the eyes is also related to the different mode of looking of lovers. In their look they lose themselves in the other's eyes; the dangerous intimacy is rescued from violence and rendered benign.

The eyes, too, carries connotations of superior power. Thus, God has a been likened to a ubiquitous, all-seeing, all-searching eye. No wall or secret, no hiding place nor hidden thought can resist its merciless, merciful power. Eternity watches time down to its last shameful detail. But the terror of this eye is not all, for it gazes on things in peace, looking serenely on being with the look of blessing. Here we find the celebrating freedom of the surveyor of worlds, superior to the world in its rejoicing in the world, the benign beholding of the Creator resting on the seventh day.

Of course, superior power can be abused, and this too is disclosed in the eye. In our brazen looking we can be too forward, too prideful, too stiff-necked. The dart of the eye releases its look as a weapon. It is to counteract this conquering side of vision that a necessary modesty has frequently been enjoined. This moderation comes to us in the guise of the modest mien. There the prominent feature is the eyes turned down — not cast down in abjectness but rather turned inward with a certain reserve and reticence. Contemplatives of old recognized this hubris of the eyes (Sartre understood it very well), their insatiable concupiscence, when they practiced what they called "*custodium oculis*," custody of the eyes. Thoughtful, mindful, inwardized eyes become the guardians of our deepdown dignity, a dignity that is violated by pride's insolence.[6]

In the measure that it displays itself as an ordered, dynamic, well-balanced whole, every vital thing (not just the human body) exhibits living aesthetic form. Non-living things manifest aesthetic form too, though the form is just there, quiescent, not actively proclaiming its presence. The aesthetic proclamation of presence, the dynamic drawing of attention to self by sensuous attraction, is not just a matter of increasing biological power. In many respects our biological prowess is inferior; many other animals outdo us in the range of sensuous attunement of eye or ear or nose. They sense a presence, where we feel nothing but the vacant wind; they see a prowler haunting the darkness which for us in only black night; they scent the coming of the thunderclap, while we balm heedlessly in the sleepy sun. Biologically they are on the alert while we just picnic.

Nevertheless, we discover an increasing delicacy and refinement of aesthetic form when comparing the human to the animal body. Compare again the subtlety of the human nose to the biologically more powerful snout of swine. Or compare the exquisite perfection of the child's ear to the elephant's floppy tobacco leaf. Not that the latter lacks its own peculiar perfection; instances of perfection are so abundant in nature we frequently fail to appreciate them. Yet somehow a child's ear — and this sounds like paradoxical hyperbole — approaches a certain acme of perfection. Here is matter overcoming its own materiality and preparing itself to become a vessel of spirit. The human ear is matter become inwardized, matter become a form of receptivity fuller than the physical. It is not just a listening device, nor a mechanical receiver, nor just an organ of biological alertness. It may stand ready with a different vigilance, as in the admonition "Those who have ears . . ." Hearing is a free opening of spirit: we may assent (we lend our ears); we may refuse or resist (we stop our ears). Hearing is a measure of character.

The human body is nature's very art, a moving living artwork. It is more than functional form: the ordered adaptability of the organism fitting it for survival and biological prospering. It is more even than aesthetic form: the beauty of formed harmony that we delight to behold in its attracting thereness. Here aesthetic form becomes *expressive form*: beauty that beatifies life, a creation of nature that itself becomes creative. In the human body the aesthetic form draws attention to itself through the expressive form that proclaims and utters its presence. If the human self is nature's artwork, here with its original expressive powers, this art is *doubled*, and a new world begins its birth. Expressive form is witness to this new awakening in the middle, this astonishing leap above the erstwhile silence of being.

In the body as expressive form, the content of the human spirit is concretely shaped and made present. We now move beyond aesthetic immediacy, for expressive form is the beginning of the *self-mediation* of the aesthetic. This self-mediation will occupy us more fully later, but for now we must continue to dwell with the body as expressive form. Thus, a hand waves—this is not just a chunk of matter propelling itself through space, but a gesture that carries and communicates a world. Thus, this soundless word might greet our homecoming; it might bid farewell at parting; it might dismiss with noiseless contempt; it might beckon with seductive allure. A wave of the human hand opens up, mediates worlds of human relations. (As a philosophical failure to see this, I think of the mindless simplicity of G. E. Moore's hand waving, as if *that* refuted idealism: on the contrary, his hand was not a hand simply but an entire philosophical position, that is, a living embodiment of the truth of the idealism he thought he was realistically refuting.)

For the expressive body is an entire system of communication. As we move from plant to animal to man, we witness a deepening "interiorization" of the sense of self. But with this deepening grows an increasing freedom of "exteriorization," that is, of expressive and communicative power. Again the *face* is the true focus of the body's expressive power. Hence, it is the first place wherein we try to read the person. The face is what first draws or repels us; we study there for hints alerting us to the presence of singularity. The faceless crowd, rightly derided by Kierkegaard and Nietzsche, is the betrayal of our singularity as bodied forth in the face.

Of course, we often read most into the voice, for it possesses great conquering, dominating power, indeed discomfiting power. It might even destroy our attraction to aesthetic beauty, as, for instance, when a squeaky, rasping sound, coming from a beautiful face, tempts us to laugh. Alternatively, the beauty of voice, the beauty of spirit it bears, can win us, even when we are spontaneously repelled by externals. A delicate, gentle voice in an ugly face draws us back again, astonished. The word is the acme of incarnate beauty, for in it the human spirit in its entire range becomes most freely expressive of itself. For this reason poetry, when the great artist vanishes into sheer voice, might be held to be the most expressive artform.

Let us briefly consider what art shows us of the body's expressive power, namely, how the expressive body becomes charged with a sense of the significance of the *whole*. Again we are pointed to the double mediation of the metaxological. For the expressive body cannot be contracted into a closed material monad; its own self-mediation becomes expressive of the larger world of otherness that it inhabits; in expressing itself, it is also the bearer of the otherness; in this sense it is an aesthetic microcosm, a particular concretization of the community of being. In some sense all art is a celebration of the body's expressive power. This is evident with arts like dance. Some thinkers, R. G. Collingwood for example, held that all language is originally dance: expressive, imaginative gesture.[7] Originally, too, dance seems to reveal a religious, magical significance. In its most obvious forms this was connected with fertility, which earlier humankind invested with incomparable sacred significance. The dance served to renew the religious mystery of bodily origination and genesis. Even today the secularized dance can create something of the archaic aura of sacred sex. If solitary individuals dance together, by that act they become partners in the dance, partners in an energy of being beyond their solitudes. The dance extends beyond its ritual limit, such that all life, in the expressive beauty of its reaching beyond, is a kind of dancing that stretches out of solitary subjectivity to the whole of otherness.

In painting, the bodily medium has been refined to a surface upon whose face color and form work, once again, to evoke an entire world. Even the most transitory, evanescent, momentary moods, say, of light, can be contemplated here. The painter then may hold still for our gaze the fugitive beauty of the sensuous world. One thinks of the strange serenity of that light playing in Vermeer's paintings. The human body as expressive form even comprises a distinctive genre in painting, marking once again human singularity: the nude.[8] The nude is not raw naked corpulence but insinuates the mystery of human flesh—that this flesh radiates with the quality of presence. To capture this shimmer of radiant presence is the work of genius. One thinks of the peculiar delicacy of human skin, and painting's efforts to portray its subtle, all but incommunicable shades. Words may fail to describe the color of skin in its nuance, yet painting may present to our vision this elusive lustre.

Sculpture is another witness to the body's expressive beauty as an aesthetic microcosm that in its own self may mediate a sense of larger otherness. Consider freestanding figures of the naked body. Statues of the Greek gods stand before us in their repose and serenity. The quality of spiritual presence is also rendered in the figures of wrestlers, boxers, warriors, athletes. The Greeks presented the body in the light of their vision of its idealized perfection. Everywhere the celebration seems to grow out of the motive of reverence. Even their attitude to the athlete was not devoid of a religious note. The great athlete was gifted of the gods, his bodily prowess a treasured bestowal of the divine. To portray the body in its idealized perfection was simply an act of gratitude for this gift. Bodily beauty was a presentiment of perfected humanity, which, in turn, was not radically distinguished from the gods themselves as images of immortal perfection. Beauty could be a reminder that being might be other than our present domestications of its original power. Stendhal later implied something similar in calling all beauty *"une promesse de bonheur."*

It is significant that the Greek celebration of the athlete declined with the decline of religious belief. Celebrating the athlete, the community celebrates itself; losing faith in its gods, its dream of perfected otherness, it loses courage and assurance in itself. One might say that the body is a kind of liturgy (in the Greek sense): a festive work of public celebration. Nor is this intimacy of gods and body confined to Greek paganism. Despite many severe ascetical strains throughout its history, for Christianity the axis round which history revolves is incarnation, absolute word and flesh at one. Reverence for the body as a sacred space is granted to our flesh, seen as the house of the Holy Ghost. Even the suffering body might become a ceremonial life, a sacrament.

If we compare all this to the modern mechanization of the body, we discover a shocking alteration in the sense of our sensuous presence to being. This relates to the neutralization of the charged otherness of being, spoken of at the outset. Thus, Descartes, one philosophical father of modernity, thought the body a mere machine, an automaton used by a separable soul. This Cartesian mechanization has been pervasive in modern culture, and the view has been called, by Gilbert Ryle, "the dogma of the ghost in the machine." In time the ghost ceased to haunt the machine and a mechanical view of the whole self prevailed. Recently this attitude is less accepted, as more organicist, holistic views have emerged. Modern science first treated the body as a fairly simple machine, but the more it knows about this "machine," the more intricate, infinitely intricate it appears. The sway of mechanistic attitudes is still not broken, as we see, for instance, in the way conventional medicine is often more a matter of advanced technology than the ancient art of healing. Even in cults like "the body beautiful" the residue of mechanism works hiddenly. Even while denouncing mechanization, this cult does not pass beyond a superficial exteriority. It fails to attain the depth of beauty where the body, as it were, shines out from itself and reaches to become the expressive form of spirit. The interpenetration of body and mind still remains enigmatic, as does the interpenetration (I would call it metaxological intermediation) of bodied mind and being's otherness. What also remains enigmatic is that quality of radiant presence that art, though it has never explained it, has always profoundly acknowledged it.

II. AESTHETIC SELF-MEDIATION

Beauty and the Adorning Self

We have just suggested how the immediacy of the aesthetic body as expressive can mediate an entire sense of a significant world. I now want to dwell with my second theme: the explicit self-mediation of the aesthetic body. I will consider the phenomenon of adornment as indicating the self's power of *being-other*. For with this we find the opening of the self to a more complex, *pluralized* identity. Not only is the body spontaneously an expressive form, but we also *work* on it as adorning beings; our bodies are wrought into artworks, that is concretizations of mind in sensuousness. We see the aesthetic again as a form of being mindful closest to bodily being, showing there the *poiēsis* of emerging mind. We also will begin to see the aesthetics of the ethical.

Consider here how the animal's contentment with itself shows no discontent with being to trouble its seemless immediacy; its being does not loom before it as a question; it just is. With us something more turbulent surges up; our being is questionable to itself, hence we conjure up the image of another, fuller humanity—we dream of ourselves as *other*. Therefore, something essential about our singular being is disclosed and hidden in self-adornment, for it shows us as *living superfluously*.

What does this mean? Animal desire seeks definite objects—food, shelter, and sex. It repeats itself—now briefly satisfied, in a moment it will spring up dissatisfied again. It repeats itself in a circular way—the animal moves through the round of nature, alternating endlessly between lack and repletion. The animal is nature's naked immediacy, bare and unadorned. Suppose we are deprived of clothes and shelter, evicted from fellowship, unhoused in the rough elements. Would we then have the thing itself? "Thou art the thing itself," Lear cried, "unaccommodated man is no more but such a poor, bare forked animal as thou art." But such a divestment is a violence to us, indeed a violation. We deprive the self of its being human, when we reduce it to such a raw, naked essence. As Lear also cried: "Our basest beggars/ Are in the poorest things superfluous / Allow not nature more than nature needs / Man's life is cheap as beasts' " (King Lear, Act II, sc. iv, 263-266).

The sensuous in us, human flesh, is not a mere outside, a house of straw. It is an outering revelation of an energy of being not itself exhausted in outerness. It is a fragile display in which inwardness shines and comes to communicate itself. Our sensuous being is itself superfluous life—the incarnation of a "more." It bodies forth something more than just body; it is the incarnation of being mindful. Human sensuousness is free sensuousness.

Again the human face is the perfect example of freedom emergent in embodied form, given its amazing plasticity of expressive power. Freedom emerges in our sensuous being as a surplus, an excess that is not initially controlled by self-conscious will. It is the spontaneous eruption of original power that loosens and breaks through the hard crust of nature's necessity. Such freedom gives us the power to imagine forms of human possibility beyond those actually given, allows us to image an ideal in sensuous shape. In that we can image the ideal, idealize the real, we are beings who do not have to accept being as a fated given, but who can transfigure it into a pool of possibility, a promise of novelty and improvement. We impose new form on the material given us, including the materiality of selfhood itself. This idealization articulates a new image of selfhood, liberates our surplus power, originates the realm of culture as the human cultivation of the human.

Some individuals are gifted with natural beauty. Beauty flowers in them. But always time's battering must be granted. Beauty of nature is fugitive, and soon care of self is needed. The body, nature, must be covered, preserved with a new nature, a new creation. To safeguard our essence, we must adorn ourselves. Perhaps we first safeguard ourselves for primitive reasons of preservation against enemies: threatened, we threaten, painting the face with the mask of the savage beast. To terrorize the threat we *become the painted image* of the preying, blooded beast. But this process may be freed from ulterior motive and become an end in itself. Self-preservation is a self-mediation closest to biological need, but there are self-mediations free of biological necessity. I paint my face, and behold the simple slash of color opens up an entire world, an entirely different consciousness. I become the image transcribed on my face; I am transmuted into the life of otherness in the image itself.

Indeed as adornment is increasingly done for its own sake, it becomes a free play of forms, not tied to an extrinsic purpose. Its imaging of otherness may do less violence to the face, cease to distort it into sub-human form. We may dream of otherness in terms of powers more ultimate than the vital, blind organic energies of animal excitation. The adorning self now detects delicate subtleties in the face. The face becomes a suggestion, a sign, the faint trace of virtualities of spirit hidden within its surface folds, the hint of ultimacy. Adornment sets out to highlight these traces, to follow the beckoning of this hint, to coax from human contours the image of god-like beauty. Idealization breaks with any tendency to brutalize. It rather becomes an act of the *divination* of the human. In our sensuous being divine presence may lie in wait. Adornment may serve to release this sensuous divinity in the striking presence of rare beauty. The nobly beautiful face gathers to itself our wandering vision, nurturing our nature on the serene harmony of the secret god.

Thus, adornment is an aesthetic self-mediation but it produces a *doubling* or pluralizing of identity. Consider here the phenomenon of the *mask*. We both are as we appear and are not as we appear, that is, we are masks. Being aesthetic is here related to the emergence of "being true." The latter is complex, since the self being true to its own intermediate being discovers itself, not only in relation to others, but discovers itself as the power to present itself as other than itself. Human selfhood reveals an original power of *self-othering*. Thus, with the mask, we come across a distinction between "seeming" and "being" that allows us to deceive and dissimulate. We mask ourselves in our appearances, such that our identity becomes opaque and enigmatic, even twisted. We reveal self obliquely, and sometimes have to be unmasked, so elusive can be our ambiguous inwardness. We inwardly hide our own ambiguous otherness in response to the ambiguity of the otherness surrounding us. Thus we often think of masks negatively. When Hamlet replied to his mother: "Seems, madam? Nay, it is. I know not "seems," . . . . But I have that within which passes show," he was invoking this negative side of masking. As outward seeming, the mask is a potentially deceptive show of self that masquerades as something other. Hamlet was also calling on the element of mystery: the within that passes show, the truth impossible directly to reveal, the innerness of self, indeed its inward otherness, beyond all showy exterior display.

But the mask's ambiguity, like that of "being true," is doubled-edged.[9] Consonant with the double mediation of the metaxological sense of being, the mask also makes apparent, *brings out* into the open what would otherwise be lost in labyrinthine inwardness. A person dons a mask and is suddenly transformed. The shy, gauche person becomes a flamboyant actor. The mask liberates, releases from normal social constraint. Normal self-consciousness may paralyse efforts at self-revelation, or even merely being oneself. The mask may put a thin paper barrier one and others but it miraculously lifts the psychic veil that repressed presence. One thinks of the anonymity granted revellers at a masked ball. All rigid roles are suspended; being becomes fluid again and, as in childhood, open to magical transformation.

Of course, it is the actor who knows most intimately the power of the mask. A mask creates a new identity, catapults the actor into the different world of an other self. It originates a new self, makes impersonation possible, the injection of living energy into a merely imaginary role. It actualizes an imaginative possibility; the appearance invents a reality. It makes possible the multiplication of identities, showing forth the open potency of the unfinished self. In fact, the first actors wore actual masks; the mask was the persona; the actor was agent of the mask, servant of the persona. Now an actor, shedding the physical mask (though never entirely, as the use of make-up shows), must make himself into an invisible, imaginative mask. His service to the persona becomes interiorized—inward imaginative identification with the role of the other. In this imaginative interiorization of the mask, the actor takes the persona to heart. The role then is played from within out.

I stress that this pluralizing of identity can *open* the self to even the most radical *otherness*. Thus, some masks present the power of religious mystery, the holy in its terrifying and overwhelming enigma. We gaze on those ritual dance masks on display in sedate museums, but even there demonic power seems to emanate from them. We wonder at how much more primordial must have been this power when the mask came alive in its proper setting, in the sacred dance itself. The dancer dons the mask of the ritual animal and he *becomes* the animal power; he dons the god's mask and his dance *is* the god dancing. The mask releases the dancer from quotidian consciousness and makes him the receptive vessel of power lower and higher, powers savage and ecstatic. In the religious mask archaic man danced his identity with the energy of the whole. The mask itself becomes the presencing of unmastered otherness.

Beauty and Dignity

Thus, adornment is far more than any escapist wallowing in languorous sensuousness. Emerging from the immediacy of our metaxological intimacy with being, it forms the outerness of self into an incarnate presence of meaningful inwardness. Moreover, there is an implicit *ethical* aspect to this mediation. We witness the appearance of an indispensible ethical feeling: the sense of *dignity*.[10]

Dignity is the irreducible sense that the human self has an inerasable worth, even despite the indignities that nature or fortune might heap on it. Dignity and beauty belong together in that the latter is the aesthetic counterpart to the ethical sense of dignity. Adornment is not just an alteration of a mere externality, but brings with it changes of character; the outer transformation brings an inner shift. At the origin of exterior self-adornment is an upsurge of interior self-consciousness that presupposes our ability to see ourselves as if from an external perspective. Here again the self doubles itself; it is both the subject and object of vision, the seer and seen. Beholding ourselves as in a mirror, beholding *ourselves* in the mirror, we see ourselves as we imagine *others* to see us, thus growing aware, through an imagined sense of the other, of individuality in the round. Adornment thus is an aesthetic self-mediation that includes also the self's imaginative intermediation with others.

Beauty is thus especially important to a being with a developed sense of self, a sense of special worth that extends beyond nature's limits. Adorning is our husbanding of natural beauty, our prolonging of it beyond the lavish squandering and quick dissipation of nature itself. Nature seems to care little for the particular beauty of *this* individual. It gives beauty with such astounding generosity as to seem thoughtless, even careless. Its luxurious excess extends to the whole, such that its reckless bounty almost comes to this: what if one beauty dies, a myriad will spring up to replace and renew. This reckless generosity towards the whole seems like indifference to the individual, an equivocal proliferation that is neutral to the worth of any individual as individual, a refusal to absolutize any particular.

Yet the human self, nature's most individualized this, *singles itself out*. We will to perpetuate the beauty given us individually, preserve it from encroaching age, prevent the decay that quickly sets in if nature has its way. When nature has had its way beyond a certain ripeness, we say that the growth has "gone to seed." The flower gives up, surrenders its individual beauty for the perpetuation of the species. At the moment of full bloom, the flower sings to the world its ripeness. Its beauty is its singing thereness, but this beauty is a swan song. The beautiful individual goes under and broadcasts a promise of renewal; in going to seed it sacrifices its individuality for a thousand future flowers. But we want to circumvent nature, even cheat it, by turning the power that both generates and scatters into a different, more singular perpetuation. We try to maintain, sustain a ripeness in adornment. We too "go to seed," but think of this as a kind of failure, a failure to cultivate the self, or care appropriately for it, a failure to respect the dignity of flesh.

Nietzsche said that the one thing needful was to give style to one's character. Many of us are like the flowers, and delight to see our being perpetuated in the fresh beauty of offspring: children are songs of continuing beauty. But human perpetuation insists on more than carrying forward of the species; we crave self-perpetuation, individualized self-perpetuation. Adornment ministers to this desire. This is not a question of reducing the ambiguity of becoming to one univocal identity, as if nature as genesis were a duplicitous equivocation process. It is one of gathering selfhood in an identity whose very pluralization mirrors its metaxological intermediation with the otherness of becoming.

So it is a simplification to see adornment as just narcissistic self-obsession. Quite the opposite: to be capable of self-adornment implies liberation from narcissism. Narcissus has no sense of himself at all. He failed to recognize himself in the mirror of the still pool, falling in love with what he did not know was his own face.[11] Narcissus did not drown for love of himself but because he *failed to know himself* in his reflection; he drowned in ignorance of himself, or what comes to the same thing, in his impotence to imagine any otherness. Self-adornment liberates from narcissism because the pure narcissist, in his absolute self-immersion, is oblivious to the possibility of being-other, of self-othering, and hence to the call of the other as other.

The narcissist is swallowed in the immediate undifferentiated self; he cannot stand back from self and imaginatively leap free from this envelopment and so envisage an other self. Without the image of such an other, ideal self, the very possibility of self-adornment is excluded.

Adornment can be a concern for self without being an indulgence of self. We adorn what we think might look better. This impulse emerges from self-discontent. We feel that if we look better, we might *be* better. Beyond univocal identity and equivocal difference, appearance and reality work together in a *dialectical mutuality*. Our appearance discloses our reality; but when we adorn ourselves, the reality tries to catch up with the appearance; we endeavor to be as we look, as our actual self strives after the ideal self it envisages.[12] For instance, a change of clothes can bring a changed person and thus confirm the adage: clothes make the man. Clothes alter mindfulness of self because they carry aesthetic alterity, articulate the inescapable presence of others. So they effect one's entire comportment towards the world. How one wears cloths, though they be tattered rags, may reveal a complete demeanor towards being, one's own and that of others. For instance, we speak of "shabby gentility." This is a dialectical concept, a *coincidentia oppositorum*. The "shabbines" and the "gentility" seem mere incompatibles, but the point is *how* the "shabbiness" is carried. In some cases the "gentility" shines through and catches up the faded garments in the light of a special dignity. "Shabbiness" can be worn differently. It can be worn without grace, cheaply. But sometimes patches can be worn as badges of sartorial panache.

Hence, clothes are not simply artificial protection against the unruly elements to compensate for bald bodies. They may define a kind of self, may communicate the color of a personal presence. They testify to a self in dialectical mediation with the other who, in fact, the dressed self has imaginatively interiorized. They may even create a kind of self.[13] If one dresses in certain types of clothes, one finds oneself becoming that type of person. So especially for children "dressing up" is a fundamental imaginative exploration of the human world. Likewise, actors bring this exploration to the level of art when they dress up. The best actors are the most adept adorners, those who dress up the self *in imagination* itself, those who inwardly transport the self into another being, or alternatively allow the other into the inner "space" of imagination. Clothes are social, cultural concretions of dialectical and metaxological mediations between selfness and otherness. This transport of selfness into otherness or otherness into selfness can occur also when we assume the uniforms of different professions. For clothes are roles, clothes are acts that imply a world. Put on the soldier's garb, and the self struts tough; shelter the pate with a judge's wig and how easy it is to thunder verdicts; ring the neck with a clerical collar, and the melting devotee all but swoons into piety.

Despite the release from pure narcissism in all of this, there is no denying conceit and vanity. Conceit comes from an excessive self-consciousness in the form of an immoderate self-regard. The vain person is one fooled by its own mask, one who fools itself with its appearance, takes the mask, the appearance for the complete self. It preens itself in its appearance, vanishing without residue into its own surface. When reminded that, after all, this is surface, the vain person reacts with inordinate touchiness—testimony to the developed sense of self. Vanity is paradoxically both an amnesia of otherness and yet inordinately touchy about the other's opinion. The vain self, obsessed with its own difference, is really indifferent to real difference. It vanishes in that fleeting glimpse of itself it caught in the shop window. Though the vain one is always looking into the mirror, it never sees into the mirror. Always looking at itself, nothing but itself, in the end it sees nothing of itself. Where there is only self, there is no self.[14]

In a word, vanity and conceit are degenerate forms of dignity. Dignity is the proper pride we take in ourselves in the doubleness of our intermediate being; that is, both before others and in inner relation to ourselves. We delight in beautiful form as the sensuous shape of dignity and develop a cult of manners to dignify our doing. The cynic, indeed the Rousseauian, might scoff and ascribe this to fustiness and falsification and artificiality. But without artifice, the human being is not human. We beautify the world when we turn energy in excess of animal vitality to the creation of delighting forms of life. What is crude may be refined, especially the body; the world itself may be made to embody a more human ideal.

It is not just the will-to-power that fuels this desire. The will-to-power is not negligible, but we are capable of a self-expression more civilized than the impatient, brusque will to assert ourselves. At our best self-expression is inseparable from openness to otherness such that we are capable of a *chivalry towards being*. Beauty then becomes a bestowing presence, the *gracing* of life itself. No longer impelled by nature's necessity, this is something gratuitous but in an entirely positive sense. It wells up from gratitude to being, even in its otherness, which we salute in the generous expenditure of our own being.

When the exuberant energy is untried, it naturally takes the form of youthful self-assertivenes. Thus, youth resorts to *outrageous* adornment: hedgehog hairstyles, safety pins through the nose. It does not work by seduction and allure but by affront to the installed decorum and the elders. The outrageous adornment gives notice to the other: Look at me! I am a self! I stand out! I am different! I make myself ugly! It is a kind of shout for dignity—a contradiction in terms, I know. But youthful energy cares little for contradiction. It wills to assert itself in its own otherness, announce its arrival to the stale elders by confronting them with the shock of the new. Wise cultures temper the energy but do not smother it. They change its self-assertive form into more civilized shapes, thus also rejuvenating the old forms with the flush of new blood. They try to match the calm beauty of sustaining form with the urgent energy of life itself. Of itself beautiful form becomes sterile, while raw energy quickly turns barbarous. Between these extremes civilized life seeks a wedding of beauty and energy (see chapter 4 on ethical civility).

The common word "cosmetics" reveals something of this marriage. We usually think of "cosmetics" as synonymous with "untrue appearance," as a false face on a hidden flaw, a gilding lying on the unsightly. But again the negative view is incomplete, and taken alone is untrue to the richness of aesthetic ambiguity or doubleness, as the Greek word "cosmos" shows. Cosmos is an adornment, but it also means the beauty of a well-formed, living harmonious whole. For some ancients, all of being was such a cosmos, such an adornment; the whole was beauty itself. Thus, the deeper meaning need have nothing to do with a "cosmetic" counterfeiting through vain externals, but with the shaping of self and its being into an artwork, its self-creation as a microcosmos, a whole of beauty imaging the beauty of the whole in its otherness to the human. When self-adornment attains such a level of being our own *poiēsis* of being, to be thus adorned is never to be narcissistic but to be cosmopolitan in this sense—a harmony of the human being, itself in harmony with being other than the human.

III. ART AND THE AESTHETIC MIDDLE

Imagination as Metaxological

It will be helpful to take our bearings, both recapitulating and anticipating. Thus far, we have focussed on our intimacy with being; against our neutering of otherness, I spoke of the charged body as aesthetically self-activated and self-mediating in adornment. The energy of our being as intermediate emerges in the aesthetic body as a mindfulness that is implicitly both self-mediating and open to otherness. This excess of energy that surges up in our aesthetic being is given *express* articulation by imagination. In fact, imagination's mediating power is implicit in all previous discussion without being made a focal theme. We now do this, since imagination offers a link between the wider sense of being aesthetic and artistic activity as one of its more concentrated expressions.

So let me anticipate my overall argument in the rest of the chapter: First, imagination surges up in us as an original articulating power that is rooted in the intimacy of being. It also show the double mediation of the metaxological: imagination is metaxological. Its doubleness can be artistically articulated thus. On the one hand, art can be seen in terms of *imitation* (the artwork is an image of what is other to the self), or on the other hand, in terms of *creation* (the self is original and the artwork is an image of the original self). These two possibilities reflect the sides of the other and the self that the metaxological holds together in a complex, non-reductive intermediation. Nevertheless, there is always the danger that one side will try to reduce the other to itself in order to master the middle through itself alone. Hence below I will say that a certain unturning of the screw of "creativity" risks a paradoxical cultural bankruptcy through a reduction to self-mediation of the double mediation of the metaxological. For if imagination (understood as "creativity") becomes interiorized in a too *subjectivistic way*, the self is separated from the other, becomes its dualistic opposite, and in the extreme becomes ontologically unanchored from the primary intimacy of being.

The latter provides the immediate metaxological ground of the human being's own self-mediation, despite the self's claim to be independent of that ground. This claim proves finally hollow. This hollowing happens with the historical unfolding of the Cartesian construction of being. Instead of being the paradigm of creative selfhood, and the acme of original self-mediation, the Cartesian self becomes ontologically hollow, and its unanchoring produces the metaphysical malaise that now raises our "postmodern" cultural disquiet about the already noted "death of art." But what is dead, should die, is the self ontologically deracinated from the metaxological matrix of being. At the end we must return to this in terms of art's intermediation with otherness.

With respect to imagination itself, as with respect to the aesthetic body, philosophers have tended to distrust it as something other and at odds with the logical mind. Some have implied that to imagine is to mistakenly take our fictions as facts, and so to fall into falsity; to imagine is to "see" as something what is nothing. Spinoza, for instance, implied that to have too lively an imagination is to risk bondage to illusions. Hume, to name another, calls poets "liars by profession." The import seems: to reach truth is to surpass mere imagination, to sober up the self for reason. Others are perhaps more sophisticated. Even when Plato gruffly attacked the poets, he did so because he perceived their *power*. Despite the ambiguity of images, it is all but impossible to be extricated from their sway; our being and the image seem to be ineluctably twined together.

Other philosophers acknowledged the necessity of images and not grudgingly. Imagination is seen to be an indispensible power. Vico, the great other to Cartesian rationalism, rightly saw in imagination the original activity by which we articulate ourselves and our world. It is the primordial naming, articulating of being. For Vico (Hölderlin, Nietzsche and Heidegger would agree) languages were originally poetic, as were the first human beings. An imaginative outlook, not self-consciously known as such, but simply lived, pervaded their entire sense of being. The world was one vast, vital drama, sympathetic to hope and dread, peopled with mythic powers, a work of living poetry. Afterwards as human beings settle, imagination cools, abstract thought advances and disenchanted rationality contemplates the dead obstinacy of things. Poetry precedes prose, even though science in time supplants myth. The sun that was a shining god for the first golden humans becomes for us iron latecomers just a conflagration of gases.

Though the prosaic mind develops from the poetic, the child sometimes turns cannibal on its parent. Then prose is split off from poetry, reason from imagination, science from art. The result can be dualism again, even enmity. As we saw before, dualistic thinking confuses our being in the middle with an equivocal process that must be reduced to univocal manipulability. The necessary double mediation is reduced to a univocity that services our will to master rationalistically the ontological engima of being in the middle. Thus, earlier in our century, we see this dualism in the way the positivists (A. J. Ayer, most famously) drew a thick line through the forms of human activity, placed empirical science and mathematics on one side, the meaningful side, and then consigned to outer darkness, by a kind of epistemological excommunication, other activities like art, religion and ethics.[15] They even banished most of what traditionally passed as philosophy—though when the positivists thought further about this, they became embarrassed by their own philosophizing, since it inconveniently turned out *not* to be an instance of science.

If thinkers like Vico are correct, however, to suppress imagination would be to stifle the primary source of all culture, whether scientific or humanistic. All knowing and hence every advance in civilization originates in the image. All original thinking, including scientific thinking, is first imaginative. In science imaginative thinking is first dismissed as "speculation"; then it is found that some "speculation" does strangely coincide with the real; only later we forget that the successful "speculation" had its origins in imagination, and become ungrateful to our first source. Imagination is a smithy wherein the first spark of mindfulness is struck. The image is the beginning of articulate mind, and though it may not be the end, everything subsequent is impossible without this beginning. Rational concepts themselves are not the complete opposites of images but images metamorphosed by reflective mind and by further self-conscious consideration.[16]

How is imagination a beginning? This question again concerns our singularity. An animal responds to the stimuli of its environment, registering what is before it in terms of its needs for protection and sustenance; absorbed in its environment, it makes with it an unselfconscious marriage. But we can free ourselves from such an enveloping immediacy, distance ourselves by *not* reacting to stimuli. Imagination reveals the power of freedom by which we first so distance ourselves. It initiates desire's *express* dialectical self-mediation and its metaxological intermediation with otherness. On this score, Kant's well-known distinction between reproductive and productive imagination is important. Reproductive imagination is the ability to join together previously given sensory images; working on already given material, impressions received and retained, it is a kind of sensory memory that preserves and rearranges the old but does not bring anything new into being. With productive imagination we do not find just the retention and ordering of old impressions but the generation of new images that lack a complete precedent in previous experience. Productive imagination gives birth to something that is not completely explicable in terms of prior impressions. It originates images from the self's own productive resources of being, free images that cannot be fixed to given sense impressions. Such free, productive origination seems to be a mark of human beings.

In strict terms imagination is transcendental: a necessary condition of the possibility of articulate experience.[17] The importance of this cannot be understated. Imagination can be understood metaxologically and not just in terms of subjective idealism. For it opens up the express sense of difference wherein we begin to contemplate the contours of otherness. Imagination gives us our most elemental and primordial freedom. It contributes to the articulation of the middle, lets us range in mind over the whole of creation and not be confined to our local little feeding patch.[18] It liberates an excess of being in us, makes more of us than organisms in bondage to the environs. With imagination we are not determined by external stimuli, but begin to determine our being though the power of its own self-differentiating and self-mediating spontaneity. The energy of being coursing through us is not spent in organic, animal purposes. Imagination emerges from the free articulation of the aesthetic body where the original energy of being becomes surplus. (Thus it originates the adorned self.) It is a kind of ontological overflow, an excess of energy that lifts itself above bodily necessity. As such imagination is the birth of mindful being as self-aware and open to the other as other.

Thus, mind as imaginative is not stopped before the given facts of sensory experience but roams beyond or within or beneath them, seeking more than their glaucous thereness, seeking the significance of creation. Beyond the immediacies of an environment, imagination opens a *world*, a human space of mediated meaning. Moving us into a realm of ideals, it mediates between body and mind; partaking of both body and mind,[19] it emerges from the first and concretizes the second. (In later chapters we shall see that since imagination is an articulation of desire closest to our bodily intimacy with being,[20] from it will also arise the darker images of religion and ethical images of blood.)[21] Imagination offers both an Ariadne's thread to the underworld of the inarticulate, and a song of Orpheus that calls us beyond our nocturnal caves of being to the ideal space of free mind. It allows us to envisage the other, indeed is always secretly originary of openness to otherness.

Thus, while productive imagination is crucial for all forms of ideal activity, it is especially important for art, which can idealize being, and transfigure its sensuous presence into the image of a golden world. Valéry was getting at something like this imaginative envisagement of transfigured otherness when he called the poetic word the "golden coin" of language. (The golden word is, so to say, the linguistic standard of intrinsic worth; other words are mere means, of instrumental use only.) Even art's depiction of ugliness need not be itself ugly. Artistic perfection allows us to see imperfection calmly, like still gods embracing all creation. Nor is this to forget *breaking otherness*, for, as Rilke says, the angel is terrible.

Being Imitative, Being Creative

Imagination's original opening to otherness relates to the ideas of imitation and creation, two fundamental ideas in the tradition of reflection on art. The first corresponds to art's imaging of external otherness, the second to its imaging of internal otherness. The metaxological requires the togetherness of both. Imitation is a more complex relation than commonly held, but it risks a *dualism* of image and original; art as creation actually develops the mediation implicit in imitation, meeting the problem of dualism in a concept of art as a *dialectical* self-mediation of mind in sensuous expression. But when this dialectic tilts excessively towards subjectivity, as in modern notions of "creativity," we can subjectivistically distort the aesthetic middle as properly *metaxological*.

Imitation has been the dominant idea in Western aesthetics, if we understand dominance temporally. It has an old and noble line, and art has been seen as imitating nature or eternal form or ideal beauty. Appeal to creation is more common now, at times in debased form. All one has to do is boil a bowl of tripe and one is credited with "creativity." Creativity has become a catchall for conceit. The accompanying denigration of imitation runs: be an original, don't be an imitation; imitation is second rate, only reproducing the old without producing the new; as mere copying, it just duplicates an original already complete in itself and so is only an *impoverished* version of that original; imitation is a mere parasite. So arises the dictate that we must cease "being like everyone else and be ourselves," cease being imitations and become originals. Imitation is merely reproductive imagination, while being creative shows the more primordial power of productive imagination. As Emerson famously said: Imitation is suicide.

Yet if we look closer, imitation is a far more complex and fundamental aesthetic mediation and hardly deserve its bad name. I put it this way: without a foundation of being like everything else, we could never become ourselves, for the selves we would become would be vacuous. One can exhort someone to become himself until one is blue in the face, but unless one starts by imitating others, that is, by being open to otherness, one will never stir from the spot. "Being oneself" amounts to "being nothing," however much one panders to vanity and suggests that the person is an absolute original.

In fact, the opposition of imitation and creation—one passive and unfree, the other active and spontaneous—is entirely misleading. To be able to imitate is to possess the power of imaginatively identifying with the other, a power far more complex than simple reproductive imagination. An imitating being has the fundamental capacity to be other to itself. Consider. I am Peter but I imitate Paul; if so, I am no longer plain Peter; that is, through imitation I have imaginatively put myself in the place of Paul, identified myself with an other self; yet in becoming Paul, I still remain myself, Peter. My identity has been *imaginatively doubled* through a creative appropriation of an other, a difference. Imitation is neither passive nor reactive nor identical with naturalistic copying; it is a form of imaginative acting, an opening to and mediation of otherness in which we become the other, giving ourselves up to its difference.

Consider an accomplished mimic. He may seem to lack a rigid univocal identity and definitive individuality, for he is forever borrowing the character of others. (Keats said that the poet has no identity.) The mimic is the plastic power to body forth the selfness of others. Imitation here reveals the original power to be open to otherness beyond any limited, univocal identity. By imitating being that is other than oneself, otherness as such is offered a first welcome into our otherwise little self. So imitating is a fundamental act of sympathy, of identifying with realities other than the self, of participating in their different lives. It articulates and consolidates our belonging with being beyond ourselves. We connect with things by making ourselves like to them, sharing in their special lives by coming to grasp them from within. As Aristotle saw, human beings are the most imitative, the most fluid of beings (especially the child). Our potential openness to otherness is boundless—we even try to imitate God. Imitation is a fundamental communication in which beings otherwise different are related together. We, the most imitative of beings, are God-like because most capable of kinship with being in all its otherness. Art may be one concentrated instance of this kinship, this fellowship.[22]

A primary reason why traditionally art was seen as imitation was that it opened contact between the artwork and the larger extra-artistic world. (Thus mimesis and cosmos were intertwined for the Pythagoreans.) As imitating nature, say, the artwork was an image of something other, hence not totally self-contained. Reflecting a more encompassing whole, indeed resistant otherness, it could illuminate the world of being. This view of art is in terms of something not itself artistic, a non-artistic other, hence the question arises: If art is justified on terms other than itself, what other is the final arbiter? Some have proposed ethical ideals, like Plato: art should image ethical goodness. Others, Left-Hegelians like Marx, have suggested political purposes. If you are a reactionary, art becomes a glorification of the powers that be. If you are a revolutionary, it becomes (Marcuse, Adorno) a harbinger of the powers that will be. If you are a revolutionary gone to seed (Lukács disguised as a Stalinist), art becomes socialist realism. Others again recommend that art should subserve religion: art celebrates God's glory. In the aftermath of Romanticism art even tried to make a religion of itself. Yet throughout the ages these two have not lacked affinity. I do not mean the poet being servant of the priest but that both may speak out of a shared sense of the mystery of being. The artist need not serve the priest, but both may serve this mystery.

The important question with art's defense as only imitation is: Since this defense can predominantly stress something other than art, is it more a defense of that other than of art itself? The danger with imitation is to oppose dualistically art and its non-artistic original or other, and then to reduce art to this other. Then art as an articulation of free mind is compromised. In place of a dialectical or metaxological mediation of art and its others, we reduce their relation (conceived as dualistic opposition) to one side only. The fact is that though art is indeed complexly related to the world of otherness, it also makes it own rich world. Indeed imitation itself confirms this. An imitation is an image of a model, an original with a life of its own; but the image, too, has its own life, the doubled identity that I noted above. This latter is something standing in its own right. So if I mimic somebody, my imitation depends on the original, but the more accomplished my imitation, the more it takes on a life of its own. It is finally impossible to dualistically oppose image and original; the image becomes an original in its own right, becomes an original image—a unity of what are opposites for dualistic thinking.

This is why we can be *threatened* by someone successfully imitating us. The successful image is too much like us; it *is* us. It seems to drain away our self-subsistence and stand totally in our place. There is a kind of dialectical reversal of image and original. For a perfect imitation seems to make the model *redundant*, because we can now see the original *in* the image. The better an imitation, the more it draws attention to itself, the more it arrests aesthetic astonishment. It presents itself as more than simple imitation; consummate imitation presents itself as a *creation* in its own right.

Some version of art as "creation" has dominated aesthetics since Kant, but the view was not unknown before this. Ancient peoples honored the poetic power, wondering about its perhaps divine source (the poet as shaman, magus, sage). They showed a hesitation here, a reluctance restrained by reverence. The power to create was the god's privilege; we must be content to be a creature—a result made, not a making source. Romanticism (concretizing Kant's productive imagination in the general culture) helped destroy the taboo on ascribing divine qualities to human beings and rushed over this ancient reverence. We are creators, it is claimed, even capable of rivalling God. Today we may be uneasy with the religious language, but one way or another we have slipped into the habit of thinking of ourselves as "creative."

In a reversal of the old opposition of image and original, creativity is again pitted against imitation. Where imitation asks submission to external norms, creativity insists that our activity contains its own norm. The view is: the self expresses itself in activity with its own intrinsic norms; hence it is not to be judged by external standards but provides its own justification. Thus are precipitated movements like *l'art pour l'art*. The self now becomes the center of concern, not, as before, the world of larger otherness; at the best, the self is seen as an *inner otherness*. Not surprisingly, some aesthetes, like Oscar Wilde, tried to make themselves their own greatest creation. Alternatively, art may seek to probe its own internal resources (as in "self-reflexive" art today), rather than render homage to anything beyond itself.

The undeniable truth here is that human activity does point to the self as an originative being whose activities come to be marked by immanent norms. Art, too, comes to exhibit such internal standards when, as a form of sensuous self-knowledge, the artist, and mediately his audience, know themselves in the creation. Thus, art is a *dialectical self-mediation*: the artist originates a work that is other to himself but in that other, the self actualizes *its own* original power, hence in the artwork as other it comes to recognize itself. The work as other is its own creative power as self-othering. This is dialectical because there is a creative interplay of self and other; it is self-mediation because the self comes to mediate with itself, know itself in the work as a sensuous other.

This dialectical self-mediation has a significance wider than any individual self. It is a mark of civilization that it lives by such internal standards. With civilized selves, standards of excellence do not have to be enforced from without, for they constitute the innermost core of civilized life. The civilized self lives them effortlessly for they are the life blood of civilization. But civilization, like genuine creation, is born of tension. Dialectical self-mediation risks asserting that *only* the self mediates the relation of self and other; it risks the self dominating the other in a spurious self-sufficiency or autonomy that is actually closed to otherness. Creation tries to win our openness to otherness and the promise of wholeness despite the contrary seduction of closure and the forces of dissolution. Creation is not a matter of merely asserting one's originality but of being honest about recalcitrant otherness, grappling with the fluid original power of our being, turning it from amorphous force into forceful form.

This risk of closure to otherness is not always avoided in our notion of creativity. We now intone the term "creativity" like a sacred password to some Holy of Holies, but while we chant this mantra, the danger is that self-absorption get substituted for self-knowledge and we shirk the intermediated condition of creative tension. For originative power is not a private possession but something given to us. What is given, precisely as gift, preserves our link with the other as other.[23] The creator betrays this original power if he encloses it within a shuttered selfhood. The nature of creative power is not just to commune with itself but to communicate itself. It does not realize itself in that swaggering self-assertion that sets itself against the rest of creation. Our opening of ourselves is our openness to what is other. Man is not "creative." Man cooperates in creation.

To avoid this closure of creativity, we must recall that the more perfect an imitation is, the more it presents itself as a creation; the richer the image, the more it is an original itself, an original image. If the artwork is such an original image, it can be said to seek the togetherness of these two sides: it articulates an original world of its own; it images, in complex mediations, the world of larger otherness. Between the work and the wider otherness there may be metaxological ebb and flow. This means that imitation and creation need not be radically opposed; imitation is an incipient form of creation; creation is imitation completing itself. One displays our ability to liken ourselves to things other, the other shows us to give expression to originative powers of our own. As a togetherness of imitation and creation, art testifies to our originative power and participation in the universe of otherness. It concretizes our self-relating openness to otherness, trying to hold together in the original image the inward otherness of the self and the otherness of being beyond the self. As an original image, the artwork is a creative double that aesthetically concretizes the actuality of metaxological being.

Thus also we avoid the extremes of passive representation, and sheer creativity from nothing. Where the first deflates art to an unoriginality below its real power, the second inflates it to an original power indistinguishable from God's. In the middle of these extremes, art's imaginative formation is double: a dealing with the vagueness of innerness, as well as the indifference of outerness. This aesthetically expresses the double mediation of metaxological being. We are often burdened with an inchoate sense of significance that asks to be expressed, but as long as this remains inward and private, it is all but insubstantial. To assume fully an articulated life it must be made concrete by being externalized. Imaginative formation shapes the inner formlessness through dialectical self-medition, such that our being come to genuine expression, perhaps for the first time. What is inward may shine outward.

But imaginative formation is not just single self-formation but double formation: a mediation of both the self in its inward otherness and what is other as beyond the self. In its dialectical self-externalization, the self is gathered to this second otherness. This otherness may seem alien and opposed, but in the middle way we try to name this, the foreignness of being. A great work names being thus. We contend with the darkness to put a small cosmos where before for us was only a large chaos. What is outward now shines with inwardness.[24] A reciprocal interplay occurs between inwardness and otherness in which neither side is reduced to the other, yet there may come to be a community of both in their very distinctness.

I stress that the artist need not be a dialectically dominating self stamping itself on otherness. The artist does not just superimpose a fixed form on sluggish matter, for at first neither he nor the matter are univocally fixed or fully defined. Both come to definition in the act of origination itself. The form of an artwork comes to emergence in the metaxological interplay of artist and his material. Imagination mediates a transition from formlessness to form, both in the inward self and in outer otherness. Indeed that the artist first has no fixed univocal self or form is at the source of views that couple art with inspiration, vision, intoxication, dream. Ordinary perception stabilizes the self, setting it apart from otherness, often in dualistic opposition to it, but imaginative formation returns our sensuously emergent mindfulness to a point prior to this fixed stabilization and dualization. Inspiration is just the breakdown of this stabilization and dualistic opposition. It is the unweaving of the fixed univocal self, the releasing of the inner otherness in the upsurge of an anterior, dynamic power that does not belong to the self like private property, for it *is* the original power of being emerging into articulation as the aesthetic self. Inspiration returns to the immediacy of the metaxological where the original power of being is "more" — "mine," yet not mine, intimate yet other. Against the dominating self, inspiration deconstructs the will to dominate otherness.

Thus, the similarity of madness and inspiration has been often noted, by

Plato in antiquity, by Schopenhauer in post-Kantian aesthetics. Both relate to the breakdown or deconstruction of the self trying to dominate otherness and the upsurgence or breakthrough of the anterior, dynamic power of being that may possesss us but which none can possess. Madness is inspiration, but inspiration often without the redemption of imaginative formation; inspiration sucked back into chaos, the dark origin, not emergent from it.[25] Imaginative formation, by contrast, harnesses the original power of being erupting in such moments of inspiration, and anchors in the artwork its otherwise overpowering energy.

IV. LOSS OF THE AESTHETIC MIDDLE

Excessive Subjectivity: Creativity as Negativity

Since the metaxological community of being is not a static structure but evidences a dynamic interplay of self and other, we can differently stress its different partners, hence lose the full complexity of the aesthetic middle and the above creative doubleness. An attenuation of the double middle relates to a certain view of creativity and to the inhospitality of contemporary conditions to being aesthetic. The dominance of "creativity" since Romanticism has ironically contributed to this inhospitability, leading to a paradoxical neglect of beauty, arguably the central aesthetic concept since the Greeks. I have discussed the matter elsewhere, but these remarks are necessary.[26]

We find that words like "interesting," "exciting," "original," have replaced beauty, while the ugly has been replaced by words like "boring," "dull," "derivative." These words refer primarily to *our* emotions. To alter Kierkegaard: Beauty is now sensing subjectivity.[27] Greek mimesis was anchored in being, considered in its otherness to the self; Romantic and post-Romantic "creativity" stresses the original power of subjectivity, but sometimes to the denigration of being as other. The first, while acknowledging otherness, may not be fully adequate to the metaxological as soliciting the self's original power; but the second exaggerates this original power, diminishes respect for otherness, and so distorts our place in the metaxological. What I will stress is a certain open aesthetic dialectic of trust and distrust towards the other. We will later see religious and ethical versions of this dialectic. The doubleness of the metaxological allows both an aesthetic yes and no to being's otherness. In the first instance, creation becomes the generosity of being, in the second it can become a distrustful negativity which, uprooted from the metaxological community, can become an ontological aggression towards the aesthetic intimacy of being.

Related to the second possibility we find a stress on art's *specialness*, but as divorced from being aesthetic in the wider sense I have delineated. Art becomes *the* aesthetic: self-sufficient unto itself, marked by intrinsic norms that forbid trespass from religion or ethics or philosophy or science. Art hands its others, turns to itself as is own other. The Romantics often set out to explore this special realm (e.g. in Schlegel's call for a "poetry of poetry") but the theme reappears in contemporary "self-reflexive" art, which is less original than it claims to be. Its forgotten roots are in Romanticism where priority is given to aesthetic subjectivity and the endless task of probing this, down even to the wastes in the abyssal self. Art will serve no other, none but itself alone. Unanchored from any ground in the otherness of being, the self risks its own loss in a labyrinth of inwardness. Admittedly, in the nineteenth century creativity was still tied to traditional ideals of organic unity; tempered by such an ideal of wholeness, aesthetic subjectivity anchored itself in the work of beauty. With time, however, in the dialectic of self and other, a certain excessive subjectivity comes to the fore and all but beats otherness as otherness into nothing. This is prefigured in Romantic Irony and is tied to the ambiguous legacy of Kant's transcendental imagination. Many Romantics were the aesthetic heirs of Fichte who, with a more radical doctrine of the active self, claimed to be Kant's true heir in transcendental epistemology. An imperious aesthetic ego, sometimes a tyrannical subjectivity refuses, in the name of the putative higher freedom of imagination, any limitation that otherness as otherness might impose.

In doctrines of Romantic *genius* this specialness of the aesthetic was coupled with the strong, even exaggerated individualism of modernity.[28] The genius becomes an exemplification of originative power, the acme of original humanity, and art asserts itself with a fervor not far short of religious. The Romantics carried this heroic individualism to a limit by deepening the sense of self in the direction of inwardness; the self become an entire world unto itself, a profound abyss. Now the problem is not this deeping of inwardness but its unanchoring from its metaxological intermediation with otherness. This unanchored inwardness always seems to outstrip all possible wholeness. (This problem will recur in being religious and being ethical.) Traditionally beauty was such a harmonious whole to be admired by the contemplative gaze, offering an aesthetic equilibrium and resting joy. If restless inwardness shuns this aesthetic peace, it must fail to find its own objective correlative in being as other. Its aesthetic creativity becomes ungrounded, its freedom floating. Thus, Hamlet is prototypical of the modern self in that his elusive innerness overflows every possible external manifestation, just as also his outer action is stymied by excess of self-consciousness. I quoted Hamlet before: "Seems, madam? Nay, it is. I know not "seems". . . . But I have that within which passes show." But the aesthetic is the realm of "seems," of "show," of appearance and sensuous manifestation. What if we become saturated with suspicion about sensuous show? Inevitably we invite the decomposition of the aesthetic. One thinks of Hamlet's own unsurity whether we are the noble acme of creation or just the quintessence of dust.

By elevating an ungrounded aesthetic "creativity" into self-sufficiency, we invite a paradoxical reversal of faith in the aesthetic. Selfhood is set in dualistic opposition to being's otherness, and their creative dialectic is undermined by subjectivistic suspicion. In opposition to otherness, subjectivistic "creativity" becomes negativity. But the self's sense of superiority over all externality not only plants seeds of suspicion about the poverty of all otherness to satisfy it; the same suspicion also *turns back on the self* when it lives through the consequences of its unanchoring from otherness. There follows a hollowing out of subjectivity itself as the spirit of suspicion becomes progressively universalized and equally regards the self as well as the other. If "show" or sensuous manifestation is in principle suspect, it is not many steps to the bankrupting of the aesthetic, one all the more likely, given the initial enthusiastic faith invested by subjectivity in art as a kind of this-worldly salvation. In our search for the "interesting," we end up "bored." But boredom is only our subjectivistic camouflage for spiritual death, or more kindly, the aesthetic nihilism of our self-obsession.

Though honoring itself as "creativity," this aesthetic restlessness risks being a sheer striving without any gathering goal. Such restlessness without end (I think of Hegel's "bad infinite," or Kierkegaard's figure for aesthetic possibility, Don Juan) inevitably breeds despair, first concerning otherness, then concerning itself.[29] The Promethean effort to realize the ontologically uprooted self ends in a strange elusive malaise; the "creative" self is nagged by the suspicion that along the way to self-realization something essential was lost or missed, bypassed or even betrayed. Certainly it is fashionable to denigrate Romanticism, but that is not my point. Romanticism was a great constructive movement, not some petty pining for a lost perfection or anaemic nostalgia for a world well lost. What is now denigrated is really a vulgarized, sentimentalized Romanticism. But we still live, ungratefully, off the capital accumulated by the great Romantics. The great Romantics (e.g. Hölderlin, Wordsworth, Keats) divined the problem, while we at times seem to have forgotten, or run away from it. The point is to stem the hemorrhage of spirit that occurs when an excessive subjectivity asserts an undue dominance in the intermediation between the self and the other. This dominance breeds an aesthetic closure to being's otherness and hence undermines the aesthetic middle itself.

The outcome of this dominance is not always creativity; it may be a petering out in impotence. Nothing seems to stand its ground before such an ungrounded self, infected as it is with a spirit of unbounded suspicion.

Interestingly, the three thinkers honored as the masters of modern culture—Marx, Nietzsche and Freud—have been titled by Ricoeur the "masters of modern suspicion." But suspicion alone can never provide the basis of genuine creativity. On the wings of suspicion, the aesthetic ego elevates itself into the absolute creator, but it flies on the wings of Icarus and suffers a fall: initially self-assured in its suspicion of otherness, it now becomes corroded by an ontological insecurity that nothing seems to allay. There may arise an endless quest for novel stimulus but this soon proves boring to the jaded ego in its insomniac superiority over all objects. Not a great deal has altered in the aftermath of the Romantics. After Nietzsche's notice that "God is dead," we are now told that "Man is dead." A purposed purposelessness, a rationalized absurdism denounces and dismantles all that was and is. Initially modern consciousness retreats from otherness as objectivity to inwardness as subjectivity. The end of this withdrawal seems to be the evaporation of all absoluteness, whether other or inward.

So we find a progressive radicalization of the unanchored self's negativity, an apocalyptic negativity calling itself "creativity." This reaches an apogee in postmodernism. I am not criticizing postmodernism in so far as it tried to renew our openness to otherness. But too often postmodernism is only late modernism, that is, a parody of modernism. The latter, in turn, saw itself as ironically debunking Romanticism, forgetting with the ingratitude of cultural heirs that already with Romanticism, irony defined an entire aesthetic comportment to being. Parody seems to be a very current aesthetic strategy,[30] but such parody is only irony pushed closer to frivolity. Parody is uncreative, parasitical irony. Better, such parody presents the semblance of creativity but only by being parasitical on the creativity of another. Here we find a further variation of the problematical relation to otherness arising in the wake of the repudiation of mimesis. The "other" of aesthetic irony and parody becomes the *predecessor* that now has to be debunked, lest precedent curb the pure inward freedom of the divinely suspicious genius. The latter experiences all the anxieties of influence, as preceding others becomes threats to its uncertain stake to originality.

The Cult of Novelty

The point is not only relevant to the mandarins of high culture. So let me offer one brief sketch of a widespread simulacrum of "creativity": let us call it, the "cult of novelty." This cult appears with boredom, when everything is passé, when there is flatness, a staleness to our sense of being. To make the flatness fade, to put sparkle into the staleness, we set out in search of novelty. Novelty surprises us, startles us with the unexpected and, like the Apocalyptic Lord, it says: Behold I make all things new!

But what if the boredom is only palliated by spurious originality? Then the underlying staleness is untouched, only the surface effects briefly altered. What then? We may refuse to dwell with the boredom, refuse to risk what it might reveal. Instead our endless search for newness masks the deepdown tiredness of spirit in an orgy of self-narcotizing excitation. The bored self drowns itself in ever new provocation that briefly energizes it but overall leaves it numb and anaesthetized.

When the word "creativity" drops from every lip, one lives in expectation of meeting genius around every corner. This talk is cover for impotence, a perverse parody of creativity. The cult of novelty looks askance at what went before it, simply because it went before. Everything has to be absolutely novel, so away with the old and obsolete! It exploits the clever expedient of upgrading the present by downgrading the past. It ushers in the relevant new with a million manifestoes declaiming the irrelevance of the old.

But such stirring war cries of the avant garde are ambivalent: along with true originality, we are just as likely, perhaps more likely, to get aping. Everyone must be absolutely "novel," "different," "original," that is to say, everyone must be absolutely the same. To be novel becomes the supreme stereotype.[31] Of this a million copies are reproduced, all identical in their loud empty "difference." Moreover, these copies are utterly uniform because they all copy absolutely nothing. This absolute originality is absolute poverty. Creativity unanchored and absolutized reverts again to mimesis, but mimesis destitute of any original. Creation from nothing creates the image of nothing.

Strangely enough, the cult of novelty (contradicting itself—but what does it care about contradiction?) makes its one *rule* of the dictate that everything must be new. The rule is there should be no rules. Thus, it generates a ceaseless transition from one novelty to the next. But the devastating paradox is that nothing ever changes. For its basic rule is fundamentally a principle of *obsolescence*. The cult of novelty, by its self-contradictory logic, must make all novelty obsolete. It is therefore only really possible as a *cult of decay*. It must camouflage its underlying impotence by ceaselessly changing the scenery, mistaking this change for a different drama.

If genuine origination is like a dialogue wherein we face the awkward question of the other without flinching or switching the subject, the cult of novelty is like mindless chatter which, to give the illusion of conversation, always shifts topics at the moment the difficulty should be faced or the recalcitrant otherness allowed to be, or the revelation respected. This ceaseless chatter gives the semblance of wit, ingenuity, ease and inventiveness, but under the surface all is humorless, ill at rest, and given to sterile mimicry. Everything is said but nothing is being said. Here is aesthetic self-conceit dressed up for high-minded show, chanting snappy slogans to beguile the gullible. It will even sing fake revolutionary jingles—for the self-congratulation of the establishment.

V. ART AND METAXOLOGICAL OTHERNESS

Art and the Community of Others

The metaxological sense of being calls for a break with imperialistic aesthetic subjectivity and a restoration of the intermediated community of original selfness and being's otherness. We need to remark on this, first in relation to social otherness, then in relation to a wider sense of ontological otherness that returns us to the intimacy of being with which we began.

The above aesthetic unanchoring develops from a self-assertive selfhood that exaggerates its own individualistic creativity by setting itself in dualistic opposition to all otherness. But an important factor in this unanchoring is the way modern society problematically shapes the relation of the aesthetic self to its *social others*. The modern artist is often reduced to a solitary self *cut off* from social others. In his *Defence of Poetry* Shelley once likened the poet to a nightingale who sits in darkness and sings to cheer its own solitude. Romantics like Shelley have been dismissed by skeptics for supposedly indulging the feeling of adolescent loneliness; yet history tends to side with him. The modern artist has been driven into a stony, often unchosen solitude. Here are some key episodes of that "history" in sketch.

One mark of modernity is an instrumentalization of being such that art's claim to intrinsic value does not often enough find social support. In the nineteenth century, the artist found himself at odds with what he saw as the vulgar commercialism of capitalism; driven from the marketplace, he made common cause with fellow artists. This may alleviate the solitude but only temporarily, for the inevitable outcome is the formation of a clique that inclines to be inward looking. The gulf between artist and his social others can only widen. The clique, however, with the courage of crowds, begins to make noise, especially sounds disparaging of the philistines. The solitary artist becomes defiant of his social others. The latter first react with derision when their stale habits of perception are not confirmed, but in time the disenchanted artist wins out because there is a chink of disquiet in the jeers of his detractors, and this chink only enlarges when he shows himself rebel enough to fight. The rebel artist wins in making the philistines ashamed of their previous perceptions.

Does this effect a genuine intermediation of artist and his social others?

Not necessarily. The audience is now receptive perhaps, but when it is too receptive it becomes merely passive. Making the audience feel unsure of itself, the artist may think he is now licensed to inflict outrage on it. He thinks he shocks his social others but really he is in collusion with them. He becomes stale because his passive audience has failed to fight him critically: it has failed to become a properly *collaborating* other. In turn, he tries more and more shocking things until a saturation point of outrage is reached. The social others are now numb, the artist still as solitary as Shelley's nightingale, only the sweet sound has vanished and the voice has begun to croak.

All along commerce (the economic shape of the calculative, instrumental mind) haunts the stage, impatient for its entrance. A passive audience, unsure of its desires, will buy almost anything, if you insist long enough on the worth of your worthless wares. Because an audience has been readied, made submissive, entrepreneurs of art emerge. The social others become exploited as a market for a commodity. First the artist was in revolt against art's capitalization; now he ends up being paid absurd prices for his productions. The artwork becomes an investment, a security against inflation, a stock in the ballooning rapacity of capital. A think of beauty is a joy forever, Keats sang; now it is a hedge against the market, a good place to park excess yen.[32] Yes, the entrepreneur may mediate between artist and society, but in the way a procurer mediates between client and gigolo—the price for the beauty must be right. The artist who used to shock becomes a panderer—and the best panderers are those who shock most. Shelley's nightingale completes its itinerary through solitude, finishing up a Television Celebrity, a famous image of nothing, fatuously fluttering about the bright caves of electronic glitter.

This "history" seems to teach two extremes to be avoided, both following from neglect of the metaxological community of being. The first extreme is to so *distance* the artist as a singular self from a community of others that art is made the privileged preserve of the coterie of isolated geniuses. The artist's excessive singularity then turns him into a kind of a detached god, an ataraxic aesthetic creator. He cuts his roots from the communal soil of others, but without sap from this ground in social otherness, his vigor will wither. Either he becomes so obsessed with himself as to prove of no interest to others, or as above, he floats like a flickering ghost on a mechanical screen.

By contrast, the second extreme is to so *submerge* the artist in society that he has nothing distinctive to offer; his necessary otherness as singularly originative is then sacrificed. Excessive sameness takes the place of excessive singularity but the result is again monotone and bland. The sources of creation atrophy. Indeed in modern society excessive sameness and singularity tend to be found together. Modern society tends to atomize communities, breaking them down into aggregates or collections of separated individuals. In this atomization, every self is encouraged to be absolutely different, just to "be itself." But since everyone wants to be absolutely different, everyone turns out to be absolutely the same. After all, one atom is indistinguishable from another. The artist's position in modern society, alternatively a rebel against his audience and an exploiter of it, is one expression of this atomization.

This atomization is really a reduction of the self and the other to univocal units that can be instrumentally manipulated. Thus, it undermines the bonds joining us together in community. It either sets us totally apart, as if each were a self-contained entity in competition with every other, or else it lumps all together as indistinguishable atoms of a collection. In the first case, community is weakened because the individual is separated from its fellows and both are bundled together in external association. In the second case, community is made tenuous since the individual is merged with the others and so lost to itself in the crowd. These two options broadly correspond to the main modern forms of social organization, communism, and capitalism. Where the first breeds conforming atoms, the second breeds competitive ones. Both weaken the metaxological intermediation of self and other (cf. chapter 4).

Since art participates in this intermediation, its creative power is weakened without some community of others. As Tolstoy insisted, art is essentially communication, but this occurs only with a proper intermediated balance between the self and its fellows, between its distinction from others and its engagement with them, between its solitude and its solidarity. To communicate is to be fulfilled, nay it is to be, by reaching out to otherness. It is to utter meaning, not before a mirror reflecting or mediating oneself alone but in intermediating with others, in neighboring them. Thus, artistic meaning requires the community of others, not only to ground and support, but also to crown and consummate the work. Without the reader the writer is truncated, as is the painter without the other's discerning eye, the musician without the attentive ear, the dramatist without the public performance. Paul Klee said we lack the strength for the great work, for there is no people.

The artist may communicate an individual vision, but if this is purely subjectivistic, something fails. Communication is grounded in significance shared. Particularity of vision must touch something transcending particularity, something hitherto unspoken in the people but now being brought to light. Not just communing with himself, not just communicating himself to his audience, the artist in the middle is midwife to his others, in their communicating with themselves. In his own self-knowledge he aids his others towards their self-knowledge. Community is then the convergence in the middle of a plurality of self-mediating, self-knowing beings. Mediating between a people and its sources of secret significance, the artist names, opens their hidden sense of being, draws notice to what before was obscurely felt but not directly depicted. He is one with others by being spokesman for the sense of life that is at work in the intimacy of being but that is otherwise busily unspoken.

This does not mean telling a people only what it wants to hear. Something is struggling to be born but dishonesty will abort the birth. The sources of significance elude easy saying, for in them may be mixed some alarming secrets (the intimacy of being is not pure light). A people may recoil from these secrets, shudder to recognize itself, disown its darker side and cling to a censored image of itself. Since the artist insists on a true image, he must grapple with the recalcitrance of the community of others, as well as celebrate his solidarity with it. Some societies that refuse to confront themselves will scourge its artists for daring to be candid. When the artist is so silenced, a people tends to dissipate its vigor in evasion. The artist must be cunning enough to disarm this resistance. He must have already conquered the resistance in himself and made himself a witness to honesty.

Granted (again as Klee implied) today we often lack a sense of wholeness and are unable to divine our deeper community with our fellow human beings and with being in its otherness. Then aesthetic honesty is sometimes forced to give expression to its own alienation and fragmentation. Indeed traditional images of beauty might have to be shunned as mere escapism: aesthetic opiates for the consumers of sensations. The artist may have to mirror the revolutionary (cf. chapter 1) and subvert established tastes; he may have to refuse beauty's consolation and celebrate dissonance without harmony, fragmentation without unity.

It is not only in art where today we find such celebration of disunity. The danger here is mere surrender to disunity. Disunity may offer, as Adorno implies, a genuinely creative opportunity. But if all we offer is only a mirror image of the alienation, then art canonizes the decay. Art's protest becomes an empty negation, if there does not flicker within it some dream of wholeness. Rilke puts it thus (*Sonnets to Orpheus*, I, XII): Hail the spirit able to unite us!/For we truly live our lives in figures (*Figuren*). . . . Without knowing our true place/ We yet act out of real relatedness (*aus wirklichem Bezug*). The elemental necessity of being aesthetic cannot be eradicated, nor art's promise. This promise is bound up with our bodily rootedness in being and our community with the other, and every protestation of absolutely autonomous creativity is itself made possible only through this prior ontological rootedness in community. We need to reawaken aesthetic mindfulness of this ground that, notwithstanding our claims to absolute originality, always supports us.

Aesthetic Mindfulness: Art's Tolerance of Otherness

To close this chapter I want to speak of this aesthetic mindfulness. Art offers us a way to the metaxological community of self and other through an intermediated sense of wholeness, midway between the closure of "Hegelian" totality and the fragmentary incompleteness of "Wittgensteinian" plurality (cf. introduction). I will make two points, first concerning art's transcending of the instrumentalizing of being, and second, concerning its tolerance of otherness.

A strange obstacle to aesthetic mindfulness is that we seem *saturated* with art. Art today seems both remote and crowding. Remote: the divorce of artist and public makes the former seems careless of communication, except to the "art world,"[33] while the wider public takes refuge in the old, already canonized masterpieces. Crowding: everywhere we are surrounded, smothered even, with images plucked from art's realm, for example, in advertising that plunders art's treasury for the extraneous purpose of selling soda pop, jeans, and women's lingerie. Great music is packaged as "musak"—a vaguely present, tediously pleasant hum of background sound; great painting becomes insipid ornamentation, wallpapering we hardly perceive in passing; courtesy of technology, we seem surfeited with cultural decor.

But this very ubiquity produces a startling peripeteia: art vanishes in its surplus availability, becomes absent in its massive presence. As consumers we voraciously use up art like any other convenient commodity, a pleasantry to palliate a void. Excess of stimulation produces defect of attention; saturation of the senses produces our aesthetic enervation. Against this, aesthetic mindfulness insists that we stop; attention must be arrested, brought to a pause. We literally need to be brought back to our senses in their aesthetic receptivity as opposed to susceptibility to stimulation. (This is one reason I began with the aesthetic body.) Great art calls for silence, for slowness; it must be taken in intervals. One cannot rush through its gallery and take in what is there with a quick sweep of minimal seeing. It insists on quality of attention, that we dwell with the rich thing itself. It claims concentration as its right. It asks especially for *patience* in perception. When we solely crave the sheer immediacy of the "happening," attention is quickly corrupted into anxious, harried seeing, that is sightless seeing. Mindful intimacy is born of patient perception. Art needs distance, respect, aloofness, in order to be allowed to speak to us out of the quiet spaces of its otherness.

This means that aesthetic mindfulness must be freed from the instrumentalization of being. The instrumental mind attends to being only as a means to satisfy its pragmatic aims, and must needs narrow its focus to what it can handle from the inconstant, indefinite flux, to what can be bounded and filtered to our use. But something escapes beyond. We label things, handle them more efficiently but they recede into a kind of invisibility. We are not interested in their elemental thereness or otherness. We want to eat them, barter them, secure our future; we want to dominate others through them. What we use this way, we do not fully mind.

Consider: The apple in my hand disappears from sight; for I am hungry and must consume it. I bring it into such closeness with my needs that it must vanish in being consumed. I crush it with my mouth. And so it is not an apple; it is mere food, a means to an end. Its being I make relative to my desire. But now I am free and stand back, not driven by need. I push this other apple away, place it at a distance. It is not food now; it is just an apple. I have no interest in devouring it; I let it be. It exists, exists indeed in its own right—its being in its otherness is not just relative to me. For the first time I look at this apple because it exists simply for itself. The direction of my mind ends there and does not glance away. Its being there arrests me, stills the hurry of practical worry, releases a freer mindfulness. I begin to contemplate what before I ungently consumed. I see more. I discern something coming to appearance that before was unshown. It is there and other, a strange suspended presence. It is other, yet intimate. I reach for my brush and make the first stroke of a still life.

The instrumental mind specializes our sense of being, economizes the imagination, prunes it of useless excess. But the truth is that great art is rare and offers sparse consolation to the standardized perceptions of our egalitarian age. Great art evidences a different economy of mind, one that restores and enlarges imagination beyond utilitarian parsimony. It joys in sheer seeing, seeing for the sake of seeing, seeing freed from ulterior motivations. It baptizes what practical desire leaves nameless, and jolts us out of the rut of use. I mean something other than Oscar Wilde's dictum: "All art is quite useless." The dandy and utilitarian are not unalike; for both art is beyond utility but in one case it is an amusement for relaxation, in the other an entertainment for escape. Art's uselessness is rather a kind of metaphysical appreciation of the thereness of things just in the inexhaustibility of their being there and in the intimacy of their otherness. This we value for itself, letting it be with delight, surprised by joy in its otherness.

How does this relate to my claim about an intermediated wholeness? One can say that aesthetic mindfulness is a bounding of attention that is releasing rather than constraining. It is not that art is or could be formless; the point is rather the character of freedom that aesthetic form gives. An aesthetic whole is a paradoxical "open whole," for it marks the sensuous space of freedom. Much of experience is a muddy flux of happenings, a passing pandemonium, but one might claim that *all significant* experience partakes in some measure of artistic form. We are in the ebb and flow of happening, the streaming of being that mostly is not expressly gathered. Attention is needed to discriminate this elusive becoming, to make us singularly mindful of its appearing. In rising above the inarticulate immediacy of our being in the middle, imagination *is* aesthetic mindfulness, for it disrupts the homogeneous flux, congealing knots, eddies, patterns in the flux. As a synthetic power, it gathers a flux of immediacy into discernible, meaningful wholes. Such gatherings stud all significant experience, indeed testify to its poetic character. What we normally call art carries through in a heightened manner the quest for such unities, better communities, for they image a togetherness of self and other.

Thus, the artwork can offer an enclosure for aesthetic mindfulness without implying any totalizing violence. This relates to the fact that all perceiving, as Nietzsche among others saw, is perspectival. To occupy a perspective is to be somewhere *between* the absolute vision of a God that encompasses the totality and the scattered consciousness that is fragmented in the dissipating flux. Aesthetic framing may occupy this intermediate perspective. Framing is most evident in the painting within whose spatial borders attention is gathered. Music tends to frame in time; the ebb and flow of feeling concentrated and heightened in the rhythm of musical form. Likewise, the stage sets off an arena for the drama of human action. The cinema screen, by setting a limit to our wandering perception, focuses us, opens us. In all cases the frame gives space for mind, what Bullough called "psychical distance." (This distance from the anxiety of everyday desire was a point of metaphysical importance for Schopenhauer.) As subversive of instrumentalized framing, aesthetic framing is significantly different to what Heidegger called the *Gestell*. For it is akin to a contemplative concentration of mind, releasing wonder before the density of giveness, feeding a hope that all perception is not profane.

Aesthetic framing delineates a significant appearance, forms an emergent open whole, making it distinctively stand out against a background. Hegel and Nietzsche agree that some of the greatest of such appearing wholes are statues of the Greek gods. They repose within themselves, defining the surrounding space by their assured presence, charging that space with sacred presence, making it appear as "there" through their combined energy and equilibrium. But such wholes are not to be seen as falsifying univocal units, for the enclosing work of the frame need not lead to closure. Externally the frame is a boundary, but internally it may dissolve the psychic barriers repressing mindfulness. As a framed whole the artwork opens us out. The frame is a fenestration: at once an enclosed opening and an opening of mind beyond closure. (Recall that the artwork as original image is double: the aesthetic frame as intermediate whole facilitates both dialectical self-mediation and metaxological intermediation with otherness.) The whole into which we look is an opening to what is other. Like finally arriving at the seashore, we greet a limit, but the limit opens us, draws out the eye to a boundless horizon, to the space of free being.

I do not speak literally: the frame is not so much a physical limitation but metaphysically names a concentration of attention. True, modern art has often broken the frame literally. It does this sometimes to deny art's isolation from its others, sometimes to subvert the commercial packaging of artworks as commodities, sometimes to question the very ideal of wholeness. The literal frame deconstructs itself, but in so doing it serves metaphorical framing, namely, a different concentration of mindful attention.

Here deconstruction has recently attacked any quest for unity. As Adorno (a serious Left-Hegelian deconstructionist before post-Heideggerian deconstruction) says in parodic inversion of Hegel: the whole is the false. One can accept the disquiet with fragmentation, and especially the dismay with the totalitarian pretension of instrumentalized reason. But it makes no sense to deny our ineradicable exigency for significant "unity," which I read here not as "Hegelian" totality, but as our metaxological community with being in its otherness. The deconstruction of wholeness is itself parasitical on wholeness, and only makes sense if its external negativity secretly hides a dream of even truer wholeness.[34] Otherwise our protestation against alienation becomes indistinguishable from acquiescence in the flat prose of the world. Instead of the functionary prose of the system we get the shrill prose of the protester; or worse, we get a parody of messianic fervor that likes to shout its negation in the ear of the others that it takes to be complacent. Here the beautiful soul de-idealizes itself into the ugly soul—the anti-aesthetic vengeance of aesthetic homelessness. But in all this we still remain gripped in the vice of the utilitarian world, where everything seems to be only a means and nothing an intrinsic good, and where the recollected eye of contemplation earns no respect.

Hence, aesthetic wholeness as intermediate is not at all antithetical to openness to otherness, since the imaginative power that gathers becoming into significant "unities" is the same power that enables our identification with difference, our rapport with creation. In its quest of unities, art's resistance to instrumentalization (art as middle is not a mere means) follows from what I called its "tolerance of otherness." This tolerance calls to mind the doctrine of art's disinterestedness of Kant and Schopenhauer. But tolerance is more clearly freed from any implication of "indifference" or "neutrality." Tolerance of otherness is not negatively defined as non-interest; it is an active respect of the other, a courtesy to its being, an engagement with otherness that is not dominating.

Let me illustrate it through the difference of aesthetic and logical mindfulness. Logical mind prohibits contradiction in terms of the law of excluded middle: *either* A *or* not-A, but not both A and not-A. The result is a reduction of equivocity to univocity, a sundering into opposites, where to accept one position necessitates rejection of its other. From this intolerance of contradiction, art seems strangely exempt. But it is not simply equivocal; rather art allows a non-reductive mediation of the ambiguity of the middle. Though beauty and the ugly seem to be the logical opposites here, ugliness is not outside beauty's embrace, for in art the representation of the ugly may be marked by its own complex beauty. I do not mean bland harmony but beauty that includes the deepest pain. For instance, a depiction of Christ's agony seems to be excluded from beauty if we think in terms of a Greek god. But when great art depicts this grief, it includes within beauty what is beauty's negation. Beauty can be there, there even where death is.

Art is a tolerance of otherness precisely because its imaginative range allows of an openness to *all* possibility, including the terrible. It rejects nothing for the sake of abstract principle alone. Individual works will involve a definite selection or emphasis, but a great work strains to be inclusive of possibility; even possibility it cannot directly embrace, it may still let open, maybe suggest indirectly. It does not promulgate a dogmatic answer but rather articulates the shape of the deepest questions and concerns. Thus also one work need not contradict or negate another. The word "tolerance" (from "*tollo*" meaning to carry) indicates this willingness to bear all; nothing need be alien to it; rather the alien may be generously welcomed. True, tolerance can become frivolous in the dandy indulgence of the aesthete, or in the search for the merely shocking. Like the cult of novelty this vacuous tolerance soon stales into blankness. This explains why, at the opposite extreme, protest art, which is narrowly partisan, fails to remain fresh long but seres and yellows like the newspaper.

This tolerance evidences a vigilance to individuality as a thereness recalcitrant to complete encapsulation by the abstract logical universal. The general concept isolates a particular happening, say, of jealousy, but does not dwell on this particular happening as particular. It defines an example of jealousy as *one of a kind* and fits it into relation with other happenings of the same kind. From features common to all instances of the same kind, it generates a general concept to cover, hence to classify all examples of the same kind. The aesthetic mind is struck by the *that* rather than the *what* of a particular *thisness*.[35] There is an otherness to the "this" that resists encapsulation in the abstract generality of the logical concept.

The jealousy is Othello's. To name the intimacy of its particularity, in its very inward thisness, we need something other than logical classification by abstract concept. Thus, in the work *Othello*, we meet something that stands on its own, something *sui generis*. From the point of view of generalities *Othello* deals with realities that are as common as dirt, yet it makes of them something completely its own, something not to be repeated. The work is tied to a unique image, and its tolerance of otherness respects this tie.[36] It does not abstract from individualized difference, is not descriptive of generalized events but is expressive of a particularity in its richness. It remains intimate with the happening in its textured aesthetic concreteness, nor does it seek to reduce its otherness.

Does this tolerance leave us with an aggregate of pointillistic particulars? Not necessarily. For tolerance is again evident in that art's *universalizing* power has been noted as often as its individualizing concern. Though Aristotle formulated the law of contradiction, and thus the intolerance of opposition marking logical universality, he also suggested another universality in his famous words: poetry is more philosophical than history. Poetry discloses a universal import unencumbered by irrelevancy, while history is cluttered with contingency. History is sometimes an aborted effort to be intelligible, what Joyce called "a nightmare" from which he wanted to wake, what Eliot spoke of as an "immense panorama of futility and anarchy," what Hegel termed a "*Schlachtbank.*" Time craves transfiguration.

By poetic universality is not here meant a controlling abstraction that is superimposed on thereness by instrumental rationality; it is emergent for the aesthetic as patiently mindful of the otherness of the concrete "this." If we look at a great painting, say, we see a particular "this" but we do not just stutter "this," "this," "this"—as if it were blank being and nothing more. In letting it be, we come to see more than indifferent presence. The more we dwell with it, the more mind is arrested, the more the "this" shimmers with an always other meaning. The painting is a rich "this" and as a double image it does two things, seemingly opposed: it gathers our gaze, concentrates our mindfulness; but when we are caught up in its frame, it radiates beyond as a beckoning to more. It is not an impoverished particular but a particular cosmos. Its universality precisely springs from its being just such an individual universe, full with a compacted meaning we cannot fix to this or that univocal meaning or set of class concepts. Something there is still not encapsulated. This compacted fullness chastens the logical impulse to analyze and abstract. It also compels us to ponder a universality other than the merely abstract, what Vico called "an imaginative universal," or an aesthetic embodiment of what Hegel termed the "concrete universal."

I am saying then that aesthetic tolerance, anchored in the particular artwork, metaxologically mediates a sense of being in its recalcitrant, inexhaustible otherness. The dynamic power of being comes to form in a particular work, and collects itself into an intermediate whole with more than individual significance. Or rather: the individual is not negated here, but its fullest meaning extends beyond closed individuality. The work as an

aesthetic "this" both rests in itself yet radiates beyond itself (those who break
open the frame want to stress the latter aspect, against a self-enclosed, smug
aestheticism). Unlike Leibniz' monad, it is *not* windowless; but like the
monad, it is an individual that in its intermediate being reflects the universe
of otherness from its particular point of view.[37] An imaginative cosmos
shows forth a poetic universal in the Greek sense of *poiēsis*: a coming into
being, a coming to emergence in a work that stands there and embodies
appearing mind. For instance, Rembrandt's great self-portraits show the
aesthetic thisness of an individual face. But this is no univocal identity but a
pluralized, polyvocal presence. It is both a completely particularized
presence and yet an other, universal face of suffering sympathy—a
forgiveness that will not judge but by which we sense ourselves as judged.

The call of the community of being can itself be embodied in the
pluralized identity of the ontologically rich individual. Art's tolerance of
otherness is born in imagination's free play that opens up the space of the
possible wherein we identify with the different, see with the many eyes of
others, including suffering others. When Hegel called the artwork a
"thousand-eyed Argus," he implies this concretion of plurality in the
particular work. And when Aristotle defined mind (*nous poiētikos*) as the
power to become all things, he offers us a way to think of the great artist's
largess of imaginative mind.[38] We might see the grand style as instancing this
unified yet polyvocal tolerance, as incarnating an aesthetic version of what
the Stoics called "*sumpatheia ton holon.*" An artist in the grand style forces
nothing of himself on his audience. As with Shakespeare, the creator is
content to vanish into his creation. His voice is the community of the voices
of otherness. The promise of plurivocity is realized in an aesthetic
communivocity.

Thus great drama may make the whole of humanity its possible theme,
including the contradictoriness inherent in being human. In the very unity of
our being we are often opposition itself, but poetic universality embraces
more than the abstract logical universal in embracing the human in the
intermediated wholeness of its sometimes divided, contradictory being. Its
yes is to the contrary, plurivocal fullness of concrete being and not to the
logical, univocal consistency of abstract thought. In logic there are fallacies
but negligible comedy; in art we have the cruel tolerance of the comic, its
explosive yes to being, spanning scorn of the ridiculous and sympathetic
derision of stupidity. The tragic, too, has its torn tolerance: compassion for
the failure of greatness.

What I am calling poetic universality is beyond the dualistic opposition
of univocal individuality and abstract universality, beyond the dualistic
opposition of self-contained inwardness and estranging otherness that we
found in inadequate views of imitation and creativity. It is also at odds with

the unanchored selfhood and the impoverished sense of otherness that serves as the spur to its pretense of originality. As soliciting an emergent mindfulness, tolerant of otherness, it points us again to being aesthetic as itself the *poiēsis* of being, which is neither the work of inwardness nor externality: in the middle, it is being itself that flowers in being aesthetic, that is, in the sensuous show of the overdetermined power of being given to us in the rich appearing of its thereness. The fundamental issue, as we now see it, is not at all the flowering of this power in the self, but the proper rerooting of this flowering in a recharged sense of being's otherness.[39]

This rerooting requires renewed mindfulness of metaxological being. This reminds us that real creative power is the generosity of being. What ontological deracination yields is the void energy that fuels our talk about the end of philosophy, the death of art, the death of God. These "deaths" are related to the *Entzauberung der Welt* that some think is the destiny of modernity. Art must be reluctant to acquiesce in this supposed fate which, if welcomed, would signal its own slow suicide. Yet it too has sometimes fallen under the spell of disenchantment's evil eye. One is reminded of Kafka's Hunger Artist who draws attention to his own negative novelty by sterilely subsisting on a diet of nothing. The Hunger Artist takes no food from the other, but in fact he is absolutely dependent on the *notice* of others; when this notice is withdrawn, his hollow self-sufficiency becomes evident and he wastes away. Faced with the deadened world, art first looses its disenchantment on otherness as transcendent and seeks refuge in inwardness. But when inwardness is hostile to otherness and ontologically ungrounded, it must inevitably become disenchanted with even itself and succumb to the neutralization of all being, the disenchantment of the whole in which art becomes anti-art. As long as the worm of nihilism battens on its power, art will find itself debilitated in the struggle to regain a sense of otherness in its ultimacy. I now turn to being religious where we are forced to ponder just the mythic mindfulness of such ultimacy.[40]

CHAPTER 3

Being Religious

Being religious and aesthetic are alike in that metaxological imagination works in both in our transcendence of indifferent thereness. As there is a sensuous show of charged significance in the aesthetic, so in the religious there is a *poiēsis* of being in the form of a show of the sacred, a hierophany. The hierophany is not our doing, but we name the sacred and say "It is there." Religious imagination, as an original identification of ultimate difference, tries to name the absolute otherness of the holy. But here we tend to find a stronger claim for the truth of the image; compared to art's tolerance, religion shows an impassioned urgency of ultimacy (as I will call it) that often bewilders and appalls rationalistic minds. The urgency of ultimacy reveals the self-transcending of human desire, as a restless intentional infinitude in search of actual infinitude in otherness itself (see *Desire, Dialectic and Otherness* on this).

Driven by this urgency *homo religiosus* finds it hard to say: here is one image among others. He is tempted to say: *this* is the image of the ultimate; as *the* image, it *is* the original, and hence the simple truth. Being religious is at first the unself-conscious poetry of absoluteness that is ambiguous about, even a denial of, its own *poiēsis*. Its image making both reveals and conceals the absolute original, both expresses and dissimulates its own imagistic character. Art often accepts its own imagistic nature, even to the denying of its own seriousness (not often enough do we find a *religious ironist*, whereas the aesthetic ironist is not uncommon). A great artist lives being aesthetic as a way that is absolutely serious, but few can be aesthetic with this urgency of ultimacy. Being religious is a more democratic art of ultimacy.

Religion is also one of philosophy's most challenging others. Hence, the arc of thought traced in this chapter will be double: both open and questioning, a balance of respect and iconoclasm. This doubleness is not only required by philosophy as metaxological but is actually continuous with a dialectic of trust and distrust in religion itself. As an overdetermined way of being, the religious calls for interpretation; thought takes shape *in* the religious as itself a form of our being mindful in the middle.[1] Being religious, like being aesthetic, exhibits the metaxological sense of being. Both inhabit the middle in their differently mindful ways.

Since the metaxological middle is not a static structure but a dynamic process of being that separates and relates, differentiates and brings together the self and the other, it can be manifest in a plurality of ways. Overall I will focus on the immediacy, the dialectical self-mediation and metaxological intermediation of the religious middle. There is no simple linear passage from immedacy to intermediation, since all being religious is implicitly mediated, which is not to deny relatively more immediate forms. Since metaxological intermediation is dynamic it can also be contracted as a way of being and misunderstood as a way of mind. As with being aesthetic, it will be helpful to begin nearer to religious immediacy and make sense of the emergence of forms of mediation, whether of the self or the other or both together.

My remarks are divided into five stages. First, I start with an immediate immersion in what I call the "double image" of sacrality. Second, I discuss the mediation of the double image as unfolding through a dialectic of trust and distrust towards what I call a "releasing disillusionment." This dialectic is an *open* one: properly it is a metaxological intermediation rather than a closed dialectical self-mediation. I call it "dialectic" because its "dia" or dyad is continuous with the double image in the middle. Likewise by releasing disillusion, I mean precisely that: a release from illusion that is also a freeing of mind into the truth of the image—the image is understood to be an image.

Third, I remark on this release in relation to divine names and the sense of mystery as helping to mediate a less ambiguously anthropomorphic sense of the divine. The result is not a reduction of equivocity to univocity, nor a "demythologization," if by this we mean to extirpate the image. The result is a deliteralized dwelling in the essential doubleness of the image, namely, its rich ambiguity rather than logical equivocity, an ambiguity that both reveals and conceals. Ironically one must insist against both the religious and logicist fundamentalist: the image must be taken imaginatively, never literally: only this preserves the openness to otherness.

Fourth, I turn to religious mediation in selfhood itself as trying to interiorize the deliteralized but not reduced truth of the image. I look at the mystic and prophet as exemplars of such religious selfhood. Finally, I discuss the dangerous ambiguity of the dialectic of trust and distrust as evidenced in warring religions. This is one of the source of modern atheism and the attenuated sense of the religious middle, though even here ambiguity persists. The religious may be problematic like art, but both will spring up multiformed, maybe camouflaged, maybe corrupted, as long as we remain human beings.[2]

I stress in a prefatory way that my primary focus is not on a metaphysical exploration of the God of monotheism but on a comportment towards being in which the sense of the holy predominates, a sense not exhausted by the theistic God. The monotheist may hear some metaphysical echoes in what everywhere I call the "absolute original."[3] The absolute original is not here made the focus of thematic attention, though it constitutes the unstated ground of the metaxological community of being. To make it the focal theme would require a volume to itself, for it is the ultimate other that always resists thought's claims to absolute self-mediation, breaking its every closure on itself, recharging thought with ever renewed ontological perplexity. The absolute original precedes, grounds, exceeds every effort to name it, philosophically, religiously, ethically—which does not mean we ought not to try to "name" it. The absolute original is beyond all images, yet in our intermediate being we need images to articulate our sense of its being. We must avoid what Vico calls "the conceit of scholars," namely, mistaking the later development for the original ambiguous phenomenon. Prior to the theistic God, mythic images articulate the context of emergent mindfulness which, though forgotten, is never entirely erased. If it is forgotten, we risk abstraction—a kind of senile religious thought without roots in the primordial sacral otherness of being.

This context, grounded in the absolute original, is the metaxological community of being: the complex intermediate that holds together the being of self and of otherness. Initially we have our immediate being in this middle and the being of otherness as sacred swamps the being of self: the whole is the holy.[4] But since the metaxological also includes the self's original power, we can increasingly articulate the sense of our own otherness. A certain dialectical balance of self and otherness may come to be in which we and nature coexist in accord (say, in the aesthetic beauty of the Greek god). But an increasing self-assertion of our own otherness can attenuate our sense of the middle, dim our sense of divine otherness, and dedivinize nature. We may try to recuperate the sense of sacred otherness within human inwardness (e.g., Christianity); vanishing from external nature the divine is interiorized. But the self-assertion of our original power may also produce the same ontological deracination in religion as in the aesthetic. If this happens inwardness itself becomes dedivinized, and the human being merely another disenchanted thing among other profane things. We may seem to be left with nothing, but the metaxological is the always already thereness of original being. Having passed through the releasing disillusionment, we need a recuperative mindfulness of the metaxological, beyond the naiveté of the first origin.

In sum: the open dialectic points to a tension of opposites in the middle. If in the religious middle, a dominant self-mediation tries to subordinate otherness, it may produce a forgetfulness of sacral otherness. The metaxological as dynamically intermediating allows the possibility of this negative outcome. To understand this possibility is not to endorse it as the final actuality. A less negative outcome is possible: the shift to religious inwardness is not a domination of otherness, but a living of metaxological openness in selfhood itself. Beyond the immediate sacred otherness or animistic exteriority of less differentiated religions, deeper than the dominating self-mediation of secular modernity, the self can live and safeguard in inwardness a metaxological respect for being in otherness. The affirmative outcome of releasing disillusionment is not abject obeisance, not overweening self-assertion, but perplexed openness to, patient readiness before the absolute original as the radical other.

I. THE IMMEDIACY OF THE SACRED

The Double Image

Let me first consider what I call the "double image," the religious significance of which will recur throughout our discussion.[5] As driving our transcendence and envisagement of what is other, imagination is at the source of all culture, and so too at religion's birth. We confront the ambiguous middle but only a measure of meaning is vouchsafed. We ask more questions than we are given answers, press for more than is presented to us. The inevitable gap between our reaching and grasp is especially evident with the religious urgency of ultimacy. We go anxiously into an undetermined end, not knowing if we step into light or dark, or melt into nothing. Origins are shrouded in similar obscurity: Is the beginning a benevolent dispensation or only a random eruption of chaos? We guess at an answer but we cannot freeze our guess into a solid certainty. The one certainty in the middle is our inexorable movement between origin and end—time's slide cannot be stopped: this surety stirs up all other unsureties. Since a gap remains between what we know is the case and what we believe might be, when we ask urgent essential questions we cannot answer directly, we must perforce imagine. In the gap between the given and the intimated, ontological perplexity excites us into religious imagination.

We saw that imagination is metaxological, implicating a certain community of self and other. Thus, religious imagination is not merely individual but the mythic memory of a people bound together over time. No "psychologizing" of religion is intended that reduces it to individual subjectivity. (This is not to deny the eruption of astonishing individuals of singular religious imagination.) Behind the backs of individual self-consciousness, often out of the memory of the immemorial, religions flower in the middle space between a domesticated present and a dreamt of otherness, for in the sensed insufficiency of the domesticated world, there is felt the lure of a more demanding, yet satisfying otherness. In this dream of otherness, being in the middle presents the face of an enigma, an enigma doubled in its effect on us through the sense of our own estranged condition. Religious imagination displaces the terror of such enigmas, and generates an ideal significance for the ontological strangeness of being at all.

Hence, mythic images of origin and end are especially responsive to our metaphysical turbulence as tossed in the middle. They try to weave together first and final things, and knit the wavering human into the larger play. Time past and time future float from us as fragments, but the unmastered otherness of supersession stuns us into the thought of eternity. Religious imagination is not confined to a dead present but broods over a story in the process of being hatched, spreads itself over a pregnant present, spanning a receding heritage in memory, anticipating our destiny in hope. To crack time's riddle, mythic imagination rises through and above time, rendering homage to its dream of ultimacy in images of eternity—the egg splinters into brittle shell but inside an eagle shakes itself for flight.

Here there will *always* be inherent ambiguity. Our sacred dreams, as Ricoeur saw, are always amenable to conflicting interpretations. Thus, religions have been proclaimed as the acme of truth and decried as error's deepest abyss. This conflict springs from a twofoldness in imagination itself. First, imagination can be equated with fantasy, understood in a negative sense. Or it can be viewed as a positive agency, an ontological power possibly revelatory of being—the ability to body forth powers of being that otherwise remain nameless. The image is always and essentially double.

If we see imagination in the first way, as the flight of sheer fantasy, we think of it as creating images that are incredible, unbelievable pictures with no coincidence with actuality. Doubleness is seen as duplicity or deceit. This is the view that religion is riddled with *equivocity*; the univocity of logic will shows its contradictory essence. Fantasy projects illusions, nonexistent things, figments, nothings. Religions have been rejected as fantasy worlds in this sense. Thus, with Feuerbach, Marx, Nietzsche, religion is said to project an illusory world over against the "real" world, with the illusory world then given a status more real than the "real" world itself. Undoubtedly, at times the "other" world has been held as more real than this, compared to which this present universe counted almost as nothing. Hope of the "other" world eclipsed enjoyment of this one and we take flight from the complex tension of metaxological being. On this view, religions are our most powerful fairy tales, but when one ceases to be a child, one ought to separate illusion from reality, and confine oneself to the hard school of actualities. This view claims to be realistic, though to those clinging idealistically to religious images it appears reductive. It refuses to let the dream continue and shakes it with harsh temper. Religion's doubleness as ambiguous becomes equivocity, which univocal reason reveals as illusory.[6]

By contrast, the second view sees imagination as more than constructing fantastical nothings but as a power that draws from the well of being, as articulated in the original energy of the self itself. The point is not to reduce equivocity to univocity but to mindfully dwell in the doubleness of the metaxological. Should imagination dip deeply enough, it may meet with what is unthought on the crust of "realistic" awareness, disclose our attunement with a more originary power of being. This second view points towards a religious appropriation of the *ontological* significance of transcendental imagination. By imagination as ontological I do not mean a "representation" of an "object" in the "world" (this is Kant's reproductive imagination), but as revelatory of the original power of being as emergent in the inward otherness of the self, in the self as inward otherness. It is not first an intentional epistemic consciousness of "objects." Originally it has no "external object," for it reveals the coming to appearance of the original indeterminate power of being in the self. But against subjectivism,, I stress not so much the immanence of self as the original power of *being* in its inward otherness. It is the same power of being (it is not "mine") that originates the world of "objects" as external others. Thus, the divine power is better "imaged" by the inward indeterminacy of free creativity than by the same power as frozen into a static external "object."[7]

The religious image is never just a sensory image, but an articulation of original imagination understood in an ontological sense, hence a *mediating spiritual representation* of extraordinarily compacted significance (recall Vico's imaginative universal). In this sense, religious imagination is not just a *transposition* of an image from the secular to the sacred, the immanent to the transcendent, the finite to the infinite, as if the first were the given originals. Rather, given being (the finite, the immanent) *is* the image of the sacred in the sense of its hierophany or manifestation. The sacred is there for us in the image, "in" but not mastered; hence the sacred as original (in itself) remains still elusive and mysterious. As above implied, mythic images especially tell of the origin, for original imagination is not under will's deliberate control, but returns us to a point prior to any dualism of self and otherness (cf. chapter 2), the point of an original emergence or appearance. Religious imagination divines the place of the original show of the sacred. The time of the origin is said to be in *illo tempore*, the world itself being born or reborn, heaving into shape in a *poiēsis* of being, offspring of nature naturing, still unworn, still ungrimed.

In a sense we *live* in a world of images: the image is an apparition, a coming into presence—as much of the original power of the self as of the power of being in its otherness. We ourselves are images in the sense of manifest concretions of the original power of being. The ancients were closer to this coming to appearance *in statu nascendi*, as it were. We may be now more differentiated, but we often lack the metaphysical astonishment before presencing itself, being as process of apparition. We live forgetfully in domesticated thereness, sediment of the process of apparition. The original state was promiscuous perhaps, but ours often is amnesiac. We are a fugue of being, though the sediment of time is rich with signs. The image as such is a carrier and promise of culture, *cultus*, that is, a religious community of being. Cultus, worship itself can be a dramatic imaging of divine life in which the worshipper participates.[8]

The second sense of imagination as ontological is truer to the metaxological sense of being, and so must be kept to the fore, which is not to deny the first sense entirely. For human beings will dream; this is our nature. Our dreams may be the thoughtless wanderings of a lax consciousness, or they may be our mindful struggle with intermediate being as we try to envisage the ultimate. (The Aborigines actually call the time of the origin "The Dreaming.") Religious people are touchy lest their loved ideals be identified with hollow fantasy, but this risk must be run. The crux is to separate empty fantasy from ontological imagination. Often when we dream religiously these two are mixed: weeds grow on the same ground as wheat; idolatry worships in the same sanctuary as sanctity.[9] Unquestionably religious imagination at times produces a species of madness, an afflatus that is not divine. Yet this same source may issue in an impassioned, cosmic sanity. One thing is clear: those who dream, like Marx, of ending all religious dreams, themselves only dream the impossible—they dream of putting an end to dreams.

Ancestor Worship and the Sacred King

But we have already moved ahead too quickly, for skepticism of religious imagination is a late development. Archaic man immediately senses the divine; it is there—from the origin being is holy. We *become* aware of otherness, and concomitantly of our own being, but original otherness is charged with awful presence. Being aesthetic captures this in the archaic sense of the poet as priest. As Vico saw, originally poetry and religion were indistinguishable; the imagination that later becomes more aesthetically differentiated is first mythic mindfulness—an intimacy with being insepara- ble from the sacred. The developed articulation of the self in its difference, its loss of proximity to the immediate thereness of the holy, leads to a dimming of the sacred charge of the overdetermined origin. But, historically speaking, it is we secularized latecomers who are anomalies, not the norm. Atheism is a sign of lateness, of imaginative debility, of spiritual senility—yet perhaps as inevitable as age or decay are.

By "immediacy" is not meant sensuous immediacy, for as we have seen, there is no such "pure" immediacy. Immediacy is always in some measure mediated, hence by "immediacy" I imply a certain givenness of metaxological being prior to our explicit self-mediations. By sacred immediacy is meant forms of religion, which though complex cultural formations, are *lived in* spontaneously prior to skeptical reflection, hence prior to a more distancing mediation. Let me consider two manifestations of sacred immediacy: first, the sacred intimacy of the human family in ancestor worship; second, religious intimacy with the earth itself in sacral kingship. These testify to sacred otherness, and the mythic picturing of the whole, as both *beyond* individual will. They have a metaxological resonance in that both imply certain communities of being. Later we look at how distrust of this intimacy attenuates, even ruptures the rapport with the holy, leading to inevitable skepticism and self-assertion of our will.

Ancestor worship invokes our ineluctable relatedness to primal origins. As well as trying to bind up time, ancestor worship sustains a sense of the intimacy of all being, by viewing origins in quite elemental terms. Father begets son, who in turn as father begets son, and so on and on. Thus over an indefinite stretch, we find a blood chain of procreation and descent in which the individual loses its isolated particularity. There is an actual fleshed bond binding one to the community of one's ancestors, even though these be now sheltered in death. This blood bond with the dead generations lifts one beyond lone particularity, carries one along in the life blood of time itself. In ancestor worship the self feels its kinship with the whole, a kinship expressed with proximate intensity in the family bond, in the ties of consanguinity. In the familial piety of the ancient world, the hearth (*hestia*; Latin, *vestia*) was the religious center, middle of the house—here one was at home. Here also one might say that the idea of monogenism (regardless of its scientific truth) has the strong symbolic value of religiously naming the family of all humans.

This elemental bond is evident in that literally the dead are held close to the living; they might be buried in the garden, or be admitted to the pantheon of household manes. Thus, it seems that ritual burial is distinctly human; indeed for Vico it is one of the inaugural acts of human being. Ancestor worship is a denial of death's finality; the dead are deified, not annulled; they are not discarded but there besides us. Living and dead are held together in the continuity of generations, in an embrace spanning both sides of the great dark.[10] Human transcendence outstrips the finitude of its own middle being, gripped by a sense of life other than this finitude. Ancestor worship points to the urgency of ultimacy in familial form. Consonant with the double image, we also find the ambiguous note of fear, fear of the Fathers. The dead are besides us but they are also just like us, given to bouts of rancor. We love life but the dead envy us our life. They watch our joy. Though ancestor worship seems like a worship of death itself, it is a way of clinging to life in which the living generously give the dead a share in its sweetness; it is also gratitude for the gift of our being that the dead themselves made possible. Sometimes, as in Celtic mythology, the Land of the Dead is also the Land of the Living (*Tír inna mBeo*; also called *Tír inna mBan*, Land of Women), an apotheosis of what is festive, gay and rejoicing in *this* world. We wake the dead.

Ancestor worship may seem in decline, but many religions offer some displacement of this awe of age. In its place is put respect for the wisdom of the Elders. A halo is hung on the traditional teachings; what the Elders believed was holy, is yet holy and will still be holy. The consent of generations gone becomes the embrace gathering strays to the faith of their fathers. Western man thinks of the exotic Orient, but variations on the theme, loosened from old religious links, spring up even in scientific cultures. The point will recur: even scientific cultures that pride themselves on a rational secularity evidence, beyond every univocal reduction, an upsurge of the "religious," albeit in displaced or disfigured form.

Thus Age itself, the Old, the Primordial, is deemed venerable. We find this when lovers of culture revere the old Masters, even when sportsmen toast the Greats of time past. Or suppose in a Museum we look with more than detached scientific curiosity: sometimes we are filled with a shudder of strangeness, carried across the chasm of years. The ancient thing fills us with awe, with a memory of primeval emotions, with feelings recalling the reverence of a ritual. The ancient thing sparks off something deep in the soul of even the most secularized self. We feel in the presence of the mystery of time itself. A Greek vase may do this; or perhaps an old bronze Poseidon, caked with time, dredged from the ocean bottom; or perhaps a black stone that radiates an aura of undeviating endurance. The feeling might be released by an Egyptian mummy—those vessels of death intended for eternity. Some mundane thing might occasion it, such as the yellowed photo that fixes an incommunicable moment now long dissolved. That moment once was—once and once only it was. Involuntarily we find ourselves wondering; where is it now, is it "anywhere"? The ontological perplexity at religion's root is released, metaphysical wonder at the moment's sheer being there, its once-there "is": the enigma strikes home that this had being, was something rather than nothing.

Ancestor worship knits the self into the flesh of the *human family*, but being religion in its immediacy also knits the self into the *flesh of the earth*.

In earlier sacral ages, nature was not a dead mechanism but was lived in as if it were the aesthetic body of divinity.[11] Sacral kingship is an important manifestation of this religious intimacy of being. We can contrast this intimacy to the dedivinized nature of science.

Consider. A catastrophe occurs, the crops are blighted. The people cast about for cause; the sacred has been offended. The plague descends because the king debauches himself. But even in his personal vice, the king is holy, a sacred representative of the people, standing between them and their gods, a divine man. The king in riot is a sacred stain. But the hidden powers exact a savage justice, even on those individually innocent. A people shares its king's guilt, which in fact concentrates its own guilt. Disease, war, floods are retributions for disorder in the kingdom. Indeed the king's sacredness was enacted through a ritual marriage (*hierogamy*) to the earth. Perhaps the most famous case is Oedipus: here the pollution that haunts his human family also stains his marriage to the earth. The Theban family's fated sins also blight the wedded land, and turn it into the waste land. If blood has been spilled and stains the earth, ritual cleansing will purge the pollution, catharsis will set right the balance. Sacrifice, indeed of the king himself, will expiate the offence, and the atoned earth return again its fertile yield.

In the attunement to being emerging here, nature's powers are not radically different to the powers that drive us humans. Nature is a *community* of quasi-personal powers. If evil happens, then evil *intent* must be cause—some just pretext for the malice, some inherent grim justice to counterpart my transgression. The gods' justice seems to enclose as much darkness as we ourselves do. But consonant with the double image, this attunement evidences also a redeeming side. Since the powers are akin to us, and we are given to benevolence, so we may gain the gods' goodwill. Evil powers may struggle with the good, but sometimes the good will win, and being is bathed in golden blessedness. Victory may be provisional, yet despite strife, a home is provided for human beings. The world is not an indifferent, neutral alien, but as alike to us, it offers an habitable kinship. It was literally seen as a religious middle. (In the ancient world, pre-Ptolemaic religion saw the earth as center of the cosmic womb, or navel or *omphalos* of the world.) Even the hostile powers are not completely alien, for these too are like us; we and they belong together. In this belonging we recognize and purify our own darkness.

Consider, by contrast, a different attunement in which this tension of otherness in the double image becomes reduced to rational univocity. I am sick, but I go to my doctor, not my shaman; my sickness is scientific, not expiatory. The crops fail—I consult my agricultural advisor, not beg my priest's blessing. An earthquake convulses the country; but we do not accuse the political leaders of degeneracy. Instead we calculate it as the outcome of indifferent forces—forces as much indifferent to human evil as to good. Even if we call a catastrophe an "Act of God," we mean nothing religious. We mean something incalculable yes, but indifferently incalculable, not charged with the meaning of religious punishment. (Still, it is worth recalling that the Japanese Emperor was a god until the end of World War II. Loss of the war was also the loss of his divinity.) In this second dedivinized world, nature is an organization of univocal, impersonal forces, not an ambiguous community of personalized powers. This second world has been called an "It," in contrast to the first religious world that is an ambiguous "Thou." The universe begins to lose some of its terror, but it also loses its mysterious intimacy. It ceases to arouse religious reverence and is made an object of scientific curiosity and technological exploitation.

Publicly now we inhabit the second world. But we must ask if the will to univocity of instrumental mind has conquered the ambiguity? Throughout this chapter, indeed this book, I argue against the objectification of being that turns the metaxological into a univocal "It." If to be is to be metaxological, any reduction of the middle to univocity, while giving us objectifying control of aspects of the middle, also represses or distorts other, not so easily objectified aspects. Thus while the public world is an "It," privately, in the submerged archaic self, there persists traces of the old tangle of chaos and terror and mystery. Suppose one be subjected to repeated, unmerited misfortune or senseless sickness. At some point one will buckle and a question will be uttered that is senseless, scientifically speaking: "Why me?" The indifferent worm that gnaws its cancerous grave at the heart of my being, knows nothing of me as an irreducible, irreplaceable "I." It carelessly gluts its life on I, its host's death. I might plead justice Job-like, or toss defiance at the forces grinding me down. But scientifically we cannot make any sense of the fact that we humans are the only animals who *knowingly* shake our fists at the *empty* sky. All said scientifically, does the battered heart, be it rebellious or resigned, stretch out only to a heartless universe?[12]

II. THE MEDIATION OF THE RELIGIOUS MIDDLE

The Open Dialectic of Trust and Distrust

This elemental question only makes sense to the religious heart. But it shows the worm of doubt stirring *within* the heart of religion itself. Already we are broken off from the first intimacy. In some sense this is inevitable with the emergence of explicit mindfulness. I now look at a dialectic of trust and distrust that follows, and indeed a sense of dipolar divinity and piety that comes from the double image. As already stated, this is an open dialectic: the "dia," dyad is not closed, hence the dialectic is really a metaxological intermediation in the between. I retain the term "dialectic" here because of its traditional connotations of "struggle," and the "tension of opposition." Such tension is here at stake, leading to a stress on religious self-mediation. The alternatives presented here are: either a reduction of double to single self-mediation, and hence a closure to religious otherness of a self that tries to absolutely dominate the enigma of the between; or the living in inwardness of a religious respect for sacral otherness, a respect that keeps the dialectic richly double and hence open to the metaxological sense of being.

This dialectic is evident in that the question posed above can be asked either by the realist or idealist who will tilt our gaze in different directions. The realist does not flinch before the brute resistance of things; the idealist prides himself on not being arrested by the same resistance. The realist says: "This is!" The idealist retorts: "This is not, but it ought to be!" The idealist is heard to murmur: "I dream of more . . ." His talk is peppered with wistfuls like "Perhaps," "Maybe," "If only," "Who knows." The realist rudely replies: "Wake up, you yearning innocent—I told you so!" The idealist points us beyond to a hidden heaven, the realist reminds us with sweet glee that life is hell.

The realist looks like the metaphysical tough, but the idealist plays a more difficult part. It is easier to deflate every extravagant desire, to jibe at every "ought" not yet realized, to prick every intimation of unseen otherness. The realist points out our descent from apes but does not assist us take wing with angels. So realists never make revolutions; they recognize the brute nature of existence but, mired in what is taken as being's univocal obviousness, they do not perfect existence. By contrast, many religions are different ways of gathering up our idealistic zeal. Each has its glimpse of paradise, its picture of perfection, its anticipation of Elysian fields, its *Tír na nÓg*. The concept of God is perhaps the extremity of trying to picture perfection. Of course, idealism becomes saccharine when it fails to offer a lodging for the realistic principle, what we might call "religion's Satan." To be credible, a religion needs its Devil's Advocate.

Inevitably, then, the double image is manifest in the tension between realism and idealism. Besides heaven, there is hell; besides salvation, sin; besides Eden, the twisted jungle of the lapsed world; besides the beauty of being, the fault that runs through things and threatens to crack the cosmos. Indeed many religions, in trying to incorporate the realistic principle, have difficulty in preserving the divine unstained. The most radical form of the difficulty is this: if God is good, why is evil rampant? When it comes to evil, religions have tried various ways, theodicies, of giving God an alibi, none completely convincing. Religions are caught in an unavoidable conflict between the idealistic and realistic ways. Periodically even the realistic principle dominates the tension of the middle in this way: Then the ideal is postponed to an always elsewhere heaven, while the world remains defiled, vile, to be dominated with contempt.

An untempered idealism does not brace the self, and lacking salt's bitter savor, proves unpalatable. Innocent idealism cannot win; defeat is part of our lot, an episode in our education. In being religious our intimacy with sacred otherness coexists with the possibility of our radical estrangement from the holy. But a cynical realism, which battens only on the latter, cannot win either. This is defeat, passing itself off as the voice of weary experience. An enduring idealism must endure defeat. Put otherwise: Necessarily, as we develop a more mediated sense of being, there arises a condition of *metaphysical distrust*. We know the precariousness of our finitude in the middle. The love of being in our own being, when threatened, can turn into opposition to being in the being of the other. The lamb does not trust the lion, the hen the fox, the fly the spider. Animals betray this distrust either by fleeing their enemies or devouring their prey. But in the animal kingdom there are no idealists, hence no religions. But we human beings have many ways of dealing with this metaphysical distrust, religion being one of the most crucial.

Some religious attitudes just give vent to this distrust; they hate the earth, realistically recognized, for not being their ideal heaven, dreamt of unrealistically. Other religious attitudes struggle to overcome the distrust; they do not flee the real but try to realize the ideal, loving the earth for its promise, even in the frailty of its grandeur. They will to realistically enact their dream of perfection, for the ideal is just our willing participation in the perfecting process itself. Human beings alone have religion, for they alone self-consciously contend against metaphysical distrust, struggle against this condition of their own being, struggle to transmute it into its opposite. Realists are right in the recognition of distrust, but wrong if they fail to fight it.

The central expression of this dialectic of trust and distrust, as I implied, turns on the question of evil. Here the double image appears in a sense of a *dipolar divinity*. The matter can be expressed in more abstract philosophical form or in mythic terms. It is perhaps *the* stumbling block to religious trust, the place of radical rupture to our spontaneous intimacy with sacred otherness. Evil confronts us with a kind of negative otherness, resisting our will to completely conquer or conceptualize it.

In illustration, consider Leibniz' thought. Here we find a metaphysical "idealism," not without a certain plausibility in logic, producing unparalleled theological optimism. Leibniz held that God, in his infinite wisdom, and out of all the possibilities open to him, created the best of all possible worlds. Given God's goodness and omnipotence, what God made must be good.

Even though we cannot see as God sees, from God's vantage point the world must be maximally good. What seems evil to us is like the shadow in a beautiful painting—necessary to the light, contrast and harmony of the whole, and so from the standpoint of the whole (God's standpoint), good. Leibniz' *Theodicy* became one of the most celebrated works of its time. But in 1755 on All Saints' Day there occurred an "Act of God"—the famous earthquake of Lisbon, the great catastrophe that shook the satisfied minds of the time. Later Voltaire was to contemplate this disaster in juxtaposition with Leibniz' optimal assessment of things. The famous result was *Candide*, another work that attained celebrated status. Indeed this dual celebrity of *Theodicy* and *Candide* strongly underscores our double need: both to dream the absolute dream that is God and to debunk that same dream. The best of all possible worlds contains incalculable suffering, the grief of which no idealistic metaphysical theory can conjure away. We try to comfort someone in distress, but there are times when to say, "All is for the best, God knows," borders on the blasphemous. And yet we struggle to say "It is good."

The difficulty is traditionally put this way. Is there a lack of congruence between God's goodness and power? God is held to be both omnipotent and absolutely good. Yet the persistent recalcitrance of evil causes us to wonder if God is impotent to prevent what to us is appalling. Since he is omnipotent, how can he tolerate the evil so opposite to his nature? If he is all-good, he seems powerless; if he is all-powerful, he seems heartless. This is an abstract, philosophical way of putting the problem, but there is an older, more imaginative way. When mythic men were perplexed at divine goodness and power and how the two conjoined, they spoke about the Wrath of God. We moderns, supped on a milder, milkier diet, like to think of sweet goodness and forget the awful majesty of incomprehensible power. Our ancestors tasted acid. All things, even the highest, have a terrible, dark side. The dark side of the ultimate power they called the Wrath of God.[13]

In metaphysical distrust we deny the finitude of our intermediate being by willfully seeking to overreach all otherness. We overstep the boundary of our due lot, but Nemesis restores the proper order. Like Nemesis, the Wrath of God humbles us, dwarfs us in our overreaching pride. It shakes us out of our easy contentment with finite things; it batters our conceit. But there are times when justice seems lacking, radically absent. The innocent suffer absurdly; just and unjust are indiscriminately destroyed, without any reckoning of merits. In the Lisbon earthquake it seems the greatest casualties were in the Churches, while the brothels escaped unharmed. Some humans try themselves to become the Wrath of God: the urgency of ultimacy reduplicates the orgic god in human selves who, in willfully pursuing sheer power, end up as rulers lacking in justice, that is, tyrants. The similarity with the Wrath of God is uncomfortably close. In natural catastrophes, disasters, we come to know what we sometimes call the "tyranny of things." This seeming likeness of tyranny and God's power is one contributing factor to modern skepticism concerning religion. God the Father seemed to stifle the power of our freedom, a jealous heteronomy squashing the promise of autonomy in the middle.

The same "tyranny of things" and divine justice are barely distinguishable in the old mythic image of the Flood. The Deluge unleashes nature's destructiveness. It swamps all things, drowning them in terror. Everything is to be feared as extinguishing our fragile particularity. In the Garden of Eden, the myth says, nature was trustworthy and the original humans were at home, at one. But how can one trust nature in Flood? One becomes conscious of not being at home, of being estranged. Difference as cleavage erupts in Eden, considered as the immediacy of sacred nature. It is necessary now to be on one's guard. In a moment one might be washed away. Nature now as sacred immediacy is rupturing rather than harmonizing in community. It breaks down the community of being that before its power built up. Here we are at sea, claimed again by formlessness, by untamed powers. But this destructive power does not baptize being; it simply annuls.

After this wounding result we cannot entirely suppress our doubts. Even Noah's Ark is but a frail bark barely surviving, a tiny hope in a vast waste of water. The Flood swells ontological distrust rather than admiration. Henceforth there is no unself-conscious trust. Everything has become tainted with suspicion. We mortals watch our step. Joy comes only despite our alert constraint. We do not sing spontaneously. We sing to appease the savage powers.[14]

The Double Piety: Sacred Terror and Gratitude

The above dialectic not only reveals a suspicion that the divine may be dipolar but is also concretized in religious piety in two ways, namely, in sacred terror and gratitude. As itself double, piety has a negative and affirmative side: sacred terror corresponds to metaphysical distrust; piety as ontological gratitude corresponds to a deeper trust in being. In the religious middle, the overpowering otherness of being evokes our terror and our thanks.

If religious idealization elevates being above bare thereness, this elevation does not commence with something univocally noble but with the primal emotions of terror and awe. The ancients said *primus in orbe deos fecit timor*, and modern writers like Otto have reminded us of the *mysterium tremendum et fascinans*. However far any idealization or further mediation of being develops, it never totally shakes off the vestiges of this origin.

I sit in the gloom where twilight tantalizes the fantasy. Crispness of perception is frustrated as I populate the darkness with things half-seen, things half-guessed. In the clumpy blackness I make out a threatening presence—the heart's fear finds there what it imagines—the anger of the underworld. Against the gathering fear, I whistle in the dark and prayer is born. I survive the night and cast my morning gaze towards the zone of terror, not at all surprised that the power now borrows the form of a blackthorn bush. I ponder the devious malice. In my calculating prayers to the benign power, I resolve guardedly to placate the dark one.

Vico is one of our great teachers here. The sky is broken by a shaft of lightning, the silence rent by a thunder clap. The human being, small against the powerful elements, drops to the ground in dread. We bow before the bright bolt from the sky and call it Jove. We wonder what grim mystery rumbled in the thunder. In naming the lightning Jove, as Vico powerfully teaches, the human animal ceases to be feral, and the germ of metaphoric, social, civil life is sown. The trace of feral being may linger for millennia, may simply sleep as a possibility, to be reborn, transmuted with a vengeance, who knows when, who knows how. But the lightning bolt, named as Jove, makes us different, makes us human. Religious terror first makes us human. This is the first piety, the first respect. The world is articulated by a difference, an otherness we cannot comprehend; indeed we can barely stammer it out. The lighting bolt *is* Jove. Fear of the Lord is the beginning of wisdom.[15]

The above pictures often have been said to give us the essence of religion. Piety is the placation of terror. This is *one* side of the truth of the dipolar image. It is impossible to avoid some metaphysical distrust in the middle in the face of the overpowering otherness of being. Being religious is bound up with our *suffering* being. Consider our finitude: I am hungry and cannot find food by day; in dreams I feed on the food of gods. I am sick and my case is terminal; I alleviate the pain with hope that elsewhere I may be whole again. I am brought low by indigence for which there is no remedy here; I redeem my threadbare existence by suffering it with steadfast faith, storing up treasures in heaven. Undoubtedly religions minister to our sense of lack in the middle. The unknown unsettles us and arouses trepidation; in faith we have an antidote for fear. We can make sense of intermediate being up to a point, but here and there baffling events are enfolded in a mystery that we seem unable to penetrate; we give a religious name to our bafflement and baptize it as the supernatural.

We find this in what we might call "exile religions." Exile religions emphasize our homelessness in the middle, our unhappiness with the world. Existence itself is said to be exile. It is a punishment, not a privilege. Life is retribution for a fall. So we pay homage to God by humiliating ourselves. Our life becomes servility to strange and tyrannical forces. The vigor of our souls is reinterpreted as the pride that produces downfall. The bodies that keep us healthy become our shame. Our sacrifices cease to be feasts and dances and instead become ceremonies of complaint. We become little different to the worthless worm, thrilled by grief, enraptured by misery, ecstatic in our own abasement. When human beings feel thus about being, their prayers come out as a hosanna of groans.[16]

This exile side of religion is not currently in vogue. Hostile critics of ascetic religion, like Nietzsche, have detected a subterranean will-to-power in such pious negativity. Moreover, defenders of religion tend to maintain a polite silence about the questionable aspects of exile religion in the past, especially its fostering of self-hatred, disguised as devotion to divinity. Exile religion has faded perhaps because of our forgetfulness of finitude. More so than our forefathers, we moderns seem at home with the world of finite things. We seem to have pushed back the boundary of mystery. We have extracted some of the powerless horror from sickness. We think we have silenced nature into submission with our own atomic thunder. We think we have distilled the energy of the lightning bolt.

One need not defend the self-hatred that exile religion can foster, but one can see that such an extreme response does release and articulate the urgency of ultimacy. Given the tension, indeed fragility of our being in the metaxological, some such response is inevitable at times. We need a less hostile rejoinder to our strangeness in being. This also means rejecting the metaphysical thoughtlessness that is the contemporary will-to-power, its self-congratulatory complacency, *its* flight from strangeness, its shallow incomprehension of exile religion as one flower of the ambiguous depths of our being. There will always be undefeated terrors, chinks in the armor of our confidence behind which we breathe the ancient vulnerability of our ancestors. No matter how successfully we become, in Descartes' words, "masters and possessors of nature," we remain suffering animals. We suffer physically and metaphysically. In the unsheltered night all confidence is quickly dismantled. Death brings us our greatest terror, our undefeated dread. When the old, exile religion tried to overcome this terror by offering up this death, its piety at least tried to stand fast before the darkest power of all. We are no different and have not done much better. We still sing with gusto in the dark, but no longer name a god.

But there is another kind of singing. We may break on otherness, but the *other* side of the dipolar image says that piety can be more than the imagistic displacement of metaphysical terror. Since we live ambiguously in the middle between extremities of debasement and ennoblement, servitude and freedom, poverty and plenty, religion reproduces this ambiguous doubleness in symbolizing the extremities as hell and heaven. Besides exile religion and the piety of terror, we find gods that reflect our intimate joy in the bounty of being. For the otherness of the sacred is not only terrifying, it also welcomes our festive celebration. Religion includes the whip, the hairshirt and the groan of servility before savage powers. It is also marked by the feast, the potlatch, by dancing, by alleluia and amen.

After all the open dialectic also offers the promise of metaphysical trust from which can be born on ontological gratitude for being as such. An inspection of the several senses of "piety" points to this other side. Certainly one view identifies piety with superstition—a toothless crone or Crazy Jane jabbering away in an empty church. But we speak also of filial and local piety, and these reveal a sense more positive. Filial piety signifies the special bond of loyalty and respect between parents and children, a spiritual bond based on the physical kinship of blood (cf. ancestor worship). Local piety signifies the special loyalty for one's own place, one's home—a spiritual kinship again closely tied to a physical reality (cf. sacred kingship as wedded to place). The horror we feel at crimes like parricide and treason shows how deep these pieties still go. A like sense of a kinship or bond or community of loyalty can be found in religious piety. As has been pointed out, by Augustine among others, the roots of *"religio"* imply a binding together, a bond of connectedness. Religious piety, in this sense, acknowledges our metaxological link with powers of being more ultimate than ourselves, signifies even in the doubleness of our intermediated being our intimacy with sacral being, not our estrangement from it. Such piety is not born in ontological poverty but in a sense of due justice, in praise of the powers that vitalize and beautify and perfect creation.

Unlike the piety of terror, here in this second affirmative possibility, one is not rent by an excess of disunion. The powers of otherness do not tyrannize over the middle but mould its possible perfection. One is granted to approach these perfecting powers, taking due upright pride in one's participation in their promise. Here a god is not envious of us actualizing mind in daring thought; nor interested in magical tricks to stupefy the credulous; nor cranky about insignificant details like a fussy fishwife; nor a lonely hearts succor, playing tease and hard to get with human aspiration; nor so insecure in himself that he must enforce an abdication of their wills by his supine devotees.

Besides gloomy gods there are laughing, noble gods.[17] Noble gods are not symbols that discharge our complaint against life, but condensations of our metaphysical gratitude for being. The absolute is no sourpuss. Being showers its bounty on us. It bestows us with power, beauty, fertile springs, full harvests, the dawn song of a blackbird. Its gifts seem too much, unmerited by us, a motiveless benevolence. With grateful modesty one will want to share the bounty. One will want to thank, to give in return, to return a gesture of generosity. Whom is one to thank? Certainly not oneself; there seems no one. We condense our gratitude on the images of the gods, and through these channel our thanksgiving to the ultimate powers.

But gratitude can be linked with a kind of pride, and here, too, we find ambiguity. Noble gods humanize, civilize a people's pride. A people finds itself full of power, vigorous, fertile, successful, admired by strangers. It is tempted to overreach, to be too full of itself.[18] But a pride that overstretches power weakens this power instead of enhancing it. Again in the urgency of ultimacy, the self can become orgic. Thus, hubris becomes the primordial fault, the *prōton kakon*. Pride becomes barbaric, uncivilized, when we do not keep to our proper measure; instead of elevating a people through its gods, it causes a fall. Noble gods restrain our self-assertion, idealize it, substituting beauty for our brutal pride.

If noble gods tend to be witnesses to our gratitude to being, gratitude itself is rarely unalloyed and frequently mixed with resentment. Envy lurks in impure thanksgiving, hence gratitude almost inevitably alternates with apprehension before a god's ferocity. Gods seem to show brutal qualities when their devotees show the like brutality. Contrariwise, as a people becomes more civilized, the more idealized become its gods, the more they image the ideals of perfection a people harbors and hopes to realize in its way of being. One thinks immediately of the theomachy in Greek mythology, the transition from Chthonic and Titanic gods to the Uranian and Olympian. As this idealization continues, gods tend to progress from the physical to the spiritual; they rise from the earth (Gaia is the mother of Uranus in Hesiod; earlier Greeks imaged themselves as earthborn), are elevated to dwelling on the Sacred Mountain, and from there they vanish into the Sky, beyond the Sky. At some point divinity may be idealized out of physical existence entirely.[19] Think of the contrast of, at one extreme, the Celtic fertility figure, Sheila na Gig, or a lingam and, at the other, the invisibly present, yet never materially mastered, Paraclete. Since we continue to be priapists, by and large, in our daily dealings, it may seem that the divine has simply disappeared in the idealization. When we think of gods at all, we may do so with a crude sense of spirit—gods become like ghosts, or dematerialized matter, what Hobbes called "spooks."

This shift from earth to sky, the Chthonic to Olympian, images the shift from immediacy to mediation. The opening of space between earth and heaven is a mythic image of the differentiation process. This also allows a possible alienation from immediate intimacy with sacred otherness—the space of otherness seem to become *empty* (e.g., the sublunary world in the Ptolemaic system; or the infinite spaces that made Pascal—a thinker of the middle between nothing and infinitude—afraid in Copernican cosmology.) Thus, an unsophisticated atheism easily springs up as we develop the idealization and express intermediation that goes with civilization. For this idealization may be approached from *without*, that is, in terms of commonsense realism; then the intermediation will look like atheism. For this view, dominated by a sense of physical thereness, the traditional gods are like things, or beings like other beings, albeit more magically powerful.[20] One thinks of the charge of atheism against Socrates. It was Socrates' sophistication of spirit that fueled religious suspicion. Though sophistication is tied with the ideal of *sophia*, it also invokes the sophists' worldly skepticism and this is not always distinguishable from merely destructive debunking. On the other hand, if we understand the idealization from *within*, there emerges a more subtle mindfulness. To the superficial glance such a nuanced mind (again I think of Socrates) will look atheistic, for this mind is skeptical of the physical images of the gods that some idolize (the fundamentalist faithful) and that others curse (the militant atheists). The nuanced mind realizes that any increase in civilization must bring an increased possibility of atheism—precisely because of the necessary skepticism that civilized selves have of any physical images of the divine.

Because of the double image, the dialectic of trust and distrust and piety's doubleness, many believers tend to be schizophrenic, certainly dualist: materialists in their lives, spiritualists in their worship. If they cannot find a way to join these poles, they often revert to the material side, the gravitational pull of the given reality being too strong. When they cannot pin spirit down to a physical image, they eventually tend to doubt the reality of spirit. In this sense, the believer is not very different to the ordinary atheist. The atheist has simply chopped off one side of the dualism. Such believers are only embryo atheists, while such atheists are but stillborn believers. The otherness of being in the metaxological middle is dualized in the sense of an unmediated opposition of body and soul, matter and spirit, inner and outer, sensuous and supersensuous.

By contrast, the civilized self (that is, one mindful of the complexity of the metaxological middle) neither abandons the ideal of perfection, nor stifles the skeptical impulse. Skepticism as metaxological (cf. chapter 1) can be just the questioning, seeking desire, the opening to otherness that is the starting point of any quest for perfection, absolutely necessary for our first awakening. We might not get beyond the first awakening. We might be torn apart by the negativity of our doubts, arrested by a coarse realism or an unripe spiritualism. The civilized self as metaxologically open tends to be neither spiritualist nor materialist. He understands the need for sensuous images but will not bow before them. The sensuous is seen as a possible embodiment of spirit. Likewise, his sense of spirit is not on the level of spooks. Spirit is the perfection of the sensuous, its capacity for the idealization of intermediate being, the power that may transfigure it and make it the original image of being's own inexhaustibility.

Gods variously name this inexhaustible power of being, a power neither merely sensuous nor spiritual. Thus reverence can be metaphysical gratitude for this power and what it gives. Ontological gratitude stays true to the metaphysical value of the metaxological middle. And since the energy of being in middle is neither univocally internal nor univocally external, the civilized self may be equally attentive to the abyss within and the wonder of the world without. Both the self in its inward otherness and the outer otherness of the cosmos may serve as places where the reverence of ontological gratitude finds anchor. In this sense civilized religion become embracing and tolerant. But, as I suggested at the outset, it is also *disillusioned*. Partly springing from nostalgia for innocence before sophisticated but cankerous doubt, many think of disillusionment as a bad, regrettable thing. But disillusionment need not be regretted, for in the sense intended, to be disillusioned is to be freed, to be released from illusion. The disillusionment of this civilized, metaxologically open self can be a positive condition of being and mind.

III. METAXOLOGICAL OPENNESS TO SACRED OTHERNESS

Naming and Not Naming: The Problem of Anthropomorphism

This releasing disillusion seems to negate the religious but it really offers a further opening of the sense of sacred otherness. It mediates a less closed anthropomorphic sense of the divine. It allows both the fuller self-mediation of the religious middle, but also its *non-closure* in terms of human self-mediation, resisting every anthropomorphic reduction of divine otherness. The perennial problem of anthropomorphism relates to this releasing disillusionment, for the latter demands a deliteralizing of the double image to preserve its essential openness to otherness. I first remark on anthropomorphism and names, then turn to the middle way of mystery as trying to further mediate this openness without compromise of the metaxological relatedness to otherness.

Our discourse about the divine unavoidably imbues the gods with incongruous human qualities. Consider the utterance: Vengeance is mine, says the Lord. The desire for vengeance is a primitive impulse that civilized human beings try to outgrow or at least curb. To ascribe this to a divine being may be metaphorical of its dark side, its wrath, but it also risks reducing this being to a state less than civilized, conferring on it a detestable rancor. The mindful self expects the absence of such base human characteristics in a being supposedly higher than human. We envisage the divine as an ideal beyond present imperfection, but our vision here seems to be a reflection of ourselves. Instead of escaping into the "beyond" as through a window, the glass into which we peer only gives us back our ugly face. In our images of divinity we collapse their doubleness into ourselves and find again our own twisted self. Far from being free of our imperfections, the gods seem only to reduplicate them. They seem human-all-too-human.

Xenophanes noted the difficulty in antiquity. Jews and Christians believe God made man in his likeness, but Xenophanes noted the opposite and reversed image and original: gods were like the men who revered them, not the other way. An Ethiopian's gods are snub-nosed and black, while Thracian gods have grey eyes and red hair. He satirically wondered what might happen if bulls and lions and horses had hands; would they perhaps draw gods like themselves? The implication seems clear: man makes gods in his image. If we recall the two senses of imagination mentioned before, with Xenophanes we meet a rationally differentiated self, but one placed at a distance from religious imagination as *ontological*. The stress now falls on the image as *our* projection, not as an original upsurge of manifestation. *Our* articulating otherness has begun to grow in its distinction from the articulated otherness of the sacred. In the metaxological community of being we do not see immediately the otherness of the sacred but primarily ourselves. Better, we see the sacred as only the self in its *own* otherness. The dialectic of distrust and trust now can take the form: rational distrust of the image, primary trust in our own reason.

The problem arises whether you are antagonistic or sympathetic to religion. Xenophanes found the antics of the gods of Homer and Hesiod blasphemous; their quarrelling, licentiousness, lying would be intolerable among us, so it is *impious* to envisage the divine thus. Such gods are images of imperfection, hence *religiously* unacceptable. Being religious "demythologizes" *itself*. For Xenophanes sought to free the idea of god from these imperfections. His satire on Homeric gods was the negative side of a religiously affirmative struggle to conceive of a One, non-anthropomorphic God. Later Plato, in his *Republic*, attacked the gods in similar terms, and with a similar intent, namely, to purge the divine of human imperfections. I note, too, the aesthetic aspect of Plato's "demythologization." The criticism of the poets in the *Republic* is often misunderstood because we impute to Plato modern "aestheticized" notions of art. But the Greek poets knew nothing of *l'art pour l'art*; they were guardians of the images of the sacred. Plato was deeply aware of the image's profound power in art and religion, indeed of the complex intertwining of these two.[21]

Among those hostile to the holy, Marx is a classic example of one trying to explode rather than purify religion on just this problem of anthropomorphism. Taking his line from Feuerbach, the gods, he argues, have human characteristics precisely because they are the products of human power. They are the projections of this power away from man and anchored in an alien object, an "other" being. The power we falsely ascribe to the god as other is *our* otherness and henceforth must be returned to humans, not to purify the idea of God but to deflate the divinity entirely. Not surprisingly, Marx reduces the Hegelian dialectic between the human self and the divine other to the self's own dialectic with itself, to a *singular* humanistic self-mediation (cf. introduction). Marx, in fact, advocates an immanent, secular anthropomorphism: instead of projecting itself into another world, the human self must project its power onto this world and knowingly, that is, atheistically, work to perfect life here and now.

There is always the articulation of an image, I agree, but this is never simple self-projection. Even when it includes the latter, the image is not "projected" into nothing but on to the "screen" of otherness. The question here is: Is otherness exhausted by our own otherness, or is there *an other otherness*, irreducible to our own? I argue here, as before, for both sense of otherness and their complex metaxological community; hence I also argue against either their dualistic opposition, or the complementary reduction of one to the other. In fact, this metaphor of "projection" breaks down. A true image is not only a mediation of self-reflection, an image of us, but also a metaxological intermediation of otherness, our image yes, but our image of otherness, attentive to its otherness simply as other. If the theory of projective imagination is not to be completely discarded, it must be freed from an interpretation that stresses only one side of the image, its powers of self-mediation. The image's other side, its intermediation of otherness, the image as opening us to otherness, indeed the image as the other opening itself to us, is absolutely essential (cf. chapter 2). Put otherwise, being religious is not a merely human product, nor contrariwise an external superimposition by an extrinsic divinity. It is a complex conjunction, indeed community and intermediation of the two in the double image. The religious image is a community of being. Thus, we must transcend both theological and humanistic dualisms; these are abstractions from the doubleness and hence complementary in their neglects, the first of self-mediation, the second of real otherness; both reduce otherness to dualistic opposition, now from the side of transcendence, now from the side of immanence.

Granted, anthropomorphism is not avoided by religions—for example, Judaism and Christianity—which insist that we are the image of God. For even here the images of God must always carry traces of the here and now. To cite an important example: God is called "Father." Without denying the depth of meaning possible with paternity, clearly fatherhood also is a mundane thing, a common finite relation. Obviously God is not Father in this sense. Is our use of this language subject then to what Anthony Flew called a "death by a thousand qualifications?" Finite categories inevitably bend when applied to a being said to be infinite.

Sometimes the result are comic (comedy has religious significance; cf. chapters 5 and 6). A teacher tells my son that his "real" father is in heaven. I am nonplussed and say to my son: does this mean I am only a stand in? If so, what role have I, the natural father, seeing that I pay the bills? When I look at the mother of my son, I am made uneasy to think I might be just an earthly proxy, possibly being upstaged by some ghostly doppelgänger. There is the dark side too. Good fathers stay close to their children, do not abscond once having dropped their seed. Yet sometimes we suspect we are abandoned. The father is derelict, the maternal earth is desolate and we fear our ontological illegitimacy. Are we then—shuddering thought—God's bastards?

This problem of mindfully purifying the double image extends to whether we can name gods or God at all. Though some religiously refuse us the right to name the divine, nevertheless there have been many names: Zeus, Yahweh, Allah, Brahma, Siva, Ahura Mazda, Dionysus, Jesus, Uwoluwu, Quetzalcoatl, and so on. Some polytheisms are so generous, Shintoism, for example, that the gods are thousand-titled.[22] Other monotheisms, grown austere with insistence on the pure One, pare the name down to almost nothing. We find the two extremes: gods as thick as shoals of fish, bearing each a different name; no gods at all, only the One, and at that its "identity" utterly elusive, perhaps even melting into Nothing.

What happens in naming? In naming we try to arrest the flux of happening, isolating something from the flow of manifestation, thus calling attention to and identifying it. To put a name on something helps us abbreviate the act of discrimination by which we situate something and hold it separate in the flow of appearing. Because names can abbreviate discrimination, they also allow us to label things conveniently. This convenience, in turn, can detract from real comprehension of the thing named. Then we nominally manipulate the labels as if they were self-sufficient realities and lose sight of the thing itself as a presencing in the flow, *the thing as other* that the name was originally intended to identify. Thus also names seem to offer a degree of control. Ancient peoples believed in the intimacy of name and thing: to know the name gave one power over the thing. Indeed the ancient respect for the poet relates to fear of this magical power of words; the true word is essentially sacred, hence an image with ontological power, hence also dangerous.[23]

Given its character, naming presents special problems in religion, particularly in monotheism. Can we name God, if this is to identify, pin down God's being? If so, do we not rob God of mystery, power, and transcendence? The name seems then to be the fundamental violence on otherness. We seem to reduce the infinite to finitude, turn it into a manipulable thing, as if to call on God were to summon a genie from a bottle. Alternatively, in invoking the sacred name we risk the descent of the dangerous, destructive power of its bearer.[24] Judaism has been especially guarded. Other religions may be on first name terms with the Most High, but it insisted that the divine name not be uttered. Perhaps it might be pronounced on momentous occasions, but in time even the old name became blurred and its exact pronunciation disputed. The name was too mysterious and powerful for us. What "names" we have come by indirection, through a burning bush, or a voice in the whirlwind. By directly naming the divine we objectify it, turn it into a finite object, turn it into something it is not.[25] The name is a shelter for identity, but God has no univocal identity, hence no name. The name leaves God's otherness out.

Are we then only allowed to gesture mutely towards a *Deus absconditus*, or the Nameless in the secular manner of a Samuel Beckett? But the trouble with the Nameless is that it dissolves into the nebulous, and thence into nothingness. Instead of univocal identity, we get merely equivocal, that is, unmediated difference. Without some name the divine seems to disappear. But then our silence breeds indifference to otherness. One might have recourse to the Buddha, seeking salvation in Nirvana on the path of extinguished desire, but this, too, is to distrust all names.

So: If we name, we miss; if we do not name, we miss. Either way something seems lost. In one case, we forfeit something by speaking, in the other, by being silent. I do not see a way out of this dilemma if we insist on one of its horns and ask for an either/or between speech and silence. We must live in and with this tension, mindful of its stress. We have to name otherness in a way that names our failure to name otherness. From the dilemma there even arises this paradox. When a religious person, precisely because of reverence, refuses to violate the divine by naming it, the divine may vanish in this anonymity, and being religious dialectically turns into its opposite—atheism. Strange as it may sound to some, there is an atheism whose source is religious reverence.[26]

In sum: The name cannot be a univocal identity, for this collapses the difference of the human and the divine. Nor can it be equivocal, for this fails to mediate their difference. Not can it be only dialectical, for the danger here is the reduction of divine otherness to human self-mediation, or indeed the subsumption of human difference into an absorbing god. The name must be metaxological: a non-reductive "identity" that intermediates with, that is, *lets be, while intimately relating to*, the sacred other as other, thus also guarding human difference as free difference.

The Middle Way and Mystery

The dilemma of the name simply articulates our intermediate being—the image is double because we are double. In the middle we can say "either/or," or "both/and," as above, or "neither/nor," as we will see below with the mystic. But the religious urgency of ultimacy always tempts us to tilt to extremities. The metaphysical stress of the middle is difficult to live; it requires a strange kind of strained equilibrium, that is, an equilibrium we must seek to attain, strain to keep, again and again. It is equilibrium in process, never a finished product.

If we consider this middle in relation to sacred speech, we immediately note opposite claims. For it is said often that no one has seen God, yet in unguarded moments of fear or wonder, we do speak of God. But whence can come the substance of such speech? Is it like empty gossip about others not known directly or only by hearsay, the idle chatter of a quacking mouth energetically delivering nothing. Serious thinkers have always wondered if religious language is words without matter, edifying but vacuous verbiage.[27] Not many are bold to claim privileged conversation with Deity, though some imply they lie deeply in the Lord's bosom, catching voices in the air, being drawn through the night by dreams. Generally the limit of our claims is granted. This reflects the above dilemma and is in some respects a compromise between extremes. It is a middle way between complete ignorance and knowledge, between the gnosticism that asserts it knows all, and the agnosticism that claims to know nothing at all. One might recall the intermediate character of the ideal of wisdom and its characteristic mindfulness (chapter 1).

This middle way implies: we cannot have direct knowledge but we can home on the divine by way of indirection. We may approach the heart of the matter obliquely, not through random hearsay but through pointers, through symbols, through analogies, even with all their limitations. Speech about the divine is necessarily representational. This middle way can seem like a bland compromise, and sometimes it is. But understood in its richest possibilities, it is fraught with tension. The naming of otherness that also names its own failure must walk a ridge between extremes, and so always risks toppling over into either of these sides.

On the one side, the risk is that religious representations are fantasies, images without real reference to an original, images of nothing except our needy fear. This repeats a previous objection: No one has seen God because there is nothing to be seen. Fantasy fills up this nothing with configurations of its own creation; let fantasy itself contract and the gods will melt into insubstantial air. On the other side, the middle way runs the opposite risk. A zealous person might say: if we can approach indirectly, why not directly too? If we have oblique familiarity, why not face-to-face knowing? Why not go the whole way and cease to tantalize ourselves with mere anticipations of the absolute? Why not complete knowing, stronger, why not become as a God? In the first case, God is absorbed in us; in the second, we are swallowed by an absorbing God, snatched into the all-consuming life of eternity's vaporizing fires.[28]

Established religions, with a developed sense of worldly prudence, are alarmed by the second possibility, even more alarmed than by simple atheism. For it takes religious imagery to the extreme. This not only can breed fanaticism but can also bring to light the instability built into *all* religious imagery right from the beginning. Established religions hedge their bets, and generally postpone the fuller knowledge until after death. Now in a glass darkly, then face-to-face—a riskless wager, Pascal might agree. On this side of death they admonish their flocks not to stray from the middle way, but now made suitably safe. The counsel is to steer straight ahead, veering neither to right nor to left, blinkered if necessary against the seductive abysses of either side, ears stoppered against the Sirens of atheism and fanaticism.

A less domesticated sense of the middle way, one truer to the genuine self-transcendence of the religious urgency of ultimacy, can bring a less disingenuous sense of mystery. Religions are not born in the shadow-less noonday of logic; they are born in darkness and to alleviate darkness. The rationalist looking for all-embracing clarity is sorely disappointed. Religions may be born in darkness; I do not say they must end there. What they feed on and tenaciously defend is this sense of mystery. From the standpoint of analytical thought, being religious is a waywardness, a dissidence. This is what disappoints the rationalist insistence that being conform to a rigid, univocal logic. Being religious refuses such univocity and rebels. Superficially the insistence on univocal logic seems correct. For the category of "mystery" gives every impression of being entirely negative, a null concept and cunning subterfuge for nescience. It lies beyond our logical will to capture being in a concept. The mysteries of a religion seems merely the exotic, Freudians might say, pathological tablets of our ignorance.

The instrumental mind calculates being as a problem to be solved, not a mystery to be celebrated, yet one can speak of an affirmative sense of mystery. Our rational concepts are generally appropriate for finite objects, but a less nugatory sense of mystery emerges in the intimation that being is not exhausted by the world, considered as an aggregate of objectified, finite things. Since our concepts are tied to finite things, our minds are checked here, arrested before a limit.[29] This arrest may precipitate the struggle to bring to mind what exceeds the aggregate of objectified things. Thought itself is not exhausted in objectifying concepts. Finite being may even become a conspirator with the sense of mystery, a collaborator pointing to something it fugitively intimates yet also guards in hiddenness. Mystery, in this sense, is not just our lack of analytical concepts but an extension or stretching of the call to be mindful of being, forcing a revision of the narrower instrumental rationality. At the limit thought opens to an unlimit and stutters into deeper speech.

This sense of mystery is again tied to the imagistic mindfulness of being religious.[30] An image is an image of some other; it need not encapsulate the original other, yet it is not completely cut off from it, but is always intermediate, as Plato's *Sophist* teaches. It is neither identical with its original, nor absolutely different, it necessarily both reveals and conceals. Just so the gap between image and original can be interpreted variously. As we saw, some say this space is empty, hence, to be rationally consistent, here we do not even have images, properly speaking. What is before it is what it is and nothing more. This is a univocal realism: it calls a spade a spade, and that's that.

Now the religious sense of mystery relates to what is differently, doubly: Bread is bread yet not bread, wine is wine yet not wine. Being before us is both itself yet betokens something other; appearance hides as well as manifests, hence draws us into a metaphysical space where the attuned, perhaps alarmed, self stumbles onto something more. Like Alice through the looking glass, behind the glittering surface lies amazing difference. Turned in the gap between image and original, a middle world is shaped that is both itself and not itself, what it appears to be and something other or more—the world itself is the double image. The profane eye meets a blank, stops; the world is too much with it and it sees but the sedimented thereness. The imagistic eye, meeting the same blank, sees a silent enigma, perhaps a hieroglyph for deciphering, perhaps the uncarved block of the Tao. The world is not too much with it and in the opening of metaphysical space an other otherness comes to meet it.

Though the divine can never be completely encapsulated in created things, through and indirectly in them it can still be approached. As a doubled image, finite being is a to-be-interpreted *poiēsis* of the original ground. Finite things have being but are not ultimate or absolute; they image in their intermediate being the ultimate ground. They shimmer in their lack of fixed self-subsistence and make a dance of symbols that tells of something other or more. In the finite we divine the infinite—the religious cipher is the middle agency spanning their divide. The lack here of analytical concepts is made up for in profundity of representations. Consider but one image that inscribes the sense of metaphysical mystery in the very earth itself: the Neolithic burial ground at Newgrange in Ireland. This is a huge mound, and in its heart is a burial chamber. I call this construction a religious image because it pictures a sense of the whole in its otherness, especially as this concerns our end, death, and its place within the cosmic cycle. This "picture" of the whole is concretized in the mythic forming of the very earth itself. Nobody knows exactly when such microcosmic mounds were sunk in the engendering mud. They were sunk by a pastoral people with a highly sophisticated sense of the movement of the heavenly bodies. For in midwinter, the grave of the year, exactly at the winter solstice, following the year's longest night, and at the day's dawn, the sun pierces a gap readied in the roof, enters the mound, moves along its entrance, and gradually bathes the burial chamber in light. The light is within the earth briefly, about seventeen minutes or so. But the meaning of this brief entrance spans time. These "primitives" erected on the earth a still enduring icon of eternity in the very bowels of death itself.[31]

Nevertheless, the sense of mystery is polysemic and comes in many guises, so cannot be celebrated without discrimination. In one form we glut ourselves on bizarre obscurities; in another we frown on any excess of fantasy and make an enigma of emptiness. Reaching into the space of the cosmos, shuddering to think its silence is void, even the silence becomes a suggestion of mystery. Because religious representation mediates between the hidden and the manifest, it require mindful interpretation. Such hermeneutical discrimination (as it might be called) follows the releasing disillusion and its need to find direction by indirection, that is, by intermediation. We do not directly behold but divine a presence; we need an image to hold what we divine; imagination and divination are linked. Religious discrimination is divination that enjoins a proper mindfulness concerning all representation, a guarded attentiveness that hovers between yes and no, suspended but moving between acceptance and perplexity, an open dialectical, hence metaxological doubleness that holds trust and distrust together in order never to close out otherness.[32] Consider a Hindu ceremony: the worshipper takes refuge in a doll, and for the ritual's duration, the figure *is* the god; but when the spirit passes, the figurine reverts to its character of clay. The ceremony ends with the devotee discarding the doll. It is drowned in the Ganges, an emptied vessel that served its brief purpose to incarnate the god but which now is nothing but impotent plaster. The Ganges, sacred river of the gods, because also a graveyard of idols. The very destruction of the religious image itself images religious respect for sacred otherness.

Without the intermediation of informing inwardness religious images appear as straw dogs, as relics of the dead, detritus of a mode of being once vital but now exciting no awe. We see the bones of saints and shake our heads that past believers could frantically tear to pieces the still warm body of a saintly self, with the intent of thereby coming closer to the divine. The religious urgency of ultimacy can rise to a crescendo of blind frenzy. The scientific rationalist is here like a sober latecomer, straying into an intoxicating orgy: it strikes his univocal mind as too much. Yet sometimes, despite time's passage, an aura of the sacred persists. At Stonehenge, for example, no battle cries now ring in the air, no songs of agony and exultation accompany sacrifices to the gods. The Sun rises as it always has, and floods this circle with its golden balm. In the silence this pagan enclosure still speaks out its former saturation with a sense of the divine. Even the grey latecomer might be moved by this memorial to some mystery immemorial.

With the sacred we are not prone to patience. The urgency of ultimacy makes us equate the image with the original and eradicate the necessary gap of the between. This is where idolatry originates. One Greek word for image is "*eidōlon*," from which derives our "idol." When an image becomes an idol, it is we who create the change by collapsing an essential metaxological difference; it is not the thing itself that is an idol. An idol is a finite thing worshipped as though infinite. It is not things that make idols but worship, our worship. We worship the image for itself and not for what it represents. Idolatry is really a *lack* of discriminating religious imagination, of metaxological mindfulness—the image is taken *literally*, as if it were completely the original, univocally identical with it. Idolatry is a refusal to abide with the sense of mystery. In an ironical way, idolatry can share the realism of secular univocity; both turn mystery on its side and try to flatten the double image to a single meaning.

No religion is free from the risk of idolatry, because none can continue without the sacred image. What of those religions that refuse to name a God? Here being religious is being silent. My point remains. The necessary "image" of this mode is not a physical thing but just the reverent, expectant silence itself. Silence is an image, for it is an overdetermined comportment of a living self that calls for interpretation. Silence is the silence of a self, and a silent self is an icon. A silent self *says something* in and through its silence. Religious silence is one of the most charged of all silences (cf. chapter 5 on silence and otherness). In fact, this "image" is physical too, since the religiously silent self is an embodied being whose very mode of concrete presence communicates a meaning, albeit a meaning also withheld.

The recalcitrant ambiguity of a silent self can be one of the most important ways of respecting the otherness of the divine.[33] This otherness gets flattened into univocity more easily when the image is an external thing, or a sensuous representation, or a ritual that can lend itself to mindless repetition. Images of the sacred are necessary, but since they inevitably becomes stabilized, reverence can become fixed and shackled to them, in bondage to them. Religions spawn idolatry because we resist being reminded of the impermanence of our images, even those of the Holy. When they become empty, we find it difficult to discard them; they become fetishes: invisible chains the believer cannot snap without reawakening the old ontological terror at the unknown.[34] Instead of articulating the sacred, the image becomes a barrier against mystery, a secure landmark in a familiar landscape. Every religion can be the womb of idolatry when it becomes too solidified, too established, too univocalized. This is *inevitable*, given the ambiguity of images and our haste for the putative ontological security of univocity. Established religions tend to oblige us with assurances. They do not always ask us to wait. They film over the gap of mystery. A religious self might be wary of religions.

IV. RELIGIOUS INWARDNESS AND THE METAXOLOGICAL MEDIATION OF OTHERNESS

The Mystic and Religious Inwardness

Let us briefly take our bearings. Our discussion allows us to see that discriminating mindfulness requires an appropriating *inwardness* in relation to the image itself. Such mindfulness is ultimately metaxological. The image, as it were, has to be taken to heart, hence the quality of the self in its inwardness becomes crucial. (The "heart" is the spiritual middle: the metaxological community of being lived in religious inwardness.) Thus out of religious immediacy, the dialectic of trust and distrust breeds a necessary skepticism that turns the double image back on itself, such that the otherness of the sacred is less vested in nature's externality than in the self's inward otherness. In the mediation of religious immediacy this is the development of *homo religiosus* as self-mediating; but this self reveals a more radical openness to otherness in inwardness itself. The dialectic of trust and distrust, inwardness and otherness now continues in the context of the inwardizing of religion as trying to guard the deliteralized truth of the image. The positive outcome of the dialectic is the need to live in inwardness and in social selfhood a metaxological respect of sacred otherness. I now look at two exemplary selves, the mystic and prophet, the first in relation to inward otherness, the second in relation to the eruption out of inwardness into social otherness.[35]

The mystic may be the one who, *within* being religious, most radically responds to skepticism about representation. Here is a religious skeptic who doubts the sufficiency of *any* finite representation. But here also the releasing disillusionment flowers into a religious inwardness that is committed to the unconditional character of our essential togetherness with the unconditional, more commonly called the "*unio mystica*." Superstition fixes the god with a name, treats it as one thing among others, to be managed by magic words. Mysticism proceeds to the opposite extreme. God, or as some like Eckhart have better said, the Godhead beyond God, is never a finite object among other objects. Every effort to name Godhead, reduces Godhead. Hence every name is not the name. A certain silence, a certain reserve is best. The mystic claims to experience "something," but the significance of this resists full articulation. It is said to be ineffable, though mystics ironically have poured out floods of strange words to say what cannot be said. But in the end, the word of the mystic says: words fail. All language buckles under this strain.

The logically-minded rationalist is cautious, if not hostile. If we cannot articulate mystical experience, there is no sure test to decide its genuineness. Every fake can utter such claims, but if they resist reason, we cannot discriminate the mountebank on the make from one genuinely gifted of God. Orthodox religious minds share this suspicion. If mysticism is beyond ordinary articulation, it cannot be institutionalized or controlled. It cannot be subjected to the human authority of an organization, for it claims a source beyond all finite authority. Hence mystics have met with more hostility from their fellow religionists than from skeptical rationalists. They have met torture, indeed death.

The mystic is an extremist who pushes a certain line of thought to the limit, but there is mindfulness in this way. The goal is said to be beyond all finite things, hence no image from finite things will get us there, so the mystic is skeptical of all representations, including those to which his coreligionists cling—hence *their* suspicion of him. He deliteralizes the established representations. We must deconstruct the representations, or rather use them as a ladder that crumbles as we climb it, to a space of divine emptiness beyond all representing. To come to stand in this space, everything inessential must be stripped away. The mystic will say: Godhead is *not* this thing, is *not* that thing. The path is a "neither/nor," a way of *askēsis*. But the intent of its negation is to edge towards the frontier of finite intelligibility and open a space for the infinite. There one is unhoused of the palaces of corrupt consciousness, naked before a power that is not a thing at all, a power that looks like *nothing* to minds engrossed in finite things. One passes through negation to release in oneself an affirmation of the absolute power. Here radical skepticism concerning finitude is not in the services of a purely destructive nihilism but is the purifying, penitential side of what, from the other side, is a positively saturated sense of the unsurpassable mystery of Godhead. I think of the poverty of Assisi as he danced—naked and singing and on fire.

The mystic is an extremist not so much in wanting to desert the middle as in deepening the self's inwardness there: selfhood as an inward otherness must be deepened towards the absolute other. Thus, the logic of mystic mindfulness tends to favor an *inward* voyage of discovery. What serves as the ship of our passage is the inward "self," understood as resisting any objectification or reduction to the finitude of external things. The mystic finds more within, the trace of transcendence; the promise of infinitude is secretly at work in the essential, original self. Mystical negation tries to break down within inwardness itself the obstinate opposition between the resistant self and Godhead fixated as alien. The resistant self treats its selfhood as private property and the other as estranged. The sense of mystical togetherness finds, deeper than this opposition, a kinship or community between original selfhood and Godhead. Mystical negation decomposes the crusty, congealed self, and lets the indwelling divinity shine forth there. Inward otherness becomes the place of meeting or metaxological community with the absolute other. This may mean the rupturing ingression of otherness into self-mediation whose "breakdown" now becomes a "breakthrough." (Eckhart speaks of a *Durchbruch*.) The other beyond self-mediation breaks open the possibility of a new transformed self.[36]

Again the claims are extreme, even dangerous to the more sober, institutionalized religionist. For if the ultimate dwells within, if inwardness itself can embody metaxological community with the absolute other, what need has the original self of stone temples or priestly bureaucracies? The temple is our flesh. This can be a provocation to a more orthodox humility. Granted, mystic negation can grind the self down to nothing, as in nihilistic asceticisms that fail to find the affirmative intermediation of our community with God. But the result can also be the opposite. If the absolute power can be released in us, why then we are no grovelling wretches. Being nothing and being divine come very close.[37] The human self may not be *the* absolute, but there may be something absolute about it. Institutionalized religions tread warily, for such conclusions easily fuel the primordial flaw, our pride. Instead of the Adamic self restored, they fear a new Fall.[38]

The Prophet and Social Otherness

The upshot is that the dialectic of trust and mistrust that we saw before with respect to divine otherness (The Wrath of God) and nature's otherness (The Flood) can now find a lodging in the citadel of religion itself. Idolatry shows that religion can work against the grain of its own best intentions and produce a spirit paradoxically forgetful of spirit. Yet the tension between mysticals and conventionals (as we might call them) shows the impossibility of remaining in absolutely pure inwardness. This tension points towards the prophet as a further exemplary form of religious selfhood.

The original urgency of ultimacy often gets dimmed or distorted in being passed down through a tradition. A tradition may also develop an original vision in a manner augmenting the first inspiration. Yet with time's passage the truth of a religious vision is often asserted on the authority of time or tradition itself. The awe of age in ancestor worship is appropriated by priestly castes claiming their authority on the basis of a chain of inheritance which they trace back to the original revelation or founder. Bureaucrats of salvation manage the deposit of faith, husband it for the ages, but thereby also try to make manageable the always unmastered spirit.

Consider this dialectic between religious skepticism and the appeal to authority in this story about that gentle religious skeptic, the Buddha. Sleeping under a mango tree a hare was suddenly jolted awake by a noise, and in alarm concluded the world was ending. He fled the noise; other hares, alarmed by his flight, were also told of the coming end. The panic grew into a stampede. The host of hares fan past the Buddha who did not take to his heels; he sought their grounds for expecting apocalypse. Each hare pointed to the one before him, and so on back to the original hare. In turn, he recounted the big bang of the world ending. On returning to the mango tree they saw the thing on the ground—the fruit just dropped, the banal culprit of the catastrophe. One recalls another story, a profane fable for wise children—Chicken Little.[39]

The original hare, vulnerable to alarm, is credulous; he leaps before he looks; he believes he knows the answer before even stopping to ask any question. The hare's followers accept on trust what they are told; they believe; the moving authority of the original hare is enough. The Buddha, by comparison, is moved by a genial doubt, not by anxious faith fuelled on images of doom. He is not hurried to premature answers. Where he can know the truth, he refuses only to believe. But his searching can cause disquiet. He refuses to join the rush, but it is hard to refuse the refuge of crowds. At a crucial moment he stands outside. The hare is a gentle, timid animal, but sometimes the herd in flight is a pack of jackals or hunting dogs. The Buddha might have to pay dearly for his difference.

And then again, one very reasonably objects, is there not something obstinate in resisting such a *consensus gentium*? Surely there is no smoke without fire? Surely, if all the hares agree the world is ending, the world must be ending? Suppose further, that chain of hares stretches back through millennia? Who is Buddha enough, original self enough, to snap that chain? The Buddha can easily be seen as a wrecker. But let this not trouble us. After all, the revered Buddha is long dead; and, as we all know, there are no more hares today.

But what if the first is not the Hare but (like Buddha) a real religious original? This is the difficult question concerning the prophet, who as an exemplary self, does not retreat, like the mystic, into inwardness, but is driven beyond inwardness into social otherness. Social life has rare peaks and exotic abysses, but mostly it is a level plain with scattered bumps to stop us dozing. We fight shy of extremes and opt to make metaxological being into a more temperate, even tepid median; uncontrollable elements are to be kept to a minimum. Likewise the divine is consigned its defined places as an original inspiration solidifies into an established institution that domesticates the urgency of ultimacy. But upheavals cannot be entirely suppressed. The divine deserts the spot we allot it and invades the secular spaces. The upheaval can be a mass movement, as recently with Islam. But sometimes it is concentrated in a single representative. An individual of unusual, powerful inwardness erupts out of the homogeneous mass and becomes a singular exemplification of the energy of transcendence. Decades after his death, sometimes sooner, he is called a prophet.

The prophet is the genius of religion, its original hero (cf. chapter 1). We tame the divine, and go blandly about the rituals, frozen in a routine. Discontented with this sclerosis of the ultimate, the prophetic self finds itself under the sway of enthusiasm. Derived from the Greek "*en*" and "*theos,*" enthusiasm means to be "in the god." The prophet is in the god, filled with the passion that something humanly ungovernable is coming to emergence in and through his person. Yet despite the prophet's singularity, this emergence is not merely private: his inwardness tells of the universal call of all human relatedness to powers of being more ultimate than the human ("*pro-phetes*" does not mean to "foretell" but to "tell forth"). This enthusiasm is not the product of will. On the contrary, the prophet finds himself singled out, blessed with a calling he may curse. He feels sent—by the Other—to the community of others. Again this self is not a univocal self but a religious witness to metaxological community.

There often is a clash between the prophet and the establishment. Here religious distrust meets religious distrust. His skepticism of the stale status quo is met with the skepticism of the assured establishment. No prophet is recognized by his own, it is said. For his own people know *his* doubleness—his human, all-too-human roots. If you have cradled a crying infant, later it will be hard to see the representative of divinity. The people will mutter: "We knew his father and his father's father." The prophet as neighbor is only an upstart with notions, an upstart to be put back in his place. We revere only dead prophets, those whose threat has been interred by time.

Thus, the people's ancestor worship threatens to smother him. He will retaliate by claiming to speak for the truth of the ages and steal the thunder of the fathers. If he sets forth on a public mission, he looks like a raucous madman in the marketplace. (Jesus' family seemed at times to think he was mad—with an idiot wisdom? [Mark 3:21–22, John 8:48]; Hosea seemed foolish and mad [Hos. 9:7]) So begins his fight against the idols of the tribe. He becomes a pioneer advancing beyond the stale morality of the old sect. First, he will be seen as a smasher, an iconoclast. In time he will find devotees, for he refuses resistance to the energy of transcendence he releases. Eventually he will gather numbers to himself. His disciples will themselves coalesce into a sect and petrify the prophet's original energy. The sect will make a new tribe with new idols, the prophet himself being their chief Golden Calf. The time will be ripe for a new liberator, a new destroyer.

As with the mystic, the question is always how to tell the true prophet from the false. It is easier to discriminate the dead, when their heritage has the firm form of yielded fruit, But when alive, the false prophet, no less than the true, will make extraordinary claims. Yet one will peddle sick wonders, the other may be a pathway to health. How do we tell the difference? There is no certain univocal answer. The will to univocity in the injunction "Believe me!" will not wash. The true and false prophet both will say: "Accept what I say as true, for I give it to you as guaranteed by a higher authority." But why not imitate the people and return the upstart to his place? The prophet might say: The Voice of God has spoken to me. We are often uncertain if this Voice is really the Devil's. The Devil is surely likely to say: I am the Voice of God. Was Hobbes right when he tartly put it: when someone says God spoke to him in a dream, this means that "he dreamed that God spake to him."

The genuine prophet has to suffer—suffer the *necessity* of unbelief. This rejection is part of his ordeal of initiation, part of his releasing disillusionment. There is no univocal standard. This does not mean that all is equivocal. It does mean we cannot avoid the dialectic of trust and distrust. But we cannot *close* the dialectic with an absolute certitude that rids us of all risk. Rather the metaxological demands that we live with, though mindfully mediating, an ultimately irreducible ambiguity.

V. THE PROBLEMATIC RELIGIOUS MIDDLE

Miracles and Sects

Is belief undermined if we lack a univocal standard and religion is plurivocal? This raises the issue of the problematic religious middle that will concern us for the rest of this chapter. We must briefly look at two common ways to stave off doubt: miracles and sects. The first seeks the support of an external criterion whereby it tries to reground an immediate certitude of belief. The second tries to reconstitute immediate certitude but by retreating into a closed self-mediating religious group wherein the urgency of ultimacy seems to circulate.

Miracles obviously are tied to a sense of sacred otherness. They are said to be wondrous happenings of divine intervention. But they occur in the public realm, hence offering external certification for the prophet's claim to authenticity. This appeal tends to happen when the worm of doubt has already fattened itself on a disenchanted self and world. In a sense, for archaic man there are no miracles, for all of being is immediately a miracle: the show of the divine. Only when the divine vanishes beyond the world, when the world takes on the character of a law-governed cosmos, an ordered totality unto itself, and when within this totality our sense of our own difference, that is, alienation, is developed, does the issue of miracles assume its accustomed shape.[40]

Philosophers, prime agents of disenchantment, are hard put to leash their suspicious minds. In nature's normal course, dead bodies do not rise, nor cold stones weep. Their suspicion follows the rational faith (there is a little irony here) that nature as a whole is governed by laws that as universal do not allow radical exception. Miracles are claimed as precisely such radical exceptions that interrupt nature's course with a shocking irregularity, overriding the laws governing the whole. Skepticism arises from this seeming suspension of reason. But some theists can be as just as incredulous as atheists. They are alarmed lest God be seen as capricious, as not respectful of reason and law, as Himself given to irregularity. Such theists are afraid that God will embarrass them.

The voluntaristic theist stresses God's omnipotence, saying that He can alter nature, as He wills, since nature is subordinate to His will. God now wills one set of laws but can as easily suspend them and allow deviation, even create a different set. But then law seems to be the expression of arbitrary fiat: the ground of law seems lawless. There is the difficulty too, that God's own will seems to become contaminated with arbitrariness. The result can be a sense of God's ultimate irrationality or absurdity.[41] (There is a *voluntaristically* mediated residue of the Wrath of God at work here.) Admittedly, on this point some believers like to throw sand in the eyes of the rationalist. *Credo quia absurdum*, and this *quia* drips with scorn. They glory provocatively in religion's recalcitrance. I think of Luther's fideistic disdain for reason—the Greek "whore," whose eyes the true Christian should tear out. I think of Kierkegaard's sometimes absurd celebration of absurdity. It is as if some brew of contempt for reason and exultation in absurdity constituted a perverse "proof" of God, felt in its truth along the pulse of fideistic blood. If we think it enough to assert thus vehemently our belief, we but mirror our arbitrary God. (There is a *fideistically* mediated residue of the Wrath of God at work here.)

There are other theists who criticize this view and, in a rationalist as opposed to voluntarist mood, stress God's omniscience rather than omnipotence. God's mind spans the whole, knows the whole. Miracles are part of this whole, and so not deviations from divine reason but unusual manifestations of it, unusual, that is, for us, not for God. Thus, Augustine sees nature as manifesting God's will, but this will is not arbitrary but the expression of ultimate reason and wisdom. Hence miracles are not contrary to nature but contrary to *our* knowing, which is limited. Relative to God's knowing, everything is in order. The irregular is included within a larger providence, the exception is reconcilable with a more embracing design.

Beyond such philosophical and theological subtleties, in the appeal to miracles there resurfaces the need for otherness of a marvelous and surprising character. The demythologized world induces spiritual anorexia due to a malnourishment of otherness; our self-starvation in relation to the sacred brings its backlash of feeding on the occult. A sense of the miraculous feeds on a strong contrast between the ordinary and extraordinary, the mundane and transcendent. The steady stream of grey standardized experiences seems to be pierced by a rupturing light of strangeness. The religious person with a literalistic mind, the fundamentalist, treats this strangeness as a simple, unambiguous, albeit wonderful fact. Likewise, the scientific fundamentalist, with a complementary literalistic mind, treats any such strangeness as amenable to simple factual verification. But whether scientific or religious, the literalistic mind, which thinks the standard of truth is some simple univocal thing "out-there," is part of the problem, not any solution, The abiding enigma *that being is* remains occluded.

Suppose in pursuit of a literal, univocal standard, one calls for evidence, for testimony, for trustworthy witnesses, believing that these will be the standards of truth "out-there"? Suppose we say: Look! See if the marble Madonna weeps; see if the unmoved stones move. Yet one person sees the unseen; another stares out with eyes that bend on vacancy. Seeing is never simple. The believer sees the stones as moving; the unbeliever sees the stones as stones. In a single act of seeing may be implicit a whole world-view, an encompassing way of attunement to bring: one sees things as a manifestation of the divine, the other sees things, well, just as mere things.

Since seeing is always complexly mediated, there is a tradition that sees miracles as signs, not just as freakish facts disrupting nature. Signs, it is admitted, are ambiguous, not literal or transparent. They are like a language requiring interpretation, hermeneutical tending. Nothing is absolutely settled by this, however, for ambiguous signs can be subject to different readings. The religious person may read miracles as signs revealing God's word. The antireligious rationalist will see them as signs of our ignorance and credulity. The Machiavellian politician may read them as gambits in a game of secular power. The psychoanalyst will read them as a language of the unconscious. The obvious wonder dissolves in a Babel of competing voices. Scholarly hermeneutics helps us understand the different voices, but of itself it cannot determine if, in the whirlwind of babble, the divine voice speaks. That determination must come from a different source. The metaxological sense of being insist again that we live with, though mediating with the deepest mindfulness possible, an ambiguity irreducible to any univocal certitude. Since there is no logical calculus or system or objective certitude, there may even seem something *idiotic* here, but this too is double-edged (cf. chapter 6).[42] One must mindfully decide in fear and trembling, though one is tempted by the reassuring refuge of the sect.

For failure of the external wonder to allay doubt, and dismay of the babble of disagreeing others, can drive unsure religious inwardness away from the ambiguous middle into the closure of the sect. Massing under the banner of a prophet, or pretender to prophet, the sect offers to provide an immediate *social ground* of a new assurance. Where the prophet feels called to preach the neglected truth to others benighted and is secure in his mission, these others insecurely lack direction and crave consolation. He insists on his truth and names God as his guarantor; to the unsure others, his insistence is an augur of success. Let him but win over a small core of disciples and already he is on his way to founding a cult. With the cult comes social courage. Increasing numbers crowd out the doubts of the waverers. In no time at all we have a sect, complete with its own language for reading the divine.

This reflects our natural tendency to group, but the religious sect has an added burden, a charge heavier than the secular group. It proclaims itself as the children of the Bagwan or the Swamis of the Shining Path or Followers of the Force or Reapers of the Ripening of Time or some such. Despite proclamations of universal significance, sects are always limited groups. They exist by separating themselves off from the mass of others—something the prophet does individually. The doubleness of the religious middle is reduced to a dualistic opposition—a division into the Enlightened and Darkened, the Chosen Few and the Swarm of Sinners. There is no such thing as a universal sect, for by its nature the sect is exclusive and particular. There cannot be a catholic sect. (This is not to deny the possibility of a particular community being a living witness to the promise of universal community.) The sect lives on its intolerance of those who are different, its spirit a state of siege against dissenters, though it calls this state of siege the way of salvation. Its temple is a coop.

Radical suspicion and absolute self-assurance are lodged together here in this social sanctuary of religious inwardness. The sect risks becoming a closed self-mediating faction—in fact closed to otherness in its exclusive claim to represent God's absolute otherness. Thus, it may conceal the seed of bigotry. Milky churchmen will bleat that this is a minor, inconsequential factor in our enlightened times. Yet sects often plead for tolerance when in the minority, but do not so often extend tolerance when in the majority. The same sect that yesterday was victim, today sits in judgment, yesterday harassed, tomorrow harassing. The plea of tolerance springs from the sly expediency of the oppressed sect, a plea withdrawn when it becomes the overweening sect. When the sect, early on, was in the minority, its members were made martyrs. Later on, when the sect ascends to power, its members make martyrs.

For the sect tends to be composed of fanatics, individuals who must insist that their way is *the* path to truth. Religion's plurivocity is reduced to fanatical univocity. Religions are born in the energy and enthusiasm of our transcendence as it encounters and is converted by strange powers. This energy is, in a sense, simply what we are. It allows of genuine articulations; selves and communities can exemplify, live the Holy; likewise the human family is sold short if the call of the neighbor remains unheeded. It is the energy of transcendence, the urgency of ultimacy, that radically opens us to the other. But fanaticism lets this same energy run wild: the will to religious univocity produces religious equivocity. For this loosing shows the fanatic as outwardly self-assertive but secretly as deeply insecure. His cruelty to himself and others matches the need to see himself reflected in the confirmation of others. Religion provides the vehicle of his will-to-power, the expedient by which he can dominate. And because he wants absolute security, he is intolerant of disagreement: differences must be reduced, indeed blotted out within the group; dissent must be crushed. There can be no mediation with the "equivocal" other. The other to be obliterated is the enemy "out-there."

Thus, too, the notion of "heresy" invariably springs up. For heresy threatens the sect's security, homogeneity. But heresy is often a category of power, not a category of truth. The heretic is reviled, branded the foul agent of darkness, cursed as a renegade of God. (Heresy is from *hairesis*, one meaning of which is to take or choose sides: again we see dualistic opposition produced by an oscillation between univocity and equivocity.) He is declared anathema, apostate, in a ceremony of majestic vilification. One thinks of Giordano Bruno running afoul of the Roman Church for an unorthodox God, or of Spinoza being subject, again because of an unorthodox God, to the solemn curse of his Jewish community in Amsterdam. But this holy show of excommunication is often a complex, colorful, almost operatic means by which the sect tries to get its own way. A universal sect is a contradiction in terms; sects are always particularistic. To become universal is to rise above sectarianism. Some walk out of the stockade and embrace the stranger.

Warring Religions

Thus, the dialectic of trust and distrust can be at work in the very inwardness of religious community itself, even when it claims universality for itself. If it cannot get beyond the mentality of dualistic opposition that goes with an oscillation between the univocal and equivocal senses of being, this internal social dialectic can bring religion to the verge of its own self-deconstruction. Sectarianism reveals the perennial danger of religion warring with itself, even despite the conflicting parties' claims to be catholic. The sect reduces the double image to the simple one: for us is the truth, for the others untruth. Being religious risks its own self-contradiction when any sect proclaims itself as the universal body, taking its particular image of truth for the truth that brooks no rival.

Here the wars in Western religion between paganism and Christianity and within Christianity itself are still significant.[43] These wars tell of complex *historical* concretizations of the failure first to tolerate, then affirmatively mediate the ambiguity of metaxological being, and finally to remain faithful to the promise of community, of communivocity offered there, always offered there. "War" gives up on the plurivocity of the religious middle: instead of the intermediation of otherness, it seeks its violent domination, if not eradication. Thus, monotheistic religions make claim on a universal God but the living of the claim can be intolerantly totalitarian, not tolerantly universalistic. The universal becomes the suppressor of otherness, not the guardian of openness to difference or the community of being in its otherness. The tension between the ideal of a universal claim, indeed promise of universality, and the actual practice of an intolerant particularity, also bring us to the problematic presence of the divine in modernity.

Much reaction to the word "paganism" is conditioned by millennia of Christian criticism, some would say defamation. Paganism has its modern defenders, notably Nietzsche, and Christianity itself has been criticized, not to say defamed, again notably by Nietzsche. But whether we defend Christianity and attack paganism, or vice versa, between the two is an uneasy relation, sometimes erupting into outright hostility. Traditionally Christianity has had a tendency to be a religion of two worlds, frequently disparaging this world and elevating the next. Though it claimed to reconcile God and world, often it split apart heaven and earth and set the two in opposition. Sometimes it introduced this enmity between the City of God and the City of Man, Augustine's terms, into the very heart of man himself, sundering him into two worlds, that of spirit and flesh, and setting these at war. The flagellant, who whips his body for love of God, is the living incarnation of this war. Some say that this was not true Christianity, perhaps due to its confusion with an ascetic Platonism or gnosticism. But this war with the world was accepted in the past as a significant version of Christianity. It is not easy to give a bland, post-Nietzschean interpretation to the injunction to pluck out the offending eye, or that it is better to enter heaven without one of your parts than burn forever in the fiery pit, or that there is some special dignity in making oneself a eunuch for the Lord, an injunction Origen took all too literally. We are in a different world with paganism when it elevates into symbols of reverence parts of the body, such as the phallus, that Christianity considered base, objects of shame rather than awe, literally *pudenda*.

This war with the world in part explains the old hostility. Paganism is a religion of the world. Its gods people the earth, and are intimately bound up with a divining of powers beyond us that are alive throughout nature, powers that are more than the individual and that course throughout a vital community. A Christian may worship Jesus, but since Jesus as an earthbound self has gone, the empty grave points to a *Deus absconditus*. A pagan will pay homage to the visible Sun itself. A Christian may make a cult of the Virgin; a pagan may revere the earth itself as a generous Mother who joins in hierogamy with the Sky Father, through the sacred King, to make nature fertile and full of growing, As the Ionians had it, all things are full of gods; earth, sky, sea, air are gods or full of gods (cf. above on sacred immediacy).

Judaism and later Christianity depopulated the world of gods. There are no gods, there is only the one God (cf. above on anthropomorphism and idolatry). Everything else is a foul idol, a dark power that the One God demands we conquer. Nor is there any one image or representation to capture this One God, though Christians will say, not without difficulty and indeed the accusation of blasphemy from Judaism, that Jesus *is* God. The One God is everywhere and nowhere, and in Christianity incarnated as this particular self—at once, absolute pure spirit and a paradoxical fleshed absolute. Yet if nature is depopulated of gods, and the remaining One cannot be imaged, divinity loses its intimacy with the external world. And while divinity may instead take up dwelling in our spirit, in the inner self, the outside world is silenced and an uncanny emptiness comes to reign.

It is only a few steps from this depopulation of the world of gods to the ascetical Christian war on dedivinized nature. It is only a few further steps from a Christian war on the world to an Unchristian war. If there is nothing to be reverenced in external otherness, what is to hold the human self back from unleashing its brutal impulses on it? Christianity did restrain, not by a god in the external world, but by a God external to the world. It also restrained because God spoke to the interior self and could take up abode in the inner temple. But what happens if the inner God is felt to vanish like the outer? The mediation of external otherness as sacred has been already attenuated, but the internal otherness of the sacred is now in question. The inner self ceases to be a temple and goes the same way as the pagan gods Christianity originally conquered. The self becomes a cold, abandoned sanctuary. We are left with the dark gropings of the psyche inside, the blind forces of a dedivinized, indifferent nature outside, and the meaningless collision of these two. We seem to find ourselves in a position not dissimilar to ancient paganism, at the mercy of uncontrolled currents of the demonic psyche within, threatened and tantalized by the forces of nature without. But we lack this redeeming feature of ancient paganism—its reverence. Instead, with the technological hubris of a secular will-to-power, we pillage the disenchanted earth, unmindful of any piety of the whole.

Christianity struggled with paganism because of a divergence in concepts of divinity. Here again the outcome of the social dialectic of trust and suspicion is the branding of rivals as agents of darkness. There is a tendency to think of paganism as synonymous with atheism, but this identification is totally untrue. The atheist denies all gods and God, whereas the pagan is full of gods. Every hearth or nook of nature, even every tree or rock or mound of earth might have its proper god. In many respects the atheist is fundamentally modern, possible only *after* Christianity and its depopulation of the world of gods. The Christian denies many gods for one God; the modern atheist, parasite on monotheism, continues the denial, only now it is the One God that is repudiated. In contrast with the atheist, the pagan, I was almost going to say, is your true Christian!

The incongruity, of course, is that the identification of pagan with atheism is a Christian slander. The slandering operated in the opposite direction too. In Rome when Christianity appeared as a possible rival to the established religion, the pagan *status quo* reacted in no other manner than by cursing the Christians as atheists! This is perhaps inevitable in situations of religious rivalry, especially when religion was taken with a more fundamentalist seriousness, that is, when religions were more intolerant of opposition. The Christian was both right and wrong. He was right because the pagan worshipped gods that to him were no gods—hence the pagan's "atheism." He was wrong in implying that the pagan denied the divine. This was simply false. The pagan interpreted divinity differently, and in a manner intolerable to Christians.

Likewise, the pagan was right and wrong in branding the Christian an "atheist." The pagan set store by the traditional gods of family and people, gods of hearth and nation. His religious piety intertwined with familial and political piety. To be disloyal to familial and national gods was not simple religious impiety: it was also political treason. Unlike the modern secular separation of state and Church, religious impiety and political treason were inseparable, for both involved a break or repudiation of a sacred tradition of loyalty. (Socrates' treason, his "atheism" coupled in a seemingly contradictory way with the crime of "inventing new gods," is to be understood here.) Christianity transgressed the ancient code. In depopulating the external world of gods, it also denied the gods of the hearth, and claimed an allegiance more ultimate than the tribal or political. It claimed a God more universal than national and family gods, and consigned the latter to the status of superstitions. This made the Christian an "atheist," a blasphemer, a destroyer, in the eyes of the pious pagan. The pagan was right in that the Christian denied the pagan gods. He was wrong in implying that the Christian had no god at all. In their different denials, paganism and Christianity were sometimes mirrors of one another.

Likewise the term "atheist," as used to discredit an opponent, is often the sign of a struggle for *power*, political power. It is not always a measure of the quest for ultimate metaphysical truth. This same struggle for power can occur within the *same* religion when that religion splits into factions, the "orthodox" as opposed to the "heretics." Since this enemy—the foe within the walls—is the most terrifying enemy, the heretic is seen as more dangerous than the atheist. The atheist is the person who, because of his suspect loyalties, must be excluded from power. Nor is this controverted by the practices of modern "atheistic" revolutions. The "atheistic" revolutionary merely reverses the rules of the traditional power game. This reversal is literally part of the meaning of revolution: to turn around. As we know in our time, revolutionary regimes that have worshipped at the shrines of Marx or Lenin or Stalin or Mao have systematically tried to extirpate the traditional believer from power, from life. The "atheistic" revolutionary excludes the "believer" from power for the same reasons as the old exclusion of the "atheist," namely, suspect piety. So, too, the systematic savagery used can be seen as a perversion, a complete corruption of the religious urgency of ultimacy. This savage corruption approaches what used to be called the mystery of iniquity.

Though conquering paganism, Christianity never totally extirpated it. It evolved the strategy of bending old foes to new purposes. The old pagan customs, like visiting holy wells or blessing the fields or rendering thanksgiving at harvest time, coexisted alongside the more distinctively Christian rituals. The Celtic goddess Brighid became the Christian saint Brighid with some of her earthiness expurgated. The heathen shrines were usurped when they could not be suppressed. A god dies to atone for the people's pollution; in his death the people are purged; in his rebirth the people rejuvenates itself. This story is not original to Christianity, and is found in many ancient cults. Adonis, Attis, Osiris, Tammuz are just some of the dying and rising gods. The Greek god Dionysus, god of wine and frenzied intoxication, is torn apart and destroyed; but he also comes to life again, fertile and young once more in the vegetation of new vines. Trees, for instance, in their power to die and resprout were reverenced by ancient peoples. The Christmas tree is an ancient pagan evergreen close to the hearth of the Christian remembrance. Christ's Cross is the tree of life, the gallows of a dead god, driven into the earth, uplifted in offering to the heavens, making a fourfold and crossing of all the corners of the cosmos, an *axis mundi.* Religious mindfulness divines the kinship across the differences. Those who watch winter and spring in the world, those who know winter and spring in their souls, understand well that these images symbolize a structure universal in life itself: that in the middle world death and birth flow into each other, that night and day revolve patiently together, that coming into being and passing away are inextricable episodes in the becoming of the original power of being.

In the modern era, Christianity has been shaken in its ascendancy as a previously stifled paganism emerged to reassert its rights. We can compare the modern self coming to birth in the Renaissance with the Medieval Christian being left behind. Renaissance man wills to be scientist, poet, thinker, painter, architect, ambitious conqueror; the Medieval Christian is a monk humbly expectant of a reward elsewhere, a theologian not a freelance thinker, submissive to divine, alias, ecclesiastical authority, not insistent on his own divine rights. Renaissance man blends together Christian and pagan. Indeed some hold that the Protestant Reformation instinctively divined and refused this pagan power of the Renaissance. It sought to unmask the Catholic cunning with its genius for survival through compromise, which allowed vestiges of the old pagan gods to mingle with the Christian deity. Protestantism renewed the war on paganism in its war on Catholicism. The luxurious Catholic incense that carried the perfume of the East, and that lifted the soul into the airy heights of Cathedral towers would be replaced by an austere, Northern puritanism, and a bare, squat, functional house of prayer. The rich and jewelled vestments give way to grey daily wear or the unadorned cassock of black.

The outcome of the war is not the elimination of ambiguity but its perpetuation in new form. At the beginnings of modernity the war of Christians with each other did much to make thoughtful persons wonder if the urgency of ultimacy had not turned into madness, and if we ought not to turn away from its religious form or make *anti-religious* war on it. In the last two centuries and in the wake of the Enlightenment, Christianity has come under strong and repeated criticism, a good part of which involves it own self-deconstruction. Some thinkers have repudiated its otherworldly side, like Marx, and more recently some Christians, under the rubric of Liberation Theology, have joined him. Other thinkers, rationalists not revolutionaries, have fought its resistance to modern science, Other have struggled with its ascetical spirit and its suspicions of things bodily. Others have taken issue with its sometimes ambivalent attitude to art, and in neo-pagan fashion tried to reinstate the poet as a kind of priest; the aestheticism of modernity harbors a not so secret religious strain.[44] Ironically, it has been the sons of German pastors, some of the German philosophers of the nineteenth century, who have done most to disturb Christianity, and especially Protestantism in its self-assurance. Nietzsche, son of a Lutheran pastor, put it most succinctly when, instead of mingling pagan and Christian, he went to war against the Christian in the words: Dionysus versus the Crucified. He reminded the Christian of the old pagan truth. Gods that lose their tie with the earth, with the actual life of man here and now, eventually become anaemic and wither away.

Sacramental Earth?

Where are we now? This extended discussion of "war" was to show how opposition to otherness (in many complex forms with social, political, economic, cultural implications) can reduce what is at play in the metaxological community of being. It was also to reiterate the fragility of our mediation of the promise of this community. The result, however, need not be entirely negative, for part of this promise is selfhood itself as affirmatively concretizing in inwardness the metaxological respect for religious otherness. In one sense, the whole point (analogous to my point about aesthetic mindfulness at the end of chapter 2) is to become reminded of such mindfulness.

Thus, as I have presented it here, a developing mindfulness shows the following. Originally the divine is immediately, powerfully there, and there arises no question that all being finds its origin and end therein. Moreover, we have our own being in its existential truth in the enveloping aura of the holy. But the same energy of transcendence that places us in the space of the holy also in time is the womb of our restless questioning. We eat of the tree promising knowledge, and eventually come to wonder about the reverse possibility: is the sacred our image, not we its image. We spread our wings for a new flight, daring to pride ourselves with being the absolute original. Our differentiation, the promise of our otherness grows and we enter in a mediated way the space of mystery. As we saw, in that space of differentiated articulation, we risk a rupture with the originating experience of the holy, risk the dying of the light though we call this death enlightenment.

For one can even try (like the modern Prometheans such as Marx, Nietzsche, Sartre) to make oneself a closed dialectical self that rejects God's otherness and says: I am the absolute original. This is a fundamental violence to metaxological being, untrue to its double mediation, an antireligious version of the self-inflating "creativity" whose final bankruptcy we saw in being aesthetic. In fact, the dialectic of trust and distrust remains open, irreducible to either side. In this sense, the dialectic is just the play between these two and so, properly speaking, is not a dialectical but a metaxological intermediation; that is, the play of the middle cannot be reduced to our dialectical self-mediation for the irreducibility of otherness (whether the self's inward otherness or the transcendence of God) tells against every effort at closure. The *dia* or double of dialectic opens into the *metaxu* or between or "inter" of the metaxological. The *dia* is reflected in the doubleness of the religious image, but this double is not reducible to an equivocal dualism between human beings and God; nor is it reducible to a univocal unity of the sort the fundamentalist religious person performs on belief and that the literalistic atheist performs against belief.[45]

Knowing evil and good, there is no simple going back to the first immediate thereness of the sacred. Is it possible to pass through Ezekiel's valley of dry bones and be returned to the mystery of being, but at a different level of intermediated mindfulness? This mindfulness tells us that the sacred is itself the image of ultimacy—the ultimate is the absolute original that no image can ever exhaust. Such mindfulness is radically different from the debunking anthropocentrism that we are used to in modernity and that now tires us. Nor is it a nostalgic return to the first immediacy, a return behind complexly differentiated self-consciousness that would sacrifice its troubled mind for thoughtless immersion in the flow of images. Yet it grants the sense of ultimacy that discloses itself, ambiguously but plurivocally, in the images. Having passed through modern anthropocentrism it cannot turn its back on the necessary self-mediation and self-determination that modernity has rightly, though onesidedly, recommended. As molding the space of religious mindfulness, self-mediation, in its releasing disillusionment, now patiently awaits its metaxological reopening to radical otherness. It is ever mindful of our place in the intermediate, where the point is not unreflective immersion in images of the sacred but recovery of the meaning of the sacred.[46] With their grand flowerings of profound sacred images, great religions are born, develop, and die. But ontological perplexity is perennial. The sense of sacred mystery gives religious expression to this perplexity which, though mythic imagination ages, always cries for reawakening to a deeper metaphysical mindfulness.

I say this as philosophically alert to the anaemia of being religious in technological societies. The cry "God is dead" is merely a loud, poignant ejaculation in a vanishing, or amnesia, centuries old. But we have forgotten that experiences concentrated in such plaints have long had an essentially religious meaning. The death of God is hierophany in radically negative form: the negative otherness of the absence of the divine. The "breakdown" that happens here may also be the possibility of a "breakthrough." Many religious traditions have spoken of the necessity of passing through forsakenness, abandonment, nothingness to become properly mindful of the divine. The twentieth century has known repeatedly the harrowing of hell, so deeply that it seems to have lost the hope of it as a penitential prelude to rebirth. But we should not be so conceited as to think of ourselves as pioneers in the dark bourn of religious destitution.[47] Yet we seem to have lost the memory of such night symbols. We run from the religious meaning of death and the desert. We have become the bemused spectators that joke at the passionate despair of Nietzsche's Madman in whom the horror of our murder of God had sunk home. Instead of trembling with grief at the vanishing of the god we have become blandly, even chirpily at ease with the desolation. We are having a nice day, though the sun is black and the moon and stars are blotted out. It is the dead of night and we party. We do not wake the dead.

In their objectifying will to reduce the ambiguity of metaxological being to mere equivocity and thence to manipulable univocity, scientist and technicist minds (cf. chapter 1) have produced a disenchanted earth. Can we live with the univocal deadening of the earth, the reduction of its plural voices to a cybernetic monologue? But even the meaning of our nothingness is charged with religious significance: the suffering, dying god is a religious cipher that implies the sanctification of the earth, a transfiguration of being there, a hallowing of time. Being religious, as recollected in the inwardness of the metaxologically open self, may help midwife the reemergence of sacramental earth. Out of that inwardness, it will issue its charge: renew reverence for being; recall a sense of the sacredness of life; reactivate a proper piety of being there.

The earth has been neutralized, univocalized, made mere indifferent matter for instrumental use. If we are to allow the earth to offer more, to let its many voices speak once more, some reawakening of religious astonishment is require. This is not a plea for obscurantism but for simple acknowledgement of the elemental things that change being with meaning beyond the instrumental (cf. chapter 6). This mirrors the need for aesthetic recharging, noted before. As is the aesthetic body, so being in its otherness is a liturgy: a public work in the services of the festival. In the bleakest times religious mindfulness will break out of its new exile, for its dissidence in the instrumentalized world of univocalized being can never be entirely suppressed. Certainly one must guard against its reemergence in grim, violent forms, *its own* Witches' Sabbath.[48] The time may not be ripe, but if our destiny is passive conformity to the dictates of the time, our lot is as the lost. Religious mindfulness can ready itself. It need not be a foolish virgin.

In the interim the importance of being ethical cannot be overstated. Here the emergent charge of absoluteness is guarded in the self under obligation to the good. We can flatten the resilient earth, pretend to be its technical kings, and seek to evade or delay or pawn off to posterity the consequences. We cannot flatten being ethical without more immediate, dire consequences. The result is quickly uproar.

CHAPTER 4

Being Ethical

That I consider being ethical after being religious may seem to reverse Kierkegaard's evaluation of their ultimacy, but these ways of being are not rivals for ultimacy, nor to be opposed to being aesthetic, Kierkegaard's third other. All three tangle together, and while differently configured, their senses of ultimacy are akin. The more mindful we become, the more reluctant we are to separate them absolutely. Aesthetic beautification is not unrelated to ethical dignity, just as emotional attunement may be ingredient in our moral discernment. Likewise the religious is truncated apart from its own ethical dimension; it has been, and still is for many, the major mediator of the ethical. And though the ethical has its own life apart from philosophy, the latter implicates a necessary ethical concern. In being ethical we are constrained by ultimacy in relation to the other as a self of inviolable worth. Aesthetic and religious respect for otherness are wider than this, not so directly focused on the other self as moral.

In this chapter, as in the previous two, the overall movement will be again from immediacy to dialectical self-mediation to metaxological intermediation, though we shall see that the last really supports the whole movement. This movement follows the fourfold sense of being (cf. introduction). The human being as ethical desire finds itself in the middle where the demand of metaxological community issues its charge. Again there is no "pure" immediacy, if by this we mean to exclude mediation, though there is a relative immediacy of the ethical. This "immediacy" can be dominated by the *univocal* sense of being: desire become engrossed in extroverted gratification with particular objects. This univocal sense reduces the full sweep of desire's transcending power in the middle. It breeds its correlative in immediacy, namely, *equivocal* desire that cannot settle on any definite satisfaction for desire's ambiguous restlessness: here discontented desire flits from particular object to object, endlessly. Such ethical equivocity points to the need for an explicit mediation of the ethical middle. The ethical self desires to be a *dialectical self-mediating* whole involved, out of its own integrity, in *metaxological interplay* with others. The "immediacy" of the ethical middle is then revealed as the implicit promise of the to-be-mediated community of being. This requires both dialectical self-mediation and metaxological intermediation with the other, considered as an end in itself.

My remarks will again develop in five stages. First, I will remark on the dualism of being and the good and say that some more immediate sense of the ethical whole, if only metaphoric, is prior to abstract principles, as is the need for images of the genesis of the ethical self in its implicit intermediation with the other. Second, I will remark on the genesis of the ethical self as self-mediating in the break with natural innocence and look at the ethical charge on the self that it be other, that is, ethically shape itself in accord with an ideal self. I will remark on practical wisdom as intermediate and on the importance of work in mediating ethical dignity.

Third, I will turn to the emergent sense of the self as an end in itself, and how ethical inwardness makes possible an opening to the community of otherness, wherein all are to be respected as possible participants in a universal formation of ethical being. Fourth, I will consider this formation as an ideal pointing to a certain constitutive solidarity at work in the ethical middle. I will consider the metaxological intermediation of ethical being in relation to different social others. Ethical will is socially formed such that we find a moral version of the religious intermediation between trust and distrust: in ethical trust of the other we will find an openness, ranging from love to civil respect; in distrust of the other we will note the power of closed self-insistent will, at war with the other as other, a war that can be declared or cold. Finally, I remark on ethical intermediation in relation to the recalcitrance of the malign(ed) other.

I. THE IMMEDIACY OF THE ETHICAL MIDDLE

The Dualism of Being and the Good: On Mind and Giants

Since Hume moral reflection has often opposed facts and values, the "is" and the "ought," or more generally, being and the good. Being aesthetic first gave us pause concerning this opposition; being ethical causes us to reject it. The ethical, as care for the good, is a way of being, articulating what we are in a manner that from the outset shows a configuration of being always already charged with the good. The ethical is an articulation of being as good, the charge of being in us that we become, actualize, the given promise of the good.[1]

A major source of the dualism of being and the good is a "Cartesianism" where the self is unanchored from being and infected with a sense of opposition to homogeneously indifferent things. We have already questioned aesthetic and religious versions of this. Though Cartesianism is currently under attack, its presuppositions often persist in moral discussion. The human being is seen as the desiring self of utilitarianism, calculating its satisfactions on the scales of pleasure and pain.[2] Descartes' thinking thing is transmuted into a desiring thing that calculates how other things can be used for its optimum satisfaction. But the ethical self is not any objectified thing; and though it is a being of desire, this is poorly rendered in the utilitarian hermeneutic; its roots are pitched much deeper into being. As being aesthetic and religious articulate the sweep of human transcendence, so being ethical participates in the restless dynamisn of desire as an ineluctable thrust to the unconditional good. Being ethical is a mode of being mindful in praxis wherein care for the goodness or worth of being is nurtured.

Besides utilitarianism, Kantianism is also important in recent discussion. Kant's reiteration of the moral unconditional is to be respected, as well as his deeper sense of desire and rationally mediated will. But his moral self, charged with the categorical imperative, tends to be abstracted from the context of ethical origination. Kant's moral agent is the end result of a process of ethical mediation, is consequent on a certain understanding of ethical agency as rationally self-mediating (autonomy). To avoid abstracting such self-mediating agency from its ethical concreteness, we need attention to being ethical in its ambiguous immediacy. To be deeply mindful of the moral charge, we need some self-knowledge of ethical emergence, even in its primitiveness. Otherwise we risk an artificial narrowed self, an *abstract* moral agent—one who sees the ethical as finding abstract moral principles for use as logical devices to then solve problems, almost modeling moral mind on a technicist sense of reason. Deeper than such abstract principles a more tacit mode of moral comportment must be presupposed.[3]

If the ethical involves a certain care for being, morality is ultimately metaphysical. We value according to an ontological sense of being, the self-knowledge of which we often lack. This lack is the ethical amnesia of what we are. Ethics tends to abstraction if the abstract self is unquestioned. The modern Western individual has many characteristics of this abstract self: unanchored from being, estranged from the deeper metaphysical sources of its own energy of being, concentrated on the "self" as an insatiable void of calculative appetite, sensing the other as an always possible threat to its own loudly asserted autonomy. The sources of this abstraction of self include the ontological presuppositions of science/technology and its tendency to objectify all being, the capitalist ethos which sees the earth as merely a use-value, a resource for exploitation for economic profit, the bureaucratization of daily life and the flattening of sanctuaries of intimacy produced by an unbridled managerial mentality.[4]

A first way to undercut the dualism of being and the good is to recall that human communities are already complex, social embodiments of value. Community is always, already an ethical "immediacy" for the individual: we find ourselves, prior to will and choice, in a particular community as a dynamic ethical middle, that is, as a forming, constituting mediating social givenness of ethical others. The utilitarian and Kantian selves testify to an ethical uprooting that takes the character of a certain abstraction from the forming culture that socially embodies a community's sense of value (later I will speak of this in terms of what I call "ethical civility"). But any uprooting from social otherness is untenable since the very condition of the possibility of both utilitarian and Kantian selves is a certain kind of community of being. Both attenuate such community in their explicit pictures of ethical selfhood (though each also generates forms of ethical civility from a relatedness to otherness that they seem at first to deny). The other we must include in our calculations for utilitarianism is supposedly like ourselves— another predatory individual; in Kantianism the other seems to threaten heteronomy (the law of the other, the *heteros*) and so endangers the pure autonomy (*auto-nomos*: law of the same) of the formal universal self. But both such selves are derivations, not originals—derivatives from the metaxo-logical community of being, one emphasizing appetitive selfhood, the other the formal self of pure practical reason. Neither is adequate to the concrete self in ethical intermediation with the other in metaxological community.[5]

But we need to question the dualism at an ontological and not only social level. Our kinship with being is deeper than the opposition of the abstract self (albeit socially objectified) and indifferent things. This kinship has an immediate intimacy (cf. chapter 2)—it will be subsequently mediated, indeed the mediation may even *turn against* the kinship and misinterpret being's otherness as a dualistic opposite. But we ourselves are one determinate formation of the same energy of being that courses throughout the entirety. In us this energy strains towards self-consciousness, becomes self-aware, expresses itself in intelligent activity. Our physical powers provide the conditions, the seed bed as it were, out of which our powers of mind emerge; but the self is not a sheerly material entity, nor a pure detached mind; as an actual configuration of material energy, it is the possible mindfulness of the meaning of this energy. Bodily being, having attained a degree of astonishing complexity, stands there with a new presence difficult to reduce to exclusively material terms. Something emerges; mind makes a startling appearance.

The more complex the body's internal organization, the more we discern traces of sleeping intelligence, and the more likely its bestirring. No roses would flower, no lion prowl, no eagle soar, if its being were utterly mindless. Each has and fulfills its being only because it is in accord with the intelligibility of being. Nevertheless, we ascribe mindfulness to the human being in a fuller sense. Scientific reductionists will suspect anthropomorphism in the thought of being as is accord with mind; but this suspicion, one suspects, it also secreted from a Cartesian bifurcation of mind and matter. Others, theological rather than scientific dualists, fear we will be robbed of our special privilege. This fear seems to stem from metaphysical conceit, and the buttressing of this by an ill-digested understanding to the religious reminder that our responsible privilege is to husband the earth. Cartesianism merely changes this husbandry into mastery and puffs us up into technical tyrants. So monkeys and parrots, rats and killer whales live being's intelligibility? Instead of alarming our conceit or inciting it, the human self, even in its distinctiveness, need not be in estrangement from the rest of creation. A profound kinship with things is engraved on us. This might be cause for joy and for ethical respect.[6]

We ascribe intelligence preeminently to the human self as complexly mindful of the power of being that makes it what it is. The human self is an explicitly mindful being. Mind is not known thus intimately or explicitly by plant or animal: they are relatively passive to mind, locked into an intelligible pattern or structure. We are also passive to intelligibility, and especially our organic bodies as unfolding according to guiding orders not of our own creation. But we are active intelligence. The wakeful energy of our being becomes an active minding. Now we are not carried along by the immediacy of the stream of happening but shape the stream and mould its future form. Therein lies our unprecedented wile, also seed of our ethical being. All being mindful is ethical.

Traditionally here philosophers distinguish between speculative and practical mind and are captivated by the former. "Theory" originally comes from the Greek "*theōroi*": delegates sent by the Greek cities to the religious festivals, regal spectators enjoying the games from above, not bruised in the painful agon below. Speculative mind has delighted philosophers who have seen themselves as watching the play of life, with the freedom of Olympian gods. Our destiny is to activate the Olympian mind and to know, without quarrel or railing, the original mind or cosmic *Nous* that is the rudder of all being. While speculative intelligence contemplatively enjoys being as it is, by contrast practical intelligence, while a form of being, sees how being might be different to what it now is. It is transforming intelligence. It does not rest in the present but looks ahead to goals to be realized. It assesses their worth, examines the means to achieve them, constructs the expedients to bring them to fruit. Practical intelligence is mind in the services of our desire that *being be other*, that we ourselves be other. It is rarely Olympian but busily sweats at the base of the slope. There we dream of success but also we wrangle and clash and brood on defeat.

With this we witness a hint of dangerous ambiguity, for our kinship with being grows into our very difference, namely, our distinctive power to be mindful of this kinship. Our ontological kinship with being in its otherness is not, cannot be a univocal identity. With mindfulness we cease to be absorbed in nature and must endure the tension of being between: like and unlike the rest of being. Thus, like any animal, we are driven by need; animal instinct gives desire firm, univocal direction, but in us instinct is often slack or blurred—practical intelligence must firm up this slack and focus this blur. The dangerous ambiguity may seem to imply that all desire and being are equivocal. But nature and necessity conspire to make us cunning. The mediation of immediate being and transcendence of mere equivocity emerge as a task.

We are not immersed in the present moment, but time stretches before us both beckoning and frustrating, at once receptive and resistant to desire. Our awareness of future threats checks the exuberance of animal vigor and makes us vulnerable; for self-consciousness can lead to a loss of vital poise, and sap the spiritedness essential to bold deeds. Yet intelligence also overcomes its own paralysis, steps into the void it opens, making weapons to balance its new knowledge of dangers. Some thinkers have seen *all* intelligence as constructing such weapons against nature and time's hazard, but this is too sweeping. Nevertheless, calculative intelligence, the planning of means and ends, is essential. Besides its new means of defence and destruction, it also devises instruments of production, tools to ease the burden of animal drudge, to increase control over secure food supplies, in short, to guarantee the future. Calculation itself spreads in widening circles, solidifying mind in artificial social structures, distancing us from the raw crudities of elemental nature.

Prudential moralities generally and utilitarianism in particular rightly draw from the presence in being ethical of calculative intelligence, but the latter does not encompass ethical mind in its fullness. This fullness is an achievement, the product of a process of development, for though we are born innocent, we must *become* ethical. Here we have the risk of soul-making: being ethical involves a *poiēsis* of selfhood, the self-becoming of the human being in praxis with respect to its ideal perfection. This ideal, like prudential morality, will come later, but we need first to ask why we cease to be innocent, amoral animals, and become complex ethical beings with both the promise of goodness and the betrayal of debasement. How does an innocent child become the adult that is ethically noble or ugly?

In our distancing from the elemental crudities, our dangerous moral possibility takes form. Consider the infant's eye: it is innocent; hence it gazes at us, and we can gaze at it without danger of violence, a gaze impossible with adults. But at some point the eye becomes the presence of inwardness, the insistence of selfhood. It becomes the bearer of moral possibility. Will is the self. The "I am" is an "I will": a standing there of self where existence is insistence of self. Nor can we completely include the "I" as will in any closed system. Why the human eye becomes the embodiment of refusal, a saying of "No," is of deep philosophical interest.[7] "No" manifests "myness"; to say "mine" is to say "no"—the self surges up as affirming itself, affirming itself as itself, as different, hence as power to negate, say "no" to the other. Here is will appearing: will against the will of an other, will perhaps against the being of another, or against all being–other—as in the tantrum. (The tantrum is a metaphysical drama in miniature.) This leap from the eye that is empty of insistent inwardness to the willful, weaponed glare is a qualitative break in which being ethical has its birth.

If we are rooted in nature, then out of nature we see an emergence of ethical value beyond the dualism of "is" and "ought." To reject dualism is not to deny differentiation, but here, as it were, we must follow Vico rather than Descartes. Thus, our distancing from raw crudity can be approached through the persistent fable, one the ancients often took as historical fact, and that Vico helps us see as ethically significant, namely, that the first humans were outlandish, monstrous beings. In the beginning there is no innocence, nor is there any being ethical. There is sheer power—power without justice. Physically the aboriginals were far more powerful than we; they were Giants. Sometimes they were seen as survivors of the Fall, retaining some of paradise's primordial power but as deformed into lust and cruelty, into the furious rage of impious blood. Sometimes Cain's seed were thought to be Giants, Cain the first to spill a brother's blood.

Consider the Greek Titans—the offspring of Gaia, mother earth, and Uranus, the sky god. One myth tells how in time Earth incites them to revolt against Uranus. They are led by Chronos (Time), the youngest Titan, who castrates Uranus with his sickle and so ends his reign. Another Greek myth tells of the Giant's revolt against Zeus. Zeus, chief of the Olympians, had confined the Titans to Tartarus, the underworld. Infuriated by this imprisonment of their brothers, the Giants waged war against the Olympians. In time, but only in struggle, their savage power is tamed. Indeed Orphic myths speak of the *origin of evil* as due to a free act, ascribed to a race of Titans, *before* the beginning of history—man is a degenerate descendent of that race. Nor is the power of Giants over the imagination now spent. Children are still tantalized, terrorized by tales like Jack and the Beanstalk, where the Giant, stupendous in physical power, makes a meal of more meagre men, sating himself on warm blood.[8]

Such stories reveal the sense that human, hence ethical beginnings were partly savage and brutal. While different, the Giants are still like us. Their grossness partakes of animal, sub-animal powers, ethically thoughtless powers. Yet their largeness, their Leviathan powers, call to mind other majestic, awful powers that humans think divine. The Giants mingled earth and sky, animal and divine powers in a promiscuous, blind form. They image a kind of promiscuous univocity of gods and beasts, hence image the potential equivocity of human desire caught in the middle between higher ideals and lower powers. They present an image of the gross originals who have yet to card the chaos, and bring to light a more temperate, civilized self. The process of time itself is ethically important as eventually mediating and domesticating the coarse origins. The gods, not easily, conquer the savagery, and time comes to throw up a more moderate humankind. In one tradition a Flood was loosed to swamp the Giants who wandered the earth, plundering at will, lawless in life, drunk deep on savage power. Their rage was insolence towards the great divinity itself. To warn against lawless pride, to erase the infamy, the Wrath of God unleashed the Deluge.[9]

With the aid of divine powers and the cunning of intelligence, time diminishes the earlier barbarism. Though not destroyed, the Giant's prodigious power is humanized. The civilizing process as an ethical intermediation of otherness diverts this power from joy in destruction to the construction of life giving more enduring joy. The civilizing process beautifies the brute, but the work is never complete in that desire's elemental immediacy is never completely mediated. Rumors, indeed traces of chaos linger in the clear air. Those after the Flood were uncertain if some Giants had not retreated safely to mountain tops, unsure whether even now, Giants fitfully slumber in caves. This might seem quaint, but it reminds us of the ambiguous power to create *and* destroy at work in human desire. One dreads the coming round of the epochal gyre, as it spirals back to its beginning, and at the close of the civilizing process threatens Vico's *second* barbarism of reflection. Will postscientific Giants, Prometheans of scientific enlightenment yet spill from technological caves? We await new Olympians and relive in fresh guise Plato's old fear of Thrasymachus—the dread of power without justice (cf. below).

Shame and the Other: On Feeding and Dining

The Giants were shameless. They gave vent to their power without ethical respect for themselves or others. But respectful attention to otherness is at the birth of ethical selfhood (the religious counterpart is fear of the Lord). This can become extraordinarily refined, but it is present even in our most elemental, natural needs. Even in desire's immediacy the mediation of self and other is at work from the start. Here I will consider how our desire for food shows the mark of the other and how dining can serve as metaphorical for entire ethical comportments to being.

Intent on the risk of enemies, the opportunity of prey and the seasonal rut, the animal eye is immediately directed on the other; but its gaze is cast away and absorbed into the environment. The human eye is also directed on the other, but it knows that the other's eye is directed back on it. It is not absorbed into the environment, for another eye comes to meet and confront it, catches a gaze and casts it back. Certainly animals confront eye to eye, but with us the encounter is a richer reciprocation, ultimately a metaxological intermediation. In the encounter that returns our regard, self-consciousness is born, for this return is known—the other eye is acknowledged as the presence of an other self-conscious self. Thus, in the mingling of many looks, self-consciousness (the self splits into two sides—knowing and being known) emerges into definition. For if my gaze were absorbed and not reflected back, I would not know my difference. This knowing is self-mediating but also ambiguous: it places us in the middle before the other. There I know joy in another's greeting, for greeting leaps across emergent separateness. But I also know shame; the other's gaze awakens my naked vulnerability. Then instead of meeting the other's look, I want to hide, to vanish into the original univocal homogeneity of the indifferent, comforting environment. For the other makes a call on me, a demand on my difference. The call is alarming. It says: never more can you be just naturally innocent. It demands we answer for ourselves by being ethically good.[10]

Here the story of the Fall helps. Absorbed in the innocent perfection of Paradise, the original humans did not know themselves. The apple of divine knowledge brings self-consciousness; they become aware of *another* looking at them; God's gaze judges them. Sensing their nakedness, they cover themselves with shame. The story of the Fall denies any *smooth transition* from self-absorbed innocence or narcissistic immediacy to guilty awareness of self and other, that is, self-awareness mediated through guilt before the other. There is a rupture, a wound, a breach wherein freedom's terror and promise awaken. There is a *shock* of ethical otherness. (In one traditional view evil is an absence of good; all being is good; evil is non-being; the rupture is the possibility of our will of nothing, will in radical refusal of being, nihilism.) In innocence there is the possibility of freedom, but in guilt one *already is in* freedom's actuality.

That is, freedom is an emergence in desire's immediacy wherein a *doubleness* breaks through: the self becomes a forked awareness caught in tension between self and other. We may be tempted to see this tension of the metaxological as equivocal and turn the difference of self and other into an unmediated dualism, even war of opposites; or we may intermediate with the other to form an ethical community. In every case, as free of immediacy, desire will always subsequently live this tense doubleness—at once seeking its own fulfillment and also called to openness (ranging between fear and love) to otherness. Even Thrasymachus (in Plato's *Republic*) cannot deny this shame, for essentially he advocates strategies for avoiding shame, that is being found out by others—and he denies the gaze of a divine other. The Ring of Gyges fantasy (one has a magical ring of gold that makes one invisible) implies that no other's eye can judge one; one can see all others (like God) but the others cannot see one and reciprocate the look. Plato profoundly asks: would the invisible one then be ethical? Would one's desire become tyrannical?[11]

This threat of shame percolates through all social relations. How we deal with it marks our transition from raw nature to more humanized life. We know our animality but aim to deflect it, beautify it. This aesthetics of the ethical (or the mediation of value in the sensuous body) would never occur if we were solitary beasts. As essentially social, we finds intolerable the shame arising with the judgment of others. Out of the union of shame and beauty emerges the moral sense of modesty. Thus, the idealization surrounding our sexuality is astonishingly involved, as is our beautification of our dwellings, or our use of clothes. But let me focus on our transformation of the need for food, because this need is clearly instrumental and necessarily tied up with survival value. Since I want to deny that ethical desire can be interpreted in purely instrumental, or use values (as "utilitarian" views imply), it is very significant that at the most needy, elemental level of survival, we are *always already* transcending the instrumental, even when inextricably tied to it.

Our transcendence of the instrumental in the instrumental itself is evident in our relation to food. This relation is not ethically neutral. We tend not to devour food in the raw; we "prepare" food; we cook. Thus, we distance ourselves from animal appetite and grace our needs with the rituals of the meal. We make ourselves different through the instruments that separate us from unadorned nature—the dining utensils that beautify a table; a silver spoon, a cloth, a bowl of roses. In a sense, these mundane objects are the bearers of our humanity; they not only refine our being; they define it. The animal feeds, but we dine. There is food in the animal kingdom but there are no dishes.

Indeed the meal can carry our ultimate ideality and have the character of religious ritual, with its reverence and concern for our joy of being. Thus "companion" is derived from "*cum*" and "*panis*," meaning "with bread," that is, "bread together with an other." To be a companion, to break bread with an other is one of the deepest symbols of a shared humanity. To share a meal, to participate in an *agapē*, defines the essence of human fellowship. An agapeic feast is the realized promise of the metaxological community of being. A basic animal need is transfigured to bear our ethical destiny to share being with others.

Thus we see the implicit mediation of the other *in* the self-mediation of immediate desire. Levi-Strauss reminds us that the transition from the raw to the cooked signals our emergence from nature and entrance into social, cultural life.[12] We are what we eat, Feuerbach said, repeating the German folk wisdom—*Man ist was man isst.* I would amend this and say: we are *how* we eat—nor is this "how" ethically neutral. Eating may be a physiological pleasure, but dining is a mediation of value. For though eating and drinking seem immediate, our culinary habits are humanly mediated, and so incipiently ethical: hence their power as metaphors for entire ways of being. Consider the following contrast of vegetarians and carnivores, taken as ethical metaphors.

Here again we find metaxological ambiguity. Since stories of origins point to the first emergence of difference from univocal identity in the articulation of the middle, here we find stories about origins that are the complementary, dialectical, opposite of the myths of Giants, namely, the view that our ancestors were herbivores. The story is that at some decisive point a switch in diet occurred from solely fruits and vegetables to flesh, and thus was inaugurated a great change in human history. With the eating of meat, the speculation runs, human beings had available more concentrated sources of energy, and this in part accounts for our gradual increase in power and mastery over the external environment. If you like, human beings became human when they first learned to kill. How the scientist interprets the factual evidence on the first humans is a complex affair. This aside, the contrast between vegetable and meat eaters is ethically suggestive. How we eat seems to have an essential connection with our definition of ourselves. This contrast is not just a metaphor of two instrumental ways of coping usefully with nature's necessity but images two different attitudes to being as a whole, evaluations of being-other, imaging indeed two different ways of ethically dwelling in the metaxological community of being and of organizing social existence. We might call these, vegetarian and carnivorous society.

What am I talking about? Vegetarian society would be one organized around nature's basic, immediate necessities. The vegetable is the sign of innocence; it is just there, rooted in its place, at home in its growing, in harmony with soil, sky, sun, and air. The vegetarian self would live in tune with earthy innocence, would know what is needful and desire nothing more, primitively at peace with its original being. So also in the vegetarian ethos no significant violence is involved in harvesting plants. Vegetables are more easily masticated and digested, hence there follows a deeper organic harmony with itself of the metabolising self. Do I jest? Consider that "Paradise" (*paradeisos*) simply translated the Hebrew word for "Garden." Consider also Epicurus in the Garden as pointing to vegetarian ethics in the ancient world. And today longing for vegetarian society is widespread, growing out of an implicitly ethical protest at contemporary society. Witness the political rise of the Greens in Europe. The romantic yearning for nature, its characteristic ethical and metaphysical emphases, reached the dietary level even in the nineteenth century, but it makes an entire economic market now.[13]

The vegetarian ethic emphasizes simple wholesomeness and constant, recurrent necessities, and so would seem to offer the stability of bedrock essentials. But there seems no way we will be satisfied with immediate simplicity, given the inescapability of ethical mediation. Even in terms of immediate desire itself, the itch for luxury, hence unnecessary, artificial desire cannot be stifled; alienation from the norm of simple nature is inevitable. The *carnivorous* society is born in this necessary alienation (othering) from the necessary. The carnivorous society is the community of inordinate eaters. I mean this metaphorically, though Western society seems to be literalizing the metaphor in the prevalence of the obese self. In carnivorous society desire is in excess of natural necessity. It wants more and more; it is insatiable. This mirrors the diet: flesh gives more concentrated energy, hence the carnivore has surplus, excess. This finds expenditure in desire for the unnecessary.

Instead of the univocal peace of the vegetarian, the carnivore makes war on the equivocal, threatening other. To eat the carnivore must kill; its life is supported by violence on the other. For the carnivore to digest, the metabolism must work and strain the harder: external energy is sustained by internal turmoil. Do I jest again? But can we be skeptical about the connection between stressed life and carnivorous life. After all, the doctors of carnivorous society are surgeons, not herbalists. This society is one of hunters, warriors, competitors. Life is essentially active struggle, not placid rumination. Surviving is killing. We identify it when we say: dog eats dog; *homo homini lupus*. In the ambiguous middle, the destructive power of desire constructs itself by negating the other: all being-other is a dualistic opposite to be devoured. The carnivore is never innocent but builds himself by destroying another. Nor is he fastidious about the prey as long as it can be ingested. Power reigns overall, not peace.

Such ethical images are often more revealing than impoverished abstractions. But, in fact, these metaphors do have philosophical respectability. They surface in the classic text of ethical and political thought, Plato's *Republic*. There Socrates gives us one image of the good community, a polis ethically devoted to primitive essentials very like the vegetarian society. The origins of society, Socrates claims, lie in a conjunction of human need, individual insufficiency, and the different capacities of persons. An essential society will exploit these aptitudes to serve the essential desires. Like the vegetarian society, Socrates pictures this community as constructed on minimalist lines. Its people will have few luxuries, and will dine on uncomplicated, wholesome fare like figs, nuts, and beans. Without poverty or war they will survive to a ripe, untroubled old age, enjoying all their days in robust rustic purity.

It is unclear how ironical Socrates is in offering this image as the ideal. Glaucon tartly comments that with such fodder it looked like a city of pigs. So Socrates goes on to picture society as we know it now. All we need do is load luxuries on this simple life. Then the city will have to be enlarged to embrace the new profession supplying such luxuries. People will become restless with acquisitiveness, clamoring for more possessions and casting about eyes of envy. Inevitably this society will go to war with its neighbors to increase its power and wealth. Meanwhile, its citizens, gorged on unhealthy sauces and spicy delicacies, will require the services of medicine to aid overtaxed digestions. Two new professional classes will be necessary: soldiers and doctors. These will express socially the corruption of the previously peaceful and healthy community. This fevered city is roughly the carnivorous society.

We might lament the advent of the fevered city and hanker for rustic repose, but the fevered city is inevitable. It is the communal embodiment of the relentless misery and hope of our desire. Animal desire meets nature's necessity and rests content, but ours has a more insatiable momentum, is infinitely restless. Often it proves difficult to distinguish genuine and false needs. Desire creates its own needs, and on attaining one goal cannot resist demanding more; our happiness is our unhappiness. We simply are excessive desire. What do we really want? To separate out the tangle of desire is hard. We use our skills to satisfy need; but these skills can also be used to make objects for barter and exchange. Skill makes more objects than we need. In producing more and more, it creates new needs and the itch for luxury leading to the fevered city. We produce surplus and desire surplus, so that natural need and artificial desire promiscuously mix. From the univocity of vegetarian desire, desire itself seems to generate from itself its own feverish equivocity. This ineradicable ambiguity of desire made Kant despair of finding the moral unconditional in terms of happiness. It impelled Nietzsche and Sartre to deny that man has any "nature" at all.

The fevered city perplexed Plato, but its capitalist version appalled Marx.[14] The invention of money only makes efficient the exchange of goods and streamlines the production of desires. We first do not have a set of simple desires and then find money to meet them. Given money, we acquire or invent the desires necessary to spend it. Money is the economic embodiment of social power, hence it carries the mark of others—especially, for Marx, the exploitive others. Money mediates in advance the possibility of even expressing, much less satisfying, immediate desire. Money leads to desire's multiplication, for it is paper power requesting to be realized in gratified desire.

Given our excessive desire, once we are infected by the fevered city, the corruption tends to stick. How can we be kept down on the farm, when we've seen gay Paree; once dazzled by the bright lights, the dull pleasures of the brown barnyard pall. Yet the fevered city must find its doctor, doctor itself. There is no cure in desire's negation, as Schopenhauer thought, for this would be to negate the human being. One must pass through desire's different forms and learn to discriminate the best. No doubt some cures demand surgery; others, less cruel, nurse the redirection of desire towards the better. There may be new health, not in retreating behind desire's infinite plasticity, but in reaching through it, in sifting its forms and letting the dross discard itself. In the middle there will be insomniac tossing before this fever breaks.[15]

II. THE SELF-MEDIATION OF THE ETHICAL MIDDLE

Free Desire: What Is To Be Done?

Thus far we have seen that even in what looks like immediate desire, ethical self-mediation is already at work. We must now turn more directly to self-mediation, both in relation to freedom and the question: What is to be done?; then in relation to practical wisdom as intermediating; then in relation to work as the worldly embodiment of practical mind that shapes our ethical self-mediation.

Desire's excess, as we saw, shows a break with immediacy. Desire is excessive because it is free. But such desire can be full of self-opposition: it may release lust for luxuries, inessential things, yet this craving is but an expression of our essential freedom. Something essential to us, namely, being free, licenses us to evade what is essential. And just as we drive beyond natural need, so we have the peculiar power to suppress, even turn against such need. Hungry, we decline to eat, whether for religion's sake or fat's; in heat, we refuse an embrace. In deferring gratification, in repressing impulse for a later good seen as greater, desire is free. Animals are never ascetics.

It is through the power of imagination that desire rises above the momentary satisfaction. Here the eye of ethical assent and refusal is born. By the eye of refusal, I do not mean the eye of animal aggression but the presence in the human eye of ethical will. Here we see the express differentiation of the ethical self out of the flux of immediate desire, a differentiation necessary for its express dwelling in ethical community as metaxological. For will is the present self as affirming the particularity of its thereness; the ethical will is our being as willing—our yes or no as self, as spirit, to being, in ourselves, in otherness. By contrast, animal aggression is a yes to its own being by a living being that is not yet ethical selfhood. This too expresses our being, our proper self-insistence which Spinoza's calls *conatus essendi*, and which Nietzsche wanted us to acknowledge against a self-deceiving altruism or self-negating asceticism.

Ethical will is not just this self-insistence, though it is related to it, and though the ethical self (the artist and saint too) works on this self-insistence as the dynamic matter (Freud calls it the Id) of its own self-formation. We *are* self-insistence; existence is self-insistence. But our being ethical is the struggle to widen the yes to being that is particularized in our self-insistence, widen it to all otherness. Only in this widening do we rescue will from the deformation of selfhood resulting from the turning back of this self-insistence into a closed self-sufficiency, a closure that is really a parody of absolute autonomy. In a word, the yes to being that is animal aggression, becomes the yes that is "I" in human desire, a yes that must open to the universal in ethically responding to the call of the other. This remains to be seen.

The ethical eye is born in original imagination through which the self begins to sense its difference from the being of otherness. This sense of difference awakens in us the intoxicating power of refusal and absolute self-insistence. Thus, as at the origin of freedom, imagination is also at the origin of evil. Hence, also the first freedom is not that of the developed self-conscious will. I said we first *sense* our difference, we do not properly know it. Thus, we do not first control imagination by will-power; freedom is first an upsurge of images from the roots of our being, not a deliberate act of control over alternative choices. Freedom is a given necessity of our being; our being is self-articulating in terms of images of the ideal self we desire to be; but the images that are spontaneously articulated reflect our intermediate being and hence include both the self of mindful goodwill towards the other and the self of boundless willful rage at being, in Plato's metaphors, the just king and the tyrant.

These ideal projections of human possibility are extreme developments of desire's excess: they image a perfection of and defection from the promise of human transcendence. These extremes point us back to the ambiguous middle where the beginning of our promise is dark. The beginning of our difference is bewildering. In a sense, the origin of evil is prior to self-conscious freedom; for if it were a result of self-conscious freedom, we would already have had to possess the knowledge of evil, which at the beginning we do not. There is a paradoxical freedom in which evil seems to *happen* to us. We here seem to be strangely free and spellbound at the same time. As implied, the images of evil are the upsurge of our being: they articulate what we are; in free imagination we find welling up images of blood from the abyss of our fevered being. Evil "happens" to us at the origin before self-conscious choice; yet the spontaneous upsurge of images of blood is what we are, though we do not "choose" it; we have here a "freedom" before "free-will." The myth of the Fall is again indicative. The first humans had to eat the forbidden fruit before they *knew* evil, yet they did the evil, and in a *freedom before fully knowing*—hence their guilty surprise at their nakedness. They were already *in* evil, before knowing it. Such a freedom before self-conscious knowing arises in the freedom of original imagination.[16]

If I seem to stress the image of evil, imagination also has its affirmative side, as we saw with the double image in religion. Free desire articulates our intermediate being as intertwined with productive imagination that is the generative source of our possibility of being other. Desire imagines something other and more than our present state. Hope is the imagination of desire that shows desire to be other than, more than sheer immediacy. Imagination frees desire by grounding its self-mediation; yet as an original identification of difference, it opens desire to the other as other. Ethical imagination is metaxological: it grounds both our self-mediation and openness to the other as other.

Here I stress how it mediates a practical selfhood with an articulated sense of temporal being. I suffer now, but time stretches before me, an untested pool of possibility. I can plan that time, seize its opportunity. I hope the future will reward my waiting with delight greater than present deprivation. It is said that we are the working animal; we are also the only animal to demonstrate ambition. But just so free desire is hazardous. Breaking up the regimentation of instinct, it gives us the scope of an empty stage where we must choose. But choice is uncertain and the chance of satisfaction in doubt. One may be defrauded by hocus desire, untutored in choice, free in essence but lost, bewildered in act. Free desire may take the poison for the elixir. Or it may rise above necessity, coaxing externality into congruence with our more intimate selves. Desire may flower into liberty that begins to order nature. Free desire itself is called to order by practical mind that gives it a direction, and releases its energy towards fulfilling goals. Practical mind orders the initially undefined potentiality of desire, or rather it is desire's own self-mediation that insists that immediate desire give up its aimless play and get down to doing mindfully the world's work. Practical mind is desire making for itself a new, man-made necessity.

Here arises the fundamental question "What is to be done?" In raising this question, we become selves of action, doers of deeds. Desire leads to doing wherein desire is clearly not only immediate but self-mediating. The latter process is not ethically unambiguous. The calculative prudence of utilitarianism is but one interpretation of the ambiguity. The thrust of transcendence of desire in the metaxological is much more enigmatic than such calculation. Our doing grows out of our being (the scholastic adage was *operari sequitur esse*). As active animals, we do our being; doing need not be opposed to being, though given desire's free play, we can act in ways contrary to our being; to be free is to be able to negate one's being as well as affirm it. Thus to ask "What am I to do?" is also to ask "What am I to be?" because our being is not a finished fact. Our being is initially the power to be, a promise of perfected selfhood, not an accomplished product. "What am I to be?" is directed to a future form of selfhood, an ideal of selfhood and hence arises from a deep sense of our being as temporal. In the opening of the space of our difference the germinating acting self faces the unmastered becoming of time.

To ask "What is to be done?" not only presupposes a differentiated agent but an opening up of the temporality of middle being, of the dynamic becoming of our being in the middle. "What am I to do?" shows the temporal nature of all doing. This is a question out of the past, uttered in the present, directed to the future. We slide on rolling time and find no final stasis, for the future is open and incomplete. Through this mundane question peeps a possible *metaphysical distrust* of time. We are finite and offered no guarantees; our intermediate being is not self-sufficient; the being of otherness is beyond us and unmastered; our difference, albeit self-insistent with respect to its own being, fills us with the fear of death. This metaphysical distrust, sensed prior to self-consciousness, comes upon us in the original imaginal freedom prior to knowing freedom: the sense of our finite being as coming into being out of nothing, in the suspense of the middle but suspended over its own future nothingness. This metaphysical suspense precipitates what Kierkegaard called dread and Sartre the vertigo of freedom.

Human desire is initially self-insistent and affirms its own being; but because of our finitude, the otherness of being may appear as a threat to our being, and hence something to be attacked or negated or dominated. What we have here is an *ethical dialectic* of trust and distrust at the level of self (we will see later a similar dialectic in relation to the other; we have seen aesthetic and religious versions before). The ethical challenge put by our distrust is to overcome a self-insistence rancorous about its own finitude and turned against the other as curbing its claim to absolute autonomy. This means granting the fragile vulnerability of our being in the middle and attaining a metaphysical trust in being. If our deeds are rooted in this trust, then a response to otherness need not be hostile, nor need the proper self-assertion of our being be but the compensating aggression of our ontological lack. Our deeds may be the ethical perfecting of our being, pursued in respect of the other. The risk of freedom responds to the finiteness of intermediate being where the hardest ethical affirmation gives utterance to the metaphysical trust: being is good. If human doing cannot be anchored, in some measure, in such trust, then the ethical ultimately degenerates into

Thrasymachian power without justice, an ethical defect of being, or a tale told by an idiot without idiot wisdom.[17]

Practical Wisdom and the Intermediate

"What am I to do?" Does this ask us to determine the indeterminate, to close the open, to round off the incomplete? Or does it suffice simply to get by? The open future is unnerving; it allows some free play, but we may lack the assurance to trust our ingenuity. Many things are possible, but to realize any possibility, especially one untried, involves gamble. Like a sudden blur of fog or an abrupt plunge into night, the void openness of the future may precipitate panic—a dissipating energy of being overcome with alarm at its own intolerable ethical charge. "What is to be done?" One stares at nothing definite, attacked by nerves at taking the next decisive step. One dreads to venture forth for fear that one may wander.

Becoming seems equivocal and deprives us of any univocal answer. But beyond the quest for unambiguous univocity to freeze the temporal flow of our being, and beyond the surrender to equivocity that scatters the self abroad on the flux, several responses are possible. I will mention three responses relevant to the middle. A first one is merely to muddle through. This is the way of drift and bump and reaction. This way is not to *do* anything, and so is not action at all. It relies on accident not action. It does not decisively answer the question "What am I to do?" but takes the next step by the blind leap, by unsighted, lurching impulse. Human action becomes swamped beneath waves of chance and happenstance. It drowns its metaphysical distrust by a retreat from otherness to immediacy. Examples might be hedonistic immersion in pleasure, or a retreat from the ethical to the aesthetic, in Kierkegaard's usage.

A second response swings to the opposite extreme. It seeks for inviolate rules of behavior, categorical laws to cover the lawless future completely. We must act in conformity with certain norms and standards and not swerve or deviate from the code of commandments. We must standardize behavior and domesticate the unpredictable. We must plan, we must calculate, we must progressively reduce risk. Everything immediate must be completely mediated, everything spontaneous systematized. Mediation here means *rational self-mediation*, for it is being's otherness that is seen as ambiguous and recalcitrant. Examples might be: Stoic ethics that retreats into inwardness and a self-mediation there supposedly beyond the unpredictable, disruptive power of external otherness; Kantian ethics with its stress on duty and the formal rational self-mediation of the categorical imperative. In this second strategy, the risk is assimilating the unknown to the already known, the novel to the well tried, and we never really make a leap.

Very generally, at the first extreme one is all pliable impulse and no principle; at the other, one is all starchy principle and no impulse. In the first we get concrete chance and irrationality, in the second rigid rationality and abstraction. In fact both these seeming opposites simplify the complexity of ethical intermediation with otherness. The first forgets, rather flees from ethical otherness into a narcissistic self-absorption; the second buffers itself from otherness by a rigoristic self-mediation, more concerned with its own rational self-consistency than with an open ethical mindfulness of otherness as other.

There is a third possibility that tries to avoid these extremes and remain true to the middle. What the ancients called *phronēsis* or practical wisdom reflects an ethical mindfulness that respects intermediate being. Human beings are neither beasts nor gods but are in-between. Practical wisdom is an embodiment of metaxological mindfulness. Neither retreating to mindless immediacy (a danger with the narcissistic hedonism that complements calculative utilitarianism), nor closing itself up in empty, formal self-mediation (a danger with Kantianism), this ethical mindfulness intermediates with otherness by trying to wed the particulars of experience with principled mindfulness. In the nature of the case, being ethical is always tied to concrete acting: a way of being in which we try to do the concrete good. Hence practical wisdom as intermediate cannot be an abstract, rigid rationality. It issues from a concrete, originating mind. Its principle must be openness to the other and the unknown, but also the attentive look before any leap.

Nor need it yield a bland, insipid mean, since the metaxological relation of self and other is always fraught with tension, plurality, and potential conflict. If necessary, practical wisdom must dare untried solutions to problems without precedents. Least of all does it insist that human action be sanitized of all ambiguity, as if the ethical self could be bound by a univocal mathematical concept (as Aristotle denies with respect to the mean). Its whole point is to live well, discerningly, in the ambiguity of the between. Sometimes the ambiguity can be clarified, sometimes ambiguity inevitably remains after all efforts at analysis and mediation. Sometimes practical wisdom cannot solve a dilemma but has to suffer the undecidable and the loss or sorrow that must ensue on an agonizing choice. Practical wisdom as intermediate may even confront forms of otherness on which its desire to mediate breaks. This may extend even to the tragic.[18]

At its best, practical wisdom is a self-mediating openness to otherness in being willing to deal with the nonstandard, with situations not yet governed by rules. It does not just conform to tested rules; it may also originate new rules. There is an originative dimension to this middle mindfulness. What is to be done cannot be determined completely in advance. It demands the ability for rational *extemporization* in the concrete situation. Thus again it reveals ethical imagination at work. Only given ethical imagination can practical wisdom get down into the midst of the intricacies of real predicaments in their very otherness to precedent cases. This need not imply anarchy with respect to principles. But principles do not simplistically carry the recipes for their own concrete application in the middle. Nor do they apply themselves there. It is the concrete self that, as a principled self, open to the otherness of the concrete situation, applies the principle. This application is not itself a principle but something more. The metaxologically open self embodies ethical readiness for this "more." Without the self being ethical in a concrete sense more than just the possessor of principles, principles themselves would be ethically formal and impotent. Intimate alike with principles and particulars, practical wisdom as intermediate is discerning about the ready made, but also ready for any new good still in the making.

Thus the question "What is to be done?" now becomes "What is it *best* to do or be?" where the latter seeks to envisage the best or ideal ways of being human. Though impossible to assign priority to one form of the question, in one sense "What am I to be?" is basic, since the ethical is *a way of being*. What kind of self, character am I to become? But this self-becoming, what we are to be, is shaped by what we do; doing is a way of being ethical such that, as Aristotle saw, habitual action shapes character. Practical wisdom looks to the shape of human selfhood that makes, and hence is, a concrete union of mind and the good. Such an ideal self would mindfully live the good.

Since practical wisdom cannot be abstract, we recognize it, again as Aristotle saw, by identifying the self who is its outstanding embodiment. This is a matter of a concrete Who or Thou, not one of an abstract What or It. It forces us to ponder the existence of ethical exemplars, heroes, the ethical originals we are to imitate. Being ethical has here its *mimetic* dimension, hence again implicates a relatedness to the other. We learn the good by being *shown* it by one who lives it. Ethical mimesis involves this show of the good. In the mimesis of the shown good, the self lives out its ethical debt to the good others who have already tried to show the way.[19]

Work, Ethical Self-Mediation and Dignity

Though such wise ethical being is an ideal, great exemplary humans have approximated it, and hence it is not an empty "ought." To realize the ideal is the imperious "ought," the obligation our particular form of selfhood lays upon itself. It is what we are to be, hence what we already are, the eruption of the demand of fuller human promise in our present complacencies or compromises or betrayals. This is the matter in terms of the ideal, but in terms of its realization, *work* is closely connected to the ethical self-mediation implied in the question "What is to be done?"

That we alone work is indicative of an implicit link with the ethical. I do not mean what is called the "work-ethic," but rather the intimate connection of work and practical mind. The ethical as a way of being is an *energeia*, a being at work of selfhood within social otherness. (*Energeia* means literally "at-work" (*en-ergon*); consider also the connection of actuality, actualization with work in the German *Wirklichkeit*.) As a way of being, it is a doing of our being; work shows a dialectic of doing and being. Work is an expression of practical mind, its individual and social embodiment in an ordered set of actions. It is an intelligent direction of the energy of our being, its organized expenditure with a particular purpose in view. This expenditure has been variously understood. In line with the doubleness of our intermediate being, it has been seen negatively or as a positive power. Neither view can be dismissed, for one tells of our troubled break with vegetarian being, the other of our struggle for dignity in carnivorous circumstances. One tells of work as a struggle with natural necessity, the other of the dialectical self-mediation of active freedom and our sense of ethical dignity. Let us look at these two views.

The negative view is linked with a certain religious view and to our lack and finitude. Work is seen as punishment for the original sin, retribution following the Fall from primordial innocence. By their pride the first humans forfeited paradise and, consigned to worldly exile, are placed in subjection to harsh necessity. If we will eat, now we must sweat and groan and toil, reminded of finiteness, made humbly mindful of dependency. Work will be a necessary evil chastening our foolish feeling of infinite freedom, our deluded desire to be a god. This retributive view often goes with a nostalgia for the paradisal state of innocence without toil. Paradise would be ease and rest, pleasure in the bounty of being not bought by any expenditure of energy. It would just be the vegetarian enjoyment of nature generously nourishing us without any calculation of cost.

This longing is not confined to the Judaeo-Christian tradition. Pagans also pictured perfection as beyond plod and drudge (see Hesiod's *Works and Days*). In the Golden Age the world is effortless fertility. Horace envisions the Island of the Blessed thus: the land, unploughed, produces corn; the vines, unpruned, mature and ripen; olives and figs unfailingly mellow; goats come to milking without the need of herding; the hollow oak oozes with sweet honey. Nature is a surfeit of plenty, an unsolicited and limitless largess. But *now* a harsh wind blows over Nature. Her groves grow wild and her fruits breed bitter. To reap from her unordered tangle we must work. We must cultivate her chaotic powers and coax them to subserve our desire.[20]

This contrast of paradisal ease and worldly work throws important light on the opening up in the middle of an ethical sense of time. Paradisal ease is an image of the good life, but bathed in the nostalgic light of magical childhood. But though imaging the good life, it is, paradoxically, ethically innocent, amoral, just because it lacks a developed concept of time. Paradisal ease, like the gratified infant at the breast, is the quasi-eternity of sheer pleasure. There we enjoy the moment, and the moment of pleasure is all we know. Paradisal man, like the lilies of the fields, neither weaves nor spins. He knows no care because he is cared for. He gives no thought to the morrow, for he is plunged deep in the bliss of the undying instant. Nor do we have to seek the death of difference in sex, for we are already in the rapture of union.

Work, the necessity of work, appears with the dissolution of this rapturous univocity of the paradisal moment. So also does our suffering difference and the lust for sex.[21] We know our incompleteness, know we are exiled to time. We cannot simply *be*, we must learn to *do*. Tomorrow comes into view and with it the future's fret. It is this sense of the future that makes one a worker. One works because one knows. One know one's fragility and vulnerability. Besides nature's bounty, one knows its unpredictable harsh turns. One knows what little one can count on, what one must secure through one's own strategies. We work because we worry.

That we suffer from metaphysical distrust is again ethically relevant. With work we cannot univocally accept what is, as it immediately is. The metaphysical worry of our anxious temporality insists on our altering being that is into something other, being as we would will it to be. Thus, also work can be wrath, that is, ontological aggression against being in its otherness. Differentiated self-consciousness confers on us an extended sense of time and a disquieting sense of the future. Worry incites efforts to fill that empty future, to make it safe. Our anxiety before tomorrow causes us to toil today. If tomorrow can be secured, or better, the day after tomorrow, perhaps we may taste again the healing moment of ease and forget time's uncertainty. We labor under the shadow of death.

This is a negative view of work as penitential product of paradise lost. But given human doubleness in the middle, we can assume a different ethical relation to time. Suppose we dim the memory of a forfeited Eden, and awaken to ourselves, our powers of being still virgin? Suppose we hope for a gain and cease to brood on a lapse? Some such temporal redirection inevitably happens in our ethical maturing when we put aside nostalgia for narcissistic innocence and face the ambiguous future. With this redirection of temporal mindfulness, work may begin to offer an essential good, not a necessary evil. Instead of expiation for pride, it may become central to our endeavours to dignify our existence.

We confront external nature and must gain support from it but are resisted; yet we do not bow before the rebuff; we refuse to let nature swamp us and try to reshape it into closer conformity with our desire. We accomplish this reshaping though work. That is, through work we struggle to stamp ourselves and perhaps a sense of the ideal on nature. This transforming process is begun when by the intelligent use of natural materials we create tools. Tools are the material embodiment of our practical ingenuity, extensions of our body that give us extra dexterity and control in ordering nature. Extending our bodily power into external nature, tools use matter to conquer matter. Thus they lighten the burden of toil, allowing will to bend nature's otherness to itself.

In this way work enables us to remake nature in agreement with our own nature. Work is ethically important because it expresses in action and in the very doing of power the reality of what we are and what we purpose to be. For not only does it let us stamp our press on nature, it aids us to a deeper understanding of ourselves. Work is a process of *dialectical self-mediation* in this sense. In it we confront the otherness of the material world but are not paralysed by a sense of its opposition. In working on it we objectify our power in the external world; hence the external product of our power is the public, social object in which we begin to realize and recognize ourselves. Work dialectically mediates the dualistic opposition of humans and nature and shows to us that we are what we produce. It is not just the making of an external product, but a dialectical process of *self-making*. Analogous to the dialectical self-mediation in art, the product here can be selfhood, a certain self-*poiēsis* of humanity in the deed.

We are what we do. And though modern technology has made clear the destructive potential of some forms of mechanical work, it is *we* who are the destructive doers. Destructive work reveals our ethical nature in negative dress: it is we who are *the* destroying animal. In what we destroy we know ourselves, our ethical darkness. Contrariwise, in the worthwhile things we make, we recognize ourselves in the realization of our affirmative promise. Whichever way, work not only actualizes, realizes our power; it also shows the nature of this power and so mediates the comprehension of our own character. In making or undoing something, and in knowing what we make or undo, the human self comes to know itself.

This affirmative concept of work sees it as progressively releasing our freedom. At first an unavoidable necessity, work progressively may elevate us above necessity. Positive, humane work need not humble us but show us rising above limitations, giving us pride and assurance in the worth of our powers. Indeed the more humane work becomes, the more it becomes a new kind of necessity. Then it is not just a means to an end, a necessity imposed on us as extra, but becomes an end in itself, a necessity demanded by our dignity and humanization. Initially we expend ourselves in work to overcome natural necessity; subsequently, we may do so because it is necessary to the essential realization of our being. In this fuller sense, humane work may be our free self-realization. This is the releasing work we find, for instance, in the work of art.[22]

Are the two senses of work held together in the middle? Though we seem to be far from toil as punishment, in a way we here return to that beginning, or at least to a transformation of the theme. For what is the most positive work but the endeavor to perfect existence? And what is paradise but the symbol of perfected existence? But with the second sense we do not hanker nostalgically for a lost paradise, but launch out into the unknown, confident in our powers, ready to realize them to the limit, not suppliants to a prior perfection but patient builders of the better. The future sense of human possibility of the second sense of work indicates an origination of self-responsibility in time in that it shows the future as partly within the self's will. It is the same willing "I" that takes responsibility for its future "I," in projecting its chosen possibility into the time to come and working for its realization. This self-responsible projection of the willing "I" reveals the nature of the human as, in every sense, *the promising animal*.

Admittedly, the ethical scandal of much human history is that most people are confined to the first form of work, and in our day, without any divine sanction. The tedium of the assembly line, the standarization of work into a mindless routine, are by now stock examples of this dehumanization of work. Nor is our technological mastery necessarily work as ethical, for its hubris over otherness is often a violent humanistic mastering, devoid of any respect. Marx saw the possibility of the second kind of work, and (drawing on Hegel) he analyzed its character very well. He and Hegel also saw rightly that properly humanized work, work that does not radically block the realization of the human, is one of the great ethical issue. If our work is degrading or empty or disabling, profound repercussions ensue throughout the totality of being human. Modern work may enable economic profit but it may disable humans, disable community. It may not rise to the level of free service consecrated to the other. It may concretize human power, but that power, especially as articulated within certain social orders, paradoxically makes human beings powerless. Though Marx is right to emphasize the solidarity of human beings as workers in opposition to disabling social orders, he did not always escape a hubristic humanism in relation to nature. The community of human beings as sources of acting power need not imply tyranny over the otherness of being. Being ethical has to grow beyond any such tyranny.

The modern world witnesses the dominance of an insistent instrumental intelligence but being ethical is more encompassing, insists on a larger view than allowed by a pressing practicality, and is not inimical to modes of mindfulness not immediately practical. We are not always helped by the preference of much modern philosophy for practical intelligence, coupled with a contempt for the ancient preference for speculative mind. Thus, Descartes disparaged Aristotle's "idle" speculations and aimed to contruct a new practical science. Putting aside Hegel's metaphysics, Marx demanded that philosophy do more than interpret the world; it must change the world. Olympus is to be leveled in a crash of rubble. The voluntarism of much post-Kantian thought, and some characteristic emphases of contemporary pragmatism reveal a similar stress on the practical, seen with too strong a sense of its opposition to the speculative. Ordinary people often unwittingly reduplicate the reflections of the thinkers they affect to despise. They want intelligence to be useful, that is, to service everyday desire. But the dignity of free desire is not to be engulfed by the busyness of the day.

Work as implying an ethical relation to time entails a process of perfecting. This means the attainment of appropriate wholeness in the middle, the intermediate wholeness of the sort we saw with the artwork. When work becomes a merely instrumental devouring of time and a mindless drive into the future, it can produce a totalitarianism of instrumental life. In the frenzy of such totalized instrumentality, works cease to mediate ethical dignity and becomes an *escape* from intermediate being, a flight from the self-knowledge and openness to otherness demanded there. Work drugs us against time. We still labor in the shadow of death, but the frenzy of instrumental life deadens us to its shadow.

I said at the outset that being ethical involves a general comportment to being that takes care for its worth. Morality is ultimately metaphysical: it grows out of a pervasive sense of what is ultimate in being, articulating especially what desire and will prize as of ultimate worth. To further the realization of human promise, practical intelligence (as calculative mind) must be itself grounded in this prior sense of being ethical. When it is, it may provide the base for a further freeing of the energy of our being.

For once practical necessities are met, the human being may dream of more. Danger is past, everyday desire is content, the will is resting. Pure, idle curiosity may appear and mind take a more contemplative form. Mind may itself become freed into the spiritual spaces of ideality, released from the worry of daily work and any ontological wrath towards the limiting conditions of finite being. This idealizing freedom goes into the creation of culture, and indeed civilizes the very process of practical life. Here, too, may emerge work as a free service dedicated to the other. In so far as being ethical cannot be abstracted from this civilizing process, we also see its inseparability from the particular aesthetic styles, the forms of being religious and the tacit or explicit philosophical wisdom of different cultures. Moreover, free mind is reflective; besides driving into the future, it also turns back when the work is done to ponder the work's meaning and itself. It involves a *recollective* self-mediation of desire in communion with otherness, one that tries to gather up into a new ideal wholeness the energy of being that drives forward practical life itself. Art, religion and philosophy (as Hegel saw, and Schopenhauer) are works of free mind in this sense. They are recollections of the human being, gathering its energies into a fresh wholeness that both frees desire and is beyond its fret. Nor are they closed to otherness but respectfully name what in otherness is of intrinsic worth.

III. ETHICAL INWARDNESS AND THE MIDDLE

Persons and Intrinsic Value

Our discussion of work again shows us the transcendence of the instrumental (the dignifying of self and perhaps respect for being in its otherness) *in* the instrumental itself (work as useful). Work may mediate a sense of ethical dignity and so point us beyond the instrumental sphere to what cannot be reduced to a mere means. The sense of dignity points to a certain internalization of value in selfhood itself, or good character. It points to a sense of inner otherness, ethical inwardness as an end in itself, never to be reduced to a mere instrumentality. This is important for our concerns henceforth, namely, with the turning of self-insistent desire to the ethical other as a value in itself. The inwardizing of inherent value allows respect for the intrinsic value of the *other* and so mediates a sense of ethical community as metaxological, that is, as grounding a mutual mediation of self and other, never exhausted by any one singular self-mediation.

Let me situate my remarks by recalling that in the history of ethics a fundamental distinction is repeatedly made between instrumental and intrinsic goods. An instrumental good is valuable as a means to an end. The value of wealth, for example, resides in its usefulness for a good that it does not itself encompass; properly used, money may enable one to pursue fulfilling life, but there is nothing inherent in it necessitating its proper use or preventing its abuse. By contrast, an intrinsic good is worthy in itself and for itself; it is an end, good in itself, not a means to something beyond itself. Health is a simple instance. We can ask what health is good for, in the sense of what else it empowers one to do, but being healthy requires no justification beyond itself. To be healthy is simply the realization of the proper power of one's being, and as such is self-justifying. Health is simply physical well-being. Another example is truthfulness. A cynic might inquire: what is truth good for? And in a sense truthfulness is good for nothing, but precisely because it carries its own worthiness. Genuine honesty is a perfection of character that justifies itself.[23]

Many philosophers have sought for goods that might be unconditional, sifting the myriad possibilities that tempt desire. All possibility that is pursued is perceived as good; is there any good that will not only be perceived to be good, but be actually good? One person sees carnal pleasure as good but this gratification is tinged with regret; brief satiety brings brief joy, but prolonged satiety arouses tedium; this satisfaction also disquiets and breeds incessant, inconstant desire. Wealth and honor have also been seen as inconstant: wealth entails no guarantee of moral discrimination, indeed one can be wealthy and insufferably stupid. Likewise, honor may involve the conceit of an infantile, secretly sucking self; it is dependent on the undependable opinions of shifting others, as Aristotle reminds us. Is there any good radically desirable for itself around which might be discerningly ranged other more or less relative goods?

Different candidates have been nominated. For Aristotle only happiness (*eudaimonia*) passed muster, for it supremely is desired for its own sake; we desire everything else for its sake. Aquinas held that happiness was the supreme good from our side, but he pressed the question: what supreme good as *other* need we possess to be absolutely happy? His answer was God, though in fact God is not a "thing" that we could ever "possess." As with Augustine, our heart's do not come to rest until they rest "there." With a philosopher's passion, Spinoza rejects fame, wealth, sensual pleasure as intrinsic ends, though he tolerates pleasure as a means to the end of health, and wealth as a means to the end of life, health, or the advancement of art and science. For Spinoza, the singular good was perfection of character in enjoyment of the eternal truth, attained in the mind's union with the whole of nature (in our terms, metaxological community with being in its otherness), or otherwise termed by Spinoza *amor Dei intellectualis*. Kant returned the ethical focus to the self, claimed that only the good will was of unconditional worth. One might happily satisfy ones desire, yet without good will one would be morally lacking. Likewise, a person without a good will might follow a right course of action, not because of its ethical rightness but only because he dreads the punishment of God or the father figure or society. The action is diminished by the absence of the genuine moral motive. Good will is an ethical absolute *interior* to the self, making possible the moral worthiness of its every action.[24]

Aquinas locates the ethical absolute in the transcendent, Kant stresses its immanence in the self. In seeing God as the supreme good, Aquinas rightly reminds us of the otherness of radical ethical perfection to the finite self. In speaking of the good will as the moral unconditional, and so pointing us to an absolute interior to selfhood, Kant rightly recalls us to the intimacy in our being of the charge of ethical wholeness. The modern sense of freedom is more Kantian that Aquinian in its strong stress on uncompromised autonomy. Heteronomy is ethically taboo. For the metaxological sense of being, the good will is crucial, as a mediation in inwardness of the ethical unconditional. But the concretion of the good will's freedom is never in abstraction from its metaxological interplay with its other, its *heteros*. We need a view of ethical freedom beyond the religious heteronomy that threatens to dwarf human autonony, and beyond the pure human freedom that risks insisting on itself at the price of spinning dizzily in a formalistic void. Ultimately one cannot evade the question of the absolute in its otherness.

In fact, the difference of Aquinas and Kant need not exclude an overlap with respect to the ethical person as an end in itself. For traditionally the person's unconditional worth emerges in relation to God. In the eyes of one's fellows, one might seem of limited worth, if not worthless; in God's eyes this does not obtain. As God's image every human partakes of the divine life and is marked by infinite worth. In the humanistic framework, the reference to God is diminished, if not dropped; being ethical asserts its autonomy from being religious. Yet there persists the view that the person is of intrinsic worth; its very being is a value; it is not an instrumental thing, and is to be treated accordingly. This is absolutely essential to safeguard the inviolate ethical inwardness of human selfhood.

To grant this is not to deny that often the person is treated as a means. In practical life one may be used by, or be useful to, others. The butcher, the baker, the candlestick maker, these we use, for they are useful. But our use of others ceases to recognize the person as person when the other becomes a thing whose ethical dignity is discharged in indifference. The extreme case is slavery. Slaves are persons treated as instruments, extensions of the master's will, themselves treated as devoid of will. Their ethical claim as persons, their being as ethical inwardness, is denied. As Aristotle put it, a slave is just a "living tool." A more extreme case is not just using others thus, but "eating infants"—on a purely instrumentalized view of ethics, Jonathan Swift's grim "modest proposal" of capitalistic cannibalism is the most rational thing in the world.[25]

Of course, those with a low view of human motivation reduce all our intermediation with the other to instrumental exchange. Every self may be made a pliable tool if the pressure or enticement is enough; everyone has his price, the cynic intones. One may even treat *oneself* as a means; as we say, one sells oneself. If this selling exceeds a certain limit, it transgresses a moral bound, and we then say that one has sold one's soul. One has failed to act in accord with the intrinsic dignity required of one by virtue of being a person. One has reduced oneself, reneged on ethical inwardness, relativized its unconditional core.

Admittedly, it is impossible always to treat persons exclusively as intrinsic ends, yet we need not reduce them to mere means and close off other claims. I may use the butcher, but in this I can dignify the instrumental relation with the quality of a further respect, even if this extends no further than cold courtesy. To treat others solely as useful tools entails an externality foreign to human interplay, indeed an objectification of selfhood that deforms its non-objectifiable inward otherness. When the other is a thing out there for convenient use, our ethical kinship is distorted. Even despite their difference, even despite any antithesis of master and slave, both are human beings, each is the same. To recognize the other as an end in itself is to witness to a basic ethical community, despite external divergences in power or prestige. To grant the other this intrinsic worth in being granted this worth by the other, is to grant the ethical intimacy of all human beings.

There is no denial of the necessity of instrumental exchange: we need and use each other—the hand washes the hand. But our relatedness to otherness is not exhausted by this. Ethical respect for the other as other is possible. This respect releases, lets be, the other as other. The very *being* of the other as person defines its dignity in terms of its own nonreducible inwardness and its claim on us. This follows from what we might term the metaphysical worth of personhood. To be a person entails the promise and to some degree the realization of certain powers of being, but also it points to the concretion of an ontological perfection. Too true to our own self-insistent being, we crave that others acknowledge this claim about *ourselves*. Our touchy dignity is stung if this claim is refused.

To be a person is to be an appeal—an ethical appeal for dignity. This appeal radiates in the middle from the "I" as well as from the other: it transcends any dualistic opposition of "I" and other. Beauty, as we recall, sensuously prefigures this ethical appeal: the aesthetic work of self on self is not instrumental. As adornment asks the other to recognize my special self-ness in the body's allure, so the ethical appeal asks for respect of our very being as a different center of free dignity. In this appeal we ask of the other the hard trust in our own freedom. We do not always reciprocate the recognition or trust, or heed the other's appeal. That we ought to reciprocate, treat others as ends as we would have others treat us, is implied in the Golden Rule and at the basis of all personalist ethics. We should recognize the other, as we would ourselves be recognized—worthy of dignity by virtue of our very being. This is not a respect we earn, but one we are offered and should offer.

IV. THE ETHICAL INTERMEDIATION OF OTHERNESS

Ethical Will and Otherness: Two Loves

We can now address the double mediation between the self and the other that marks their ethical togetherness in metaxological community. We must ask how, given desire's self-insistence, the self can thus ethically turn to the other as other? One objection, formulated perhaps most strongly in Kant's critique of "eudaimonism," is that morality makes demands of obligation *beyond* desire's self-interest. Kant hits the target if desire is reduced to the sensuous appetite of classical empiricism and utilitarianism. But one cannot avoid desire: the issue is not desire's circumvention but a profounder conception of it as articulating the ontological energy of our intermediate being and so as always already containing the seed of ethical will.[26]

As I implied at the outset, the human self is a configuration of the energy of being that itself is neither material nor mental, though it is manifested as both. This primordial energy surges up in us and desire is one of its articulated expressions. Desire emerges in our bodily being, crosses between body and mind, expressing the primordial energy in the form of a certain striving awareness. To desire is to be driven by internal exigency, yet also it is to reach out to something other than oneself that one needs or lacks or loves. It testifies to the self's power as both demanding its own satisfaction and stretching beyond itself to things or selves other than self. Desire expresses the power of being but this expression is not single but double. Desire reveals the power of the self to be or become metaxologically open to the other. It forks into two basic forms, one that insists that the self be gratified (self-mediation), the other paying due heed to being other as other (metaxological intermediation). This inherent doubleness grounds the difference between an instrumental relation to the other and one that grants the other its intrinsic worth.

Because of such doubled desire we find, as it were, two loves. First, the human self loves itself: this is its nature and nothing else. From this standpoint the man who hates himself is perverse. Selfishness, I know, is repudiated by all civilized people as a failing that the mature self surmounts. By basic self-love I do not mean such base selfishness. I mean the fact that every being, in its own way, is marked by an insistence of energy and wills to preserve and continue its own being; every being affirms its own being. Selfishness is a refusal to acknowledge the legitimate claims of others; but this basic self-love is the legitimate proclamation every entity makes about itself: this I am and as such I will to continue to be.

Spinoza's *Ethics* exhibits a very acute sense of this ontological self-insistence, though in Spinoza what empowers our move beyond it is not entirely clear. I prefer to put the point thus: this basic self-love is simply the love of being expressed in this particular being, this individual unity of selfhood. The ethical and metaphysical stress falls on the love of being. Those who make a show of horror at "selfishness" are hypocritical on this score. They either dissimulate their own basic self-love, or else they fail to know themselves. It is a perversion of being if a being does not love itself.

To own to this is ingredient in health. This is not disproved by the fact that we often hate ourselves, in some cases to the point of violent self-annihilation. This proves rather the free nature of desire, its ability to deform its own basic intentionally, to turn against and destroy what its deepest insistence loves.

The second love, arising from metaxological desire, is not our love of our own being, but may extend to the whole of being different to the self. Within the heart of selfness, I know that my own being does not, cannot exhaust the fullness of being. Desire is witness enough to this: we desire what we lack, as Socrates reminds us, but the sense of lack is impossible without a corresponding sense of some other fullness to requite the lack. The immediate, unarticulated sense of the absent other and whole is implicated in the lack of desire from the outset. Thus, even when desiring something for ourselves and giving rein to our self-insistence, we realize that our selfness cannot stand alone. Ontologically we are the immediate need of otherness; indeed selfness is first formed by this need.

The self is never a windowless monad, as Leibniz has it. Throughout the entirety of being there is no such thing as a windowless monad. Leibniz rightly insists on the unity of selfhood, but this is an open wholeness: every whole is implicated in a necessary relatedness to its others in the metaxological community of being. Every whole is the more open in the measure that the powers of its characteristic energy reveal richer participations in the power of being: the more true to metaxological being, the more open the whole. That openness may be potentially infinite or unrestricted with the human self as whole—a fact that mirrors the infinite restlessness emergent in its characteristic desire. The energy surging up in our being breaks open every self-enclosure, thrusts further than the individual as lone and aims at the full otherness of being beyond itself. The call of an unrestricted openness to being's otherness breaks through even in the dialectical self-mediation of self-insistent desire. Then we find what I call the "second love": the self does not just love its own being, it loves being simply as such.

This implicity universal openness nourishes the seed of ethical will. Put otherwise, no finite self can be completely defined in itself nor so self-sufficient as to derive the sources of its being from itself. Finite selves, as it were, tread water on the supporting sea of the infinite otherness and are what they are, even in their unique particularity, by virtue of participating in this. This is not to deny to finite beings their *individual* wholeness, but to say that the energy of their individual being is their share, that is, metaxological participation in the energy of being itself. It is this absolute energy of being that ultimately we regard in the two loves. The two loves as forms of ethical desire must be called metaphysical in this sense: they express our fundamental kinship with being, in ourselves and in our bond with being other than ourselves. But the second love is the more ultimate because the more embracing, the more universal in being open to the full otherness of the community of being.

The Golgotha of the ethical will is the self-transformation of first love into second love. This transformation answers the question "What am I to be?" with a dread command: "Be other! You must change utterly!" But strangely, being other is just to be what we are, to become our promise. Thus, if we look back at our discussion to this point, we can see two fundamental turns. The first turn is from innocent desire to insistent will that thrusts us into the ethical. Now in the second turn from first love to second, we meet the demand for a conversion of the will; but unlike the first turn which is a rupture, this second is a breaking through—the breaking through of a more universal willingness in the particular will itself.

Willingness implies an entire comportment towards being, both of the self and the other. The will's transformation here at issue implicates the entire self. Hence it is not just the product of a deliberate act of will, nor a respose to an injunction like "Act rationally!" To the contrary, reason and deliberate will themselves reach their roots down into sources of selfhood that do not always come to explicit self-consciousness or self-mediation. Rational acts of will are often but the daylight side of a more opaque, pervasive willingness. This willingness may be a deep ethical readiness, ingrained in the very texture of our character. The breaking through of second love into our particular deeds, of metaxological openness to otherness into desire as self-insistence, presupposes the hidden transformation of our very being as willingness. "Be other!," as implying "Be what you are!," pitches its ethical command at the very ontological roots of our self-being.[27]

It is no easy task to realize any of the power of second love, and perhaps only a few scattered individuals have come anywhere close. These are selves who have ceased to fear for their lives, and thenceforth sacrificed themselves in love of the other, sacrificed in the literal sense of "making sacred" their self-being in its being-for-others. They live being as an ethical sacrament. Such selves have been the great ethical and religious heroes like the Buddha or Jesus or Francis of Assisi. But none is exempt from the call of second love. Most often second love is collapsed into first in a manner that corrupts both. Though self-love is essential, it can be bent from the proper affirmation of its own being when it refuses the express flowering of second love as the proper affirmation of the being of others. In this bending, base selfishness begins, that is, desire that in trampling on the other's claim comes inevitably to distort the self's claim.[28]

The two loves, as articulating desire's self-mediation and intermediation with otherness, are not to be abstracted from the communal embodiment that organizes their energy into forms of social will. When the first love predominates individuals insist on themselves and relations are governed by self-interest. At best we find wholesome struggle and rivalry where the self-assertion of one person spurs another to emulate and excel. But such rivalry is only possible if one grants some *respect* for one's rival, that is, it requires some expression of second love, love of other-being. When the love of self-being closes in on itself, competition degenerates into a self-willed struggle for mastery of the other. Enmity infiltrates the fray; hostile others become threats to self-interest. Sharp envy emerges, resentment festers—well understood by Nietzsche and Scheler in its subterranean rancor toward the worthy, excelling other. The individual, now aggressive rather than rancorous, or rather rancorous in outwardly explosive mode, becomes intent on securing his own base against all otherness, even if this means the overriding or negation of all others. If the other cannot be dominated, it is to be destroyed. The ethical intermediation of self and other collapses into their war in carnivorous society.

By contrast, the formation of social will correlative to second love is held together by a trust deeper than the distrust whose necessity we must allow, even while overcoming it. In the first form competitive individuals will assert "mine," but in the second a cooperating people will try to say "ours." The common good comes to subordinate the claims of particular self-interest. In general also we find two corresponding attitudes to property: in one private property is socrosanct; in the other the idea of property is more widely vested in the community. Actual societies, reflecting desire's doubleness, will mingle or mediate the claim of the two forms. In all societies there will be some recognition that self-interest cannot be allowed unbridled play. To secure social order it must often be subordinated to the good of the larger whole. The laws of a state, the duties and rights of its citizens, will check and restrain and punish, if necessary, the vehement energy of excessive self-will. This is not to justify the totalitarian state that tries to stifle the energy of individual self-love. As a society grows in civility and tries to live the ethical promise of metaxological being, mindfulness will transforms the initial energy, power and will. Civilizing society tries to transmute sheer power into genuine justice. Increasingly, it will even admit more tolerantly individual liberty and refrain from completely sacrificing it to the exigencies of the larger whole.

Civilized, metaxological society will not insist on extirpating one strain of desire, but acknowledging its double nature, will extend within the community the rightful space of individual liberty. Of course, sometimes a dialectical reversal can result. Civilized trust in individual liberty can breed a condition of *distrust* towards civility and liberty themselves, especially if the latter liberty fails to find its way beyond the exploitative instrumentality of first love. At a certain acme of civilization individual liberty is enshrined as an inalienable right; but this very liberty can slacken the restraining bonds of civilized life. The result may be a return or regression to a barbarism wherein the individual is atomized and defines its freedom as *opposition* to every other individual. Civilization guarantees individual liberty, but when this becomes excessively licensed, civility itself becomes infected with nascent civil war. Elements of this are evident in modern Westen democracies, as MacIntyre notes, but Plato noted the same thing in Athenian democracy. Men glare balefully around them, though their faces hold smiles. None casts the gaze of cold eyes beyond survival and aggrandizement.[29]

Ethical Civility and Otherness

In our discussion what is at stake is the promise of metaxological intermediation within ethical community: a plurality of ethically self-mediating selves living in respect of the worthy being of irreducible otherness. This community cannot be reduced to *one* dialectical self-mediating whole, for at a very basic level, even the ethically self-mediating person is *double* and is hence the bearer of its *own* irreducible otherness. Metaxological community as an ideal asks us to realize the ethical promise of second love.[30] But both desire's doubleness and the dialectic of trust and distrust mean that there are factors inherently recalcitrance to this promise. This recalcitrance is a kind of negative otherness. Hence we must look at ethical will's turn from the familiar other to the stranger, and from the civil to the criminal other. With respect to the differentiation of more intimate and strange others, what I will call "ethical civility" is central in transforming our relationship to otherness, especially in social conditions inhospitable to the promise of metaxological community.[31]

In relation to the differentiation of social otherness, we must remember that the being-for-self of modern individualism is not some primordial condition but a late development, resulting from a protracted historical process. Nor can individuality (even modern autonomy) avoid marks of its own natural genesis in the family bond. These traces can never be erased, not because we remain children, but because they define what we are. The primary place of intimate community is the family, and though we develop beyond this, we never entirely shed its radiance, or in some cases, its disfiguring effect.[32]

Consider here this radiance of familial terms into the wider social otherness. Thus, in the Middle Ages when equality was viewed in religious terms, humankind as a whole was seen as descended from the original Adam, and God the Father knit the heterogeneous plurality into a universal family: before God all were brothers and sisters. Not surprisingly, in trying to imitate on earth the Kingdom of God, as in monastic community, fellows in this divine work called each other "brother" and "sister." By contrast, modern man tends to substitute politics for religion; the Kingdom of God is displaced by the Kingdom of Man. Nevertheless, the urge to call our neighbor "brother" has not evaporated. We need only think of the triple slogan of the French Revolution whose ideals still project their light, or shadow: Liberty, Equality, Fraternity. As in the Middle Ages, equality is still linked to fraternity, only these are not now primarily seen as gifts of God, but as rights and bonds the freeman enjoys with other freemen. Again the longing for the human family lives on, but expressed in secular, political terms.

A Cartesian self, abstracted in its isolation from the otherness of being, can make no sense of this longing for brotherhood. Perhaps this is one reason why the language of fraternity is now strangely absent in advanced technological societies. Nor can utilitarianism fully comprehend the call of this belonging. The Cartesian, the utilitarian, the technicist would never seem to have lived in a family or been loved by one. (Who mothers the *Cogito*?) As the most elemental community wherein one is known by others and comes to know, nay, *be* oneself, the family is the primary originary matrix of social otherness from which concrete selfhood emerges. Cartesianism, utilitarianism or technicism cannot comprehend this genesis or origination: they take the derivative (the atomized self) for the original. But it is the bond with the other that is original, not isolated, opposed selves. The latter are derivatives trying to snap themselves absolutely free of their originating social source. Such freedom is the fugue of communal origins, obliviously dependent on the fact that first love is really a particularization of second love. For here we find first love ambitious for closure on itself, all the while honoring its distorted exclusivity with the moral rhetoric of autonomy. Ethical mindfulness cannot be uncritically mesmerized by this distortion, admittedly prevalent; otherwise our reflections reduplicate it in abstractions.[33] The danger is all the more in that the values of the instrumentalized world can invade and disfigure the family.

The family is a natural community in the sense that none chooses by free will to be born of certain parents, to be reared and defined by their care. No one contracts to be born; our origin through otherness is a given. Family is literally educative (*e-ducere*) in drawing us out to be selves. Here the elemental "immediacy" of the metaxological reasserts itself as an originating and grounding community that is already at work in mediating our identities as relational, even though our explicit self-understanding seems to deny such mediations. Obviously, the family takes different forms in different societies, but beneath the differences are the elemental ties of blood. Thus, the family tends to be seen as a kind of natural, organic whole; no estranging separation is felt between oneself and this whole. Parents and relatives, sisters and brothers, these we encounter face to face. We meet their anger in breaking the social code, but we can directly seek forgiveness and reinstatement within the whole. Social being seems within our embrace and to embrace us, complex but not completely beyond our power. Most especially, we feel ourselves as not alone but buoyed up by the intimacy of others in the most primitive intimacy of blood—the latter involves an elemental destiny beyond free choice, pointing literally to our being related to others in the very flesh itself. When politics is charged with the language of brotherhood it tries to carry some of the elemental resonance of this primitive intimacy. It exhibits the impulse to rescue social life from the burden of alienating solitariness, to return us to community within a sympathetic social whole, to make political institutions themselves the embodiment (the body politic) of this deep commonness between man and man.

Of course, when communities develop beyond a certain complexity, differences arise that cannot be intermediated in familial terms. The stranger shows scant respect for the dignity of familial intimacy. Unable to encompass the complexity of communal being, the family comes to be defined by contrast with other public, less personalized modes of common life. Here at the level of otherness, we meet the dialectic of trust and distrust, previously met at the level of self. This dialectic is unavoidable. A child may feel alarm at stepping outside the family into other social contexts, for he may meet no new wholeness there, only jarring estrangement. Some children scream with refusal, or become mute with apprehension, on first arriving at the gates of school: brothers vanish, and the blood sings with the shock of strangers. For now social relations cease to be intimate natural ties and become a web of distancing artificialities. The stranger does not understand me, takes me for a rival and plots. Alien stresses erupt; bonds break; factions form; power groups grow and conspire. In the suspicious public glare, the person is not loved. There are no brothers.

One reason why the language of "brotherhood" never entirely deserts politics is because we cannot suppress the desire to reconstitute a sympathetic social community.[34] The given promise of metaxological community as immediate and elemental cannot be finally repressed. The artificialities, the strains, the coldness, the enmities of public life might not be eliminated but might be mitigated. The pursuit of fraternity embodies the hope of accomplishing this mitigation. Granting the appeal of this hope, in practice the word "brother" is not always enough. The actual embrace of our love is always limited. In addition, a complex society increases distance between its members and the ties of blood, in that these become essentially private, an asylum to be protected, not the germ of an empire to be extended. Thus, inevitably the ethics of otherness demands a substitute or complement for fraternity and natural love. One such ideal I call ethical civility.

What is involved in this? Beyond the exclusive intimacy of family, when differences between strangers emerge, these must be mediated. The mediation of civil selves seeks such a harmony. There is need for an ideal, a prescription of how we might be in relation to the stranger, how better we might be in relation. Ethical civility sets up a model of exemplary public conduct in which due weight, proper justice is allowed to others. If one cannot be friendly to one's fellows, one can still be civil. One may relate to them according to forms of decorum and respect, deference and consideration, graciousness and solidarity. Civility tempers our apprehension before the stranger and diverts the temptation to contempt of the other. It moderates public behavior with often unwritten rules of reasonableness. The civil self epitomizes ethical mindfulness as this moderating reasonableness.

Ethical civility is not merely an optional etiquette. It is not unrelated to aesthetic cultivation and religious respect. Nor is it unrelated to the Greek *paideia*, the German notion of *Bildung*, and the cosmopolitan ideal of Stoicism.[35] This latter embodies universal ethical ideals, seeing the self as a citizen of the cosmos that is itself a universal community. Beyond the kinship of Greek with Greek, Jew with Jew, Roman with Roman, the cosmopolitan ideal proclaims the kinship of all humans and of the human with all otherness. This shared humanness transcends the divide that separates and sets in dualistic opposition the master and slave, for in both an absolute ethical inwardness is to be respected. As we have already seen, both the self and the other as self-mediating persons are to be respected as ends in themselves, bearers of an irreducible, not-to-be-violated ethical inwardness. Nor need ethical civility be mere outside form; it can be the social radiation of ethical inwardness. It can be spirit and heart, not just letter and rule. At its best it mediates ethical inwardness and is its communal safeguard and keeper.

At the other extreme, ethical civility is essential to midwife the very *emergence* of the individual from the condition of barbarism. As the tales of Giants remind us, the human being is born barbaric and only realizes its humanity through appropriate cultivation. Ethical civility makes possible the harmonious actualization of the powers of a plurality of selves. Hence, we must stress that the civil self is no self-creation, complete unto itself, but is the outcome of a civilized state already at work throughout social otherness. The civil self is a particular manifestation of the civilized state, individualizing its conditions and realizing its requirements in his person. He may represent, "stand for" ethical civility which, in turn, has become the second nature of his habitual character. The family, too, is essential in this process in that the bond of blood may charge the process with deep dynamic intimacy. Growing to be ourselves, we become our elders. We imitate their otherness, even if later we may sometimes also deconstruct it.

Ethical civility itself calls for a more widely diffused social mimesis, which humanizes the wildness through ideals like these. Differences are not to be dealt with by brute force or by resort to rudimentary vengeance. In some cases they are to be resolved through law that stands above parties in dispute and subjects both equally to its impartial assessment. Law provides a civilized substitute for vengeance by embodying the moderating standards of justice of a society.[36] This is the ideal, I know. The civil self realizes this ideal by abiding by the law, by respecting the equality of all according to its fairness. This need not extend to the rigid regulation of all action but is quite consistent with the demands of tolerance—another ideal nourished by ethical civility. With regard to the many differences that do not engender conflict, one lives and lets live, for such differences do not impair the social bond but add the spice of surprise and heterogeneity to the forms of common life.

Ethical civility tempers with justice the aggressive and destructive expressions of power, promotes the pursuit of happiness and the good, welcomes the self to be at home with his community. Where a community frustrates these attainments, ethical estrangement results. Devoid of ethical civility it deforms the demands of justice and undermines the very state of being a civil self. If society has only partially degenerated, the self may be ready to rebel; if corrupted to the core, he may become a revolutionary. In ethical crisis the self might have to become a warrior of justice.

It follows that no community is ever merely a neutral framework to be exploited as power and will permit, nor a disinterested context within which the individual works out an exclusive satisfaction. Community is ethos, namely, always already an embodiment of the ethical mediation of otherness. It is an abstraction to view community as an instrument of individual desire, as always a means and never an end, or as abstaining from preference in ethical norms that putatively are left to individual will. The purely formal tolerance implied by this view is really a disingenuous indifference, for ethical norms are necessarily smuggled surreptitiously back into the communal context; or rather some norms are so taken for granted that they are not perceived as ethical preferences at all. Ethical civility is less oblivious to and hypocritical about recognizing the inescapability of ethical norms being embodied in social praxis itself. It denies the implied separability of self and the community of others. The civilized state is not just a means to an end, or instrument of individual desire, but the communal embodiment of fundamental moral and political ideals, all flowing from the basic respect for the ethical other as other.

This respect repudiates the atomization of the social bond into an aggregate of freelance individuals of exploitive desire. Respect for the other as an inviolable end expresses the ethical bond that always holds us together. The freelance individual is only possible because of this bond and the dimming of ethical respect into simulacrum tolerance, namely, indifference to the other as other. The freelance individual is the complete lie of self-subsistent autonomy; for take away the social source propping its instrumentalized desire, and it retracts to a void inarticulate self, a mumbling, better, shouting insistence of striving thereness. The freelance self is what it is (first love) in virtue of what it denies any self can be—a giving source supporting the other as other (second love).

To see society as ethically neutral goes in hand with a reduction of the other to a mere means, with a totalized instrumental sense of being. This is a dangerous abstraction, for we are tempted to remake society in its image, and then take what we have made as an eternal fact. No society, not even technological society that tends to embody this abstraction, is ever ethically neutral. Even the abstract ideal of instrumentalized desire is itself an ethical ideal that is prescribed as most conducive to happiness and in accord with our being. But our being is metaxological. If we understand what this means ethically, every civilization is the social embodiment of some idea of the good; essential to the civilized state is public commitment to its concrete implementation. An ethically neutral society would hardly deserve the name "civilized," for its attenuates just that public commitment. When society is an embodiment of the ideal, the self's commitment to it is justified; it is itself a manifestation of justice. The self loyal to its ethical civility is the guardian of the good already realized there, and a fastness of its promise for the future.[37]

On Justice and Power

Genuine ideals are never merely regulative; in naming the living actuality of our ethical promise, they are constitutive. Again the dualism of "is" and "ought" is not to the point, in that as ethical desire we are the drive for the ideal, for the self-becoming of what we ought to be in the midst of community. One could agree with Hume that there is no logical deduction of "ought" from "is," were the "fact" at issue not the human self, and were one's concern simply with logical deduction. But the open fact of our metaxological being (the "is") is ethical desire for the worthy, the valuable (what "is to be"). The imperative of the ideal is the constitutive charge of the ethical that immanently articulates the unfolding of our desire as human. Far from being a sentimental singing of "sweetness and light," the constitutive idealism of the ethical self, as free desire, allows the possibility of its own failure and deformation. We must consider this.

The metaxological sense of ethical being involves no blinking of the "reality" of our refusal of the ethical charge of second love. Hence also ethical civility entails no blinking of carnivorous society. Our double view of desire, in fact, demands we acknowledge both sides. Ethical mindfulness also means self-knowledge of our refusal to be ethical. There is nothing wrong with power per se; the difficulty is its ethical mediation. Rightly understood, virtue is power, as Aristotle and Spinoza imply.[38] The peace of ethical civility is sought in the full knowledge of the devastating possibilities of civil war.

In some fashion, every society tries to order its subjects' energies along the lines of unsurprising, domestic forms of behavior. It regularizes human power, making us predictable, disciplined, liable to control. It extracts the sacrifice of alarming eccentricity to safeguard the concord of the daily. Inevitably there is leveling of sheer particularity, and blunt, unmediated differences. But there is always a contentious recalcitrance that can never be entirely erased. Every person, in its deepdown self, thinks itself someone special, someone different. This sense of difference grows out of the inward thisness of the self's own otherness. On the ethically affirmative side, the self's sense of its own intrinsic dignity follows from this inward otherness. But the ambiguity here is that this inward otherness is, by its very nature, resistant to the pressure of certain forms of social renunciation. Some social sacrifices seek a self-denial, repudiation of the kernel self-insistence that ontologically defines the being of the self. Nor need social pressure take the form of rational persuasion. Persuasion works only if there is a prior willingness, that is, if the self has already opened itself to the renunciation.

Most often the pressure takes the form of force. This may be overt, it may be subtle. Often a hint of threat is enough to unlock the needed fear. Then fear of being different provides the power to dissolve difference; we then simulate a sameness to preserve ourselves against external threats. But since we are still devoid of the self-transformation coming from ethical civility, our essential ontological self-insistence continues to foment, now taking the form of conformism, or else worming its way to a subterranean source. This is the truth of Nietzsche's view of herd man, or Thrasymachus' view of the lambs; they camouflage their self-insistence as altruism. Dostoevski lays bare the rancor towards others, indeed being as a whole, stemming from this impotent subterranean self-insistence, resentful and spiteful because of its own self-suppression. In the Underground Man he shows us this self-insistence, full of arrogance and abjectness, swinging between hatred of others for not recognizing its specialness or dignity, and hatred of itself for cowardice in not giving direct expression to its own secret will-to-power.

It must be said, and said again: this is what we are. But it also must be said, and in our time again and again: this is not all we are. Desire's metaxological doubleness means that our self-relation and relatedness to others are always permeated with dangerous ambiguity. To be ethical in the sense of *phronēsis* is to be discerning with respect to this ambiguity. We see this ambiguity in common ways we talk about our ethical and political relatedness. On the one hand, our relations will be understood in "idealistic" terms. It will be said that communities are formed because no individual is self-sufficient; as Aristotle said, we are by nature political. Our being, in its essential expression, is defined by our relatedness to others. So even if we do sacrifice some of secret desire, the price spent is repaid with interest; we only sacrifice part of ourselves to gain greater benefits from participation in the larger community. One need not subscribe to any contract theory, but it does touch the truth that our relatedness to others is often infected with hidden self-interest. We give up a little freedom for ourselves to attain increased liberty with others. On an initial investment the social bond gives a return far exceeding the first outlay. On the other hand, the language of calculation is noticeable in this effort to idealize our self-interested relatedness to others. The element of "realism," even in this idealized picture, cannot be concealed. The sacrifice of self is calculated.

Now suppose someone insistently refuses to be a joiner? There will be those who see through the "idealistic" rhetoric of the "contract," those who think that the preservation of their insistent particularity will pay them better, perhaps even those who, protecting *another* idealism, will find a deeper dignity in their free difference. It then becomes less easy to gild relations. Against the sheer obstinacy of refusal to join, the social tolerance of difference will quickly sour. This will be true even of societies, like Western democracies, that shout their unswerving respect for the differences of individuals. The plain message of this shout will be sameness. If the message is not heard or heeded, sanctions will be introduced, all with the aim of quickly bringing the rebellious individual to heel. If still unbending, rebels can be broken when they cannot be moulded. The beckoning hand of friendship swiftly twists itself into a fist of force. The hand that before caressed, now sharply slaps.

Men abide together. We abide one another. The very word "abide" carries the doubleness of desire in the metaxological. On the one hand, we "abide" the other, when we really cannot "abide" the other. That is, we barely tolerate their difference, when really we would be rid of it, if at all possible. On the other hand, we "abide" *with* the other, when we dwell by their side, finding ourselves at home there, committing ourselves to them in loyalty, offering to the other our willing constancy, finding the same offering of willingness reciprocated. To abide together thus is to make an abode for selves in just community, an ethical shelter.

Thus, our metaxological "togetherness" is itself the concrete union of harmony and conflict. Were our "togetherness" pure harmony, "togetherness" would itself vanish, for it is possible only given the differences of those who are together. To erase differences entirely might melt a many into a mass but would not constitute a community. This is the collectivist error—totality without differences. Paradoxically, pure harmony—were it a complete, dissolving conformity—would destroy the very basis of common life. Needless to say, we also destroy common life if differences are turned into unrelieved oppositions, as we find in certain forms of predatory individualism. We find such opposition in Hobbes' *bellum omnium contra omnes*, or in Sartre's claim that the essence of human relations is conflict. Hell is the other indeed, if the other is merely a threat or curb on my asserted absolute freedom. Such freedom is an absolute in the void, or a void absolute, that is hell. Socrates, however, rightly pointed out that some unity of harmony is necessary even among a gang of robbers, if they are to be successful even as criminals. Otherwise they could not properly organize and pursue their crime. Among successful thieves there must be some honor. The pursuit of injustice is parasitical upon some just order of harmony. Without this order the conflict between human beings becomes an enmity that first will devour its antagonists and then finally itself.[39]

Social relations are living tensions that reflect our intermediate being, tensions in which self-interest and care for others must be encompassed in a balanced order. Friendship and force, harmony and hostility, faith and distrust strive together in the middle. The living tension affords no bland balance or mean. Ideally the tension tips towards trust, but realistically an ineradicable suspicion tilts unrelentingly the other way. This intertwining in tension also effects the promise of ethical civility. Everybody may gain *if* the laws are good, and *if* they are respected and obeyed. But both these "ifs" are wild cards in the game. The laws may not be just; even if just, cunning self-interest will still secretly sprout. The laws will not be standards of justice but treated as instruments of self-advancement, weapons in a cold war against others. They will be denied intrinsic respect; the game will be to break the law and escape retribution. Instead of ethical civility we resurrect Thrasymachus with the Ring of Gyges.

Hence, laws as standards of justice will call out for sanctions. They must *impose* themselves against opposition. People see the lawless escaping with immunity and ask: If one gets away with lawlessness, perhaps most others do too, and so why not me also? If this ethical mistrust becomes widespread, laws become suspect and their power to civilize is blunted. To stop the slide into lawlessness, the threat of punishment inevitably emerges as a brute barrier. For even at the heart of ethical civility the Giants will continue to work their mischief. Law civilizes our brutality but never completely defeats it. In the ideal they embody standards of justice, but in the real order they call upon the threat of force to protect themselves against the brutal force out of which they initially emerged. Idealistically, society would persuade us to love justice; realistically, it must enforce conformity, albeit outward conformity, to its standards of civility. So also in the practice of its ideals, a society will sometimes betray these ideals, but with the best intention of enabling their continued realization. This seems to me an unavoidable conflict or antinomy: to humanize man's brutal power, man must turn this brutal power against himself, albeit in the name of civilized ideals. Power must be used to defeat the abuse of power. But what protects the corrective use of power from itself being abusive is not at all univocally clear.

No rational Hegelian *Aufhebung* or Marxist Utopia that claims to pass absolutely beyond this aporia into final social harmony offers itself as an unproblematic solution.[40] The aporia is not a mere provisional equivocalness but rather a constitutive ambiguity calling for the metaxological mindfulness of practical wisdom. Law asks for obedience and respect, but when obedience is coerced through the fear of power, respect is decreased and in the long run ethical civility is weakened. Our free desire resents (resentment albeit expressed in perverse refusal) the non-recognition of its dignity by the other (non-recognition albeit buttressed by the massive authority of power). Free selfhood has to find, or be offered, a place of consent within the palaces of power. If the sanction is enforced unjustly, the law, far from being preserved in its respect, becomes infected with internal instability. It is almost impossible in some situations of conflict to know in advance whether the sanction will not itself be swamped by its own use of brute power, or whether it will preserve a precarious stockade of civilization where the jungle fails to penetrate. The very notion of an ethical "stockade" goes against the metaxological call of universal openness to otherness. But the difficulty always remains while ethical civility uses or has to use the weapons of its antagonists to preserve itself. Then the despoiling jungle is *within* the fragile clearing, roots itself in the civilized stockade itself. Adapting Rousseau, we must sometimes be forced to be civilized, but force and civility strain against each other. Justice must emerge freely from power, but how can justice use power, and yet be above power?

V. ETHICAL COMMUNITY AND RECALCITRANT OTHERNESS

Malign(ed) Others: Criminals, Wolfmen

This question brings us to an extreme, namely, the question of social others that seem recalcitrant to mediation within ethical community. Some selves inevitably fall outside the social normalization that mitigates the destructive possibility of difference. Some fall outside by virtue of exaggerated powers, developing their energies to extremes and ending up as marginals. The poet, philosopher and saint might be seen as benign marginals, though sound commonsense will call them misfits. The poet can specialize imagination beyond the normal, perhaps to the point of an overripe, decadent sensibility. The philosopher can develop reflective thought, sometimes to the point of lostness in abstraction. The saint can awaken our sleeping goodwill to being in the direction of the universal, though his serene amen on the all will look like a blind benevolence, an agapeic idiocy.

By contrast, the criminal falls outside by epitomizing an ethical recalcitrance that the law finds difficult to normalize. Society makes a different norm for the criminal but one on the margins of ordinary society. The outsider here is an outlaw, for the powers the criminal develops are destructive of common life. The criminal is not a misfit merely, but a danger, worse, an enemy. He is the never defeated, carnivorous self that ever survives untempered even in ethical civility, ineradicable descendent of the Giants even in these later times when humans are normal sized. The criminal is the other that is hated, the malign(ed) other.

The ambiguous doubleness of the middle is again evident. Because the despised other is an other, the criminal also draws our interest, and in a hidden manner, the hatred other may also be loved. Thus the criminal was a *sacred* figure for archaic man, an other who, in order that normality be restored, must be *desecrated*. So also thinkers and imaginative writers have sometimes displayed an almost inordinate fascination with the criminal, as if he were *their own* dangerous other. We come across it in Dostoevski's *Crime and Punishment*, a profoundly revealing work that explores the tangled recesses of moral guilt. Nietzsche gave thought to the "pale criminal," investing him with some of his own contempt for mass man. Nietzsche's "splendid blond beast" as *homo natura* carries some of the criminal glamor of the wolfman. One also recalls Sartre's apotheosis of "Saint Genet," though interestingly enough, criminal Jean Genet, when he had become an acceptable, literary celebrity, did not at all appreciate Sartre's canonization.[41]

This mingling of fear and fascination with the felonious self also marks the dutiful, law abiding citizen. The criminal interrupts, ruptures normalized life, sometimes displaying an outstanding daring, or cunning or perhaps desperation. We dutiful ones cannot remain cold, we who quieten our desperation and talk ourselves out of daring. We rummage for deeper motive for this otherness, this abnormal difference. We scan the face in the dock for remorse, plot the psychology of the accused, allow ourselves the costless luxury of judgment.[42] Sometimes the fascination becomes a romanticization, a glamorization. The outlaw is not really an outlaw; he really is Robin Hood; the official supposed to embody the law, the Sheriff of Nottingham, is really the villain. Genuine justice has retreated to the unpoliced margins, the green forests. From them will spring the criminal as society's savior, for the green man is a vegetable god. The criminal that seems to be a carnivorous self is secretly a preserver of vegetarian ethics. Indeed this mythology of the outlaw may embody an ethical response, a needed utopian protest, an outburst of indignation against social conditions that deprive one of ethical dignity.

The criminal's ethical otherness meets with different responses. Two common responses hold that the otherness can be mediated, albeit in different ways. First, a liberal view traces the criminal's fall to poverty of social background; he is essentially reactive to intolerable circumstances. Remove this degradation and the social source that generates the criminal will also vanish. Society is the disabling otherness, not the individual criminal's refusal of justice for the other. This view, correspondingly, tends to diminish the element of retribution in the law; prison is to reform, rehabilitate, not to punish, penalize. A second, less liberal view traces his fall to something *within* the criminal himself, namely, his perverse free will: essential responsibility belongs to him as a being of ethical inwardness. No external condition, no social otherness forces one to crime; rather in the flawed choice of the inward otherness, we uncover the source. Many have been exposed to unjust conditions, but most have not become criminals; nothing external necessitates. These two views see the criminal as falling outside the communal norm, but think that, except for adverse external circumstances or an internal aberrant choice, he would otherwise want acceptance within the normal community. Whether due to free inwardness or conditioning social otherness, the criminal otherness can still be mediated, whether through punishment or rehabilitation. Thus, the criminal is the *deviant* who, as deviant, refers back to the norm, and indeed in breaking the norm tends to indirectly justify it. The fact that he "falls" indicates that there is yet, as it were, a state of social "grace."

But just as being ethical is not exhausted in social normality, we must ask if there a third kind of criminal, recalcitrant in a deeper degree, one who does not just deviate from an otherwise acceptable social norm, one who would smash all such norms, and not just for "rational" self-interested gain but for the sheer pleasure of destruction? Are there criminals whose recalcitrance is ingrained in the texture of their being, those who make a virtue of their complete refusal—of any norm? Is there a self of satanic refusal, like Milton's Lucifer who will say "evil be thou my good?" The liberal utilitarian cannot help. Consider what is termed the "hardened" criminal. We often mean by this someone in whom the criminal impulse has *become* ingrained. This "hardened" criminal may once have been innocent; the liberal can offer an interpretation of this "hardening." But is there a different, more radical "hardness," almost if there was never any innocence to be lost? If there is such a one, he is not thus by bad choice that can be corrected, nor necessitated to crime by social conditions that can be alleviated. He would be destined to crime, the way another might have a vocation for priesthood, like Pinky the child Satan of Graham Greene's *Brighton Rock*. One thinks about the motiveless malignity of Shakespeare's Iago. One asks about a person in whom, as if from the outset, the wrathful self had surged up and swamped in images of blood the self of second love.

This third possibility fascinates us as one who personifies *radical evil* with respect to ethical community. He seems the complete negation of social grace, the absolute repudiation of normalcy, a living waste of lawlessness, a wild will that cannot be tempered with justice. He is a Lucifer before the law, or the perverse form of the Wrath of God. What fascinates us is the pure freedom of absolute refusal, or the absoluteness of the will in its negating power. The "I" here is absolute willfulness, but like Milton's Satan its absoluteness is a mimicry of divinity.

Admittedly, many people too quickly see the complete criminal in any slight deviation. The thought of the outsider brings terror which, in turn, we visit on persons strange and out of the way. This terror has its source as much in us as in the other. But most things that are terrifyingly strange are merely unfamiliar and a brief tolerance will make them domestic and benign again. Patience will disarm these bogus alarms. Many deviants would welcome domestication with a little tepid friendship. Generally, they meet rebuff and are consigned again to the margins. Thus, in their mutual interplay the normal self and the deviant come to define each other dialectically.[43] Thus, one reason why some intellectuals have idolized the criminal is because of their own contempt for those who sit in judgment. Secretly the Judge may harbor as much evil as the criminal displays openly. King Lear, wise in his madness, saw this. The dog denies the wolf in himself and sits in judgment on his brother. The irony is that such intellectuals, with their burning contempt for bourgeois normalcy, become avant-garde Judges.

The complete criminal is one wholly other to, I almost said, your decent deviant. The decent deviant can be placed, but the complete criminal calls from wastes of nowhere. The complete criminal is the wolfman who makes a virtue of his vice. The dog in his kennel hears the wolf howling in the wilderness. He is disturbed by this voice from the desolate, sightless night. He is attracted and repulsed. Attracted: after all the wolf is his brother, even if untamed. Repulsed: this kennel is cosy, and besides, the meals of tomorrow are safe. Should the dog remember his own security, he will hate the wolf for unsettling his quiet. I cannot see us approaching the perfection of the ethical without acknowledging our fraternity with the wolfman. Being radically evil is a limit possibility in being ethical: a negative otherness against which all "mediations" seem to break, an impasse of ethical failure.

How is one to deal with the impasse? Beyond this "breakdown" the only "breakthrough" seems to be "forgiveness," "pardon." These are "intermediations" beyond "mediation," in the sense of "sacrifices" of the natural tendency, springing from the self-insistence of first love, to hatred of the malign(ed) other. Forgiveness is an unweaving of this hatred at the limit of all "mediations." In the risk of the latter's failure, it is a breakthrough of second love, the simple love of being as good, open to the promise of the other, despite the other's radical negativity. It is a breaking through into trust, though this trust may not be reciprocated or be abused. What unconditionally breaks through in real forgiveness is the ethical promise of trust as an ultimate openness to the malign(ed) other. This is a promise without guarantees, almost impossible for us to rationalize. It takes us to the boundary of the ethical. It asks too much of us, an excess, an agapeic idiocy, but finally it alone make metaxological sense.

Dostoevski's Christ knew deeply the heart of the criminal, but also the heart of the Grand Inquisitor, the Judge.[44] In the Grand Inquisitor's condemnation of Christ as a criminal, Dostoevski gave us a most profound symbol of the forked doubleness at the heart of ethical desire. For here we see the togetherness in the perverse middle of the ethical opposites: cold hatred of the good, masked as the good; forgiveness of all evil, execrated as evil. We might rest relieved if the wolfman were out there. But suppose we carry the wild into the sanctuary of ethical civility? Suppose there is a Siberia of spirit and that the damned are its frozen dead, though in their social lives they survive too sleekly? What if the wolfman is the manicured self beside you at the symphony?[45]

The Gyre of Energy

I conclude this chapter with what (with a bow to Vico) I call the gyre of energy. This will serve to recapitulate and be a metaphor for the ethical rhythm of rise and fall in terms of the fourfold sense of ethical being. In the beginning there is virgin energy, in the end there is energy again, at first fulfilled but soon souring in exhaustion. In the middle there is the struggle to shape the energy of being, whether of inwardness or otherness, and give it just form. Here is an attempt to plot its gyre.

Though placed immediately in the metaxological community of being, the energy of our being begins as barbarous power. In the *univocal* insistence of primitive desire, the barbarous self feels the energy coursing through its being. It gratifies that desire, again through energy, energy discharged in assertive will. Obstacles to the expression of the energy of self-being, barriers to elemental drive are smashed down when not surmounted. But barbarous energy is indiscriminate. It is driven energy, not directed energy. Barbarous energy is all rudimentary drive, but because it lacks any definite ideals it is not clearsightedly desire at all. It is driven towards everything but beyond a few needful things, does not mindfully seek anything else in particular. Univocal drive easily dissipates its power in an *equivocal* scattering of energy. The future is merely the void expanse wherein it discharges its rude marauding will. Excess of energy, frustrated by its own blindness tends to turn to violence. Energy becomes wild will. Vandals, and I do not just mean the Teutonic tribe, are caught in this gyre of barbarous energy and repeat its destructive cycle.

The energy of being becomes discriminately directed when it takes the form of mind. It escapes endless oscillation between univocity and equivocity. Intelligent energy gives eyes to blind drive and cultures the insistence of rudimentary will. The energy of our being becomes ethical in the form of *dialectical self-mediation* and *metaxological intermediation* with otherness. With this, desire discriminates itself into the two loves—self-love and love of others. Mindfulness civilizes energy. Initially energy is self-centered, but civilizing mind expands the discernment of this center. It expands it by undertaking projects of practical intelligence: the jumble of nature is progressively subdued and on it human order put. Barbarous energy is formed, transformed by human work that taps nature's power, expands human potency, gives aimless desire a definite direction, mediates our dignity and the humanizing of time.

Mind humanizes barbarous energy by both bending it back upon itself (self-mediation) and intermediating a more radical respect for otherness. It allows energy to reflect upon itself, become informed by self-knowledge, but also mediates increasing openness to otherness. The deepening in the middle of our self-knowing openness to otherness hears the call for an ethical concord of the individual and community. Elementary communities tend to dissolve the individual in the community, thus minimizing the outbursts of the barbarous energy. As it becomes more settled and secure, civilized community will become more mature and assured, and make growing room for the just liberty of the individual. But in this space for individual liberty, barbarous energy may swell once more. Here we confront the sting of freedom. That is, the idealization of primitive energy effected by civilization, on reaching a rich formation, threatens to dissolve once more into the mother power of sheer vehement self-insistence. It is for this reason that democracies are vulnerable to fascism and to totalitarianism that either repress the barbarous energy or earth it, diverting it into a rigidly regulated social whole. Unfortunately the barbarism is then only concentrated in the tyranny of the leader or distributed by him throughout the social whole.

Thus also civilizations when old are vulnerable to the untried, unweary energy of being of young barbarians. In the constant flux and reflux of the universal impermanence, societies rise, societies fall. They rise on the crest of the elemental energy of being; they form, harness, direct the energy; they are dissolved again when they exhaust their particular sources of power. A new tide swells that swamps the old forms in its new formlessness, making a compost to fertilize another beginning. An ethical hero may emerge, witness to an absolutely startling sacrificial benevolence. This is a rare singularity, a reminding sign of absoluteness.[46]

Below that peak but at the height of its civilized life, a community tries to marry power and justice. But even here the form of justice may stifle the sources of a people's power if, say, a managed society is paralyzed by the rituals of bureaucracy. This paralysis may even mask itself in the hyperactivity of instrumental selfhood, but the frenzy of instrumentalized life may spring from ontological exhaustion. This "dynamic" paralysis may equivocally mask itself in slogans about "progress," "expansion," "growth." Stasis may be sustained for long ages but always with diminishing vigor. Eventually the energy is choked, the form becomes an empty rubric. Sometimes the scream of exhausted life is shrillest at the climax of choking, and we are taken in by this deceptive, deadly burlesque of the energy of being. Sometimes the crumbling of foundations takes place in silence. No one knows until later when, perhaps under the onslaught of an external enemy, as if suddenly, the hollowness of the old life is exposed.

C H A P T E R   **5**

Being Mindful: Thought Thinking Its Other

Being aesthetic, religious and ethical are different configurations of being mindful, a term used before without being made an object of explicit reflection. Philosophy, too, is a distinctive mode of being mindful. Taking cognizance of these ways of being, I turn again to philosophy as metaxological mindfulness, that is, as thought thinking both itself and its others. An impatient reader may demand a univocal definition of being mindful. None can be given if mind is metaxological. Nor can mindfulness be fixed at the outset. As a way of being that thoughtfully relates to the otherness of being, it cannot be confined to any one mode of thinking or to philosophy itself. The being of mind is not that of a thing but of a mode of activity, plurally articulated. To be mindful is an exigency that issues its imperative in every significant way of being, including those other to philosophy. In this and the next chapter we will see the breakdown of that insistence on univocal identity that would pigeonhole philosophy and its others in the interests of preventing philosophy from being contaminated by its others. Listening to the voices of otherness, philosophy's own voice must become plurivocal.

By its nature philosophy risks being merely abstract thought. In pursuit of the meaning of being, the philosopher can become unanchored from being, producing an abstract reflection that is ontologically deracinated. This is hard to avoid, for essential to the philosophical quest is a no to merely blind, immediate immersion in ways of being. This need not preclude a more ultimate yes, but such a yes has to win through to a more nuanced understanding of the essential ways of being. The skepticism necessary to all philosophical thought can degenerate into a merely debunking negativity. But as we have seen, the unanchored negativity that can result from the dialectic of trust and distrust is not philosophy's preserve. The aesthetic courts it when it tries to swallow its own tail in postmodern irony. It lurks in the precariousness of religion as reduced to an inwardness, so lost in itself that it fails to find a home in the natural cosmos or in the public community actually sustaining this inwardness, Kierkegaardian protests notwithstanding. We ethically risk it with the abstract calculative self of utilitarian desire. Being mindful points to something more than any such unanchoring, be it aesthetic, religious, ethical, or philosophic. What is called for is a mode of being mindful that in reflective thought is beyond merely debunking negativity, restorative of a sense of metaxological being in its elemental thereness.

I speak of thought thinking its *other* with explicit self-consciousness that the philosophical tradition has tended to privilege thought thinking *itself.* Consider Plato's view of thought as the dialogue of the soul alone with itself, or Aristotle's *noēsis noēseōs*, or Descartes' *cogito me cogitare*, or Hegel's post-Kantian reformulation of the matter in terms of the self-generating and self-thinking Idea. I am concerned with thinking the otherness of being as resisting categorization in terms of any dualistic opposition of inside/outside, subject/object. Thought thinking itself is necessary and unavoidable; this is the self-mediation of mind. But in this self-mediation, the other of thought is manifest within thought again; hence no simple dualistic model of interiority/exteriority will work. The very being of the thinking self, even as self-mediating, exhibits its own *inward otherness.* Thinking here does not yield a Cartesian self-transparency, for the otherness of the thinking self resists encapsulation in clear and distinct concepts. The question is: In granting this resistance, can we break through to a bond between this inward otherness and the other otherness of being as such, a bond deeper than any dualistic opposition? I will say yes, but we must pass through a breakdown of monological thought, or imperialistic subjectivity, and of fixated objectivity. In this breakdown there can occur a breakthrough of the original energy of being in both the self and the other that is prior to their objectification and dualistic opposition, that supports even this opposition, and that ultimately is beyond any such dualism as an excess or transcending "more" that is never absolutely encapsulated.

This ontological bond between selfness and otherness cannot be fully articulated in terms of univocal identity, equivocal difference or dialectical self-mediation. This bond is what throughout I have called the metaxological community of being, of which we have seen aesthetic, religious, and ethical manifestations. This community is not a bland medium but the place where we must face the *extremes.* So in this and the next chapter, I explore the limits of thought's effort at absolute self-mediation, and how metaxological otherness always breaks through such self-mediation. There is a nonobjectifiable sense of being manifest in innerness and outerness and in the different ways of being as metaxological. The limits of self-mediating thought in relation to being's otherness force philosophy to the limits of middle being. Such limits are not just "out-there." They are "in" the middle, in so far as there we must deal with our own inward otherness and our participation in being's otherness. As a way of being mindful, philosophy must be true to thought in its doubleness. If we try to reduce the metaxological middle to closed self-mediation, we invite a breakdown of the middle. This breakdown can be both negative and positive: negative, in unweaving the closure of hubristic self-mediation; positive, in allowing a breakthrough in the middle of the universal energy of being, universal in the sense of grounding the community or togetherness of beings. Within this community is possible an open wholeness of being, intermediate between Hegelian totality and Wittgensteinian diversity (cf. introduction). In breakthrough there is an eruption of the absolute in the middle that unsettles the middle and thrusts our intermediate being towards its ontological extremes.

In this chapter, I pursue the matter in three metaphysical meditations on these related themes: being logical, solitude, and failure. The first meditation concerns a sense of being's otherness as resistant to conceptual instrumentalization, otherness emergent as much within such instrumentalization as beyond it. The second meditation concerns the breakdown of monological thought in the very inward otherness of self-mediation. The third meditation concerns the suffering of otherness at the limit of instrumentalized selfhood and the possible release there of deeper mindfulness. My point in the first will be that mindfulness cannot be exclusively determined as being logical: thought rocks back on its own limitation in relation to the otherness of being that resists complete logical categorization. Yet this does not destroy but deepens our sense of the metaxological community of being and mind. Likewise, in the second and third meditations, solitude and failure bring thought, as pretending to total self-mediation, close to a breaking point. Indeed solitude and failure have always haunted philosophy as bringing its self-mediating thought to a breaking otherness.

In all previous chapters we tried also to understand the possible deformation of the different ways of being mindful. We must not now forget the potentially nihilistic aspects of this and turn our back on the difficulty. We must stand in the negative, as it were, and not flinch before its sundering power. We must ask if, in allowing the negative its play, there can come certain moments of fundamental reversal in the midst of the negativity itself; ask if the latter's sundering power must lead to nihilism, or whether breakdown leads to an affirmative breakthrough of the metaxological community of being. This chapter then will be something of a negative way. But this breaking on otherness need not imply thought's utter humiliation. Becoming mindful of being broken we may break through into something other. Hence the next chapter will speak of being mindful as thought *singing* its other. These two chapters must be taken together as addressing the double requirement of metaxological thought. This chapter will primarily ask about the limits of instrumentalized mind and being; the next will concern those breakthroughs that transcend instrumental justification and name the intrinsic worth of being.

I will not labor the notions of the univocal, the equivocal, the dialectical in the quasi-linear fashion of previous chapters. Nor will I overtly organize my reflection in terms of the movement from immediacy to self-mediation to intermediation. By now we have sufficient sense of these as systematic ordering concepts. I am now concerned primarily with the limits of self-mediation in relation to the complex space *between* self-mediation and our intermediation with recalcitrant being. We must hover ruminatively in the ambiguous space between limitation and release. There the appropriate mode of discourse is not simple straightforward conceptual analysis that would reduce the ambiguity to systematic univocity. The plurivocity of metaxological thought, in relation to the limits of self-mediation, and to the plenitude of original being as in excess of dialectic, is reflected in my stress on *metaphysical meditations*. Such meditations imply the contemplation of nonobjectifiable limits, and the search for more releasing thought that sings the otherness of being.

I. FIRST MEDITATION: BEING MINDFUL AND LOGIC

Logic, Mind and Unruly Otherness

Philosophers have an inveterate tendency to think of being mindful as being logical, but if we respect the otherness of the different ways of being, this has to be reconsidered. While philosophical mindfulness demands fidelity to logos, I will say that neither mind nor logos can be reduced to instrumental rationality. The latter in a first movement formalizes itself in abstraction from being, and in a second movement exploits its categoreal forms as logical tools for the manipulation of being in its otherness. Fidelity to logos breeds a deeper mindfulness of the community of being and thought in which there appears the failure, certainly limit of instrumentalized reason, and the need for a more patient thought respecting being in its otherness. First I will remark generally on the distrust of logic. I will remark on the self-mediation of analytical thought (corresponding to univocity) and the other that Nietzsche called "woman" (corresponding to equivocity). In a second reflection, I consider being as a disruptive otherness, and in a third reflection I ask about this disruption in relation to the issue of power.

In our time we find a distrust of logic, or if distrust is too strong a word, certainly an ambivalence towards it, even among philosophers. I mean logic in a broad sense, logic as epitomizing a general rationalizing approach to being. Logic in the specialized sense is a particular discipline, akin to mathematics, concerned with the forms of valid reasoning, a discipline which has seen a great flowering in our century. Distrust of logic in the broad sense articulates a wariness of all claims made on behalf of reason. What is striking is that this distrust is pervasive in an age whose life-forms are massively mediated by the sophisticated products of logic in the specialized sense — as in the invasion of, certainly encroachment on, all being by the "cybernetic revolution." Among the sources of this distrust is the fact that we have witnessed barbarous deeds on a monstrous scale defying every rationalization. We have known war on a global scale and in the face of its brutality, logic seems frail, naive, ineffectual. War undermines our sense of the reasonable nature of things and saps our confidence in rational thought. This confidence was still relatively innocent in previous centuries. Especially during the Enlightenment, the so-called Age of Reason, widespread faith in Reason saw it as a benign universal power present in all. Moreover, it might be applied to life to ameliorate the conditions of existence. Against the confusions of ages-old ignorance, the prejudices of corrupt customs, the fanaticism and superstition of religions in strife, logic was a mighty force to make life more humane, a revolutionary power which, cleansing heads of darkness, would inevitably culminate in progression to a better state. To be logical was to be borne along and washed by waves of Progress.[1]

We now know better. The Age of Reason was an age of innocence, that is to say, an age of stupidity. Out of pure reason exploded again and again pure unreason. Dostoevski squats on our shoulder in the figure of his hideous, toadish creation, the Underground Man, and sneers: the innocent babes! the pure innocent babes! The Underground Man is the incubus of Enlightenment reason, the haunting night terror that Enlightenment cannot exterminate. More soberly, we now know that progress bequeaths its ambiguous heritage, its dark other. Gain here brings loss there; what once we discarded with alacrity now returns to nag us with nostalgia. We do not see the pearl in hand and, rushing futureward, frenzied with faith in Progress, it spins loose beyond retrieve. Should we try to stand still, the momentum of the impersonal rush would crush us. Mixed with the bread of Progress we are sometimes handed stones. The check of their barren weight stalls our flight. In the pause is sown our reluctance for logic.

In the nineteenth century, a reaction had already set in against this version of reason, with its now familiar overtones of technicist control and calculative exploitation of the earth.[2] The heart asserted its rights, often against the logic of the head, and Romanticism unloosed the unruly. *Aufklärung* dialectically gave rise to Romanticism as its own other and, as we shall see below, the dialectical interplay of the two does not complete the process of Enlightenment, but rather furthers the self-deconstruction of logicism. Many thinkers may now scorn both Romantic unruliness and

Enlightenment logic, but though soured by the excesses of both, we still bob in their backwash.

We can neither abandon logic nor worship it. We cannot worship it because we are still brushed with Romanticism. We know the wild side of humankind. We have witnessed the masses of wolfmen running as numberless packs, otherwise called nations. Only inexcusable forgetfulness can blind us to the crack in the bright mirror and the glimpse of black things that crawl below. Nor can we abandon reason. Instrumental mind can bypass the heart of the matter, but we cannot sink face-flat into soggy confusion. We dream only in short spurts; at other times it is imperative to be lucid and alert. Calls to celebrate the irrational eventually croak, but we still hunger for reasonable order in being. To be mindful in the sense I intend is not to sacrifice but to enrich reason, deepen it in its bond with what reason itself cannot absolutely encapsulate. To speak alertly the heart's turbulence is not to be just swamped by it. In a sense, reason's other is internally related to reason; but it is so, not as an other to be logically mastered, but as an other that always unsettles from *within* all of reason's own claims to absolute self-mediation.

I here note a certain oscillation between a logicism operating under the aegis of univocity and an anti-logicism permeated by equivocity. Today the heart's turbulence may seem muted, if not silenced, to the extent that precision of thought is associated with computers. For these are technological materializations of the kinds of reasoning amenable to logical formalization. In fact, the issues here are older than the "cybernetic revolution" that only culminates the development of a mode of logical thinking that has been a dominant, recurring potentiality for the Western mind. This is the element of truth in Heidegger's view of the technological *Gestell* as the latest episode in thr story of Western logos. I disagree with Heidegger's *totalization* of the tradition as an imperialistic "logocentrism," yet what is intended by logocentrism is undoubtedly a primary configuration of mind in that tradition. But great philosophers such as Plato and Hegel are reminders of a wider mindfulness, exemplars of what I called heroic thinking (cf. chapter l) for whom reason cannot be boxed into the polemical category of logocentrism. With such thinkers logos at its best lives ambiguously in dialogue with its others, especially art and religion, and therefore as participant in metaxological being. There is no univocal totalizable tradition; rather we find a plurality of possibilities in incessant interplay. Undoubtedly now a technicist, calculative reason asserts a sway over the mind, but this version of reason exhausts neither reason, nor being mindful, nor can it do justice to philosophy's metaxological interplay with its others.[3]

To illustrate this oscillation between univocity and equivocity, I shift from the pomp of world history and the epochs of being, and put the matter in terms of a contrast between Nietzsche's woman and the type that ordinary parlance playfully dubs the logic-chopper. The logic-chopper, if not quite a Platonic archetype, is certainly a recurring type, a recognizable reduction of being mindful to a certain analytical, one might say, legalistic precision. We find shades of the type in Zeno's dialectic, in the sophist's eristic, in the method of *diairesis* of Plato's Eleatic Stranger, in Socrates even, in Abelard's medieval dialectic of *sic et non*, in present day analytical philosophers. There is here the risk of caricature, but the recent polemic regarding logocentrism, I suspect, feeds of an even less sophisticated strawman. The logicist names a type who insists on an ideal of univocal precision in terms, often regardless of the case being argued. He casuistically divides up the case, confident of the numberless distinctions he introduces, as sure of the confusion of others as in his own efficient and unfaltering power to clarify. Casually toss him a question and like a dog worrying a bone he will tirelessly set to work, taking apart, analyzing, probing for tender ambiguities, triumphantly detecting gross fallacies and specious reasonings in his rival disputants. He is a virtuoso of technical analysis, a hardheaded, no-nonsense man of mind. The lips curl in a slight sneer of superiority when the dread judgment is pronounced on the devastated opponent: your ideas are "woolly." This is the ultimate put down for the analyst, naming the failure of the logos of the other to attain univocity.

We can be soothed, even consoled by this logical assurance. I am all vague perplexity, but this manicured surgeon of puzzles brings a sharp scalpel to my cancerous muddle. (Someone once said A. J. Ayer had a stainless steel mind.) We are a mass of fudgers, but he calls a spade a spade, trims words of their nebulous waffle, pinions our deceits—colorful butterflies encased for categoreal display, alas now dead. The logic-chopper is a species of warrior.[4] If we find ourselves on the same side in the conflict, we feel protected and secure. If we do not take sides but are a neutral third party, his cool virtuosity still attracts. Even when we are victims of his dialectic, secretly we cannot helped being awed, or better, cowed by this self-assurance of logical expertise. If he makes his opponents uneasy, he seems securely at ease with his own mind and its capacity for univocal clarity. Logic puts him in the fray but also places him above it. Being clearheaded, being in control of what one means by one's words, being on guard to seductive equivocation, not being a vague mind that wanders: these are virtues drawing us to the logical mind. We love logic because we love definiteness.[5]

But there is an insistence on being logical which, when we think about it, is slightly illogical. Given the apotheosis of univocal logic here, it is ironic that we react ambivalently. Why should our admiration have its undertow of unease? One thing his univocity should *not* do is make us react with *equivocity*. And yet we are filled with ambivalence. Something about this cool mind leaves us cool; it has cast the net of univocity into the teeming seas, but the catch it draws does not empty the ocean.

We are perversely equivocal about his univocal logic, mindful of the obstinate ambiguity of the otherness of the human and of being. Moreover, this tincture of reservation cannot be specified with univocal precision. Instead one asks: Is the central clarity of the univocal mind not surrounded by a penumbra of shadow; around its stockade of definites, is there a jungle of indefineables, never to be completely beaten back? As we know, a hardheaded analyst in one thing is often a soft sentimentalist in another. With the head of iron goes a heart of mush. But there is no "logic" to the latter from the standpoint of the former. Thus, for instance, the concept of "wooliness," used as a standard of unclarity, is itself a very "wooly" concept, not univocal at all! The standard by which univocity is judged is itself equivocal. It can happen, too, that we become so intoxicated with the intricate casuistry of discourse that we snap our contact with concrete being. We spin a web of words, but the gnat we spiders entrap is only ourselves.

This logicist is prim and proper about univocal concepts, but awkward with the recalcitrant indefinites of being.[6] We murder to dissect, Wordsworth said. Like a butcher, precision cuts (*praecisio* from the word to cut) a carcass along the joints. Organs vital to the living being are cast aside as cheap. The heart becomes a cut called "offal." If mind is exhausted by the univocal logic of analysis, was Pascal right to distinguish *l'esprit de finesse* from *l'esprit de géométrie*, and say the heart has reasons of which reason knows nothing? Something of this lies behind Nietzsche's judgment: dialectic in rabble. Something of it lurks in his teasing question: Suppose truth were a woman?

Thought thinking itself comes face to face with an other that resists and mocks. Univocity flips over to equivocity. The Nietzschean and now the Derridean presents woman to philosophy as the unruly other that breaches its logical self-possession. The conceptual closure of analytical self-mediation is burst and thrust beyond itself. Here intuition is often said to be a mode of mind opposite to analytical discursiveness. Women, it is said, is more intuitive than man, and this contrast is often expressed in quite physical terms. The man is logical because his thinking is hard, thrusting, aggressive; the woman is intuitive because her senses are soft, yielding, receptive. Man is mathematical form, woman is passive matter; man is Uranian and loves the gods; woman is Chthonic ("imitates the earth," Plato says) and loves man. Man prefers to fight his enemies in public, and logic is always a public weapon; woman gets her way through the inarticulate cunning of intuition. Man needs the subtleties spelt out for him; woman registers nuance effortlessly.[7]

This metaphorical contrast is implicit in the post-Heideggerian judgment on the tradition of philosophy: its logocentrism is really "phallogocentrism." We find it also in feminist criticisms of philosophy. In the unstable opposition of univocity and equivocity, an emphasis on the rigid unity of the first is quickly superseded by stress on the unmediated difference of the second. But this unstable oscillation is a recurrent possibility, as is evident in the fact that the contrast of the logical and intuitive is an old theme. Even granting philosophy's predilection for logic, one finds crucial acknowledgments of modes of mindfulness that strain against, if not transcend the limits of logic. Recognition of this strain and imperative of transcendence are essential to being mindful as a thinking, not only mediating with itself, but genuinely open to otherness. The other of logos can be granted by logos as its own unsettling limit.

Certainly philosophy appears to be a masculine enterprise *par excellence*, an adventure for the logical warrior who spends himself in the combat of argumentation, in the "cut and thrust" of dialectic. The sexual imagery, as metaphors of ways of being mindful, is difficult to suppress. We find feminine genius in religion and imaginative literature, but the great philosophers have been men, indeed mostly bachelors, Socrates excluded, until the married philosopher became more common since Hegel. Despite his sly insinuation, Nietzsche, too, laughed at the married philosopher as a comic grotesque; even Socrates' marriage was a joke, Nietzsche thought, his philosophical irony. Is it not true that past philosophers have sought to master themselves in ascetic solitude, and rivaling the priest, spoken suspiciously of the seductions of woman? Schopenhauer's diatribe against woman, a hyperbole not without venomous *Heiterkeit*, is only the most celebrated, excuse me, notorious instance of this genre.

And yet, Schopenhauer's misogyny notwithstanding, the intuitive principle was never entirely absent or banished. Indeed Sophia is often figured as a woman, a beautiful goddess. Parmenides, father of Greek logic and the univocal sense of being, is guided by the *Heliades Kourai* (daughters of the Sun) until the goddess, *Thea*, taking his hand, leads him on the way of truth (*Alētheia*). Plato, for some the archpriest of ascetic philosophers, says that the highest mode of mind is *noēsis*, intellectual intuition. This is higher than the logical discursiveness and mathematical ratiocination of *dianoia*, which is below *noēsis* on the divided line. This can be read to imply a subordination and transcendence of logicist univocity. *Dianoia* without *noēsis* would cause a degeneration of the Platonic philosopher into the logic-chopper. *Noēsis* is marked by a receptivity, a submissive openness to truth that is given from beyond, or that erupts from the order of transcendent otherness. This suggests that at the level of *noēsis* truth for Plato is woman; logos is not at all "phallogocentric."

Properly speaking, Plato's philosopher is beyond genital definition: a being of eros who, though driven by eros in the *metaxu*, is at the end beyond eros. Notice, too, that Plato's philosopher-rulers belong in a qualitatively different class to the warriors, the class most likely to pillage and rape if their will-to-power is not tempered by a superior wisdom that respects truth as other to human power. Truth is to be neither male nor female; truth is not to be ruled by the genitals. Philosophy's eros is not just the epiphenomenon of testosterone. Even Schopenhauer sought a will-less knowing, that is, a truth beyond the genitals which were, as he said, the metaphysical organs of the Will. This at least is the promise of the ideal, though in the realization, admittedly, the philosopher can be a conceptual codpiece.

Consider this further example. Did not Socrates, the hoplite, submit himself to a female sage, Diotima, for instruction in love's mysteries? Did he not compare, in mindful mimesis of his mother's profession, his own philosophical practice to that of a midwife? The midwife must have power to read the ambiguous signs of pregnancy, an intuitive power.[8] What appears in the middle is ambiguous; the ambiguity must be discriminated; but this means metaxological discernment, not an oscillation between univocity and equivocity. Similarly, the Socratic thinker must be able to recognize and identify those individuals with the promise of giving birth to more than a wind-egg. This is a hermeneutic matter of divining the complex character of the one before us, not a matter of arguing a general case. Beyond any logical definition of the philosopher in general, it requires a concrete identification of *this* individual as genuinely philosophical. Without this prior discrimination, subsequent argumentation may be formally valid but it also may prove contentless and sterile. To thus recognize a concrete "this" is not only to discriminate the middle's ambiguity, but is already to be beyond thought thinking only itself. It is to be concretely discerning about the other *as* other.[9]

But we find a caution about, even alarm at appeals to intuition because of the character of its claim to know. Frequently intuitive knowing is said to be immediate or direct. As the other of analysis, it is said to be knowing without concepts, sheer "seeing" without further justification and articulation. This seems to be its beautiful simplicity: it claims immediate certitude. But this is also its difficulty. Inevitably one will ask for an account (*logon didonai*). But this is already to move away from intuition per se, to move from immediate to *mediated* knowing. One may reply that one's insight is *self-evident*. This self-evidence might seem to satisfy the claim to univocal clarity; in fact it seems to generate a new equivocation. For since to some rational others, the intuition is not self-evident, one may either repeat the claim ("I know and that's that"), and then it seems an arbitrary assertion; or one may say that reason has nothing to do with it, but then too the intuition seems capricious. Intuition as putatively univocal now paradoxically seems equivocal; it seems to undercut the possibility of a shared community of different minds; no mediation between one mind and another seems possible. Intuition, then, seems purely idiosyncratic, something felt along the pulses which, nevertheless, cannot be pinned down, and which, moreover, seems to vanish when subjected to closer scrutiny. On its own, intuition sings dumb. It is this blank knowing of mute intuition, if you like this enigmatic dumb blonde, that draws and makes uneasy the masculinity of the logical mind.

Thought as analysis seeks to mediate the ambiguity of the immediate. This is to the point. But the logicist risks turning thought into the closed self-mediation of analytical discursivity. The issue is whether this mediation of ambiguity is to be effected solely under the aegis of univocity, and whether it can be effected purely by the self-mediation of thought thinking only itself. The answer is no, because to think its other, thought must become metaxological intermediation and not remain dialectical self-mediation. The answer is no, not only because Nietzsche's Lou Salomé says no, but because of the way Molly Bloom says yes.

Eros is not only difference, it is also congress. What separates, also comes together, Heraclitus said; truth is *sunousia*, Plato implied, being with, intercourse. Thus, as a logos of the metaxu, as metaxological, philosophical logos (from the verb *legein*) can mean both a "laying out" (the Greek *analusis* can mean a "loosing," "releasing"), and also a "gathering together." We can come upon this truth of the metaxological when mindful of its otherness to purely formal thought. This is not a matter of rejecting logic *tout court* or of repressing what is genuinely at stake in "intuition." It is a matter of freeing both from a false sense of opposition that in the end hinders philosophy from thinking what is other to any formal category.

Nor need the logical and intuitive be so dualistically set against each other. Though the goddess *reveals* the truth to Parmenides, she nevertheless enjoins him to judge the truth with logos (*krinai de logoi*). Every "seeing" at some point may evoke its appropriate interpretation, every significant immediacy its intermediation. It is tedious always to have to give an account, but intuition, be it genuine, will struggle to preserve and articulate its own significance. To be the mindfulness it implicitly claims to be, it must do more than merely assert itself. The thought that thinks its other is its helpmate to unfold its compacted meaning. For a genuine intuition can be like a dense, abbreviated discourse. A thoughtful logic may bring out its structure or contours of intelligibility, as an acid bath develops the hidden, and hitherto suspended picture in the photographic negative. An insensitive logic, with excessive acid, will not develop but only destroy this hidden picture. Then it is not dumb intuition but dulling logic that is responsible for the resulting blank print. Analysis is a necessary form of mind, but mindless philosophical analyses produce such white concepts, such albino notions.

Logic, Being, and Mindfulness

When the analyses of the logicist yield albino notions (i.e. empty univocity), the suspicion surfaces that thought and being are so radically different as to present a dualism precluding all mediation. Equivocal difference seems to have the last word. A Kierkegaard will retort to a Hegel: there is no identity of thought and being; logic and life are opposites without mushy mediation, conflicting poles of an antithesis that ever resists synthesis. Kierkegaard and Hegel are very relevant to the previously noted distrust of logic. Ironically a major source of this distrust is Hegel's apotheosis of logic, his so-called panlogism. Panlogism sees the whole as the concretion of the logical Idea as absolutely self-mediating thought. In Kierkegaard's wake, existentialists and other reject this concretization of logic as a wrong logicization of the concrete. Something about concrete being remains recalcitrant to the logical Idea: the very concreteness of its being there, which is there, not as a thought, but simply as being.

Unlike Hegel, we balk at seeing the real as the rational, and the rational as the real. We distrust logic because we have grown suspicious of idealism. The irony is that this suspicion surfaces when rational thought, *logic itself*, reaches a certain sophistication of self-consciousness. The famous words in Goethe's *Faust* say: Grey is all theory, green alone life's golden tree. Hegel himself said: Philosophy paints its grey on grey at dusk. Grey is the old age of thought when mind, though it be beyond its suspicion of woman, beyond its suspicion of life, becomes radically *suspicious of itself*. Logic comes to distrust its own former idolatry of logic. Previously philosophy saw its purity in the whiteness of its notions, now it senses the void, or its own death, in its contradictory eros to be beyond eros. What now disturbs philosophy is not "phallogocentric" power, not feminine fertility, but conceptual sterility. The nihilism of theory is not white or black but grey.

In one sense this outcome is risked by every activation of mind. This activation, opening us to being's otherness, is inevitably rupturing. Prior to this rupturing, and apart altogether from the old age of thought, we are bound to being as involved participants. Life is a drama that draws us into its development, and initially we do not distance ourselves; we are in this drama; we are this drama. With logic distance appears. We resist the part thrust on us, find one part tedious or unworthy, covet another part more. We question the play as a whole, begin to argue with being and with ourselves. Like a grey-headed adolescent Hamlet, we are sicklied o'er with the pale cast of thought and find ourselves estranged. Logic can sow distrust, even disgust.

This tension of being and logic is inevitable. But we need not see it as dualistic opposition or equivocal difference. The immediacy of being envelops us and carries us in its flow; but there are rapids in this river. Now we hit a rock and are jolted, or we run aground on a strange shore. The immediate continuity of simply being is disrupted. In this rupture we are impelled to think. Here I am, but where is here? I am lost, I am at a loss, I must think. Thought is urgent now. Can I restore the continuity of being, my community with its otherness? In the disruption of its flow, self-consciousness begins to dawn. Thought is sorrow. It is tied to the suffering of being. Urgent thought emerges in the gaps of living that sheer living itself seems unable to bridge. At the points of transition, thinking can be most intense, because life is most interrupted. Then we must be mindful in a concentrated way. For in such passages we perhaps may find the hinges of meaning on which a door to deeper thought may either swing open or slam shut.

In the wounds of being mindfulness originates. But just for that reason to mind being can be terrifying. Being ceases to be a comforting womb. The human being stands out, mindful of its own inward otherness and the other otherness that envelops it. I mention two recurrent responses to the opening of this gap. One extreme response is to magically think the gaps out of being by throwing ourselves back into immediacy with a frenzy. But this frenzy is only the hysterical side of our terror before thought. Instead of bridging the gap thoughtfully, we throw a tantrum in the vacuum, and call our tantrum "love of life."

Then there is this other extreme. Matching the simulacrum of Romantic inspiration that is mindless immediacy, we find the simulacrum of Enlightenment that is pure mind, voyeur logic. Matching the Maenad philosophy, we have the thinking of the catatonic god or the cybernetic peeping tom. Here, rather than refusing the gaps in being by immersion in vehement immediacy, one diminishes the suffering of such ruptures and intrusions by standing *above* the middle. One completely detaches oneself from every disruptive otherness. This tends to be a hidden motivation of the logicist (Nietzsche is right—though this disciple of Dionysus also courts a Maenad philosophy). In this second case, thought and being are again separated, but now logic is transformed into a self-contained formal system. It becomes a mode of mind that is hygienic, abstract, removed. Logic makes its own world of concepts, and has nothing to do with the otherness of being. It declines any dealings with the discontinuities of otherness but instead makes itself discontinuous with otherness.

In one case, a frenzy of irrationalism claims that being and mind have nothing in common. In the other, an opposing but secretly complementary rationalism turns frenzy into asceticism, yet the same divorce of thought and being obtains. We have, as it were, a life that is promiscuous and a logic that is puritanical. But promiscuity and puritanism are in hidden complicity. So this frenzied irrationalism and sterile rationalism call forth each other, feed on each other, feed on what the other fears or neglects. Instead of bringing about a mindful intermediation in the between, these opposites cause one to swing violently back and forth, alternatively making thought empty and being senseless.

Neither extreme is adequate to the metaxological community of being and mind. Neither mindless immediacy nor a purely formal self-mediating mind is adequate to being's otherness or to mind's own recalcitrance to complete self-transparency. Undoubtedly there are forms of abstractive thinking that can be corrosive, forms of stilted self-consciousness that stifle vigor. These forms literally makes mind abstracted, as it comes to share in Hamlet's condition: oversubtle, distracted, paralyzed before the living choice. Such decomposing thought tries to set apart neatly into simpler elements what in itself was first complexly whole. We gain a clearer view of a collection of abstracted parts, but we lack the original whole. But without this whole the parts are indistinguishable from fragments.[10] Such decomposing thought can arouse suspicious of *all* thought. Commonsense then will say: thinking too much is dangerous; the point of being is not to think it but to live it; we are advised *to be*, not to think. Had Hamlet not weighed being against non-being, he would have simply been, and let be—a happy but dull dummy, not the epitome of metaphysical unease.

Against the formal security of logicist thought and the insecure, domestic security of unreflective commonsense, something dangerous *does* erupt in thought, something disquieting and terror-tinged. The danger cannot be avoided, for we have no choice. We cannot but be thinking beings; we are commissioned to metaphysical mindfulness. Every effort to stop thinking about inward and outer otherness is only an evasion, a twisting of what we are. Existential immediacy, logicist self-mediation, unreflective common sense, all court an untenable dualism. Our thinking is born in the complex concreteness of our being as participants in metaxological being. Thought is not imposed extraneously but a development arising immanently from the peculiar kind of intermediate beings we are. Being wakes up in us and shows forth the power of a singular being—the human being—to become both self-minding and other-minding.

Every other thing has being without questioning its own being, but we can knowingly probe our own internal intricacy and become the promise of knowing alertness to all otherness. Other forms of being are caught in the centrifugal swirl of immediate being, but we can become directed on our own being; and this, not to become self-enclosed, but to articulate a mindful gathering of self and otherness in and despite being's dispersions. We are alarmed by thought because it makes us different in the flow of immediacy, but, alarm or no, we are different, we are difference, and again not because we must be dissociated from the rest of being, but because we exhibit the power of middle being in more complex form. We are the promise of mindful being. We do not just exist; nor are we the power to think. We are thinking being, being thinking about itself and the rest of being. We are the promise of a community of thinking and being.

These are simple, elemental things to say, but we easily forget how astonishing they are. I do not think that this enigma of being become self-minding and other-minding in the human being has been dispelled by philosophers, though, in fact, it is what sustains all understanding and explanation. It emerges in the intimacy of the aesthetic body, yet all explanatory discourses are grounded on it. Scientific explanation forgets its own unexplained ground, but even such forgetting is unintelligible apart from this enigma. Commonsense forgets this enigma because it is caught up in extroverted busyness with things other than the being of its own accompanying self-presence. It is so absorbed in external otherness that it loses mindfulness of itself as a relatedness to otherness. Not all philosophers have been forgetful, perhaps especially transcendental thinkers—though here the recurrent risk has been for thought to close in upon itself in formal self-mediation. If we succumb to this temptation, we forget that thought itself, no matter how abstract or self-mediating, is still a form or way of being.

If the human self is the promise of a metaxological community of being and thinking, this means that thinking that only fragments is bad thinking. It also means that a human existence that merely is and nothing more is incomplete. With the self in the full, being requires thinking to be articulate, just as thinking requires being in order to be concrete. Without the other, each is unwhole. Thus, also there is a sense in which we, by our very essence, transcend the dualism of being and logos, life and logic. Man is the logical animal, *zōon logon echōn*, as Aristotle's famous words say. He is the living being who manifests, stronger *is* "logos." The mindless way we repeat the phrase "man is the rational animal" dulls our philosophical perplexity before the astonishing living being of logos.[11] Christians privilege Christ as the Word, the Logos. But there is a sense in which *every* human being is the word made flesh. Every human being is a speaking incarnation, or as put above, the promise of metaxological community of thought and being. This is not the privilege of one but of all. The thinking human is a kind of living logic, a logic that need not be just decomposing.

Logic, Otherness and Power

The basic issue here not only concerns the recalcitrant being of selfhood, but also the perplexing otherness of the power of being itself. A vital question is how we are to understand the source of being out of which mindfulness itself emerges and into which it puts its root. Here we must note another crucial source of contemporary suspicion, namely, the belief that beneath logic's surface lies a darker, more primitive power. Logic is suspected of being a mask for more elemental powers, a disguise of non-logical forces. For in the interplay between promiscuous irrationalism and puritanical rationalism, reason not only grows suspicious of itself but eventually claims to *see through its own mask*. In a word: Pushing through to its own limit, logic begins to *deconstruct itself*.

What happens is that in the reflective movement of thought by which thinking turns back on itself, logic pierces the crust of its own rational consciousness and finds the shifting abyss of the unconscious. The discovery of the unconscious is often attributed to Freud, though Nietzsche is widely recognized as his precursor. What is not widely recognized, a fact significant here, is that it was Schelling, at one level a defender of idealist thought, who was one of the first to take the unconscious seriously. The unconscious makes a strong entrance *within* the conceptual framework of idealist logic, not outside it, nor simply in existentialist reaction to it. Schelling already was *both* sides of the dialectic. Schopenhauer (despite his hatred for Hegel's idealist logic, he is not altogether unsympathetic to Schelling) only brings further into the open (well before Nietzsche) the secret of the unconscious. The ultimate source for him is what I have called the "dark origin."[12] I mention the historical point because it clearly exemplifies the philosophical dialectic. This dialectic is allowed by the nature of middle being itself; it testifies to the decentering by being's otherness of any putatively autarkic subjectivity or self-sufficient thought. Its danger is a retreat to a dualistic oscillation between univocity and equivocity, or the deconstructive celebration of merely equivocal thought. Though finally inadequate to metaxological being, this philosophical dialectic is not at all unique to the twentieth century. Holders of that view suffer from historical-philosophical myopia.

In this self-deconstruction of reason, logic becomes seen as a tool to manipulate what is beyond reason, like a hammer we use to beat reality into level submission. It is said: Logic objectifies being, reifies, hence falsifies its becoming. If we follow this line of thought we would agree with Schopenhauer and Nietzsche: logical reason is a secondary phenomenon, camouflaging something more primordial. It is a manifestation, one among others and with no eternal, Platonic privileges, of a dark, blind Will (Schopenhauer) or our will-to-power (Nietzsche). By means of logic we reduce the promiscuous plurality of things to manageable, calculable categories. The origin of logic, then, is not in the pure desire for truth but in the impure need to make uniform, to control, to equalize, to regularize reality. This is nowhere clearer than in Nietzsche but, due to reason's self-deconstruction in the wake of idealism, the attitude pervades contemporary culture. Logic is our cunning cowardice before the contradictory, contrary character of what is. It is in flight from the terror-tinged thought of absurdity. But far from this flight being now commended, absurdity itself is said, in a strangely self-contradictory way, to be the ultimate truth of being.

There are metaphysical assumptions to this view. We meet the view when the real is understood as sheer flux, a process of pure becoming. Reality, it is said, does not stand still; it is ever in motion, always generating ceaseless change. This is the world of Heraclitean becoming, but devoid of Heraclitean Logos. Nothing remains the same in such a flux, nothing static; the process of pure becoming sweeps away every permanence. Now the metaxological sense does not at all deny the universal impermanence; but it does deny that becoming is pure in the sense of being absolutely devoid of intrinsic order or structure. If the latter were so, we would be completely at sea; we would always founder in the flux. Our reaction would, and ought to be, complete terror. We would sink in an ontological swamp—ousia would be ooze. There would be no supporting earth, only insubstantial waves in endless transformation, a world of shapelessness, lacking all signs of order, a world different to distinguish from chaos, that is, not a world at all. I recall Aristotle's response to extreme Heracliteans. Philosophical logos would degenerate into fluxgibberish.[13]

In the middle of things, we do not find ourselves in such a chaos. We *do* find ourselves in a world of endless transformation, but in the midst of the process the striking fact is *transformation*. There thought seeks a logos of the *metaxu*: in fact the metaxological community of being supports our logos, as thought thinking both itself and its other. The world of becoming is itself a middle, an intermediate: it mingles order and disorder, stability and change, regularity and surprise. The process of becoming is an intermediation between the original indeterminate power of being and its crystallization in determinate patterns and things. We find a dynamic intermediation between indeterminacy and determination, not their dualistic separation into opposites without mediation.

The devotees of pure flux are the contemporary opposites of the defenders of frozen stasis, but both are one-sided, hence each is half-right, half-wrong. One offers us frozen ousia, the other flowing ooze. In the past the upholders of stasis might be found in the Eleatic camp, to a modified extent among the Platonists. The devotees of flux today tend to congregate under the banner of Nietzsche. (Schopenhauer is a Plato who, via Kant, was on the way to becoming Nietzsche!) When they assert that logic is a form of will-to-power, they articulate a definable reaction to this mixed, double, intermediate nature of the world of becoming. But they reduce the ontological middle to the side of flux, a revealing reduction since one of their chief objections to logic is just its purported reductive urge. They just reduce differently, all the while claiming really to be more "open."

Unrepentant, Nietzsche will jeer (and do not say Nietzsche does not jeer): humans, being cowards, cannot endure the uncertainty of flux, hence introduce their discriminations into it. This, he will insist, is *our* doing, not the doing of being in its otherness. The order we see in the intermediated world is not an intrinsic feature of that world itself (see Kant) but a product of our will-to-power. (Nietzsche's deep continuity with Kantian and post-Kantian predecessors is striking, despite his pretense to unprecedented discontinuity.) We blend our own desire for order into the intrinsic disorder of the given. Without us being would be a tangled jungle; logic domesticates the wilderness. All concepts become instrumental constructions we make to still becoming's uncertainty. If they help us discriminate the flux, they also are inevitably abstractions that remove us from the deepdown real, put us at a distance. Thus, reason creates a cushion of abstraction between vulnerable consciousness and the raw real. Logic must invariably be a falsification: it fixes in a formula what cannot be absolutely fixed, freezes and hardens what by its nature is absolutely fluid. It pins down something that really immediately escapes, and we are left with its shell rather than substance.

Nietzsche does help us put the question: Is logic, philosophical logos, simply mind's way to play the tyrant with what is? Significant cases give the lie to this view. Nietzsche's own courageous entry into the dark labyrinth of the will-to-power, his willingness to turn the corner of the unknown, though he meet the Minotaur and be devoured, instance an intrepid will to truth that is willing to let itself be *broken* for truth. Likewise, the rational self's suspicion of *itself* is very revealing: one is willing to find *against oneself*; one might be wrong; one is open to being judged as being in the wrong. There are time's when one is willing to sacrifice one heart's desire if the logic of the case goes against one. Dishonesty is intolerable. One would be radically honest with oneself, even into the night of nihilism itself, though this honesty will cripple one with serious matters like power, or money or sex or success. One will not play that game. There is a nobility of truth beyond tyranny in this submission to being in its otherness, whether it elate one or throw one down. There is a suffering of truth transcending what one might will truth to be.

Even if logic can be of use to a subtle will-to-power, this hardly tells the full story of what being mindful means. Rather it tells of the reduction of mindfulness to a calculative rationality by which we try to lord over a recalcitrant otherness. We must question any reduction of mindfulness to rationalized will-to-power, not only with respect to being mindful, but with respect to what it means to be. As we saw, will-to-power is ancilla to the ontological view that being is pure becoming, formless flux, that is, simply chaos should we take away our interventions that mould the real to our desire. But is being so formless in itself, is otherness so void of order or its own inherent mediations, without our rationalizing or mediating interventions? In the wake of Kantian epistemology the order in being as other is often interpreted as only a construction of human activity, all but nothing apart from our mediations, but suppose we return to the intermediate nature of becoming above mentioned? What if we must break with the dualistic separation of self and other implicit in both Kantian and Nietzschean epistemologies and which allows the active self to throw its grid of abstractions upon an otherwise indifferent, passive thereness?

In fact the thereness of being as other, even in its becoming, exhibits order, pattern, regularity as intrinsic features of its own nature. This, like the becoming self-present of being in the self, is extremely simple, and yet its very elemental character makes it the most evident and the least noticed, hence something deep and enigmatic. Given the nonsense sometimes uttered after a poorly digested meal of post-Kantian epistemology, it is unbelievable that one has to reassert seemingly simple truisms like this. We do not create this order of the universe. We are products of it, participants in it. True, it may be given to us to name that order. But to Adam it was given to baptize creation, not to give birth to it.

For being mindful as metaxological is first of all a way of being, not a creation of being ex nihilo. Mindfulness is itself grounded in the character of being. That is why the above views of logic and anti-logic do not approximate being mindful in the sense I intend. Their implicit presupposition, that carries into their entire articulation of the matter, does not really question the uprootedness of thought from being. Such ontological deracination is undoubtedly a marked feature of the modern mind, which for that reason is often deeply deficient when it comes to being mindful. It is blinded by the proximate success of its own calculative conceptualizing of being. But even this success is parasitical on a deeper energy of mind and being, on their metaxological community, which is distorted in the very act of being thus exploited. Metaphysical mindfulness can acknowledge that the ground of being is original and other. It is other, not necessarily as a dualistic opposite or as nothing. It is the unmastered other to thought which is yet necessary for all of thought's mediations. Hence thought must try to think this other of thought without having to claim either complete self-mediation or total conceptual comprehension of the other as other.

Mindfulness as a way of being is not to be described as a way of world-making, Nelson Goodman's term,[14] unless we free such a term from a false constructivist epistemology. Of course, human beings do make "worlds" for themselves, intelligible orders within which they give articulate expression to their sense of being, its fears as well as its ideals. In the formation of societies and cultures, in the cultivation of land, in the creation of works of art, in the rituals of religions and the reflections of philosophies, the human community is engaged in the task of building a civilized order of being that will answer in some measure to its deepest needs, and at best its openness to being. None of this is to be denied. But the power of being is not, nor can ever be, exhausted by any order we construct. Beyond human order, the real exhibits order that is not of our own making. We see it in the wandering of the Planets, which do not wander at all. We greet it in the cyclic recurrence of nature's seasons. We silently live our homage to it with every rising of the sun and every setting. We meet it when a seed sprouts, reaching down into the dark earth for roots, stretching out for growth, up into the bright air. We marvel at it when a new human being issues into being, a virgin presence already a world unto itself.

The flux as intermediated becoming is shot through with this order. Deny this and we are just disabled Heracliteans, swamped by fluxgibberish, our ears stoppered against logos in its otherness, while we chatter on mindlessly about our own "creative subjectivity." Again the matter is very elemental. Let a person get a stomach cramp and this chattering of "creative subjectivity" soon ceases. The spasm in the gut recalls us to an order of otherness right at the heart of our incarnate being, an order silently there and at work even during all the transcendental talk of our so-called world-making. We are sustained by this order in the organic order of our bodies. The order we make is grafted onto another order that we ourselves do not produce. Try as we might to bend its otherness, we must still respect it.

So we cannot just say that reason superimposes a net of order, a grid of false intelligibility on the universal impermanence. The opening of mindfulness comes to find the contours of intelligibility in the universal impermanence. Reason does not just construct its own fictitious order; being is at work (being as *energeia*, *Wirklichkeit*) to construct its own intelligible order. Being mindful seeks the point of intersection of open reason and this ontological order, a wakefulness of self in attunement with this order of otherness. Indeed one of philosophy's great questions arises from the perplexing fact that sometimes the categories of mind are deeply appropriate to the order of being, an appropriateness hard to attribute entirely to conceptual projections of subjectivity or any of its post-idealist surrogates or replacements, like Nietzsche's will-to-power, or Wittgensteinian language games, or Derridean *differánce*. A thinker develops a set of ideas, concepts and categories on their own terms, and is astonished to find they fit, not just with themselves, but with the order of otherness. Ancient Pythagoreanism might be cited; in our day the genesis of Einstein's theories is often cited. The dream of reason wakes up and finds it was no dream, wakes up and finds itself astonishingly at home with otherness.[15] Put in our terms: thought seems to mediate only with itself, but its self-mediation, on deeper reflection, turns out to implicate its ontological bond with its other. This undercuts the dualistic opposition of thought and being's otherness. There is manifest a community of mind and its essential other, being. The ground of this community of logos and being is the metaxological community of being.

Being mindful is on the way to such being-at-home with otherness. It is not just our fabrication, suiting our convenience, so as changeable as new conventions may dictate. It makes us ponder a sense of reason beyond convention and power. Interestingly, Marx is not unlike Nietzsche in identifying reason and power when he famously said: The ruling ideas of a period are the ideas of the ruling class. But are there ideas transcending the rulers and the times? Is it power that justifies some ideas, or rather some ideas that justify the exercise of power? The reader may sense the ghost of Plato in such questions. Nowadays it is fashionable to try immediately to exorcise this ghost. Instead we should ponder the anomaly of Marx's own ideology. The logic of his ideas was intended to speak most powerfully to those who themselves were powerless, the proletariat. Perhaps, then, their persuasiveness springs from some source beyond any appeal to ruling powers; for example, the ethical promise of the metaxological community of human beings?

If, in fact, Marx's ideas about ideas were correct—that the ruling ideas are the ideas of the rulers—then there could never be a true revolution, that is, a transformation of given reality in the direction of better, fuller reality. There could only be a shuffle in those holding power (usually carried out with blood). The power of some ideas—ideas like justice, or freedom, or truth—must transcend political power or not reduce to human power in any ordinary sense. They are grounded in inherent requirements of the metaxological community of being. Otherwise political power itself is both blind and unjustified, the ultimately capricious expression of mere force. This view not only makes logic senseless—so also it makes power.

II. SECOND MEDITATION: BEING MINDFUL AND SOLITUDE

Solitude and Inward Thisness

The theme of my second meditation is solitude. Instrumental mind takes for granted, in a potentially mindless way, the beings that are given, and goes to work with its categories on what is there, devoid of metaphysical astonishment before the *that* of its being there at all. It bustles with activity, but just this its virtue may crowd out an essential otherness. To restore mindfulness of this, one must stop thinking in that mode, stop thinking that instrumental thought exhausts the energy of thinking. Silence, patience, a different ontological vigilance is needed. Solitude may prepare an opening for different thought, for a celebrating mindfulness of being.

No escapist nostalgia is intended, for my concern is still with thought thinking its *other*. Post-Heideggerians charge that philosophy has always been monological and in solipsistic retreat from otherness: solitude and monological thought, they claim, go together to make a univocal logic infected with secret will-to-power over being.[16] Against this critique of the so-called metaphysics of presence, I will say that solitude can be a breaking of monological thought at a basic level of absence and emptiness. Even when thought thinks itself, it finds the necessary breach of any monological circle and the unavoidable call that it think its other. There is an essential recollective "innering" in being mindful (see the German *Erinnerung*): this "innering" can take self-mediation to the limits of self, hence it need not be "subjectivistic," but may be a way to think what is other to selfhood and its mediations.

Solitude can reveal a *double* mediation, that is, metaxological intermediation of an otherness that is no thing, a nothing. On the one hand, what I call the "ineluctable particularity" of the self's inward thisness breaks monological thought, for it reveals a resistant, constitutive otherness of singularity right at the heart of selfhood. This explodes any pretension to master the being of selfness. On the other hand, the "place" of solitude also resists complete conceptual mastery. I will speak of the desert as a negative otherness, and of city and country solitudes as mundane "places" charged with this often unnamed otherness. Solitude may open mindfulness through absence in presence, transcendence in intimacy, otherness in what is elementally close.

The importance of solitude was granted by the ancients and medievals (I return to this), and by some of the great thinkers of modernity (Kierkegaard and Niezsche). In the faceless mask of mass man lies a bottomless well of anxious solitude that seeks, but does not always find, something of spirit to fill his emptiness. As escape we drug ourselves with busyness. Solitude must be faced and accepted, in its terror and promise, to conquer the dread loneliness of atomized individuality (see chapter 4). What of the deep truism that man is a social animal? Unavoidably we are in company, beings with others; yet "being on one's own" asks for thought. Some thinkers, Hobbes perhaps most famously, have held that our original nature is to be solitary, predatory beings. Necessity drives us to a pact with others, to obviate our vulnerable loneness. Solitude is natural, society an enforced artificiality. If one could, one would hunt for oneself alone; but most cannot. The few who can are the solitary eagles; the many who cannot are the flocking lambs.

This view of our original being, though supposedly pointing us back to origins, rather is prescient of the competitive atoms that pass now for individuals and the masses they make and miscall communities.[17] Selfhood, metaphysically speaking, is always *within* a basic bond with otherness, as we saw differently with being aesthetic, religious and ethical. My focus now is not on solitude as a primitive "state of nature" but rather as emergent into mindfulness with sophistication of selfhood. In "primitive" societies there may be little space for this, but the need to "be on one's own" is increasingly acknowledged with more civilized conditions.[18] The "individual" is not a ready-made unit, given fully at the beginnings of social relations, but its being an "I" is supported by the complex differentiation of the social homogeneity. Solitude seems an aberration from social life, but in fact civilized life calls forth a sophisticated solitude that is not just a cutting off from others—a merely negative idea. The deeper an individual becomes and the more it selves, the more its need to be alone—not to feed any narcissistic infatuation with self, but to renew self in powers of being deeper than either self or society.

Paradoxically, this sophisticated solitude can become a metaxological opening to what is other, through a recovery of something ontologically elemental: namely, the *inward otherness* marking the ineluctable particularity of the self as self. This haunts even a melting mass or mob wherein all seem the same, each an interchangeable unit, an anonymous number. (Here, actually, is the quantitative operation of univocal thought, reductive of internal difference to uncomplex sameness.) On the outside a mob self seems just an excited, hysterical shout, but inwardly even the mob self feels itself, however minimally, to be a single one, inarticulately feels itself as itself, divines itself as an irreducible, all but incommunicable center of being. We are a unique point of view on being, one that is inescapably "mine" and not another's, a point of view necessarily "mine' because unavoidably anchored in selfhood as *this* self. This does not preclude a community of being between the "I" and others. Yet for every self the world is *its* world, even despite the seductions of drowning itself in an absorbing mass. But this sheer fact is not a determinate "what," hence extremely hard to utter discursively. We relish the world as "mine," indelibly marked by an elusive taste or savor of selfness. Let my opinions be exactly the same as all the others, yet the sheer fact that *I* hold them, this is mine and mine alone. This ineluctable particularity of self I call its "inward thisness." It is found at the source of all solitude and at the ground of singularity.

Being mindful of inward thisness, our singularity even within all bonds with otherness, implies the justice of some existentialist criticisms of the "System." The "System's" apotheosis of logical universality may blind it to concrete selfhood in its singularity, and as Kierkegaard saw, ease the path of thinking towards an abstract, mindless objectivism. (Behaviorism enjoins literally this mindless objectivism.) Often it is the artist who resists this flattening effect and remains faithful to the richness of singularity in its very singularity. That being aesthetic is a mode of being mindful is nowhere more evident. An analogous refusal to betray such singularity is evident in ethical respect for the person as an end in itself. Generally, inward thisness is passed over, smoothed over in the normal run of things. This is true, not only of any logical system but of any social system, precisely because of the extreme difficulty of even naming it, much less communicating it. Though social exchange diverts us from inward thisness, this savor of self informs even such diversions. We may devise different evasions, social and logical, but there is no escape from this singularity.

Because it is an elusive inward otherness at the border of graspability, we encounter fear of solitude. A common logic will allay this fear, and this is not unnatural. Everyone has felt the fear of being abandoned. We shudder with recognition at the Ancient Mariner's words: "Alone, alone, all, all alone / Alone on a wide, wide sea / Nor any saint to take pity on my soul in agony." Many fear death less than dying alone, with none to care. Thus also, solitary confinement is an extreme punishment. It wounds a self to be forced to be thus absolutely alone with itself. The point of this confinement is to *break* the self in its singularity. To be alone with oneself thus is to be alone with *nothing*. This penal solitude is just short of death.

A systematic univocal logic cannot command mindfulness of this "nothing," for this nothing is something *idiotic*.[19] Such impotence of univocal logic is mirrored in reverse in the following striking anomaly of modern mass societies, the most systematically organized societies, in a sense the least idiotic, most rationalized societies, ever devised: the coexistence of an overheated rhetoric of individuality and a pervasive dread of solitude, dread of the idiocy of inward thisness. We solve this antinomy by "doing our own thing" in droves. But this "solution" only deepens the contradiction, bringing it to the border of the comic. Mass man, the system self, flees from solitude, but the paradox of its flight is that it is a decampment into a more despairing solitude. The individual caught up in the crowd is absolutely alone within the crowd. We witness reiterated emptiness in the socialized solitude of massed glee.

Fear of solitude assumes different forms in democratic and totalitarian systems. In the latter the solitary is suspect for his refusal to be just one of the masses. Every aspect of his privacy may suffer encroachment. The stock image here is the all-seeing Big Brother from whose baleful eye there seems no escape. One is watched lest one dissent, for any solitary is a threat to the norm. One is driven more and more inward, into an enforced, exiled solitude. Temples of unspoken solitude may survive in the inward inviolability of free thinking. (A torturer wants to destroy the inward otherness.) Sometimes all that can be done is watch and wait, and even then honest vigilance is arduous.

By contrast, in democratic systems the laws acknowledge certain rights of privacy that should not be violated. In principle, but within limits, one is allowed to be alone; in practice we too often find a technological destruction of intimacy. Everywhere the electronic media intrude with their brash publicity and the attitude that "nothing is sacred." With this attitude, nothing has the right to be left alone. Most are left alone because they are unknown. For others we have frivolous versions of the All-seeing Eye: for the famous, the powerful, the celebrities, for those in the Eye of the Public, we have the gossip column and chat show. This is a relatively trivial invasion of privacy compared to the totalitarian crushing. True, many in the Public Eye fall over themselves to exhibit eagerly their tedious "thisness," to make a public show of their shallow selves. This show of intimacy seems indistinguishable from a destruction of intimacy. To the discomfited who wish to be left alone, you say there are the libel laws. But the pursuit of justice through these channels sometimes gives the plaintiff just the publicity he sought to avoid. Too late the slandered person learns that silence *was* golden. Recall the rueful Kierkegaard after his merciless barracking by the *Corsair*. But then Kierkegaard did lead with his jaw.[20]

Negative Otherness and the Desert

There is then something "negative" about solitude that we shun as an eluding absence rather than a masterable presence. By contrast with the Pythagorean brotherhood who, listening for an unsounded music, made a liturgy of morning silence, we switch on the radio first thing of the day to catch a crackle from the air, anything to fill the void space of silence. Being mindful has to think through such a negative otherness, as we might call it. The point is not negation but the release of remembrance of what it is to be. The being of self is a hazardous becoming; solitude opens a space of negativity where, against our immersion in things and the perpetual risk of self-forgetfulness, concentration is trained on the bypassed being of self. With nothing to engross one, we may strike through to a deeper energy of selving. The mind must go down to the inward place/noplace of darkness, sit still in the cavern of its own nocturnal depths, endure its suffering passage through its own meonic contraction.[21]

Here any simplistic opposition of solitude and community, being for self and being for others, makes no sense. The inward otherness of the self and surrounding otherness of the "place" of solitude are inseparable. Thus, the morning silence of the Pythagoreans was the silence of a *Koinōnia*, a fellowship. Thus also, the essential self-discovery enabled by solitude is sometimes socially ritualized, say, in initiation rites. To enter into maturity and partake of adult life, a youth is severely separated for a space, as say the Aborigine boy on walkabout. Alone with himself and with nothing but a hunting weapon, he is committed to the desert. The desert, vast physical expanse of negative otherness, tests him on a threshold, partners his entry to mature community. In his wandering he will face and endure danger alone; he will fight for himself alone; alone he will suffer the terror of no external support, beyond his cunning, courage and indomitability. He might be destroyed but in surviving alone with himself he earns the right to be called adult. The survival is not just physical; it is the youthful spirit that must not bow or break; it is character or "self" that must come through its own breaking. The desert overcome, better, the desert won over and made a friend, makes a new self.

Interestingly, the first Western settlers in Australia called the desert "*terra nullius*," land of none. But we must mark an essential *reversal* between merely empty "aloneness" and community. In calling it *terra nullius*, the settlers were partly right about the negative otherness, but wrong in their blindness to the deeper being of the place/noplace of the negative otherness. For the Aborigine all of the land was a complex sacred site, a place of community that bound one to the ancestors. On walkabout the self passed along the ways of the ancestors that were articulated by what were called "songlines." That is, in the time of the origin, the time of the Dreaming (cf. chapter 3), the world and the places charged with special sacredness were *sung* into being. The ancestors were the singers of the original, originative songs. The space of seeming emptiness, of solitude, of silence, is the place/noplace of a community of being held together by the songlines. The songlines are the ways of being that support and finally exceed the seeming emptiness. The solitude reveals original being as singing. The community of being sings in the solitude.

The desert, as the noplace of meonic contraction, is the place of paradoxical sterility. As a negative otherness it offers stony conditions in which only a strong self can flower. Superficially it presents an environment barren of life but closer intimacy yields nuance. Strange exotic forms of life flourish in these forbidding circumstances. The desert tests the versatility of things, reveals how tenaciously things cling to being, despite exposure to the most scorching of negativities. A self that endures it, nay thrives on it, is released from encumbering dependencies and is to that extent freer. In the desert's necessity, it is in inwardness that freedom puts down its root. Outside we find a burning blank, but within inwardness the desert opens up an oasis. The enduring energy of being sings even in the negative otherness.

There is nothing "subjectivistic" about this inwardness. Consider solitude as preparing a new beginning in being religious. Here stress is put on the need for *retreat*. Of course, retreat can become total, turned into a mere flight from the world. But this is not inevitable. In many religions retreat, and its supporting solitude, are episodes in a larger drama, serving the advancement of that drama as a whole. One retreats in order to advance: first to advance inwardly, then to advance again on being as other. One retreats to return with new strength for transfiguring. I again think of Francis of Assisi—a self stripped to its essential poverty, but singing and fired with this new energy of being.

Essential here is a contemplative comportment towards being in which a more radical otherness than even our inward otherness is to be saluted. In the ancient and medieval eras, the contemplative mind needed little defense. Logos, reason, theōria were not radically instrumentalized as in the modern era but held the promise of a mindfulness that was self-justifying because it was its own end. The contemplative attitude epitomized our highest freedom, the freedom to mind what is of ultimate worth. This was consistent with a comprehensive vision of the cosmos and our place therein. The human being was not the measure of all things; our being was measured by more ultimate standards of perfection, indeed only reached the acme of its own fulfillment in being receptive to the ultimate powers. The contemplative mind activated just this receptivity. There were intimate issues between the human being and the ultimate that could not be resolved anywhere but within the individual, in the final solitude of its opening soul in its relatedness to the ultimate.[22]

While the importance of the active life was not denied, it did not enjoy the supremacy it has in the modern epoch. Thus, the premodern (in this case medieval) distinction between the *artes serviles* and *artes liberales* already implies something not unlike the "postmodern" critique of instrumental reason. The servile arts dealt with work and our laboring efforts to meet nature's necessities. The liberal arts were the arts of liberty, of leisure, including those we today call the humanities. The servile arts were instrumental skills, useful as means to different practical ends. The liberal arts were intrinsically valuable; their very exercise or activation completed and dignified an essential human potency. In their perfecting of the human being they required no justification beyond themselves. They articulated a contemplative mindfulness, devoid of which human life lacks an essential nobility and dignity.[23]

The changed picture of the modern world is striking. No doubt, previous eras made possible this nobility only for the few, and too often, as Marxists never fail to point out, on the backs of the many. One need not defend slavery to defend the contemplative mind. To the contrary, it may be only with its aid that ethical mindfulness begins to dawn about the scandal of slavery. Even granting the past restrictiveness, one need not urge an apotheosis of the servilely activist mind. For the latter the liberal arts, the humanities, the arts of being human as opposed to being a functionary, are not acknowledged as essential but tolerated as luxuries, as extras. Where the contemplative mind survives at all, it does so on sufferance. It survives on the margins. The contemplative discovers himself an outsider.

In some ways being "outside" is an essential source of its strength. Thus, in "contemplation" we hear the word "temple," and the religious resonances that sound there. In ancient times a "temple" had to do with the demarcation of space, the setting apart of one region from another. Originally, it seems, it had to do with the founding act that set off a city: a drawing of a limit wherein religious and civic piety intertwined. Contemplation carries an akin connotation of a basic act of spacing. It implies a release from the thoughtless immediacy of being, not at all to avoid being, but to "see" it with needed distance, to see it more freely, that is, with pressing pragmatic involvements provisionally out of play. To be involved with things without pause or respite is to risk being lost, not only to oneself, but to the very things consuming one's attention. One looks too long without distance but one ends up no longer seeing. Differentiation vanishes, as does discrimination, in the sense of mindfulness that discerns differences, nuances. Contemplation, by contrast, introduces rupture into habitual seeing. This rupture, this "setting apart" is a necessary act of differing, of distancing, without which the rejuvenation of thought is impossible. Like the body, the mind needs rest to be refreshed. The differing act of contemplation, purging mind in the solitude of inward thisness, reawakens metaphysical astonishment at the being there of being, in its inward and outer otherness.[24]

That this has nothing to do with any narcissistic infatuation with an isolated, precious subjectivity is clear even with extremists in solitude, such as the early Western contemplatives, the desert monks. The term "monk" comes from the Greek "*monachos*," meaning someone who lives alone. It is related to words like "*monas*," meaning a one, a self-sufficient unity, a monad. One might suspect *monological* mind but in fact the "*monas*" internally splits into a dyad, a unique dyad. This is not a dualistic opposition but a togetherness in inwardness of the self and its ultimate other—in Augustine's terms, the dialogue of the soul alone with itself and God.[25] This dialogue opens up the space for absolute community, the community of spirit.

Here flight to desert solitude sharpens religious mindfulness whose initiation is the inward spiral of the soul coming before its always there God. God is always there in inwardness, but not necessarily known as there. This coming before the ultimate in inwardness has been described as the soul "alone with the Alone" (Plotinus). In desert solitude the soul's recovery of itself serves the rediscovery of something more ultimate than itself. In plumbing the depths of its own reawakened inwardness, it greets, is greeted by the ultimate ground of its own being. In the abyss of inward otherness, through the narrow pass of meonic contraction, ungrounded in the negative otherness, the absolute otherness of the ungrounded ground is divined. This ungrounded ground is not "up" or "down," "inside" or "outside." It is nothing and nowhere, just as the soul's own Mount Carmel or Scellig Mhicíl is a place that is noplace. The mind of the desert self is exceeded by itself and its ultimate other, yet the desert self is alone with itself to belong more intimately with what is more than self alone.

Technicist thought will dismiss this as all mysticism (cf. chapter 3) but the issue is worth more serious thought. If we compare Western and Eastern solitaries, the former aimed to pass through the self as an intermediary on the way to God. The self is a pathway to this ultimacy. Eastern mysticism seems to concentrate on the self differently and in some ways seems directed to realize what I called the self's ineluctable particularity, its elusive inward thisness. Thus, some yoga techniques will ask one to free oneself progressively from absorption in external objects. By exclusively attending to just one thing, that thing in its congealed material thereness will begin to dissolve. One will become aware not of *what* one perceives, but of the fact *that* it is I who am perceiving, am the very process of perceiving itself. By attention to breathing, for instance, by sheer attention, sheer mindfulness, progressive self-awareness becomes gathered self-consciousness that realizes selfhood in its inward thisness.

The classic formula of this realization is "Thou art That," "*tat tvam asi.*"[26] For the external observer this is not a very descriptive formulation for it is empty of determinate content. It is an empty statement, a nothing that mirrors the emptiness out of which it was gathered. But from within this emptiness, the nothing or indeterminacy is said to be charged with intense significance. It is "seen," not logically deduced, a charged experience, not a conceptual construction. Mysticism is this guise, it might be said, has nothing to do with a leap into some other world but is merely the proper mindfulness of an otherness that is right now present to one, proper mindfulness of what is and what one is. But this "presence" as nothing is peculiarly resistant to fixed objectification, just as this "is" is recalcitrant to encapsulation in finalized, determinate categories. Stated with maximum concision: The "is" of "I" is not just "mine." In naming the enigma of inward thisness we are made mindful of the enigma of being as such. Nor need we see here a self-nihilating dissolution in an absorbing god. Rather in the ontological bond of original selfness and the absolute original, the "I" of second love (cf. chapter 4) is awakened to mindful participation in the metaxological community of being.[27]

Eastern mysticism might seem more indulgent of the self than the Western form, welcoming a subtle self-absorption instead of the release of self from itself towards God. But this contrast does not take us far enough.

Eastern self-realization is, one might say, self-deconstructing. For when one knows "Thou art That," a peculiar liberation from isolated particularity is recorded. At its deepest the "self" is never an isolated unit or atom. Selfness is the very "stuff," the essence of being as a whole. Selfness is never "mine" in any exclusive sense, for the whole of being is "self." The other, initially a stranger, even an enemy, is "self" and so is my kin. Or conversely, as Rimbaud said: *Je, c'est un autre.* "My" self is one turbulent wave on the ocean of being. "Mineness" becomes an illusion if I treat it as an irreducibly self-sufficient ultimate. At this conclusion singularity as a sheer isolation vanishes.

Hence in both Western and Eastern solitudes we discover this crucial reversal. In the West, mystical solitude is converted into the conversation of the soul with God. In the East, mystical solitude brings with it the unweaving of the illusion of isolated selfhood; the particular self overcomes its solitude by coming to mindfulness of its being as partaking of a more universal life. Solitude is necessary to overcome illusion. But absolute solitude is just that very illusion that mystical solitude must disperse.

Country and City Solitude

I said before that the "place" of solitude intimates an otherness that eludes conceptual instrumentalization: the otherness of inward thisness cannot be abstracted from the otherness of its being placed. It is here we find the double mediation of metaxological being. Solitude as restorative is not a mere absence or void but an event or happening that may open mind, letting the otherness of being play upon our patient quiet. Nevertheless it eventuates differently in different contexts; occasion enters silently into its distinctive shaping. This sense of occasion was present with the negative otherness of the desert. But just as the "mystical" might seem merely esoteric, so this desert setting might seem merely exotic. To charge esotericism and exoticism is to miss the point. The "commonplace" can also bring home to us the elemental power of solitude to renew mindfulness of the metaxological. "Ordinary," exoteric configurations of solitude also offer what resists encapsulation by instrumental reason. Philosophical mindfulness (which is not unreason) cannot think the meaning of what it is to be without heeding the charge of their otherness. What we cannot encapsulate in a concept, we must nevertheless try to name.

Consider two "commonplace" solitudes: country and city solitude. With the first we meet the nonhumanness of nature, its sometimes sublime, sometimes appalling otherness. Nature's silence seems like indifference, yet it need not be a repudiation, nor identified with human loneliness. Within the silence a *meeting* with otherness may be offered. We encounter the elemental powers that storm us in their wilder forms, steal into us in gentler calms. To be opened to the elemental powers of earth, sea, sky, and air is to be quickened with primitive vigor. The abstractions of instrumental reason have no time for this. Yet within this quickening, time peculiarly slows down: nature's inexorable roll unruffles the self with its undying rhythm. We need not be lost in this but find ourselves participant in a vaster play of powers. Within this play our role may be undefined, even dark; we may be devoid of grand destiny. But sometimes *just to be* within the play is gift and meaning enough. A sense is granted of the marvel of just being; one is thankful just for being. In unbeguiling gratitude one is restored to one's own being.[28]

The shaping of solitude by place as other to the self is here evident; this "place" is also its timeliness or untimeliness, its proper season. Thus, in nature's different season's, a different silence will be given. In winter the solitude is at its most cold and nonhuman. One is dwarfed under the empty night, by the vast ice blue of the ether. The elemental powers sing our vulnerability. We are admonished to shield our nakedness, or perish. The emptiness delivers a cold caution: consult mortality in overreaching, beware to take a temporary coziness as guaranteed. One is taught care and respect: care for the frailty of the human, respect for the encompassing might of the natural. Yet the infertile solitude is not dead. Ice grips the world, winds blow through it, rains rinse it clean. The infertility purges. The soft fall of innocence alights on things with snow.

Spring solitude brings the mood of return, of recognized restoration. Winter biding surrenders to a shaking, uncongealing, a new awakening. Solitude heaves with the earth as it rises up in the elemental sap of its stirring powers. The quietness over things is different too. First there is a flutter of freshness. Soon things more insistently sing out their presence. The insistence grows to a raucous chorus and the silence is cluttered by a choir of outbursts. Have you watched a flock of starlings? Here you have it. I see the starlings picking the earth in a still straw field. Now they are jerkily busy when—abruptness itself—up they fly and are scattered away—light specks of black energy—fugitives from a startling something I cannot sense, a silent otherness that, staying hidden, seems nothing.

Summer solitude is other again. Something is suspended in the shimmering heat, a musk is on things, a somnolent earthiness. Dust hangs in the pollen air, and the floating heat makes the earth itself lift up, as if it too would float away into the ether. One must slow, as a dreaminess, even lethargy settles on the elements. Out of the basking earth brief flashes of irritability flare and slowly subside. The enveloping floating density of air makes nature seem as if it were swimming through the hot elemental energy itself. Dog days force us to the shade, our stable selves are melted into magma, the pitiless sun finds us out and brands us.

Autumn solitude lifts the oppression. We move less slow. Intimations of ending arise from the stubble fields. Signs of completion are ingrained on the ancient earth. Ripeness is scattered in the elegiac air. Solitude savors the satiety in things. Soon the plump fruit will drop, and if unharvested, will rot. Consummation is a fall, for the completion we celebrate carries also a death. Autumn solitude broadcasts the bursting fullness of the elemental powers but also sends out the harbingers of their coming withdrawal. Between the ripeness and this retreat, autumn asks for a valedictory solitude.

Thus the occasion, ordinary perhaps but elemental, modulates the happening of solitude. Its "place" may produce a silence of multiple shades, from that of the sheer vacuum, of nothingness, to that of infinite richness, of ripeness itself. The silence may be full of significance, or be a sinister, malignant emptiness. Thus, too, the nonhuman otherness of nature brings its danger. It may drag one down into a silence that negates, a silence that we embrace only to be engulfed and drowned. Nature's solitude may reclaim one without restoration. The anonymous thereness swallows one, makes one "nothing" in an invidious sense: the drowning weight of thereness is reductive of the "I," effects the vanishing of its difference into inarticulate homogeneity (Aristotle called this "*prōtē hulē*"). To guard ourselves we seek the balance of the bustling city.[29]

Though country and city both may be indifferent, one startles us with the indifference of the nonhuman, the other shocks us with the indifference of the inhuman, the inhumane. In both the possibilities of a metaxological community are differently at stake. Through the nonhuman indifference of nature we may meet the elemental powers; in the inhumane indifference of the human, we cast out greeting and meet with nothing, or worse, the hostility of refusal. City solitude is then the happening of an absence—the solitude of Eleanor Rigby, a waiting in loneliness for we know not what, a Godot that will never come. We are expectant of the other's presence, but are brushed aside with an avoidance. The presence that should be there, is not. City solitude is then the solitude of disappointment.

I stress there is no denying the genuine gathering found *only* in the city. But when one is cast outside this gathering, the exclusion is all the more stressed with pain. Where we should be with or encounter the others, we confront and counter the stranger. This city solitude creates an absence that first makes us anxious, then disquiets us with guilt, then fills us with frustration, and finally drives us to the verge of rage. Anxiety: one is ill at ease when one should make contact but cannot, caught in a hiatus between what should be and what is. Guilt: in the hiatus one is perplexed: what have I done to provoke the empty space? Am I answerable for the silence? Frustration: no answer echoes back, only the mocking question repeated without reply. Sold short, let down, one festers with rancorous impotence.

Rage: impotence boils over in angry refusal and the silence is burst with a sudden thunder of violence.

Such random violences are the extremity of response to malignant solitude, but we may find less baleful stages on the way to such unexpected explosions. One develops the subtle art of not noticing. One sees but one must seem as though sightless. Eyes move restlessly everywhere, but one avoids the other's eyes. To make eye contact might be mistaken for a gesture of aggression. One sees everything and one sees nothing. Fear is suspended in the silence. Likewise, one cultivates the art of not being noticed. Faces refuse to smile, for smiling faces are seductive lures that draw attention to themselves. Smiles make one vulnerable; they are the elemental bodily gestures of openness, of welcome. Smiles are the flesh of community. They stretch wordlessly across the gap of silence and arrest the other's attention. One avoids this, hiding behind inscrutable frozen features. One will not be detained by those gestures through which the winning silence greets us. Stonily we brush past, hurry on our way to an elsewhere, another nowhere.

There is a lunacy, a folly that responds to such malignant silence. Malignant silence becomes a negative otherness on which the self is broken. One tries to talk to another, discovers no reciprocal response and the desired dialogue dissolves into monologue. One may entirely shut up, shrink into an interior wordless world. Or one tries to make up for the absent other. Speaking in the place of the wordless other, one will talk for two. The interior monologue splits into a compensating dialogue, the self breaks asunder into many voices, into Babel itself.

This is the opposite extreme to the mystical solitude in dialogue with the divine. The self is not decentered towards its solidarity with the other. The fractured self mutters to itself, many-tongued. Shards of worlds swirl around in the jabbered chaos of such hurled mutterings. Suddenly the voice will wildly shout out its presence, for though crazed, it is still an ineluctable particular of inward thisness: "I am the Madwoman of Cork! I defy you, implore you, pitiless emptiness, with my shout in the street! Here I am, lunatic and all, a self gone berserk, but I still stand here! Fasten on the fact! I am the thing itself!" The voice rises into stridency as the alarmed people watch from a safe distance down the road; the voice rises into empty space, soaring madly into vacancy; the rising voice collapses, and the shaken silence is restored.[30]

Of course, there are benign city solitudes. One does not demand of the other but something is given in presence itself. There is an unnamed community of being in the silence itself. One finds oneself moving at ease in a streaming crowd, contented with one's thoughts, alert to the surrounding show of strangeness, bobbing in its flow, unconsciously blessing its sparkling eccentricity. Or one sits in a restaurant, simply watching others, overhearing conspiratorial talk of mundane splendors. Or one sits in the upper deck of a bus, like some serene god on Mount Olympus, arrested by sunlight caught in windows, or by a glimpse of gardens tended behind walls, caught in the intense mindfulness of sheer motiveless looking.

Also, the city plays host to the guest solitude of nature. At dusk nature's silence wraps itself around the city. Twilight brings a sudden suspension, a stillness between two worlds, an unnoticed gesture from the encircling emptiness. The pace pauses, the strain slacks off, the bustle begins to subside. The night envelopes the city in its embrace; lights flicker on to meet it. Similarly at dawn, before the bustle, another envelopment occurs. Again there is a brief moment of suspension before, unobtrusively, the day slips in. Soon the noise machine will clatter into life and stimulate senses to the verge of enervation. But now something other seems possible—things hold a promise of guiltless freshness.

The city day is bounded by two silences, one of release and resting, the other of renewal and awakening. So dawn and dusk can be the least distracting times. At sunrise we are touched by the light itself that is not yet immersed in the myriad of things it will later illuminate. Things present themselves as silhouettes, tinged by the pure light that gives them presence. At the day's decline, sometimes the light can crowd the air, a kind of thronging light, thick like a dense multitude, murmuring and expectant before a departure. Previously silhouettes, things now become shadows, pointing above and beyond themselves to the last rays, like gentle dreamy reminders, telling of what they need by day and await through the night.[31] We name but do not master the silence. The silence, properly minded, reverses mind: it is the city, not nature, that is the guest.

III. THIRD MEDITATION: BEING MINDFUL AND FAILURE

Philosophy and Failure

Such naming can break into thought singing its other. I return to this. The theme of my third meditation is: thought thinking its other in mindfulness of failure. As solitude implies, there is a mindfulness beyond instrumental reason that is still mind and not just the irrational. In our time, speculative or contemplative mind is often forgotten in the pervasive instrumentalization of reason. Philosophy itself shuns perplexities resistant to such instrumentalization. In a sense, mindfulness calls for a kind of metaphysical memory. Indeed the Latin *memorare* just means to keep in mind. To keep something in mind metaphysically implies a recollective movement of thought in which the self gathers its being to itself, but in this self-gathering, the whole self find itself charged with unrestricted openness to otherness. One should not understate the strain put on self-mediation by the charge of this metaxological intermediation. Our mouths say "openness to otherness," but the voice will be letter, not spirit. Simulated highmindedness will empty the ideal. But swelling self-satisfaction, covert or overt, has nothing to do with answering the call of this ideal. Thought *breaks* on otherness. We ask: what then can it glean from the negativity of failure?

I first remark on philosophy and failure. Then, I consider radical failure; I look at an ancient and modern response, and suggest a third possibility beyond ancient resignation and modern defiance. Finally, I consider art's power, in tragic and comic form, to name and transfigure failure. Again my point will not be merely negative. The breakdown of the instrumental may prepare a possible breaking through of a different energy of mind and being in excess of any instrumentalization. We are reminded of being's unmastered otherness in the middle; acknowledging the limits of our self-mediation, a different inhabitation of the middle might be granted.

The instrumental mind, given its "optimistic" bias, its faith that there is no problem it cannot solve, will suspect morbidity in our theme. Yet philosophy has always reflected on failure's meaning. Socrates' view of philosophy as a life-long preparation for death testifies to an obsession with the knowledge that being as given to us must eventually fail. The philosopher least of all should shun this. Becoming mindful of death, its shadowing of all finite being, may make one honest about the universal impermanence.

True, this honesty can become nihilistic when, in the failure of finitude, being as such is denounced as metaphysically worthless, as a valueless thereness. Here existential philosophies of the absurd only continue this very ancient concern with failure, though the mood now is more willfully defiant than quietly resigned. But honesty about the failure of finite being may also occasion an opening to being in a more ultimate sense. This openness is part, I think, of the Socratic-Platonic appropriation of failure. Ancient skepticism (Hegel calls it "noble skepticism" in contradistinction to modern, empiricistic skepticism) may involve a similar preparation for openness to something more than failing finitude. As we will see, the Stoic ideal of the ataraxic Sage involved a very important strategy for dealing with the ultimacy of failure. Salvation in Christian theology offers a religious answer to our suffering of ultimate failure, interpreted as a sinfulness, or radical disability of the ethical will, that human beings themselves cannot redeem.

The history of post-Hegelian philosophy has yet to be written as a plurality of philosophical and anti-philosophical responses to ultimate failure. The massive concern of that history with the problem of finitude is clear indication of the fermenting of failure in contemporary thought (see chapter 1 on the "end of philosophy"). The so-called death of art (see chapter 2) epitomizes this sense of failure with respect to being aesthetic. Contemporary worries about the future of the ethical relate to the failure of utilitarianism to radically answer the issues of modernity and its ontologically unanchored self (see chapter 4). The concern of post-Hegelian philosophy with failure is especially evident in relation to being religious. Here the "death of God" (see chapter 3) is the scandalous sign blazing over the entrance to ultimate metaphysical failure. Heidegger's concern with finitude, with (following Hölderlin) the god's failure, with indeed the failure of the *logos* of the metaphysical tradition, carries us through the entrance. (I have argued elsewhere that philosophy has *always* being concerned with the possible failure of the *logos*.)[32] Existentialist absurdism passes into what it hopes is the Holy of Holies, only to find the sanctuary empty. It quickly dissimulates its disappointment into defiance and, trying to be a strong Nietzschean nihilism, absurdly celebrates the ineluctability of failure. This absurd celebration of failure cannot eventually hide the fact that it amounts to little more than metaphysical, sometimes anti-metaphysical whistling in the dark.

The mood of existential bravado wears thin with the post-Heideggerian deconstructionist. As the new high priest of exotic textual carding, he takes up residence in the sanctuary of failure. But as more ironical, more world-weary than the existentialist, as tired of the metaphysical absurdity of being, he prides himself on exposing the ultimate failures covered over by the great affirmative metaphysical texts of the Western tradition: logos must fail. He does not *live* Nietzsche's strong nihilism; with excessive philological self-consciousness, he parodies it instead; he puts it on paper, not into life. The text is failure, failure is in the text. The tradition of philosophy as a treasury of texts fails, but it is other. But let the deconstructionist apply his deconstruction to himself and he will find the self-reversion of failure. The failure of the other will boomerang and return to haunt him. Deconstruction first finds the failure in the other, but it must eventually find itself a failure, deconstruct itself, should it be honestly mindful of itself.[33]

Given these few historical reminders, let me focus on the matter itself. First, we must be mindful of success. Since no self is a complete whole, it is our nature to strive. In this respect, Nietzsche was right in calling man the unfinished animal. Modern consciousness here rightly stresses the self as activity. Our striving expresses the will to initiate significant ventures and to carry them to successful outcomes. There is joy in such venturing; striving itself delights, for in it we are party to an expansion of the self. The human being is an incomplete nature, but essential to our given being is power, power to pursue proper wholeness. To strive is to envisage a desired goal and to stretch the self to it. Transcending our limitations, we become concentrated in our endeavors and channel our energies towards the ends we elect. If we attain the end, our venture is crowned with success. Success entails not only the energy of pursuit, the excitement of search itself; it also points to the satisfaction of purpose attained. Our activity comes to something, some consequence, and the prior pursuit is not vain or inane.

Such success gives purposeful meaning to our desires and acts. Success evokes stock images in our society: a well paying job, two cars, a house expensive enough to require a burglar alarm. These are particular images of success, relative to the special conditions of certain societies. But it is wrong to restrict the sense of success to such particular conditions. Conditions being different, success might mean many different things, including the exact opposite of economic satisfactions. One might commit oneself to abnegation and poverty to liberate oneself from bondage to material goods.[34] One might count economic success as spiritual failure. To reject economic failure is not simply to court failure as such; is to court a different success, more elusive and singular perhaps, but a kind of success nonetheless. Indeed is it possible at all to pursue *pure failure*? Is this not a contradiction in terms? Suppose we attained our purpose here? Would not the achievement of pure failure be itself an example of successful purpose? Would not pure failure be thus an instance of success? Success in some guise seems to be an imperative written into all our endeavors. Success is accomplished purpose; and while different selves pursue different purposes, all selves purpose. A basic thrust towards or exigency for purpose seems ingrained in all activity, transcending all the particular purposes that express our individual desires.

Success is not simple. It conjures up the sense of satisfaction, but in this may be submerged much suffering and struggle. Success is an end, not a beginning; it comes to crown long effort. Out of strife striving grows; success often is conquered strife. Success is something *won*, often in wrestling with a resistance. A barrier rises before us; we may succumb to its obduracy; alternatively, we may slide around it, or surmount it, even smash it down; we say no to its obduracy with greater, more unrelenting stubbornness. Into success is written the scar line of limitation surpassed. But such surpassing does more than surmount a barrier blocking us; it rebounds on the self. We become aware of ourselves, conscious of our capacities, proud in the feeling of our new powers. Success is essentially self-mediating in engendering the sense of self-esteem. We grow in our own eyes, the phrase has it; we also grow in the eyes of others. Success brings both self-respect and the respect of others; we are esteemed. In the eyes of others we detect subtle shifts, all of them confirming one's new view of oneself. In the resulting self-assurance, not unnaturally, one may be seduced into believing that destiny lies securely within one's palm. Why then did William James call success the "bitch goddess?"

To answer this question, we must distinguish different forms of failure or breakdown. Any breakdown indicates these aspects: the "breaking," that is, the threatening of the self's wholeness, its being subject to a strain beyond the limit of self-mediation, one that may fragment or shatter its integrity; the "downing," that is, the reducing, the diminishing of its energy, its being—death is the extreme of such diminishment. We might distinguish three forms of breakdown that we can call: "physical" breakdown, "psychical" failure, and failure of "purpose." These recall but do not exactly reduplicate Plato's still helpful tripartite articulation of the psyche in terms of *epithumia*, *thumos*, and the *logistikos*.[35]

Physical failure relates to our being as a bodily organism. The body has an integrity, a wholeness of its own that we call health. When sickness hits, this wholeness is put under stress, disrupted. The body is laid low and fights to recover its energy. Illness is of extraordinary interest precisely because it reveals a negating counterthrust to the inherent exigency of the body to express its energy and insistently maintain its being. Against this counterthrust to its life, the body doctors itself. All medical skill is only an ancilla to this self-doctoring. Illness is a breakdown *within* the self-mediating, regenerating process of healthy life. Of course, there is the radical physical failure that passes beyond this regenerating process that names mortality as the inexorable destiny of our aging. But even here, so absolutely insistent is the energy of our being that many religions have hoped for a real regeneration beyond this dark divide.

Contrary to a superficial impression, philosophers have *always* been obsessed with the body, with sickness. The body is a privileged place of unavoidable failure. Their generally ascetic strategy is precisely a way to want always to be in advance of our necessary failure here. The asceticism that says the body is of no account shows a reverse image of this obsession with bodily failure. Such failure shadows all claims of spiritual self-sufficiency. You have to be obsessed with the body, treat it with ultimate seriousness, to undertake the negation of the natural involved in many ascetic practices. Asceticism is an attempt to negate the negation, here seen as the body, but this negation must inevitably reaffirm, even while allegedly suspending, the body's insistence of being.[36]

The second form, psychical failure, is implied when we say that one has lost one's nerve. The body may be perfectly healthy, but unless the psyche can summon a certain excitement or verve, it proves impossible to initiate, much less carry to term, challenging ventures. Without this emotional excitation the self is flat, insipid, listless. Action becomes tedious, an attitude of bored indifference descends. This happens, say, at a certain stage of adolescence: the youth cannot get "psyched up." Psychic failure can be illustrated from competitive games. At a certain point one side *gives up*. At a decisive stage of a game, and for perhaps inarticulate reasons, it ceases to fight back. Something happens that causes it to lose its heart. To have "heart" is not sheerly physical, nor completely intellectual, but something between. To lose "heart" is to become quickly demoralized; it is a failure of morale. The rest is merely waiting for defeat to work its full. Nor is the need for "heart" confined to the field of games. Its necessity is pervasive in human life, in individuals, in families, in cities ("heart" here is civic pride), in institutions ("heart" is something like *esprit de corps*), in states and nations ("heart" here is patriotism). The religious urgency of ultimacy (cf. chapter 3) is perhaps the most fundamental form of "heart." Without "heart" all these slowly wither. They become hollow from within, devoid of the emotional drive to continue and overcome.

These two forms of breakdown, physical and psychical, are initially below the threshold of self-consciousness. The third form, failure of purpose, occurs above this threshold and is the shadow of previously discussed success. One clear-sightedly intends an end or goal, but instead is frustrated. Failure of purpose is one's failure as a planning, calculating, rationally self-conscious agent. As self-determining, self-mediating beings, we define goals and work to fulfill them. But the intention turns awry, the plan comes unstuck, the agent lacks the required resources, the purpose cannot be effected. Failure of purpose is perhaps most easily named, since it occurs in the light of self-consciousness. But it may bring us to confront a limit recalcitrant to the grasping of instrumental rationality. Physical and psychical failure are elusive, often shrouded to self-consciousness. Yet all three are interrelated: body cannot be abstracted from self-conscious mind, nor either of these from the psychic energy mediating between them. Thus, psychic failure from an emotional shock can lead to physical breakdown; ill-health may lower emotional vivacity and the power to think straight. Hypochondria may even be a metaphysical ailment, a sickness that is no sickness, a sickness of spirit.[37] Thus, too, the absence of steady goals may cut a self adrift—with nowhere to drive itself, its emotional energy can explode into aggressiveness or dry up in aimlessness. Lack of purpose can precipitate a physical demoralizing, eating relentlessly into the will to live.

At this third level, instrumental mind as entirely self-mediating seems to hold full sway. But clearly this is not true. Failure here hints at deeper roots and demands a mindfulness more embracing than instrumental mind, one that breaks through any closed self-mediation. Resistant otherness erupts *within* the circle of closed self-mediation. A manifestation of otherness as metaxological, that is, unmastered by the self, is impossible to avoid. Thus, if we consider the calculative rationality which, in its abstraction from being as a whole, dominates modern societies, it is no surprise that the apotheosis of its success yields an obsession with failure of the first two forms. With respect to the first form, witness our unprecedented obsession with the body and the ballooning of doctoring into big business; with respect to the second form, witness the invasion of everyday life by the "therapeutic culture."

Thus, the cult of instrumental success is forced to exorcise the demons of physical and psychical failure. Its divinity calls these demons forth from the deep, but its exorcism sometimes only exacerbates them.

Radical Failure: Modern Success and Stoic Strategy

The instrumental self is suffused with a glow from its sense of success. In confronting limits, it is assured it can deal with every one. Any negative is but a prologue to its corresponding positive; every resistance is but another test proving its surpassing power; its own incompletion is merely the unfinished present of its future promise. Being mindful, however, demands a deeper understanding of "limit." We are essentially oriented to success, one can agree, but the meaning of this orientation is more opaque than the instrumental self can comprehend. Ripples from a different wind ruffle this bright and shiny self. The negative frequently strikes its wound deeper than any such optimism can heal. Failure asserts its paradoxical power, and perhaps, too, its wisdom. Certainly many failures are of a provisional sort: barriers that with time will be overcome, temporary blocks on our self-creation. But there are more intractable failures, radical failures that bring us up short, and though we ceaselessly bid them move, they will not budge.

Most ventures mingle success and failure. Most purposes are never realized in exactly the way initially envisaged. One gains something here, loses something there, is surprised on this, has one's expectation strengthened on that. But flanking this mass of ambiguous ventures, two extremes of failure stand out. The first is born of lack of venture, of absence of pluck. Anxiety, apprehension incapacitates us from the outset. We fear even to try, for all trying risks breakdown and defeat. This failure shirks such risk, but also paralyzes those powers properly spent in seeking. It is the failure of the anaemic self, the neutral (cf. chapter 1) who would bury the talent rather than gamble with its use. Indeed it often masquerades as a cautious prudence: if you gain nothing, at least you lose nothing. But this is spurious, for you lose something really essential—the daring necessary to make some return on one's gifts. This cautious prudence is really the rationalization of a profound cowardice before life's chances.

The second extreme of failure is something different. Instead of daring nothing, it appears when one is risking everything. One sets before oneself a consummating goal. One demands everything from oneself. One throws oneself into the venture with an "all or nothing" attitude. But having done this, and nothing relevant having been left undone, one finds that all one's efforts, as we say, "come to nothing." All the striving proves fruitless, as the consummating goal collapses before our reach, a beckoning mirage decomposing into desert sand. Unlike the success of the activist self, here our concentrated efforts, all the expansion, expenditure of self, do not surpass a limitation. We come across a limit on which we break.

The result can be a contraction of the self, a shrinking of our being back into itself (consider how in being deeply disappointed the self seems to shrivel up, retract from the expanse of being in its otherness). We confront negative otherness in radical failure, but the ensuing meonic contraction of selfhood seems to lack any redemption. This extreme failure brings with it the danger of a self going under. Failure engulfs us, threatens to drown us. We sometimes say: the person was crushed by disappointment. "Being crushed" expresses well that blocking of zest, that congealing of hope, that dissipation of energy following such failure. The person may even wear failure in his physical features. A bend in the body, a slight slouch, communicates in gesture the entire plight—the look of being beaten. You can tell by the way he carries himself, that is, by the fact that he does not carry himself at all—he *drags* himself.

In the case of great failure, this experience of being crushed extends far beyond this particular act or that particular enterprise. I have thrown myself entirely into a venture, but in failing I am thrown back upon myself completely. But I alone cannot mediate the failure, master its negative otherness. It is my entire selfness that is crushed. I experience a terrifying, sinking feeling that my existence is not necessary, that my being is superfluous. Not only do my actions "come to nothing"; my very existence "counts for nothing." My failure becomes a cracked mirror that mocks my former proud boldness. The ineradicable precariousness, insecurity, contingency of my nature beats on me, beats through me.

As previously with solitude, one is here tempted to see such failure as just the absence of significance, an unmeaning void. Yet both "negativities" must be faced. Not to be mindful of failure, is not this the real failure? The question is crucial since the modern world tends to banish or taboo the actuality of such failure, at least in its public, official rhetoric. For modern activist selfhood sees itself as solving *problems*.[38] What is a problem but a difficulty that, in principle, can be tackled and some solution devised? The possibility of some solution is inherent in a problem; our calculative, technical, manipulative powers will do the rest. Assured of our power to control, we gloss over, even disguise from ourselves, forms of failure not amenable to "problem-solving." Our mighty refusal of failure thus becomes a more subtle form of failure—an evasion of the full impact of our finitude.

On one level we are undoubtedly justified in fighting against the limitations of the finite. It is part of our dignity and glory not to rest content with being but a finite object. But even a fighter comes to know his opponent, to respect his enemy, forms even a bond with his destroyer. This intimate, disquieting mindfulness is lacking in what we can call the modern cult of success. This cult tends to push failure away from its focus of attention. Failure can be given no significance, so those who are deemed failures are shunted aside. The most elemental functional failure, bodily failure, we find in old age; hence age enjoys no inherent respect for the cult of success. Frequently to be successful means health, wealth, youth, no matter how vacuous. Age, sickness, death, whatever slips outside the norm is forgotten, unnoticed, unmentioned. A web of silence is woven around the nameless ones. A failure is a non-person. A failure is *refuse*: what is rejected, refused.

The modern cult of success refuses to reintegrate the negative otherness of failure back into success. So it misses the opportunity to give to failure a further significance and to success a less shallow conception. Related to this is the predominance of the language of work and function. A success is what fulfills its functions; a human success fulfills certain social and economic functions. Success here, however, is confined to the recognized, widespread functions. Compared to the Greek version of the notion (e.g., humanity's *ergon* in Aristotle's *Ethics*), human function is itself flattened, excessively standardized. Functions not recognized by the widespread flattened standardization are denied the status of success: instead they are named as eccentric, as marginal. The whiff of difference the outsider brings is to be sniffed with suspicion. If it brings disrupting otherness, it is greeted with alarm. It is a threat to success.

Indeed, success in this functional sense comes to serve as a standard of reality, of *realness* itself. Something is real if, as the phrase has it, "it works." Realness becomes correlative to pragmatic function. Since failure is the breakdown of what works, it is the intrusion of the unreal. Even scientific theories, speculative and theoretical, it would seem, have been yoked to this functional standard: a "true" theory is said to be one that "works" (this view always begs the question, I think). Beyond the specialized areas of science, it also becomes a pervasive standard throughout life. A person who does not "work" is not just a failure, but is perceived to have diminished realness. Not surprisingly, people who seem not to serve "socially useful" functions—like the unemployed, those who cannot work, or perhaps the retired, or those who do not leave the family or home for work—all these are seen, and come to see themselves, as reduced in realness. The come to be seen as "counting for nothing." They are and have being, but their being is seen as its opposite, as nothing. When they acquiesce in this verdict, and themselves perceive their own existence as counting for nothing, a spreading corrosion of spirit can set in. They are unreal, hence they make themselves unreal; they are nothing, hence they will confirm their nothingness. It may take a heroic will to resist the depression and despair.

In the measure that the cult of success can lead to the self's reduction to despairing nothing, we find an *ethical* failure to acknowledge the other in the intrinsic worth of its being (chapter 4). Hence it helps to counterpose to this modern cult of success a classical response, namely Stoic strategy. In the latter the intimacy of being ethical and being mindful are very evident. For the Stoic, being mindful takes the form of trying to safeguard the ethical integrity of the inward self in the very midst of failure, in fact, in the midst of the ethical failure that passes as success. One meets failure and sometimes one can do little about it. The appropriate response, the Stoic says, is resignation. By accepting failure, resigning oneself to it, one gains a little success, a little moral victory. So one might attain, if only inwardly, the composure that failure tends to crack. Thus Stoic strategy is primarily directed inward. It tries to detach the inward self from the defeat of its outward action and suffering. At least the inward self can remain calm and at home with itself. Externally the entire world might be collapsing, everything else might count for nothing; but the Stoic sage would preserve an inviolate temple of interior composure.

There surely can be great nobility in this Stoic strategy. Stoicism is, as it were, the aristocracy of self-mediation. It is grounded on a clear recognition of the ethical inviolability of the inward self. It answers the summons of this ideal, nobly so, because its fidelity to the ethical ideal takes shape within social contexts notably inhospitable to being ethical, contexts that might easily serve as rationalizations for the violation of the ethical self. That the others may be ethically vile is no excuse that I be equally vile. Stoic strategy tries to find ethical significance in the extremity of disappointment. It pushes the experience of "counting for nothing" through to a deeper ethical level. It finds a way of shrugging off failure, a way of saying: "It does not touch me, the real, essential me. I say no to failure by refusing to treat it as absolute; thus I guard the ethical peace of the inner man." For there are necessities in the nature of things against which it is unreasonable, nay ignoble, to rail. The ancient Stoic (like his modern heir Spinoza) responds to failure by nodding towards Necessity, saluting it. Thus he tries to reverse failure into success. Failure becomes the occasion that discloses human foolishness, and so, if we attain the right mindfulness, becomes the doorway to wise peace.

Still, something in Stoic resignation lets us down. Stoic nobility follows its commitment to ethical self-mediation, but in retreating inward it risks closing the circle of self-mediation in a way that wills *not to suffer otherness*, or to minimize its impact where unavoidable. This is enshrined in its ideal of *apatheia*: non-pathos, non-suffering. But radical failure means we cannot avoid suffering otherness in the form of a negativity that self-mediation cannot master. We can imagine the Stoic saying of failure: "It is beyond human control. Let it be." But this simple phrase "Let it be" harbors the entire ambiguity. It can be uttered in various ways with different tonalities. One mode of uttering it, makes it into a gesture of *turning away*. "Let it be"—it is not worth the candle; we do better without it. This makes it a slogan of rejection, of repudiation. Here we *may* find a secret contempt or disgust. "Let it be"—here we *may* discover the desire to be rid of being in its uncontrollable otherness. We cannot conquer all the obstacles of life; but we want to preserve our pride; we do so by saying that the fight itself is not worth it.[39]

Stoic greatness lies in its desire to stare the negative in the face. But its stare sometimes squints. It becomes sightless before the horror, and does not outstare it. For the Stoic response to failure is partly a pretence that failure does not really exist. So surprisingly, it is not unlike the modern cult of success. It separates the inner self and outer world; its aristocratic self-mediation attenuates metaxological intermediation with otherness; real failure, it implies, is *only* the moral failure of the inner self. But this is to consign to unreality forms of failure that, in their recalcitrant otherness, pass beyond human will, and that (like tragic failure) are supremely real precisely in their revelation of radical otherness. Having separated the inner and outer, it is easier to convince oneself of inner triumph. But if the outer does not test the success of the inner, every kind of hypocrisy and self-deceit might be possible. Of course, the noble Stoic wants to avoid just this, but his detachment risks an ancient version of what in the modern era is radically unanchored subjectivity, with all the attendant lack of being-at-home with oneself and with being. The experience of failure is intimately bound up with the fact that the outer action does not, cannot fulfill completely the intention of the inner self. Thus it is never enough to separate the inner and outer. This separation, in fact, is only a redefinition of failure.

To deal with failure means, in part, to surpass this separation and bring inner self and outer action into harmony. More: it is to surpass the alienation of inner otherness and outer otherness in renewed participation in the metaxological community of being. Stoic strategy tries to win by retreat, but this can be but another kind of defeat. For Stoic resignation, having retreated into the inner self, must find the resources for return, that is, for advance outward. But to advance outward again is to refuse to be simply resigned. Thus, the danger of the Stoic "Let be" is that it may become nihilistic. It may become a subterfuge that puts the gloss of nobility on despair. And in fact in Stoic resignation the note of despair is never entirely absent. Marcus Aurelius, for instance, never ceases to admonish himself forward with maxims and moral exhortations. But a tiredness, a despair, a disgust with life surfaces repeatedly. He is intent to keep himself clean. But since the inward self and outer otherness are set in contrast, the effect is to impute a kind of uncleanliness to everything else but the self. For all the nobility of Stoic resignation, it is not entirely free of the note of negation. When its "Let it be" cannot rise above this, its strategy with failure turns out to be a highminded defeatism.[40]

If in the Stoic "Let be" there may lurk a possible defeatism, even despair, there is a somewhat different way of saying "Let it be." This second "Let it be" is not a turning away, a repudiation; instead it gives utterance to a deeply affirmative acceptance of being as metaxological, hence as unmastered in its otherness. It does not leave finite being aside as worthless, but moves towards it with a new openness. "Let it be": this now becomes a kind of blessing of being. Yes, I may count for nothing, as radical failure reveals. But being is not therefore to be greeted with disgust or contempt. Despite *my* failure, it is still good, most good. Unlike the Stoic withdrawal, this second "Let it be" steps beyond, while preserving, the caretaking of ethical inwardness and says yes to the being of otherness as good. In the inner otherness something breaks through the estrangement of inner and outer otherness.

Nor should we be unfair to Stoicism, since the great Stoic might also be seen as blessing all being, in so far as he holds the cosmos to be an unsurpassably perfect whole. Stocism sometimes distinguishes the wisdom of the Sage that is divine and the knowledge of the philosopher that relates to the necessities of life. Despite the Stoic's withdrawal from being as an external other, it is in this sense of the cosmos that we find his metaphysical amen to universal otherness. This is the point. In the second mode, "Let it be" says I am willing to affirm being as it passes beyond my own failure. Radical failure need not necessitate despair. My pride counts for only so much, as in a certain sense does my inward self. What is more important is that I go to greet what being gives with joy. "Let it be" in this second mode moves from resigned, noble defeat to the willingness to be reconciled with all that is, to say "yes" even in the darkest and most destructive failures.

This second "Let be" breaks through from nowhere in particular and for no particular reason, like a gift out of nothing. But its gratuity engenders a gratitude to being and a response to failure that is neither the modern cult of success nor classical resignation. It is linked to what I can only call a kind of religious reconciliation that has passed through the releasing disillusion I discussed before (chapter 3).[41] I am talking about affirmation that does not turn its back on the negative, but that affirms while standing in the very sundering of the negative itself. I say reconciliation because, unlike resignation, this amen is more rinsed of the note of defeat. To be resigned is often, as we say, "to give in" — an inward collapse of the hollow self. To be reconciled is a different kind of yielding: it itself may yield a breakthrough beyond breakdown. To be reconciled, say, with an enemy, is not to "give in" to him and so to negate oneself. It is to assume a new demeanor to what before was seen only as hostile, and to discover a hitherto unseen side to the "hostile." To be reconciled is not to "give in" but to "give up" — give up, that is, an untenable way of being. It is not simple surrender, but a surrendering of oneself to what passes beyond the defective way of being. It is itself a suffering passage beyond this deficient way.[42]

Such reconciliation is not completely quietistic. It does not deny the truth of ethical inwardness of Stoic composure. Nor does it downgrade the rightness of the self actively giving expression to its own being—this rightness is the core of truth in the modern cult of success, a truth it distorts in turning activist selfhood as self-mediating into the absolute. Failure may have another meaning beyond modern success and ancient resignation. The failure is not denied but its absoluteness may be mitigated. There is a way towards transfiguring failure that sees breakdown as the negative process wherein the self comes across its own limit in an otherness it cannot master. But to come across such limits need not be destructively negative, for through it may arise a mindfulness of that radical otherness, whether inward or outer, beyond our utmost limit. To accept that one breaks on one's utmost limit may push one to ponder on an otherness "beyond," "beyond" in being more primordial than the self as a standard of being. To grant this boundary here is to break through to metaphysical wonder about its "beyond."

If failure forces no such reconsideration, we have learnt nothing. But radical failure may be the dark side of our exposure to the "beyond" in which the recalcitrant otherness of being appears in the mask of nothingness. The shock of such exposure concentrates the self, makes it mindful. It rocks us back on ourselves, and in the inward desert of "counting for nothing" may occasion both deeper self-knowing and the patient opening of thought to what lies beyond our power. In place of the old restless, stressed striving, a new acceptance may dawn. A fresh affirmation may rise from failure, our demeanor to defeat wresting a triumph from defeat.[43]

The profound desolation of radical failure may thus be a purification of the abyssal sources of metaphysical mindfulness. Just as subsequent to sickness, the return of health may refresh every perception, so radical failure may be the dark threshold of a dawn. Even the experience expressed in the words "we count for nothing" can offer a bitter wisdom, a bracing wisdom. The outcome might be a new, shakened honesty about our ultimate achievement. It might also be a new benevolence, a taste of second love, a new compassion for all things, including the downcast, the forgotten, the downtrodden, the forsaken, the rejects, the lost. One has tasted a little of their abandonment and come away from it chastened.

Art and Failure

As one of philosophy's significant others, art is revealing in regard to failure. So let me conclude with art's power to name, transfigure failure.

Failure can brings us to a limit beyond our control that bluntly discloses our finitude. What we do with this disclosure beyond lamentation? Do we risk any other gesture? But even when we cannot surmount or eradicate a limit, we have the power to give voice to its otherness, to articulate its impact. Somehow the act of expressing what is recalcitrant binds us significantly to what seems so to oppose us. Art, in the variety of its expressive power and as a tolerance of otherness (see chapter 2) is one of the most subtle strategies with failure. It allows us to say the otherness that limits us without destroying our dignity as self-mediating beings. Often indeed it offers a complex exploration of dignity in encounter with such limits. It also illuminates the second "Let be."

This might seem strange considering, say, the Greek idea of art. Thus, Aristotle sees art in terms of a specialized skill, a *technē*. What more reveals our power to control or manipulate, our power to fight all failure? Often this is just the idea we have of the artist as craftsman, as master. The master craftsman seems to plan out his product in advance. Then through his skill, he simply superimpose his preconceived plan on his chosen material. Perhaps initially his material may resist him, limit him, but in his struggle with it, he eventually manages to dominate it. Thus he subdues it to his own purposes, stamping it with his victorious seal. What could be a better image than this of the human self as master of its fate?

This has some plausibility if we are dealing with fairly simple artefacts, the making of a chair perhaps. Even here, though, the craftsman comes to know that one cannot *force* the material in a direction contrary to its nature. The material in its otherness must be known from within, respected intimately. Otherwise it will break under the violating hand, whose brusque imperiousness thus defeats its own purpose. Craft involves coaxing and compromise, as much as control and mastery. Ingrained in the simplest material are *its* limits, which become one's own limits in the crafting act. This means that artist and material are not defined exclusively by the artist's dominance. Rather in his efforts to determine and shape the material, the artist finds *himself* shaped and determined by it. In the aesthetic interplay between artist and material, the artist is not the sole commanding master; the material issues its call too. So much so that many artists will speak of their work as coming to follow *its own* course, as *shaping itself* in a manner not fully in the power of self-conscious will. The material presents the artist with certain *necessities* whose recalcitrance must be granted before any release through them or from them can be gained. Any freedom the artist may yet attain will be reached through this creative struggle with necessity. The struggle must respect necessity. There is no escape from limits, yet our granting of their necessity need not squash freedom but may crystallize some its fullest determinations.

The greatest challenge is with the richest, most complex material, that is, when the artist deals directly with the matter of human existence itself. The human being struggles with itself, struggles with itself as its own promising, chaotic material. We shape ourselves, articulate our own otherness. We probe the line of limitation and necessity internal to our own being. We seek to make free the sources of affirmation lying beyond that line. Our struggle with ourselves, the human interplay with the human, is expressed most profoundly in *dramatic* art. A drama is a complex web of interrelations wherein humans have nowhere to turn without confronting the limitations of someone other. In the intermediation of the human, drama articulates the inescapability of the other as other. Hence dramatic art, particularly tragedy and comedy, images some of our most significant struggles with radical failure.

While there are many theories about tragedy and comedy, both are especially revealing about failure. This is obviously so with the tragic. Here we are not dealing with the petty pains of life; we are confronted with great suffering, spiritual suffering, indeed sacred suffering. Radically resistant otherness intrudes on the human self in a dark and destructive way. Yet in the failure of man we see suffering in its power to ennoble man. Like all drama, tragedy deals with the interplay of the human, but the interplay here reveals a collision of powers that catch and rend the hero in sublime and terrible conflicts. He suffers a dark limit that stretches, strains and eventually shatters him.

Character is destiny, the saying has it. In tragic drama character and destiny cooperate and collide at once. It is the resistant otherness of destiny that decrees ultimate suffering. A course of action is within the choice and power of the individual. But the cunning of other powers nests in the same course of events. An initially unknown necessity conspires to travel *incognito* the same path as the hero. Working with and through his chosen acts, it brings him face to face with himself and with the bounding finiteness on which the old self is broken.

What occurs at the boundary offers tragic transfiguration of the failure. Aristotle thought that the hero works out a fatal *hamartia* or "error," but it is wrong to think of tragic failure as simply his failure of will.[44] We do not say: "if only he had previously willed differently, this would not have come to pass." There is no consolation on this level in the tragic, for we sense from the outset, with a sinking feeling of horror, that nothing human can aid this hero. He must be brought to nothing by the doom that already begins to effect its inexorable work. It is the constraint of a dark necessity against which he often unwittingly runs and is destroyed. But in this destruction there is an ennobling, a sacrifice, a redemption of the failure.

The term "sacrifice" is entirely appropriate, since it literally means to "make sacred." Being is ultimately sacrificial: all self-being goes under in the universal impermanence, but in this perishing self-being many become being-for-another. Tragic failure makes sacred. In this any victory may be pyrrhic, since to rise above radical failure the hero must go down. But in this death there is not resignation. There is exultation, the exulting that Nietzsche knew and Yeats. We who watch the conflict participate in the blessing of being that is won out of destruction. We share in the sacred purgation of the hero. As Aristotle's catharsis indicates, we, too, are reconciled to a conflict without finite resolution; accepting the failure of finitude, we come to know a brief, bitter leaping joy. Tragedy confronts the terrible pathos of great failure, but in the heart of failure it affirms. Despite the extremity of his suffering Oedipus would say: All is well. In Hamlet's foreboding there flickers the sense: the readiness is all.

Some think of comedy as tragedy's antithesis, one light, the other serious. But comedy, too, is a dealing with failure, in some ways more inventive and sophisticated. Put simply: there are no comic heroes; comedy does not need nobles for affirmation; it is more *humanely universal*.[45] It releases an affirmation of even mere humanness. As with its affirmation, so comedy itself abounds in failure. There is not one central flaw, but rather a promiscuous myriad of human absurdities, especially in the form of pretension and self-deceit. Comedy shows our absurdity as "coming to nothing," shows being human as risible. It brings down, indeed explodes pretension, dissolving in laughter the constriction of being that failure brings. Failure is not ultimately serious; what is ultimate is the sheer energy of being that laughter discloses. Laughter is self-forgetting, Olympian, God-like, redeeming. What we treat as ultimate is not ultimate; laughter exposes its absurd, illusory character. It makes the failure inconsequential. It, too, is nothing. And where failure cannot be healed, laughter at least makes us forget it.

Comedy is a kind of *metaphysical commentary* on finiteness and failure. We will *always* and *inevitably* fail. Sometimes we laugh with failure, sometimes at it, sometimes with bitterness, sometimes more gently. Laughter, of course, can become nihilistic, a violent disgust with being that is nevertheless parasitical on the power of being for its negation. It depends on *how* we say "It is nothing." A laughing "It is nothing" can be a healing "Let it be."

Laughter explodes with the joy of energy before the absurdity that is being human. There is no denial of the absurdity; but laughter destroys it while accepting it; it transfigures it by letting shine through it, break through it, a forgiving energy of being that is other to finite failure, a healing outburst of unanticipated plenty[46]. Even "just being cheerful," "putting a smile on things," may be deep rejoinders to failure. I am absurd. But what do I matter? I shrug and laugh. I *am* laughing; I am *being* laughing; but the "I am," absurd or not, never exhausts the power of being. The energy of being of the laughing "I" is not "mine"; it passes beyond me. I laugh at my defeat; but in laughing I pass beyond myself. The laughing of the energy of being outflanks me. Transcendence laughs. Laughter is the benevolent face of nemesis.

Comedy is a brief but abundant truce with the darkness of being; we cannot say for sure if beyond the end all will live happily ever after; yet for a span and within the middle, we are reconciled with the bounding dark otherness. If comedy is a festive truce with darkness, we bless it when it comes; tragedy, in the beginning, does not bless, but endures and comes, in the end, to bless. But there is something absolutely elemental about laughing. It reveals an essential promise of being human. For a defeated, disappointed self finds it extremely difficult to laugh. To laugh would be to destroy the disappointment, and this we strangely hug. It would be to unlock the flow of energy that the disappointment of failure congeals. In laughter we briefly taste the return of infinite, irrepressible energy, the energy of being that unfailingly plays a subversive comedy—promise of the folly of idiot wisdom.

CHAPTER 6

Being Mindful: Thought Singing Its Other

I now consider being mindful as thought singing its other, the preparing nocturnal side of which we saw in thought breaking on otherness. I will be more directly concerned with the possibility of being beyond breakdown, of our opening to metaxological being in breakthrough. Hints of this already have been given, for example, in the eruption in laughter of a more primordial energy of being beyond failure. This breaking through cannot be completely systematized. It cannot be technically manipulated, predicted or guaranteed. It is an episodic shaking eruption of what slumbers or is repressed in our domestications of metaxological being. Though it cannot be ordered, it can be named. What erupts is the original power of being that variously figures itself forth in the aesthetic, the religious, and the ethical.[1] As the power of being, it is not ours; yet it is configured through us, both coming to self-awakening and yet transcending any particularization that falsely claims this original power for itself alone. I speak of the naming act of philosophical mindfulness as thought *singing its other;* for in singing we meet an outpouring of articulation of enigmatic affirmative power, even when the song airs the grief of suffering being.

As in the last chapter, I deal with being at the limit in the metaxological middle, beyond self-mediation, but now with more emphasis on affirming thought. Facing the limiting otherness we find ourselves othered, altered, indeed reversed. We are dispossessed of the securities of self-mediation, but opened to being in a non-possessive mindfulness. My focus is on the radical between: radical in the sense of the extremes in the middle, in the sense of roots, grounds in the middle. I am concerned with metaxological reversals. These are not dialectical reversals in Hegel's sense, where plurality is included in one self-mediating whole. There is no final reduction of the interstices, the caesuras of being. In the tension of extremes, beyond all self-mediation, we find ourselves crossing back and forth between the limits of intermediate being. What happens in crisscrossing these gaps, intervals of being? Does a song of being somehow spark across these gaps? Is there a breakthrough in the breakdown of seamless self-sufficiency, a crisis of being and a reversal of mind, a destruction that is a renewal? Can we follow the process of coming to nothing to a renewed coming to being, beyond nihilism?

In a return to the elemental givenness of metaxological being, beyond instrumentalized mediation, we find in the interstices a breakthrough of the energy of being as infinite and overdetermined. How to affirm this? A certain metaphysical praise is needed, but this becomes nebulous and would dissipate into nothing if not particularly "placed." We cannot encompass the infinite (contra Hegel's infinite as dialectical self-mediation). We are metaxological participants in its grounding otherness. But there are determinate disclosures of being as full — finite revelations of what is beyond all finite determination. What is disclosed may seem like nothing, for it is not a determinate object, but a breakthrough of the overdetermined power of being in the very thisness of the charged occasion or moment. There is no dialectical encompassing of the absolute or the whole, but there are moments of absoluteness in which we are made whole. Our saying of these cannot be a determinate proposition, but is more like a song — as an episodic breaking through of festive thought. Such breakthroughs are *idios*, revealed in particularities outside all systems of abstract generalities. They may lead to general reflection perhaps, but must be named in their thisness. In order not to forget *the this as this,* I have to move between particular and general. Nor is this easy for philosophy, for it reveals its inescapable need of the poetic.

Again we must take our stand between closed Hegelian totality and the fragmentariness of Wittgensteinian or deconstructive plurality. The finite occasion as overcharged with otherness is suggestive of the infinite energy of being as the radical other. Art, religion, ethics may be ways of being mindful of this. I am trying to think beyond their bureaucratic separation, itself a product of instrumental mind. To respect their transcendence of the instrumental, philosophical saying has to be more than a set of determinate propositions. This is disconcerting to philosophy. But if philosophical language is dealing with being as infinite energy revealed in the finite event, it is logical for it to be open to such overdetermined discourse, discourse as much metaphorical as conceptual. This would be festive thought.[2]

If philosophical thought can sing, the episodic nature of breakthrough implies a like episodic aspect to this singing. In a sense this whole work is thought singing its other, an effort to ring the ontological powers of philosophy's others, while not reneging on philosophy's own voice. I do not now offer a finished symphony but variations on metaxological themes, strains of which have found voice in previous chapters. The lyrics of such philosophic song may cause us to jettison jargon; yet intricacy of thought can be intimate to their simplicity. The echoing and concordance of my themes will appear in what follows. First, I consider the plurivocal character of being mindful by asking about the ontological suggestiveness of the element gold and the pluriform thought it requires. Then I turn to singing and the healing naming of the elemental it can effect. Then I ask what song of thought, what mutability canto, is possible in the breaking of being that time and death inexorably effect. Finally, I ask if the breakthrough that can come points to a sense of festive being and what I call "idiot wisdom": a powerless power beyond the will-to-power of instrumental thought. Are there self-justifying moments of golden being? Thought must sing their gift, as best it can.

I. SONG OF GOLDEN BEING

The metaxological view means that being human is being in interplay: the ways of being—aesthetic, religious, ethical, philosophic—cannot be reduced to some simple unitary essence, even though formations of being mindful are found in all. Being mindful enjoins us to ponder the crisscrossings of these different ways. I first pursue such pluralized pondering in respect of the singular instance of gold. I want to reiterate the plurivocity answering to metaxological being, but relevantly to the intrinsic worth of being, even in all the plurality.

Hegel once said that philosophy does not merely console; it must reconcile, transfigure being. Being mindful tries to be such golden thought. But the realist will rightly ask: Is this not wishful thinking? Is not being just "out-there," a thing neutrally objective, while thinking and value are merely subjective processes? Mind can conjure up a myriad of fantasies, but solid reality stands out there, plainly evident, comfortingly unambiguous. Being is univocal: there is one essential meaning to which all others reduce, must be reduced. The logicist says: a spade is a spade, and should be called a spade. As Bishop Butler put it: Everything is what it is, and not another thing. The unadorned thing stands before the mind, and other than the one literal meaning, everything else is decoration, mere metaphor.

The realist has a proper conviction of being's otherness and its givenness to mindfulness. But that givenness, even in its otherness, is bound up with a metaxological relatedness of being to thought. The bonds between mindfulness and being are complex; we need plurivocal thought, which includes in itself the power of metaphysical metaphors, to be open to being's plenitude. Openness is thoughtfulness, even to the elemental, and need not be naive. To name in the singing sense I intend is not to clamp on being a rigid, univocal designator. The point is not to deny being its own proper "unity"; this, however, turns out to be a dense "unity," in fact, a community, requiring a plurality of modes of thinking to make open for us its intricate significance. The "metaphorical" modes of mind need not be wishful thinking but real unveilings. To metaxological mindfulness being is not given indigently as bare literal prose.

Thus, the elemental "unity" of gold unfolds its compacted significance in a plurality of articulations that call for pluriform thought. Gold is gold. But this bald proposition remains poverty-stricken and hardly begin to articulate the wealth of meanings that shimmer before the mind when we hear the magic word: gold. As tantalizing us with a plurality of possibilities, gold is metaphorical of the presence of being itself in its welcoming yet resistant inexhaustibility. It is a determinate thing which, when thought about, takes on an indeterminacy wherein the human self discovers the plurivocity of its own indeterminate being. All the ways of being, aesthetic, religious, ethical, philosophic find a voice there. Gold is, one might say, the metaphysical metal.

When the literalist mind names one basic reality, it sees gold in material terms. It is just one of the elements, a primitive physical irreducible. However, beyond this univocal meaning, gold carries the suggestion of far more. (Even the elemental, we will see, is not a univocal concept.) For it brings to the surface the idealizing powers of mind which, in turn, liberate gold into an otherness: its materiality is also ideal.

As a first instance of this ideality, consider gold's use for *economic* exchange. Human beings might have confined themselves to exchanging one thing for other things in the give and take of practical life. Such a literal-minded mode of exchange proves impracticably cumbersome. Seemingly simple, such a univocal economics become snarled in inefficiency.[3] Gold becomes a means of facilitating exchange. Thus, gold is *ideal* in being more than any material thing, by standing for the worth of many things. It is not simply a thing but the value of things. To see its ideality is to see its intimate intertwining with desire. It helps meet practical need but its ideal power ranges beyond any particular good or need. It functions as a standard of value, of desirability. Modern economics, I know, has tried to break with the gold standard. But paper standards are just the less poetic standards appropriate to a prosaic, utilitarian age.

Even so, gold retains its archaic, metaphoric power. It provokes not only the prose of domestic desire but also the poetry of more extraordinary longings, desire itself in its restless expanse. As a supreme standard of value, it prizes open great vistas of yearning. A telling example is the famous quest of El Dorado. When adventurers boldly set forth in quest of El Dorado, visions of fabulous gold provide the physical counterpart to their own limitless, insatiable desire. Gold precipitates a kind of *absolute desire*. The seeker of El Dorado is drawn into an impossible quest for a nonexistent treasure, but is progressively consumed in the rising expectation of his radically deluded desire. El Dorado may be an illusion, a dream that turns to nightmare. Nevertheless it reveals something elemental about desire: its hunger for absolute worth, its thirst for absoluteness.

That a thing has more than one meaning makes the literalist mind uneasy; that it carries opposed meanings makes it despair. This happens with gold and absolute desire. Gold also invokes the opposite to the standard of worth. This occurs when it is seen *religiously,* as is appropriate with absolute desire (recall the religious urgency of ultimacy). If we treat gold as the absolute, this view goes, we inevitably break ourselves on a mirage. El Dorado is really the graveyard of desire. A finite thing beckons as if it were the infinite. A self whose absolute desire is drawn by this seduction, investing it with the urgency of ultimacy, must inevitably destroy itself. In gold's ideality we behold the temptation to idolatry: the adoration of the finite as infinite, and the consequent desecration of both. This precious metal is religiously base, a source of evil of appalling power. The Golden Calf is the most famous instance; it is the paradigm of the ideal as idol. When Moses was in delicate communion with unseen ultimacy, his waiting people grew anxious, impatient and fashioned a seen, secure god. To want to fix the god thus is the idolatry of the univocal mind. The Golden Calf is the false god diverting desire for the absolute into deluded worship.

Splitting the univocal unity of the literalist mind, gold precipitates *double* desire and separates its direction into two contrary extremes, extremes joined by the fact that each beckons with a different version of the absolute. Mindfulness must be properly discriminating about this complex, tensive "unity." Mammon is a god—gold as the supreme standard of value; Mammon is never a god, only filthy lucre—gold as the paradigm of the idol. We fail to find a single, univocal meaning. The literalist mind will suspect equivocation and logically unacceptable contradiction. Rather we should say that gold becomes a symbol of the strain in desire, a symbol of the fork in our intermediate being that divides us and forces our decision for ultimacy—for one can absolutely serve only one absolute.

Gold's bewitching power lets us idealize given reality into images intense with significance, but such images, while not univocal, are not sheerly equivocal. The metaxological sense of being is reflected thus: in the plurivocity of such images we find a community of akin meanings. We find variations on the common theme, namely, our intimation of *perfection of being*. (Variations on this theme will recur throughout *all* this chapter.) Thus, we speak of a golden boy, a sunny boy, and mean by this a child marked out by special gifts. A golden child is one lavishly gifted by fortune or the generous gods. Similarly, a golden voice is one that approaches perfection, resounding for us hearers as a reminder of the hidden order of perfection.

Or consider Yeats' Golden Bird of art's perfection, singing of "what is past or passing or to come" (*Sailing to Byzantium*). Consider the golden crown as the emblem of the king. The crown symbolizes the authority to rule the kingdom, the power to gather a people into a community. This symbolic weight was all the more momentous in other ages when authority was held to stem from the divine. In temporal affairs the golden crown mediated between peoples and their gods (*their* laughter was itself golden). In spiritual matters the halo is the golden crown's analogue. The halo shows a human to shine with ultimacy, to be a living embodiment of perfection. The halo is God's golden glow. I think of the golden background of eternity in some sacred paintings. I think of the golden Buddhas of Burma, their shine of serenity.

This connection with perfection is evident in the way the ancients saw gold as the sole pure mineral. Liquid gold was the elixir of life, possessing the ultimate power to heal and rejuvenate. Yet all our dealing with perfection is fraught with ambiguity, hence with peril. Thus, the Golden Bough Aeneas plucked at the bidding of the Cumaean sibyl, served to allow his passage to the *underworld*. Moreover, if we wrongly seek complete identity with perfection itself, we risk destruction. Hence the tale of Midas. King Midas was granted the wish that everything he touched would turn to gold. The result, first delightful, finally proved intolerable. The ultimate impoverishment in the midst of massive wealth was his impotence to eat the food he touched. The food became gold, but the golden food cut him off from life's renewal in the humble element of daily bread.

Again, as an image of perfection of being gold often takes on magical meaning. It carries extraordinary power. In many fairy tales, say "Jack and the Beanstalk," the Goose who lays the Golden Egg plays an important part. Jason's search for the Golden Fleece, the barriers he has to surmount, the hostile forces he has to encounter and conquer, all testify to the dream of extraordinary power. The philosophers themselves, sober, cold contemplatives, have not been immune to its excitement. (Pythagoras was fabled to have a golden thigh.) The search for the philosopher's stone is their dream of extraordinary power. Should the stone be discovered, base metal might be changed to gold, dross be ennobled. The search for the philosopher's stone embodies a dream of mastery over the elements, a vision of power to transfigure the world, a dream shared by rhapsodist and technicist thinkers. It discloses one of desire's deepest dreams: to bring being and desire into concordance, such that when we reach beyond ourselves we meet no estrangement, only what fulfills and joys.[4]

A recurrent, perhaps irrepressible imaging of perfection is the myth of the Golden Age. Many periods have believed the Golden Age to be an actual time, but one need not be historically literal. It may never have been in univocal time, yet as a mythic norm of happy life, it can serve as an imaginative criticism of the present, a standard to show up the shortfalls of the now. The myth pictures a pristine present. "Once upon a time

. . ."—the words transport us to an immemorial time, a time out of time as now undergone by us clock-harried latecomers. This image of perfection articulates a vision of primordial contentment that, paradoxically, generates a restless discontent—discontent with the univocal present that would blossom into the quest for something other than our tamed temporality.

The myth has many variations, but Hesiod's *Works and Days* gives one of its first notable expressions. Hesiod separates time into different periods, each epitomizing a different way of being, each marked by its characteristic metal. In the First Age the newly minted originals were a Golden Race. Loved by the gods, they also lived like gods. They existed without toil, at ease with themselves and the world. They enjoyed themselves directly from the generous fruits of fertile nature. Without pain they lived, without pain they died, passing through death to become good spirits. The Golden Age was the unsullied time of Chronos (Roman: Saturn), the earth festive with a kind of vegetative, sacramental innocence.

The next age gave birth to a Silver Race. Here we have a slight decadence from the gold, but for all its slightness the fall from the origin has set in. In the Bronze Age men were further hardened, brazen, violent. The Bronze Race were warriors but their very toughness was their doom; they destroyed themselves. This was the carnivorous age: "They ate no bread," Hesiod says. Hesiod claims that the next age brought a restoration. Heroes flourished, for divine favor was dispensed again. Chronos was king once more and they lived on the Island of the Blessed. This age is not graced with a characteristic metal. It is an interim before the final fall, an autumn before the winter of now began to closed its cold vice on time. The final age generates the Iron Race. We are the Iron Race: workaday, devoid of divinity, lustreless. Crime and discord, avarice and deceit are our lot. In suffering we survive.

Hesiod viewed the Golden Age through pessimist's eyes. The story of time is a tale of tarnishing. Becoming means declining, decaying, degenerating. History falls away precipitously from a primordial rich source (involuntarily one thinks of Heidegger, a philosopher of the country to Hesiod's poetry of the rustic). The self awakened to the dull iron of the present looks back to the golden beginning, homesick for Arcadia. But the Golden Age can be approached from another temporal direction. Then we have eyes for the future and do not lament the lapse of the past. What once was, may again be possible; what once was will come again. Now one speaks of regeneration, not degeneration—one looks forward to a return, a restoration. When the Golden Age is in the lost past, we come across Arcadian thought; when it is in the coming time, we meet Utopian thought. A Golden Age is the hope of transfiguration that excites the Utopian. This he longs for, works for. This is his expectation, his prayer: that the tarnish be removed from time, that the bright lustre of being again shall shine.

Arcadian man pines for the past glory of a lost Golden age; Utopian man longs for its second coming. But I am interested in the myth as asking us to think of *the present as other*. Was the White Queen right when she said to Alice: "The rule is, jam tomorrow and jam yesterday—but never jam *today*"? For Utopians and Arcadians are both tempted to escape the present: one by flight into the future, the other by retreat to the past. But the Utopian hope may be a dream of nothing; there is no gold at the end of the rainbow; the future may be steel. The Arcadian, by contrast, can feed on an infertile nostalgia, screening the memory of the barbarous, titanic beginnings. But despite these temptations the myth might still reveal a cry for something rich, right now. Sometimes we are seized by moments of wholeness when an elemental innocence and joy are aroused. In this light the Golden Age need not be time's evasion but the mythic, memorial mindfulness of a qualitative presentness: we are to behold the world, now, existing, partaking of perfection, manifesting something inexpressibly good. The ancients themselves understood the episodic nature of this festive presentness. The Golden Age was thought to return for a day in the celebration of the Chronia festivals of Attica (Greek ancestors of the Roman Saturnalia), celebrated under Chronos, god of time and the Golden Age. Celebration of festive being was for a day but the day could recur.[5]

In this light the dream of the Golden Age can be seen to want to safeguard, perpetuate what I will call the acme moment of being. Such moments are moments of *kairos,* of crisis and opportunity. They are not defined by clock-time as quantitatively measured and successive. They are qualitative ruptures: emergencies in the sense of moments of emergence. As crisis-critical (Greek: *krinein),* they discriminate time, judge, demand mindfulness. The *kairos* is a breakdown that opens heterogeneous time; but in the peripeteia or reversal that may ensue, the ruse of heterogenous time offers a breakthrough into a "So be it," a "Let it be," an "*Ita est.*" There is a consent, a singing "I will." Such moments are absolute in the sense of absolving, releasing. Such moments of absolution occur, pass, cannot be fixed. They arrest gratitude but seek no freezing or closure of time. The fugitive benediction manifests the generosity of being. We return to them in memorial mindfulness. This is not sentimental nostalgia, nor is it imperialistic; it is grateful re-thinking of an otherness that will always elude us, exceed us.[6]

In relation to such moments, the Arcadian produces a pastoral idyll: he immobilizes time, as it were, in a snapshot of perfection, which as thus immobile must become monotonous. For the moment fades, must fade. The Utopian knows this, but is so eager for the second coming that he too rushes over and forgets the present. He becomes so consumed with the future that he is blind to perfection in the present. He is so ready for the future that he does not savor the replete present nor recognize the advent of the moment of ripeness. He is always looking elsewhere, though all around him might crowd many images of releasing wholeness.

Great works of art are such images to keep us in mind of the acme moment of festive being. They are not escapist fantasies that distort the time process; rather they sift and winnow time and let the chaff blow away. Thus sometimes we gain rare glimpses of the promise of perfection when we meet the reality of ethical goodness. We encounter a good person. We may not be able to analyze the precise constituents of their ethical character, yet somehow we feel sure of superlative moral worth. We do not know quite *what* makes him or her good, but we sense for sure *that* he or she is. The good human appears before us, a living perfection of essential powers. Not surprisingly, Plato speaks of the noblest natures as having golden souls. He views the good human being as imitating, partaking of Goodness itself. He or she is a likeness of the Good, a temporal realization of what is absolute, a particular representation of its unsurpassed perfection.

Plato resorts to the most famous philosophical image that shows golden thought: the Good is like the Sun. As the Sun is to the physical world, so the Good is to the intelligible realm; as the Sun is the supreme source of light, illuminating the visible cosmos, so the Good is the ultimate source of truth, making intelligible the entirety of being, even while itself beyond being (*epekeina tes ousias*) in its otherness to things. The Sun is the origin of life, for without it nothing would be generated or grow or ripen; likewise the Good is the very engendering origin of being, without which there would not be the world we know. Far from Plato being the world-hater of Nietzsche's caricature, he mythically says (see, *Timaeus,* 29e–30a): the god made the world as close to perfection as was possible. As the Sun radiates over things and casts its glow, the Good itself throws a golden mantle over the entire universe, on beauty and the ugly alike. It shines even on the filth, transfiguring its defiling thereness without its own steadfastness being shaken. The good self, as it were, catches this brightness in its being. In ethical deeds it reflects the light intensively, may even come to radiate its very presence.[7]

In the iron age of univocity, the scientist conceives of the sun as just a ball of blazing gases. It is this yes, but we now see more. This "more" relates to the call for a recharged sense of being's metaxological otherness, variously spoken of in being aesthetic, religious, and ethical. There is something simple in this call, which is why we often fail to thoughtfully heed it; yet the meaning of what we here acknowledge, and the metaphysical metaphors articulating it, might require interpretation without end. It is not for lack of mindfulness that peoples in disparate places and times have worshipped the sun as divine. But apart altogether from economics, religion, myth, morals, philosophy, we return to something very elemental when we experience the healing power of gold in the balm of sunlight. Or should we say: sometimes the physical and the metaphysical come close, matter itself coming to shine with import?

Gold is ingrained in our being. There are grey iron days when we go about our business, dulled and grim and overcast. But there are golden days when we soften and cease to be brazen. We melt and become malleable. We become open and receptive and full of golden laughter. We walk through a golden world, brightness showered on us out of the blue ether. Such golden days bring great satiety, but also great longing. We are saturated with well-being. And though we know that this fullness must fade, we would that it were held in suspension, we would that it was eternal. The physical world itself in its elemental being-there precipitates the acme moment, the moment of releasing wholeness full of compacted significance. We might not be able to say satisfactorily what such moments mean, but that they occur is undeniable. We return to these moments to harvest their memory and to praise. They occur to be mindfully recalled or sung.

There is a place in the South West of Ireland called *Dún an Óir*, Fort of Gold. On an autumn afternoon, near the feast of Samhain, I recall climbing the promontory at *Dún an Óir*. The climb was through boggy earth, watery on the hillside. On the height stood a ruined coastal station, looking one way over the bay and back to the land, facing the other way into the maternal ocean, the limitless Atlantic. The height hovered in the air between earth and sea and sky, their conjunction in a massive rock. The late sun spilled over the height as we ascended, but the shadow was increasing on this side of land and harbor. Just before attaining the top we were wrapped for a time in sober shadow. One step further and (in sudden moment) we were in a reversed world — a golden world at almost the furthest reaches of the Western world.

The sun was a revelation. But we were not given this gift without some call on us. On the height and on the side of the sun, the cliff was sheer. Gulls and crows hung there in the silence, a thousand feet above the silent wash against the wall of rock below. More used to the level plain, to us this vantage was vertigo. The gut knots at this height, but holding itself together the spirit exults. We saw the light there, the pure golden sun luring us with its hypnotic eye. There was nothing to distract: the vantage was surrounded by air, by the open, by nothing. There was nothing in the way. Sky and sea merged, the water itself becoming a golden liquid. The air too, empty of obstruction, was a liquid gold. The ground on which we lay — to stand was impossible on the rim of this cliff, and to lie down was almost to bow in reverence — the ground on which we lay was invaded and enveloped by the sun, now beating almost on a level with it.

Time brought on the night. It was late, and later we had to go. We returned to look out a number of times but had to turn and descend into the somber, evening land and its brown mud. This side was darker now, the sun being obstructed, and me bearing down, like a priest with a monstrance, the memory of the other side.

II. SONGS OF THE ELEMENTAL

The Elemental and Otherness

Some will say: a philosopher should not talk like this. But who is giving the orders? And who is talking? My point is: the plurivocity of metaxological thought concerning the overdetermined being of gold moves us towards a sense of otherness that asks to be sung. But let us ask what song itself implies.

Singing is an event of highest interest. Compare a singing being with something inanimate. The wind blows around a bush and makes a whir or low burr, but neither the wind or bush properly sings. But a bird chirps, a thrush sings out again and again a line of lush notes, and we sense a presence there that was not manifest before. Something is coming awake in singing life. Physically speaking, the advent of song is dependent on complex physiological structures, but this is not my point. It is rather that song is a witness of affirming presence. Song is like a kind of birth. The bird's song is an unselfconscious, effortless celebration of being. Even Kant seems to have a sentimental spot for bird-song: we never tire of its warble, though if a human being whistled the same notes repeatedly, we would soon find it tedious. Kant was not so sentimental about all music. He was cautious of music's power to move us without words and all their conceptual apparatus. He objected explicitly to music's intrusiveness, the way it affects us without any by-your-leave. Kant was very irritated with pious neighbors who insisted on so singing their hymns that he could not escape their devotional stridency. He compared music to a dandy pulling out a perfumed handkerchief: everyone, regardless of willingness, has to endure the odor diffused everywhere.[8]

The human being, even more than the birds, is an astonishing singing being. Song provokes mindfulness because it comes from sources of being where the calculating, controlling will does not hold sway. Song simply surges up, wells up from some hidden root of our being. The flesh becomes free in the song and voices its presence. A self sings, but something about song is beyond complete self-mediation. We have the phrase: a person *breaks into* song. Song is a primordial language of selving in communication with otherness (Vico saw the first languages as singing).

Obviously our song, compared to bird-song, is more complex. There are many kinds of song: work songs, ballads, war songs, hymns, festal and funerary, and so on. Whole *worlds* sometimes rise up in a song. One finds oneself (again the involuntary) humming to oneself; the song is an expression of our being at home, or at odds, with the world. It is not a chirping or warbling, but the articulating of a whole sense of being. We sing ourselves. Rilke said it: existence is song *(Dasein ist Gesang)*.

Song is not only physically elemental for us, it also seems to have a natural affinity for the elemental passions. This is especially true of love and fidelity, evanescent desire, betrayal, loss, endurance, sex, grief, frivolity, lewdness. The love song testifies to passions that recur, elemental essentials so commonplace as to seem banal but which give lives their deepest and most intimate charge. If we go by song we see how little changes in this passionate elemental. I think of a ballad called "The Dark Eyed Sailor": a woman waits the seven long years, keeping one half of a broken ring, expectant for her sailor to return from being at sea. As one might expect, her William does return, only first to disguise himself to test (again!) her fidelity. But the broken ring symbolizes the sundered and yet healed whole (literally a symbol in the Greek sense: two parts of the same whole, later to be rejoined in mutual recognition). A great ballad of the elemental pain of betrayal is *Dónal Óg:* love betrayed is also the theft of God.[9]

The manifestation of the passionate elemental is very evident in operatic song. If one were unmoved, there can be something exaggerated, almost ridiculous in operatic singing—pulpy *prima donnas* with throats the width of Hell's maw. Yet we are moved and in the great aria the simple truth, in the overwhelming power of human passion, is sung out to—I say not to the audience, but to the very empty air itself. The passion is simply announcing itself. We talk about the audience, but the agony and delight in some of the great arias breathe a different air. It is the human voice overreaching itself in a song that speaks to the human heart but knows also that the human heart does not know itself. It is a confession of the elemental in us to a confidant, a beloved, who is not there, and may never be there. But we sing and are somehow healed.

I speak of the elemental. What I mean by this relates to a mindfulness transcending instrumental reason, to a renewal of our being in the middle, through a refreshed relatedness to being in its otherness. But there are ambiguities here demanding attention. An ambiguous reflection of the elemental is the following.

As Western society has advanced towards technological perfection, there has surfaced repeatedly a strong fascination with what still seems "outside," "other," namely, the primitive, the savage, the still untamed.

This fascination is evident in art, say, where the prehistoric paintings of Lascaux and the art of Africa have evoked admiration. We might think of Gauguin's search for a pagan paradise in the South Seas; or of the scientific anthropologists entry into tribes unchanged for millenia; or of the urban dweller longing to break out of the concrete jungle for the real jungle of pure wilderness. The idea, in modern form, is as old as the discovery of the "New World" and the virgin frontier it presented to European man. These new worlds seemed uncontaminated by Europe's stale oldness. Freed from the weight of tradition, we might regain paradise. The noble savage in happy pagan innocence beckoned without the repressing moralism of Christian Europe. Here supposedly we would live by the senses, not by calculative reason. Life would be more like play than work's drudge—the vegetarian society. The Golden Arcadia would be free of the servitudes of the old social order where master subjugates slave, for now each would be equal in pure pristine humanity.

The Communist Utopia, where the state will wither away, has something of this desire for the primitive, only the Golden Age is projected into a post-technological future. The Romantic will to return to nature expresses the desire, as does their cult of the child, carrier of an intimation of immorality. The more complex society becomes, the more comprehensive the success of instrumental technique, the more systematically complete its self-mediations, the more the desire grows to get behind its facades to some pure source, stripped of the occluding accretions of civilization. This search of the primitive is itself often very artificial, as when the anthropologist invades the primitive with all the gadgetry of advanced technology. We both venerate the savage and fear it. The pure savage is a myth, a fairy tale. Shakespeare early saw through the ambiguity when in the Brave New World of the *Tempest* he gives us the savage side of nature sans rosy myth—behold Caliban.

We must be mindful of Caliban, cousin of the Titans (cf. chapter 4). The elemental must be freed from false Arcadian nostalgia and from empty Utopian expectation. Yet the idea of *renewal,* or beginning again, does call to something deep in us, something other than the conflict of old and new, pagan and Christian, Europe and the New World, Western civilization and the undomesticated rest. The idea of renewal concerns a basic ontological need. It has to do with the elemental as something essential, something perennial, something we are always losing, something for which we sometimes long, something we sometimes regain. It is simple yet elusive, clear as daylight yet mysteriously stirring, ageless yet recurrent. The heart must be stirred to divine it.

Listening to some old ballads we sometimes hear the elemental—so simple, so elegant, so powerful—yet without insistence—as if singers were more directly in touch with something irreducible. Now we have to force the pace to rise above the noise—but that, of course, destroys the elemental which, as it were, bespeaks just itself, without artifice, without the need to call attention to itself, without self-insistence. For the elemental is such that its expression is just its simple being. There is no disjunction between expression and being—as if a pure voice of innocent song just rose from the heart of being, as if that song were the most natural thing in the world, were the very nature of things.

Children have something of the elemental. Lovers, some; poets, some. Holy ones have it. Christ Fools, like Dostoevski's Idiot; or Francis of Assisi, first called *Pazzo,* Madman by his neighbors; what the Irish call *duine le Dia* (a person with God; naming the simple-minded, the idiot). A mother's love can be the elemental. What the Andalusians call the *Duende* is related to the elemental.[10] Philosophical natures can be possessed by the elemental but they tend to lose it in abstractions; some try to think their way around to it again, concrete metaxological thought releasing it anew. Athletes sometimes have it: a great runner might describe the perfect race as the experience of nothing, a strange clear sleep of energy. This is related to the elemental.

Innocent Dionysiacs can have it; modern Dionysiacs tend to corrupt it, forcing the orgy. You cannot work at the elemental, force it by your will. Sky Apollonians have it more so. Girlish nuns can have it; boyish priests; a person in grief, a mourner; musicians. Politicians, bureaucrats, ecclesiastical officials have a tendency to betray it. A person laughing at a joke—the disjunction between being and expression goes; not a person telling a joke—the disjunction is not fully overcome; telling the joke one is not in it, in the elemental. A cry in the wilderness is it. A self whose being breathes thanksgiving. Lose the elemental, life greys.

Consider, too, the smile as a living song of the elemental. The human smile is one of our metaphysical marks. To my knowledge, no other animal smiles. We think of the Chesire Cat, but nonfictional cats do not beam. We would be astonished, nay alarmed, if one did. Yet for us distinctively to be able to smile, complex biological conditions are presupposed. Only because of the complex composition of the many facial muscles, and the power of intricate coordination the organism possesses, is the smile possible. But again, the smile seems to emerge *spontaneously* in the human infant (around two months). A smiling elder bends over the cradle, and as if by a preestablished harmony, the infant smiles back. Spontaneously self responds to self, beyond any control of conscious will. The smile seems to imply a kind of fit, or rapport, between the still innocent infant and the welcoming face of another human. The expression of self is its simple being, but this expression is simply concordance with the other.

The smile is the fleshed immediacy of the metaxological community of human beings. That is to say, the smile is elemental; it is elementally human.

It is not confined to any one culture or type of society. It is our being to smile, especially when another welcomes us, especially in the presence of another smiling face. It is as if, beyond our will, the smile is a shining out, a radiation through us, of a deep affirmation of being. The smile is a salutation of being, an elemental greeting of benign otherness.

Similar considerations apply to laughter: a spontaneous eruption of the elemental energy of our being. Of course, the smile can be subsequently shaped, subjected to later cultural accretions. Laughter too can be culturally shaped. It takes on different shapes in different groups. In some "refined" groups, for instance, it is taboo to guffaw. We learn to smile crookedly, put on false smiles. With our growing sense of inner difference, we separate the inner and outer, and manipulate the outer expression, though this may be untrue to inner being. Interestingly, this is hard to do with the smile. Suppose someone is glum, his face a turndown and turnoff. But we coax a smile, faint at first, then more expansive, finally a reluctant beam. Presto, magic: the inner being too is relaxed, released, freed again into the energy of joy.

We often resist, refuse this energy. Hamlet said: one may smile and smile and be a villain. We *use* the smile, instrumentalize it. We turn into a means to an end what bodily is a natural expression of an elemental affirmation. Commerce exploits the smile for noninherent purposes: to disarm, cajole, sell to the unwary buyer. The smile is for sale, for selling at a price. It is distasteful to be face-to-face with a salesman, false smile pasted on the features, a mocking grin of patent insincerity, and then to be chirpily wished: Have a nice day! It is not the smile that repulses, but the fleshy mask of mindless glee. Or think of the exploitation of canned laughter by television: this is a miniature of ontological insult, a technical playing around with the elemental human response, which is to laugh with laughter, to be at one with the other in laughter. It is a macabre thought, full of ontological irony, but actually some of the laughs in canned laughter are laughs of the dead.[11]

We warm to a warm smile, a true smile. The self is there elementally in his body, affirming its being, open through its smile to what is other. The power of this smile can be astonishing. I see the Buddha's enigmatic smile: a shining silence that saying nothing, says everything.

Defiant Simplicity

The elemental is scorned by some philosophers, for instance, by those who make a fetish of technicist mind or by those who make an idol of world history. The first sterilize being; their "logocentrism" is secretly terrified before the unmastered song of being. The second betray our existential intimacy with being,[12] failing to acknowledge that the upsurge of the elemental can be more than a privatized therapeutic blowing off of emotional steam. Its reemergence can affect an entire attitude to the world. In certain times when life becomes a complex of artificialities, overlaid with unreal accretions and routines soullessly perpetuated in endless grey iron days, we can lose the sense of our elemental community with being. We cease to find ourselves in the drama of the everyday. Nausea and ill-defined disgust set in. There comes a breaking point when this becomes unendurable. Something deep in us is driven to an extreme. We are tempted by a kind of recuperative desperation. At the limit the urgent attitude springs up: All or Nothing. The self seeks to return to itself in a kind of pristine simplicity, as if the traffic of daily noise is too unceasing and the longing ear aches for restoring silence. In the emptiness it seeks an opening for freedom, space for the simple.[13]

Thus, in antiquity Diogenes the Cynic threw off the entangling social abstractions and sought to descend to the concrete simplicity of the natural human. He literally stripped off the adornments of convention and tried to live as a free animal might. Diogenes was the dog-philosopher (*kunikos:* cynicism from *kuōn,* dog, hound) whose life was a desperate protest for the elemental in us, a protest through which shone a kind of nobility in crudity itself. The defiant simplicity was not a mere willful stubbornness. It was an ethical protest. The protest was not just on behalf of the self, but on behalf of our elemental community with being in its otherness. The point struck home and his fame spread throughout the civilized world. He sought the gold of elemental being by defacing the dross coinage of the empire. There is a story that Alexander the Great came to him while he lay basking in the sun, offering him any favor he wished. Diogenes' reply was to ask Alexander to get out of the way between himself and the enjoyment of the sun. The light of the sun: simple, elemental, absolutely necessary, golden even on the vanity of empires.[14]

A different example might be Francis of Assisi. Poverty here celebrates the sacramental earth in singing a canticle of the sun. The brotherhood, sisterhood of all being is elemental, extending to solidarity with senseless suffering. As with Jesus, the defiant singing simplicity of Francis was an agapeic idiocy. In a famous encounter Francis kissed a leper: he overcame the natural revulsion of self-being to the diseased other. This might seem like sick masochism, but it is a conquering of the repulsion of first love (cf. chapter 4) to the sick other. Self and other are bound together in second love. The kiss of life was not the courting of death, but the attempted conquering of the fear of death. And Francis experienced *joy:* the breakthrough of a love of being beyond all breakdown. This is idiotic in terms of the first love of self-being. But since one comes to nothing, honest love of life has to come to terms with death. There is no mastery of death, but one might surpass its fear, be released to an acceptance, an elemental "Let be." Francis' kiss showed him as a being beyond death in a loving of being beyond death, in his own willingness to die.

Or consider Luther. Against what he saw as the falsifying formalism of Roman Catholicism, here the simple piety of the inward heart seeks to regain its stature of absoluteness. No longer can an ecclesiastical hierarchy claim the role of necessary mediator between us and the divine. In elemental purity of heart, the individual stands alone before the divine in immediate simplicity. There is no hiding for the soul in the multiplied folds of artificiality. The simple sparks off a religious revolution.

Modern romantics, in Rousseau's footsteps, represent a similar, though more secular simplicity. The cry of "Back to Nature" expresses the restless desire to extricate a more pristine self from the toils of social facades, from false, soiling conventions.[15] The quest for the resurrection of the elemental emerges not at the beginning, but at the end of a long process of complexification that freezes the human face into a lifeless social function. The power of the simple strikes through to a place of primordial selving where, renewing our participation in the metaxological, we are reattuned to the otherness of the startling cosmos. Nor need simplicity of spirit be simplistic. We might think of the lives of Socrates or Jesus or Gandhi. There is a simplicity so deeply rooted that it will topple the established world. For the established world is despair.

Loss of the Elemental: Denatured Being

Admittedly the renewal of metaxological being can be derailed both in relation to nature and the self, the intimacies of otherness and of innerness. We can lose the elemental, even when all our talk is of new worlds and of finding oneself again. Thus, in regard to nature, a guiding inspiration of modernity, the New Time (*Neuzeit*), was to be a renewal, renaissance of our naturalness, in distinction to Medieval supernaturalism. But the modern self does not find itself as at home with nature as expected, and tries to secure its own being by technological will-to-power over its otherness. A will to sanitized life infiltrates our instrumentalized being. Is this a revenge against nature for its previous undomesticated prodigality? Premodern man marveled at this prodigality, but also suffered its sometimes indifferent, destructive power; mother earth mediated, as it were, the Wrath of God. We visit a vengeance on the otherness of this God, but the wound is self-inflicted, for our mastery results in one of the deepest ever devitalizations of being.

Consider this simple example, the fact that the *nature show* is one of the most popular types of television program. This is paradoxical because most Westerners live in cities—much of their lives is artificial, indeed, denatured. The modern city seems to fulfill the dream of technopolis: complete self-mediation in an entirely man-made environment, not only in its shapes, usually mathematical or geometrical, but in the very materials shaped by us there. Granted, there are differences between cities. Growing up by a centuries-long process of accretion, mathematical structure is not so evidently imposed in European, old-world cities. Because the New World city is often laid out in blocks (geometrical squares) and numbered in neutral mathematical terms (123rd street, 5th avenue etc.), New World visitors to old-world cities are often disoriented by the higgledy-piggledy amorphousness of place. European streets wind in nonmathematical shapes, like random labyrinths grown up without the guiding hand of any dominating, overarching architect. One can be easily lost in such cities, if being lost is defined in terms of mathematical coordinates. Yet some older cities have a different quality of intimacy. One can be at home there, even though one might be more easily lost, mathematically speaking. One can be humanly lost in the mathematical city, though in physical terms one knows, without any equivocation, one's place upon the neutral grid of the urban space. One can number one's place even, as if one were a mathematical point defined by numerical coordinates on a homogeneous geometrical space.[16]

This paradoxical popularity of "nature shows" is also revealing: beyond the mediation of being by man-made mathematical structure, it hints at a kind of undernourishment for otherness. Nature is other. We need this other, even when we claim to master it or bend it to our will. Denatured selfhood, deprived at the root of what makes even artificial life possible, cries out for some sense of this other. Its cry is like a longing for Eden that the electronic image tries to soothe. The technical self responds to the undernourishment in terms of its man-made world: it literally has a nature *show,* not nature itself. Nature is processed as an electronic image. In some way this appeases the longing for nature's elemental otherness, but it can also be deceptive. The facility with which we can switch on the screen and immediately have nature packaged for consumption produces a falsification of the world of otherness in (you might say) its very fleshed thereness. Nature is made antiseptic, sanitized, even when the image portrays, say, the mystery of birth. Our remove is perpetuated. We might get a better sense of nature's astonishing sprouting power from contemplating a humble flowerpot or a stray dandelion that somehow cracks through the ubiquitous asphalt.

I offer another illustration. In a recent survey of changes in the Irish countryside over the last 150 years, the findings indicated that the countryside remained almost unchanged from the early nineteenth century until some time in the 1960s. Since then rapid alterations have set in, constituting almost an explosion of change. This is a significant image of the astonishing change in outlook, incubated in Western society for centuries, but glaringly concentrated in this instance. These changes relate to the entire outlook of modernity, especially its characteristic attitudes to nature. Nature is viewed as an indifferent materiality which is neutrally there, and which we may use this way or that, use as and how we please. Oblivious to the metaxological community of being, nature is an externality over and against us, to be mastered and subdued, to be exploited for utilitarian ends. If we carry this to its logical end, nature exhibits nothing inviolable or intrinsically valuable. All value and worth issue from what we do with it, how we stamp our own seal on the otherness of being. Instrumentalist self-mediation is supreme. Everything depends on the expansion of power, and the efficient exploitation of natural resources. Centuries of modernity are concentrated in the last twenty years in Ireland as the available technology has made easier less constrained exploitation. The land becomes of value mainly as it adds to economic well-being. Its yield is subsumed into the international markets of global capital.[17]

Something here is disquietingly at odds with the old love of the land. The land once bore traces of the sacramental earth to which the people were married.[18] Now the land is not even land; it is a resource. The word "land" is not spoken like a comforting gesture of home; it is but a label for "use value." Shall I name the land? Secret country lanes, sheltered universes of muddy ruts, host to the superfluous color and gaiety of butterflies, promise of the bursting blackberry; hedgegrows giving harbor to worlds of wildlife; marshy edges along a river taking its natural bend; a massive rock, the presence of dense being, squat there in the middle of a meadow, where winds make the wheat flow around it, like a golden shimmering sea; an oak tree, angular on the sloping hill, towering up in an inconvenient place, like a letter dropped into time from the alphabet of an alien, undeciphered tongue. What are all these in the language of instrumentalist power? Nothing. Worse: when they stand in the way they are to be erased.

A different power intrudes into the land. Ultimately what intrudes is the power of a changed philosophy, a change in the way of looking at being in its otherness, a loss of metaxological mindfulness. This philosophy, this changed comportment towards nature, materializes its weakening of such mindfulness in the power filled world of technology. The countryside carries the change, sometimes in the ugly form of scars. The mindful self is no luddite. But the "hard-headed" technicists, with hearts as metallic as their thoughts (the metal is not gold), are not to be let disguise the potential devastation. If the land is just neutrally there, can you love it, can you hate it? You can use it, exploit it brilliantly. But can you respect it in its otherness, can you be rooted in it with constancy? If the land belongs to you, but you do not belong to the land, can you make a real home there, an abode?

Here a mindfulness of responsibility for the *future* is often enjoined on us and rightly. But suppose philosophy also demanded a kind of *posthumous, mindfulness:* a thinking from the future when we are dead, about the ontological worth of the present, imagined from beyond death as our past. (The Irish call death *slí na fírinne:* the way of truth.) Such a posthumous mindfulness could not be subsumed into instrumentalized mind, as responsibility for the future is sometimes subsumed. For it would *reverse* and escape entirely the instrumental relation of means and end: it would seek the ends, the justified values of being that are incarnate in the present. Nor would it have any ulterior motive, since it would be beyond the fear of death and hence be metaphysically honest in a way that instrumental reason can never really be (instrumental reason is driven by the fear of death).[19] Radical honesty serves nothing but praise of the worth of being, truly worthy being. This elemental honesty is simply being mindful as thought singing its other.

So imagine this: what would it be like to die, and come back to your home after a hundred years? Would you like to see everything changed, utterly changed? Would you be dazed? Would you be lost? What would you mourn? What are the nameless, intimate things we now love, and which in our post-humous return we would delight to greet again? Or rather, the intimates of being that might greet us, like old, trusted friends? These things have no name in the technicist's vocabulary, no price in the economist's world. Yet they give charge to life and worth of a different sort. What do we love now, that its loss or desecration would grieve us to the roots on our return? If we cannot name any golden thing, anything that now blesses being, anything that we would want to perpetuate into the future, perpetuate even beyond our death and regardless of death, has not life become metaphysically bankrupt?

Let me illustrate such posthumous mindfulness in terms of this story from Irish Saga: the story of Oisín in *Tír na nÓg.* Briefly, Oisín was the son of Fionn mac Cumhaill, leader of the warrior band, the Fianna. There was something strange and other about Oisín, for his mother was not a mortal. He was famous as a warrior, more famous as a bard, singer of songs, teller of tales. The story is that he was carried across the sea with Niamh on a White Horse, at Rossbeigh Strand, not too far from *Dún an Óir,* to *Tír na nÓg,* Land of Youth, the Celtic Island of the Blessed. He stayed there for three hundred years, though he felt no time passing. But he grew homesick for Ireland. He especially longed for his father and son; also the land, the sights, sounds and smells of home. He was allowed to assuage his homesickness, only under the proviso that he not touch the land of Ireland. If he did touch the earth, he would immediately turn into an old man. Time and age would catch up with him. He crossed back over the sea but found that all was changed. His family and companions were long gone. In the interim Ireland had been Christianized by Patrick. He traveled around the country and marveled at the smallness of the men since his heroic time. The story is that he came upon a group of men unable to lift a boulder. He bent down from his horse and shifted the rock with ease. Alas the strap on the saddle broke, Oisín was pitched to the ground and immediately became an old man. The burden of time descended instantaneously; the magic horse vanished.

In this story we first have a familiar longing of temporal beings for eternity, imaged in the first movement across the maternal sea, origin of all being, to *Tír na nÓg*. Oisín left home for pagan eternity. This images the first homesickness of mortals for the immortal. *Tír na nÓg* is the vegetarian paradise, the garden apotheosis of ripe life, the atemporal immediacy of deathless eternity. It is the Golden Age as statically beyond time. But the deep enigma here is the *second* homesickness. How does one become homesick if one is already at home, lost in the immediacy of eternity? How can one grow homesick for *time,* if absorbed already in timeless perfection? More thought provoking perhaps than the first movement across, is this second movement back, the crossing into time from eternity. From out of the timeless rapture of eternity, arises the enigmatic longing for the things of time. What is this love of the temporal? Is it for what is elemental, what is home in time? Why did the earth, the land draw Oisín home. Is the land the sacramental earth? Was it just his loneliness for his father and son, for that bond of community in the flesh itself, generational community as fleshed time? To what did his longing show him to belong?

Oisín moves back and forth between two worlds, and at one level, the recrossing makes no sense: *Tír na nÓg* is the land of vegetarian perfection, the sleep of the elemental in which there seems no chink of difference through which might start up any longing for something other. Nevertheless the longing for time, and for a return to time, does start up. And when Oisín crosses back, he moves in a middle between time and eternity. In this middle there is a new exile and a reversal. This condition of being between, of crisscrossing and liminality, is a turning, returning, a being turned. What interests me about the return is the turn about. I ask not simply about *what* he sees, namely, that the universal impermanence marks all things as changed: not what he sees, but *how* he sees; how he looks, and how things look to him. These looking eyes are not of time or of eternity, for they come to look on the beloved land with the eyes of an "afterlife."

Oisín discovers that he is as dead, as if returned from the dead. He is mindfulness as posthumous. My question is: what kind of eyes are those that look on life from this death? Such eyes are *double:* they have lived in time and beyond time; now they have returned to time *differently,* since their return is from beyond the first lived time. Thus, Oisín is said to be *i ndiaidh na Féinne,* after, post the Fianna. *Oisín i ndiaidh na Féinne* is a phrase still used in Ireland for someone who has outlived his contemporaries. Such individuals should be dead. Their generation is dead, but they live on. How are we to comprehend their posthumous eyes? The most obvious answer is to say they are dead eyes that look on loss; but this does not go deeply enough. They are only eyes of loss because their more radical nature is that, knowing their impending nothingness, they are on the look out for what is good in time, what is worthy to be praised and perpetuated. I see them as many-sighted eyes, eyes in search of the occasion of greeting, when one can thank, and renew a community of being with the elemental things that charged one's being there with its sense of intrinsic worth. Lament of the lost becomes praise of the golden that once was and that, as absent, may haunt what still is present.

In a sense, all memory as such a mindfulness is outliving thought. It is beyond death, not in a timeless eternity but a beyond within time itself. Memory is not "outside" time but reveals time's own other in us. Memorializing thought may be an immortalizing praise of the between, precipitated by its extremes of loss. The self as exiled is metaxologically between two worlds. But an exile knows a death, a grief, a rupture—to be outlived in time itself. Oisín in fact became a *double exile;* both in his own home and in the eternal. He is neither here nor there—yet he is both here and there. Posthumous mind, as the metaphysical imagination of being dead, involves mind in a step beyond time, and so is both in and out of time. It involves a *doubling of the self* between the here and the beyond. In looking on life as if dead, the self discovers distance in time, outliving time, rummaging through time for what made it good.

In one way we do this all the time: the present in its plentitude is lost to us; we love it; we do not see it; we are too close to it; it lives us. Metaphysical memory is love of the earth, love of time, homesick for what is golden in time. In the crossing of time and what is beyond time, we neither have simple temporality nor static eternity. We have something between being-at-home and not being-at-home. Nor do we have simple nostalgia but a doubleness of mind, a redoubling of mind. We have irreducible love of the elemental and the texture of its ontological otherness. We have honesty, but saddened by a grief that is released towards the other. One is looking for an otherness only visible from distance. The elemental is normally lived in and almost impossible to think. Mostly it is brought to mind through absence, like a beloved that one grieves and appreciates only when gone.

There is also this doubleness of posthumous Oisín. He is between age and youth, but he lives these extremes differently in relation to time and eternity. When young he showed not being-at-home in time as home, showed the condition of being between time and eternity by longing for the stasis of the perfect moment, *Tír na nÓg.* But death is the way of truth through which we live the extremes differently. Oisín's return brings a fall, a being reversed. There was disorientation in time even before the fall into decrepitude, age. My question again is: How differently does he see when he sees loss? Does he love what was, but as living it innerly, as if it still was contemporary? Does he begin to sees it because of exile, as if for the first time, and last time? In its invisibility does something become more innerly visible to memory? When aged beyond all mortal aging, is he life-in-death, death-in-life?

Yet Oisín is not a Struldbrug. What does he laugh at, laugh with? What marvel astonishes him, what folly saddens? Is there gaiety before this death; can there be laughter after it? Must he not sing the earth differently? For he has been to the eternity of youth, but now on the edge of vanishing, he is not looking for the golden world in static eternity. The last looking is for golden being in the ephemeral. This search looks differently between here and there. In the final reversal of age beyond age, the negative under it all is acknowledged. But is there a homesickness for time, an elemental love for time and for the earth as home? Is there not a metaphysical nostalgia that is love of the mortal?

What, you ask, is all this about? I am getting at a mindfulness of time and the earth that cannot be understood in instrumentalist terms, or in terms of any simple nostalgia, or any vehement immediacy of the moment, or willful drive to futurity. The point is especially relevant to any instrumentalization of time that sees its value only in relation to the future.[20] This point could be made in relation to a number of modern thinkers (Marx, for instance, as well as capitalist instrumentalizers), but I cite Nietzsche as an extreme example. Nietzsche is both brilliantly insightful on the issue of time but disastrously wrong in his apotheosis of the future. What I intend by posthumous honesty releases us from the metaphysical lie of this glorification of futurity. The apotheosis of the future risks being the apotheosis of empty time, of nothing. Instead of overcoming nihilism, it produces a new nihilism. Unlike Nietzsche's notion of willing backwards (see *Zarathustra*, II, "On Redemption") for the sake of willing the redemption of what was beyond his will, and hence releasing him for the future that he believes is within his will, my invocation of radical honesty beyond death is concerned with intrinsically worthy being (past, present, as well as what is to come), and with being in its *otherness* and not as merely within our will. The point is not at all a nihilistic devaluation of being, but precisely the opposite: to become participant in metaxological being as given, to praise. Nietzsche wanted to be a yea-sayer, but he willed being to be as he willed, hence his intoxication with futurity and frustration with pastness and presentness. Hence, too, his relentless nay-saying against what went before as a curb on his will to absolute freedom.

There is a radical contradiction between Nietzsche's will to be (as self) *the* absolute source of worth, unconstrained by otherness, and his consent to fate, that is, to the radical otherness of being as it passed beyond his will.

The consent to radical otherness is incompatible with his absolutization of a self-projective subjectivity. There is a reversal here that makes absolutely no sense on Nietzsche's terms—this is true regardless of whichever side of the dilemma we use to approach the question.[21] I try to get beyond this dilemma, because what is to be affirmed is the metaxological power of being which itself passes beyond the dualism of self and other, as we saw previously (e.g. in chapter 4 with second love). The metaphysical imagination of posthumous mind forces us to consider: freed by death from the lie of selfhood closed on itself in grandiose but monadic self-congratulation, the released self asks: What in being do we love for itself? There are also reversals, peripeteias, but they are not meaningless. They make sense in terms of the mindful affirmation of metaxological being, thought singing its other.

I will return to the issue of time and perpetuity, but I implied previously a *subjective side* to the loss of the elemental and denatured being. Nietzsche's absolutization of projective selfhood reminds us of a bankrupting of being's intimacy by a certain excessive subjectivity (cf. chapter 2), or mindless mind wrongly taken as the antidote to mindless objectivism. Here we sometimes behold the nemesis of Kierkegaard's proclamation: "Truth is subjectivity." This seems in shocking contradiction to the traditional idea that truth is objective, reached only in overcoming the waywardness of subjectivity. Kierkegaard seemed to reverse this hallowed belief, even to endorse "untruth," if only this "untruth" was the truth for impassioned subjectivity. There were complex motives for this claim. He was reacting to the Hegelians for whom truth was so objectively universal as to extinguish any significant place for the concrete individual and the elemental, inward thisness of its being. Kierkegaard found this unacceptable, for it implied that the Hegelians could stand in for God's mind and survey the whole, despite their finitude. This was especially ridiculous with religion where the individual's relation to God and its authenticity could not be objective, since it was essentially and elementally a relation of self to self. To think of all truth as objective would be to deny the ineradicable personal, inward, that is, "subjective" dimension of such a relationship.

One sees the point of the protest. World-historical reason loses sight of the elemental and our existential intimacy with being. Existential intimacy is an idiocy that the categories of world-historical reason cannot exhaust. But something like Kierkegaard's dictum can become a kind of dogmatic "truth," with consequences as ridiculous as those he protested. The stress on subjectivity can be amplified with a vengeance, in a manner entirely devoid of his seriousness and profundity. The self is made vacuous instead of deep. The elemental is lost in a devitalized selfness, oblivious of its own middle being, uprooted from otherness.[22] Instead of its being appalled at its own triviality, its vacancy is sanctioned. The self is not brought back to the elemental thereness of its being in the middle, but rather loses itself in its search for stimulation, for sensation. Its idiocy is not wise.

This narcissistic search is tyrannous. I offer two simple examples, again from everyday life. Suppose elemental wonder is aroused and expresses itself as the desire to know. One is not interested in opinion, one's wonder is openness to truth. What is on offer? Without a blush one is propositioned with a *"learning experience."* Notice where the emphasis fall—on one as having some kind of experience affecting one's subjectivity. Truth has become subjectivity indeed. In fact, "learning experiences" often evidence the "teacher's" anxiety that the "student" not be bored; what is important is the "enthusiasm" or "excitement" one feels. We find nothing of what the despised Hegel called the "strenuousness of the concept" (*Anstrengung des Begriffs*). "A learning experience"—hype and vapid ferment; nothing of the patience, discipline, struggle with blindness and stupidity, all things which concern a genuine "learning experience."

Turn from hunger of mind to elemental bodily hunger. When I am hungry I want food. Food is something external to me, something objective, which I need and on which I am dependent. I swallow the food and, of course, it becomes part of me, but it is real food I am eating, not just an experience. Consider now this widespread culinary pimping: come, consumer, and enjoy a great *"eating experience."* Food, as objective, has been swallowed (metaphorically) by subjectivity and has now become a pale shadow of its previously robust reality: not grub, an "eating experience." (Do you have to be hungry to have an "eating experience"? Is the pervasiveness of obesity in Western "subjectivistic" societies related to a nonrespect for the real physiological conditions of being?)

Notice the stress falls again on the self savoring the experience rather than on the food. We are only a step away from obsession with how one feels, not with what one really eats. Subjectivity becomes reduced to a set of feelings to which external things must pander. One might even imagine a machine feeding electrical impulses into the brain to stimulate a "real eating experience." The world in its otherness becomes a cosmic vibrator, there just to help our precious subjectivity throb a little more exquisitely. Truth as subjectivity now means: truth is an intense throb. The loss of the elemental, the trivialization of truth, of selfhood itself, is complete.

III. SONGS OF DEATH AND TIME

Sleep, Death, The Elemental

But death is elemental and deflates this throb. Death is a breakdown of being, a radical failure in which the "I" in solitude faces the negative otherness of its own nonbeing. All self-mediations are put in question, every domestication of metaxological being disrupted. Like Socrates, the philosopher must become the song bird of Apollo and ask what music can be made on the eve of death. Socrates also said: to survive as a philosopher, he had to live the way of an idiot (*idioteuein*).[23] The song of the elemental is an invocation *de profundis,* but what are those depths?

As a first step beyond the lie of denatured subjectivity and devitalized nature, consider our elemental need for sleep. In this is suggestion of death, and a coming to wakefulness of death. We spend about a third of our lives sleeping, but philosophers rarely give it thought. Yet it is an absolutely necessary other of mindfulness. Deprived of sleep, we weary, grow anxious and irritable; we may hallucinate, even go mad. This is a stark and elemental contrast: waking man, full of the thought of himself, busy about the world sure of his dominion of being; sleeping man, now a vulnerable organism, frail consciousness sunk into a well of darkness, not even a thinking reed, almost a breathing vegetable.

Though various researches have been undertaken, sleep remains a philosophical *terra incognita,* a no-man's land the ancients thought was an opening to other worlds, not given in waking. How is sleep related to the mindfulness of being?[24] Sleep eclipses consciousness, and brings the loss of awareness of distinct selfness. What status has selfhood then? Is a sleeping being selfless? Or is there an original unity of being deeper than the distinction between waking ego and dormant organism? Even if selfhood is suspended in sleep, "something" seems tirelessly active. Even in deepest sleep, certainly brain activity never ceases. There seems a paradox here: an alertness of energy below the level of consciousness, an "awareness" of which we are not aware. It is as if sleep returns us to the underground of our being, to a ground or depth or grave of being beyond consciousness, yet making consciousness possible. What is this original, nocturnal source of selfhood that ebbs and flows, day after day, night after night? And when we emerge from sleep, is it like a reconstruction of an ordered world in consciousness? Is it like being reborn every day? We emerge from the womb, not of the mother, but of just being, emerge into a world of meaning above and beyond mindless being. Waking recapitulates the stages of being born and becoming a mindful self. Instantaneously, say at a big bang, the waking self surges back into its body, a tidal wave of awareness flash flooding the estuaries of the flesh.

We need sleep to heal and restore the tired body, but what of the mind? To be capable of mindfulness is our great joy and heavy burden. But we can endure it only intermittently. Suppose one were awake *all the time?* Suppose one could not forget? A general reaction would be horror. We cannot bear ceaseless mindfulness. Plato slept; Descartes slept; Hegel slept; Nietzsche slept; Derrida sleeps. Or suppose one possessed a pure mindfulness, just flowing endlessly, without goal or purpose? Most would see this as just endless boredom. To be infinitely mindful, without escape — but we want to be distracted from self-consciousness, longing for sleep when there is nothing to do. Sleep is a limit, a mark of finitude, a daily death necessary for mindfulness. Is it like an inescapable metaphysical nostalgia: the longing to be absorbed into the undifferentiated whole? We seem to need *not to be,* not to be aware of our being or being as other. To be resurrected in the morning, we must die every night.

We cannot endure or sustain uninterrupted mindfulness of the metaxological community of being. If God could be thought, compared to our sleepy selves, he would be absolute wakefulness, never tired, never weary, never bored, even though absolutely self-aware. Because we sleep, need to, desire to sleep, we can barely conceive the idea of God. Suppose God were to sleep; think of God nodding. The world goes mad. The pilot at the rudder is drowsy and the ship is wrecked on rocks. The thought of absolute alertness, mindfulness never sleeping, is almost intolerable to us. If *we* were God, we could not stand it. We would smash the world, run aground just to sleep. God simply loves being, but we do so on and off. A God sings wakefully but we desire to die.

The elemental need of sleep, then, is the nocturnal side of a troubling mindfulness that springs up with wakefulness. All things but man live, as it were, the sleep of elemental being. The rock on the mountain, the tree on the forested slope, the flower and the summer grass, all of these are there, just there. They exist and that is all. Existence is enough. They have no mindfulness, not of themselves, not of another. The rock does not know the mountain, nor the slope the tree, nor the flower or grass the wind that makes them dance. Together they exist, an unmindful, innocent brotherhood.

Our mindfulness brings a new disturbing world. It brings a wonder before things, a wonder tinged with metaphysical terror. Animals are conscious; they thrust out and explore, ferreting and rummaging, attentive to the outside. We are conscious but also self-conscious: the rummaging bends back from the outside and sifts within the inner being. In all this ravening, high and low, there is uncanny disquiet. Unconscious things exist purely, unknowingly showing forth the simplicity of just being. Mindful beings exist in a middle that is close to an edge, exist doubly, in themselves, outside themselves, aware of gaps, within themselves, outside themselves. The privilege of being mindful carries with it the pain of knowing death.

This emergence of mindful being is one of the great enigmas. Whether we see it as a "materialistic" or "mentalistic" event, it still bears a kind of signature of death. How so? All consciousness is consciousness of something. To be aware is to be aware of being, whether outside oneself or within. Thus consciousness always entails an awareness of *difference*. To be aware of oneself is to be aware of what is not self, the other.

Self-consciousness is a kind of break or rupture: awareness of what is not self brings us to a dangerous edge where we stumble across the limits of self and the uncertainty of alien otherness lying in an unknown beyond. Although placed in the middle, our awareness of this vast otherness of the world brings home to us the fragile individuation we specks of self possess.

Mind knows a world beyond but what is beyond is also partly beyond our will. We cannot conjure up or wish away this world. We meet a limiting resistance, a weighty presence that counters our fantasies of divine omnipotence or the magical overlordship of things. We *receive* from the other, as mind finds itself checked by, impinged upon by existence external to itself. We always find a degree of passivity, of receptivity. In this sense mindfulness is always a kind of *suffering:* we undergo the experience of what is other, we do not actively create it from nothing or ourselves. Thus, mind always involves an element of *pathos.*

There is revealed an irreducible space between the self and the other. Into this crack all insecurity and pain and frailty send down their sharp roots. Thus, mindfulness necessarily brings a sense of the alien, the other, the strange; alienation and estrangement are intimately lodged in its condition. Fear and anxiety, for instance, seem to be present in all conscious being, part of the price of this gift. Since in us mind develops into self-consciousness, not surprisingly we have the most developed sense of anxiety, the most acute sense of nothingness and death. The mindful human self is the most harried, the most metaphysically stressed form of being.

If insecurity pitches its roots in the crack of consciousness, the self also sends out shoots of growth to bridge the chasm, to alleviate the sense of estranged difference. Being mindful counters the danger of any otherness that is excessively alienating. We find a kind of rage for plenitude to balance the corrosive awareness of limits. The desire for knowledge itself tries to surpass the gap of self and world, to step across and so mitigate the limit that separates. We try to stitch a trellis of connections across the abyss that seems to open between us and being. Along with mind springs up a restless energy that wars with death. Mind becomes itself transcending, self-surpassing. In it lies coiled a passionate unrest for the absolute. There arises a desire for the deathless, an eros for the eternal.

Unconscious things play out brief lives in the deathless but always unknowing of death. We cannot go back to the consolation of unconsciousness. We know: and there is no step back or behind from this. There is no shelter from being mindful, though humans have variously sought asylum in drink or power or sex or wealth or work. Some live through their unsheltered condition, live out of it. Out of it arises much of our greatness in art, in politics and ethics, in religion, even in philosophy. We arrive too late for innocence and too early for paradise. In the interim of metaxological being, the unsheltered self's greatness is its will to knowingly immortalize.

Age: Elemental Time as Fleshed

Death then is the intimate other of being mindful. But time is the dissolving and threatened death of the *pure immediacy* of the elemental. Singing thought is one mode of its *mediated* reaffirmation. Other beings live, are in this pure immediacy of the elemental. Time, minded by us, scatters this — but time is also the ground of its regathering and immortalizing — elemental being not just lived but lived and loved.

Throughout the philosophical tradition the nature of time has always presented a peculiarly elusive problem. Its otherness to thought is captured in Augustine's well-worn words: I know what time is when I do not think on it, but when I think on it then I do not know what time is. Put in our terms: I live time as elemental but when I try to think time, as elemental it is always other to thought. We are forced to acknowledge the universal impermanence as other to thought.

In the interim of the metaxological, all being seems temporary. All things tell of mutability and inconstancy. Nothing abides; everything submits to devouring time. Again the most shocking sign of this is death. Things not only grow, they also decay, not only come into being, but also pass out of being. Death stamps its seal on this, the frail, intermediate being of things. The human being knows most intimately the fatality of this stamp, even despite our powerlessness to pin down pervasive time. We are the animal most mindful of the mutability, a witness from within to the devouring time in the watched aging of our flesh. So also we are the animal who rages against time. Conversely we the only animals who exhibits vanity: the desire to be eternally young and loved.

The metaxological sense of being points to a middle between time and time's other. It is not that time is defective or unreal, a succession of shadows all without abiding substance. Nor ought we dismiss time as nothing, to escape to an abiding reality beyond time not cursed by change. Time manifests the negative — a statement that would be read differently by Plato, Hegel, and Nietzsche. The dualistic Platonist enjoins us to be detached from time's tyranny and be reattached to eternity. The Hegelian identifies time and eternity in a dialectical *Aufhebung*. The Nietzschean renames eternity as the recurrent circle of time. All are mindful of the negative, albeit differently. But though time may be the negative process, even as breaking down it is the issue of the power of being, and so a sign. It is a sign of something breaking through. Time is not only negative process but the appearing of being's original power. It hints at something more, a memorial becoming to remind us of the otherness of being, of which our own self-becoming too is an issue.

Plato's famous words are: time is the moving image of eternity (*Timaeus*, 37d6–7). I read this as saying: time as image is moving because original—an original image of eternity as more original, that is, the ultimate dynamic energy of being. It is not that eternity as original is static and frozen; it is that the dynamism of time is itself the moving original image of a more primordial dynamism. (Plato's word for time is "eternal image" *aiōnion eikona*, 37d9.) The philosopher tries to follow the direction marked out by this image, not so much to pierce beyond the flux, but to be ready for the advent in time of the more, the acme moment. One has to find a middle between nihilistic drowning in time and a despairing flight into static eternity. The acme moments are interrupting emergencies in time itself; as ruptures they break down the false face of domesticated time; but only because something more is breaking through in the very tornness of time itself. These moments must be mindfully named, sung in mutability canticles, woven by thought into the tapestry of singing supersession.

I am not talking about mathematical time, clocked time, which treats becoming as a homogeneous, quantitative continuum. I am talking about our intermediate being as itself the intimate mindfulness of qualitative time. We can think this innerness of time in terms of *age as elemental time*.

Consider. No one is completely immune from the fascination of his own face. This image in the glass ensnares us. I do not say this in the posture of narcissism. I do not marvel before the mirror. The mirrors doubles me, others me, brings before me the double edge of minded time. For what I see startles me. What I see unnerves me. I see age. Those older see youth; those younger see cranky oldness; I see age—time's otherness in the face. We are all right and yet each of us is entirely wrong. For there is nothing to see out there really, hardly anything. A line, a hint, a shadow, a ghost of an absence. A whisper of "now once but never again, never more," a tender rustle of finality. But nothing really.

I am rebuked as morbid. But I know. What I see is not "out there." My outward gaze is not out there at all. I would "see" age even if I never looked outside, even if I never stole glances at myself in mirrors. The mirror is within and its shine is a tarnished sparkle of inwardness. Or rather, there is no mirror at all, only a conviction silently stirring that barely, now, struggles to the surface in words. Let me be straight: there is no face, there is no mirror—only eyes casting into lustrous darkness, their own globed darkness. Eyes? Windows of the soul? No, not now. Now: an abyss of inward otherness. The eye: only a delicate gloss on darkness.

I do not see age, Rather I am aging. I see nothing. Nevertheless, the ghost of an irreversible process passes through me, unsettling all the tidy order, like a random wind passing from window to window in a neat room. The sigh of an absence lifts and settles, and the empty air shapes itself again into still and calm. I am aging. A process passes through me; I am that process now; the process passed beyond me. What I find I lose again just so, even now in this very act of finding it.

What is this that is everywhere and nowhere, a nothing that is yet in all? Age is not a thing. We cannot manipulate it like a thing. We cannot pin it down, take hold of it like some solid substance. Nor is age simply a condition of the subjective mind. Age, of course, has some thing-like qualities, as implied, for instance, by images like "the rock of ages." Also its manifestations are related to subjective state, as when we say a person is "old before their time," though stress or worry or brooding on the negative. But of itself aging seems a peculiar in-between process, half-way between the neutral indifference of a thing and the personal involvement of a self. Age, mindfully understood, reveals our being as a between.

For like the otherness of things, age *happens* to us. One does not choose to age; one undergoes, suffers the passion of transience. Age is the temporal, intermediating process as ingrained in our very flesh. Age is the very flesh of time. It is our physical destiny, fight it how we will. Yet like personal self-consciousness, aging reveals the peculiar intimacy of being in the case of humans. It does not come on us from outside but grows with the interior burgeoning of the sense of self and its inward otherness. It is so close to us that we hardly notice it till, a stretch of time having elapsed, we scent the missing shade of youth and search, eyes peering into eyes, the self sounding deeply its own unfathomed self, for the beckoning gesture of some other destiny, itself as evanescent as the youth that is dead. Aging is more intimate to the self that is the surface self we turn to others and even ourselves, namely, the personal ego, the mask of our being. Like sleep, it is both between and beyond neutrality and personality. It is neither neutral nor personal but somehow both.

All this follows from our peculiar relation to time. For us time is more than a detached process we can mathematically clock with quantitative precision. Flowing in an evanescent present, we reach out to the past in memory and the future is expectation, trying to span in the middle what has been and what will be, what is passing away and what will be coming to pass. Time is the interiorized process of the self where we struggle to gather what inevitably will again be scattered. The process, the struggle, the scattering, all are issues of the original power of being as metaxologically articulated. Aging is the primordial experience of this interiorized time, not the clock ticking the seconds away with metallic deadness. In aging time happens to us, and yet we are time itself: the surging swell of its forward, expectant energy, the elegy of its fall and mourning ebb.

Other things do not age thus. They do not know time's irreversibility, unmindful of the destiny of time for finite beings, death. ("Never" is a crushing word.) Even when we do not put this knowing into words, or repress its surfacing in self-consciousness, we "know" it in an inarticulate way. We know the radical boundaries of middle being. We perhaps are simply this mindfulness of time, living its bitter wisdom most profoundly in our own aging. To come to age, to come of age is our destiny. So when I see age I see nothing at all, yet I see a hieroglyph of more. I see that the end was present in the beginning. In the quickening of the eyes, in the transient glimmer of those globes of emptiness, I behold aging as a fitful, grieving struggle to be born.

Reversed Generations

We are born to difference but not to absolute self-sufficiency, for in our own otherness is traced the heritage of a larger otherness. We can see this in a second kind of fleshed time that always exceeds the self, namely, the *line of generation*. Publicly, Western societies insist on the self: Religions say the self is a special creation; political philosophies hold that each human is marked by inalienable rights; moralities insist that each person is an end in himself. Privately, we all have a special sense, unique savor of our selves; we taste ourselves from within. We feel our difference inwardly, even when outwardly it is ignored or mocked or trampled on. Our intimate self-relation makes each of us a distinctive organizing center of experience. Our inward thisness is a world and a window on the world. But despite our sense of inward absoluteness, we are threads woven into a fabric of metaxological *relativity:* our very being is relatedness to others.

In the elemental bond of kinship, such relativity is written in our very flesh. We may not be mindful of this, but our bodies bear living relations to the dead and the coming. With shock one looks at a decades-old photo of an ancestor, confronting in this image of the dead the same presence now playing on the face of the living descendent. The genetic thread throws up a sameness of physiognomy, a persistence across generations of enigmatic presence. The sameness, the enduring face belongs absolutely neither to the dead nor to the quick, but is the signature of genesis itself, the flourish of its deepdown power of origination. This power of genesis distributes itself in an endless web of relations that are infinitely spread out. The particular self, the "I" is just one knot in this web that is stretched out and out and out and lost in backward time. The astonishing thing is that, despite this, every "I," every individual knot of oneness, takes itself as "absolute" in its own way.

It is difficult to properly comprehend the metaphysical place of the "I" in this web of metaxological relativity. It is perhaps easier to think of a place, a physical place where, say, a family has had its habitation for centuries. I think of the Percy family in Northumbria, which has inhabited the same castle and lands for over seven hundred years. One senses the generations passing and passing, the numberless lives lived, the dead bound to the living, the living to the dead, and both to the yet unborn. Most of us do not have this privilege of a place to easily picture the passage of generations. Our place in the metaxological web retreats beyond our memory, beyond all grasping. Yet the power in the web works on. When we think of this power, the individual "I" seems to dwindle to nothing, like a brief ripple on a restless ocean. Yet it is the destiny of the "I," the knot in the web, to live, to try to live close to absoluteness. We are spellbound by the illusion that we are absolute. Yet the partition between this illusion and truth is thin. The call of the absolute erupts in every living "I." The ultimacy of the whole metaxological web is reduplicated in each knot in the sense of absoluteness of the "I." This enigmatic doubling and redoubling is the roll of the ocean. On the surface of this deep, we are like swimmers treading water. And there seems to be no bottom or shore.

Again I am not offering an abstract theory of time but trying to name a significant reversal in time. We suffer time as heterogeneous, as other, but singing though need not lament its peripeteia. A canticle of mutability is not a whistling in the dark. In our breakdown the peripeteia may be timely for our breaking through. So consider the following peripeteia of age and generation. What I will sing is a certain reversal between self and other.

A child is the virgin experience of difference. But a birth is the beginning of reversal. For nine months the fetus lives as close to absolute sameness or identity as ever a human will. It floats in vegetable oneness with the dark aqueous womb, a flower of paradise still drowned in the mother salty sea. In being born it is delivered over to otherness, and wawls out its self as the raw presence of fresh difference.

Time matures the child in a perpetual oscillation of sameness and difference. Sameness: the blossoming self identifies itself with others, imitates, emulates, desires to be like the others. Difference: the seed of its individual selfhood insists upon its unique ownness, wills to follow its own path and not another's. If sameness smothers, the self becomes a drab clone, its selfhood vanishing into anonymous conformity. If difference is absolutized, the individual becomes a wayward, a stray, an eccentric or a mere freak.

Children bloom into adults who are blithe about the specialness of their own being. Often they think of their ownness as radically distinguished from their parents. To become themselves they say "No" to what their parents were or are. The adults, these grown up children, see themselves as the "new generation," putting the stress on their "newness," growing hazy about their participation in "generation."

A wave breaks over these bathers bobbing in the wash of time. Extremities cross and meet in the middle: the womb and the grave, the young and the dead, birth and perishing and perpetuation. A reversal different to birth begins: reversion to a sameness that is not chosen by the individuals, but that is thrown up, unbidden, by the ceaseless tide of generation. The grown children become parents of their children, but in the process again become their own, older, parents. The hidden thread of generation weaves a pattern of perpetuation no individual can oversee or master overall.

I voice this metaxological reversal, as if I were being turned time and time by a cycle of generation in which one participates but never commands. I am watching my son playing on the strand. The sea in its whoosh and thud and retreat voices a rhythm of constancy in incessant change, an immemorial order sung out of the womb of all. I see him, concentrated in effortless play, the presence of a human self before the unmarked boundary of the empty horizon, building castles to be destroyed and rebuilt in ceaseless oscillation with the relentless wave.

I am father of difference in this other self that, as son, is sameness: blood of blood, flesh of the same flesh. But slowly there breaks the awareness that my eyes are not my own. It is my father who is looking out of me: the eyes benevolent in quiet delight in the absorption of the other in play. I cannot see my face, but I know that it is my father's eye that gazes and knows. I have the awakening that this same eye reaches back beyond my father to numberless generations, now and ever anonymous to me and him. The same eye of generations, belonging to all and none, travels from me to the shore, passes through my son and beyond, and perhaps its passage will outlive all our deaths.[25]

Reversed Time

Let me approach the reversal in another way: not by becoming mindful of fleshed time in age and generation, but by *reversing fleshed time in the mind*. Time lives us forward, beckoning us with the seductive ambiguity of futurity. True, we can be captivated by memories and lose ourselves in nostalgic reverie. True, without a sense of the past our present would lack ballast and we would be little different from amnesiacs. True, now and then the richness of the present so engrosses us that anxiety of the future is stilled; we come to rest, if only for a small span, within the deep now. But mostly in the middle we see being as passing into what has-been, with futurity the inviting possibility of the not-yet-in-being. In intermediate being, we pass beyond the past, through the present and into the future, which never is: we always move towards it, we never reach it, we never overreach all time. The stages of this inexorable forwardness are: birth, growth, maturity, decline, decay.

As we saw, a dominating future can feed an instrumentalization of time: present and past are merely for the sake of the future. Since being mindful involves a break with this instrumentalization, we must try to think time otherwise. In line with previous peripeteias, my suggestion is that we imagine ourselves in a reversed becoming. What if the experience of time were the reverse? Suppose we were born old and the sweep of life went backwards? What if we were to experience the course of becoming like a film being rewound: from old age to middle age to youth to childhood to the womb and then our vanishing into nothing?

What interests me is how we would experience the beginning and end, and how this might make us mindful of what in *middle being* is of intrinsic worth. *Now* we think of ourselves as nothing before we are born (that is, if one does not believe in reincarnation). *Now* we fear we will be nothing after death. At least in the Judaeo-Christian tradition there is little worrying about the possibility of our *pre-existence*. But if time were reversed, would we not worry about our possible existence *before* old age, before this life, before birth? Would we not then worry about vanishing into nothing by going through the womb? As I say, preexistence does not seem to greatly worry Westerners now. But if preexistence does not now worry us, why should nonexistence worry us after the womb, that is, in our reversed world? There are many who believe in life *after* death, but why not life *before* birth? If one, why not the other? Logically speaking there is as little reason to exclude one as the other. Why not think of death as one thinks of birth? My sense is that if you reversed time, you would get the same *clinging* to being, perhaps even more tenacious clinging, as the reversed human sped towards its childhood.

In normal time, *now,* age can partially free us from that clinging. There are some elders who have had enough, who calmly wait for death as a release. But reverse time: think of maturity and middle age and their fever for success; think of the adolescent, the child, the infant growing more attached, more powerless, more dependent, more vulnerable, as it broaches its own vanishing into nonexistence. In fact, in reversed time the self's sense of its own vanishing would vanish also. The child thinks it is eternal and initially it finds it impossible to think of death at all. The child's time is the undying day—the living of the elemental as a pure given. In the womb we would be as close as we could ever be to the pure now, pure immediate being without past and future: the vegetable eternity of a flower of paradise. Reverse time and the idea of death would become absurd. Would time itself appear as the process of the death of time? Reversed time would lead to the dying of death, at least as a concept we could think.

IV. SONG OF BREAKTHROUGH

The above is a speculative fantasy, but it has its point: the reversal, thought through, might arouse the elemental mindfulness of simply being. A truly mindful self knows what it is to be torn from this immediacy of the elemental. But we must think through the matter, we cannot just lay it aside—rethink it now shaken, chastened by the cut and grilling of skepticism. We play our brief lives between nothing and nothing, but in the metaxological between Spinoza's famous words come to mind: nevertheless, we feel and experience ourselves to be eternal (*sentimus experimurque nos aeternos esse [Ethics, Pt. 5, 23n]*). The question is: Can we make any sense of this "nevertheless."

Death, as minded by us in its metaphysical intimacy, reveals the inherence of the extremes in the heart of our intermediate being. Our intermediate being is the place where coming into being and passing out of being flow into each other. Our being as middle is the place of intersection of being and death. Mindfulness brings the intimate knowing of this intersection. We are not here dealing with a determinate "problem" at the frontier of positive knowledge. This is an essential question that will always remain a question, remain open to further question and deepening: a present, intractable perplexity always elusive of complete rationalization, yet always forcing us to return to its enigma, constraining us to question again and again without the satisfaction of one definitive, univocal answer. Does the longing for a beyond simply express our self as transcending being, a will to surpass present limitation to a more complete condition of being? Is there a sense in which our transcending always moves within the shadow of a beyond. One voice says: This transcending ends in death. Another answers: Why even now does the momentum of this transcending not stop short at this end? Why here should our reach exceed our grasp? Another says: If this excessive reach touches nothingness, is our being but an excess overreaching into an emptiness?

Why does the thrust of transcending strain beyond death, even if only in dreaming? Is the dream of deathlessness, even through a dream, profoundly significant? Among the things of nature are we the only animal that dreams thus? Are we then the ultimate in freakishness since we knowingly refuse nature's limit, dreaming of the absolutely unnatural, namely, deathlessness? Or are we too captive to physical images, and the beyond has nothing to do with any quantifiable space? Suppose it had something to do with a different quality of time? Do we not have this experience: Something was there before us all the time, but it was beyond us all the time? To be awakened—is this to break through to different mindfulness of what is there: the beyond as the present of profound import, being there seen now to be a dense, unsurpassable inexhaustibility? Are the peripeteias of time the radiant instants of opening, releasing wholeness? We cannot say with absolute, univocal clarity what such acme moments mean, but they do come upon us. That they occur, this is undeniable. What they mean we are not sure and always remains on the verge of definitive grasp. They are beyond us yet they strike intimately home, pierce the crust of uncomprehending consciousness. Do they too die the death of consciousness when we as individuals fall? Or are they signs, within the devouring supersession of time, of the transcending otherness of being, which is not itself superseded?

These essential questions pose an unremitting perplexity we cannot either escape or finally settle. They cannot be brushed aside as meaningless, nor yet put to rest with one definitive solution. Such questions importune one, induce a kind of metaphysical migraine. We must mindfully return to them again and again.[26] They are not to be posed with the immoderate measurelessness of the modern will-to-power, for they moderate the conceit that we are the absolute measure of all. We cannot measure time as age or generation, for we are this limit; our being is other to our own will. The point is patience in the metaxological middle before this otherness, humility before the beyondness of the power of being and our own being. And yet this beyondness sings in us.

Consider once more the elemental fact of our intimacy with sheer being. Are we not the voice of a powerful, fleshed insistence on being? Do we not exhibit the drive to persist in being and fight what threatens destruction? Spinoza's ghost comes again before us. No doubt some individuals express this insistence on being in a more powerful will to live. But all life recoils from death, anything that hints of its negation, where even miserably to be seems better than not to be at all. An intense, even insatiable insistence on being holds the human being together into a self. This makes us to be the present unity of existence we are. This expresses the unique energy of being that individualizes us into a distinct self. This unity of distinct being is not just the construction of social relations, as sociologist might have it, or the fluctuation of psychic energies, as psychologists might have it. It is the core ontological power of our being that is manifested variously, participant of the metaxological community of being, shaped too, in social relations and psychic process.

Is this core insistence of being just a provisional formation of material energies that will in time dissolve and return to the amorphous flux? Why should a temporary formation of material energies so insist upon its own being, the selfness of its own being, in the way we do? For if we are that provisional formation, these energies become very strange here. In the human self, they seem to desire an absurdity, their own deathlessness, and in the form of this unique individual that is, it seems, unavoidably deathbound. How can material energies self-consciously desire their own deathlessness, not as material energies either but as energy of selfness, as humans do in their longing to immortalize?

The insistence of being clings to the sheer sweetness of life itself: we savor this sweetness, though often we hardly notice it—just being, the honey of just being. Take away this savor of being and the dull insipid residue is appalling. Perhaps everyone experiences this sometime—a life flat, stale, loathsome—death-in-life itself. Whoever has known this, and also known release, recalls the experience with shudders. The golden honey of being sweetens time but also troubles thought.

What is here named is a certain love of being: being is good and it is good to be. But this insistence of being is not to be seen as a self's hostility to being's otherness. Rather it is a particular selving of the love of being as metaxological. The promise of a certain universal affirmation appears in the particular affirmation of the being of the "I."[27] So it is necessary that the insistence of being be purged of a monadic self-will: only then will its breakdown bring a breaking through.

This is implied by the peripeteias of time sung above. For the endless supersession of time as the otherness of the universal impermanence alternatively repulses and draws us. It seems to swallow us up and snuff out our being in insignificance. There is something boundless in the immensities of sublime nature. We glory in this sublimity, yet in it we also shrink in stature. It serves to remind us of the chill of death that will settle on all human endeavor. I find incredible the statement of Lucretius that the being of the world is least remarkable or surprising: *non est mirabile*. This is a neutralization of ontological perplexity, passing itself off as blasé philosophical maturity. Look up at the night sky; see the cold englobing immensity; try to measure the night. Can you encompass that black expanse, specked with an infinity of stars and galaxies and perhaps other worlds? Humans once thought that the stars were eternal, but now, for all their galactic stillness, we know their fugitive being. Indeed given the void spaces of this cosmic immensity, the heavenly beauty we see from the dark earth may right now in fact be nothing. We grow fearful of this otherness of infinite space, this seeming indigent endlessness of the cosmos, which causes the self to dwindle to nothing.[28]

Not only infinite space, but also unceasing time stirs us out of inertia, refuses us all false sureties. We have this experience with the unexpected. We try to master time by anticipating the future, making plans to deal with unwanted eventualities, buying insurance to cushion the impact of the uncontrollable. But no plan can help with the essential negativities of life, like suffering and death. The unexpected finds the chink in the armor of our anticipation. It disrupts; it interrupts; it ruptures steady life. It comes down on us like a doom to whose hints we were hithertofore unattentive. The process of becoming devours our efforts to stabilize life and puts us adrift at sea, like a Noah after the Flood. For all the surface bravado we respond to what is radically unexpected with bewilderment. The unexpected first brings down its terror; then it may be apprehensively anticipated; finally it may be greeted and met. In meeting with it and in contention with its bane, a gratitude for being may be born and a will to generate beyond oneself. We are bestowed with the creative power to continue, perhaps even augment the line of life. Though finite beings will meet their end, nevertheless they *are* now. We appreciate the fact that they are at all, that we, too, are gifted with being at all. Death itself may reinvigorate an unwilled passion for being; readiness for its advent may release life's moments of ripeness.

Time as an unmastered other appalls us because it both supports all our creative acts yet mocks the perdurance of every deed. Thus, the fact that time's infinitude can be seen either as a vacant abyss or as an absolute richness is mirrored in two of our most characteristic attitudes to death: either as the portal of nothingness or a promise of radical otherness. In the middle, of course, we tend to waver between these poles, our experience of metaxological being coming to us as a mixing of the extremes. On the one hand, we know the feeling of being almost nothing in the terrifying infinity of the cosmos. On the other hand, we cannot escape the deepdown affirmation, often hidden from explicit consciousness, of our being unbrokenly bound to the cosmos. This second aspect is revealed perhaps in the way primitive peoples, closer in some respects to the primordial springs of life, find it all but impossible to conceive of death as an absolute cessation or negation. It seems they do not know death in this way. Freud's speculation that the unconscious is convinced of its own immortality, invites the question: Could it be that what is deepest, sleeping and most hidden in us is an affirmation of being beyond rupture?

Mindful selves live *after* self-consciousness. This comes out in Pascal's great anguish before the fearsome, infinite spaces. We are forced to face the negative full on. We are forced to seek an affirmation that is not naive. Again death and the suffering of time's infinity are our instructors, herding us unwillingly towards an extreme and radical limit. They offer the opportunity for simple honesty, calling forth from us an "all or nothing" response where we may finally take stock of where, if anywhere, we stand. We are broken off from the unconscious immortality of the primitive, of the child, of paradise. We are tugged between the void infinity of nothingness and the full infinity of the absolute original. Between these extremes finite selfhood is caught by, tripped by death. We sojourn and wander in the world between. Yet in the great affirmation to which we can rise, we somehow pass through the void infinity and say our simple yes to the startling, strange infinity of all that positively is.

In such affirmations it is not the "I" that is affirmed. The "I" of isolated self-consciousness dwindles in prominence. It hardly counts, and certainly does not insist on its own importance. It becomes again the vessel of a great outpouring of energy that belongs to no one, yet that surges through all. Perhaps in such affirmations the mute immortality of the primitive, the concealed eternity of the unconscious, flares up again through the torn experience of self-consciousness and bespeaks itself for the brief moment. This tornness of suffering being uncloses a chink in self-consciousness through which the primordial energy breaks through.

In some great works of art and philosophy, we get the sense that the primordial energy breaks through and communicates to us its abiding ultimacy. There are great ethical lives and rare religious heroes that epitomize this breakthrough. Some are torn open more profoundly than others; these, in winning through to the simple yes, often have to suffer most.[29] Not that this breakthrough is only for an elect elite. It can occur through love or through sickness, in drunkenness or in dreaming; it can occur in grief, in laughter, or rejection, or forgiveness; it can flare up from forgotten time in the patience of the night that insomnia imposes. This breaking through may be the deepest drama of the everyday: how each readies himself for this opening out, how the most anonymous soul, in the unnoticed, nameless details of daily life, makes way for the blessing of this breakthrough, blessing it in turn whenever and wherever it comes to greet him.[30]

V. SONG OF FESTIVE BEING

The purely instrumental mind will suspect something idiotic in this breakthrough of metaxological being. This breakthrough, however, is not merely private. This we now will see in terms of festive being, for this entails the breakthrough of a *communal* rapture of the elemental. But here an accusation against philosophy currently goes around and the buzzword of its indictment is "nostalgia." I hear its hiss. I have been hearing it all along. I must first try to coax this cacophonous sound into song.[31]

I grant dangerous ambiguities concerning the mindfulness of metaphysical memory. Recall my critical remarks on Arcadian thought. Recall also that earlier eras knew well that *et in Arcadia ego:* death too is there.

Nostalgia itself is an ambiguous mood that moves most at some unguarded moment. The taut reins of everyday life slacken and some presence— forgotten, absent, buried, long dead—resurrects itself in the spaces of memory. The present greys and the vista of time elapsed adds sparkle to remembered events, now gone by. We yearn for what we once had, what now we seem to have lost, the long ago we now long to regain. Memory is a magic power; it selects; it allows only a portion of the past to pass through its filter; it can consign the pain part to a neutralizing limbo of forgetfulness. It transforms, sometimes deforms: the past event, when it was present, was fraught with tension, with ambiguous uncertainty and chance. But now, that past remembered, and the bygone event is laundered of the stains of concrete happening and almost transfigured into a destiny. Memory seductively whispers, time almost had to be that way. Behold yesterday's grief turns out to be all for the best. Thus retrospective memory heals time through omission. Yet when we turn the rosy retrospective back to the present and try to launch such a benign time again into the future, memory is soon grounded in the plain prose of everydayness.

Nostalgia, then, may be a fertile womb of sentimental falseness. But it is wrong to turn a completely cynical eye on it. Out of the mood sounds the muffled echo of an authentic strain. Nostalgia often flashes up when present reality fails to meet our longing for the perfection of being. Since this longing cannot be absolutely stilled, it must find some outlet for its dream of fuller being. The past allows the space for imaginative roaming. Memory need not always conjure a fantastic perfection out of nothing. For the past both fetters and frees. The past was, is punctuated by actual moments of great satiety and consummation. Memory of these may be paradoxically *progressive:* through their recall, it may make room for hope. Perfection of time did once, does still briefly flare out, and for the arrested moment all is transfigured. Time may give this gift again; time may just be this gift. When the present times are insipid, past transfigurations stand forth like peaks in a flat desert landscape. They are what memory inevitably tends to recall. The indifferent times literally make no difference. Nostalgia, I suggest, can feed on this deep need for difference, shaping itself around the contrast (albeit partly imaginary) between present and past.

With some avant-garde intellectuals, nostalgia is a bogeyman, seen in an opposite light—as a flight from difference, a mere escape from the tensions of harsh presentness into a more primitive state of sameness and oneness. "Nostalgia" is a kind of effigy they use to terrorize their opponents. "Nostalgia"—they can hardly utter this buzzword, so deep in their distaste—is regressive, a cowardly, cowering longing for the womb. Instead we must lash ourselves to the mast of the present, launch ourselves away from the seductive sirens of the past. This nostalgia is said to be the metaphysical condition of Western man. In his religions, Western man has repeatedly longed for community with God; in his philosophies, community with being or nature or self. If you dream of wholeness, if you quest for the metaxological community of being—as all great philosophies and religions have done in some sense—you are dismissively charged with "nostalgia," where this amounts to a metaphysical indictment.

There is an element of playacting here, avant-garde fanfaronade. Grant the ambiguity of nostalgia and all the risks of dishonest regression. Put aside philosophical profundities. Dig beneath the cultured histrionics. What is so shameful about releasing wholeness—and this without any betrayal of metaxological being? Why should not a true self dream of being's perfection, even in the middle—dream of better fulfilling the promise of metaxological being? My thought is always other to absolute truth, yet the otherness of truth is the intimate kin of my exiled, outsider thought. Then why the guilt when an exile longs to return home? We are unaccommodated under the unsettling elements, but are we not native to the world, native to being as home? Amidst the ruins of time, can one sing the well-being of the world? Why should one be in bad conscience when the elemental desire sings in one's blood, simply to be at home with being.[32]

We touch again on how metaphysical memory relates to a posthumous mindfulness: that is, as in time, yet beyond time's devouring supersession and drive to futurity. For in regarding what is behind us, memory can release the essential to be kept in mind. It tries to see what was there, is there, without instrumentalizing it, or reducing being to the scheme of an ulterior purpose: to remember its being as elemental. Such memory is many-voiced, full of the voices of otherness. This is "nostalgia" in the deepest sense: homesickness, memory of home. This "love of one's own" need not be the tyranny of the Same. Home may name the deepest community of being.

Such being-at-home entails a breakthrough beyond time's functionalization. Here metaxological mindfulness, as thought singing its other, reminds us of festive being as a liminal condition that is metaphysically elemental. Freed from false nostalgia, festive time makes us mindful of being as a feast or agapē.[33] In the ancient world, as I mentioned, the Attic festivals, the Chronia, offered to humans the taste, if only for a day, of the life of the Golden Age under Chronos. But in modernity the fetters binding the instrumental self are fast. For us, I think, it is far more important to loose those fetters than to posture about "nostalgia." For our world, as mobilized supremely for purposes of work, is in fugue from festive being. In order for something to assume reality in our lives, it has to work. One is often defined by one's function; without work, one may be without identity, even deprived of dignity in one's own eyes. Our sense of time, shaped by instrumental work, produces an amnesia of agapeic being. An efficient schedule organizes our day, carves the continuum of time into manipulable, productive units. The workweek, "real" time is counterposed to the weekend, idle time, where we are allowed to recuperate only to resume the cycle on grey Monday. Secretly, of course, real time for many is the weekend, the space of time outside the regimented cycle of the pragmatic, productive workday.

In the increasingly effective success of work, there arises this first reversal. Successful work tends to make work redundant. It expands the space for leisure, idleness, luxury. The working week shrinks, the weekend extends. In all this, however, work still, not enjoyment, holds the first place. The leisure we have dangles dependently on real work, being made possible by it. Thus, for the instrumental self under the sway of the sovereign work ethic, the weekend can prove strangely disorienting. It simply does not know what to do with spare time. It has time to kill and it kills time. A restless boredom descends like a mysterious malaise. It should be happy, free from work, but instead it is miserable. The order of days has collapsed, the external scaffolding of functioning being gone, and no joy is discovered in pure, inviting idleness. There is no Sabbath.[34]

The weekend is a modern institution, tied up with the modern rationalization of work and being. Throughout history a more profound sense of time is manifested in the happening of the festival. Festive being breaks through the closure of the functional system of instrumentalized life. Interestingly the festival is now treated with renewed seriousness. The idea is something like this. Today we live in a post-industrialist age, a post-work world, an age founded on technology's success in lifting the oppressive weight of dehumanizing toil. As this outcome increases in its effects, the claim is that we must learn, relearn the proper enjoyment of being, to order time in ways free from the dominance of the workweek. The restoration of the festival signifies the admission of this other concept of time, the development of a non-pragmatic, indeed a more aesthetic, poetic comportment towards being.[35]

The festival is nothing new. Neither old nor new, it is elemental. In previous ages when work was an imposed necessity, a curse, the festival stood out as a time of communal rapture or reversal, a time of consummation, even transfiguration. The Saturnalia (Greek: *Chronia*) were such reversals, where the working social order is turned topsyturvy and the servant mocks the master without fear of reprisal. One thinks of the Dionysian celebrations or the Irish *Fleadh Cheoil* (Feast of Music) as interruptions of the domesticated world of work time, eruptions of great communal rapture and intoxication. I think of Samhain: time of intersection of time and eternity, this world and the other, the juncture, crossing, the complication of the living and the dead; a time in time out of time, of carousal, chaos, dissolution and renewal. One thinks of the harvest festival blessing the year's yield and completeness; of Easter transfiguring the sacramental earth with jubilating, spring shouts of renewal.[36] One thinks of the Wake as the celebration of festive being on the occasion of death itself. James Joyce thus called the funeral that wakes a "funferall."

But unlike the modern weekend the festival is not a mere end-game, tacked on to the "real" workday world—a mere adornment, concession or consolation. Festivals punctuate the time process itself with a calendar of key points of birth, passage, finality, and renewal. Festive being reveals a metaxological between: an interim that is both a middle and an extreme, between time and time's other. Festivals are within time as recurrent in the calendar of the yearly round. They are outside time, celebrating the perennial essentials that give memorability and meaning to the full course of the year. The festival ritualizes a more concentrated, intensive sense of time, where the devouring future is stayed for a brief span, where the grief of the past is submerged in the present enjoyment. The solitary individual is lifted out of weary isolation, the normal successive sense of days is suspended, the meaningless supersession of moments seems conquered. In the rapture of the community, something is loosened out in us and we exhilarate in enjoying, in an elemental way, the simple earth.

In the modern rationalization of time the weekend gets its instrumental justification from the workweek; working time possesses the primacy. In the festival, by contrast, we experience time as other. Festival time does not simply borrow its meaning from worktime. Often, in fact, festivals give a new meaning to worktime, say, when a spring festival consecrates human labor for the coming sowing. For modernity, efficient work, aided by powerful technology, is the primary transformer of nature. With the festival, however, nature and the human are transformed in a different way such that everyday work becomes a secondary mode of transformation, drawing power from the first festive transformation. The original power of being itself is festal.

Not surprisingly, festivals point to something essentially religious, testifying to the sense of a special time that releases the more ultimate, transtemporal powers. Festivals ritualize a more sacred time, lift time out of the more secular flow, making a world of celebration unto itself.[37] Mundane pursuits can even appear extremely silly. During a street carnival a businessman in bowler and brolly bundles by; the celebrants see this busy brolly as comedy, and jeer amiably. This bowler is out of the swing of things, stiff, uptight, stressed, straitlaced, missing the fun. Carnival time can be a forgiving exposure of diligent pretension.

When we speak of festival time as holidays,[38] important dates specially hallowed, we find again the consecration of time within the flow of ordinary chronology. The cyclical, periodic character of festival being is here important. Repetition reveals the mystery of renewal and continuity; it extends to the present the welcoming meaning of the community of the whole. Yes I may be low now in winter, but the sun will course round and exult again in the spring sky. True I will age forwardly, singularly, but children will repeat again and again the circle of creation. I will go under, but the round earth will roll, and another will set out, pass through and pass away. And each key transition may be celebrated with its proper rite of passage. The individual does not say: "What an insignificant speck I am in this embracing drama," but: "I am in and of this drama, yes, insignificant or not as I, but yes, yes, it is good." Festivity deals out this largess of consent.

Festivals free from the tyranny of linear time. Day follows day, week week, year year, interminably, literally endless, stretching out into empty indetermination. Festival time bends back upon itself. This is time when remembrance, reminding is vital. Each year the crucial time is remembered; and when the celebration is over, memory guards the hope of recurrence. Memory becomes like a tabernacle of living mind that shields something consecrated, houses it till the next time of its proper reappearance. Hiddenness now nurtures the gestation of the again coming epiphany. When we have danced and drunk ourselves to the verge of exhaustion, we do not collapse and weep with weariness. There is peace, a catharsis both of emptying and of satiety. Things will settle into normalcy the day after, but already the secret powers prepare their appointed reemergence.

The festival is very important for embodying, enacting the drama of community. The atomic, functionary unit of separated selfness haunts the urban, suburban world. He works and retreats to rest. But let there be a festival and the dreary utilitarian aloneness dissolves. Festivals not only give expression to an already existing community. They make a community, create it as a coalescence of celebrants bound together in their play, in their being together as metaxological, as beyond mere functional interplay. During a festival a person is both a participant and a spectator, engaged in the middle, yet mindfully standing at its limit. As participants we are part of the celebration. Yet a key part of the celebration is just being there, there where the enjoying crowd is, just watching the others, and in watching the others, coming to see ourselves, understand ourselves, be ourselves as gifted by joy in being. Festivals are the self-knowledge of a people that rejoices in being's otherness. The solitary individual forgets himself, is snatched out of his confined selfhood by the energy of the surrounding surge, carried beyond himself and welcomed into a larger life, into the very largess of life.

VI. SONGS OF IDIOT WISDOM

Folly and Mind's Other

The basis of festive time is a kind of metaphysical amen to given being as a promise of perfection. This is what Vico would call a golden thought. But such golden thinking and its amen to the well-being of the world look like idiot wisdom. Is this the epilepsy of thought or the ultimate ectasis of mindfulness? Is it a seizure, a rapture? Is festive mind a saturnalian excess of thought? Plato's divine madness (*mania*) [*Phaedrus*, 244ff.] is not to be forgotten by singing philosophy. For there is a peripeteia in the mindfulness of festive being, namely, its dangerous proximity to folly. Folly is mind's own otherness that decenters every closed self-mediation. In it we find the breakthrough of more radical otherness in the depths of the self's own inward otherness, manifesting in the middle an extremity of otherness that subverts every claim to self-sufficient self-mediation. Folly, too, is elemental— elemental being as out of the center, as ontologically eccentric.

Contemporary society shows a strong concern with disturbance of mind, down to its pervasive institutionalization. It has bureaucratized, formalized rationalized its dealing with what seems the complete opposite of all system, reason, form and mediation, namely, madness.[39] It tries to systematize rupturing idiocy. There were times when madness was not thus rationalized, when the ambiguous power of the alogical and metalogical was differently approached. In earlier societies, the madman was as much an object of fascinated awe as of terror. Madness could sometimes be a gift of the divine, the madman a messenger whose words, springing from strange primordial depths, uttered an oracular truth from beyond everyday rationality. Alternatively, the madman might be possessed of darker, dangerous demonic powers. Measures to hedge the destruction, rituals to exorcise the possession might be taken. But the madman was not simply locked up or shunted aside, even in his difference and turbulent strangeness. He might move in out of the normal community, a reminder of disruptive powers and the strangely exciting enigma of those unloosed, unanchored souls like Crazy Jane or the Madwoman of Cork.[40]

The fool at the medieval king's court is a festive ritualization of this ambiguous mixture, this side-by-side existence in our middle being of the disruptive powers of the metalogical and the sovereignty of the ruling authority. One thinks of the intimacy between King Lear and his Fool. They are not like estranged others but like brothers, twins. The Fool is licensed to say what the King knows out of the hearing of rational mind and that initially he cannot acknowledge overtly—that in giving away his kingdom, the King was a real fool. The King himself must be broken, become a madman before snatching any crumb of bitter blessing from exposure to cruel ingratitude. When the mad Lear becomes "God's spy," he is and sees as if he were dead, and breaks through to an idiot wisdom, deeper even than his Fool's. Posthumous mind becomes idiot wisdom.

But the difference between fool and king here is no absolute divide. The fool has his licensed wisdom, itself granted as essential to the proper functioning of the rule of the normal. This coexistence in the middle is also acknowledged in the Saturnalian feasts that turn the normal order upside down; for a brief crazy hiatus, the Lord of Misrule is given his head. Respected figures of power and authority are treated as the fools, jeered at by erstwhile subordinates. Madness—what would normally be madness—is allowed to rule. The fool is put on the king's throne. Yet this madness is recognized as necessary, profoundly salutary for normal sanity.[41]

Royal politics is rare today, but some leaders might metaphorically be called kings. A true statesman is regal in ruling with vision not trapped by the power politics of huckstering. This "king" is not the tyrant but the healer with a just care for metaxological community. His wise worldliness transforms the will to dominate. He symbolizes the well-founded order of the everyday and its powerful flare of majesty. Every system, and not just traditional monarchies, tries to capture for itself some of this flare. But while guardian of the whole, the king is not the whole. The whole also includes the fool's disruptive power; sometimes it must welcome his destructive incursion. The fool is the messenger of finitude, the indispensable put down of pretence, the necessary shock that reminds of absurdity. He is the shaker of everyday foundations, harbinger of the mockery of the death we cannot sidestep. He is the visitor of paradox and strangeness, the carrier of enigma into the well-secured palaces of power, the voice from death, from beyond death, the laughter of posthumous mind that brings us back down to earth.

Modern politics silences the fool and his mocking song of otherness. Even worse: in some systems he is relabelled a dissident and consigned for psychiatric rehabilitation. Modern politicians do not welcome besides them their railing sobering jesters, reminders of pretension's folly. There is dead solemnity. To allow the fool his outing might affront the touchy respectabilities. Modern politics might break through its own instrumental-ization of communal being with a new festive ritualization of the licensed fool. We have countless court flatterers, armies of Osrics, but where are the irreverent gravediggers?[42]

This separation of king and fool makes the madman the absolutely other as *hostile:* we lock him up. There are destructive disruptions that every society, including premodern societies, finds necessary to restrain or quarantine. The hectic in us is stoked into a fevered darkness and the deranged soul risks ruin. What can also happen is that the social segregation of the mad "other" splits into two separate spheres what, in fact, are two dimensions of a unitary reality that is *within* the overall community or the individual self. The fools are not just "them," in there behind the walls, while we, out here, preen ourselves as pretender kings. We repress the inherent ambiguity, our double nature in the middle as both king and fool, only for this doubleness to resurface in the apartheid form of the sane versus the mad. Madness institutionalized is madness elsewhere: managed, rationalized, sanitized. But too vehement a will to repress the arational sometimes reveals that rationality itself has gone mad. The precarious ambiguity of human life is denied. Reason cuts itself off from its roots in the metalogical. But the mind is not made any the more secure by this surgery. Its metaxological power in often truncated.

There is a sense in which we are, in the ambiguity of our intermediate being, both king and fool in one: the middle that is between and yet joins, the divine and demonic, the sovereign and wretch. As king, man is nobility; as fool, cruel honesty. As king, he is exemplar of the ideal; as fool, harsh recall to the real. As the togetherness of these contraries, we are stressed and defined by the tensed doubleness of these inseparable extremities. This powerful paradox is one reason why the Christ figure exerts such a sway. In the middle space between time and eternity, this figure is the contradictory conjunction of king and fool. The fool mounts the hill to the Place of Skulls with the noble majesty of the king. The debased reality is the lofty ideal, lowness exalted to highest preeminence. In fact if God's kingdom is where first shall be last and last first, divine rule looks like the reign of the Lord of Misrule. It looks like an anarchy of reversal. Again we see paradoxical conjunctions of contraries: worldly impotence is true power, great authority resides on the neglected margins, ludicrous death may be deepest majesty, the despised criminal is to be accorded infinite respect. If instrumental reason is king, and truth its monopoly, all of this is pure folly.

The Reticence of Power

Folly is mind's other before which, not only the instrumental mind, but all will-to-power is humbled. Will-to-power over being's otherness is essential to modern instrumental selfhood. Such power over otherness is thought to give meaning to our freedom, to the expression of our being, to our sway over being. Such power is like an aggressive arrow shot from within out, the thrust of a weapon that from within finds its outward target, making its scarring mark on being. It is like a gesture of defiance that insists to the other: I have touched you, mastered you; take note, I am the Lord.

This defiance is not defiant simplicity and now appears to us as unwise, blustering folly. But in festive folly as other to will-to-power, we can be shown a different reticence of power. This reticence does not well up from an aggression towards being as other that would force it to acknowledge us and recognize our will. Nor does it spring from a depth of ontological insecurity that has to strike out at the other only to confirm itself. Since the modern will-to-power is so like this, one asks if it covers over a secret, festering impotence, a slackness of spirit, a despair. To alleviate the inner lethargy, the self explodes outward. In trying to subjugate the world, the inner slackness finds itself released, feels that it *is* something after all, proves itself in some way against the world of otherness. Without this outward explosion of energy, the inner lethargy might be sucked into an implosion of despair, and the self snuffed out in a kind of inner black hole. If the modern will-to-power is partly a defense measure against inner despair, there is a peculiar impotence, helplessness, metaphysical lostness in all the grandiose strutting.

By a reticence of power, a different sense of power, I mean a breaking through of self-being that does not have to compensate for the emptiness of its own inner abyss. I mean an outpouring of innerness that hides its own otherness. The human self maybe as deep, as unfathomed as an abyss, but some selves gives expression to their being earthed in powers of being transcending their limited selves, sources of power rooted in the grounds of existence and their consent to the metaxological community of being. This is related to the "letting be" that can spring up in the experience of "counting for nothing," to breaking through the confine of any monadic self-insistence and the reversal of its closure in an abandonment of freedom. As an image of this, I think of a boxer, one with the power to injure, to maim, to brutalize his other, his opponent; but this boxer has nothing to prove. He is a dancing boxer; his hands, legs, weaving and leaping are laughing expressions of being. This ludic body might well be turned into a weapon, but instead the warrior is a kind of poet of the flesh. He may be confronted by an opponent; but where he could easily ram through the blow and damage, he merely lets the glove glance lightly on the delicate skin. In that touch, terror and joy may pass to the opponent, and this may be enough. Beauty deflects the fatal blow. The boxer dances away.

Some will see this as weakness, thinking that power is nothing if it does not humiliate the other, bring the opponent to his knees. Has the boxer failed to prove himself by "letting off" his enemy? Has not the reticence of power shown itself as doubly powerful? It has shown itself as physically powerful; being "left off" and the terror withheld, amply testify to this. More importantly, it has shown its power in its ethical, indeed aesthetic forbearance. Eastern masters know this. The karate master is a potential killer; his whole body, nay even his flicking hand, is disciplined into a living, lethal weapon. But the master will veil the power to kill. The presence of the fatal power is there, clearly communicated by being unexercised. Playfully before danger, warnfully before a threat, the master briefly reveals what may be beyond the veil and then draws back. The inscrutable face returns to its uninsistent thereness.[43]

The bully is the opposite. He has the physical power, even psychological power to terrorize the other. But this is often coupled with moral cowardice. Thus there is impotence in his use of power. The bully has to prove himself through the weakness of others. Let him face an opponent of ethical courage, and the hollowness of his victories is intimated. The ethical presence says: in your bullying you will come to shame yourself. Without saying it that presence shows: I am the mirror in which you may see your shame. The reticence of ethical power consents to powerlessness.

Like the reticence of physical power, there is a festive reserve of spirit. Some thinkers so hide the suffering of their struggle that to the beholder the result seems effortless. The surface looks seamless, but this is a veil drawn over turmoil. The surface only says: those who have ears to hear let them hear . . . and leaves the blank space there, the space of freedom that welcomes rather than forces the other.[44] I think here of the enigma of Spinoza's *Caute!*[45] Other thinkers are more concerned to be admired, to call attention to themselves through "shocking" ideas, instead of being the patient prism through which the light passes, refracts and scatters its infinite brilliance. These are philosophers on show, sometimes Nietzsche's spawn, philosophers who seem to need to be noticed. Nietzsche himself is an ambiguous case. He rightly says that truth that guides the world comes on dove's feet, yet he might be called the "shouting philosopher." He swung between the reticence of power and the need to make others notice how brilliant he was (he was brilliant).[46]

There is a stereotype of the philosopher as the pedestrian technician of conceptual surfaces. Everything must be out in the logical daylight, no dark background, no unplumbed depths, no receding mirror on mirror in the abyss of mind: the univocalist logic-chopper will fit the type. But the most interesting thinker is masked. Everything does not have to be said on the surface. Festive mindfulness is masked thought (Plato's philosophical plays dramatize the festive agon of masked thought).[47] Such philosophers know this themselves. They do not need the psychoanalyst or the deconstructionist to remind them that a dark background is the necessary other to the bright foreground of conceptual enlightenment. The bright foreground is precisely the veil of the reticence of power, a grille separating the cloister of deeper mind.

Such thinkers ask not to be read exclusively on the surface. This is precisely not to read, to glide on the glassy sea, not to plumb the cold murk below, where the eyeless crustaceans float by and exotic fish, so cut off from the sun, they have to generate their own light. There is a certain power of spirit disturbing to expose, dangerous to place on open view. It must be masked lest one take fright at the terrible. The honest thinker must look the negative into the face, Hegel says. The impulse is to recoil. It seems difficult, even impossible to transfigure the terrible without falsifying it. Tragic art comes close to this: to bless being, in spite of terrible things; to be honest about the negative without rancor, even with thankfulness for being. Art's tolerance of otherness sings being, even in the tragic.

The reticence of spiritual power may mark a lifetime of struggle with the terrible, composed into a new noninsistent power: a thereness, a presence that does not clamor but that draws because of something else. Again this presence is easily misinterpreted as weakness. But it is not that at all. It may be a kind of well-less acceptance, a wisdom that looks like idiocy. This letting be of things is easily mistaken for neutral indifference but really it is an unwillingness to falsify or force reality to conform to one's conceptual mediations. This face of foolishness is again deceptive. It may be really a wise seeing and festive consent. Some artists have this reticence of power. Mozart, for instance, has been seen as light and airy, a cheerful child, mindlessly serene. But he does not put himself on show, nor exhibit the self-insistence that on the odd occasion grates in Beethoven. He lets the music be, but the bright surface both reveals and conceals everything. It manifests nothing but the music, but what is manifest comes from a country of mystery. Here there is just a ripple, a vanishing disturbance on the waters, but this is enough. Lesser artists will grind out the dissonance. Real light, pure light is the darkest of things. It illuminates us, dazzles us, but also blinds if we look directly into it.

Idiot Wisdom

In the levity of festive being, the heart is lightened. In the play of laughing mind, thought sings its other and leaps in the terrible. So, too, it toys with the idea, startling though it be, that wisdom is identical with idiocy. To become wise is to become an idiot. I do not think only of edifying paradoxes about the first and last, the wise and foolish. Strange irony, philosophical mind points us in the direction of idiot wisdom. How so?

Philosophy has named itself the search for wisdom. And wisdom entails some fulfillment of the desire for knowing. Yet what if we attained a breakthrough into such wisdom? Knowing implies a relatedness or community of knower and known. What would our breakthrough into such metaxological mindfulness mean? While we still seek wisdom, there is disjunction between knower and known, the self and the other. Suppose one radically fulfilled the desire for knowing? Would this mean an overcoming of the disjunction of knower and known, a surpassing of the dualistic opposition of self and other? But if we totally surpassed this opposition would not the result be a kind of idiocy? Would wise metaxological mindfulness not look mindless?

Consider these cases where passing beyond opposition seems to yield a supreme idiocy. Thus, mystics have claimed a oneness or community with

Godhead, dissolving all self-insistence in the decentered ecstasy of the *unio mystica*. The separation of opposition is said to cease. Do not mystics think up the most exalted idiocy, surging on wings of enthusiastic intimacy with Godhead? Some become unrestrained blatherers about the ineffable, while others mope in what looks like autistic silence regarding what is beyond mere mortal words. Idiocy or wisdom? If we come back down to earth and think of lovers: when they experience the two in one and breach the skin wall of separateness, in a shudder of rapture they seem to lose their minds. Instead of worldly calculating care, they break out in all kinds of silliness. Wise idiocy?[48]

What is this idiocy? More universally, idiot wisdom would manifest a form of second love, love of being as elemental. This need not imply the loss of differentiation or otherness, or the abnegation of selfhood through its disappearance into an absorbing god.[49] The breakthrough of idiot wisdom is into a consent to the metaxological community of being. Its mindfulness might seem mindless, idiotic, but only in the bad sense from the standpoint of instrumental reason. It is a recovery *after* alienated difference of the metaxological community of being as elemental. It implies an otherness at the heart of mind itself that yet is the end of mind: thought so other it does not know its own thought ("know" here in the sense of being mastered conceptually), thought always in excess of itself and its own self-mediation. Thus, one senses that some of the great philosophers did not "know" in Cartesian concepts what they were doing. This is paradoxical since philosophers have always prided themselves on such self-knowledge. Great philosophic mindfulness, nevertheless, feeds on an otherness beyond the determinate categories of mind, while mind itself is the self-conscious flourish of an excess of being that is prior to, informs, and yet surpasses every determinate thought. One does not think: one is being thought.

What might happen if metaxological mindfulness set at naught the dualistic opposition of self and other? Since the other would not then be radically opposed, you would have the simple pouring forth of benevolence, perhaps even the foolishness of turning the cheek. Also without the sense of opposition, the stress of striving would not persist. You would enter a state of calm will-lessness. Insistent desire would be suspended, you would have no hurry to and fro. Peace would replace willfulness. But would not the absence of anxiety look like the vacancy of the idiot's face? The face would not be battered or worn by care; the eyes would be soft, almost in a daydream, a reverie of benevolence; the wrinkles from the weathering of hostile difference would be smoothed out. You might be either a dead man or a child, or if the latter, forgiveness and forget would quickly follow every hurt.[50]

Without willfulness ambition would seem senseless. But a goal-less man, a person going nowhere, one who as the pious put it, accepts the will of God—what is this? Thereness with unstressed receptivity, acceptance without tension, vacant, empty, sheer openness—the idiot? I am not talking about the *idiot savant* who is a real imbecile overall, though a genius in one particular respect. I am talking about a kind of universal idiocy, a kind of heedless love of the whole. Do I hear an inaudible yes, the murmur of an unqualified "Let be," like a God accepting all, including the evil? Accepting the evil? Would not such an amen spell ethical idiocy?

I have this image in mind from *Aguirre: The Wrath of God.*[51] Aguirre leads a mutinous band of *conquistadores* down the Amazon in search of El Dorado and its mythical gold. The silence of the jungle unnerves all and Aguirre forces an Indian slave to play his pipes: music to fill the still vacancy of nature that in its sheer thereness Western man cannot tolerate. In Aguirre's face one sees the tortured eyes of a baleful self, a satanic willful inwardness—a Thrasymachus in nature's jungle. After playing and soothing the indifferent silence, the Indian slave looks out into vacant space, his eyes untroubled by the tangled inwardness of the willful self. That empty innocent gaze unnerves me. I am unsure if these vacant eyes are an idiot's or a wise primitive's, or both. Or am I the idiot to ponder this gaze from nothing onto nothing?

And we philosophers, we shake ourselves loose from this look, we bristle and we say: we *seek* wisdom. But we also show a strange reluctance to belong fully to it. Why do we hug the middle ground between the beast and the god, as Plato has it? We pride ourselves on our lack of hubris in remaining mere mortals. But do we remain philosophers, that is, searchers in the middle, not because we lack wisdom and respect its divinity, but because we are terrified by its idiocy?

Notes

1. See my *Art and the Absolute* for a reading of Hegel that tries to acknowledge a more open dialectical interplay between art, religion, and philosophy; also "Hegel and the Problem of Religious Representation." These indicate the basis of my reluctance to accuse Hegel of any simple monism.

2. The whole book develops the position, but in relation to Hegel see especially the introduction and chapter 5.

3. On this see *Desire, Dialectic and Otherness*, chapter 3.

4. Some commentators see Descartes' resort to God as an epistemological weakness. If the philosophical task is purely for thought to think itself and if God is an other, this may be so. But if thought must think its other, then Descartes' discovery of the idea of God as absolute perfection, shows his commendable willingness to think the absolute other in inwardness itself. There are subtleties here connected with the "ontological proof" that might be metaxologically illuminated. When Husserl takes as his motto *ego cogito cogitatum* rather than *cogito ergo sum* (see *Cartesian Meditations*, p. 50 and *Paris Lectures*, p. 14), it is not at all clear that this is an improvement on Descartes. For Descartes' *sum* keeps us in mind of thought's bond with being, and hence the promise of otherness. Husserl wants a more self-sufficient closure of thought thinking itself, though the doctrine of the intentionality of consciousness inevitably strains against any such closure.

5. My emphasis on being aesthetic, religious, and ethical recalls Kierkegaard's stages of life's way and Hegel's triad of art, religion and philosophy. In distinction to these triads, I note my *fourfold* concern: philosophy is also a way of being mindful. My difference with Hegel follows the metaxological view that there is no *one* dialectic that subsumes the others: philosophy does not subsume the otherness of art and religion into its own self-thinking thought. Nor is there any simple progressive relation between philosophy and its others, nor any totalizing *Aufhebung*. Kierkegaard insists on the otherness of religion; his danger is setting this otherness into a dualistic opposition to philosophy, especially as identified with Hegel's panlogist thought thinking itself. Such a dualistic opposition is untenable if philosophy is metaxological, hence open to the *thinking* of otherness. Kierkegaard has a sense of the other as resistant to philosophy; Hegel has a sense of philosophy's own

self-mediation in relation to its others. Philosophy as metaxological and plurivocal may still find a qualified place for both these emphases, while avoiding dualistic opposition in regard to the first, and dialectical subsumption in relation to the second.

6. To keep my discourse manageable and in interplay with the matter itself, I have developed some points in the notes. These contribute to the plurivocal thought of the work: they contain, as it were, a series of subterranean conversations with the views of important others. Hence some notes are not just bibliographical.

7. See my "Can Philosophy Laugh at Itself?"

8. Since the philosopher is a participant in the metaxological community of being, the latter cannot be completely objectified by him, made an "object" out there for the conceptual mastery of thought thinking itself. One cannot master what one depends on ontologically, for such putative mastery would again instantiate the ontological dependence and hence refute itself. So neither the metaxological community nor the participating "I" can be completely objectified. This participatory character is very evident with the aesthetic, the ethical, and the religious, but needs to be remembered by the philosopher. One cannot totally abstract from such participation, for abstract thought is itself a certain mode of participating in the middle. The philosopher as being mindful cannot escape implication in the other ways of being mindful.

CHAPTER 1

1. The work of Rorty (*Philosophy and the Mirror of Nature*; *Consequences of Pragmatism*) is a focus around which controversy has most recently swirled concerning the self-images of philosophy. The internecine conflict in the body of sages sometimes reaches the level of professional war (see *Proceedings* of the American Philosophical Association, 60, # 2).

2. Since the "end of philosophy" has been an issue since Hegel, those who think the recent debate is new suffer from historical myopia. Thus, Kierkegaard, Marx, and Nietzsche are thinkers on philosophy's end, the first in contrast with religion, the second in relation to political revolution, the third in relation to tragic art. (Later chapters will advert to other related "deaths" in art, religion, and ethics.) In recent Continental thought, the issue is associated with Heidegger and more recently Derrida (*Margins of Philosophy*). In Anglo-American thought, positivism can be seen as one "end" of philosophy. On its ordinary language successor see, Ernest Gellner, *Words and Things*, p. 20, for the "euthanasia" of philosophy; also p. 173, on "the withering away of philosophy." Gellner does not go back as far as Hegel. His book appeared in England in 1959, and is a devastating polemic against linguistic analysis, far superior to Rorty's recent sallies. One comes to realize the power of entrenched professional position, given the survival of many of the objects of Gellner's critique. Stanley Rosen's, *The Limits of Analysis* has superior philosophical substance; see my

review. See also J. Rajchman and C. West, eds. *Post-Analytical Philosophy*; and K. Baynes et al. eds. *After Philosophy: End or Transformation*.

3. See my "Plato's Philosophical Art and the Identification of the Sophist." Also, *Sophist*, 268c, the sophist is a mimic of the wise, *mimētēs tou sophou*.

4. This might seem tart, but it condenses a whole attitude to what are sometimes called "recursive arguments," which Aristotle's *ad hominem* criticism of skepticism (e.g., *Metaphysics*, XI) already articulates: the skeptic implicitly assumes in his logos what his logos explicitly denies; if he wants to talk rationally a necessity is already imposed on him, a necessity he epitomizes even when he denies it. The contradiction is not just propositional but a living contradiction between proposition and performance. Implicit in my remark also are considerations from the philosophy of transcendental self-reflection: the misological skeptic cannot sustain his logos in confrontation with the demands of transcendental self-reflection except by continual epistemological squirming. Spinoza had it right when he said that truth is the measure of itself and its opposite, and when he tartly said in *On the Improvement of the Understanding*: "Such people do not know themselves . . ." One thinks of Augustine: we blithely lie to others, without compunction; but we absolutely hate to be lied to by others. Francis Bacon is an essay "Of Truth" says of the skeptic: "Certainly there be that delight in giddiness, and count it a bondage to fix a belief . . ." You cannot talk philosophy in the company of this giddiness.

5. See Plato's *Symposium* 200ff. on the intermediate nature of the philosopher; *Meno* 80e–d, *Lysis*, 218 on the paradoxes of knowing what we do not know. This is not Plato of "Platonism," caricatured by Nietzsche and recently identified by Rorty with Philosophy, supposedly now dead (Big P Philosophy: below I call this "heroic thinking"), as opposed to philosophy (small p philosophy: the thought of what below I call "the neutral"). This Plato of the *metaxu* and eros does not reduce conceptually the ambiguity of the middle to a set of abstractions. As *philos*, friend, the philosopher is not *turannos* or *dominus* who tries to make truth a possession, a property. A *philos* respects the other.

6. See Kirk and Raven, *The Presocratic Philosophers*, on Heraclitus' contempt for the poets, frs. 57, 42; on his contempt for learning without wisdom, fr. 40; on his contempt for Pythagoras as "polymath," fr. 129.

7. This is an old philosophical strategy. See *Hippias Major* (285d–e): Hippias specializes in genealogies of heroes and antiquarian lore. Socrates teases him about reciting the list of Archons from Solon on. Stone dead to the irony, Hippias says: "Why I can repeat fifty names after hearing them once." On the sophist as a polymath see *Sophist* 232a. In *Encomium moriae seu laus stultitiae* Erasmus mocks the scholar—himself. Kierkegaard has strong words for the scholars, especially the Hegelians, though if the *Earliest System Program* belongs to the young Hegel, with Hölderlin he was contemptuous of the *Buchstabenphilosophen*. He wanted to be a teacher of the folk (*Volkserzieher*), not just a professor. See H. S. Harris, *Hegel's Development*, pp. 57ff., 510–512. Hegel also speaks of the "spiritual animal kingdom" (*Das geistige Tierreich*) [*Phenomenology*, pp. 237ff.], and remarks on

those who swarm to a new "matter," *Sache*, like flies to freshly spilt milk (p. 251). In his *Philosophy of Religion* he likens historical theologians to bankers always handling someone else's money, never creating their own wealth; or to blind men handling the frame of a beautiful painting but never seeing its beauty.

8. My point is not to deny the importance of philosophy's history, but the stress falls on the history of *philosophy*, not on the *history* of philosophy: philosophical perplexity is the perennial *Sache selbst*. Unless one brings a philosophical mind to the hermeneutical dialogue with tradition the result is unphilosophical history of ideas. See my "Hegel", History and Philosophical Contemporaneity."

9. In Kierkegaard's *Johannes Climacus* there is a joke at the expense of the professorial scholars who do not take doubt with lived seriousness. The dangerousness of philosophy is evident with Socrates (and before him Anaxagoras); even Aristotle was brushed was the danger of losing his life. One thinks of Bruno's execution, the attempted assassination of Spinoza. Kierkegaard invited execration in the *Corsair* affair and did not escape without scars. Nietzsche (the younger Schopenhauer too) felt he was being killed with silence; now he is the object of raging research.

10. Is Professor Derrida a real shark? Or a postmodern Alexandrian? He seems to be an original (but of course deconstruction denies the possibility of originals) generating a thousand clones—strange epigonal champions of difference, an endlessly disseminated mimicry of Derrida. Derrida himself is a peculiar mix of cautious textual scholar and intoxicated original thinker, at least violent interpreter. Working both sides of the street, his ambiguity generates influence: the sober scholar ("rigorous" is a favorite word) speaks to the work-ethic of the academy, the wilder thinker to the secret desire to be "creative," "revolutionary," "original," also percolating through the academy. If we subtract the textual exegesis, what would the original thought look like? The deconstructionist will reject the question, since "creative thinking" seems to be identified with hermeneutical aggression on the texts of others (the scholar as revolutionary warrior in a *guerre de plume*). If I misread the deconstructionist, pray do not hold this against me, for, as they say, there are only misreadings. But the simple question has to be put in relation to this logomachy, this "creative scholarship." What human voice is to be heard here? Could one reverse Pascal's expectation and say: I sought a human voice but found an author? But, of course, the deconstructionist says there are no authors. As the absent author, Derrida then would be the invisible shark, the noumenal shark. But, of course, Derrida's voice is *ubiquitously present*, especially in the writings of his commentators. And why anyway must philosophical thought be always *parasitical* on the *texts* of others, including Derrida's own texts? In the "textual revolution" is the deconstructionist a scholar with a bad conscience: resentful of his dependence on texts, the work of others, does his own lack of creativity overflow into aggression, interpretative violence towards the texts of others? All the while the deconstructionist is battering the text of the other, he chants the mantra that unwittingly damns him: "openness to otherness."

11. The philosopher as technician even reproduces God in his image: I think of the clockmaker God of the deists of the eighteenth century; the calculative reason of the eighteenth century Enlightenment produces a clockwork world and a technicist God. Leibniz' God reminds one of an *infinite technicist* in his absolute calculation of universal compossibility—though since knowledge of *final causes* is included in this calculation, a wisdom in excess of technical or efficient causation is also implied (see note 14). Marcel and Heidegger both are critics of the rationalist hubris that technique risks. See W. Barrett, *The Illusion of Technique*.

12. I think also of figures like Descartes and Bacon who wanted a complete break with the then book philosophers (the scholastic Aristotelians) and a different redirection of mind to the book of Nature itself.

13. There are passages in Carnap, *The Logical Structure of the World*, p. viii, where his description (without irony) of the logicist philosopher reminds one of a technicist god, reducing the given equivocity and totally reconstructing the physical world. See David Weissman, *Intuition and Ideality*, pp. 75ff. The technicist reduction of being to univocity reveals the implicit conceptual imperialism of "logocentrism," as Heidegger would put it. See chapter 5 on logic and being mindful.

14. Leibniz' search for a universal characteristic is extremely revealing concerning the intertwining of the technicist mind and the sense of larger metaphysical purpose, showing a kind of noble simple-mindedness. In his search for a universal calculus, Leibniz the rational technician draws on more than the technicist dream. In his desired reduction of all equivocity to univocity, the primitivity of the latter is likened to a kind of *Adamic* language (see "On the Universal Science: Characteristic" in *Monadology and Other Philosophical Essays*, pp. 11–21). From the simples that would be "a kind of *alphabet of human thought*," everything follows by a kind of calculus. "Such a language would amount to a *Cabala* of mystical vocables . . . language of *magi*" (p. 12). Silence would be imposed on the sects: if there is disagreement all one has to say is: Let us calculate! (p. 14) Leibniz wants to avoid the equivocations of natural language; mental error is identified with error of calculation (p. 18). The instrumental nature of the characteristic is evident in that it would be an *organon* for *every* subject matter (p. 19), with benefits for the perfection of mind and body (p. 17). Leibniz' reference to Adamic language and Cabala, as well as worldly betterment, are post-Cartesian echoes of an older, less instrumentalized tradition that we find, say, in Plato's *Statesman* (305) where philosophy and royal art are discussed. This philosopher king is related to the figures of the revolutionary, sage, poet, priest, hero, as much as to the scientist. Nor need we read Aristotle's sense of logic as *organon* or instrument as logicist imperialism, since he acknowledged other forms of mind, as also the alogical. I think also of Pythagorean number and its being connected with music and mysticism.

15. On ethics and calculative self-interest, see chapter 4. I cite one episode from R. J. Lifton, *The Nazi Doctors*, pp. 178–79. One of the killing doctors, ghastly arbiters of life and death said: We were professional functionaries; the killing was entirely a technical question; the pure efficiency of the process was the concern; the

word "ethics" simply did not exist. "*Nein. Ethisch spielt überhaupt—das Wort gibt es nicht.*"

16. See R. Rorty, *Consequences of Pragmatism*, chapter 12 "Philosophy in America Today." He quotes Hans Reichenbach whose book *The Rise of Scientific Philosophy* "maintains that philosophic speculation is a passing stage, occurring when philosophic problems are raised at a time which does not possess the logical means to solve them. It claims that there is, and always has been, a scientific approach to philosophy. And it wishes to show that from this ground has sprung a scientific philosophy which, in the science of our time, has found the tools to solve those problems that in earlier times have been the subject of guess work only. To put it briefly: this book is written with the intention of showing that philosophy has proceeded from speculation to science." Such views are now criticized, but one must not forget the imperialistic, even implicitly totalitarian, intents of "scientism" in the past: scientism as the belief that *all* the fundamental problems will yield to positive science, bringing the progressive amelioration, perfection of the human condition, for example, Condorcet, Comte. Comte's scientistic parody of Catholicism, with its priesthood of the scientists, now seems quaint, but it is very consistent with scientistic imperialism. True to scientistic univocity, Comte did not see the laughable nature of the parody. I stress: to criticize scientism is not to reject science. Scientism is a philosophical interpretation of science, an unacceptable interpretation of a genuine but not absolute human enterprise.

17. H. G. Gadamer, *Truth and Method*. P. Feyerabend, *Against Method*, and recently *Farewell to Reason*. In "The Overcoming of Metaphysics through the Logical Analysis of Language," Carnap says: "What, then, is left for *philosophy* if all statements whatever that assert something are of an empirical nature and belong to factual science? What remains is not statements, not theory, nor a system, but only a *method*: the method of logical analysis." Reprinted in *Heidegger and Modern Philosophy*, ed. M. Murray, p. 31. Carnap does recognize a likeness of traditional metaphysics and art, though he judges this to the detriment of philosophy: it is poor art. Rorty treads similar terrain, I think, only he reverses the plus and minus signs: something positive is seen in philosophy's relation to literature, and something negative in philosophy's obsession with the technical and scientific self-image. In Continental thought this issue took form around phenomenological method and hermeneutics, and now the deconstructive radicalization, indeed attempted dissolution of the latter.

18. On metaphysical astonishment, see *Desire, Dialectic and Otherness*, pp. 183ff. Inward otherness will reappear in different forms throughout the present work, but see chapter 5 on solitude and inward thisness. A classical example here is Socrates' turn from nature to *logoi*, as recounted in the *Phaedo*: the enigmas of nature must await a response to the issue of self-knowledge, as Socrates asks: Am I a Typhon, a monster swollen with excess, or a being of more gentle or divine nature? This is the resistant otherness of the soul, its being beyond itself.

19. The manifesto of the Vienna Circle called for a *Wissenschaftliche*

Weltauffassung, a scientific world view with no insoluble mysteries: unanswerable questions are to be put aside as no longer scientific. Whitehead, co-author of *Principia Mathematica*, said towards the end of his life: "The exactness is a fake." The cultural assumptions of science are now being more critically explored; Nietzsche was one of the first genealogists of science. On the enveloping context of science, see Kuhn's (*Structure of Scientific Revolutions*, p. 44, n. 1) endorsement of Polanyi's notion of "tacit knowledge." The figures of scientist and revolutionary are here wedded, and indeed the scientist and hero—the revolutionary hero corresponds to new *rupturing* paradigms, models, originals, exemplars in thought; paradigms are implicit anticipations of the whole.

20. In discussing the Anaximander fragment, Heidegger says that all thinking is poetizing. Marcuse, Adorno, Gadamer also importantly underscore the aesthetic. See Vico (*New Science*, pp. 69ff.) on the poets as the first sages. When Shelley called poets the "unacknowledged legislators" of the world, when Pound called them the "antennae of the race," they were brothers of Vico, as indeed were Yeats and Hölderlin, for whom the poet was sacerdotal and heroic. On Rorty, the strong poet (Harold Bloom's phrase) and the utopian revolutionary, see his articles in the *London Review of Books*. It is a nice irony to find Plato anticipating Rorty: poets "are our fathers, as it were, and conductors in wisdom" (*Lysis*, 214a).

21. Heidegger is concerned with this common care when he says: Language is the house of being; the thinker thinks being, the poet names the holy. Socrates' turn to *logoi* shows him a guardian of articulation: not only an analytical guardian, but also (since the whole human being is at issue) a musical (cf., *Phaedo*, also *Republic*) and rhetorical guardian (cf., *Phaedrus*). Without the latter philosophy would be *dianoia* without *noēsis*; the scientist-technician paradigm would wrongly dominate.

22. One does not have to be a follower of Leo Strauss (see, *Persecution and the Art of Writing*) to see some truth in esotericism: all great thought is by its nature esoteric, that is, masked, reticent, holding something in reserve. It is nurtured in a silence, silent even in speaking, esoteric even when being exoteric. A Cartesianism that foolishly thinks it communicates in absolutely clear and distinct concepts blinds us to this elementary fact. Everything does not have to be laid out; great thinkers are hard, not obscure, but it is simple commonsense to acknowledge that this is not evident at all.

23. Such spiritual seriousness is evident, for instance, in the torment of dark truth that we find in Aeschylus and Sophocles; also in Dostoevski. (Plato mentions sacred fear in the *Laws*; one is reminded of the proximity of beauty and the terror of the sacred—Rilke relived this.) Nietzsche called for an artistic Socrates in *The Birth of Tragedy*, but is not altogether wrong in criticizing "Socratic man": Socratic dialectic does risk superficiality. But it was Socrates' death that redeemed his thought, making us wonder: was there hidden in this life of thought also the *suffering* of truth, the *pathei mathos*?

24. Wittgenstein identified the ethical and the aesthetic in the *Tractatus* (6.421). A logicist saint for the Vienna Circle, later apostate of pure positivism, he saw the

poet in the philosopher: "I think I summed up my attitude to philosophy when I said: philosophy ought really to be written only as poetic composition." *Culture and Value*, p. 24.

25. I refer to the idea of being as perfection—an old theme in philosophy, with myriad ramifications, metaphysical, ethical, aesthetic, religious. See *Art and the Absolute* where I speak of the transfiguration of the ugly in relation to aesthetic theodicy, with particular reference to Hegel and Nietzsche. The issue haunts the notion of being in *Desire, Dialectic and Otherness*. I return to the golden world in chapter 6.

26. See A. Danto, *The Philosophical Disenfranchisement of Art*, chapter 7, "Philosophy/As/And/Or Literature." Significantly Danto begins with a citation from Hegel's *Aesthetics* but does not succumb to the raillery once *de rigueur* for analytical thinkers when even the name Hegel was mentioned. Hegel, *the* object of philosophical derision for analytical thinkers, is incubating his nemesis of the technicists. Against the lie that philosophical discourse is the "plain prose" of technicist mind, see Danto's amusing list (p. 141) of the astonishing variety of literary forms produced by philosophers. I implied that for sound commonsense Zeno's thoughts are outlandish, mad, show that logic is mad. See Danto (p. 143), again amusingly, on contemporary analytical speculations of "fictive reference," confirming my point that to sound commonsense many philosophical thoughts are so *other* as to seem mad, since they ask, as Hegel said, commonsense to walk on its head. Philosophy's concern with the thought of nothing is an old example of this speculative madness.

27. Hegel's use of the word *Gottesdienst* in his philosophy of religion is the most familiar one. See *Lectures on the Philosophy of Religion*, p. 79; also, my "Hegel, Philosophy and Worship"; but he also used the word in his *earliest* published piece—on art and philosophical speculation as a divine service, see Hegel's *Difference*, pp. 170–72. Hegel also calls philosophy a *Gottesdienst* in the *Aesthetics*, I, p. 101. On Wittgenstein and the priesthood, see B. McGuinness, *Wittgenstein: A Life*, p. 274. See Plato's Seventh Letter (especially, 341d), also *Theaetetus* (175aff.). The picture of Protagoras in *Theaetetus* (166d) reminds of Rortian edification: the sophist is a physician, a therapist; opinions are not truer but better; the philosopher is a like a freelance consultant, like a lawyer—Rorty's all purpose intellectual, name-dropper. Compare to Socrates' service to the god in *Apology*, on philosophy as catharsis in *Phaedo* (67), and the accompanying god in philosophical midwifery (*Theaetetus*, 150d), or the image of initiation in the mysteries as a metaphor for philosophy (*Phaedrus*, 249c–250c). Husserl invokes Augustine in *Cartesian Meditations*, p. 157. Josef Pieper (*Leisure*) sees the connection of philosophy and cultus; Gadamer dwells on the connection of *theōria* and the festival (*Truth and Method*; also *The Relevance of the Beautiful*). See chapter 6 on festive being and philosophy as thought singing its other.

28. It is not only those who want to abolish Christianity who despise the priest,

like Nietzsche. Kierkegaard wanted to restore Christianity, but he despised the priest as a state functionary, as a bourgeois civil servant (see *Attack upon "Christendom"*).

29. Freud says in *The Future of an Illusion* "Our God—logos— . . ." Later in *New Introductory Lectures on Psychoanalysis* (1933), in "The Question of *Weltanschauung*," he sees religion, not art or philosophy, as the greatest opponent to the scientific *Weltanschauung*. The issue lurks in Hegel's more complex doctrine of absolute spirit in terms of the dialectical relations of art, religion, and philosophy; in the Heideggerian critique of Western thought as ontotheology (theology is one of the conceptions of *prōtē philosophia* in Aristotle's *Metaphysics*); in the use of the term "mystical" as a jargon word of abuse, not only by analysts and empirically-minded thinkers, but also revolutionary thinkers like Marxists.

30. An extended interpretation might be offered on the dialectical twists, not to say reversals, not all of them holy, made possible by the classical formula for fideistic insolence to thought: *Credo quia absurdum*. The fideistic insolence is a religious inversion of the logical insolence of the *reductio ad absurdum*: it is an *elevatio per absurdum*. One interpretation of the formula implies the following (logical) incoherence: the absurd is not really the absurd *per se* but absurd only to finite thought; really the absurd is its opposite, namely, the most meaningful thing, as the mystery of the ultimate above finite thought. This logical incoherence has a significant dialectical consistency.

31. Thus, the connection of politics and religion is clear in Plato. Socrates was executed because religious impiety was also political treason; to question the gods was to question and possibly undermine the foundations of the polis. This is also why Plato in the *Republic* is so obsessed with the images of the gods in laying the groundwork for his ideal polis. It is clear in Spinoza's *Tractatus Theologico-Politicus*: political kingdoms accord with concepts of God. It is clear in Hegel and his atheistic heirs, like Marx. See Heine's magnificent ending in *Philosophy and Religion in Germany*. Heine is very indebted to Hegel in plotting the modern movement from religion to philosophy and from philosophy to politics. He really just recounts what Hegel said in his lectures on the philosophy of history concerning the inner dynamic of the movement from the Protestant Reformation through the Enlightenment to the French Revolution.

32. Marx uses Hegel's idea of the inverted world in relation to religion and revolution (*Early Writings*, p. 43), but his language is full of warrior holism. He stresses "war," "weapons," criticism with "indignation" and "denunciation" (p. 46), "hand to hand fight" (p. 47). His reference to Luther (pp. 52f.) is almost exactly the same as Hegel's. Extremism is evident in an all or nothing attitude (p. 56), "desire to be everything" (p. 57); revolution "upsets *the whole order* of things" (p. 202). The connection of philosophy and politics is admitted with Rousseau and the *philosophes* as preparatory for the French Revolution. On the connection today, see F. Dallmayr, *Critical Encounters: Between Philosophy and Politics*.

33. The utopian thrust of revolutionary politics (shared with some religions) can issue in a political parody of religious ultimacy, not to say blasphemy. Mussolini

spoke of Fascism as the "church of all the heresies." Hymns and prayers were composed to Hitler, to Stalin; see Aryeh L. Unger, *The Totalitarian Party: Party and People in Nazi Germany and Soviet Russia*, pp. 188–91; also Robert A. Pois, *National Socialism and the Religion of Nature*, p. 28. Consider Che Guevarra's famous remark on the abolition of the intellectuals as a class—something the Khmer Rouge did with a fury of destruction against anyone with even rudimentary education. Transfiguring all means destroying all. Consider the madness of the Red Guard in the Chinese Cultural Revolution: fanatical idealism gone berserk, ending in destruction. Disillusion, passing through terror yields the negative freedom of aggressive violence, hatred of what is. Instead of revolutionary transfiguration, the religious urgency of ultimacy becomes disfigured in social/political/cultural form. On Marx and art, see Louis Dupré's thoughtful *Marx's Social Critique of Culture*, pp. 258–275. See Mao Tse-Tung, *Talks at the Yenan Forum on Literature and Art*, pp. 25–26; also chapters 3 and 4 of my *Art and the Absolute* for discussion of some Left–Hegelian views of art and religion: the end of art and religion is related to the issue of the end of history and so-called post-historical society.

34. When Marx said that philosophy must change the world, not just interpret it (as with Hegel), he showed the anti-contemplative bias of post-Hegelian philosophy: *praxis* is superior to *theōria*, for *theōria* smacks of priestly contemplation, conservative canonization of the status quo. He was also calling for a post-philosophical philosophy. The end of philosophy discussed previously now means: we abolish philosophy by realizing it (*Early Writings*, pp. 50–51). The totalitarian danger is that the revolutionary project will complete and abolish as distinct, not only poet and priest, but the philosopher, indeed also the scholar, technician and scientist: all these are to be subordinated to the requirements of political totality.

For revolutionary thought is *commanding*, legislative thought which says: This is to be, shall be. It anticipates the otherness of the ought-to-be. The danger here is a *dictatorial* thinking that leads to tyranny in the legislation of the ought-to-be: it destroys the otherness of present existence in justification of the future ought-to-be. Here Hegel's ambiguous, dialectical caution must be heard: philosophy does not tell being what it should be; it respects its otherness; this is not resignation; being is already in the process of becoming what it ought to be. Commanding thought risks being a violating reduction of present and future otherness. This caution has to be applied not only to Marx but to Nietzsche who celebrated the *legislative will* of the new philosopher, itself beyond good and evil. Nietzsche gives us a rhapsodic version of Plato's philosopher-king (see *Beyond Good and Evil*, sections 203–211); but Plato's philosopher does not really want to be king (see *Republic*, 347b, 520e, 540b).

35. See *Inferno*, canto III.

36. I discuss this in *Desire, Dialectic and Otherness* in terms of what I call our "intentional infinitude."

37. I return to originals and imitation in art in chapter 2, in chapter 3 in regard to the religious prophet, in chapter 4 in relation to paradigms for ethical mimesis.

38. Another reason is the modern revolt of the sons against the fathers. Modern sons first revolt against God the Father, then against the human father, then try to be autochthonous originals by becoming a freak species of mother: one capable of self-creation, auto-creation, father/mothering itself. In the interests of brevity I omit the book that might be written to illustrate this point in art, religion, and philosophy. The results of the sons' efforts at auto-creation are ambiguous. But see at the end of chapter 2 on how "creativity," unanchored from otherness turns into free-floating negativity.

39. This tale is told by Socrates in *Theaetetus* (174aff.); he paints a picture of the singularity, aloofness of the philosopher that is laughable to the many. Socrates' arrogance is clear in the *Apology*, but Plato is very sensitive to the double-edged comedy of the philosopher—the latter often cuts a sorry figure in politics, showing the blinking ridiculousness of one who has seen and has to be forced back into the dusky cave (*Republic*, 517d). Aristophanes (whose work Nietzsche said was found under the dead Plato's pillow) deeply knew the comedy of abstracted, alienated thought. Jonathan Swift's fantasy of Laputa is the great modern version of this comedy: the abstracted thinkers on the floating island have one eye turned inward, the other upwards to the Zenith (one thinks of Augustine's Platonic itinerary of thought: inward and upward). Laputan thinkers are covered with Pythagorean musical and mathematical symbols, but are always in danger of falling down and in perpetual need of flappers to recall them to their senses. Meanwhile their women make love to servants before their eyes; the women love the earth, hate the free-floating mathematical island, are rooted in being in the body. Laughter here is the nemesis of alienated thought. See my "Can Philosophy Laugh at Itself?"

40. See, e.g. *Metaphysics*, I, 2; also *Nicomachean Ethics*, 10, especially 1177b25ff. (Consider Parmenides' words: *to gar pleon esti noēma*, for thought is excess. fr. 16; cf. *Metaphysics*, 1009b24.) Many of Presocratic thinkers present this heroic profile (consider Empedocles, or Pythagoras), mingling the sacerdotal, the ethical, the mythic, the logical, the poetic—hence their attraction to Nietzsche in *Philosophy in the Tragic Age of the Greeks*.

41. On *sophia* as associated with sage, poet, priest, sophist, see C. B. Kerferd, *The Sophistic Movement*, p. 24. Not only in the Greek world is the philosopher emergent from the magus, in the early modern age the new science had roots in Renaissance alchemy and the Hermetic tradition (see M. Berman, *The Reenchantment of the World*). The issue of hero and sage is related to the issue of power and justice (see chapter 4): if the hero is power and the sage is mindfulness of ends, then without the latter we get Thrasymachus. (When Socrates confronts death in *Phaedo*, it is *phronēsis* that is repeatedly ascribed to him.) Nietzsche is Dionysian hero to Plato's Apollonian sage. Aristotle's distinction between the *phronimos* (man of practical wisdom) and the man marked by *megalopsuchia* (great-souled man) is relevant. It is not coincidental that the term nihilist was first made current by Turgenev's *Fathers and Sons*: the nihilistic son is his own *self*-hero; he ruptures his bond with the father-sage who would be the *other* as hero. The modern son loses respect for otherness in proclaiming himself the newest self-regarding aboriginal.

42. See Robert C. Neville's *Soldier, Sage, Saint*. I strongly agree with Neville's insistence on spiritual models. I see this as true not only in the case of the original hero, but in the formation of the philosophical individual.

43. Spinoza insists that wisdom means we have no grounds for railing against being. Wisdom involves *amor Dei intellectualis*. Such mindful love of God is a religious mnemonic for being as perfection, for what I called the thinker's attempt at amen. Hegel transforms the Spinozistic sage: after Kant's transcendental subjectivity, *amor Dei intellectualis* becomes the eros for absolute spirit, the absolute form of being mindful as completely transparent to itself in its own self-mediation—in Spinoza's terms, our love of God is God's love of himself. Controversy surrounds Hegel's claim in the *Phenomenology* to have attained wisdom, not just seek it. Kojève endorses the claim and as Hegelian sage has had tremendous influence on European thought. See S. Rosen, *Hermeneutics as Politics*, chapter 3. Throughout this work I argue against being mindful as closed self-mediation: thought thinking itself must also think its other, and in a metaxological way, not in the Hegelian dialectical way. See chapter 5 on the Stoic sage, failure and letting be.

44. The full passage in Montaigne says: "The soul is which philosophy dwells must, by its own health, give health to the body also. Its contentment, repose and ease must shine forth, and it must so mould the outward body to its own form that it endows it with a gracious pride, an active and alert bearing and a quick and merry countenance. The chief sign of wisdom is a constant rejoicing (*esjouissance*). Its state is like that of things above the moon: always serene." Quoted in G. Marcel, *The Decline of Wisdom*, p. 44. In antiquity Democritus was called the "laughing philosopher." Nietzsche certainly allows the laughing, not to say mocking, sage to speak through him.

45. The later Heidegger (heir of the heroic Presocratic sages, of Hölderlin the poetic-heroic sage, and of Nietzsche) lets the sage be voiced. But unlike Nietzsche, whose sage voice periodically deflates itself with high-spirited buffoonery, the sage voice of Heidegger is deadly serious, serious without relief. Consider, on the one hand, the hostility of Heidegger's critics to his later so-called vatic utterances, and on the other hand, the adoration of these utterances by some disciples. We must steer between these extremes: skepticism precludes adoration of the sage; yet, the tie of sage and philosopher is undeniable. In my view Heidegger's later utterances are far more continuous with the tradition of thought than his enemies realize (they do not know this tradition as deeply as they should, or as Heidegger did; with the exception of Gadamer and the possible exception of Derrida, his sympathetic successors do not know that tradition deeply enough either; instead they mime their sage). Heidegger wanted to be an original, you may say, a hero in waiting (a mixture of postmodern fatigue and expectancy of the coming god?). Gadamer civilizes the wilder voice of Heidegger, revealing how *continuous* is that voice with the tradition. Heidegger's striving for originality sometimes makes him miss the "splendor of the simple" he sought, which Gadamer, because of his lack of self-insistence, sometimes hits less idiosyncratically (not so much in *Truth and Method*, as in shorter pieces like those in *The Relevance of the Beautiful*).

Utterances as enigmatic as Heidegger's stud Wittgenstein's writings. In the *Tractatus* there is the famous image of his thought as the ladder we must throw away, once having used it, as well as sundry sage riddles about the mystical. Some things that cannot be *said* can be *shown* or show themselves — this is the sage appearing, as the mask of the logicist technician/scientist briefly drops. In *Philosophical Investigations* there is the famous image that compares philosophy to the fly in the bottle, buzzing. What bottle? What fly? These are not univocal concepts but riddling images, yet more memorable than any concept. When Wittgenstein speaks of philosophy as a battle against the "bewitchment" of language, he brings to mind a conceptual sage fighting linguistic spells and charms, an analytical magus. Or consider the image: philosophical problems are like bumps on the head we get from running against the limits of language. What kind of bumps are these? Again we have memorable riddles, not univocal analyses. Scholarly careers have depended on these bumps and buzzings, on the deciphering of these riddles.

I am not objecting to riddle. Certainly the riddle was seen as sacred in the ancient world (see J. Huizinga, *Homo Ludens*, p. 108; also pp. 115ff. on the early thinkers and riddling mystagogues). The gnomic riddling style of the Presocratic sages is related to the archaic form of their metaxological mindfulness as mingling ethics, politics, poetics, religion, cosmology. Even when all these begin to be distinguished, Plato will resort to riddling myth when analysis and logos run aground on an aporia. Even Hegel, high priest of the logical concept, appealed for a *new mythology of reason* in the *Earliest System Program*.

CHAPTER 2

1. Baumgarten was the first to use the term "*Aesthetica*" to refer to a distinctive sensitive cognition. But the wider sense of the aesthetic is present in the Greek notion of *aisthēsis*; also in Kant's "transcendental aesthetic" in relation to the role of the senses in all cognition. Drawing on Heidegger, Gadamer criticizes (in *Truth and Method*) the aestheticist concept of *art* also stemming from Kant ("aestheticist" here meaning art understood as an entirely special domain, separate from other modes of mind). Gadamer rethinks the ontological concept of art stemming from Hegel. The wider sense of the aesthetic is implied when Heidegger cites Hölderlin, "*Voll Verdienst, doch dichterisch, wohnet/ der Mensch auf dieser Erde.*" Vico helps us to a similar view. Strangely, I think Plato would agree with Hölderlin (he was deeply influenced by Platonic thought, of course), with the proviso that we ought to be suspicious of the poetic image: its very power makes it extremely dangerous for the psyche, religiously, and ethically speaking. Why else does Plato dwell on the poets and *ta mousika*? The aesthetic is separable from ethics and religion.

2. The "end of art" is associated first with Hegel (he does not use the term *death* of art). Heidegger returns to the issue in "The Origin of the Art Work." See, Danto, *The Philosophical Disenfranchisement of Art*; also A. Heller and F. Fehér (eds.), *Reconstructing Aesthetics*. C. Newman, *The Post-Modern Aura*, takes to task those weary in aesthetic spirit. But even with the best of intentions, polemic against the

weary is itself wearisome. All the grousings of an impoverished time get to sound like mediocrity chanting its own impotence. Very well, all one needs is one instance of present greatness or stature to silence the whining. This is a hit for the *promise* of our time. I agree with Schelling when he said that, even if art only once makes manifest the unconditional, once is enough; enough certainly for philosophical thought to ponder that manifestation.

3. See Plato's *Cratylus* (400c) for a play on the word *sōma*, which can mean body or jail—here the soul must stay until its debt is paid; there is no need to change a single letter. If we do change a letter, *sōma* becomes *sēma* (see Pythagoras), the body as a sign; this might demand a different aesthetic evaluation. The aesthetic critique of Cartesian dualism can also be a critique of instrumental reason as mind abstracted from bodily being. Being aesthetic shows mind emergent in the body and both as "value"—charged presence. Nor is nature a mere *res extensa*, it is the body of being—the other as aesthetic presence, hence as always valued thereness (see note 4). Thus, W. B. Yeats (*Explorations*, p. 325.) thought the valueless primary qualities of Locke and Newton "took away the world and gave us excrement instead," but Berkeley "restored the world." The otherness of the aesthetic body is always a stumbling block to the abstracted instrumental mind. One cannot endorse this abstraction, for the bodied self is the still enigmatic support of the abstracted mind. We never snap our bond with the body even in transcending thought; mind is the body as self-transcendence in rapport with otherness; hence the body is not a unit of materiality contracted into itself but the place of transcending imagination and desire.

4. Some philosophers have seen emotion as a primitive phenomenon to be discarded with reason's development; emotion reveals a liability to error that the truthful mind suppresses. The paradox is that it is the *passion* for truth that enjoins this suppression of passion. Of course, there is a difference between brute emotion and the intricate attunement of a highly sophisticated mind. Yet when the passion and excitement go out of thinking, the activity goes stale and flat and it is difficult to *continue to think*. Without the appropriate passion, the intellectual drive is sapped. Mindful thinking need not cultivate anaesthesia. Aristotle sees something of this when, in echo of the Pythagoreans, he states the connection between mathematics and the beautiful (*Metaphysics*, 1078a 31ff.). Aristotle refers to our delight in the visible world through *aisthēsis*. Philosophical *theōria* and wonder, grounding metaphysical mindfulness, would be the reflective, mediated counterpart to such aesthetic delight in being. On *Befindlichkeit*, see Heidegger's *Being and Time*, sec. 29.

5. This relates to the aesthetic tradition that emphasizes play (*Spiel*). Schiller saw a connection of nature and play, art and excess. One finds a suggestion of it in Kant's purposefulness without a purpose. Nietzsche's metaphor of the child's self-justifying play reunites play with the divine play of Heraclitean becoming (*pais paidzōn*) (fr. 52; see my "The Child in Nietzsche's Menagerie"). Heidegger, Gadamer, and now Derrida continue the line. On animal self-display as more than functional, see A. Portmann, *Animal Forms and Pattern*; also *Animal Camouflage*. Jesus said it all: "Solomon in all his finery was not dressed as one of these."

6. Plato thought the eyes most beautiful (*Republic*, 420d). At the opposite extreme, Sartre's view of the "Look" makes the eyes most baleful. For all his reputation as advocate of pure spirit, Hegel has extremely perceptive things to say about the body in the *Aesthetics*, for example, I, pp. 146–47, 433–34; II, pp. 714–15. One might add that we alone properly *face* the world: being brought face-to-face with the other, and with ourselves is paradigmatic for the intimacy of being as known. All being is divined as intimate otherness in our body as the face of mind, as facing being. Thus, Spinoza spoke of the *facies totius Universi*; to try to know this face is the desideratum of philosophical mind. I would add: this face in its *otherness*, not as a *totality* we can master.

7. R. G. Collingwood, *The Principles of Art*. See also E. Cassirer, *The Philosophy of Symbolic Forms*; *An Essay on Man*; S. K. Langer, *Feeling and Form*, chapters 11 and 12 in relation to the religious dance; *Philosophy in a New Key*. Vico is perhaps the first to exploit such insights. I use the word "expression" but caution the reader against thinking that I subscribe to that old-chestnut, the so-called Collingwood-Croce thesis. This thesis, as commonly presented, implied that real-spiritual expression takes place "in the head," while bodily expression was only an incidental exteriorization, a means to an end, not an end in itself. The artwork as imaginative expression was "in the head." First, this view is actually a caricature of both Croce and Collingwood; second, I do not subscribe to the subjective idealism implied by this view; third, I clearly disavow the Cartesian separation of inner and outer, mind and matter, implied by it. Being aesthetic is the sensuous incarnation of mindfulness: the expressive body is the articulation of the self as whole. This intimacy of embodiment and being mindful (the human body *is* the concrete power of mindful being) also implies that by expression I do not mean some determinate, univocal content that might just as well be expressed by a counterpart Cartesian clear and distinct idea. *What* is expressed is polysemic, overdetermined; its richness of meaning calls for interpretation. Thus, we may express a meaning for which we have difficulty accounting. Socrates noted this about the poet in the *Apology*, but unlike Socrates, I do not see this otherness as a strike against the poets. It may be the sign of an inexhaustibility that philosophy ought to ponder more deeply.

8. Kenneth Clark, *The Nude: A Study in Ideal Form*. Flesh is manifestation, shining, *Schein*, show. Even when we shrink back into ourselves, our shrunkenness still shows.

9. Thus, the mask as *disguise*, put on by those, say a bandit or bankrobber, with something shameful to hide. The mask prevents the revelation of true identity. It is appearance meant to deceive, as if it were the mask itself that did the evil. Thus, even evil is made enigmatic: we speculate not only on some secret mystery lurking behind the mask but also on the fascination of criminals who steadfastly refuse to break disguise.

10. Thus, the work of self-adornment, like the artwork, evidence non-instrumental work that is dignified in its own right. Karsten Harries is thoughtful on the ethical and religious dimensions of ornament in *The Bavarian Rococo Church*, pp.

243ff. He cites Aquinas (*Summa Theologiae*, I–II, art. 2, *respondeo*) to the effect that ornament, precious garments and vessels, special abodes, all help foster the sense of difference, specialness (I would say otherness) needful for reverence and worship. I think this dignity is touchingly revealed in the fact that some of the earliest graves show human beings burying their dead with jewelry and precious objects, as if there were a compact between beauty and immortality in the sense of the human being's outliving worth. See chapter 6 on perpetuity and thought singing its other.

11. We might think of another "loss of face"—the loss of dignity. Notice how this dignity is centered aesthetically, that is, in the show of self, in the face. Again we meet the ambiguous eyes, their power to be shamefaced or shameless, insolent, violating eyes, or respecting, consenting eyes.

12. One thinks of the Greek *paideia*, the German *Bildung*. Kant speaks of beauty as a symbol of the moral good. Schiller tries to overcome any dualism of the aesthetic and ethical: his view calls to mind a post-Kantian version of Greek *kalokagathia* that takes into account the self-consciousness of modern selfhood. The *Spieltrieb* that reconciles the *Stofftrieb* and *Formtrieb* reveals freedom in aesthetic and ethical shapes. Schelling, Hölderlin, and Hegel continue to be concerned with *Bildung*. The aesthetics of the ideal self are evident in Nietzsche's *Übermensch* as playfully uniting Dionysus and Apollo—these as mythic figurings of the *Stofftrieb* and *Formtrieb*.

13. Swift gives us the comic side. Gulliver obsessively wants to differentiate himself from the Yahoos. Hence, he conceals the fact of his hairless body, hence likeness to the Yahoos, by never taking off his clothes in the presence of the Houyhnhnms. The Yahoo is Caliban human nature, but clothes differentiate Gulliver from the indignity of such revolting, raw nature. One must remember also that clothes are the aesthetic appearance of social and political position and function. In premodern societies this aesthetics of politics was tied to hierarchical status (e.g. royal purple), while capitalism, more instrumentally than aesthetically minded, ties clothes more to money. Clothes then reflect the aesthetics of wealth.

14. At stake is an aesthetic version of the transition from infantile narcissism to self-recognition via the mirror stage. We find a loss of the seriousness of the aesthetic in contemporary narcissism where the "cosmetic" becomes a functional means of "presenting a self-image." The body's functional form is instrumentalizied as a pleasing machine, say, to be exploited by advertising. The inseparability of the aesthetic and the ethical is evident in the fact that such narcissistic aestheticism, coupled with a manipulative instrumentalism, invades the entirety of culture. Critics like Christopher Lasch, Robert Ballah and William Sullivan point to the collusion of the "expressive life-style" and utilitarian selfhood. McIntyre in *After Virtue* sees a similiar collusion of the "aesthete" seeking personal gratification, the bureaucratic "manager," and the "therapist" manipulating others. Pitirim Sorokim referred to this as "sensate culture." Kierkegaard's ethical has collapsed into the aesthetic, such that the latter too has been trivialized—something Kierkegaard saw would happen if the aesthetic did not open to the ethical and religious.

15. A. J. Ayer's *Language, Truth and Logic* provides the occasion of the *reductio ad absurdum* of positivism: the self-cannibalizing of positivism when it reflected on its own practice in tandem with an explicit principled commitment to the verification principle. But the issue of dualism of science and its others is wider. This dualism is also present in the debate about the "two cultures," the scientific and humanistic (C. P. Snow). Likewise it lurks in the wings when the manipulators of a nation's economy deride a literary, "academic" education and stampede a people towards a thoughtless awe of technology. The attack on imagination then takes the form of onslaught on classical ideals of education.

16. Whitehead recognized the role of imagination in scientific discovery; indeed he saw the closeness of the aesthetic, the ethical and the cosmological (see *Science and the Modern World*, chapter V; also, D. Sherburne, *A Whiteheadian Aesthetic*). Robert Neville, *Reconstruction of Thinking* argues strongly for the pervasive role of imagination. See also E. Casey, *Imagining*. Heidegger's *Kant and the Problem of Metaphysics* has been a provocative book on imagination as ontological. Sartre's views developed from his early works on imagination: *The Psychology of Imagination* and *Imagination*. Collingwood develops a theory of imagination in *The Principles of Art* (see my "Collingwood, Imagination and Epistemology"). Also see R. Scruton, *Art and Imagination* and Richard Kearney's wide-ranging, *The Wake of Imagination*.

17. This view of imagination as transcendental was developed aesthetically by the Romantics, who were also influenced by Kant's rendition of genius in the *Critique of Judgment*. Genius becomes the heroic exemplar of imaginative power. It is now fashionable to debunk the Romantics and imply that we are beyond imagination. I grant that on occasion the Romantic apotheosis of imagination went too far, particularly in the subjective direction (I will argue subsequently against this subjectivization for an *ontological* interpretation, with religious and ethical aspects). To deflate this inflation is to the good. But to imply that we are beyond imagination is senseless, if imagination is transcendental. The very rejection of imagination is itself parasitical on the power of imagination rejected and so the negation is self-negating. The importance of transcendental imagination is undeniable; what is controversial is our philosophical interpretation of it—there are epistemological, ontological, aesthetic, ethical, and religious aspects to this. Imagination tries to name the elusive original power of articulating being in the self, and the realization of its importance is one of the great achievements of modern philosophy. This raises the crucial problem of otherness; but imagination reveals the *inward otherness* of the power of being in the self. As imagining selves we are other to ourselves. Hence also to preserve the other as other cannot mean to suppress this immanent otherness. I try to speak of this in *Desire, Dialectic and Otherness* (see chapter 2) in terms of original selfness; here inward otherness as dialectically self-mediating always opens out to otherness in a further sense, metaxological otherness.

18. See Max Scheler's, *Man's Place in Nature* on the importance of free images.

19. That the image is both middle and double is related to problem of metaphor,

the mark of genius, as Aristotle implied. Derrida and Ricoeur tend to see this doubleness in terms of equivocity, certainly in terms of an irreducibility to univocity. Equivocity with Derrida tends to dissolve univocity in sheer disseminating difference. Ricoeur's equivocity sees the doubleness; but there is also a togetherness in the doubleness, what dialectical thought can recognize as a *coincidentia oppositorum*. The trouble with the latter (a problem Ricoeur grants about Hegel) is that it risks subordinating otherness to unity. Hence I think that the plurivocity of metaphor can be understood metaxologically, that is, neither univocally, nor equivocally, nor yet dialectically.

20. Thus, metaphor is, as it were, the body of imagination. As has often been pointed out, many metaphors can be traced to the human body: foot of mountain, brow of hill, tongues of fire, eye of storm, face of evil, arm of the law, anus of the world, mouth of Hell, face of God. Vico, for whom metaphor is first speech, gives a fine list of such bodily thoughts (*New Science*, p. 88). It is as if in first speech there were an imaginative identification of our aesthetic being, namely, our body, with the body of the world, which would be the aesthetic being-there of otherness.

21. See chapter 3 on the importance of the double image for being religious; in chapter 4 imagination as a primordial freedom points to a freedom *prior* to free will.

22. See my "Paul Weiss and Creativity," to be published. Socrates objects (*Republic*, 394eff.) to mimesis: it makes us many. In likening us to others, it prevents us from being a one-self; against the pluralism of mimesis, he seems to favor univocal identity. Socrates is wrong to think of human identity in terms of univocal unity. The power of mimesis really reveals the power of the universal in that it opens our otherwise miserable self-identity to all otherness. The positive power of mimesis, as of imagination, is just this becoming-other. The human being as an open whole can hold unity and manyness together (see *Desire, Dialectic and Otherness*, chapter 3). This relation to otherness is evident in the way ancient dances and labyrinths mimed the motions of the heavenly bodies. The religious aspect is clear in notions like *imitatio Dei*.

23. The issue of originals and the imitation of others was noted in chapter 1. The hero is an original, but if he is without respect for the other he turns into a tyrant.

24. The dualism examined at the start of this chapter is an abstraction from the doubleness here discussed.

25. See my "Schopenhauer, Art and the Dark Origin." My view of imagination as an inward otherness is not unmindful of the psychoanalytical notion of the unconscious as a like recalcitrant other in selfhood itself. Not surprisingly, modern artist have repeatedly exploited this connection, particularly in its power to disrupt our domestications of the original power of being. On folly and the breakthrough of festive being, see chapter 6.

26. See *Art and the Absolute*, espec. chapter 6 "Beauty and the Aesthetic Dilemma of Modernity."

27. I am not denying that there is a truth to "sensing subjectivity," but the difficulty is the unanchoring of that subjectivity. There is a connection here with emotivism in ethics, as McIntyre sees. Gadamer also sees through the bankruptcy of the aestheticism involved. He returns to a more Hegelian rather than Kantian emphasis. Mary Mothersill's recent *Beauty Restored* shows Kant's influence.

28. Romantic thought conferred great importance on the psychology of the genius. Though modernism and now postmodernism are in reaction to this, the popular mind still identifies the artist with a clichéd version of genius. The ambiguity here is that now the aesthetic audience is sometimes invested with powers of being creative. It is jolted from its aesthetic contemplation, asked to be a participant, not a spectator: in the demand that it recreate the creative process, creativity seems to be democratized, merely by the redefinition of the audience's role. Even critics, traditionally reactive to another's work, may insist that their critical work is creative, that is, demanding attention in its own right, not merely as a mirror of another's.

29. This aesthetic restlessness is a version of what I call "equivocal desire" (*Desire, Dialectic and Otherness*, chapter 3). I think here of Bakunin's claim that the joy in destruction is at the same time a creative joy or Picasso's remark that a painting is the sum of destructions. Compare to the ancient restlessness of eros. Consider Plato's words (*Republic*, 403c6–7): *teleutain ta mousika eis ta tou kalou erōtika*; the telos of the musical is the erotics of the beautiful. Erotics is telos-bound to beauty. What meaning can we give to this now? Certainly it implies that the statement "This is beautiful" is a judgment of value, where to say X is beautiful is to appreciate the presence of a realized value, a perfection. One can only account for the latter in terms of creation as a generosity of being.

30. Kearney, *The Wake of Imagination*, helpfully discusses postmodernism and parodic imagination. A moment's reflection shows that the hegemony of parodic imagination is a symptom of spiritual decadence. On a more affirmative sense of parody, see the *parodia sacra* of the Middle Ages. See also my "Can Philosophy Laugh at Itself?" on what I call "comic demythologizing" in Aristophanes. For all the debunking, Aristophanic "negativity" and parody—including the parody of philosophy—were not merely negative but had a profound spiritual point.

31. Rousseau is forerunner of this, as the famous opening of his *Confessions* shows: "I am unlike anyone I have ever met. I will even venture to say I am like no one in the whole world. I may not be better, but at least I am different. Whether nature did well in breaking the mold in which she formed me, is a question that can only be resolved after the reading of my book." John Donne named the condition, and its emergence from a loss of traditional coherence in "An Anatomy of the World": ". . . new Philosophy calls all in doubt . . . 'Tis all in pieces, all coherence gone; / All just supply, and all Relation: / Prince, Subject, Father, Son, are things forgot, / For every man alone thinks he hath got / To be a Phoenix, and that then can be / None of that kind, of which he is, but he."

32. I refer to the spiritual obscenity of some recent prices paid for works by Van Gogh, and the spiritual sickness of an age that whoops with glee at such prices, dead

to the incommensurability of artistic greatness with economic measure, no matter how grossly inflated. See S. Gablik, *Has Modernism Failed?*—she is good on the spiritual betrayal that can come in the train of art's commodification. Marxist aesthetics is entirely correct to protest the commodification of art. One thinks of Adorno's scorn for the "culture industry." See Wolfgang Fritz Haug, *Critique of Commodity Aesthetics*.

33. For instance, it seems that recently in America musical performers are generally reluctant to play new compositions. The performer has become a celebrity, but as such he has to take his audience into account. It seems that when composers went into the universities in the 1930s, often they composed for their peers works that were very difficult to play (worries about tenure were not absent), leading to a divorce between composer and performer, hence to a divorce of creator and a wider audience.

34. Adorno does have a notion of reconcilement (see both *Aesthetic Theory* and *Negative Dialectics*) but I find something equivocal in his way of naming it. He is unrelenting in his attack on the "identity principle," yet he knows that to even name the non-identical we have to somehow identify it, and hence perennially risk the distorting effect of the identity principle. Adorno hence tends to push reconcilement into an always other redemptive future. But if its promise is never in any way realized in the now, the promise is empty, a promise of a never-never utopia. Hence Adorno's negative dialectics vacillates between yes and no, though the resounding no to the present tends to drown out the promise of yes. When I speak of thought thinking its other I share Adorno's concern with the non-identical; but in the terms I use, his deconstructing of univocity oscillates with negative dialectic as *equivocal* thought. This opens the question of otherness, but my notion of the metaxological tries to think it through further, beyond what is *affirmative* in dialectic, namely, its essential self-mediation. A more extended study would be needed to substantiate these remarks and do justice to Adorno.

35. This inward thisness is perhaps related to Hopkins' idea of "inscape" and his poetic use of the Scottistic "*haecceitas*."

36. This is another point against the instrumentalizing of art, namely, the inseparability of form and content. Likewise the resistance to translation indicates recalcitrance to merely exchangeable sameness: strangely the very otherness of the artwork is just its singular identity. I cite one example: An early editor (Christopher Theodor Schwab) of Hölderlin changed the words "yellow pears" into "yellow flowers" (*Blumen* instead of *Birnen*) in the opening line of the poem "The Middle of Life." The instrumental mind will say: "So what!" But the power of the poem is marred by the alteration, some critics think quite seriously. For fuller details, see E. Heller, *In the Age of Prose*, pp. 70ff.

37. In this it is a reflection of our being. We are the most highly individualized beings in all creation, yet as *capax infiniti* the most capable of rising to a universal perspective. (Kant sees this universal as subjective, but Plato, Aristotle, Hegel and

Schopenhauer see it as ontological.) Here also we find an artistic mirror of aesthetic adornment where the dynamic singularity of the human is reflected in its sensuous show.

38. On the "thousand-eyed Argus," see *Aesthetics*, I, pp. 153–54. Hegel quotes (actually misquotes) Terence's *"Humani nihil a me alienum puto"* (*Aesthetics*, I, p. 46), to underscore the democratic freedom of art in modernity. Art has no fixed subject matter, anything might be its possible subject matter. One thinks also of Keats speaking of himself as becoming the sparrow that picks about the gravel; he is placed in the otherness of the bird's life. Or Rilke's "Archaic Torso of Apollo": "There is no place which fails to see you. You must change your life." *The Selected Poetry of Rainer Maria Rilke*, p. 61. On being seen and the ethical, see chapter 4.

39. This is not a rerooting in domesticated being but in the otherness of being. Hence it is an unsettling of the sedimented thereness and a restirring of original power. It is a restoration of the strangeness of being as original, the strange power of our being as originative, and our being-at-home with strangeness. Art's tolerance is really a being-at-home with the otherness of being in its inexhaustibility—hence an unsettling being-at-home in otherness itself.

40. This *Entzauberung* (Max Weber's much used term) turns the *poiēsis* of being into functional prose and is aesthetically reflected in Benjamin's notion of art's loss of the "aura." This is related to the subjective privatization of imagination in modernity and its alienation from the mythic memory of a people. In a sense this has always been the problem of aesthetic modernity, and art has always struggled against this loss. Thus, in speaking of aesthetic contemplation as a "kind of disinterested engrossment," Osborne (*The Art of Appreciation*, see pp. 23, 35) indicates how originally this idea was bound up with the philosophical and theological controversies of the seventeenth century. Against Hobbesian egotism and its calculated self-interest, Shaftesbury and the Cambridge Platonists argued that goodness could be pursued for its own sake. Likewise the term was connected with the dispute between Jesuits and Jansenists as to whether one might love God for Himself and not merely from fear of hell or hope of heaven. In both cases the question concerns the actuality of *intrinsic* goods or whether all values are merely instrumental. I argue against this instrumentalization not only of aesthetic mindfulness but also of religious, ethical, and philosophic mindfulness.

CHAPTER 3

1. Faith seeking understanding (*fides quaerens intellectum*) is the classical effort at such interpretation, self-interpretation. The tension of philosophy and piety, muthos and logos is evident in Plato's *Euthyphro*—see Carl Vaught, *The Quest for Wholeness*, chapter 3. I previously referred to Freud's phrase "our god logos" (chapter 1, n. 29)—this is an echo of Socrates. Less antagonistic than Freud, Ricoeur's well-known words are: the symbol gives rise to thought. The Hegelian *Aufhebung* is often presented as a rationalistic imperialism via-à-vis religion. In

"Hegel and the Problem of Religious Representation," I argue that Hegel's view is more complex. I am not unsympathetic to the Hegelian *Aufhebung* of *Vorstellung* into *Begriff*, provided that the *Aufhebung* is understood not as a displacement or "swallowing" of representation but the releasing of its spiritual content from an ambiguous finite form. There I also argue (contra the normal view of Hegel) for the immanent resources of the religious image to deal with the problems of its own doubleness. As other to philosophy, religion undertakes its own purification; it does not await philosophy for this. Hence, the rationalistic reduction is wrong where it conceives the religious simply as an opposite to which reason is hostile, rather than an other to which reason is akin. Likewise the fideistic reaction is wrong in neglecting the awakening of mind within religion itself, and hence, too, religion's bond with philosophical mindfulness as *its* other.

2. On the vastness and variousness of the matter, worth mentioning are: William James, *The Varieties of Religious Experience*; the many works of M. Eliade on hierophanies, comparative religion and myth; see *Patterns in Comparative Religion*, pp. 7ff. where the term "hierophany" is proposed; also *The Sacred and the Profane*; on the phenomenology of religion, G. van der Leeuw, *Religion in Essence and Manifestation*; for philosophical sophistication, Louis Dupré, *The Other Dimension*; also *Transcendent Selfhood*. In focussing on religion as *other* to philosophy, I am not concerned with any evolutionary scheme beloved of earlier ethnological students of "primitive" religion. While no serious student of religion denies that the sense of the divine develops, I focus on a dialectical, more precisely, metaxological interplay in a way of being. There is an *immediacy* to this way; what concerns me is the articulation of this immediacy, bringing both loss of naiveté and gain in reflective mindfulness. The latter may strives to be thought thinking its other, what Otto called "*das ganz Andere.*"

3. *Desire, Dialectic and Otherness*, chapter 7; on classical theism, see H. P. Owen, *Concepts of Divinity*.

4. Virgil has it: "*Iovis omnia plena*" (all things are full of Jove), *Bucolics*, Eclogue 3, 60. See B. Malinowski, *Magic, Science and Religion and Other Essays*, p. 7: "Today we are somewhat perplexed by the discovery that to a savage all is religion, that he perpetually lives in a world of mysticism and religion . . . we are led to ask, not without dismay: What remains outside it, what is the world of the "profane" in primitive life?" That the whole is inseparable from the holy for archaic man is very clear from Eliade's work (sans Malinowski's "dismay").

5. Here doubleness implies a certain universal structure of the image as both revealing and concealing. As I indicate in chapter 2, and will be clear in this chapter, I am well aware of the *polysemic* character of images. Doubleness refers to transcendental form, as it were, not to "empirical" content, which is polysemic. Students of religion talk about symbol, representation, metaphor, analogy and so on. "Image" is often restricted to a sensory image. It will be clear that this is not my meaning. After much thought I retain the term "image" for it has a certain indeterminate generality because of its intimacy with transcendental imagination in

the strict sense. Symbols, representations, ciphers, hieroglyphs and so on are "images" in this usage, that is, originations of transcendental imagination, understood in an ontological sense. This latter sense also implies their power as revelatory of being in its *otherness* to merely subjective selfhood. See chapter 2 on imagination as metaxological in relation to the double mediation; also notes 6 and 7 below.

6. Feuerbach, Marx, Nietzsche (a kind of lyrical Feuerbachian) see the religious image as a projection. If this image has any basis in actuality, it is as a distorted revelation of the *human* being. Freud (see *Civilization and its Discontents*, pp. 27–28) identifies the image as illusion, namely, its first sense as unreality; it is reproductive of our pathology, not ontological in the deeper sense. The younger Freud read Feuerbach and was influenced by his views of religion. When Marx speaks of "disillusionment" (*Early Writings*, p. 44), he merely means the destruction of the image as illusion. He does not understand the double image in the sense I mean: in the image he sees man's self-mediation in alienated form, through God as the alien unreal being; he does not see metaxological intermediation with otherness (for Marx, religious otherness is still the alienating alien, and hence a curb on man's own complete self-mediation). Here Marx is the humanistic heir and reducer of Hegel's dialectical self-mediation.

7. See *Desire, Dialectic and Otherness*, chapter 6 on being as not an object. Compare the present view of imagination to Sartre's. For him imagination relates to freedom, and freedom relates to the human being as nothingness. Hence imagination is tied to the *opposite* of being, yet it is also revelatory of self (as nothingness). Combining these two views, we find that for Sartre the image is an upsurge of nothingness (the self) as the dualistic opposite of being-in-itself. This might be true if the self were simply nothing, if desire were simply lack; but the view is seriously misleading if the self is original power to be and desire is the articulation of this power of being (see *Desire, Dialectic and Otherness* for these views). Ultimately Sartre's view of imagination is *dualistic* rather than double; imagination is radically other to the being of things, hence the opposite of being. Sartre is reactive to a simplistic sense of the "reality," "thereness" of being. He does not entirely escape something like Hume's theory of the image as a reproductive internal sensation: the "object" is just out there. He is still caught in the alienated thought of Cartesian dualism. To bridge this gap imagination becomes *magic*: not ontological, but the conjuring of fantasy by nothingness (the self as negativity) from nothing. Thus in the *Psychology of Imagination* (p. 177): ". . . the act of imagination is a magical one. It is an incantation . . ." "In that act there is always something of the imperious and the infantile, a refusal to take distance or difficulty into account . . ."

8. See "Hegel, Philosophy and Worship"; also J. Pieper, *Leisure*, pp. 40ff. on the birth of culture in cultus.

9. Consider this contrast: first, the human being as God's image, where image means a condition of being, God's signature in the very flesh, as it were, a signature the full deciphering of which resists our power; second, magic as a belief in the power

of the religious image, real power, not merely "subjectivistic," though it gives the "subject" power—harm the image, the voodoo doll, and you harm the original being. I am not arguing for a belief in magic, but the latter is a certain interpretation of the ontological power of the image. Some, like Boehme, thought of magic as true theology; alchemists like Paracelsus had dreams of divine power.

10. Recall the gap between the given and the intimated mentioned at the beginning of this chapter: ancestor worship is one refusal of this gap. Herbert Spencer thought of ancestor worship as the basis of all religion. See Fustel de Coulanges, *The Ancient City*. Rilke's Third Duino Elegy celebrates the work of the dead in the living, the "guilty river-god of the blood" (*schuldigen Fluβ-Gott des Bluts*). De Coulanges (p. 38 n. 16) notes almost the *exact* same in the ancients, citing Sophocles' *theoi eggeneis, theoi sunaimoi*; also Aristophanes, Aeschylus, Plato, Ovid. Freud views religion as tied to the ancestors in a different way, that is, as getting rid of the fear of the primal father. While Judaism prohibits parricide, Christianity testifies to the fear of the father, but any parricide is atoned by the sacrifice of the son. See chapter 6 on generation as fleshed time.

11. For instance, in the southwest of Ireland there is a range of hills known as *Dhá Chíc Ana*, the two paps of Ana (a Celtic goddess) that are still today called "the Paps." Marriage to the land in *hierogamy* (Irish: *Banais Ríghi*, the wedding feast of kingship) was part of the sacred ritual of inaugural of the Irish High King, performed at Tara in Meath (from *Mide*, from an older "Medion," meaning "middle") which was considered to be the center of the world (see R. Kearney, ed. *The Irish Mind*, chapter 2, especially pp. 67–68). Eliade, *The Sacred and the Profane* recounts many instances of this "homology," likeness between the human being and the cosmos. One thinks also of the "animism" of early Greek thinkers whose thought was close to mythic seeing, for example, when Empedocles speaks of the sea as the "sweat of the earth." In that the earth was a divine body, not only do we find marriages of king and earth in earlier religions, but also of sky and earth. Rain from the sky might be seen as semen, the earth as mother. See M. W. Meyer, ed. *The Ancient Mysteries: A Sourcebook*, p. 6: As recounted by the Christian heresiologist Hippolytus, the cry within one of the mysteries was: *Hye kye*, "Rain! Conceive!"

As the demythologized opposite, see Aristophanes' *The Clouds* for the conversation between Strepsiades and Socrates (rain comes from clouds, not from Zeus making water through a sieve). Aristophanes' Socrates is totally devoid of a sense of the sacred otherness of nature; he shows a literalistic, rationalistic mind—but see Plato's *Phaedo* and *Phaedrus* where Socrates' attitude to myth is much more complex. Aristophanes presents Socrates as identical with the sophist and the *phusiologoi*: Socrates as a Presocratic! But Aristophanes has a brilliant sense of the destructive power of thought vis-à-vis religion, even though his Socrates is monotone compared to the many-sided character that Plato presents: the gods are clouds, Zeus is booted out, Vortex is king. Yet there is a "demythologizing" in comedy too. In Greek comedy, the human eventually comes out from behind the mask; the masks of the gods are debunked. This is what I call "a releasing disillusionment," for in laughing at our illusions, we also may come to be free, come to be at home with being. Gods laugh too. See note 17.

12. In *Civilization and its Discontents* Freud denies ever experiencing the so-called oceanic feeling (Romain Rolland). (This feeling is related to the aesthetic intimacy of being.) Freud connects piety with the terror of infantile helplessness (p. 19). When I reach out of my suffering and ask Why me?, Freud would say (see pp. 70ff.) that I am punishing myself: the internalized punitive father, the superego, *will* find a pretext for its misfortune. I am suffering, hence punished, hence I *must have done* something to displease the father. Undoubtedly, there is some truth in this. But as can be said of Marx on religion, Freud elevates a minor insight into a major blindness. I am talking about *knowingly* shaking one's fist at the *empty* sky: I am not talking about the unconscious ruse of a childish consciousness. For that matter, Freud's psychoanalytical reduction of paternity is not the only possible sense of fatherhood. One suffers evil and *knows* that the ancestors are *not* punishing one. I am talking about the experience of suffering of a sophisticated consciousness. Here the psychoanalytical reduction gives an explanation that strikes me as disproportionate, on a qualitatively different level, to the metaphysical pathos of evil suffered. That Oedipus' tragic suffering in Sophocles' play is *sacred suffering*, strikes me as confronting us with such a profound metaphysical pathos that explication of it in terms of the psychoanalytical Oedipus complex seems its utter trivialization. In relation to such suffering there is something superficial, even blind about this explication.

13. I am only looking at one aspect of the rupture of religious immediacy, but Ricoeur's *The Symbolism of Evil* is a brilliant examination of its multifaceted articulation, including the orgic god, its divine *phtonos* and the tragic way of dealing with unjustly inflicted evil. The dipolar divine is evident in *Prometheus Bound*—Zeus seems tyrannical, willful, Prometheus gentler in his pity for mortals, creatures of the day; yet both are included *within* the divine (remember Prometheus is a divine being, a Titan, not a human superhero). Aeschylus' *Oresteia* shows the dialectic within the divine in the disputing power of Apollo and the Erinyes. On tragic failure as a radical breaking on otherness, see chapter 5.

Gnostics have often been attuned to the darkness of God, for instance, Boehme sees wrath (*Grimm*) as essential to God. On the dark wrath in God in Kabbalah, see G. Scholem, *On the Kabbalah and its Symbolism* p. 92. In many ways evil presents a more intractable problem for the believer than the unbeliever. It can precipitate a more genuine perplexity—though also a more facile escapism is possible. Trust in the divine raises the stakes of distrust when one honestly faces the horror of evil.

14. Of course the ineradicable ambiguity is there in so far as the Flood has been interpreted as but prefiguring baptism. Its destruction is cleansing.

15. There is also a connection in Vico between the Flood and Jove's lightning bolt, in so far as the latter was intended to bring the Giants to temperance and modesty. The Giants were sometimes thought to be the renegade ancestors of Noah after the Flood (see *New Science*, p. 73); they are related to the Cyclopes; they might be seen to reappear in the Cyclopean, primal horde of Freud. In chapter 4 I return to them in connection with being ethical. Heraclitus (fr. 64) speaks of the thunderbolt that steers the universe. Among moderns, Hölderlin, was concerned with the thunder

of Zeus; Joyce, an admirer of Vico, makes the thunder central. In each we find signs of the sacramental earth. Harries points out (*Bavarian Rococo Church*, p. 201) that in eighteenth century Germany lightning rods were objectionable to pious peasants; bell ringing signaled an approaching storm, the wrath of God; but their pastors, whose Enlightenment education helped stifle the sense of the sacramental earth, were intent to suppress the practice.

16. By exile religion I do not mean just ascetical Christianity, whether medieval or modern. Admirers of Hegel's (an unorthodox Lutheran) treatment of the "unhappy consciousness" sometimes identify it with medieval Catholicism, and in the same breath identify Kierkegaard, an orthodox Lutheran, with the same "unhappy consciousness." Most religions have some sense of homelessness, some version of fall. Gnostic religions of exile as well as Apocalyptic, Chiliastic, Millenarian movements seem driven by discontent. See the malaise of the "sick soul" in James' *Varieties of Religious Experience*.

17. One thinks, of course, of the golden laughter of the Olympians; or the smiling Buddha; Jesus on Tabor is golden. See *The Golden Ass* of Apuleius on the "Festival of Laughter." Eckhart said that divine joy is the soul laughing together with God. In this Nietzsche was an Eckhartian, unbeknownst to himself. See also the medieval *festa stultorum* (feast of fools), also the *parodia sacra*, and the *risus Paschalis* (Easter laughter).

18. For instance, when times were good the Hebrews turned to the Baals and Astartes of their neighbors, gods of earth and success; in crisis they returned to Yahweh, sky god; see Eliade, *Sacred and Profane*, pp. 126–27. On the doubleness of religion in relation to sacrificial violence, see R. Girard, *Violence and the Sacred*.

19. See G. Murray, *Five Stages of Greek Religion*; on solar mythologies, see Eliade, *Sacred and Profane*, pp. 157–59.

20. What we have here is a *reductive* sense of the univocity of being that collapses the complexity of the middle. It is reductive in that its ultimate sense of being is taken from the finite physical thing. At the opposite extreme of univocity is a kind of mysticism that also risks a collapse of the complex middle; but in this case the unity of all being, both divine and non-divine, is modeled on an absorbing god that risks making the being of the finite thing into nothing. On the absorbing god, see *Desire, Dialectic and Otherness*, chapter 1. One thinks here too how Spinoza's univocal sense of being as One Substance reduplicates in philosophical reflection a sense of the immediacy of the sacred, expressed in nature as the body of God—*Deus sive Natura*.

21. Contrary to the standard interpretation, which only sees crude hostility to the image and a logocentric anxiety to escape into the purity of the intelligible *eidos*, Plato's *Republic* can be seen as an extended meditation on, hermeneutic of the power of the image: as musical, gymnastic, ethical, religious, political, metaphysical. Hence the paradox should not confound us that in a work ostensibly rejecting images, the most memorable passages are the philosophical images: for example, the image of the

divided line, the simile of the cave, the image of the sun, the personified image of the nihilistic wolfman Thrasymachus, the image of the fevered city, the image of the ring of Gyges, to name only a few.

I am not saying that there are no problems with logos. Logos asks a question about muthos. Thus, as is evidenced by *Euthyphro*, Plato was concerned with the internal instability, the dialectic of trust and distrust, within divinity as manifested by the disagreements of the gods. In a sense, Socrates wants to overcome the taint of negativity in the divine; his "demythologization" is partly a flight of logic from the wrath of God. Beyond the dipolar God and anthropomorphic categories, philosophical enlightenment will try to wash the world of its terror. For Plato, the hostility to man of divine *phtonos* must be overcome: "God is not envious . . ." (*Timaeus*, 29e), a refrain repeated throughout the tradition, down to Hegel. But muthos also forces a question on logos in this respect: Is the image of the wrath of God one name for a radical otherness that thought may break on, even though it must also try to think it? Nietzsche will oppose Plato by opposing tragedy and logos here, but I will say later: thought must be willing to break on its other, though in thinking it, it may also sing it.

22. Prior to polynomial polytheism, in some cases the primitive powers were nameless, anonymous. Cassirer, *Language and Myth*, p. 73, mentions Isis as *myrionyma*, ten-thousand named; also the many names of native American religion, of Allah in the Koran, of Mexican religion.

23. Naming at its best is related to what I called "framing" in chapter 2; it is not an identification that lords over the thing. The latter is found in magic where names are understood with a literalistic sense of the ontological power of the sacred image. Magic is sacred will-to-power, parasitical on the power of images to have real effects. But this power is understood univocally; if I say these prayers 5,000 times, the god *must* grant my favor; the image is bound to produce univocally the same effect. Thus some element of word magic is hard to avoid, for such magic mixes literalism and imagination, or rather reduces religious imagination in its doubleness to the univocity of literalism.

24. One thinks of the unfortunate soul, Uzzah (II Sam., 6) in the Old Testament, who saw the ark of the covenant slip, just lurched to try and save it, and was struck dead for his trouble. Even the *thought* of touching the sacred proved fatal.

25. Maimonides (*The Guide for the Perplexed*, Part 1, chapter 21) points out that Moses cannot directly see God's face when He passes, but he can reflect on His works by looking after Him. He is only allowed to see the back of God. He cannot see God's face as turned to the future, cannot enter directly the process of creation.

26. This atheism is the other side of what I previously noted: that a sophisticated mind, in its skepticism of images, tends to look atheistic to the naive believer. The name tends to reproduce the double image and the dialectic of trust and distrust: on the one hand, if all is divine, we find absolute trust in appearing, hence many names; on the other hand, if nothing is divine, we find an absolute distrust of appearing,

hence no name. In the middle you can get the piling up of names and attributes, including contradictory ones: excess of names to name an excess of being that cannot be named (a mystic might say God is father/mother, all/nothing, high/low, garden/desert; Heraclitus said Zeus was fire/water, satiety/craving). Finally, in trying to speak beyond the middle, self-cancelling naming can be a negative opening of the space of transcendence, which by contrast is affirmative in its radical being beyond.

27. The problems of religious language has been a major concern of 20th century philosophers; see "Hegel and the Problem of Religious Representation."

28. These two options are evident in recent history. Some critics claim that Hegel's attenuation of finiteness risks our being swallowed in his absolute as an absorbing god; the other extreme, when *we* become the absorbing god, has been charged to the atheistic Prometheanism of some post-Hegelians, like Marx and Nietzsche.

29. The traditional requirement for intelligible speech is that it offer determinate categories in relation to a *tode ti*, a "this somewhat." Such determinate thought is always *identifying*, hence the question of its fidelity to the divine as non-identical. I do not think all naming is identifying in an invidious sense, namely, as violating otherness.

30. This sense is not confined to being religious. Aesthetic and philosophical mindfulness exhibit something analogous. The aesthetic has its version in what Keats calls the poet's "negative capability." Plato said that wonder is the pathos of the philosopher, and Aristotle links metaphysical astonishment with an akin wonder in myth and the delight in *aisthēsis*.

Gabriel Marcel is right to remind us of the difference of problem and mystery. I use the term slightly differently: mystery for Marcel is a problem that encroaches on its own data; he stresses the self-reflexive turn and its resistance to objectification. I stress more the *otherness* of being. We cannot leave ourselves out of the mystery, but the otherness of being in its very otherness stuns us into unprecedented thought. Otherness is not identical with objectivity, hence not to be opposed to subjectivity. Marcel works his way out of the subject/object opposition. I do not think the sense of religious mystery can be put in those terms at all, even by negation; but perhaps Marcel would agree.

31. See *The Irish Mind*, chapter 1.

32. Plato *Symposium* (202d11–e7): in relation to the *metaxu*, the power of eros is to interpret (*hermēneuon*) and convey things mortal to gods and vice versa; eros binds up the whole. Hermeneutics today is one of the voices that tends to accuse Western philosophy of "phallogocentrism," but there is a joke in the fact that the first Hermes were priapic! The phallus, too, was a messenger of the gods. The origin of hermeneutics is in our aroused flesh as divining. There is irony too in the fact that many post-Nietzschean and post-Heideggerian hermeneuticists revere Heraclitus, yet Heraclitus scathingly denounces Dionysian hymns to the phallus, the shameful parts. He identifies Dionysus with Hades (fr. 15). This perhaps relates to the fact that

originally the Hermes figure was a phallic stone (only later an individualized god) placed at the grave, herald *between* two worlds. This also relates to the Latin *Terminus*, serving to mark a boundary with a phallic stone.

33. In chapter 5 I return to silence and being mindful.

34. Inquisition is born in this terror, and replies to the terror with terror. The image is rigidified into an idol (see Heraclitus, fr. 5: praying to statues is like praying to *houses*); idolatry lacks inwardness; it is the inability to let go, to let be. It cannot endure the impermanence of the image, hence kill, kill, kill. To defeat the terror of difference, it terrorizes the other (witch, heretic, scapegoat). This fury of the religious burning of witches is religion's *own* Witches' Sabbath. (See Heraclitus, fr. 46: Bigotry is the sacred disease.)

35. There is a "taking to heart," or inwardizing in the aesthetic and the ethical too, but mysticism carries this in its own name: the word comes from "*muein*," meaning to close the eyes, ears. Thus, the *mystikoi* of Greek mysteries practiced religions of inwardness, secrecy, ecstasis; see *The Ancient Mysteries*, p. 4. On the complexities and varieties of mysticism see Dupré, *Transcendent Selfhood*; R. C. Zaehner, *Hindu and Muslim Mysticism*; G. Sholem, *Major Trends in Jewish Mysticism*; for recent analytical interest, with results generally disappointing, see S. Katz, ed. *Mysticism and Philosophical Analysis*.

36. On original selfhood, see *Desire, Dialectic and Otherness*, chapter 2. On religion and solitariness, see A. N. Whitehead, *Religion in the Making*.

37. On solitude and meonic contraction and on the experience of "counting for nothing" see chapter 5.

38. What I mean is the manner in which claims to be divine can produce a licentious, tyrannous self. The elect, the *gnostikoi*, the antinomians claim to be divine, hence can do anything, even evil, for this too is divine since done by a divine being (Augustine raised this issue with the Manichee elect). See Hans Jonas, *The Gnostic Religion*. The Adamic self is related to daimonic inwardness, but this is not just the divine between (eros as daimon) but the *darkness* in the self (the self as wrath). The urgency of ultimacy risks perversion.

39. There is the Great Hare in the myths of the north American Indian; see Langer, *Philosophy in a New Key*, p. 158. We philosophical children take the familiar story of Chicken Little to heart, especially given the Apocalyptic anxieties of our *fin-de-siècle*. When Chicken Little peeps plaintively "The Sky is Falling," an assorted host of animals accept with hushed glee the disastrous news and rush to tell the next. Only Solomon the Owl confronts the crowd with the stern demand of the doubting Thomas: Show me! Show me where the Sky is Falling! Retracing their course they come upon the apple whose fall started it all. Chicken Little stands ashamed; the abashed crowd of disappointed followers slinks off. While the world is as it was before—calm, there, continuing, washed of panic—Solomon is confirmed in his nocturnal aloofness.

When the fairy tale says: "Once upon a time . . ." we are reminded of the mythic *in illo tempore*. The burden of literalist time is lifted. The attack on such tales by cultural critics for their infestation by some "ism," often shows a banalization of the imagination, as if the meaning of fairy tales could be rendered scientifically in univocal "demythologized" prose. We find a flattening of experience, a moralistic vengeance that is not due to the old puritanism or asceticism but that is "scientific" or culturally "radical." What is produced is an obtuse realism that congratulates itself on its ideological righteousness. The fairy tale is a dipolar image and it is simply dishonest to repress the darkness. I prefer the old version when the wolf eats up the first two stupid pigs (a new, sanitized version has all the pigs escaping) because it is more metaphysically true. See B. Bettelheim, *The Uses of Enchantment*.

40. Against the archaic sense of being as sacred apparition, astonishing presencing, compare miracles in relation to deism. Here a clock-maker god produces a clockwork world; god is a supernatural technician whose *technē* is expressed in the mechanistic necessity of soulless nature. This powerful machine-making god is also benevolent, if you like, a technician with a touch of magic. Miracles are, as it were, his nontechnical magic, his holiday from functional logos.

41. Thus, Occam's voluntaristic God is not unrelated to modern nominalism that contributes to the dedivinization of nature and the sense of the world as a mere aggregate of valueless things to be appropriated by the human will. The issue of such a divinity was already raised in Plato's *Euthyphro*: is X pious because loved of gods, or loved of gods because pious. While voluntarist gods can lead to dedivinized nature, they can also theologically, indeed politically (that is, in terms of this world) reproduce themselves in the human self as the dark side of the wrath of the dipolar god. This is a danger in Descartes' scientific will to be "master and possessor of nature," which of course anticipates the entire project of modernity.

42. See Heraclitus, fr. 93: The Lord whose oracle is at Delphi neither speaks nor conceals but gives a sign (*sēmainei*).

43. See R. L. Fox, *Pagan and Christians*, voluminously on the struggle between the gods of Olympus and Christianity from the second to the fourth century A.D. An analogous struggle between Celtic and Christian religion is said to have taken place in Ireland between St. Patrick and the Druids. We find it in the stories of Oisín's encounters with Patrick.

44. See, for instance, H. Hatfield, *Aesthetic Paganism in German Literature*; M. H. Abrams, *Natural Supernaturalism*. This is partly bound up with a loss of a sacramental sense, which is another way to speak of being as the aesthetic body of God. In Christianity the Incarnation carried some implication of this: the God made flesh implies reconciling selfness and otherness in the divine human: flesh is the apparition of selfness, of divinity as self; its outerness is the aesthetic thereness of sacred inwardness. Sacramental Catholicism is closer to flesh; but Protestant iconoclasm in its destruction of the images of religious art took flight into the innerness of the word. If this flight is taken in a certain direction we end up with the modern alienated self—ejected from the maternal body of nature, suspicious and

repressive of its own aesthetic being, its own body. Hence Greece will always beckon as a memory of the unrepressed body, lifted to the higher guiltlessness of artistic beauty.

45. The presuppositions and implications of this paragraph might be the subject of an entire study. Thus, the basic notions of the univocal (unmediated unity), the equivocal (unmediated dualism of self and God, either/or), the dialectical (self-mediation) and the metaxological (recovery of intermediated otherness) could be used to interpret the many notions of the divine, for example polytheistic, monotheistic, emanationist, creationist, gnostic, mystical; also the metaxological could be developed into a hermeneutical reconstruction of some traditional "proofs," rather *ways*, as Aquinas tellingly calls them: thus the moral and ontological ways stress the inward otherness of self; the cosmological and teleological ways stress the otherness of the being of nature.

46. Eliade emphasizes the *mimetic* dimension to the hierophany; myth calls for repetition of *illud tempus*. Just as we saw an aesthetic move from imitation to creation, being religious evidences a similar move with its transition to inwardness. The ambivalence here relates to metaphysical distrust, and hence the doubleness resurfaces in the dilemma: either human originality tries to usurp the divine, or sees itself as free participant in a larger process of creation. The first is a dominant theme in the story of modernity, hence the problematic presence of God in modernity. The second sense of the image (not a mere projection, but an ontological power) points us in another way, which shares with mythic mimesis the respect for otherness, without the minimizing of our own originality, as often happens in the first mythic intimacy. There is no question of going back behind man's creative differentiation from the original mythic oneness. This relates to what I call a "post-romantic symbol" in *Desire, Dialectic and Otherness*, pp. 200ff.

47. Besides the modern post-Enlightenment "death of God," one must remember that the ancient world had its death of god—the great Pan died, and a cry of sorrow and lamentation filled the world. The Christian tradition attempts to appropriate the belief that God, too, must endure death to sanctify being down to its most execrable horror. To conquer the execrable, God must give Himself up to execration—solidarity with the greatest horror, the unjust suffering of evil by the innocent. This suffering is radically absurd; it cannot be rationalized, it can only be redeemed by a radically other yes, a yes that we can barely comprehend.

48. Thus, Nazism as a grim pagan religion produces a demonic world instead of a sacramental earth. The Adamic self (the "new German man") produces a new fall, presided over by the self of wrath, the "psychopathic god," as Hitler has been called. Using the bureaucratic and technological means of instrumental modernity, its effort to reenchant the world ended up with a world of iniquity. At Auschwitz the *axis mundi* is perverted into the *anus mundi*. Nazism shows traces of the sect as the closed self-mediating cult; the Jew becomes the maligned other to be exterminated. The evil parody of the urgency of ultimacy leads to the demonic idolization of race; the

totalitarian destruction of otherness produces the evil parody of sacrifice, the holocaust. The harrowing of hell turns into the efficient running of hell.

To the extent that Enlightenment rationalism cannot comprehend the real religious urgency of ultimacy, to the same extent its heirs cannot properly understand its evil burlesque in Nazism, nor the genuine energy of transcendence that can be thus perverted and turned to evil. (See most recently, R. Pois, *National Socialism and the Religion of Nature*; the conclusion of this is fatuous in not discriminating between genuine possibilities of the religious and its idolatrous deformations.)

CHAPTER 4

1. Hume's dualism of "is" and "ought" remains at the level of the *logical* difficulty of deducing a conclusion containing an "ought" from premises devoid of one. Nor is it clear (it would not be clear to many of the great ethical thinkers) that there is such a thing as the so-called naturalistic fallacy. The ethical cannot be adequately treated at the level of logical deduction. Being ethical is a way of being of a being of desire: desire is an articulation of being that is always already charged with value. This does not solve ethical dilemmas, but its recognition is an absolutely necessary first step to the *right* questions. The issue is to understand the meaning of the fact that human desire, through its own unfolding, becomes charged with the ethical ought; this becomes its being. Ethics is the hermeneutics of this charge.

2. There are also "therapeutic" and "aestheticized" versions of this isolated self. The narcissistic self wants to enjoy the moment, instead of calculating future enjoyments. On the collusion of the instrumental and narcissistic self, see note 14, chapter 2.

3. Anscombe, for one, points out that Kantianism and utilitarianism make up the two main strands of contemporary ethical debate. More recently, Aristotle has reentered the fray (see MacIntyre, Gadamer). A general reconsideration of the ethics of virtue is under way (see, B. Williams, *Ethics and the Limits of Philosophy*). Against Kant's formalism, ethos has to be concretely treated in terms of a people's *ways* of being. Such ways are embodiments of value; ethical ways are the being there of the good. "Ways" can be formalized into the "correct" or "right" or "regular" ways of doing things; then we emphasize correct form, manner, customs, mores. But a way of being ethical is not exhausted by formalization: there is a prior origin, ground of ethical forms in ways of being as metaxological communities. As I indicate below in speaking of the family, the ethical self of abstract utilitarianism is a product of disintegration, deracination: it is not original but derivative, though it is mistaken for, or takes itself for, original. How relevant here is the so-called genetic fallacy? Does not being ethical always involve a genesis, one which shapes a process of becoming or origination? Hence time and being ethical cannot be separated. This is not to subscribe to an historicist nihilism.

4. These issues have been treated by others. Ethical thought of the

Left-Hegelian variety (Adorno, Horkheimer, Marcuse) is attuned to the difficulties of the modern concept of self. See S. Benhabib, *Norm Critique and Utopia*. The work of Richard Bernstein (*Beyond Objectivism and Relativism*) is worthy of note; also that of Charles Taylor. The matter is tied up with the instrumental reason of Enlightenment. Hegel already saw the connection of utility and Enlightenment reason in the *Phenomenology*, as well as some of the difficulties that ensued when the instrumental self is not rooted in a rich *Sittlichkeit*. Instrumental mind sees the ethical as concerned to solve "problems," like abortion, euthanasia and so forth. But this puts the cart before the horse; being ethical is much more perplexing than the model of the "problem-solver" can grant. Our whole attitude to being is at stake, not just some logical consistency of principles and applications. In its busy thinking the rampant instrumental self is blind to *prior* deformations or sanctuaries of intimacy with respect to the ethical. The abstract self becomes encased in artificialities it itself produced. Freed from these, some of its "problems" may look different, even unreal.

5. Though Kant is a radical defender of autonomy, he does reconstitute respect for the *other* at the level of the kingdom of ends. This ethical respect should force us to rethink the entire ethics of the *other*, the *heteros*, and hence to break down the standard opposition of autonomy and heteronomy.

6. What I discussed in chapter 2 in relation to functional, aesthetic and expressive form are relevant here to the intelligibility of being. A plant lives inactively intelligent, growing in accord with a natural intelligibility, exhibiting in its development fundamental principles of inorganic and organic order. Animals live intelligently, conforming to what is necessary for the preservation and enjoyment of their being. These are the immediacies of intelligibility which are self-mediating in their own right, and not just as a product of human mediation.

7. On the eye, see chapter 2; on negation in relation to child psychology, linguistics, psychoanalysis and philosophy, see W. ver Eecke, *Saying "No."*

8. On the Orphic myth of the origin of evil, see Ricoeur, *The Symbolism of Evil*, pp. 282, 290ff.: The Titans murder the infant Dionysus, boil and devour his body; Zeus punishes the Titans by blasting them with lightning and creates the present human race from their ashes. Thus humans participate in both the evil of the Titans and the divine nature of Dionysus; but the doubleness is in our flesh as made from the Titanic ashes; there is a sense of good and evil anterior to conscious will.

Notice that the Giant in "Jack and the Beanstalk" has at his disposal magical ("spiritual") powers in the Speaking Harp that soothes weariness and warns of danger, but in himself the Giant is stupid and lumbering. It is Jack, moderate in stature, but wily survivor Everyman who gains the edge through cunning. Though physically vulnerable, he intelligently turns danger to advantage. This remind us also of Polyphemos (relative of the Titans) being outwitted by the physically inferior but foxier Odysseus. Note, too, that the Giant wants to *eat* Jack. This carnivorous self eats boys for breakfast.

9. The Giants are metaphorical of a "state of nature" as unregenerate, that is, still under the shadow of the Wrath of God (see chapter 3); the Giant is the self of

wrath. The Greeks thought of the Cyclopes as *apaideusia*—devoid of humanizing education and ethical civility. Hegel has an interesting interpretation of the Titans in the *Aesthetics*, I, pp. 458ff.: Prometheus as Titan embodies *technē*, power, but without ethical or political wisdom (pp. 460ff.). It is interesting that the *Internationale* sings "arise, Titans of the earth . . ."

10. Nietzsche said that man was the animal with red cheeks. One might add: the blush is physiological—value is expressed in, betrayed by the body. The shame of the self before the other is *in* the body. Blushing is the ethical immediacy of guilty judgment, as it were. The blush is the bodily flaring up of our ethical imagination of otherness.

Shame is not a puritan Christian construction. The Greeks were not prudes, but knew that shame was intertwined with our humanity. Thus, Hesiod names shame as a goddess, *Aidōs*. Odysseus appeals to Polyphemos to show *aidōs* in obeying the laws of hospitality and reverence for the gods.

11. The story of Gyges as told by Herodotus shows the connection of violence, shame and being seen by another. The king of the Lydians, Candaules, is not content that the intimacy of his marriage remain intimate, and boasts of his queen's beauty to his confidant Gyges. Though initially unwilling, Gyges hides in the bedroom to look; when later the queen discovers the outrage to intimacy and *aidōs* at being looked at thus, she demands that Gyges either kill himself or the king. Gyges kills the king and mounts the throne and queen.

In Plato's version similar connections of being seen, regicide and lust are present. One is reminded also of Freud's version of the Oedipus story where the king to be killed is the father, and the queen to be tupped is the mother. Being invisible, not being seen by another, as it were, lifts off the bridle of the superego, looses the Id in images of evil desire that well up spontaneously. Interestingly, when Freud talks about the "primal horde," there is an allusion to the "Cyclopean family" (*Civilization and its Discontents*, p. 47) which is, of course, the family of Titans/Giants. He says that shame is traceable to the erect posture (p. 46) by which the genitals are more exposed, vulnerable because visible. I think this begs the question. The erect posture explains nothing. We must *already* be *in* shame to know ourselves as visible, vulnerable to the other. This requires *imagination* in the senses indicated in chapters 2 and 3, namely, our envisagement of otherness as other, of ourselves as seen as by the other. (In Vico's imagistic terms: the thunderbolt of Zeus—also at the origin of imagination—is the flash from the eye of the absolute other, whereby is born our humanity as a living mindfulness of the distinction of good and evil.) As I will say below: imagination as primordial freedom causes the welling up spontaneously of the otherness of the dark self in images of blood. Our visibility as ethical in relation to the look of others is inseparable from this first freedom. But we learn from the look of the other that we are *already guilty*; we are startled into explicit recognition of a condition already intimate to our being. Certainly Freud's view implies that the look of the other (see Sartre) is important, particularly the punitive look of the father. Freud speaks (p. 73) of fear of loss of love of the authority figure (the father as punitive). In fact, there is a deep connection here with *Thanatos*: I see this as the aggressive, destructive side of self-will, as the wrath of self whose imagination of blood violently articulates the metaphysical distrust of being in its otherness. There is hidden meaning in Freud's remark (p. 69) that compares the struggle of Eros and Thanatos to a battle of Giants!

12. Levi-Strauss, *The Raw and the Cooked*; note the musical composition of this work; also the importance of fire as related to the Prometheus myth; fire allows us to be *civilized* carnivores, instead of wolfmen who eat raw flesh. On eating babies, see note 25 below. I consider it revealing that Sartre as radical humanist admitted a distaste for raw foods like shell fish, and a strong preference for foods marked by man's artificing hand, especially confectionery. His preference mirrors his humanism, his at-homeness with the *pour-soi* and his metaphysical nausea at nature's brute thereness as *en-soi*. His ethical humanism interwines with metaphysical and culinary desire. See S. de Beauvoir, *Adieux: A Farewell to Sartre*. Byron's Don Juan says: "All human history attests / That happiness for man—the hungry sinner!—/ Since Eve ate apples, much depends on dinner."

13. Today almost all foods clamor to have attached to them the label "natural," or "nothing artificial added." The ethical judgment is implicit in the label: I am natural, therefore good! Buy me! One need not be a practicing vegetarian to sympathize with the desire to live less estranged from the natural. Vegetarian ethics is suggested in the fact that the word "paradise" (Greek: *paradeisos*, from the Old Persian, *pairi daēza*, a park enclosed by a wall) was used to translate the Hebrew word for "garden." But the longing for the simplicity of the primitive earth is endemic in modernity, alternatively repressed and irrepressibly resprouting. Randomly I mention Rousseau, Romanticism, Gauguin, Nietzsche (stay true to the earth), D. H. Lawrence. Thus also it is wrong to call Epicureanism a "swine" ethics, if by this metaphor is implied a simple regression to animal immediacy; rather the ethical attitude to food and drink is intended as a rational safeguarding of our humanity and the pleasure of being; Epicureanism is an ethical mediation of the immediate, both wary of and respectful of immediacy. Vegetarian and carnivorous ethics are metaphors for certain mediations, showing from the outset the promiscuity of the body (nature) and culture. The same is evident in the metaphor of the social body. This complexity of mediation is not always kept in mind by modern primitives, with the result that the truth of their longing is easily distorted.

14. Veblen's well-known words describe it: "conspicuous consumption." Plato sees its origin in *pleonexia*, the desire for more or the taking of more than one's share, which the ancients also connected with *hubris*. See Marx's essay on "Money" in *Early Writings*, where Hegel's *verkehrte Welt* assumes economic shape. There is a comic version of the fevered city in Gulliver's description of human diet to his Houyhnhnm master, comedy having much to do with the violence human beings inflict on themselves. By contrast, the Houyhnhnms are vegetarians: reasonable animals completely in accord with nature.

15. Marx's vegetarian society is primitive communism; carnivorous society is class society, civil society in Hegel's sense. Marx thought class war would be the tossing of history after which the fever would break; but through his followers, the

dream of perfection brought on the nightmare of the totalitarian state. Plato thought the fever would never entirely break within the city, the cave; we will always be sick; the best times in time are remissions. See chapter 1 on their different revolutionary dreams.

16. After Freud the modern liberal should not be chagrined at Augustine when in *The Confessions* he speaks of infants in jealous rage at another infant at the mother's breast: it is only weakness of body that prevents the doing of evil! In William Golding's *Lord of the Flies*, the civilized choir boys on a paradisal island are consumed by fear of the Beast of the Mountain. When fear of the Lord, the Adults, is not there, the children—alone, "liberated" from the parental Superego—make their new Lord, but it is Beelzebub, Lord of Flies. Evil is in the choir boys, stalks among them as a presence of absence before they *know* it; when a murder is committed. Piggy, a good natured but shortsighted Enlightened rationalist, names the evil, the murder as "an accident."

Dostoevski's *Underground Man* had the perverse measure of Enlightenment, rationalist, humanistic, utilitarian ethics: man will not do what is best for him, and you can argue his rational self-interest till you are blue in the face and still his desire may be perverse and twisted. This defense of perversity as a defense of freedom might be turned into a "proof" of God *from evil*, hence turning evil against the rationalists who take it as an argument against God.

17. See chapter 6 on idiot wisdom.

18. See my "Phronēsis and the Categorical Imperative." I am critical of Kant's formalism there, but my respect for Kant is profound in relation to his defense of the unconditional dimension of the moral, and his sense of the person as an end in itself. In *Desire, Dialectic and Otherness*, chapter 6, I develop a notion of *agapeic* goodwill as instancing the metaxological respect for otherness; this is related to what I call "second love" in the present discussion. I stress that I do not see *phronēsis* as an unproblematic application of given rules to situations; this is to domesticate its improvisatory, extemporizing power. Criticisms of Gadamer's effort to rethink *phronēsis* are not always fair on this score. Granted, *phronēsis* is made problematic in societies in ethical dissolution or decline, where ethical exemplars have become invisible or where there is widespread blindness to their charge.

19. That such a mimesis is essential is not obviated by the cultural despisers of imitation; see chapter 2 on being imitative; chapter 1 on originals and heroes. This is related to the problematic visibility of ethical exemplars in contemporary society. But see below on the family as the first context of ethical mimesis. See also J. Carroll, *Guilt*, on the rise of the matriarchal family and the vanishing of paternal exemplars.

20. In Hesiod's, *Works and Days* we find the myth of the five ages from gold to iron. After the release of Pandora's box, hope and the anxieties of time contribute to an unrelenting stress on work, work, work. This golden age is related to the vegetarian community of paradisal ease. In the bronze and iron ages humans become meat eaters. (See Empedocles of the Age of Innocence, the Age of Strife.) Again elemental images are informed with ethical mediation: such images are condensed

evaluations, carriers of value, but in a way that is sometimes beyond self-conscious control. Such imaginal value can be exploited by a demagogue, or by an ethical exemplar. Hitler provides an example of the former in a relevant sense. National Socialism exploited vegetarian ethics in its emphasis on blood and soil, rootedness; but it produced a *carnivorous* version of the vegetarian ethics in that the biologistic, organic metaphors turned the Jews into the maligned others, as *bacilli* to be exterminated. To purify the infected social body a bureaucratic Moloch was created to eat Jews. To the extent that Heidegger never seems to have adequately clarified the ethical ambiguities surrounding terms like "rootedness," his critics (Adorno, obsessively) are offered an opening for repeated attack. It will not do, however, just to denounce "rootedness": its power must be understood, for good as much as for evil. Ethical freedom in its otherness is always beyond digestion by a totalitarian organism, whether vegetarian or carnivorous.

21. The connection of the "blessings of work" and repressed libido have been noted by commentators on early modernity. In late modernity we are told "you can have it all"—both strenuous work and a satiated libido in the amoral paradise of post-technological mindlessness. Nietzsche attacked the "blessings of work" as a flight from self into narcotic busyness. The connection of work and sex is already imaged in *Genesis*. Schopenhauer's thought exploits the dark connection of sex and self-will.

22. Even Marx uses the image of artistic work to dream of the realm of freedom beyond necessity (see *Art and the Absolute*, chapter 3). Thus too the Cartesian abstraction of selfhood can be reflected in work: the self is abstracted from its integrity, turned into a specialist through the rationalized division of labor of the modern process of production. The abstraction of self is reproduced in utilitarian ethics. The instrumental mind tries to totalize itself when, in fact, it feeds off a division of the human being into a set of discrete, repetitious functions, each of which can be "time-managed," calculated in its rationalized efficiency. The doing of this specialist self is modeled on a mechanical paradigm, and wherever possible the process of production replaces the human with the machine. The mechanized self becomes redundant, replaced by the machine he previously served.

Marx views Hegel's dialectic as the alienated form of work, merely mental work. In fact, Hegel preceded Marx in recognizing the ethical significance of work in terms similar to the above. Hegel analysed work in *System of Ethical Life* and in the *Philosophy of Right*; the mediating power of work in relation to desire is discussed in the dialectic of master and slave in the *Phenomenology*; the fight to the death of master and slave is a potent analysis of the dialectic of carnivorous ethics. Vico implied the importance of work in his saying *verum et factum convertuntur*, the true and the made are convertible—a saying Marx liked to quote. The medievals were mindful of the ethical sense of work (*laborare est orare*). Even the grump in *Ecclesiastes* emphasizes both the vexation of toil and the joy. One finds a strange mixture of prudential worldly widom, not to say cynical self-interest, mixed with a released ethical wisdom that is cast beyond death. "All the toil of man is for his mouth, yet his appetite is not satisfied" (6:7). Toil arises in envy of the neighbor

(4:4), yet the wise person will ask: For whom am I toiling? Work can be a service for another, beyond work cursed by greed or power. In what sense is the modern process of production a form of work consecrated for the other, service in a true sense?

23. When the cynic argues that being truthful does not pay or that honesty is not the best policy, he imposes an instrumental interpretation that makes truthfulness a means to an end outside itself. To be truthful is made a servile good, not a free end in itself.

24. There are complexities in Aristotle in his sense of perfection as *other to the human*: the life of philosophy is higher than ordinary life in the polis. When Spinoza talks of *amor Dei intellectualis*, such love is intellectual in not being self-obsessed. It is capable of rising to the universal and being open to the other as other. That there is an "existential" side to Spinoza (complementing the "Stoic cosmopolitanism" of the *Ethics*) is evident in *On the Improvement of the Understanding*.

25. On the slave, see Aristotle's *Politics*, I, 4. Again Jonathan Swift's "Modest Proposal" reminds us of the ethical power of images of eating. The horror of Swift's proposal to cultivate infants for food is its entirely *reasonable* nature, if our ethics is consistently instrumentalized. It is hard not to see it imaginatively anticipating the Holocaust. Man is meat and "appetite, an universal wolf . . . must make perforce an universal prey, and last eat up himself," as Ulysses puts it in Shakespeare's *Troilus and Cressida* (l, 3, 121ff.)

26. I think that Kant's criticism is less persuasive with respect to the Platonic and Aristotelian views of desire and eudaimonia. While not advocating all the details of the latter views, I concur with their deeper understanding of desire.

27. Second love is really first in that it is closer to the originary metaxological matrix of being that supports the self-definition of the individual. First love is derivative from this. But numerical quantity is not what is relevant here. I retain the terms first and second love with this intended meaning, because "first" can point to the single individual, and indeed its temptation to become a self-sufficient One; while "second" always contains the presence of otherness. There is also the fact that temporally we come to the ethical *acknowledgement* of second love only subsequent to our breaking through the self-insistence of first love. Ontologically speaking, however, it is the work of second love that already supports our self-insistence. [The negative (breaking) and affirmative (breaking through) sides of this second love *as ontological* will be at issue in chapters 5 and 6.] As narcissistic children we want to be loved, but as matured selves we know that to love or to know that we are loved is what truly supports the continued deepening of the ethical will. We are what we are because we first were loved, accepted. Time is the ground of ethical appreciation (memory is necessary for ethical being), of gratitude for the unnamed community of others that always supports individual self-insistence, including the black sheep of maverick autonomy.

The promise of the ethical universal charges openness to the community of otherness. This ideal is both regulative and constitutive. The promise is not just the pull of the still unfulfilled future. It is this, but also it is the ethical charge of the present and the originating beginning in what was and is. Being as process of ethical becoming *originates its own charge*: be other!, where to be other is be the good, do the good. This ideal is originating; it is mediating or forming; it is also final in that its end is to come to respect the other.

28. Schopenhauer is talking about something similar when advocating the transformation of the tyranny of will into will-lessness. Phenomenologically he is right in advocating a release from the prisonhouse of self-will, but his explanation of freedom from this bondage in terms of the negation or extirpation of will is open to Nietzsche's charge of nihilism. My manner of talking about the love of being as basic to the two loves avoids the need to speak of *extirpating* will or desire. I agree, there has to be a "death" for the release of ethical will: death of the false self of "self-will," death of fear for self as set in hostile opposition to the worthy being of otherness. This "death" is simply the life of love.

Some religious traditions are quite violent about "breaking the will." Susannah Wesley, mother of Wesley, insisted on breaking the child's will to save the soul. The danger is that this "breaking" is merely the old will disguising itself with redemptive rhetoric. The prisonhouse sanctifies itself with the language of redemption but remains a prisonhouse.

29. Hobbes obviously saw this, but his understanding of desire is trapped by first love. He does not properly understand self-love as a particularization of the love of being; a sense of self-insistence predominates as an unquestioned presupposition. Hobbes rightly sees the violence emergent from this, and is quite right about our mistrust (we lock our doors at night; none is innocent; in deeds we accuse each other all the time), is right, too, about the need for fear of the lord. But he is wrong in not seeing deeply enough that even all these warrior, police actions are supported by deformed versions of second love. Socrates has superior insight when he argues (in the *Republic*) that, to be effective, a band of thieves must respect each other, trust each other. First love is impossible without the support of second love, albeit in mangled form. Power is ultimately impossible to express as a form of being, if devoid of justice as a condition of being. None of this, I stress, is ground for Pollyanna optimism about human community. What Hobbes calls to our attention must be taken with the utmost seriousness.

30. I mentioned a possible overlap of Kant and Aquinas in relation to the person as an end in itself. In that the metaxological allows a certain ethical community between self and other, the intermediation between these two sides permits a plurality of different stresses, not all of which do justice to the community of being (which hiddenly supports the one-sided emphasis). We need to acknowledge an open dialectic between heteronomy and autonomy. This is evident in the history of ethical reflection. Thus, the side of the other as *heteros* tends to be emphasized in the ancient and medieval world. I think of the Platonic Good in its transcendence and also of Augustine's and Aquinas' God. In the latter there is a view of natural law that follows this heteronomy and introduces a law of the other, albeit elusive, into the heart of selfness itself. Receptivity to this "law of the other" (*hetero-nomos*) made the ancients and medievals sometimes more sympathetic to the ideal of second love.

The modern emphasis initially fall on the self, pitting autonomy (*auto-nomos*: self-law) against heteronomy. The reasons for this emphasis can be traced in part to the way Platonic and medieval views risked introducing *dualism* into the ethical heteronomy. In reaction to this the nominalism of the late Middle Ages and the beginning of modernity is a metaphysical and epistemological forerunner of the ethical, political, and religious individualism that has defined developed modernity. In that medieval dualism threatens an *opposition* of immanence and transcendence, out of the promise of a metaxological intermediation of these two, modernity plucks the self-mediating individual. This changes the sense of natural law. This is now defined in terms of what I call first love: the self-insistence of being (hence the power of self-interested appetite) marking every individual unity of being (this is clear in, say, Hobbes and Spinoza). But this introduces a *new dualism*: between the self and nature, now reduced to an objectified mechanism, devoid of intrinsic meaning and value; between human selves within society, for the self-will of every individual is potentially a threat to every other. We have then the condition of ethical civil war that is the social mirror for the alienation from immanent being (the alienation is from transcendent being in medieval dualism). But just as ancient and medieval dualism eventually throw us back from a dominating heteronomy onto the promise of immanent selfhood, so the development of modern dominating autonomy in the long run (we are at the end of this long run) forces us to rethink the question of the *heteros*, the other

This is evident in Kant himself: this modern defender of radical autonomy was deeply aware of the impasse of ethics in terms of first love: ethics must move beyond the self-will of the individual, hence the importance of the categorical imperative— the self as rational is promise of the universal, that is, of possible openness to otherness in ethical respect for all persons as intrinsic ends in the kingdom of ends. Granted the danger of formalism and of abstraction from historical context in Kant's way of putting the matter. But I think we must reread this metaxologically in terms of a fundamental ethical openness to otherness. This means explicitly reraising the question of the *heteros* (against Kant's pure formalism of autonomy).

This abbreviated history of the ethical points to the need for a hermeneutic of the metaxological in its pluralized promise: the metaxological itself is what supports the ancient and modern emphases. Having passed through these two, we must avoid premodern ethical heteronomy to the extent that it tends to swamp individual autonomy; we must also see beyond the modern autonomous selfhood that imperialistically tries to swamp otherness with its self-insistence. The ethical necessity and intermediation of both sides needs a new, metaxological rereading. This would require a volume to itself.

31. What I mean by ethical civility is not Hegel's/Marx's civil society—but it is related to Hegelian *Bildung* and *Sittlichkeit*. I focus on the ethical; the political needs development. But I agree with Aristotle: you cannot separate the two. This is not to deny the problems peculiar to the modern state.

32. There are many other mediating groups (chums, sororities . . .) but friendship (*philia*) is stressed by Aristotle in his classic discussion (*Ethics*, bk.s VIII

and IX). Aristotle also is interested (*Politics*, 1, 2) in the extension of the natural bonds of family, friendship to the polis, a life larger than the tribal. Though in the *Republic*, Plato is dangerously suspicious about the family's exclusivity, he recognized the bonding power of its intimacy: hence his reconstructed polis reduplicates the family by the noble lie that all citizens are brothers and sisters, kept in ignorance about their biological progenitors. Vico stressed the centrality of strong families in the institution of ethical civility. Freud's view of family is not devoid of ethical implications. The bond of generation is way beyond the abstractions of contractarian theories, an essential other that is silenced by these theories.

Hegel treats the family in *System of Ethical Life* and the *Philosophy of Right*. I am wary of the Hegelian *Aufhebung* of ethical life into world history, or family into civil society and state. There is truth in the protest on behalf of the ethical inviolability of the singular individual. Hegel does not so much deny this as an occasion he diminishes its importance, perhaps in reaction to what he saw as the excessive subjectivity of Romanticism. Hegel claims to see the concrete universal in world history, but the claim of real concreteness is controversial. If world history is the concrete universal, it is an extraordinarily violent universal, as Hegel himself knew. Hegel sees the family as outside world history, but there may be a sense in which the ethical individual and the depth of family love are *beyond* politics in terms of Hegel's level of absolute spirit, but not *below* objective spirit at the level of subjective spirit.

33. Hegel already saw through the vacuity of instrumental reason in pointing out the connection of Enlightenment and utility, of Terror and the abstract freedom of the French Revolution. As I put it, abstracted mind produces abstract ethics. Formal, ontologically deracinated reason is empty and breeds absolute paranoia of otherness (compare to aesthetic deracination in chapter 2). The other becomes a threat to pure autonomy, hence suspect. Then a lack of deeper ethical mindfulness of intrinsic ends breeds a forgetting of the love of being that sees the worth of the other as other. For second love (the love of being as good) is ontologically beyond the dualism of the "is" and "ought." Even first love is beyond this dualism, but it particularizes the meaning of this "beyond" to the self as set over against otherness. Both first and second love are ethical desire, albeit differently configured, and are beyond this split, because prior to it. In fact, a closed instrumental interpretation of first love tends to produce the split. Having produced the split, the "I" claims then to impose *its own* worth on now valueless otherness (the neutralized, devalued "is"). What is there, what "is," has no intrinsic worth; worth is merely an instrument of the projecting self, already set in its opposition to being. The fact/value distinction is an expression of this ethical/ontological estrangement.

34. Thus, the United Nations Declaration of Human Rights, with its charge of respect for the inherent moral dignity of the human being, continually invokes the human *family*.

35. Ethical civility is not just etiquette, though the latter is not negligible. It is a counterpart to art's tolerance of otherness and to the religious universal as an

openness to the other (implied by monotheism) or *pietas* of the whole (this we find in cosmopolitan Stoicism and Spinoza).

36. The intertwining in tension of ideals and realities is found in the laws of a social body. Laws regulate human behavior, especially in relation to typical kinds of situations of communal conflict. They provide rules to standardize such situations, particularly when marked by contentious ambiguity. They arbitrate for the resolution of ambiguities that precipitate conflicts. By submitting to law the subjects of a society civilize their more contentious dealing. They are given the right of recourse to social justice, given to expect some uniform and predictable behavior on the part of others. Recalcitrant otherness is mediated, though the mediation is inevitably a necessary domestication.

37. Consider the notion of civil service. This is a rich notion if one thinks of service as work dedicated to the other, that is for the community as a whole, and if the word civil carries with it the call of the universal and its respect for otherness (as implied by ethical civility). It is this meaning that is implied when Hegel calls the civil servants "the universal class." The civil service is not in principle a mindless bureaucracy of obfuscating functionaries, though in fact it may be that. What is implied by civil service is the modern counterpart to Plato's guardians, a particular group that sees beyond first love and has the care of the whole as its rational responsibility.

38. Hobbes spoke of our desire for power after power, that ceases only in death; in the carnivorous society where life is nasty, brutish and short (see *Leviathan*, I, chapter 13), desire is secretly the ontological despair of what Hegel calls the "bad infinite." Nietzsche tried to overcome this despair of power in the doctrine of the eternal recurrence, understood as an amen to the whole in its otherness to our will (this amen relates to what I call second love). Spinoza's sense of *virtus* as power oscillates between a Hobbesian sense of self-insistence and an ancient sense of rational openness to the whole as other; for Spinoza the *philosopher*, the latter is the more ultimate. For Aristotle *aretē* as the *telos* is the *energeia* of *dunamis*: excellence is the perfected being-at-work of the power of being we are. In our terms, we are configurations of the power of being: the self-mediating identity of free difference, placed in the metaxological community of being. On justice beyond power, see chapter 6 on the reticence of power.

39. Freud is revealing here in that his deeper views coexist with a superficial psychology of motives. When he speaks of pleasure and utility as the two fundamental motives (*Civilization and its Discontents*, p. 41), we have a typical Enlightenment view, which on Freud's deeper reflection gets blasted to pieces. Freud also has a very Hobbesian view of freedom and civilization (original freedom as individual power in the "state of nature"; see pp. 44ff.). His wrong starting point in "constructing" civilized society is the abstraction of the atomized individual in nature. Hence the first and second love are inevitably set in opposition: the metaphysical fact of both as individual and communal embodiments of the love of being is not understood by him, and hence the metaphysical/ethical priority of second

love is also not understood. This becomes a strange impossibility for him rather than the ground that actually sustains community, though it is disfigured in the process: love of the other as other becomes unintelligible on this view. One finds the note of realistic appraisal of human capabilities, without the deeper realization that our shabby efforts are parasitical on the deformed second love. The point is: the harmony of community is not just a prudential construct of self-interested calculating, utilitarian selves; it is a deeper ontological condition, a constitutive solidarity. Being itself is the living creative process of differentiating (hence also the possible opposition of finite beings) and communizing (hence also the harmonizing of beings in their otherness). This original process of being is metaxological.

40. In relation to the two loves, very roughly, capitalism is one particular expression of the first form, while democratic socialism, at least in ideal, seeks to realize the second. Since second love is the fuller form, democratic socialism offers an ethical ideal that is the richer of the two. First love has some correspondence to Hegel's and Marx's sense of civil society (where we find the competitive, exploitative, calculating, utilitarian, egotistic self and so on), while the second love has some partial correspondence to their sense of the political state, where the conflicts of civil society are supposedly mediated. But I do not think a Hegelian or Marxist state brings an *Aufhebung* of conflict here. Marx's solution implies the complete abolition of first love; this is an ontological impossibility, as its intractable continuation in the totalitarian state shows. But this is not to give cheap consolation to antisocialist views: against its capitalistic glorification, the problem of overcoming first love always remains. And to be fair to Hegel, the final harmony is not political but is to be attained only in absolute spirit with art, religion, and philosophy. Hegel remarks that the state cannot be an ideal work of art, and hence is always infected with caprice. See "Hegel, Legal Status and Otherness," where I raise questions about Hegel's interpretation of the rational state in terms of a dialectial self-mediating whole. I suggest a different relation to otherness in terms of the metaxological.

41. Raskolnikov commits a horrific, vile murder of an old woman who for him is not an ethical other of inviolable worth, but vermin, a louse. She is a mere means to Raskolnikov's professed end, namely, to help humanity with the aid of her money. In fact, Raskolnikov's purported ethical justification of his murder is the hypocritical, self-deceiving complement that a malign will-to-power pays to perverted virtue. Of course, Raskolnikov's radical debasement in his reduction and destruction of the other as a worthless thing also comes to reveal the cunning of the ethical: at the other extreme, a radical nobility is possible in redemptive service for the other, even *in* the desolate suffering of the spirit's Siberia. Hegel said that Siberia has no place in the philosophy of world history. Dostoevski said that the degree of civilization of a society can be judged by entering its prisons. Dostoevski spoke with witness.

Genet, one recalls, spent much of his early life in prison. His repeated experience of being an outsider, a marginal, his thievery, his homosexuality landed him again and again in situations where he was repeatedly baptized with the name "criminal." The name stuck and Genet decided to adopt his destiny; he became what he had been said to be, the criminal. French intellectuals and leaders of culture petitioned for his release from prison. The "criminal" becomes a hero; hence Sartre's "Saint Genet." We find a kind of *doppelgänger* in the recent case of Jack Abbot. Abbot writes as a kind of felonious existentialist in his book *In the Belly of the Beast*. Note again the ethical implication of the image of eating or being eaten. Abbot again murdered (in of all places a restaurant) soon after being released.

42. As a literary genre the crime novel has enjoyed unfailing popularity—the conformist is fascinated by his own opposite, the outsider who eludes, who smashes the social norm. Crime novels can be philosophically of interest, especially if they subtly explore evil character.

43. Hence the ambiguity in the terms "malign(ed) other." We can get the ethical counterpart to the witch or heretic. On the maligned other as the excluded, the repressed, the failure that fall outside the functional norm, see chapter 5.

44. The issue of power and justice also appears in the story of the Grand Inquisitor. The Grand Inquisitor is like Thrasymachus in believing in the rule of the powerful few, but inverts Thrasymachus in exercising this rule for the contentment of the many. He is Thrasymachus inverted by Christianity, Nietzsche would say perverted. For its forgetfulness of freedom of spirit, Dostoevski hated the utilitarian utopia of the harmonious ant-heap. The utopia of the Grand Inquisitor would be a vegetarian harmony of instrumental carnivores, presided over by overlords with totalitarian minds. Leviathan would be a post-historical vegetarian paradise of collectivized, carnivorous self-wills.

45. On "breakthrough" in other forms, see chapter 6. The image of the "wolf" is an everyday ethical metaphor, but it also is pervasive in Plato's *Republic* (e.g. the tyrant turns into a wolf because he drinks human blood; compare to Nietzsche's "splendid blond beast"). Recent studies show that the wolf is not the vicious, solitary predator of lore but an animal with strong species solidarity—an ambiguity appropriate to the malign(ed) other.

46. I do not mean any isolated self but an individual embodiment of the realized promise of ethical community as openness to all otherness, even malign(ed) otherness.

CHAPTER 5

1. See "An Answer to the Question 'What is Enlightenment?' " (1784) in *Kant's Political Writings*, pp. 54–60. His qualified optimistic view of reason's place in human progress in history is evident also in another short piece of 1780 "The Idea for a Universal History from a Cosmopolitan Point of View" (*ibid*. pp. 41–53). Kant did recognize the possibility of radical evil.

2. The reaction was simultaneous with Enlightenment in the case of Rousseau. Before him Descartes and Pascal are dialectical twins: the latter pushed enlightenment beyond the former's ideals of self-transparent thought and sensed the fragile darkness

of even enlightening thought. Johathan Swift was never taken in by the dreams of enlightenment reason. At the beginning of the eighteenth century he already has an extremely strong sense of the dark side of human existence, even at times to the point of nihilistic disgust with it, as in his violent vision of the Yahoo. I mentioned (n. 39, chapter 1) Swift's comic sense of the madness of deracinated scientific reason, as in the floating mathematical island. His comic insight again hits the bull when he notes that the women of these abstracted minds body forth eros. They are always trying to escape the flying island, running off with servants to the earth. On "woman" see notes 3, 6, 7 below.

3. I find a strange contradiction in the Heideggerians and the deconstructionists: they excoriate the so-called tradition for its totalizing logicism ("logocentrism," more recently "phallogocentrism") yet to denounce its totalizing, they themselves totalize the tradition! Their *Überwindung* surmounts, mounts the back of tradition. The reasonable thing to say would be: there is not one total tradition, in fact. But to admit this would be to emasculate (an unintentional "phallogocentric" metaphor) their totalizing polemic. But as I have pointed out before, the original Hermes was a priapic figure.

4. On the dialectician as a warrior of words, emergent within the context of an *agon*, see W. Ong, *Fighting for Life*. J. F. Lyotard, *The Postmodern Condition* defends an agonistic view of knowing and language in the context of the "cybernetic revolution," and the contemporary suspicion of "Grand Narratives."

5. Aristotle's defense (see *Metaphysics*, bk. IV) of the principle of contradiction in terms of intelligibility, understood as a determinate logos of a *tode ti*, is a sophisticated version of this love. Aristotle is relentless in his pursuit of those, like the epigones of Heraclitus, who sacrifice the determinacy of logos to the indefinite. I find a tension here between Aristotle's insistence on univocity and his view stated elsewhere that *to on legetai pollachōs*, being is said in many senses. I am not saying that Aristotle is a logic-chopper, though sometimes he is.

6. The logicist is proper, that is, he insists on the ideal of truth as correctness, as exactitude. This is related to the philosopher as technician (see chapter 1). Derrida has developed a critique of the "proper," a critique related to the limits of univocity; see *Spurs: Nietzsche's Styles*. The critique of reason as masculine, as "phallogocentrism," perhaps has a point if knowing is identified with an instrument, if mind is a phallus, a tool. But what if mindfulness is not a tool, and if this noninstrumental sense has always been recognized by philosophers? Plainly it has been by Plato and Aristotle, and with incisiveness by Hegel in the introduction to the *Phenomenology*. The question is often not even raised: what is a conceptual *tool*, an analytical *instrument*: what kind of tools are these? How is thought a tool at all? This way of speaking is parasitical on the instrumentalist metaphorics of modernity but it is just such a metaphorics that needs reflection and criticism. I agree that mind as instrument cannot avoid subjectivism, the alienation of the subject from being, the reaction of the alienated subject in its will to master a hostile other. But you cannot totalize the tradition of philosophy in terms of this instrumentalized version of reason. The

tradition of dialectical philosophy, for instance, cannot be fitted into the straitjacket of univocity.

What would post-phallogocentric thinking be like? Do we need a Derridean pharmakon to make the organ of logos lie limp, no longer a weapon to dominate the Nietzschean feminine flux, impotent to bang becoming into monogamous categoreal submission? This is crude, but my point is not crudity, but to emphasize that the metaphorics of this entire discussion is generally crude. All one needs is to tighten the screw of caricature one more turn and this becomes glaringly obvious.

7. See G. Lloyd, *The Man of Reason*; also Lloyd on Hegel in "Selfhood, war and masculinity," in *Feminist Challenges: Social and Political Theory*, pp. 63–76; also M. Lonzi, *Sputiamo su Hegel* (Let's Spit on Hegel). Where Lloyd sees the entire tradition of philosophy as masculine. S. Bordo, *The Flight to Objectivity*, has a more nuanced view that acknowledges the feminine possibilities of philosophy and culture prior to the modern Cartesian masculinization of thought. Boethius in the *Consolation of Philosophy* addresses Lady Philosophy. What might one make of Giordano Bruno's use of the story of Actaeon and Diana: the philosopher is torn to pieces by Diana's hounds for seeing the truth naked. Post-Freudians might see fear of the castrating female. Alternatively it might be simply the "death" that love has always been thought to be.

8. I note what might be called Socrates' "non-Oedipal" ethics/politics in the *Crito*: Socrates refuses to harm the Laws, identified as his mother/father. This is unlike the Shepherd in the Ring of Gyges story who kills the King, seduces the Queen—murder, contempt for law, power and the phallus combine. The usurper's power of invisibility allows *duplicitous control of the appearances*; this is supposed to be the crime of phallogocentrism; Socrates clearly repudiates any such crime.

9. The point about *dianoia* and *noēsis* is relevant to the distinction in Aquinas (also Cusanus) between *ratio* and *intellectus*, and the distinction in German Idealism between *Verstand* and *Vernunft*. A crucial issue between Hegel and Schelling relates to the question of intuition and the concept. Schelling claims Hegel neglects intuition (though not in his early work), resulting in "panlogism" and the abrogating of the recalcitrant otherness, and receptivity at the summit of mind; all is discursively articulated or subordinated to such articulation. By contrast, Hegel says that nothing is discursively articulated in Schellingian intuition. Commentators have discussed a tension and togetherness of logos and intuition in Husserl. Though Husserl emphasizes method, if there is not a givenness of self-evidence, all the "saying" of logos will be void of "seeing." One will have Kant's concepts without intuitions, concepts which are empty. See E. Kohák, *Idea and Experience*.

10. The type of thinking here also implies a recombinative moment. One recalls Descartes' regulations for the direction of the mind: break the complex into simples; recombine them again. (See *diairesis* and *sunagōgē* in the *Sophist*; Galileo's *metodo resolutivo*.) The issue is whether the second moment as "synthesis," really yields a genuine whole, since the first moment as "analysis" tends to *atomize* the abstracted parts and to be guided by the heuristic that a whole is but the sum of its parts. The

result: the recombinatory "synthesis" yields at best an aggregate of parts, not a genuine whole. Instrumental thought reformulates the question "What is X?" in instrumental terms as "How does X work?" It does not ask "Why is X?" in so far as the latter question concerns the being of a thing as being: an ontological question that cannot be instrumentalized. Parmenides says the judgment or discrimination (*krisis*) here is: it is or it is not (*estin hē ouk estin*). Kirk and Raven, *Presocratic Philosophers*, p. 273.

11. The aesthetic body as emergent self-presence is related to Aristotle's view in *De Anima* that *aisthēsis* also is a kind of *logos* (this is also relevant to the relatedness of intuition and logic). Though we domesticate Aristotle's phrase *zōon logon echōn*, Latinized as *animal rationale*, something of the strangeness breaks through when Aristotle says that the life of philosophical thought is a *bios xenikos*, the life of a stranger: one might say the life of otherness, or thought itself as otherness in us, thinking not just itself but the otherness of being, both in and beyond itself. Hegel's reviled saying, the real is the rational, the rational is the real, ought to be recovered in its deepest meaning here, not in terms of the flattened thoughtlessness that usually accompanies its citation.

12. See "Schopenhauer, Art and the Dark Origin." The question of the darkness of the origin has aesthetic, ethical and religious consequences, as well as logical and metaphysical consequences. Leibniz' doctrine of an infinity of degrees among monads, and his distinction between *perception* (the inner state of the monad of which the monad may not be conscious) and *apperception* (consciousness or reflective awareness of the monad's inner state), anticipate the notion of unconscious mind (see "The Principles of Nature and of Grace, Based on Reason" (1714), sect. 4).

13. See *Desire, Dialectic and Otherness*, chapters 4 and 6, on structure in becoming as intermediate. As we shall see later in a variety of ways, being mindful does entail a certain acknowledgement, salutation of the universal impermanence. On fluxgibberish, see Aristotle's *Metaphysics*, book 4: his unrelenting attack on the deniers of truth and the extreme "Heracliteans" would show the similar views of the Nietzschean deconstructionists in a like light.

14. Nelson Goodman, *Ways of Worldmaking*.

15. In the ancient world the Pythagoreans sensed that the dream of reason revealed the structure of being in the concordance of musical intervals and mathematical proportions. See Aristotle on Anaxagoras (*Metaphysics*, 984b16ff.): "His argument that as mind (*nous*) exists in animals so it exists in nature as the cause of the universe and of order made him sound like a sober man in the midst of loose talkers."

When Heidegger accuses Plato of a turn from *alētheia* to *orthotēs* as truth, the implication is the severing, violating of the intimacy of *phusis* and *logos*. Henceforth logos become instrumentalized reason—mind alienated from being—logos deformed in a distortion of its intimacy, togetherness with being—hence logos become the oblivion of being. I agree that instrumental reason is not mindfulness of being. I disagree that the instrumentalization is due to the Greeks (on *theōria* as contemplative see my discussion of solitude; on Greek *technē* see my remarks below on art, limits and failure). The instrumentalization, as Heidegger well knew, is much more consonant with Cartesianism, with its metaphysical canonization of the subject/object split. Nor is the Socratic self subjectivistic, for this self seeks a logos of the ideal as the shape, *eidos* of otherness itself—the intimacy of logos and idea is the intimacy of mind and the intelligibility of being. (See *Republic* 582e5 where the *philosophos* is said to be the same as the *philologos*: friend of logos, not the *turannos* of logos of "phallogocentrism.") I agree with Heidegger on the *togetherness* of logos and being, but much depends on what one means by logos, being, togetherness, mindfulness, or what Heidegger calls "*Denken.*" All the latter are beyond the subject/object split. I interpret this "beyond" metaxologically. Unlike Heidegger, on this whole issue Nietzsche did not always quite know what he was talking about. Why, for instance, must one interpret instrumentally or in terms of will-to-power, Aristotle's view that somehow the soul is all (repeated by Aquinas and still echoing in Hegel's *Vernunft*) or even Spinoza's uniting of the *ordo rerum* and *ordo idearum*. Too quickly the "hermeneutics of suspicion" puts a blind eye to the telescope; or in the fashionable image of the "conversation of mankind," it produces a dialogue of the deaf. It becomes closed to the *otherness* of and in the philosophical tradition.

16. Empedocles speaks of the magnificent solitude of the circle; the Eleatic sphere in its univocal self-sufficiency is a version of what I call the "absorbing god" (*Desire, Dialectic and Otherness*, chapter 1); Plato has his Eleatic moments when (*Timaeus*, 34b) he implies that the universe is one and solitary, conversing with itself, not needing friendship. The universe is like an absorbing god talking to itself, or an absolute self-mediating whole. Aristotle's *noēsis noēseōs* carries into noology the power of the circle, the ancient image of perfection. This image is pervasive throughout the philosophical tradition. Hegel's dialectical self-mediating whole exploits the image of the circle to the full. When I talk about thought thinking its *other*, in addition to the shock on thought of otherness, I imply the internal self-unweaving of such circles, that is, the power of thought to rise above its own temptation to closure. No thought, modern or ancient, is immune from this temptation, for it is the nature of thought to be self-relating, even in its openness to otherness. It is hermeneutical humbug to imply that, unlike *our* obviously unparalleled openness to otherness, the older thinkers almost always succumbed to the temptation to closure. When I hear the tradition of philosophy blockly denounced as the "metaphysics of presence," or "ontotheology," I hear this humbug congratulating itself.

17. It is not that I am simply denying this view, as we saw in chapter 4. Hobbes rightly reminds us of how we indict ourselves in the pervasive distrust we show of our neighbors; Sartre calls our attention to the hostility that hides even in smiles.

18. One thinks of a witness to betrayed human promise standing alone against the crowd, or of those moments when one must cut loose from distractions to retreat or rest within self. This is related to the issue of ethical exemplars. On silence as significant in a plurality of ways, Max Picard's *The World of Silence* is a very suggestive book. B. Dauenhauer, *Silence*, is interested in a phenomenological

account of the eidetic structures of silence. I think what is most philosophically interesting is silence's breaking down and transcending of structure. There can be no eidetic science of silence in this respect, yet philosophy must think its otherness.

19. By idiocy I intend what is implied by the Greek sense; the idiotic (*idiotēs*) deals with what is private, intimate, not publicly political. This is the intimacy of being, which has aesthetic, religious and ethical manifestations. See chapter 6 on idiot wisdom. What I mean by the intimacy of being is not "privacy" in the sense of a delimited subjective zone standing in opposition to a "public" zone. Such a zone is one of narcissistic subjectivity—the emotive complement to the instrumental self of objectified publicity. Such "privacy" can be totally devoid of intimacy. Contrariwise, a public space can be intimate in the sense I intend, as I indicate in relation to city and country solitude below. See P. Weiss, *Privacy*.

The immanent otherness of inward thisness relates to what I develop as original selfness in *Desire, Dialectic and Otherness*: as self-articulating power to be, original selfness cannot be exhausted by any determinate what; as a this, it is a singularization of the power of being whose unity is not univocal; it shows a certain indeterminacy, in the sense of being overdetermined and hence not exhaustible in terms of univocal predication. Recall that when I spoke of inward thisness and art's affirmation of singularity, I insisted with regard to art's tolerance that individuality is not the dualistic opposite of universality; for the latter is not an abstract generality imposed on the thing by a dominating instrumental mind, but a poetic universality in the Greek sense, that is, an emergent originative openness to otherness. These senses of singularity and universality are related to first and second love as outlined in chapter 4. See Heraclitus (fr. 45): you could not discover the utmost limits of the soul, even if you traveled by every way (*hodon*); such is the depth of its logos.

20. This partly explains why Kierkegaard was particularly scathing in his attack on the Public and the Press (see *The Present Age*). In the *Journals* he is unrestrained about journalists: the quickest way to corrupt the greatest number of people by the smallest number is through journalism. One comes across a debunking attitude that intimacy always implies a seamy side; so also some ostensive calls for "openness" reveal a secret "hermeneutics of suspicion" in which the will to violate the intimacy of the other disguises itself in swelling self-righteous rhetoric.

21. The term "meonic" is derived from the Greek word for non-being, *mē on*. The "nothing" of meonic contraction relates to the experience of "counting for nothing" in the discussion of failure.

22. Among moderns Kierkegaard very clearly knew this.

23. See Pieper, *Leisure*. I agree with many of the criticisms of instrumental reason by Horkheimer and Adorno in *Dialectic of Enlightenment*. Though Adorno is obsessive about Heidegger, I sense a similar tendency to totalize the entire "tradition." Even Odysseus' legendary cunning (especially in outwitting Polyphemos) becomes the prototype of the instrumental reason of the bourgeois man. Dupré has a more nuanced view, because he does not totalize the "tradition," and appreciates the respect for noninstrumental mind in ancient and medieval culture (in

"Alternatives to the Cogito," *Review of Metaphysics*, 40 (June 1987), 687–716, especially 714–16). See notes 3, 7, and 15 above.

24. Vico relates contemplation to marking the space of the sky—the expanse of void wherein auguries are to be divined. Contemplation is divining the sky for signs of Hermes and so forth. Divining is differing, mindful differentiation. One is reminded of the theme of "distantiation" in hermeneutics, there demythologized of its Vichian imagistic power. (The contemplative differing of philosophy has its place in Husserl's *strenge Wissenschaft*: the *epochē*.) Does Derrida heed its divining in following the traces of his *différance*? Or will the sky for Derrida always remain a white metaphor, an abyss of formlessness, a silence whose speech we can never decipher—because it really says nothing?

25. Do we have to read monologically Augustine's famous words: *Deus et animam scire cupio. Nihilne plus? Nihil omnino*. While Augustine is not primarily concerned with nature's otherness, he is concerned with the radical otherness of God as revealed in the intimate unmastered otherness of the inner self. His other famous words that describe the double itinerary of his quest (*ab exterioribus ad interiora, ab inferioribus ad superiora*) can be read as thought thinking its other. To see here only the closed circle of the "metaphysics of presence" is to be misled by spatial metaphors of "in-here"/ "out-there." When Augustine says that God is more intimate to the soul than the soul is to itself (*intimior intima mea*), an otherness is implied more recalcitrant than the recalcitrant inward otherness of the self. There can be no univocal "metaphysics of presence"; we cannot master our own otherness, much less God's.

26. See L. Dupré, *Transcendent Selfhood*, p. 95. Schopenhauer found inspiration for his own thought in the identification of Atman and Brahman.

27. The full intelligibility of these statements depends on the notions of absorbing god, original selfness, absolute original that I develop in *Desire, Dialectic and Otherness*.

28. See E. Kohák's fine *The Embers and the Stars: A Philosophical Inquiry into the Moral Sense of Nature*. Note the subtitle.

29. See chapter 6 on singing and sleep and the emergence into self-presence out of nature's silence. In noting the elusive intimate otherness of the "place" of silence as a happening, my intent is not dualistically to oppose city and country, nor to express nature "nostalgia."

30. That solitude breaks monologue is here shown in destructive form: the disappointment of the relation to otherness leads to a breaking, fracturing of the self. But this is a fruitless parody of the self's creative pluralization of identity (found in art, say).

31. The metaphysical symbolism of light is very old, and perhaps most famously permeates Plato's symbol of the Sun. The light as making possible the visibility of things is no thing, and if we try to grasp it as an illuminated thing rather

than as illuminating origin it will appear as nothing. Yet without this nothing, there would be no presencing of things. See, Hans Blumenberg, *"Licht als Metapher der Wahrheit."*

32. "Dialectic, Deconstruction and the Comedy of Failure." Paper presented at Hegel-Hölderlin Conference, Yale University, October 1987.

33. In opposition to deconstructionists I argue in detail (in the paper cited in note 32) that the possible failure of logos has always troubled thinkers in the "philosophical tradition." In this regard I speak of Socratic dialectic and irony, ancient skepticism, Kant's antinomies, and Hegel's dialectic.

In regard to absurdism, Samuel Beckett is sometimes considered to be the epitome of the postmodern artist (is this why Adorno almost revered him, and intended to dedicate his *Aesthetic Theory* to him?). In fact, he is the aesthetic *reductio ad absurdum* of absurdism: no longer whistling in the dark, after waiting for Godot, he is trying to be radically silent, wordless in the dark. Beckett tries to bespeak a failure of the *logos* that never quite succeeds in being a failure, for to speak the failure would be a kind of success. Hence the essentially *comic* (hence unavoidably and ultimately *affirmative*) nature of his work; see below on comedy.

34. See S. Gablik, *Has Modernism Failed?* for a salutary reminder that the spiritual success of nineteenth and earlier twentieth century artists was willingly paid for in terms of economic failure. She warns that now the artist has been sucked into the economic market with a diminishment of spiritual power.

35. This still helpful distinction need not imply any compartmentalizing of selfness.

36. For some biographical details of philosophers' obsession with bodily health, see B.A. Scharfstein, *The Philosophers*. See also E. Scarry, *The Body in Pain*. Consider Descartes' obsession with medicine—one of the fruits for which the tree of the new science will be cultivated; see R. Carter, *Descartes' Medical Philosophy*. Descartes hoped to so perfect the new science that he might extend his own life and so complete the new science. Here we have instrumental mind trying to perfect itself through a new scientific method in order to minister to the body and its inevitable failure—a different modern activist strategy to the ascetic one of the ancients. But a glance at Plato's *Republic* on *gumnastikē* will quickly remind us of the very strong concern of the ancients with the body. For many of the early Greek thinkers philosophy was bound up with medicine.

37. One might think of Hegel's bout of "hypochondria," experienced prior to his surrender to wisdom's demand that he sacrifice his individuality and give himself up to the universal. Kojève makes much of this; Bataille also mentions it.

38. Marcel has one of the most penetrating accounts of "problem." See above chapter 3, n. 30. On the other side, I think of Marx's view: "Mankind never sets problems for itself that it cannot solve." This is a view of the human mind and power that could easily degenerate into a project for metaphysical mindlessness.

39. This is not unrelated to the first extreme of failure mentioned above: failure born of refusal to venture.

40. It is interesting that just as ancient Stoic innerness seems to generate this suspiciousness of external otherness, so also modern unanchored subjectivity (say, of the Beautiful Soul which is really a *disgusted* soul, since otherness is unclean compared to its pure beauty; as the disgusted soul, the Beautiful Soul is really *ugly*) leads to a similar suspiciousness of otherness—only in the modern era this has becomes a pervasive "hermeneutic of suspicion": the spirit of suspicion becomes more methodical, more virulent when, in response to its not-being-at-home with being, the modern self *defies* (instead of ancient resignation) the otherness it sees as alienating. This is related to the will-less and willful ways of dealing with failure by ancients and moderns.

41. See the discussion of gods and gratitude in chapter 3; also the breakingthrough of second love in chapter 4; in chapter 6 I return to this.

42. When one says, "I am as nothing, I am nought," one is party to contradiction: being as nothing. Logic cannot encapsulate this contradiction if it insists that a subject (here the "I") cannot be both A (in being) and not-A (be nothing). But in radical failure we live, we *are* this contradiction. Deeper than logical contradiction it articulates the point of meonic contraction where the self may either go under into the dark night of nihilism, or pass through the *nihil* into an *ita est*. The suffering of this contradiction is a turning point of ontological crisis, crisis with the implication of its Greek root, *krinein*, to judge, discriminate, separate in a parting of the ways: the mindfulness that may choose life, or the turning away. This is the elemental ontological choice, and as elemental resists logical categorization. Reasons of being are reasons of heart, not just reasons of *ratio*.

43. One is reminded of Eckhart's "*Gelassenheit*," as indeed of Heidegger's appropriation of this. In neither is the blessing of the holy absent, albeit differently articulated in both. One might interpret the Heideggerian "let being be" as growing out of the thought of a certain failure, that is, as a rejoinder to the modern cult of success as concretized in the world of technology and its willful quest of power over nature in its otherness. One can agree with Heidegger's desire to wrest thought free from instrumental reason but not (as I said before) with his totalization of "the tradition" as "logocentrism," and his view that the technological will-to-power is its final episode.

44. *Hamartia* was traditionally translated as a fatal "flaw," but some classical scholars now imply that this was a Renaissance misconception, and that it might be translated better as "error" or "mistake." A form of failure too large to deal with here is the failure of moral will: the radical failure of the ethical self that the ethical self cannot redeem; the possible "breaking through" beyond failure that the forgiveness of evil might offer (see chapter 4 on the criminal other).

45. When I say there are no comic heroes, I do not deny that we speak of "comic heroes" like Falstaff; my point is that Falstaff is not a hero (in the sense of a

noble, dignified self) but a complete rascal and a whoreson knave. The hierarchical distinction between "high" and "low" tends to be subverted by the comic (the proverbial pompous professor slipping on the banana skin). All the conventional hierarchies of power and status are seen to fail in terms of the elemental energies of being (see chapter 6 on folly and festive being). Hence the recurrent concerns of the comic with the irresistible elementals like eating, drinking, and sex. Comic mindfulness brings us back to the vulnerabilities of our fleshed humanness, the home of the aesthetic. See "Can Philosophy Laugh at Itself?"

46. Thus, the emphasis on plenty is reflected in the fact that Comus was a god of fertility. See S. Langer, *Feeling and Form*, chapter 18. Also, J. Morreall (ed.), *The Philosophy of Laughter and Humor*.

CHAPTER 6

1. Breaking through is present but unnamed in all the ways of being; for example, art's tolerance of otherness (chapter 2), gratitude and gods, releasing disillusion (chapter 3), second love (chapter 4), or in the inward thisness of solitude, or the let be (chapter 5).

2. In "The Overcoming of Metaphysics through the Logical Analysis of Language," Carnap condescends to metaphysicans as *failed musicians*. In a sense he is right, but not in any sense he could understand. Failure, logos, and the breakthrough into song would have to be interpreted in terms unintelligible to his logicist view. By contrast, a great logician like Leibniz would understand the idea of metaphysics as thought singing its other—due, let us say, to his Pythagorean sense of the kinship of music and mathematics: the cosmos itself is a universal harmony wherein each individual seems to play for itself alone, but in fact participates in a communal symphony of being.

3. A linguistic version of such univocal economics is satirized by Swift in *Gulliver's Travels*: he pictures people carrying things around for language games. He shows the stupidity of univocity and its insistence: one thing, one meaning. His description of resulting conversation shows that instead of intellectual transparency, univocity breeds stultification. Swift anticipates the later Wittgenstein, in ways more effectively, with the power of a few brilliant comic images.

4. There is an ironical convergence of Nietzsche's rhapsodic will-to-power and Descartes' scientistic will-to-power: rhapsodic man, scientistic man imposes, through poetic or scientific will, the value on things, otherwise void of intrinsic worth. Descartes' dream of the mastery and possession of nature is the rhapsodic dream of the technicist. Hegel is not infected by this will-to-power in so far as his philosophical *Vernunft* carries into modernity the non-violating, contemplative letting be of ancient *theōria*. This is to be borne in mind in his reference to the philosopher's stone in the preface to *The Philosophy of Right*. See M. Berman *The Reenchantment of the World* on alchemy, gold and the origins of modern science.

5. I take this up again in relation to festive time. I underline its intertwining with other themes of this chapter. Saturnalia was celebrated around the winter solstice. This was the time of the furthest distance of the sun from the earth, furthest too from the Golden Age cosmically; yet this liminal time is the cusp of return, even in the night of the remotest god. (See chapter 3 on Newgrange, the religious significance of the winter solstice and the togetherness of life and death.) Some Romans connected Saturn to Janus, god of beginnings. As related to agriculture and civilization, and to Chronos, time, the theme of supersession and regeneration is played out. (Saturday comes from Saturn, *Saturni dies*: I will talk about the weekend later.) There is a connection to Christmas (the Nativity) and the New Year: birth, generation and new beginnings are central themes. The memory of the Golden Age of Saturn is also linked to comedy. On the *aurea saecula*, see Virgil, *Aeneid*, viii, 319ff.

6. I return to the issue of "nostalgia." As I intend it, memorial mindfulness is spirit, not letter, involving *"reconnaissance"* in the French meaning of both "recognition" and "gratitude." See "Memory and Metaphysics."

7. The idealizing power of gold is not unrelated to the sense of mystery as discussed in chapter 3: the sense of given being as both itself and a pointer to something more, what I called a "double image." There is a sense in which Platonic realism, in that it recognizes a sense of the ideal as other, offers a profounder ontology on this score, compared to modern nominalism and post-Cartesian dualism. These latter see given being as either a collection of univocal things or the valueless, mindless thereness of the *res extensa*. Then the pluriform sense of being engendered by mindful reflection on golden being loses its ontological suggestiveness and becomes the mere excrescence of emotive subjectivity. Those images that have concretized our sense of richest being becomes degraded into nothing. This degradation inexorably follows the total instrumentalization of being.

8. See Kant, *Critique of Judgment*, on bird song, p. 89; on the dandy and noisy hymns, p. 196. Kant, I believe, lived near a prison where the inmates were forced to sing hymns. Plato had a wary sense of the alogical, metalogical power of music: it shaped the being of the psyche, subliminally moulded the emergence of self. See Aristotle, *Politics*, VIII, 7, on the many kinds of melodies and their benefits, including ethical and sacred melodies. Ornithologists have studied bird song and it seems that some songs are tied to mating and reproduction, some to the process of food gathering. But there seems to be third singing that is other, with no evident link to such instrumentalities: song here is not a means to the end of survival; it is an end in itself: the witness to affirming presence, joy in golden being itself.

9. In *The Birth of Tragedy*, section 6, Nietzsche briefly takes up this theme: how Archilochus introduced folk song into literature and gained a place besides Homer. Nietzsche says that periods that abound in folk song are those deeply stirred by Dionysian currents. This relates to the elemental. In a later preface, Nietzsche very rightly said that *The Birth of Tragedy* itself should have been sung.

10. See Lorca, "The Duende: Theory and Divertissement," in *Poet in New York*, pp. 154–166.

11. The laughing dead: people laughing on radio shows back in the 1950s, I believe. Aristotle noted that the human being alone is affected by tickling due to delicacy of skin and the fact that humans are the only animals that laugh. I add that laughter seems possible only for a *suffering* being: one who knows what it is to be brought to grief, one who is self-conscious of finitude, mortality. Yet laughter also seems only possible for an *affirming* being: in the very face of grief itself, laughter dances over the abyss, on death. Thus, it reveals the double edge of human doubleness. Consider also our fascination with the Mona Lisa. Is there a univocal logic to help decipher this enigmatic smile?

12. Hegel may not always take "subjective spirit" with sufficient respect (Kierkegaard's criticism partly turns on what I am calling our intimacy with being), yet he has very interesting things to say about voice and song (in the *Aesthetics*). His philosophy of history is equivocal in places: we have the two sides in the view that the world-historical hero can publicly achieve nothing without passion (the intimacy of inward thisness). The ambivalence is revealingly stressed, however, in that the heroes Hegel names are usually political warriors: Caesar, Alexander, Napoleon. The real hero should be the witness of *Geist*. Certainly Luther is mentioned, Socrates a little grudgingly (compare to Aristophanes). Jesus seems to be reduced too much to a *Vorstellung* of Hegel's philosophical *Begriff*: does Hegel veer from Jesus' agapeic idiocy for fear of the spectral beauty of the *schöne Seele*? Hegel too quickly moves away from the elemental as elemental to the philosophical concept, such that his jibes against immediacy fuel the suspicion of panlogism.

I am not enjoining mindless immediacy but metaxological mindfulness: this dwells differently with the elemental in the otherness of being. For Hegel the elemental would really be outside world history, as he says of the family and religious piety. But I think there is a terror for Hegelian dialectics in this "outside." It returns to mock the comprehensive claims of the dialectical concept, understood as thought thinking itself. It is idiotic. But to be properly mindful of it is to be on the way to idiot wisdom. Admittedly, there are times when Hegel's absolute knowing strikes one alternatively as either philosophical idiocy in the worst sense, or idiot wisdom in a sense closer to the one I mean.

13. In contrast to the exploitive instrumentality of technicist mind or the self-importance of world-historical reason, see Rozanov's celebration of just sitting in a chair: ". . . private life is above everything else . . . . Just sitting at home or even picking your nose, and looking at the sunset . . . this is more universal than religion. . . . All religions will pass, but this will remain: simply sitting in a chair and looking into the distance." Quoted in G. L. Kline, *Religious and Anti-Religious Thought in Russia*, p. 70. Rozanov's celebration of the intimacy of being has a touch of idiot wisdom, as had his compatriot Tolstoy. Tolstoy's story "The Death of Ivan Illich" recalls us to the consolation of simple things.

14. Diogenes' father, Hicesias, the money lender, was imprisoned for defacing the coinage. Diogenes was his father's son in philosophical living. The stamp on a coin is emblematic of the web of entanglements that make a system of artificially created and artificially satisfied needs. To rub smooth or deface the coinage was to

deride the false entanglement, to be insolent towards the web of artificiality, to expel the toxins of the fevered city. A king sits proudly on the coinage of empire; level the elevation, erase the profile, and beneath we expose bare dross. Yet Diogenes called himself the "watchdog of Zeus": the beast's and the god's blessedness came together. Being happy like a beast, the elemental self was free of care like a god: the extremes meet. He returned to the body in a way that seemed shameless. One thinks of Jesus: consider the lilies of the field. . . . Both are different expressions of idiot wisdom (see below). Jesus implies: the reason we cannot live this wisdom is because we cannot trust. Diogenes implies: we cannot live it because we have not overcome fear. What shame does idiot wisdom have, since it does not fear the other?

15. There can be a grim side to this: the followers of the French Revolution enjoined a return to the simplicity of natural man who had, it seems, some of the virtues of Sparta and the Roman Republic; yet the return also unleashed Terror. The same thing happened with the Khmer Rouge: the return to the rustic sowed the killing fields with blood. This is Caliban loose with a philosophy to justify his marauding against thought with a machete.

It is also relevant here to remember the effort during the French Revolution to begin totally anew the entire process of naming time: the desire for absolutely new, original time, sought in the complete destruction of the past, terrorizes all reality that already is.

16. Extremely revealing is Descartes' objection to earlier science and philosophy as haphazard like the ancient town (both lack the guiding hand of one dominating architect). It is no accident that Descartes is also a philosophical instance of defiant simplicity. He shows the radical desire to begin anew of which I speak, though he seeks to fulfill the desire mathematically: to subject the otherness of being to thought that is entirely self-mediating.

17. The surveyors made use of the ordinance survey of 1835, more recent surveys, as well as some aerial photographs dating back beyond 20 years. In comparison with other Western countries, the change here is concentrated in a time the imagination can span, though similar explosions are to be found elsewhere.

18. See chapter 3 on sacral kinship, the *hieros gamos* and note 11 on place names that carry traces of the land as the aesthetic body of divinity. Plato calls the cosmos an "aesthetic god, image of the noetic," *eikōn tou noētou, theos aisthētos* (*Timaeus,* 92c6–7).

19. See chapter 4 on work and death; also especially chapter 3 on metaphysical trust and distrust.

20. See G. L. Kline "The Use and Abuse of Hegel by Nietzsche and Marx," in *Hegel and His Critics*, W. Desmond (ed.), chapter 1. To obviate the misunderstanding that my thought of posthumous mind is *only* imaginative, let me mention survivors of the Holocaust, many of whom outlive time, as if back from the dead and despoiled of the memory of golden being. Elie Wiesel's return to his hometown Sighet after the Holocaust, like a ghost listening for ghosts, provokes

metaphysical thought abut the intractable otherness of time and death—and
continuing to be. Thus he found: "The only place where I felt at home, on familiar
ground, was the Jewish cemetry. And yet I had never set foot in it before . . . This
was the only place is Sighet that reminded me of Sighet, the only thing that remained
of Sighet." See "The Last Return" in *Legends of our Time*, p. 161.

21. I have pointed out a similar unintelligible reversal in Nietzsche's father,
Schopenhauer in "Schopenhauer, Art and the Dark Origin." Remember that
Nietzsche suggests that time be counted *absolutely newly* from his *Zarathustra*: he
claims to break history in half, inaugurating the only significant part, the future. He
makes this claim both in *Ecce Homo* and at the end of *The Anti-Christ*.

22. To the extent that "postmodernist" thought rejects this trivialization of
subjectivity, I am in agreement. When subjectivity, selfhood is rejected *tout court* I
strongly dissent. Our problem is to restore otherness that is charged with significance
but also selfhood that surmounts the aesthetic, religious, ethical, and philosophical
trivialization. The postmodern protest against trivial subjectivity is subjectivity itself
trying to deny triviality by denying itself. That is, it is evasive and self-forgetful, and
hence itself not the medicine of mindfulness but the perpetuation of the trivialization.
Kierkegaard already saw the bankruptcy of merely "aestheticist" subjectivity—its
search for the "interesting" and its horror of boredom is despair.

23. See *Phaedo* on Socrates' need to make music; Apollo's swan tries poetry but
realizes that philosophy is the music to be made: this is thought thinking its other on
the vigil of death as an unmastered other. Socrates says he would have met this other
much earlier and hence been an aborted philosopher, if he had not lived as an idiot. In
Apology (32a) he says that one must be an idiot (*idioteuein*) not a political man to do
any good. Sophists are contrasted with idiots in *Theaetetus*, 154e. I note another bird
of philosophy, namely, the Owl of Minerva invoked by Hegel. Is there any
significance to the fact that owls hoot—a silent song, if a song at all, of a nocturnal
bird whose eyes are dead?

24. Brain waves have been monitored and patterns of rapid eye movement in
sleep. Psychologists have asked about the place of dreams in the whole economy of
the psyche. Freud spoke of dreams as the royal road to the unconscious, yet many
decades later the matter still seems shrouded in mystery. I am interested in sleep and
the emergence of the energy of being from *below*, as it were, an original energy
beyond the conscious self that touches death and yet wakefully shapes itself as self.
See Heraclitus, frag. 75: sleepers, too, take part in the work of the cosmos. See Job,
35:10: "God giveth songs in the night." Erasmus, *Praise of Folly*: sleep is one of
Folly's companions. See the dreamless sleep of *Turiya* in the Upanishads: the
overcoming and vanishing of the "I" in which the soul comes closest to its own native
purity.

25. There is a reversal of image and original here: the image becomes original
and the original the image; or rather any dualism of image and original breaks down,
for every image is an original, and every original is an image; the original energy of
being images itself in each; this implies that the intimacy of being, especially in the

community of being of the line of generation, points to a certain coimplication of each in all and all in each. See chapter 3 on ancestor worship, chapter 4 on the family. Thus, to think about a face can be an adventure in otherness.

26. We must not allow ourselves to be browbeaten by Nietzsche's diatribe against "afterworldsmen," skulking away from such questions in the face of his insistent vehemence. *Not* to ask these questions strikes me as dishonest.

27. This insistence of being is not just animal egotism (see chapter 4), nor am I denying that human beings can be in love with death (see Freud's *Thanatos*). Compare this insistence to Schopenhauer's will-to-live or Spinoza's *conatus essendi*. Consider Aristotle on the convertibility of one and being: to be is to be a one. One can conceive of oneness as a holding together of the *energeia* of being into a determinate wholeness. Nor does this deny metaxological relatedness; it says that in relatedness all things manifest the original power of being.

28. On an infinity of indigence and infinity of fullness see *Desire, Dialectic and Otherness*, pp. 146ff. We shrink at being unsheltered thus radically. I suggest (p. 159) that this being unsheltered might be seen as a homecoming to finitude.

29. This being torn is related to sacred suffering, the *pathei mathos* and the patient being it brings. Hesiod: suffering makes wise the simple (*pathōn de te nēpios egnō*; *Works and Days*, 218). The peripeteias of which I speak are not temporary reversals that merely serve to reinstate and so buttress the established domestication of being. Real breakthrough irreversibly makes us *look differently* at the universal impermanence. This also means seeing deformations of being as deformations. Being is other. Things will never be the same.

30. See Wordsworth, for instance, as a great poet of anonymous greatness.

31. Novalis describes philosophy as a homesickness (*Heimweh*), but one wonders if the current contempt by purportedly anti-Enlightenment thinkers reveals an attitude to the past like the Englightenment attack on the past as error and superstition. Futurity is again given an unexamined priority, with the risk of a devaluation of past and present. The issue of "home," however, is one of intrinsically worthy being, whether past, present or to come.

32. When I ask if we are native to the world, nativity carries the implication of *natus*, being born to an original home. But there is an inevitable doubleness: a togetherness of being-at-home and not-being-at-home. Metaxologically understood, these are inseparable. The feeble nostalgists diminish being-at-home because they are oblivious to not-being-at-home; their being-at-home is *sentimental* play-acting. Their opponents, *suspicious* playactors, make an unreal fetish of not-being-at-home; they do so in a manner that makes one suspect that they lack a real comprehension of what exile means. If you speak with witness, you cannot play-act with the grief and mourning of being that comes with exile. So both of these actually distort the doubleness.

33. Consider the question: what does it mean to have a *good time*? Is time itself

good, or does "good" merely refer to a quality of "subjective" satisfaction? Is there an ontological dimension to having a good time? Is festive being the same as time being good in itself? (This is what the Irish call the "*craic*"—an indefineable term for an elementally festive good time.) If a good time is only a "subjective" satisfaction, what prevents the degeneration into the consumption of time (time becomes the bored becoming of subjectivistic throbbing): beneath the consumption of time is the spiritual death of the cult of novelty that now reveals its "creativity" as fake festivity.

34. Thus, the Medievals identified sloth with despair. Sloth and despair are the death of time as festive.

35. See, for instance, Henri Lefebvre, *Everyday Life in the Modern World*, pp. 36ff.

36. Consider that "Easter" comes from the Anglo-Saxon "Eostre" (meaning "to shine"), goddess of spring. The Anglo-Saxons celebrated her coming during the vernal equinox; fire was her best gift bringing warmth, light, growing. The eggs of Easter were symbols of fertility.

37. See Plato *Laws*, (vii, 796):"God alone is worthy of supreme seriousness, but man is made God's plaything, and this is the best part of him. Therefore every man and woman should live life accordingly, and play the noblest games and be of another mind from what they are at present . . . for they deem war a serious thing, though in war there is neither play nor culture (*paideia*) worthy of the name, which are things we deem most serious. Hence all must live in peace as well as they possibly can. What then is the right way of living? Life must be lived as play, playing certain games, making sacrifices, singing and dancing, and then a man will be able to propitiate the gods and defend himself against his enemies and win the contest." This might be connected with the ethical significance of work: beyond instrumental being, it must partake of the festive. See also *Laws*, 653dff.; 828ff.: the Athenian Stranger says (828b) there should be 365 feast days in the year! Festal being is also related to art in so far as creation involves a generosity of being. Festal being is the origin of *theōria*, hence philosophy. Since the *theōroi* were originally religious delegates sent by the polis to the sacred games, they were festal human beings. Philosophical mindfulness as thought singing its other is concerned with good time, time as good.

38. When Wittgenstein said that philosophical problems arise when language "goes on holiday," he hit the truth but did not realize how deeply. He should have asked the meaning of "holiday." For him philosophical problems become psuedo-problems when they stray outside the working thought of functional realness. But the greatness of philosophy is precisely its being the "holiday of thought." This is just what free mind means. Did the engineer in Wittgenstein give his own poetic side a bad conscience? Poets play, engineers work. Kant, true to form, said he preferred Aristotle to Plato because, while Plato was play, Aristotle was work!

39. The pervasiveness of the psychotherapist, psychologist, psychoanalyst and so on, has given contemporary society the name of the "therapeutic culture." We worry about the state of our psychic health, being suspicious of irrational drives even

in the most innocuous of thoughts. Freud and Nietzsche (who with Marx, Ricoeur called the "masters of modern suspicion") have made us distrustful of consciousness, suggesting repressed tangles of murk beneath the smooth surface. Is our interest to become wiser from madness or to repress the message of madness? See Plato's *Timaeus*, 71dff. on the superiority of the mantik art as given in sleep or dreams—though the divinations of sacred sleep must be pondered and judged by the waking mind; see 85b on epilepsy as the "sacred disease"; also *Laws* 916a.

40. Crazy Jane is Yeats' wise lunatic; The Madwoman of Cork refers to the fine elemental poem of Patrick Galvin. See his *Man on the Porch: Selected Poems*. See M. Foucault *Madness and Civilization*, on the shift from medieval to modern attitudes. See the music cure for madness, pp. 178–79; the madman as hostile other, criminal, p. 228. Foucault sees a very interesting connection of madness and death (pp. 15–16): up to the middle of the fifteenth century, madness, folly entailed death turned inward and disarmed, laughed at, but the end of the fifteenth century brought a change. The structure of the present chapter is like this premodern strategy; but idiot wisdom is not a tale told by an idiot, signifying nothing. Laughter can be festive, not just the black laughter of nihilism. Again Foucault (p. 46) connects the confinement of madness with policing the requirements of labor. The incarceration of folly was a campaign against idleness. In present terms, the coming to dominance of instrumental life feels threatened by its irreverent other, festive being, and chokes both it and folly as disruptive others. But instrumental life is always shadowed by the death it futilely works to conquer.

41. Madness has sometimes been celebrated (see Laing, Deleuze) as implying an indictment of Western culture (this is analogous to the modern romance with primitivism). The "antipsychiatrist" seems to charge Western civilization: it is society that is mad, not the madman; the madman is only a rejected product, a symptom of the sickness society refuses to recognize as its own. Undoubtedly many things passing for sanity have more than a trace of collective lunacy. But an apotheosis of madness in that sense is not my point, as if there were some pure innocent light in contrast to the contaminated social darkness. Madness is a provocative, a deep disturber. The "antipsychiatrists" sometimes imply that madness does not exist, that madness is a myth. But madness, as the disordered mind at odds with the real, is real. The struggle with this disorder sometimes yields the sublime results of great art or philosophy. It can also destroy. The war is not with "them," the enemy without. To be a self is to be a site of strife—battle and battlefield, both sides battling: king and fool at odds, king and fool at one. We all carry within our trojan horse. Nor is all idiocy wise.

42. Genuine laughter has its ground for debunking the groundless. The fool is the comic subverter of conventional hierarchies and the return of and to the elemental; the power of being as preceding and exceeding fixation, breaking through in festive outburst. Philosophical laughter itself is always skeptical of idols; it is honesty about the worthlessness of the worthless. So it is close to nihilism in seeing what counts for nothing; but it is more than nihilistic in celebrating the energy of being that breaks through even in breakdown.

The Golden Age is related to the "green world" of the comic (consider Falstaff as a Lord of Misrule: his tavern as Saturnalian). Green is the color of innocence, of vegetarian rather than carnivorous life. Idiot wisdom is green. Its green is not of William James' green imbecile but of the groves where Plato says the gods really dwell (see *Phaedo*). Those groves are no-place. In the Golden Age it was believed we could understand the languages of fish, fowl, beasts of the grass, flowers, stars, rivers, earth, and heaven: the voices of the sacramental earth sang and were heard—this song is now to us, at best, a serene silence; we no longer listen or hear; there is nothing there.

43. See J. Huizinga, *Homo Ludens*, p. 97 on Chinese chivalry in the feudal age. Honor is enhanced in moderation. He recounts a battle between two noble lords, Chin and Ch'in, that was never forgot but that yet was won. It was won, though nothing on the surface was done. The unsteady gaze and unsure voice of Ch'in's messenger was enough. See chapter 5 on play and war; in chapter 6 on play and knowing, the origin of philosophy in sacred games is proposed.

44. Think of Epicurus: *lathē biōsas*; Live hidden! His ethics of being pleased with being (pleasure) is related to the elemental: gentle simplicity that was defiant in its gentleness. *Hēdonē* is the sweetness of being, the honey of being.

45. Spinoza's motto *Caute!* is usually interpreted as Spinoza's own caution, prudence. But this fails to see the ambiguity. *Caute!* is an imperative, but is it only addressed by Spinoza to himself? Is it not also a warning to *others* whose approach might misunderstand, a warding off, not so much of those who cannot think at his level of technical brilliance, but those lacking spiritual courage for dangerous thought.

46. I think of the French Nietzscheans as philosophers on show. To be fair to Nietzsche, his later shrillness is also a reaction to the dead silence that initially greeted his genuinely urgent message. The mask of Nietzsche's gaiety was the laughing face of a thinker who had deeply suffered. His madness will always disturb us, since we cannot entirely shake the suspicion that it might have been idiot wisdom. After all, he did liken himself to a buffoon. It is hard to put from mind the unforgettable scene where Nietzsche in breakdown embraces the thrashed horse. What breaks through in this breakdown? Is there not a reversal that from the point of view of Nietzsche's proclaimed doctrines is senseless, mad—the breakthrough of pity, compassion for the weak, worthless other? I think again of the sacred folly of St. Francis kissing the leper.

47. Plato's ironical stance (even more than Socrates') means that he is never univocally manifest in his appearance. We can never pin him down. His brilliant, let us call it, disappearing dialectic is more resistant than anything Derrida might ever construct or deconstruct.

48. One thinks of Don Quixote looking at Donna Dulcinea del Toboso, plain wench, as a beautiful lady: to one who looks at being as beautiful, being itself looks beautiful. Is this transfiguring idiocy? Idiot wisdom would be the woman who loved the raggle-taggle gypsy rather than the monied lord. One thinks of Jainism, especially

one of its sects the Digambaras (literally "sky-clad," compared to the Svetambaras, "white-clad"): the absolutely naked monks (they have conquered shame), peregrinators, possessionless, practicing Ahimsa, non-violence, trying to live love for all life. All life wants to live, none to suffer (see the elemental insistence on being); even worship is seen as an interference. Their point is to let being be. This is the reticence of power. The Jain practice of Ahimsa influenced Gandhi. They never fought a war in their entire history. There is a not dissimilar, though less gentle, ethical simplicity and poverty in Diogenes. The poor in spirit of Jesus—blessed idiocy?

49. See *Desire, Dialectic and Otherness*, chapter 1.

50. The Tao has been compared to a baby, or an uncarved block. See chapter 4 on the infant's uninsistent eye: idiot wisdom would be the eye of non-insistence, but *after* mindfulness of otherness rather than before. This would be like the sacred yes of Nietzsche's child who has conquered the violent will of the lion. Was Aquinas' astonishing silence at the end of his life a manifestation of idiot wisdom? (Plutarch: "We learn silence from the Gods, speech from man.")

51. This Werner Herzog film images other themes of this book: wrath, gold, eyes, inwardness, willfulness, art, nature's otherness, sacred silence . . . We have met Aguirre before in Thrasymachus, the Titans, the wolfman. . . .

Bibliography

Abrams, M. H. *Natural Supernaturalism*. New York: Norton, 1971.

Adorno, T. *Aesthetic Theory*. Ed. G. Adorno and R. Tiedemann. Trans. C. Lenhardt. New York: Routledge & Kegan Paul, 1984.

———. and M. Horkheimer. *Dialectic of Enlightenment*. Trans. J. Cumming. New York: Continuum, 1972.

———. *Negative Dialectics*. Trans. E. B. Ashton. New York: Continuum, 1987.

Aristotle. *Basic Works*. Ed. R. McKeon. New York: Random House, 1941.

Aquinas, Thomas. *Basic Writings*. Ed. A. Pegis. New York: Random House, 1944.

Ayer, A. J. *Language, Truth and Logic*. 2d ed. New York: Dover, 1952.

Barrett, W. *The Illusion of Technique*. New York: Doubleday, 1978.

Baynes, K., Bohman, J., and McCarthy, T. Eds. *After Philosophy: End or Transformation*. Cambridge, Mass.: M.I.T., 1987.

Benhabib, Seyla. *Norm Critique and Utopia*. New York: Columbia University Press, 1986.

Berman, Morris. *The Reenchantment of the World*. Ithaca: Cornell University Press, 1981.

Bernstein, Richard. *Beyond Objectivism and Relativism: Science, Hermeneutics, and Praxis*. Philadelphia: University of Pennsylvania Press, 1983.

Bettelheim, Bruno. *The Uses of Enchantment: The Meaning and Importance of Fairy Tales*. New York: Vintage Press, 1977.

Blumenberg, Hans. "Licht als Metapher der Wahrheit." *Studium Generale* 10, no. 7 (1957): 432–477.

Bordo, Susan. *The Flight to Objectivity*. Albany: State University of New York Press, 1987.

375

Carnap, Rudolf. *The Logical Structure of The World*. Trans. R. A. George. Berkeley: University of California Press, 1967.

———. "The Overcoming of Metaphysics through the Logical Analysis of Language." In *Heidegger and Modern Philosophy*, ed. Michael Muray. New Haven, Conn: Yale University Press, 1987.

Caroll, John. *Guilt: The Grey Eminence Behind Character, History and Culture*. London: Routledge & Kegan Paul, 1985.

Carter, Richard. *Descartes' Medical Philosophy*. Baltimore: Johns Hopkins University Press, 1983.

Casey, Edward. *Imagining: A Phenomenological Study*. Bloomington: Indiana University Press, 1976.

Cassirer, E. *The Philosophy of Symbolic Forms*. 3 vols. Trans. Ralph Manheim. New Haven: Yale University Press, 1953–57.

———. *An Essay on Man*. New Haven: Yale University Press, 1944.

———. *Language and Myth*. Trans. S.K. Langer. New York: Dover, 1946.

Clark, K. *The Nude: A Study in Ideal Form*. Garden City: Doubleday, 1956.

Collingwood, R. G. *The Principles of Art*. Oxford: Clarendon Press, 1938.

Dallmayr, Fred R. *Critical Encounters: Between Philosophy and Politics*. Notre Dame: University of Notre Dame Press, 1987.

Danto, Arthur. *The Philosophical Disenfranchisement of Art*. New York: Columbia University Press, 1986.

Dauenhauer, Bernard. *Silence*. Bloomington: Indiana University Press, 1980.

De Beauvoir, S. *Adieux: A Farewell to Sartre*. Trans. P. O. Brian. New York: Pantheon, 1984.

Derrida, Jacques. *Margins of Philosophy*. Trans. A. Bass. Chicago: University of Chicago Press, 1982.

———. *Spurs: Nietzsche's Styles*. Trans. Barbara Harlow. Chicago: University of Chicago Press, 1979.

Descartes, R. *The Philosophical Writings*. Trans. J. Cottingham et al. Cambridge: Cambridge University Press, 1985.

Desmond, William. *Art and the Absolute: A Study of Hegel's Aesthetics*. Albany: State University of New York Press, 1986.

———. *Desire, Dialectic and Otherness: An Essay on Origins*. New Haven: Yale University Press, 1987.

_____. ed. *Hegel and His Critics*. Albany: State University of New York Press, 1989.

_____. "The Child in Nietzsche's Menagerie." *Seminar* 5 (1981): 40–44.

_____. "Collingwood, Imagination and Epistemology." *Philosophical Studies* (Ireland) 24 (1976): 82–103.

_____. "Dialectic, Deconstruction and the Comedy of Failure."(to appear.)

_____. "Hegel and the Problem of Religious Representation." *Philosophical Studies* (Ireland) 30 (1984): 9–22.

_____. "Hegel, History and Philosophical Contemporaneity." *Filosofia Oggi*, 4, no. 2 (1981): 211–26.

_____. "Hegel, Legal Status and Otherness." *Cardozo Law Review*. 10. no.s 5–6: 1713–1726.

_____. "Hegel, Philosophy and Worship." *Cithara*. 19, no. 1 (1979): 3–20.

_____. "Memory and Metaphysics." *Seminar* 3 (1979): 21–31.

_____. "Paul Weiss and Creativity." (to appear.)

_____. "Plato's Philosophical Art and the Identification of the Sophist." *Filosofia Oggi* 2, no. 4 (1979): 393–403.

_____. "Phronēsis and the Categorical Imperative." *Philosophical Studies* (Ireland) 27 (1980): 5–15.

_____. Review of R. Kearney. ed. *The Irish Mind*. *Philosophical Studies*. Vol. 31, 374–380.

_____. Review of S. Rosen, *The Limits of Analysis*. *Philosophical Studies*. Vol. 29, 318–322.

_____. "Schopenhauer, Art and the Dark Origin." In *Schopenhauer*. E. von der Luft ed. Mellen Press: Lewistown, 1988, 101–122.

_____. "Can Philosophy Laugh at Itself? On Hegel and Aristophanes." *The Owl of Minerva*. 20. no. 2, 1989: 131–149.

Dupré, Louis. *Marx's Social Critique of Culture*. New Haven: Yale University Press, 1983.

_____. *The Other Dimension*. Garden City, New York: Doubleday, 1972.

_____. *Transcendent Selfhood*. New York: Seabury Press, 1976.

Eliade, Mircea. *Patterns in Comparative Religion*. New York: Sheed and Ward, 1958.

————. *The Sacred and the Profane*. Trans. W. R. Trask. New York: Harcourt, Brace and World, 1959.

Feyerabend, Paul. *Against Method*. London: New Left Books, 1975.

————. *Farewell to Reason*. New York: Verso, 1987.

Foucault, Michel. *Madness and Civilization*. Trans. R. Howard. New York: Vintage, 1973.

Fox, R. L. *Pagan and Christians*. New York: Knopf, 1987.

Freud, S. *Civilization and its Discontents*. Trans. J. Strachey. New York: Norton, 1962.

————. *The Future of an Illusion*. Trans. W. D. Robson-Scott. Garden City: Anchor, 1964.

————. *New Introductory Lectures on Psychoanalysis* (1933). Translated and edited by J. Strachey. New York: Norton, 1965.

Fustel de Coulanges, Numa Denis. *The Ancient City*. Garden City: Doubleday, n.d.

Gablik, S. *Has Modernism Failed?* New York: Thames and Hudson, 1984.

Gadamer, H. G. *Truth and Method*. Trans. Garrett Barden and John Cumming. New York: Seabury Press, 1975.

————. *The Relevance of the Beautiful and Other Essays*. Translator N. Walker and Editor R. Bernasconi. Cambridge: Cambridge University Press, 1986.

Galvin, Patrick. *Man on the Porch: Selected Poems*. London: Martin Brian and O'Keeffe, 1979.

Gellner, Ernest. *Words and Things*. Boston: Beacon Press, 1960.

Girard, René. *Violence and the Sacred*. Trans. Patrick Gregory. Baltimore: Johns Hopkins University Press, 1977.

Goodman, N. *Ways of Worldmaking*. Indianapolis: Hackett, 1978.

Harries, Karsten. *The Bavarian Rococo Church: Between Faith and Aestheticsm*. New Haven: Yale University Press, 1983.

Harris, H. S. *Hegel's Development: Towards the Sunlight 1770–1801*. Oxford: Clarendon Press, 1972.

Hatfield, H. *Aesthetic Paganism in German Literature*. Cambridge, Mass.: Harvard University Press, 1964.

Haug, Wolfgang Fritz. *Critique of Commodity Aesthetics*. Trans. R. Bock. Minneapolis: University of Minnesota Press, 1986.

Hegel, G. W. F. *Aesthetics: Lectures on Fine Art*. 2 vols. Trans. T. M. Knox. Oxford: Clarendon Press, 1975.

————. *The Difference of Fichte's and Schelling's System of Philosophy*. Trans. H. S. Harris and W. Cerf. Albany: State University of New York Press, 1977.

————. *The Phenomenology of Spirit*. Trans. A. V. Miller. Oxford: Clarendon Press, 1977.

————. *The Philosophy of Right*. Trans. T. M. Knox. Oxford: Clarendon Press, 1967.

————. *Lectures on the Philosophy of Religion: One Volume Edition, The Lectures of 1827*. Ed. Peter C. Hodgson. Berkeley: University of California Press, 1988.

————. *System of Ethical Life and First Philosophy of Spirit*. Editors and translators H. S. Harris and T. M. Knox. Albany: State University of New York Press, 1979.

Heidegger, Martin. *Being and Time*. Translators J. MacQuarrie and E. Robinson. New York: Harper and Row, 1962.

————. *Kant and the Problem of Metaphysics*. Trans. J. S. Churchill. Bloomington: Indiana University Press, 1962.

Heine, H. *Philosophy and Religion in Germany*. Trans. J. Snodgrass. Boston: Beacon Press, 1959.

Heller, A. and Fehér F. Eds. *Reconstructing Aesthetics*. New York: Blackwell, 1986.

Heller, Eric. *In the Age of Prose: Literary and Philosophical Essays*. New York: Cambridge University Press, 1984.

Hobbes, T. *Leviathan*. Ed. John Plamenatz. London: Collins, 1971.

Huizinga, J. *Homo Ludens*. Boston: Beacon Press, 1955.

Husserl, E. *Cartesian Meditations*. Trans. D. Cairns. The Hague: Nijhoff, 1973.

————. *The Paris Lectures*. Trans. P. Koestenbaum. The Hague: Nijhoff, 1975.

James, William. *The Varieties of Religious Experience*. New York: Collier, 1961.

Jonas, Hans. *The Gnostic Religion*. Boston: Beacon Press, 1963.

Kant, I. *Critique of Judgement*. Trans. with analytical indexes by J. C. Meredith. Oxford: Clarendon Press, 1952.

————. *Kant's Political Writings*. Ed. H. Reiss. Cambridge: Cambridge University Press, 1977.

————. *Critique of Pure Reason*. Trans. N. K. Smith. London: Macmillan, 1929.

Katz, S. ed. *Mysticism and Philosophical Analysis*. New York: Oxford University Press, 1978.

Kearney, Richard. ed. *The Irish Mind*. Atlantic Highlands, N.J.: Humanities Press, 1985.

———. *The Wake of Imagination*. London: Hutchinson, 1988.

Kerferd, C. B. *The Sophistic Movement*. Cambridge: Cambridge University Press, 1981.

Kierkegaard, S. *The Present Age*. Trans. A. Dru. London: Collins, 1962.

———. *Philosophical Fragments and Johannes Climacus*. Editors and translators H. V. Hong and E. H. Hong. Princeton: Princeton University Press, 1985.

Kirk, G. S. and Raven, J. E. *The Presocratic Philosophers*. Cambridge: Cambridge University Press, 1971.

Kline, George L. *Religious and Anti-Religious Thought in Russia*. Chicago: University of Chicago Press, 1968.

———. "The Use and Abuse of Hegel by Nietzsche and Marx." Chapter 1, *Hegel and His Critics*. Ed. W. Desmond. Albany: State University of New York Press, 1989.

Kohák, E. *Idea and Experience*. Chicago: University of Chicago Press, 1979.

———. *The Embers and the Stars: A Philosophical Inquiry into the Moral Sense of Nature*. Chicago: University of Chicago Press, 1984.

Kuhn, Thomas. *The Structure of Scientific Revolutions*. Chicago: University of Chicago Press, 1970.

Langer, S. K. *Feeling and Form*. New York: Scribner's, 1953.

———. *Philosophy in a New Key*. Cambridge, Mass.: Harvard University Press, 1942.

Lefebvre, H. *Everyday Life in the Modern World*. Trans. Sacha Rabinovitch. New York: Harper and Row, 1971.

Leibniz, G. W. *Monadology and Other Philosophical Essays*. Translators P. Schrecker and A. M. Schrecker. Indianapolis: Bobbs Merill, 1965.

Levi-Strauss, Claude. *The Raw and the Cooked*. Translators J. and D. Weightman. New York: Harper and Row, 1969.

Lifton, Robert J. *The Nazi Doctors: Medical Killing and the Psychology of Genocide*. New York: Basic Books, 1986.

Lloyd, G. *The Man of Reason*. Minneapolis: University of Minnesota Press, 1984.

Lonzi, M. *Sputiamo su Hegel*. Milan: Rivolta Femminile, 1974.

Lorca, F. G. *Poet in New York*. Trans. B. Belitt. New York: Grove Press, 1955.

Lyotard, J. F. *The Postmodern Condition: A Report of Knowledge*. Translators G. Bennington and B. Massumi. Minneapolis: University of Minnesota Press, 1984.

MacIntyre, A. *After Virtue: A Study in Moral Theory*. Notre Dame: University of Notre Dame Press, 1981.

Maimonides, M. *The Guide for the Perplexed*. Trans. M. Friedländer. New York: Dover Publications, 1956.

Marcel, G. *The Decline of Wisdom*. Trans. M. Harari. London: Harvill Press, 1954.

Marx, Karl. *Early Writings*. Translated and edited by T. B. Bottomore. New York: McGraw-Hill, 1964.

Malinowski, B. *Magic, Science and Religion and Other Essays*. Boston: Beacon Press, 1948.

Mao Tse-Tung. *Talks at the Yenan Forum on Literature and Art*. Peking: Foreign Languages Press, 1965.

McGuiness, B. *Wittgenstein: A Life*. Berkeley: University of California Press, 1988.

Meyer, M. W. ed. *The Ancient Mysteries: A Sourcebook*. New York: Harper and Row, 1987.

Morreall, John, ed. *The Philosophy of Laughter and Humor*. Albany: State University of New York Press, 1987.

Mothersill, Mary. *Beauty Restored*. New York: Oxford University Press, 1986.

Murray, Gilbert. *Five Stages of Greek Religion*. London: Watts and Co., 1935.

Murray, Michael, ed. *Heidegger and Modern Philosophy*. New Haven: Yale University Press, 1978.

Nietzsche, F. *Beyond Good and Evil*. Trans. M. Cowan. Chicago: Regnery, 1955.

————. *The Birth of Tragedy from the Spirit of Music*. Trans. W. Kaufmann. New York: Random House, 1967.

————. *Thus Spoke Zarathustra*. Trans. R. J. Hollingdale. Baltimore: Penguin, 1961.

————. *Philosophy in the Tragic Age of the Greeks*. Trans. M. Cowan. Chicago: Gateway, 1962.

————. *Twilight of the Idols and the Anti-Christ*. Trans. R. J. Hollingdale. Baltimore: Penguin, 1968.

Neville, Robert C. *Reconstruction of Thinking*. Albany: State University of New York Press, 1981.

————. *Soldier, Sage, Saint*. New York: Fordam University Press, 1978.

Newman, Charles. *The Post-Modern Aura: The Art of Fiction in an Age of Inflation.* Evanston: Northwestern University Press, 1985.

Ong, Walter. *Fighting for Life: Contest, Sexuality and Consciousness*. Ithaca: Cornell University Press, 1981.

Osborne, H. *The Art of Appreciation*. New York: Oxford University Press, 1970.

Owen, H. P. *Concepts of Divinity*. London: Macmillan, 1972.

Pateman, C. and Gross, C., eds. *Feminist Challenges: Social and Political Theory.* Boston: Northeastern University Press, 1986.

Pieper, J. *Leisure: The Basis of Culture*. Trans. A. Dru. New York: Pantheon, 1952.

Picard, Max. *The World of Silence*. Trans. Stanley Godman. Chicago: Gateway, 1952.

Plato. *Opera*. Ed. J. Burnet. Oxford: Clarendon Press, 1900–15.

Pois, Robert A. *National Socialism and the Religion of Nature*. New York: St. Martin's Press, 1986.

Portmann, A. *Animal Camouflage*. Trans. A. J. Pomerans. Ann Arbor: University of Michigan Press, 1959.

————. *Animal Forms and Pattern*, Trans. Hella Czech. New York: 1967.

Rajchman, C. and West, C., eds. *Post-Analytical Philosophy*. New York: Columbia University Press, 1985.

Reichenbach, Hans. *The Rise of Scientific Philosophy*. Berkeley: University of California Press, 1951.

Ricoeur, Paul. *The Symbolism of Evil*. Trans. E. Buchanan. Boston: Beacon Press, 1967.

Rilke, R. M. *The Selected Poetry of Rainer Maria Rilke*. Trans. Stephen Mitchell. New York: Random House, 1982.

Rorty, Richard. *Consequences of Pragmatism*. Minneapolis: University of Minnesota Press, 1982.

————. *Philosophy and the Mirror of Nature*. Princeton: Princeton University Press, 1979.

————. "The Contingency of Language." *London Review of Books* (17 April) 1986.

————. "The Contingency of Selfhood." *London Review of Books* (8 May) 1986.

Rosen, Stanley. *Hermeneutics as Politics*. Oxford University Press, 1988.

————. *The Limits of Analysis*. New York: Basic Books, 1980.

Sartre, J. P. *Imagination: A Psychological Critique*. Trans. F. Williams. Ann Arbor: University of Michigan Press, 1963.

_____. *The Psychology of Imagination*. New York: Philosophical Library, 1948.

Scarry, E. *The Body in Pain*. New York: Oxford University Press, 1985.

Scharfstein, Ben-Ami. *The Philosophers: Their Lives and the Nature of Their Thought*. New York: Oxford University Press, 1980.

Scheler, Max. *Man's Place in Nature*. Trans. Hans Meyerhoff. New York: Noonday, 1962.

Scholem, G. *Major Trends in Jewish Mysticism*. New York: Schocken, 1946.

_____. *On The Kabbalah and its Symbolism*. New York: Schocken, 1965.

Scruton, Roger. *Art and Imagination: A Study in the Philosophy of Mind*. Boston: Routledge & Kegan Paul, 1982.

Sherburne, Donald. *A Whiteheadian Aesthetic*. New Haven: Yale University Press, 1961.

Spinoza, B. *Opera*. Editors J. van Vloten and J. P. N. Land. The Hague: Nijhoff, 1914.

Strauss, Leo. *Persecution and the Art of Writing*. Glencoe, Ill.: The Free Press, 1952.

Unger, Aryeh L. *The Totalitarian Party and People in Nazi Germany and Soviet Russia*. London: Cambridge University Press, 1974.

Vaught, Carl G. *The Quest for Wholeness*. Albany: State University of New York Press, 1982.

Van der Leeuw, G. *Religion in Essence and Manifestation*. Trans. J. E. Turner. Princeton: Princeton University Press, 1986.

Ver Eecke, W. *Saying "No": Its Meaning in Child Development, Psychoanalysis, Linguistics and Hegel*. Pittsburgh: Duquesne University Press, 1984.

Vico, G. *The New Science*. Translator T. G. Bergin and M. H. Fisch. Ithaca: Cornell University Press, 1970.

Weiss, Paul. *Privacy*. Carbondale: Southern Illinois University Press. 1983.

Weissman, David. *Intuition and Ideality*. Albany: State University of New York Press, 1987.

Whitehead, A. N. *Religion in the Making*. New York: Macmillan, 1926.

_____. *Science and the Modern World*. New York: Macmillan, 1925.

Wiesel, Elie. *Legends of our Time*. New York: Avon Books, 1970.

Williams, Bernard. *Ethics and the Limits of Philosophy*. Cambridge, Mass.: Harvard University Press, 1985.

Wittgenstein, L. *Culture and Value*. Trans. Peter Winch. Ed. G. H. Von Wright. Chicago: University of Chicago Press, 1980.

Yeats, W. B. *Explorations*. New York: Macmillan, 1962.

Zaehner, R. C. *Hindu and Muslim Mysticism*. New York: Schocken, 1969.

Index